Noraenh McElroy
1995

D0495570

THE *Virgin* FILM YEARBOOK

VOLUME 8

EDITED BY JAMES PARK

VIRGIN

ACKNOWLEDGEMENTS

Thanks to the distributors, publicity companies, publications and individuals who supplied information for this book.

Artificial Eye, Blue Dolphin, the British Film Institute, Columbia/Tri-Star, Dennis Davidson Associates, Electric Pictures, Enterprise, Entertainment, Guild, ICA Projects, JAC, Mainline, Pathé, PSA, Palace, Paramount, Rank, Recorded Releasing, Twentieth Century-Fox, UIP, Universal, Variety, Vestron, Virgin, Warner Bros, Zakiya and Associates

For Cat

In-house editor
JANE WRIGHT

In-house editorial assistant
JUDITH MURRAY

Cover and design by
JERRY GOLDIE

A Virgin Book
Published in 1989
by the Paperback Division of
W.H. Allen & Co Plc
Sekforde House
175/9 St John Street
London EC1V 4LL

Copyright © 1989 by Virgin Books

ISBN 0 86369 335 0

This book is sold subject to the condition that it shall not, by way of trade or otherwise, be lent, re-sold, hired out, or otherwise circulated without the publisher's prior consent in any form of binding or cover other than that in which it is published and without a similar condition including this condition being imposed upon the subsequent purchaser.

Printed and bound by
MacKays of Chatham PLC, Chatham, Kent

Typeset by Avocet Robinson, Buckingham

EDITOR

JAMES PARK writes feature-film screenplays and books about cinema. The author of *Learning to Dream: The New British Cinema*, he is working on a history of British filmmaking and a survey of European cinema. He is also the editor of the forthcoming *Names 1945 – 2000*, a handbook of contemporary culture, politics, science and everything else. This is the third time he has produced *The Film Yearbook*.

CONTRIBUTORS

ANNE BILLSON is a freelance writer and film critic. She has contributed to numerous publications, such as *City Limits*, *Tatler* and *The Times*. She is currently completing her third book – a novel about upwardly-mobile vampires. Her interests include opera, skin diseases and bird-watching.

PETE BOSS has just completed a PhD on the contemporary horror film. He has been a part-time lecturer, contributed to *Screen*, acted as film and video reviewer for BBC Radio Oxford and played electric guitar in a variety of dodgy venues.

TONY CRAWLEY is the author of *The Films of Sophia Loren*, *Bébé: The Films of Brigitte Bardot*, *Screen Dreams: The Hollywood Pin-Up* and *The Steven Spielberg Story*. He has written on films for publications throughout the world and now lives in France, where he has a franglais rock radio show and has co-authored *Entre Deux Censures*.

STEPHEN DARK is a journalist who writes about the media, property and finance.

RAYMOND DURGNAT is a writer and lecturer on films and cultural history. Co-author of *King Vidor, American*, his next book will be *Michael Powell and the British Genius*. He has been a visiting professor at UCLA, Columbia, Dartmouth College, Oklahoma and elsewhere, as well as a staff writer at Elstree Studios in the good old days of Pathé News.

GRAHAM FULLER is film and theatre editor of American *Elle*. He also writes on film for *The Listener* and *The Independent* and has contributed to *The Village Voice*, *American Film*, *Film Comment*, *Premiere*, *The Guardian* and *Sight and Sound*.

TIMOTHY GEE became enthusiastic about movies after seeing *Mrs Wiggs of the Cabbage Patch*. In 1960 he started working in the British film industry. He has edited films for Ken Russell (*Salomé's Last Dance*), Bryan Forbes (*The Raging Moon*, *The Stepford Wives*, *The Slipper and the Rose*) and Desmond Davis (*Clash of the Titans*, *The Country Girls* and *Ordeal by Innocence*).

PHIL HARDY is a cultural historian who is currently working on a major book on Crime in the Movies, and a short volume about the 1950s. His most recent publication was the *Faber Companion to Popular Music of the Twentieth Century*. A warm and wonderful human being, he lives amongst the rolling hills of North London.

ADRIAN HODGES had a glittering early career as the assistant editor of *BP Forecourt News*, before moving to *Screen International*. He subsequently became a script executive at Thorn EMI Screen Entertainment. Following a year at Cannon Films (UK), he was appointed administrator of the NFDF, which funds the development of British feature films.

HARLAN KENNEDY is the European editor of *Film Comment*. He is a member of the Critics' Circle and of FIPRESCI, the international federation of film critics. For four years he was the London contributing editor of *American Film*, and he now writes frequently for *Emmy* magazine, *American Cinematographer* and the *New York Times*. His bearded collie, Brush, did not win at Crufts this year.

BART MILLS writes about films and television from Hollywood for such publications as *The Guardian*, the *Los Angeles Times* and *American Film*. He is also the author of a recent book on Mickey Rourke.

MARKUS NATTEN is a retired poet currently co-writing two screenplays, *The Winter Man* and *Circuit of Nerves*. He writes regularly for *Fear*, lives in the New Forest and dreams of having his own cookery programme.

KIM NEWMAN is the author of *Nightmare Movies* and co-editor of *Horror: 100 Best Books* and *Ghastly Beyond Belief*. His first novel, *The Night Mayor*, was recently published by Simon & Schuster. He also writes regularly for *Sight and Sound* and *Monthly Film Bulletin* and has an early-morning TV slot on Channel 4.

TIM PULLEINE is deputy film editor of *The Guardian*. He contributes reviews and articles to various publications, including *Sight and Sound*, *Films and Filming* and *Monthly Film Bulletin*.

DAVID QUANTICK is a regular contributor to *Spitting Image*, *NME*, *Arena*, *City Limits* and *Punch*.

TREVOR WILLSMER started his career as an ice-cream salesman at the Kingston Granada, before being asked to write a TV series on the Children's Crusade, which led to further work as a researcher and writer. Following the publication and subsequent pulping of his first novel, *Jessie*, he formed Lone Wolf Productions, through which he has produced and directed a series of short films. He also runs an 8mm film distribution company.

CONTENTS

THE BEGINNING OF THE END?

Hollywood, they say, has never had it so good. After the glorious box-office summer of 1989, its coffers are bulging. But, when it comes to fresh ideas, the centre of world moviemaking is bankrupt.

For a time at least, this poverty of invention need not threaten grosses. Audiences are reassured by the predictable. They'll queue around the block for the latest picture featuring Indiana Jones, or remake of a recent hit, because they know (or think they know) they'll be entertained by characters with whom they are now familiar.

And even when the face on the poster doesn't tell them exactly what to expect, many pictures now come guaranteed free of any real surprises. *Deepstar Six* and *Leviathan* may be located underwater, but you soon realize they are *Alien* derivatives. And when you're told that a movie features mismatched cops, it's not hard to guess how things will turn out.

Why torture yourself developing an original idea when a sequel, a remake or a ripoff can make you rich? The time is getting closer when Hollywood won't worry about new stories at all. The packaging will change – a different star, a different locale, a different piece of music on the soundtrack – but, for the rest, each film will be essentially *the same* as all the others.

That's not to say the old stories shouldn't be re-examined and re-told. *Batman*, the tale of a super-hero's battle against crime distilled through a contemporary sensibility and the rich imaginations of Frank Miller and Tim Burton, *is* a film for our times. Similarly, Alan Parker's *Mississippi Burning* shows that the buddy-buddy format *can* be used to powerful effect.

But, for the most part, what distinguishes one mismatched cop movie from another is some gimmick that can be sold in the advertising tag-line. The succession of James Bond movies may mirror shifts in East-West relations, but few sequel writers do more than look for new twists in an established plot-line..

It's no wonder that, when it comes to sequels, diminishing creative returns set in very quickly. If *Police Academy* 6 had not been pre-sold by title, it's unlikely that many would have bothered to take a look. And this declining creative vigour is bound to have box-office consequences in the end. After all, *Cocoon* lost its magic the second time around, and *The Karate Kid* staggered through round three. So, when they've flogged the last dollar out of the current crop of ideas, what on earth are those Hollywood executives going to do?

Bruce Willis might have another go at killing Europeans, although it's unlikely that a *Die Hard 2* could tap as effectively as its predecessor into America's fear of terrorism. And perhaps Tom Cruise could go on another journey across the States in the company of his autistic brother. But what would they have to say to each other in *Rain Man 2*?

Most movies nowadays have no heart. Their makers seem so frightened of rubbing an audience up the wrong way that they fiddle with off-the-shelf narrative formulae and leave it at that. Rather than exploring what really happens when humans get together to fight, amuse each other or make love, they sidestep the complex emotions with displays of choreography or special effects. These may amuse, they may even sometimes thrill, but they don't stir the emotions like a movie should.

Hollywood may have been going this way ever since *Jaws* set the fashion for big-budget entertainment and sequels, but it's surprising how deep the rot has gone, and how quickly. Whereas Jonathan Demme's *Something Wild* two years ago depicted a relationship one could believe in, Matthew Modine and Michelle Pfeiffer make love by numbers in the same director's *Married to the Mob*, and the film ends in gimmickry and jokiness where the previous picture culminated in violent passion.

And given a creative climate that places so little premium on creative adventure, it's hardly surprising that none of Hollywood's once interesting filmmakers is doing his or her best work. You couldn't watch *Tucker* or *Farewell to the King* and feel you were in the presence of directors who believed themselves to be any longer at the cutting edge.

Nor was there much in the films that pitched themselves at a 'grown-up' audience which made the heart beat faster. Audiences were offered a comedy of sexual bad manners in eighteenth-century France (*Dangerous Liaisons*), a film about how far a divorced mother can enjoy sexual freedom (*The Good Mother*), and the case against rape (*The Accused*), but there's phoniness coursing through the veins of these movies.

Everywhere people seem to have lost interest in movies that move people, and enrich their lives. The journals are full of stories about the deals, the grosses and the superstars, but they stop short of talking about the films themselves. As the big companies are put up for sale, merge and re-merge, their filmmaking divisions become increasingly minor parts of multi-media empires. Agents sew up deals for their star clients; producers gratefully accept the packages that agents have put together, and marketing men get to work on developing the plug-lines. Forgotten along the line is the fact that it's writers who will have to come up with new ideas if movies are to tap contemporary hopes and fears, and justify the machinery that's set up to market and distribute them.

Hollywood will go on because there isn't another film industry in the world with the resources, the organization and the marketing nous to take its place. But come 1992, European producers won't be able to complain that they don't have a market big enough to support major-budget film production. And if *they* could get their act together, the competition they would offer might be good news for Hollywood too.

JAMES PARK

GREAT CONCEPT, SHAME ABOUT THE MOVIE

W e've all had those presents that look great on the outside and contain damn-ll once opened. We gasp at the shiny gift-wrapping; chuckle at the witty greetings tag; swoon to the crackle and hiss of paper as we unwrap. Then we find what's inside: a small stuffed mouse bearing the legend 'batteries not included'.

For the above, read today's movie world. Great gift-wrapping; shame about the gifts. In the decade of High-Concept cinema – for that's surely the way we'll remember and define the 1980s – films are more and more becoming Grade-A promotional exercises accompanying Grade-C to Grade-Z movies.

A High-Concept film (the term is 1970s-originated Hollywood jargon) is one whose story idea can be expressed in a phrase or sentence. Its premise is so simple that listeners have taken it in before they even knew they were listening: and it's so brightly defined they can't forget it even if they try. In Hollywood at Christmas, the showpiece High-Concept film was *Twins*. Premise: Arnold Schwarzenegger (built like a destroyer) and Danny DeVito (built like a doughnut) play twin brothers. Copyline: 'Only their mother can tell them apart.' Revenue at time of writing: $100 million and rising.

The slick sell produces a slick movie, and the slick movie can produce an empty stomach. Are there any filmgoers today, sampling the likes of *K-9*, *The Dream Team*, *Major League*, *Indiana Jones and the Last Crusade* and other medium-to-large 1989 American hits, who don't sneakingly wonder why they paid five dollars to see a film they had already – in a sense – seen?

They'd seen it in the PR; the tag-line; the 'concept'. They'd swallowed the High-Concept Idea before they even entered the cinema. (It was what got them into the cinema.) *K-9*: buddy-buddy cop thriller in which one buddy is a dog. *The Dream Team*: four escaped lunatics are cured by a day on the town. *Major League*: baseball team ordered to bat for defeat bats to win. *Indiana Jones*: Saturday matinée hero rides again (and again . . .).

In the age of High Concept, the concept and its filmic fleshing forth are increasingly all you get. Near to extinct is the art of the well-crafted subplot, the swell of richly-drawn supporting characters: all those underpinnings that used to enhance Hollywood movies and make a single 'concept' neither necessary nor relevant. (What ever is the 'concept' of *Now Voyager*, *Gone With the Wind*, *Casablanca* or *The Searchers*.)

Today, though, the order goes out: we need a return on our money and we need it fast. The filmgoing public is slung a strong hook – the Concept – and hauled in. Never mind if 90 minutes later, or even nine, they're gasping on the river bank and begging for a little more cinematic oxygen.

High Concept begins life as a sales-aid to the filmmaker pitching a project. Keep the pitch short and the listener's eyes won't glaze over as you wax on eloquently 30 minutes later. Soon the cash-and-carry simplicities of High-Concept movie-marketing spread into the films themselves. Woe betide most movies today which don't boast a portable plot premise and an instantly appealing gimmick in the story or casting.

Today's high priest of High Concept is deemed to be Disney's Michael Eisner. Since 1984, the ex-Paramount head has turned the Disney studio around from near-bankruptcy to spectacular box-office success. Under Eisner, Disney's big hits – like *Three Men and a Baby, Good Morning Vietnam, Who Framed Roger Rabbit* – have all had High-Concept plots, many based on the saleable gimmick of the 'irresistible mismatch': three bachelors stuck with a baby; funny-man Robin Williams stuck in unfunny Vietnam; a cartoon rabbit shotgun-wedded to Bob Hoskins.

Under the Touchstone/Disney banner, a cinema has grown up where the High Concept is so strong a tent-pole that it scarcely matters (box-office-wise) how drab or second-hand the canvas is, nor what's inside the tent on deeper inspection.

The three films mentioned above mopped up $450 million between them. Why? Because each had a single, built-in 'You've got to see' factor. You've got to see macho playboys Selleck, Danson and Guttenberg being cute with a baby. You've got to see motor-mouth Robin Williams dealing out schtick in a place hitherto deemed Forbidden Comic Territory. You've got to see a pen-and-ink bunny romping with a flesh-and-blood actor in state-of-the-art Wonderland.

But increasingly with High-Concept cinema, we're seeing commercial energy go hand-in-hand with quality and texture starvation. A film like *Good Morning Vietnam*, for instance, is content to surround its brainwave central chemistry of star and location with a cast of enfeebled, stick-like supporting characters plus sentimental, postcard views of Vietnam.

Meanwhile Paramount, Disney's only box-office rival in recent years, is fast catching the Touchstone disease: one that makes filmmakers rich while impoverishing their films. The studio's mid-range 1989 hits – *Scrooged, Pet Sematary, Major League* – are garage-sales of gimmickry built round a single grab-you idea. Scrooge as Madison Avenue yuppie; a burial-ground that brings the dead to life; a no-hope baseball team knocking the knockers for six.

A free master-print of *Citizen Kane* (other conditions attached) to any filmgoer who, half an hour after seeing one of these films, can remember a moment of teasing ambiguity or unpredictable characterization: of echo, enigma or puzzlement.

Which doesn't mean that filmmakers – in a perpetual rearguard action to dress up their one-idea films – don't pay lip service to 'mystery': don't often try to peddle it as part of the package. A *soupçon* of tension and paradox is desirable in any ad campaign, indeed in any High Concept. It should bite you immediately, but it should also keep you itching and scratching. Just as the Disney movie machine has thrived on the comic contradictions of the 'unholy alliance', the average poster copy-line today – the simplest, most direct medium for communicating the concept – sets out to wed assertion to mystery or paradox.

'A funny movie about getting serious' (*Crossing Delancey*).
'She captured America's heart and tore it apart' (*Patty Hearst*).
'Comedy brought them together. . .Ambition drove them apart' (*Punchline*).
'Sometimes dead is better' (*Pet Sematary*).

Through the surprising, paradoxical or pull-two-ways copyline, a film's publicity can acknowledge a film's complexity — or fool you into thinking it has some — while still keeping the 'concept' simple for the punter. Indeed the more High-Concept movie salesmanship advances, the more complexity in the cinema risks being parlayed into the pat little incongruities of the ad strategy: until the point is reached when the film itself is no more than the sum of its promotional gimmicks. The tail wags the dog: the PR wags the picture. The formula for selling the film becomes the formula *of* the film.

Whole genres, or genre revivals, can be set in motion by High-Concept thinking: its love of bells-and-whistles plot gimmicks and show-off odd-coupling in the characters. Like Disney's 'irresistible mismatch' films, the slew of buddy movies emerging in the past twelve months represents the working of High-Concept star-teaming. Why Schwarzenegger alone when you can team him with the right opposite number and create a duo whose knockabout incompatibility screams 'Love me!' at the box-office: upright, bionic Schwarzenegger with streetwise slop James Belushi in *Red Heat*; Mr Universe Schwarzenegger with Mr Pizza-parlour Danny DeVito in *Twins*.

Such teamings are an impudence every audience can respond to. A single glance at the poster and they know what they're being offered: two stars for the price of one, and two stars so mismatched they'll spar happily all the way to the High-Concept finale.

The principle behind High-Concept is the same as the principle behind a package holiday: 'Here is the well-mapped change of scene you're going to get; there are no hidden extras and we think you'll like it.' And the High Concept, sold with all its high-profile publicity, commits the seller to providing the goods and services promised in the ad. Hell hath no fury like a moviegoer cheated: at any rate, one who's been groomed and drilled by the High-Concept age.

Moviegoers want to see the plot gimmicks as advertised. They want to be 'surprised' without being surprised: they want a sense of adventure without risk, bafflement or disorientation. (Hence the success of *Bill and Ted's Excellent Adventure*, a time-trip as cosy and brainless as a video-game.) And they want the actors — who are High Concepts themselves if they're stars — to do their familiar, proven thing. They want to see Tom Hanks cast as the cinema's Overgrown Kid (*Big*, *The 'burbs*) not as an anguished stand-up comic (*Punchline*). They want to see Schwarzenegger as the cinema's Comic-book Hercules: and no departures please from his 'Yonder lies da missile-compound of my fozzer' German accent. (When he tried Russian in *Red Heat*, he had one of his rare semi-flops.)

The dominion of High Concept has become so powerful that when audiences *are* surprised by the direction a film takes, chances are they'll be distressed rather than delighted. *Fatal Attraction* was first shown to preview audiences with what might loosely be called a 'low-concept' ending: a downbeat dénouement with Glenn Close committing suicide and framing Michael Douglas who's led off in the cop car.

Audiences skywrote their dismay on the preview cards. This ending betrayed the package holiday they thought they were being promised; in which an innocently erring hero fights (and surely vanquishes) the wicked witch who led him into temptation. The preview response forced the makers to go for the alternative 'High-Concept' ending: Close turning into a knife-slashing sicko and being drowned in the bath by Douglas. Now we can all cheer.

In this instance, the movie industry effectively teamed up with the public to boost the film into the higher realms of viewer-impact. The preview phenomenon is a growing part of movie-marketing strategy; it's a way of loaning a film's authorship out to the public. The public can scribble in the margin or they can – as with *Fatal Attraction* – tear out a whole chapter and demand its replacement.

Either way, the preview becomes a method not of blurring but of purifying the High Concept. For by passing a film through the filter of public responses, the makers can eliminate all the motes of difficulty, specks of ambiguity or atoms of anti-climax that might spoil a clean, strong, one-directional movie experience.

Ultimately High Concept is no more than a high-shine reformulation of the classic Hollywood principle 'The same but different'. A movie's theme, story or premise must have a family likeness to something you already know and love. 'If you liked *Jaws/Star Wars/Crocodile Dundee/Top Gun/Rain Man/ Gone with the Wind/ Orphans of the Storm*, you'll love this.' But the movie must also offer something new that has been surgically grafted onto the old. '*The Accused*: from the producers of *Fatal Attraction*, a darker story from today's headlines.' 'Jane Fonda/Tom Cruise/Bruce Willis as you never saw them before.' Dustin Hoffman as an autistic: Meryl Streep as an Australian: Robert De Niro playing comedy: Woody Allen playing serious. (Some new ideas sell better than others.)

High Concept concentrates the ideal of 'same but different' into a high-radiance slogan or gimmick. The package-holiday principle rides again – 'We promise you all the familiar comforts, clean bedrooms, TV, English breakfasts. But we spice this with a little token exoticism: local carnivals, native barbecues, visits to the blue grotto.'

Some High-Concept hits take the package-holiday ethos almost literally. The 'Wow, what a great idea!' reaction that should greet a good High Concept – indeed that almost defines it – can come from the geographical transplanting of a star to an alien environment. *Beverly Hills Cop* flies lovable, streetwise Eddie Murphy to louche, élitist Gucci-land. *Crocodile Dundee* uproots an Aussie primitive and plonks him down in teeming NY. *Witness* puts Harrison Ford among the Amishes. *Good Morning Vietnam* posts Robin Williams to South-East Asia.

What most of these films also promise, like any good package holiday, is that hero/heroine will be back home on schedule, with identity and composure no more seriously ruffled than the audience's. The star – or the series or the genre – is the immutable object. The High Concept – or what the film wants to do with the star or series or genre – is the pseudo-irresistible force.

It is no surprise that High Concept was born in – indeed born of – the age of the short attention span. It says, 'How long have I got your interest and what can I say in that time to keep it?' Neither the studio executive to whom the filmmaker pitches an idea, nor the audience to whom the studio pitches the movie, is going to listen to scrolls of explication. In an age when commercials and pop videos can tell stories in 30 seconds, the filmmaker who can't do the same across a desk or the film company who can't do the same in a movie trailer doesn't stand a chance.

But the true origins of High Concept go back even further than today's 'three-minute culture'. They go back to that turning-point in film history when the studio system yielded to the age of agents and ad-men: when Hollywood fell to the package-makers; when independent producers and maverick companies stole dominion from the old-style moguls.

Projects were once nurtured at their leisure in the hothouse of a major studio. Here armies of screenwriters could nurture the tender growths, and a constellation of contract stars could have their charisma deployed to shore up any shortcomings in the 'concept'. But as the studio system broke up, projects suddenly had to be pitched at the majors from outside. A 'now or never' element was built into the business of selling an idea. That idea had to come with a souped-up engine and lots of multicoloured bodywork. It had to come, in short, with a 'concept'.

Today's filmmakers defy the tyranny of the High Concept at their peril. Its thin, piping yardstick of excellence may condemn us, for the foreseeable future, to a world where box-office charts are topped by pop-up-book adventure epics, dimension-hopping comedies or wacky-alliance buddy movies. Of the half-dozen films that have passed the $100 million mark in America over the past twelve months, every one could be categorized 'High Concept'. Indeed every one comes into one of the above categories.

Any director today with a yen for gritty naturalism or cross-grained contemporaneity has a struggle on his or her hands. And any director with an epic vision extending beyond the purely pyrotechnic – that is, who has an epic sense of people, not just of spectacle and special effects – is as endangered as the black rhino.

Films like Michael Cimino's *Heaven's Gate* and Martin Scorsese's *The Last Temptation of Christ* – powerful in parts and/or brave in whole – are doomed almost from the drawing-board. And when Steven 'High Concept' Spielberg goes for the great humanist canvas in *Empire of the Sun*, the gulf between aspiration and achievement becomes embarrassing. We're watching a child daubing the Last Judgement with a crayon pack, and adding a takeaway moral about Innocence Triumphant that is nowhere to be found in J. G. Ballard's book.

Roll on the new Renaissance. At least as we near the 1990s there are glimmers of hope. Disney-Touchstone's winning streak is showing signs of faltering. And there are some young filmmakers out there in North America today (Steven Soderbergh, Atom Egoyan, David Lynch) whose movies embrace ambiguity, stylistic subtlety and a subversive, questing curiosity about human motives and emotions.

Maybe the day will come when complexity is once again a bankable asset. When a budding director will be able to pitch a film as a long, rich, complex, knotty, mysterious work. When it won't have to be sold as a vehicle for a star 'extending' his or her range (Meryl Streep going Danish again but in male drag); or for a stand-up comedian going legit (Robin Williams in *Good Morning Elsinore*): or for an odd-couple duo taking over the show (Arnold Schwarzenegger and Danny DeVito in *Rosencrantz and Guildenstern are Twins*).

But that age is still a long way off. The age we live in now is one of high-intensity gimmickry, fortune-cookie articulation and cute, takeaway incongruity. Anyone want to buy a screenplay about an Aussie croc-hunter transported to Beverly Hills and finding his long-lost autistic brother?

HARLAN KENNEDY

FILMMAKERS' CHOICE

HARRY KÜMEL

It has been a terrible year. I have never seen one like it. There have been only two significant films:
Bagdad Cafe
Women on the Verge of a Nervous Breakdown

SANDY LIEBERSON

There is a lack of really exciting, innovative and personal films but this would be my choice, in no particular order:
Baron Munchausen When minimalism seems to dominate the cinema, along comes *Munchausen*. The film is so dense, rich, full of spectacle and fun that it was worth a second viewing.
Dangerous Liaisons Directed with an elegance, wit and style not seen in a long time from a British director.
Heathers A spectacular feature début, taking an unusual view of adolescence in the US without being coy or condescending.
Bagdad Cafe Enjoyable with a personal and interesting perspective on the US.
Distant Voices, Still Lives Personal, powerful and lovingly made.
Salaam Bombay Probably the best street movie since *Pixote*, made with heart.
The Last Temptation of Christ By creating worldwide debate and controversy it restored the cinema's importance as a forum for ideas.
The Navigator Full of ideas and vision, beautifully crafted with a unique story.
I'm Gonna Git You Sucka Entertaining Black American cinema.
Pelle The Conqueror An almost perfect example of narrative cinema; lovingly made, full of emotion, sentiment and compassion.
School Daze Spike Lee speaks with his own voice at all times. He is one of the few personal filmmakers in the US today.
Stormy Monday A British film that competed on an international level and made it. Nice to see so much style and good acting. Loved the music too.
A World Apart A great début for Chris Menges and Shawn Slovo.
A Fish Called Wanda Everything worked!
The Runner Powerful and interesting film set in Iran. It amazes one to see the resilience of children in the most appalling conditions.

JEREMY THOMAS

Wings of Desire
Dead Ringers
The Last Temptation of Christ
Bird
The Accidental Tourist
Track 29

KEN RUSSELL

Parents Makes *Blue Velvet* look like *Care Bears*.
RoboCop The best sci-fi movie since *Metropolis*.
Withnail & I The best recent British film.
Lawrence of Arabia (full-length version) Takes over where Ralph Kirkpatrick left off.

MARK SHIVAS

Au Revoir, les enfants
Dangerous Liaisons
A World Apart
Field of Dreams
Running on Empty
Crossing Delancey
A Fish Called Wanda

FRANC RODDAM

Dangerous Liaisons A smart movie about deception and duplicity.
Dead Ringers Powerfully made, although it fell apart in the third act.
Heathers
Bagdad Cafe
The latter two are slight, but amusing, pieces. Two of my favourite films of the year appeared on TV. They were *Elephant* and *The Firm*, both directed by Alan Clarke.

THE YEARBOOK CHECKLIST

FILM

FILMS OF THE YEAR
The Accidental Tourist
Batman
Dead Ringers
Distant Voices, Still Lives
Do the Right Thing
Heathers
Manhunter
Mississippi Burning
The Navigator
Parents
Red Sorghum
Women on the Verge of a Nervous
  Breakdown
A World Apart

HIT

HITS OF THE YEAR
Die Hard
A Fish Called Wanda
Rain Man
Who Framed Roger Rabbit

FRENCH HIT

French Hit of the Year
The Big Blue

DISAPPOINTMENT

DISAPPOINTMENTS OF THE YEAR
The Adventures of Baron
  Munchausen
Colors
Farewell to the King
The Last Temptation of Christ
Tequila Sunrise
Things Change

DOG

DOGS OF THE YEAR
Dangerous Liaisons
Licence to Kill
Scandal

TURKEY

TURKEYS OF THE YEAR
Drowning by Numbers
The Good Mother
High Spirits
Poltergeist III
Scrooged
Stormy Monday
Willow

FILMS TO LOOK OUT FOR
Au revoir, les enfants
Bagdad Cafe
Betrayed
Bird
Chocolat
The Commissar
Crazy Love
Dead Calm
The Dead Can't Lie
Dear America
Death Japanese Style (The Funeral)
Earth Girls Are Easy
Field of Dreams
Five Corners
Full Moon in Deep Water
Ghosts of the Civil Dead
Ground Zero
Hairspray
Hanussen
The Hidden
High Hopes

Hotel Terminus
I'm Gonna Git You Sucka
Kamikaze
King of the Children
Law of Desire
Long Live the Lady
The Moderns
Monkey Shines
Naked Gun
976 – Evil
Pathfinder
Pelle the Conqueror
Pet Sematary
Powwow Highway
The Runner
Running on Empty
Salaam Bombay
Salome's Last Dance
Scenes from the Class Struggle in
  Beverly Hills
Shame
Some Girls
Stand and Deliver
Talk Radio
A Taxing Woman
The Terroriser
The Thin Blue Line
Torch Song Trilogy
Track 29
Virgin (36 Fillette)
Yeelen (Brightness)

FILMS TO AVOID 👎

Arthur 2 On the Rocks
The Beast
Bert Rigby, You're a Fool
Bill and Ted's Excellent Adventure
Burning Secret
Buy and Cell
Caddyshack II
Checking Out
Cocktail
Cocoon: The Return
Cold Feet
Consuming Passions

Crack in the Mirror
Cyborg
The Deceivers
Doin' Time on Planet Earth
Dream Demon
The Dream Team
Everybody's All-American
The Experts
Fatal Beauty
Fresh Horses
Ghost Chase
Gleaming the Cube
Hanna's War
Haunted Summer
Hot to Trot
It Couldn't Happen Here
Just Ask for Diamond
Les Patterson Saves the World
Manifesto
Midnight Crossing
1969
Phantasm II
Platoon Leader
Police Academies 5 & 6
Prisoner of Rio
Rambo III
The Rescue
Return from the River Kwai
Salsa
September
The Seventh Sign
Shy People
The Sicilian
'68
Slipstream
Souvenir
Spellbinder
Stealing Heaven
Stealing Home
Taffin
Tapeheads
To Kill a Priest
The Unholy
Walker
Wizard of Speed
  and Time

THE FILMS

1 July 1988 - 30 June 1989

Short reviews by Bart Mills, Kim Newman, Tim Pulleine, Harlan Kennedy,
Anne Billson, Trevor Willsmer, James Park, Stephen Dark, Markus Natten,
Pete Boss, Graham Fuller and David Thompson

FILM

THE ACCIDENTAL TOURIST

Director *Lawrence Kasdan* **producers** *Kasdan, Charles Okun, Michael Grillo* **execs** *Phyllis Carlyle, John Malkovich* **script** *Frank Galati, Kasdan, based on novel by Anne Tyler* **camera** *John Bailey* **editor** *Carol Littleton* **design** *Bo Welch* **music** *John Williams* **cast** *William Hurt, Kathleen Turner, Geena Davis, Amy Wright, David Ogden Stiers, Ed Begley Jr., Bill Pullman, Robert Gorman, Bradley Mott, Seth Granger*
Running time: 121 mins
US release: Warner, Dec 23, 1988
UK release: Warner, Feb 24, 1989

THE ACCUSED

Witnesses are found guilty of soliciting a rape after a protracted court battle waged by the victim (Foster) and the prosecutor (McGillis). *The Accused* is, for the most part, a responsible social problem picture about the rights of women to go unmolested (no matter what provocation they offer). The key flashback sequence - in which Foster dances sexily in the backroom of a bar and is gang-raped - reveals both Kaplan's origins as a subverter of exploitation movies under Roger Corman's aegis in the 1970s, and (despite its ideological claims) the film's ultimately faint-hearted feminism. Foster is brilliant as a tough but by no means saintly working-class girl. **GF**
Director *Jonathan Kaplan* **producers** *Stanley R. Jaffe, Sherry Lansing* **script** *Tom Topor* **camera** *Ralf Bode* **editor** *Jerry Greenberg, O. Nicholas Brown* **design** *Richard Kent Wilcox* **music** *Brad Fiedel* **cast** *Kelly McGillis, Jodie Foster, Bernie Coulson, Leo Rossi, Ann Hearn, Carmen Argenziano, Steve Antin, Tom O'Brien*
Running time: 111 mins
US release: Paramount, Oct 14, 1988
UK release: UIP, Feb 17, 1989

ACTION JACKSON

Craig R. Baxley, the stunt director who was a key influence on *The A-Team* making his directorial début here, injects zestful momentum into this raucous film about a black cop (Weathers) on the trail of a psychopathic businessman (Nelson) who murders his way through union heads in the Detroit car industry. Weathers, a solid mixture of brawn, wit and soulful panache, hits a confident front-man pace after second-stringing to Stallone in the *Rocky* pictures. As the body count piles up, Baxley seems intent on orchestrating a mellower, less edgy action film than the highly-tuned massacre operatics of a Stallone epic. The tongue-in-cheek violence confirms him as an amiable, if unsophisticated, understudy to directors such as John McTiernan. **SD**
Director *Craig R. Baxley* **producer** *Joel Silver* **script** *Robert Reneau* **camera** *Matthew F. Leonetti* **editor** *Mark Helfrich* **design** *Virginia Randolph* **music** *Herbie Hancock, Michael Kamen* **cast** *Carl Weathers, Craig T. Nelson, Vanity, Sharon Stone, Thomas F. Wilson, Bill Duke, Robert Davi, Jack Thibeau, Nicholas Worth, Sonny Landham*
Running time: 96 mins
US release: Lorimar, Feb 12, 1988
UK release: Guild, Jul 1, 1988

DISAPPOINTMENT

ADVENTURES OF BARON MUNCHAUSEN

Director *Terry Gilliam* **producer** *Thomas Schühly* **exec** *Jake Eberts* **script** *Charles McKeown, Gilliam* **camera** *Giuseppe Rotunno* **editor** *Peter Hollywood* **design** *Dante Ferretti* **music** *Michael Kamen* **cast** *John Neville, Sarah Polley, Eric Idle, Charles McKeown, Winston Dennis, Jack Purvis, Valentina Cortese, Uma Thurman, Oliver Reed, Jonathan Pryce, Bill Paterson, Peter Jeffrey, Alison Steadman, Ray Cooper, Don Henderson, Andrew Maclachlan, Sting, José Lifante, Robin Williams*

Running time: 126 mins
US release: Columbia, Mar 10, 1989
UK release: Col/Tri-Star, Mar 17, 1989

ALICE (Neco z Alenky)

This is very much Czech animator Jan Svankmajer's personal vision of Lewis Carroll's Wonderland -- a subterranean maze filled with weird menace. Instead of disappearing down a hole in pursuit of a stuffed rabbit, Alice slips into the drawer of a square table and the Rabbit returns in the company of some aggressive and macabre friends to menace and terrorize her – although she fights back with ruthless determination. Sometimes doll, sometimes human, she accepts what she sees with the insouciance of a dreamer. Svankmajer's rich inventiveness restores the weirdness to a story that now too often seems cosy. **JP**

Director/design Jan Svankmajer **producer** Peter-Christian Fueter **execs** Keith Griffiths, Michael Havas **script** Svankmajer, from book by Lewis Carroll **camera** Svatopluk Maly **editor** Marie Zemanova **cast** Kristyna Kohoutova, Camilla Power
Running time: 85 mins
US release: First Run, Aug 3, 1988
UK release: ICA Projects, Oct 21, 1988

ALIEN NATION

Graham Baker's futuristic buddy movie teams a galactic immigrant and cop (Patinkin) with bigoted middle-aged law enforcer James Caan in a reworking of themes from *In the Heat of the Night* and *Lethal Weapon*. Desirous to nail the non-human perpetrators of his earthly partner's demise, Caan, in between car chases and bar-room brawls, gets to learn valuable lessons in racial tolerance from Patinkin's displays of vulnerability, courage and heroism. Caan's cop is endowed with equal doses of Alf Garnett and Harry Callahan, enabling his character to run the gamut from xenophobia to inter-galactic liberality whilst lead-villain, businessman Terence Stamp, is facially inhibited by a latex construction that, like Patinkin's, robs him of any opportunity for dramatic expression. **MN**

Director Graham Baker **producers** Gale Anne Hurd, Richard Kobritz **script** Rockne S. O'Bannon **camera** Adam Greenberg **editor** Ken Beyda **design** Jack T. Collis **music** Curt Sobel **cast** James Caan, Mandy Patinkin, Terence Stamp, Kevyn Major Howard, Leslie Bevis, Peter Jason, George Jenesky, Jeff Kober, Roger Aaron Brown, Tony Simotes

Running time: 90 mins
US release: Fox, Oct 7, 1988
UK release: Fox, Apr 7, 1989

AMOROSA

Films about madness and creativity need to be told with more imaginative zest than Mai Zetterling brings to this portrait of Swedish writer Agnes von Krusenstjerna (Ekblad). Even the opening scene, in which the crazed heroine is strapped to a stretcher and carried through carnival revelry to the local lunatic asylum, is too flatly shot to conjure up the demonic forces intended. As the films runs back through Krusenstjerna's early life amongst the Swedish bourgeoisie, the disaffection she expresses towards boyfriends and girlfriends who won't give themselves up to passion seems inadequate preparation for the later verbal outpourings. Although Ekblad rises to the opportunities for bravura that follow marriage to kinky pervert Erland Josephson, the film has by this point lost any sense of where it is going. **JP**

Director/script Mai Zetterling **producer** Swedish Film Institute **camera** Rune Ericson **design** Jan Oqvist **cast** Stina Ekblad, Erland Josephson, Philip Zandén, Cathérine de Seynes, Olof Thunberg, Rico Rönnbäck
Running time: 117 mins
UK release: Pathé, May 19, 1989

AMSTERDAMNED

There's a psychopathic skindiver at large on the canals of Amsterdam, slaughtering at random - a hooker, some anti-pollution activists, a Salvation Army collector - and defying the police. Inspector Visser (Stapel), a cop with a neo-beard and a leather jacket, is put on the case, and divides his time between autopsies, cynical dialogue and romancing a museum attendant. Dick Maas, who made *The Lift*, was obviously charged by the Dutch tourist board with getting as much of Amsterdam on screen as possible. He doesn't manage to work in any tulips, but does offer a windmill scene, some Flemish old masters, lots of canals and discreet footage of the red-light district. The identity of the killer is a shade guessable, and some characters persist in doing silly things to keep the suspense up, but there is enough straight action to make up for those lapses. The powerboat chase alone is worth the price of admission, but there's also a car chase, some prowling in the sewers, a nasty trick with a speargun and a good bit of wino-drowning to keep up attention. **KN**

17

Director/script Dick Maas **producers** Laurens Geels, Dick Maas **exec** Geels **camera** Marc Felperlaan **editor** Hans van Dongen **design** Dick Schillemans **music** Dick Maas **cast** Huub Stapel, Monique van de Ven, Hidde Maas, Serge-Henri Valcke
Running time: 105 mins
US release: Vestron, Nov 23, 1988
UK release: Vestron, Jul 14, 1989

AND GOD CREATED WOMAN

Roger Vadim returns to the scene of the crime, tamely remaking his 1957 shocker. But the brisk and un-sultry Rebecca DeMornay, pretty as she is, will make no one forget Brigitte Bardot. This time, the heroine is no tease, just a modern woman with a career - in this case, boringly, rock 'n' roll. As for the story, she begins as a jailbird paroled with the aid of a local politico (Langella) because she convinces a handy carpenter (Spano) to enter into a marriage of convenience. As for sex, she has it whenever the urge strikes, as a more conventional woman might blow her nose, and with as much apparent pleasure. **BM**
Director Roger Vadim **producers** George G. Braunstein, Ron Hamady **execs** Steven Reuther, Mitchell Cannold, Ruth Vitale **script** R. J. Stewart **camera** Stephen M. Katz **editor** Suzanne Pettit **design** Victor Kempster **music** Thomas Chase, Steve Rucker **cast** Rebecca DeMornay, Vincent Spano, Frank Langella, Donovan Leitch, Judith Chapman, Jaime McEnnan, Benjamin Mouton, David Shelley, Einstein Brown, David Lopez
Running time: 98 mins
US release: Vestron, Mar 4, 1988
UK release: Vestron, Aug 26, 1988

ANNA

The story of a former Czech movie star reduced to crummy stage auditions in New York turns from bittersweet to plain bitter as she rescues her only fan - a naïve creature with terrible teeth who's come across the ocean to see her - and the ugly duckling becomes a swan at her surrogate mother's expense. Sally Kirkland was Oscar-nominated for her bravura performance as the big, blonde, bruised heroine who sacrifices her self-worth and her boyfriend while her protégée (model Paulina Porizkova) becomes a spoiled brat. *Anna*, however, becomes sillier the longer it goes on, director Yurek Bogayevicz being unable to resist overblown homages to *A Star is Born* and *All About Eve*. Best bit - writer Agnieszka Holland at her most acerbic - has Kirkland watching one of her old movies in a rep house, only for the celluloid to crinkle up before her eyes. **GF**
Director Yurek Bogayevicz **producers** Bogayevicz, Zanne Devine **execs** Julianne Gilliam, Deirdre Gainor **script** Agnieszka Holland **camera** Bobby Bukowski **editor** Julie Sloane **design** Lester Cohen **cast** Sally Kirkland, Robert Fields, Paulina Porizkova, Gibby Brand, John Robert Tillotson, Joe Aufiery, Charles Randall, Mimi Wedell
Running time: 100 mins
US release: Vestron, Oct 30, 1987
UK release: Vestron, Aug 12, 1988

ANOTHER WOMAN

Woody Allen hits the psychodrama trail again. His third 'serious' film resembles a blind date between Ingmar Bergman and Anton Chekhov. An ageing university teacher Gena Rowlands has a mid-life crisis right there in front of us -- her marriage is on the rocks, her belief in reason and the intellect likewise - an army of stars rally round to cluck or comfort, including Gene Hackman, Mia Farrow, Sandy Dennis and John Houseman as Rowlands' dad. As with *Interiors* and *September*, the film is more like a sixth form essay on Great Art than an example of it. But at least the cast ensure some flammable moments, and it's quite short. **HK**
Director/script Woody Allen **producer** Robert Greenhut **execs** Jack Rollins, Charles H. Joffe **camera** Sven Nykvist **editor** Susan E. Morse **design** Santo Loquasto **cast** Gena Rowlands, Mia Farrow, Ian Holm, Blythe Danner, Gene Hackman, Betty Buckley, Martha Plimpton, John Houseman, Sandy Dennis, David Ogden Stiers, Philip Bosco, Harris Yulin, Frances Conroy
Running time: 84 mins
US release: Orion, Oct 14, 1988
UK release: Rank, Jul 28, 1989

ARTHUR 2 ON THE ROCKS

This sequel sabotages the comic potential in Dudley Moore's eponymous inebriate. Its tenuous narrative, masquerading as a series of moral parables, fails to recall any of the vitriol and candour which made the original amusing, and the film eventually dissolves into sentiment. Despite valiant efforts from newly-weds Liza Minnelli and Moore to inject a frisson of chaos into the proceedings, the sanctimonious script, while borrowing comic pratfalls and plot from *Arthur*, relies excessively upon the assumption that the audience can still derive amusement from seeing a middle-aged affluent pseudo-Cockney falling down. This time round, Arthur renounces his Peter Pan

piss-artist apparel, discards the bottle and settles
into benign sobriety. **MN**
Director *Bud Yorkin* **producer** *Robert Shapiro*
exec *Dudley Moore* **script** *Andy Breckman, based
on characters created by Steve Gordon* **camera**
Stephen H. Burum **editor** *Michael Kahn* **design**
Gene Callahan **music** *Burt Bacharach* **cast** *Dudley
Moore, Liza Minnelli, John Gielgud, Geraldine
Fitzgerald, Stephen Elliot, Paul Benedict, Cynthia
Sikes, Kathy Bates, Jack Gilford, Ted Bass*
Running time: 113 mins
US release: Warner, Jul 8, 1988
UK release: Warner, Feb 10, 1989

AU REVOIR, LES ENFANTS

Louis Malle drops a diving bell into his own
childhood in occupied France. Through the
shimmer of time, two haunting but hard-edged
characters emerge - Malle's own *alter ego*
(Manesse) and the Jewish boy (Fejtö), who
strives to conceal his religion from both his
ragging Catholic schoolmates and the Nazis. In
a school where the conflict between compassion
and dogma writes small the world's larger wars,
life tries to shelter from history - bravely but
vainly. 'Au revoir, les enfants' is the arrested
headmaster's farewell to his boys, and it's also
Malle's valediction to a generation's lost
innocence. Full of surreal shafts of memory -
stilt battles in the playground, prayer vigils in
the dormitory, wild boars roaming the woods -
Malle paints a yesterday full of pained rapport
with today: an artist's sensibility written in the
mirror of his boyhood. **HK**
Director/producer/script *Louis Malle* **camera**
Renato Berta **editor** *Emanuelle Castro* **design**
Willy Holt **cast** *Gaspard Manesse, Raphaël Fejtö,
Francine Racette, Stanislas Carré de Malberg,
Philippe Morier-Genoud, François Berleand, François
Negret, Peter Fitz*
Running time: 104 mins
US release: Orion Classics, Feb 12, 1988
UK release: Artificial Eye, Oct 7, 1988

THE ACCIDENTAL TOURIST

William Hurt is Macon Leary, a writer of travel guides for Americans who hate travelling. His books provide life-saving information such as the availability throughout Paris of McDonald's hamburgers, and contain the advice to 'always take a book as a protection against strangers.' Macon's own psyche can focus on detail so narrowly that he seems scarcely to register his beloved son's death, which goads his wife of 20 years, Sarah (Kathleen Turner), to divorce him.

Living alone, New Celibacy style, Macon devises ever more ingenious schemes of household management, unaware that he's heading for depressive squalor and terminal bachelorhood. He's saved from this fate by the bad behaviour of his son's corgi, now ageing and neurotic. At the Meow-Bow Animal Home, he encounters Muriel Pritchett (Geena Davis), a beautiful dog-trainer from the blue-collar classes – though 'blue collar' hardly reflects her wondrous appearance: pointy red shoes like a witch of Oz, white lace ankle-socks, a smoky-rainbow dress with fluffs, frills and shoulder-pads, and tubular plastic finger-nails. Macon winces and withdraws, but she promptly spots husband material, and moves from training his dog to training him; though more casually, considerately and subtly than her eyeball-shaking rig-out initially leads us to expect. When Macon's impeccable wife comes lumbering back to forgive and reorganize her obstinate 'ex', he faces a decision which must hurt somebody and could hurt everybody . . .

The Accidental Tourist, like Lawrence Kasdan's first film *Body Heat*, wrings enormous suspense from a topical, feminist-era, interaction: between a clever, but ultimately passive, male, and womanhood with heavyweight will. But *Body Heat*, like Kasdan's earlier screenplays (*Raiders of the Lost Ark* et al.), was genre stuff, thrilling us through the 'maximum' emotions and mayhem of melodrama. *Tourist*, however, depends on intimate, elusive feelings; that is to say, it's a straight drama which is indifferent to genre types and formulae and which counts on spectator recognition of serious real-life experience.

The film is pretty faithful to the original book, a sharply observant best-seller by Anne Tyler. The characters are simultaneously normal, reasonable, wayward and weird. Critical yet affectionate, and entirely non-moralistic, the film bristles with incisive surprises: about drift versus decision; about kindly/destructive feedback within families and friendships; about how little you feel your own mind, which runs less on motive than habit; about 'incidental details' versus decisive story points.

Alongside its jokes about human quirks and blind spots and hearts on automatic, *Tourist* generates obsessive suspense: that Macon choose the right woman, and for the right reason. It's a 'bourgeois domestic drama', and though Marxists sneer at that, films like *Marty* (written by Communist Paddy Chayefsky, as it happens) extended it to the blue-collar and work-aproned classes. The 'classic' Hollywood 'comedy of manners' also had serious moments, notably the warm and mellow playing of Katharine Hepburn and Spencer Tracy, and stretched to serious, indeed sarcastic, dramas like *All About Eve*. King Vidor's *The Crowd* and George Cukor's *The Marrying Kind* both turned on the marriage-shattering death of a child, which is *Tourist*'s starting-point too. But it's a more reflective, sombre and cool film; at once comedy and, not melodrama, but mellow drama.

The dramatic comedies of 'classical' Hollywood adapted to 1970s permissiveness via such films as *The Owl and the Pussycat*. Although *Tourist* doesn't spell out Muriel's wild oats youth, a sub-theme in the novel, her gaudy clothes-sense opens the possibility, and its non-discussion *is* an attitude. As in Neil Simon's film, the big obstacle to their romance is not the lady's tramp past, but her loud taste. Both films set a fastidious writer with middlebrow taste against a sloppy-grammar woman with ghastly-glorious taste. The obstacle to their happiness is that very subtle form of snobbery – the discomfort of the educated with lower-class norms.

Through the 1970s, dramatic comedies stressed sexual changes, like wife-swapping in *Bob and Carol and Ted and Alice* and melancholic love-lines in *Carnal Knowledge*. But *Tourist* is 'post-permissive': everyone feels sexually competent and free, and has other criteria on their mind. Moreover, comedies of sexual style got eclipsed by teenage tastes, which ran to *bad*, in fact gross-out, manners, like the-prick-in-a-popcorn-pack in *Diner*. All this rather eclipsed dramas of quieter, finer feeling. But latterly TV/cable/homevideo has reshaped the market, restoring a *thirtysomething* agenda, to which *Tourist* works. The new topics range from mid-life crises, remarriage and step-parenting, to the strange relations between marriage and lifetime-friendship networks.

William Hurt achieves a fascinating variation on his 'type', a quiet man negotiating, with sensitive hesitations, our era of quiche-eating, macho-fearing emasculation. Geena Davis's eclectic costuming merits an Oscarette; its taste is so bad that it's ultra-good. You could study her outfits for ever; Eisenstein would call them a montage of shocks. Davis's on-the-button scattiness reminded me of the young Shirley MacLaine, though where MacLaine was a romantic innocent, Davis, befitting the hard-bitten 1980s, is crisply alert, deceptively blank. (She's much too good for *Earth Girls are Easy*-type rôles, and Woody Allen should check her out as a sparring partner.) Kathleen Turner is subtly ominous as Sarah, and it's a virtue of the film that it's quite hard to work out why. For Sarah's behaviour is impeccable, her aggressive-constructive discontent with Macon's psyche is entirely justified, her corrective strategies are courageous, correct and considerate. If anything, Muriel is the more scheming and demanding, pulling her man in from the happy-go-lucky that he thought was all he could bear, to the

heavy-duty follow-through she always had in mind. Yet we're on tenterhooks for him to choose the aggressive, downmarket woman as his wife.

I think it's to do with how the two women handle the injustice of the world. Sarah's perfectionistic soul gets pole-axed, Muriel is matter-of-fact. Also, Sarah severely discusses her hubby's psyche, while Muriel, less educated and therefore less prying, leaves it be. Sarah goes with the received wisdom, of Dr Ruth and Brand X feminists, that men should constantly chatter and gossip about their 'real' feelings, and cry a lot: whereas Muriel's *apparent* superficiality is closer to *Tourist*'s fatalism about how little understanding life holds.

In common with *The Hotel New Hampshire* and *The Mosquito Coast* this film also re-explores father-family relationships. All three films hint that some archaic family forms may actually be reappearing. For before the 'classic' nuclear couple with its one to three kids, large families were like mini-tribes, much more 'roughly' related. And serial monogamy (successive divorces) can go that way too. Each partner half-takes-over the other's children; the children, too, accept or reject the step-parent; and nobody really commits themselves beyond this particular life-phase. The three films ponder upon families as untidy, amorphous communities with strange customs (like dumping on certain members, admitting odd outsiders, accepting a new son as a 'replacement' for a lost son despite every difference in their individual characters).

But *Tourist* spells out no motives and points to no moral. It's pure Story. It juxtaposes rich detail with untidy patterns. For example, outgoing Muriel has the sickly son, and soul-crushing Sarah has the happily robust one. The more one reflects on the film, the more oddities and paradoxes appear. Avid for more information, I rushed to read the novel, and though it fills out many angles, it takes equal care to nail nothing down, to respect the pattern-unmaking flow of life. Unusually, film and novel connect pretty well, into a 'multi-media' slice of life. The film's omissions spring not from lesser sophistication, but from the feature film time limitations. Perhaps Kasdan's residual genre-habits do narrow the novel a little: although retaining Macon's brothers and sisters, it omits Muriel's entourage, thus weakening his discovery of lower-class gregariousness. Still, it further expands Hollywood's rediscovery of lower-class lifestyles, and of a rarely-seen slice of America's middle classes – the quiet, melancholic, reclusive people, who contentedly dwell in dark brown homes, making me think sometimes of *Lake Wobegon Days*, Garrison Keillor's sadder (and even better-selling) evocation of another old-fangled, backwaterish, 'woe-begone' America.

I hate to praise a film for being 'civilized', a term suggesting the pulseless gloss of Merchant-Ivory; while Truffaut, so famous for being gentle, generous and sensitive, often rounds things off with shotguns. So let's just say that where Truffaut leaves off, *The Accidental Tourist* begins.

RAYMOND DURGNAT

THE ADVENTURES OF BARON MUNCHAUSEN

Terry Gilliam's lavish opus (allegedly the costliest European movie ever made) is so marvellous and monstrous one hardly knows whether to call it the climax of the lunar year, or the roast duck of the decade. Or both. It works the most fascinating, and tricky, kind of fantasy; the sort that asks you to believe six impossible things before breakfast. The improbable Baron climbs up the crescent moon, like a mountaineer tackling an overhang. A set of stars drift by. It must be Pisces, since they're joined by dotted lines outlining a fish. The result is something completely different from fantasy of the *Star Wars* kind. *Star Wars* is *realistic*, in the sense that, although these space-fleets and alien planets don't exist, they're as plausible as if they did. Down to the last nut and bolt and grain of desert sand, they obey the laws of nature. Whereas Munchausen cliff-hanging in space, with dotted lines floating by, couldn't conceivably do so. And that's the charm: ladies and gentlemen, lo and behold, before your very eyes, the Blatantly Impossible-and-Inconceivable?

Although the cinema is often supposed to be a realistic art, such fancy-free fun has a long tradition behind it. In 1912, a George Méliès strato-coach chugged past constellations shaped like their names. Half the delight of Disney's Dumbo is the very idea of a flying elephant, who ascends by flapping his ears. *Who Framed Roger Rabbit* added the refinement of the Toons' super-feats obeying 'logical' rules, e.g. they can break the laws of physics only when it's funny. And weird visual 'logics' rule Gilliam's *Monty Python* animations.

As for serious literature, its nonsense tradition goes back for ever: via *Alice in Wonderland* (which revels in logical contradiction, like a smile without a face), the Munchausen tales (various German authors, 1785—1839), Dean Swift (unexpurgated versions) and Rabelais (would you believe tripe-induced indigestion making a giantess give birth through one ear?). Such ideas, even when satirically intended, liberate our soul and refresh our spirit, for they illuminate the incredibility of the world, and the naughtiness of our imagination.

Back in the eighteenth century, the old Baron probably personified a baroque heroic, pulling the leg on the Age of Reason. That's not so far from Gilliam's conception of the old boy (John Neville) as a sort of Colonel Blimp, or Sergeant Pepper, defying the rational view that 'only facts count'. His deadliest enemy is neither the tricephalic flying griffin, nor the Islamic torture-organ which plays symphonic music in human squeals; it's the rational, therefore cynical, therefore treacherous, therefore evil, Austrian ruler (Jonathan Pryce), whose city the prodigious feats of the chivalrous Baron save. So this is a tale of bureaucracy-as-tyranny, like *Brazil*, but with more comic outreach, like *Time Bandits*. Perhaps the three films together make a trilogy, about Everyman's right to personal visions, beliefs and projects, irrespective of consensus rules. At any rate, Gilliam's Munchausen, far from being a liar or leg-puller, waxes with honest wrath when a theatrical company, enacting his life, gets it wrong through mediocrity of spirit.

Gilliam's theatre/film/flashback format triggers games galore with changes of media and kinks in chronology. Often several entities are telescoped together, by a sort of visual punnery and slippage. To start with a simple example (well, simple once Gilliam has invented it and worked it out): the basket under the Baron's hot-air balloon combines features from a Venetian gondola, a galleon in full sail and an ornate dragon; you can't take it all in at a glance and you're beguiled into reading and re-reading it. A more abstruse example is the executioner who wears a blindfold while going about his head-chopping chores. Why a blindfold? Well, the figure of Justice, swords and scales in hand, wears one to prove her impartiality. On the executioner, however, it reminds us how justice is mostly fumble and blunder.

When the Queen of the Moon (Valentina Cortesa) decides to free the Baron and his friends from prison, the problem is that she consists only of her head; so how to turn the key in the lock? Answer: she clenches the key in her teeth and spins her head around, like a planet. It's as strange as anything in Tex Avery's most way-out opus, *The Cat That Hated People* (another moon trip). But Gilliam's live-action, mega-budget, state-of-the-art special effects contribute such vivid detail and solid weight that, where Avery's fine cartoon remains notional, this becomes hallucinatory, and qualifies as a see-it-on-acid cult show, like *2001*.

That whole sequence, with heads flying off to think thoughts of Godlike detachment (and megalomania), while bodies remain below, to fornicate untroubled by thought, is Pure Cinema: the psychological made visible. As for the film's visuals, their pictorial quotes should float a thousand theses. Gilliam acknowledges Doré, Bernini, Bellotto, the Villa d'Este and an anonymous Renaissance engraving that shows Death stealing a dying man's breath (soul). The spectacle almost eclipses the stars, even John Neville, that grand old stage-swaggerer too rarely unleashed on screen, and 'Ray D. Tutto', alias Robin Williams, whose agent forbade him to put his name to so freaky a feature.

Maybe there's a moral slant, running roughly thisaways. Munchausen and his gang of grand old buffers are Super-heroes, but of an Olde Worlde kind, marooned in an age of fact and reason, much like ours. The Baron and his loyal retainers, for all their semi-feudal set-up, represent man's finest spirit — a never-say-die, rough-and-ready, bonding together. Since they have no pretensions to an intellectual understanding of the Universe, the strangest states of affairs seem all in a day's work to them, whereas modern, pseudo-democratic man, cowed by narrow reason and bureaucratic routine, hardly believes in his ordinary self, let alone surpassing himself. So, in this Reign of 'Reason', things are forever falling apart: Vulcan's volcano-stokers are out on strike; heads and bodies drift into eccentrissimo orbits; Turkish army Ayatollahs bellow at the gates of Western Europe. Only Munchausen and his retainers, with their simple panache and pragmatism, keep civilization together — just. Of the younger generation, only an Alice-like girl, surnamed Salt (a pinch of?) understands what the old guard are about, and how to help . . .

Spectacular and poetic as this film's circumference may be, its centre has a hollow sound. Already *Brazil* rang faintly tinny; though I loved every moment, my showbiz companion detested it, for 'Too many explosions!'; and that's true too. The typical Gilliam transition is to blow things up, not tie them together. Whereas a scriptwise rule-of-thumb is that, the more brilliantly strange an idea is, the more it needs familiar, everyday, sober thoughts woven in (which is where the *Alice* books are so wonderful). At least *Brazil* evoked 'the way we live now'; what with police snatch-squads, post-Recession seediness, the *1984* syndrome, IRA bombs, Wimpy-type menus in luxury hotels, irate waiters, etc. But here eighteenth-century life remains remote and thin. The characters are one-note wonders, matchstick-men one can't much identify with. The story does tackle some modern topics (as when the world's strongest man renounces machismo and becomes sensitive instead; result, he's no use to anybody), but fitfully and few. Maybe Gilliam needs a co-writer of Ye Olde Schole, a believer in strict storylines and tightly-bunched themes, who will keep tapping him on the head with a hard-lead pencil, repeating 'Stick to the point, Young Gilliam!' Gilliam's imagination is so fertile and ingenious that it needn't cramp his style.

Still, if this film's centre goes slightly awry, its surface is a summit meeting. Up here, Georges Méliès meets Monty Python meets Cecil B. de Mille meets Peter Greenaway meets Dick Lester meets the male answer to Mary Poppins . . .

RAYMOND DURGNAT

BACKFIRE

Trawling the dregs of the traumatized-Vietnam vet genre, *Backfire* struggles vainly with its pretentious *noir* narrative: an unfaithful wife (Allen) schemes to drive her ex-soldier husband (Fahey) to suicide, only to get her comeuppance from a ghostly figure out of her intended victim's ghoulish past. Gilbert Cates, clearly more at home with social-issue TV specials, moves the narrative along with pedantic caution and, for the first half hour, the continually bulging eyeballs of the set-upon husband are the only startling element. The arrival of Keith Carradine, looking as if he had just wandered off an Alan Rudolph set, sparks things up with vague, unresolved hints of the supernatural. But *Backfire* short-circuits any suspense by signalling its narrative direction too quickly: the showers of blood and a collection of eye-balls in the bed linen are ludicrous rather than disturbing. **SD**
Director Gilbert Cates *producer* Danton Rissner *script* Larry Brand, Rebecca Reynolds *camera* Tak Fujimoto *editor* Melvin Shapiro *design* Daniel Lomino *music* David Shire *cast* Karen Allen, Keith Carradine, Jeff Fahey, Bernie Casey, Dean Paul Martin, Virginia Capers, Philip Sterling
Running time: 91 mins
UK release: Virgin, Sep 30, 1988

BAGDAD CAFE (Out of Rosenheim)

Percy Adlon goes to America and, following the hilarious and humane spirit of *Zuckerbaby*, shows us more of society's loose ends coming together. A large German lady tourist (the irrepressible Marianne Sägebrecht) is dropped by her husband at a rundown motel and slowly integrates herself, using her magic set, with its tough black owner and her family. Cultural peculiarities are matched by Adlon's playful use of colour, and Jack Palance's unexpected return to the screen is a gentle reminder of how the mythology of the New World is being recast here. **DT**
Director Percy Adlon *producers/script* Percy Adlon, Eleonore Adlon *camera* Bernd Heinl *editor* Norbert Herzner *design* Bernt Amadeus Capra *music* Bob Telson *cast* Marianne Sägebrecht, C.C.H. Pounder, Jack Palance, Christine Kaufman, Monica Calhoun
Running time: 91 mins
US release: Island, Apr 22, 1988
UK release: Mainline, Oct 7, 1988

BANDITS (Attention Bandits)

A girl is sent to a classy Swiss school when her father (Yanne) is imprisoned for a jewel robbery he didn't commit. She grows into a refined lady (Marie-Sophie L.), but how will she react when she discovers the truth about her Pa? Will she perhaps discover a darker side of herself? Of course she will. The charms of a young bandit (Bruel) draw her away from a dull fiancé and towards a criminal milieu. But she can't decide which man to choose until Bruel's act of implausible derring-do shows her the way. *Bandits'* air of contrivance reflects a sense of discomfort with its dubious morality. It's also one of those films where the camera's eye roves only in one direction - director and star were married shortly after filming. **JP**
Director/producer Claude Lelouch *script* Lelouch, Pierre Uytterhoeven *camera* Jean-Yves Le Mener *editor* Hugues Darmois *design* Jacques Bufnoir *music* Francis Lai *cast* Jean Yanne, Marie-Sophie L., Patrick Bruel, Charles Gérard, Corinne Marchand, Christine Barbelivien
Running time: 108 mins
US release: Grange, Aug 24, 1988

BAT 21

An atypical perspective on the Vietnam war, based on a true story, is here rendered formulaic by Peter Markle's direction. A perplexingly passive Gene Hackman is a top-level war strategist shot down over Viet Cong territory during a surveillance mission. As a spotter-plane pilot (Glover) attempts to guide him to safety, the physical reality of war is brought home to the golf-addicted colonel in several scenes where he witnesses the consequences of human slaughter which he has initiated. But despite the obvious intentions of such a narrative device, the film only seems interested in following Hackman back through the jungle. The deaths of a helicopter crew who try to rescue him are treated more as an attempt to inject pace into a flagging narrative than as an integral part of Hackman's re-education in the human cost of hi-tech warfare. **SD**
Director Peter Markle *producers* David Fisher, Gary A. Neill, Michael Balson *exec* Jerry Reed *script* William C. Anderson, George Gordon, based on Anderson's book *camera* Mark Irwin *editor* Stephen E. Rivkin *design* Vincent Cresciman *music* Christopher Young *cast*

B

Gene Hackman, Danny Glover, Jerry Reed, David Marshall Grant, Clayton Rohner, Erich Anderson, Joe Dorsey
Running time: 105 mins
US release: Tri-Star, Oct 21,1988
UK release: Guild, Dec 9, 1988

FILM

BATMAN

Director *Tim Burton* **producers** *Jon Peters, Peter Guber* **execs** *Benjamin Melniker, Michael Uslan* **script** *Sam Hamm, Warren Skaaren, from story by Sam Hamm based on character created by Bob Kane* **camera** *Roger Pratt* **editor** *Ray Lovejoy* **design** *Anton Furst* **sfx** *Derek Meddings, John Evans* **music** *Danny Elfman* **cast** *Jack Nicholson, Michael Keaton, Kim Basinger, Robert Wuhl, Pat Hingle, Billy Dee Williams, Michael Gough, Jerry Hall, Jack Palance*
Running time: 126 mins
US release: Warner, Jun 23, 1989
UK release: Warner, Aug 11, 1989

BEACHES

Bette Midler, a successful singer, is summoned from the Hollywood Bowl to the San Francisco bedside of millionairess Barbara Hershey and flashes back over their 30-year friendship. *Beaches* gives the lie to admirers of 1940s heartstring-tuggers like *Old Acquaintances* or *Mr Skeffington*, who claim they don't make 'em like this any more. Midler is more often given to singing comic songs about brassières than were Bette Davis or Greer Garson, but her character is given just as many chances to have emotional crises, overcome her innate selfishness and put down a succession of foils with waspish remarks. And Hershey, fresh from a series of silicone implants that have done a Doreen Gray trick to her face, models tasteful high fashions, swings her gorgeous hair and gets to die with dignity. The film's concept of a deathless friendship between women is rather less substantially treated by this mainstream production than it might have been by a small-scale independent. But the bravura performances are undeniably watchable even during the fade-away-and-die finale, and the early comic stretches - particularly the sequence starring Mayim Bialik as the eleven-year-old Midler - are refreshingly breezy. **KN**
Director *Garry Marshall* **producers** *Bonnie Bruckheimer-Martell, Bette Midler, Margaret Jennings South* **exec** *Teri Schwartz* **script** *Mary*

Agnes Donoghue, from novel by Rainer Dart* **camera** *Dante Spinotti* **editor** *Richard Halsey* **design** *Albert Brenner* **music** *Georges Delerue* **cast** *Bette Midler, Barbara Hershey, John Heard, Spalding Gray, Lainie Kazan, James Read, Grace Johnston, Mayim Bialik, Marcie Leeds*
Running time: 123 mins
US release: BV, Dec 21, 1988
UK release: Warner, May 26, 1989

THE BEAST

Undaunted by history or *Rambo III*, Hollywood still fights the war in Afghanistan. This time we join a tankful of beleaguered Russkies aiming a last salvo of gung-ho at the Mujaheddin. Although the khaki-clad young Russians want to retreat gracefully, their leader (Dzundza) is a bull-headed psycho who sees red rags through every gunsight. As the tank sails through the desert, the movie thunders on through plot and character clichés normally reserved for B-Westerns. Director Kevin Reynolds, whose *Fandango* for Spielberg was a promising début, has shown that he can and, hopefully, will do better next time out. Meanwhile, put that tank in mothballs. **HK**
Director *Kevin Reynolds* **producer** *John Fiedler* **execs** *Gil Friesen, Dale Pollock* **script** *William Mastrosimone, from his play* Nanawatai **camera** *Douglas Milsome* **editor** *Peter Boyle* **design** *Kuli Sander* **music** *Mark Isham* **cast** *George Dzundza, Jason Patric, Steven Bauer, Stephen Baldwin, Don Harvey, Kabir Bedi, Erick Avari, Shosh Marciano*
Running time: 109 mins
US release: Columbia, Sep 16, 1988

THE BEDROOM WINDOW

Curtis Hanson fashions a pedestrian and unconvincing thriller out of potentially intriguing material with this story of the lover of a married woman who claims to witness an assault she actually saw. Steve Guttenberg's hysterical predicament is blandly presented, as he struggles to escape the repercussions of a relationship with his boss's wife while bringing the murderous attacker to justice. If Hitchcock is the off-screen influence, as the film's title suggests, the narrative leaves little room for the kind of tortured character motivation Hitch might have overlayed on such a project. The absurd conclusion, as Guttenberg rushes to the rescue in a stolen police car, seems to have slipped in from a *Police Academy* sequel, leaving a half-developed idea stranded amidst the detritus of a stolidly-formulaic action movie. **SD**

B

Director/script Curtis Hanson **producer** Martha
Schumacher **exec** Robert Towne **camera** Gil
Taylor **editor** Scott Conrad **design** Ron Foreman
music Michael Shrieve, Patrick Gleeson **cast** Steve
Guttenberg, Elizabeth McGovern, Isabelle Huppert,
Paul Shenar, Frederick Coffin, Carl Lumbly,
Wallace Shawn, Brad Greenquist
Running time: 113 mins
US release: DEG, Jan 16, 1987
UK release: Fox, Dec 2, 1988

BEETLEJUICE

Like a two-hour reel of cartoons, *Beetlejuice* has
just too much novelty. A comic ghost story
from the ghosts' point of view, Tim Burton's
film rivals Joe Dante for hyperactivity and over-
plottedness. Alec Baldwin and Geena Davis go
off a bridge and into a hellish after-life in
which their dream home is occupied by Jeffrey
Jones' unsuitable family. Trapped in the house,
these ghosts turn out to be ineffective
poltergeists. Death's bureaucracy forces them to
call in corpse-like, bug-eating freelance bio-
exorciser Michael Keaton. He gets big laughs
but his rôle is too small to save the film from
bittiness. **BM**
Director Tim Burton **producers** Michael Bender,
Larry Wilson, Richard Hashimoto **script** Michael
McDowell, Warren Skaaren **camera** Thomas
Ackerman **editor** Jane Kurson **design** Bo Welch
music Dammu Elfman **cast** Alec Baldwin, Geena
Davis, Michael Keaton, Catherine O'Hara, Glenn
Shadix, Winona Ryder, Jeffrey Jones, Sylvia Sidney,
Annie McEnroe, Maurice Page, Hugo Stanger
Running time: 92 mins
US release: Warner, Mar 30, 1988
UK release: Warner, Aug 19, 1988

THE BELLY OF AN ARCHITECT

Another brain-teaser from Peter Greenaway.
Architect Brian Dennehy hurtles into Italy to
fulfil a top commission and finds death and
destiny waiting to meet him. While his wife's
belly grows big with child - but not his child
his own grows big with cancer. In 40-carat
images and dialogue, he rages at the dying of
light, the faithless spouse (Webb) and a Rome
where all roads lead to tragic irony. In a world
of false perspectives and gleaming perceptions,
Greenaway the game-player becomes
Greenaway the visionary. He's aided by Sacha
Vierny's photography and by a Rome whose
vast, decaying grandeur is mirror and metaphor
for Dennehy's own. **HK**
Director/script Peter Greenaway **producers** Colin

Callender, Walter Donohue **execs** Roberto Levi,
Claudio Biondi **camera** Sacha Vierny **editor** John
Wilson **design** Luciana Vedovelli **music** Wim
Mertens **cast** Brian Dennehy, Chloe Webb,
Lambert Wilson, Sergio Fantoni, Stefania Casini,
Vanni Corbellini, Alfredo Varelli, Geoffrey
Copleston, Francesco Carnelutti, Marion Mase,
Marne Maitland, Claudio Spadaro
Running time: 118 mins
US release: Hemdale, Apr 7, 1989
UK release: Recorded Releasing, Oct 16, 1987

BERT RIGBY, YOU'RE A FOOL 👎

Musical miner Bert Rigby wins a local talent
contest and is whisked to Hollywood, where he
becomes a star and dreams of restoring his
recession-hit northern home town to full
employment. Yes, it's a musical, and it's
embarrassing. While Robert Lindsay has talent
to spare, he seems miscast and self-conscious
throughout, and is ill-served by Reiner's
tendency to restage dance numbers from MGM
musicals, thus drawing attention to the film's
lack of originality. **TW**
Director/script Carl Reiner **producer** George
Shapiro **camera** Jan de Bont **editor** Bud Molin
design Terence ·Marsh **music** Ralph Burns **cast**
Robert Lindsay, Cathryn Bradshaw, Robbie
Coltrane, Anne Bancroft, Corbin Bernsen, Jackie
Gayle, Liberty Mounten
Running time: 94 mins
US release: Warner Feb 24, 1989

BETRAYED 👍

Echoing *Mississippi Burning* as it follows FBI
investigations into a bunch of violent, right-
wing fanatics in rural America, *Betrayed* deals
with a 1980s situation (its plot trigger, the
murder of a Chicago radio personality, was also
the inspiration for Oliver Stone's *Talk Radio*),
and delves into the erosion of traditional values
that has led to a resurgence of grass-roots
fascism in the US. The opening sequences, set
amidst cornfields and agrarian decline, ally it
almost with the cycle of disadvantaged farmer
films. (*The River, Country*) of the mid-1980s, and
show how the downtrodden poor whites are
turning to increasingly bizarre and unpleasant
forms of resistance. With a plotline vaguely
spun off from Hitchcock's *Notorious*, Debra
Winger is an undercover agent, manipulated by
her sharp superior (John Heard in the Cary
Grant role) into spying on the family-man
cowboy (Berenger) she has fallen in love with,
and whose involvement in a right-wing

assassination conspiracy she gradually uncovers. The film works best in evoking the folksy horror of an idyllic Klan holiday camp-cum-guerrilla training centre where the folks sing traditional songs around the camp-fire and learn the techniques of armed insurrection, or the scene in which Berenger's angelic daughter starts parroting the paranoid racist drivel she has been indoctrinated with since birth. **KN**
Director Constantin Costa-Gavras **producer** Irwin Winkler **execs** Joe Eszterhas, Hal W. Polaire **script** Eszterhas **camera** Patrick Blossier **editor** Joële Van Effenterre **design** Patrizia von Brandenstein **music** Bill Conti **cast** Debra Winger, Tom Berenger, John Heard, Betsy Blair, John Mahoney, Ted Levine, Jeffrey DeMunn, Albert Hall, David Clennon, Robert Swan, Richard Libertini, Maria Valdez, Brian Bosak
Running time: 127 mins
US release: UA, Aug 26, 1988
UK release: UIP, Apr 28, 1989

BIG

No, Big isn't exactly the same movie as Like Father, Like Son or Vice Versa, in each of which a father and son switch consciousnesses. Big is about a boy who wishes he were big and gets his wish. Waking up the next morning as 30-year-old Tom Hanks, he embarks on a stunning career as a toy industry mogul. He finds love in the person of Elizabeth Perkins, a former steely executive melted by his genuinely boyish charm. Eventually, though, maturity palls and he wishes he were little again. He duly shrinks and Perkins is left with memories of the future. Hanks' playful absorption in the part, and a plot device which doesn't entail following parallel stories, helped make this the most gripping (and successful) of the infant-adult inversion tales. **BM**
Director Penny Marshall **producers** James L. Brooks, Robert Greenhut **script** Gary Ross **camera** Barry Sonnenfeld **editor** Barry Malkin **design** Santo Loquasto **music** Howard Shore **cast** Tom Hanks, Elizabeth Perkins, John Heard, Jared Rushton, Robert Loggia, David Moscow
Running time: 104 mins
US release: Fox, Jun 7, 1988
UK release: Fox, Nov 21, 1988

FRENCH HIT

THE BIG BLUE

Director Luc Besson **producer** Patrice Ledoux **script** Besson, Robert Garland, Marilyn Goldin,

Jacques Mayol, Marc Perrier **camera** Carlo Varini **editor** Olivier Mauffroy **design** Dan Weil **music** Eric Serra, Bill Conti (US) **cast** Rosanna Arquette, Jean-Marc Barr, Jean Reno, Paul Shenar, Sergio Castellitto, Jean Bouise, Marc Duret, Griffin Dunne, Andreas Voutsinas, Valentina Vargas, Kimberley Beck, Patrick Fontana, Alessandra Vazzoler, Geoffroy Carey, Bruce Guerre-Berthelot, Gregory Forstner
Running time: 119 mins (100 in US)
US release: Weintraub, Aug 19, 1988
UK release: Fox, Feb 24, 1989

BIG BUSINESS

With its premise copied exactly from Start the Revolution without Me, (two sets of twins from different social backgrounds are mixed up at birth and meet as adults) and one major comic sequence lifted from Duck Soup, Big Business hardly wins any awards for originality. However, it compounds the unpromising premise by casting Bette Midler and Lily Tomlin in multiple rôles, when one of each (or even one of either) would be quite enough, indeed probably too much, for any film. Midler is wont to overwhelm Tomlin in either of her incarnations but isn't given enough good material to make the effort of differentiating the ruthless businesswoman from the yodelling Southern naïf. The major problem is that all concerned are obviously more concerned with the invisible effects trickery and very visible devices necessary to keep the farcical plot going far beyond the point where its basic joke has been run into the ground than in any attempt at genuine character comedy. **KN**
Director Jim Abrahams **producers** Steve Tisch, Michael Peyser **script** Dori Pierson, Marc Rubel **camera** Dean Cundey **editor** Harry Keramidas **design** William Sandell **music** Lee Holdridge **cast** Bette Midler, Lily Tomlin, Fred Ward, Edward Herrmann, Michele Placido, Daniel Gerroll, Barry Primus, Michael Gross, Deborah Rush, Nicolas Coster, Patricia Gaul, J.C. Quinn, Norma Macmillan, Joe Grifasi, John Vickery
Running time: 98 mins
US release: BV, Jun 10, 1988
UK release: Touchstone/Warner, Aug 26, 1988

BIG TIME

This eclectic docu-cocktail distillation of Tom Waits's live show is saved from tedium by minimalistic stage-set, noirish lighting and Waits's own theatrical gesticulations.. Mercifully bereft of the pomposity and self-aggrandizement of many video rock shows, Waits's kinetic visual cabaret succeeds by virtue of its own self-imposed restrictions (no visual concessions to audience adulation). Chris Blum's direction encapsulates the nicotine-ridden, emotionally-undernourished, morally-ambiguous Waits persona, as he chants solipsistic mantras of spiritual disillusion at a solitary keyboard, or participates in vaudevillian banter with the audience and lures more disciples from the valley of the world-weary and the broken hearted. **MN**

Director Chris Blum **producer** Luc Roeg **exec** Chris Blackwell **script** Tom Waits, Kathleen Brennan **camera** Daniel Hainey **editor** Glenn Scatlebury **design** Sterlin Storm, Blum **music** Waits, Brennan **cast** Waits, Michael Blair, Ralph Carney, Greg Cohen, Marc Ribot, William Schwarz
Running time: 90 mins
US release: Island, Sep 30, 1988

BIG TOP PEE-WEE

Nostalgia, nonsense and narrative collude to create a spirited sequel to the permanently childlike Paul Reubens' 1985 sleeper hit *Pee Wee's Big Adventure*. Although likeable and funny enough in its own perverse way, the film does lack the subtleties of the original. Sight-gags and circus jokes abound as Pee Wee's experiments on a farm, complete with amiable talking pig and hot-dog tree, are interrupted by a stranded circus whose entourage includes owner Kris Kristofferson and his pocket-sized wife (Tyrrell), a gallery of freaks (notably a moustachioed hermaphrodite) and an exotic trapeze artist (Golino) as love interest. The latter's impending romance with Pee Wee propels the movie, briefly, into maturity, since he has previously been romancing pretty Penelope Ann Miller. Lightning strikes twice in this divertingly-surreal, idiosyncratic romp through Reubens' meticulously sculptured universe. **MN**

Director Randal Kleiser **producers** Paul Reubens, Debra Hill **execs** William E. McEuen, Richard Gilbert Abramson **script** Reubens, George McGrath **camera** Stephen Poster **editor** Jeff Gourson **design** Stephen Marsh **music** Danny Elfman **cast** Reubens, Kris Kristofferson, Valeria Golino, Penelope Ann Miller, Susan Tyrrell, Albert Henderson, Jack Murdock, David Byrd, Mary Jackson, Frances Bay
Running time: 86 mins
US release: Paramount, Jul 22, 1988

BILL AND TED'S EXCELLENT ADVENTURE

Bill and Ted are not very smart students. They are flunking history but have enough smarts to use a phone booth as a time machine so they can shoot back to the past and get the real lowdown. And like, guess what? They get threatened with the Iron Maiden (what do you mean you guessed the joke?), join up with Joan of Arc's aerobics class and live it up with swingin' Abe Lincoln who advises them to 'Party on, dudes!' Honest, I'm not making it up. Alex Winter behaves like a man in serious need of a lobotomy, Keanu Reeves like someone who's just had one, and the whole affair is so witlessly executed that it barely makes it as a bad movie. Nothing more than a brain-dead *Back to the Future* rip-off, the film sat on the distributor's shelf gathering dust until the writers' strike left a gap in the schedules. It promptly cleaned up at the box office. I have seen the future of American cinema, and it's a downer, man. **TW**

Director Stephen Herek **producers** Scott Kroopf, Michael S. Murphey, Joel Soisson **execs** Ted Field, Robert W. Cort **script** Chris Matheson, Ed Solomon **camera** Timothy Suhrstedt **editor** Larry Bock, Patrick Rand **design** Ray Forge Smith **music** David Newman **cast** Keanu Reeves, Alex Winter, George Carlin, Terry Camilleri, Dan Shor, Tony Steedman, Rod Loomis, Al Leong, Jane Wiedlin, Robert V. Barron, Clifford Davis, Hal London Jr.
Running time: 90 mins
US release: Orion, Feb 17, 1989

BILOXI BLUES

Number two in Neil Simon's autobiographical play trilogy reaches the screen. Under Mike Nichols' direction, this one is 'opened up' more than was *Brighton Beach Memoirs*, but its tale of cadet-training days in Boot Camp still seems all mouth and little movement, with lots of dorm mirth and rites-of-passage moralizing. Matthew Broderick is the Neil Simon *alter ego*, negotiating ethnic tensions, japes in the dorm and the hurdles of a stagey script; but Christopher Walken steals the film as a flaky psycho of a sergeant. **HK**

Director Mike Nichols **producer** Ray Stark **execs** Joseph M. Carraciolo, Marykay Powell **script** Neil Simon, from his play **camera** Bill Butler **editor** Stam O'Steen **design** Paul Sylbert **music** Georges Delerue **cast** Matthew Broderick, Christopher Walken, Matt Mulhern, Corey Parker, Markus Flanagan, Casey Siemaszko
Running time: 107 mins

US release: Universal, Mar 25, 1988
UK release: UIP, Sep 9, 1988

BIRD

The story of bebop inventor Charlie Parker, Clint Eastwood's Bird is a giddy, maze-like and ineffably bittersweet melodrama about the self-flaying sax-player, in subject and structure the most complex film its director has attempted. Counterpointing Parker's gorgeous solos with his booze and heroin-racked disintegration, the movie drifts endlessly through a subterranean murk of cellar clubs and rain-slicked nightmare alleys. It's drenched in film noir, and the romantic fatalism of Forest Whitaker's hunched and heavy Bird is therefore thoroughly appropriate. But when Eastwood cuts from Parker on stage to him tormenting his wife Chan (Diane Venora) a decade later, or sends the camera on an extended hand-held solo down 52nd Street, it becomes apparent that his moody nocturne is boldly marrying narrative structure to musical form. The remastered Parker riffs on the soundtrack are a triumph of new technology .over old vinyl. **GF**
Director/producer Clint Eastwood *exec* David Valdes *script* Joel Oliansky *camera* Jack N. Green *editor* Joel Cox *design* Edward C. Carfagno *music* Various *cast* Forest Whitaker, Diane Venora, Michael Zelniker, Samuel E. Wright, Keith David, Michael McGuire, James Handy, Damon Whitaker, Morgan Nagler, Arlen T. Snyder, Sam Robards
Running time: 160 mins
US release: Warner, Sep 30, 1988
UK release: Warner, Nov 25, 1988

BLACK EAGLE

There's a F-111 fighter plane with a top secret laser plus a state-of-the-art microchip on the bottom of the Mediterranean, and the CIA wants Sho Kosugi, the top undersea material artist, to recover the lot. However, this happens to be the two months of the year that Ken insists on spending with his cute Japanese-American children and the only way the CIA can deploy him is to airlift said moppets to Malta for a holiday. While Ken is sky-diving, hang-gliding, sub-aqua swimming and kung-fu fighting all over the island, his kids get taken on tours of all the museums. At long last, the baddies think of endangering the children, and Ken gets really mad. There has to be something wrong with an action-adventure that spends more time on tourism than terrorism. Bearing all the hallmarks of a direct-to-video rack-filler, this tatty thriller looks embarrassed on the big screen. Kosugi, who has displayed his athletics in the Ninja series, is put up against Belgian bruiser Jean-Claude Van Damme, the hulk from Bloodsport, which at least promises some sort of titanic muscle-to-muscle set-to in the finale. However, the scrap that ensues is a particularly tame affair, with nary a blood capsule crunched nor a skull pulverized. **KN**
Director Eric Karson *producer* Shimon Arama *exec* Sunil R. Shah *script* A. E. Peters, Michael Gonzales *camera* George Koblasa *editor* Michael Kelly *music* Terry Plumeri *cast* Sho Kosugi, Jean-Claude Van Damme, Doran Clark, Bruce French, Vladimir Skomarovsky, William H. Bassett
Running time: 104 mins
UK release: VPD, Nov 18, 1988

THE BLOB

The gelatinous, malevolent dessert from space returns to menace yet another small American principality in Chuck Russell's visceral homage to one of the more enduring perpetrators of primal B-movie history. First glimpsed by the inevitably-curious drunken hick whom nobody but a cutesy-pie cheerleader (Smith) and a misunderstood-rebel-from-the-wrong-side-of-the-tracks (Dillon) will believe, this Blob melts its victims slowly, inventively testifying to recent advances in special effects. Modified to appeal to both new drive-in gore hounds and nostalgic pulp-connoisseurs of the original, Frank Darabont's script makes space for every genre prerequisite, including sinister priests, dates necking in the back of cars prior to blobbification, militaristic conspiratorial sub-plots and an overall metaphoric concession to the AIDS era - replacing the original 1950s Cold War paranoia with modern biological terror. **MN**
Director Chuck Russell *producers* Jack H. Harris, Elliott Kastner *exec* Andre Blay *script* Chuck Russell, Frank Darabont *camera* Mark Irwin *editors* Terry Stokes, Tod Feuerman *design* Craig Stearns *music* Michael Hoenig *cast* Shawnee Smith, Kevin Dillon, Donovan Leitch, Jeffrey DeMunn, Candy Clark, Art La Fleur, Sharon Spelman, Del Close, Ricky Paull Goldin, Paul McCrane, Billy Beck, Joe Seneca, Michael Kenworthy
Running time: 92 mins
US release: Tri-Star, Aug 5, 1988
UK release: Col/Tri-Star, May 26, 1989

B

BLOODSPORT

The Kumite is a semi-illegal international dirty-fighting competition in which martial artists and thugs from all corners of the globe get together in a smelly arena in Hong Kong and beat five kinds of crap out of each other until only one man is standing. Jean-Claude Van Damme, a Belgian muscleman with an accent twice as incomprehensible as Arnold Schwarzenegger's, is cast as the first Westerner ever to win the Kumite. Van Damme is obviously bidding for a place in the modern muscle pantheon alongside Arnie, Sly, Chuck and the others, and this vehicle finds excuses for him to demonstrate insouciant charm, stumble through laughable 'emotion' scenes, show his bum, charm a bimbo journalist, make fools of some CIA stooges and indulge in a weird relationship with a hairy buddy that winds up with an extraordinary neo-gay hospital love scene. Van Damme's shortcomings as an actor are manifold, and they are compounded by a ridiculous script, choppy direction and various offensive attitudes to women, non-Aryans, pacifists, CIA agents and homicidal Tae-Kwan-Do experts. **KN**
Director Newt Arnold **producer** Mark Di Salle **exec** Rony Yacov **script** Sheldon Lettich, Christopher Crosby, Mel Friedman **camera** David Worth **editor** Carl Kress **music** Paul Hertzog **cast** Jean-Claude Van Damme, Donald Gibb, Leah Ayres, Norman Burton, Forest Whitaker, Roy Chiao, Philip Chan, Pierre Rafini, Bolo Yeung, Kenneth Siu, Kimo Lai Kwok Ki
Running time: 92 mins
US release: Cannon, Feb 26, 1988
UK release: Cannon, Aug 19, 1988

BLUE JEAN COP (Shakedown in US)

Director James Glickenhaus here attempts to move up-market from low-budget viscera to mainstream thriller. But, having wilfully cannibalized the exploitation genre for his late 1970s hit, *The Exterminator*, he's reduced to feeding off his previous efforts for ideas. The lacklustre story of lawyer (Weller) and cop (Elliott) teaming up against corrupt policemen involved with crack dealers marries a fashionable concern (crack) to increasingly ludicrous stunts. *Blue Jean Cop* lacks the aggressive, stylized violence necessary to carry the film over its self-consciously serious plotting. A concluding sequence, where Elliott trashes a plane by riding on its landing gear, brings proceedings to a suitably over-the-top halt.

Elliott is the film's one interesting element, a grizzled Marlboro man who sleeps in porno cinemas and washes down in their toilets. **SD**
Director/script James Glickenhaus **producer** J. Boyce Harman Jr. **execs** Leonard Shapiro, Alan Solomon **camera** John Lindley **editor** Paul Fried **design** Charles Bennett **music** Jonathan Elias **cast** Peter Weller, Sam Elliott, Patricia Charbonneau, Blanche Baker, Antonio Fargas, Richard Brooks
Running time: 96 mins
US release: Universal, May 6, 1988
UK release: Rank, Dec 2, 1988

LA BOHEME

This uninspired adaptation of Puccini's most popular opera is updated to *fin-de-siècle* Paris, where the camera's strenuous efforts to take off across the snowy rooftops or down the cobbled streets of ye olde Latin Quarter are thwarted by stage-bound production values and plodding direction. Barbara Hendricks starts off as an unusually feisty Mimi, but thereafter lapses into the familiar incarnation of wilting seamstress with a terminal lung condition. As her poet lover Rodolfo, Luca Canonici makes a fair fist of miming to the pre-recorded vocals of José Carreras, who was taken ill before filming, and the other principals are convincing, if a little mature to pass in close-up for zany bohemian types. Not as effective a filmed opera as, say, Zeffirelli's *La Traviata* or Rosi's *Carmen*, but Puccini's tunes win out in the end, and one would be well advised to have a packet of Kleenex close at hand. **AB**
Director Luigi Comencini **exec** Jean-Claude Bourlat **camera** Armando Nannuzzi **editors** Sergio Buzi, Reine Wekstein **design** Paolo Comencini **music** Giacomo Puccini **cast** Barbara Hendricks, José Carreras, Luca Canonici, Angela Maria Blasi, Gino Quilico
Running time: 107 mins
US release: New Yorker, Jun 9, 1989
UK release: Electric, Dec 26, 1989

THE BOOST

Harold Becker's 'Days of Whine and Poses' screed against cocaine has no more surprises than most message movies. Hyperkinetic James Woods would seem to be the last one to need a 'boost', and he predictably goes over the top when his character binges. He plays an investment salesman who stays high until the government closes the tax loophole through which he'd been riding a coach and four. Unable to keep up the payments on his expensive drug habit, he starts abusing his wife (Young). Young, seeing where her own drug addiction could lead her, leaves him and coke behind. **BM**

Director *Harold Becker* **producer** *Daniel Blatt* **execs** *John Daly, Derek Gibson* **script** *Darryl Ponicsan, from book Ludes by Benjamin Stein* **camera** *Howard Atherton* **editor** *Mary Winetrobe* **design** *Waldemar Kalinowski* **music** *Stanley Myers* **cast** *James Woods, Sean Young, John Kapelos, Steven Hill, Kelle Kerr, John Rothman, Amanda Blake, Grace Zabriskie*
Running time: 95 mins
US release: Hemdale, Dec 23, 1988

BOYFRIENDS AND GIRLFRIENDS (L'Ami de mon amie - My Girlfriend's Boyfriend in UK)

Eric Rohmer's sixth (and last) entry in his *Comédies et Proverbes* series is a more dramatically styled comedy of relationships than its predecessors, but none the worse for that. Lonely Blanche (Chaulet) befriends self-obsessed Lea (Renoir). Despite Lea's attempts at match-making, Blanche finds herself falling for her friend's partner. A round of emotional misunderstandings and confusions ensue, all delivered with Rohmer's astoundingly consistent direction of another superb young cast. **DT**

Director/script *Eric Rohmer* **producer** *Margaret Ménégoz* **camera** *Bernard Lutic* **editor** *Maria Luisa Garcia* **music** *Jean-Louis Valero* **cast** *Emmanuelle Chaulet, Sophie Renoir, Eric Veillard, François-Eric Gendron, Anne-Laury Meury*
Running time: 103 mins
US release: Orion Classics, Jul 15, 1988
UK release: Artificial Eye, Jun 24, 1988

BRIGHTNESS (See Yeelen)

THE 'BURBS

Tom Hanks decides to spend his vacation at home in the suburbs, and starts to feel that something isn't right at the Klopek household, where mysterious holes are dug in the backyard at night during a thunderstorm and the furnace makes peculiar noises. In its twisted comic-horror approach to suburbia, *The 'burbs* is one of several films (*Parents, The Stepfather*) that set out to counter the nostalgic, family-centred vision of Reagan-Bush Americana by finding madness and monstrosity in the heart of the nuclear family. For the most part, it follows *Explorers* in its unusual narrative strategy, presenting a situation filled with threat and mystery that then turns out to be entirely innocent. In his key speech, Hanks turns on his neighbours

as the Klopek house burns with, 'Don't you see, *we're* the ones who are acting suspiciously!' The film strings out its central situation perfectly for four-fifths of its running time, but fumbles at the last moment and can't quite make the final break with traditional menace-dominated storylines. **KN**

Director *Joe Dante* **producers** *Larry Brezner, Michael Finnell* **script** *Dana Olsen* **camera** *Robert Stevens* **editor** *Marshall Harvey* **design** *James Spencer* **music** *Jerry Goldsmith* **cast** *Tom Hanks, Bruce Dern, Carrie Fisher, Rick Ducommun, Corey Feldman, Wendy Schaal, Brother Theodore, Courtney Gains, Gale Gordon*
Running time: 103 mins
US release: Universal, Feb 17, 1989

BURNING SECRET

Why Andrew Birkin, who has been waiting a long time for his feature-directing début, should kick off with this pale tale of an asthmatic boy (Eberts) who's used as a pawn in love games involving his mother (Dunaway) and a 'Baron' (Brandauer), defies comprehension. The setting is an Austrian sanatorium in 1919, but the film doesn't capture many reverberations from time or place. Brandauer shifts too abruptly from affable storyteller to calculating womanizer to carry conviction and the interest Birkin has previously shown in childhood and loss-of-innocence (he wrote a book and a TV drama series on J. M. Barrie) doesn't electrify the boy's predicament. Whatever tension is built up at the film's climax is promptly dissipated by the stream of clichés that flow from the mouth of Ian Richardson when a distraught wife and son return home by separate carriages to Vienna. **JP**

Director *Andrew Birkin* **producers** *Norma Heyman, Eberhard Junkersdorf, Carol Lynn Greene* **execs** *William J. Quigley, M. J. Peckos* **script** *Birkin, from short story by Stefan Zweig* **camera** *Ernest Day* **editor** *Paul Green* **design** *Bernd Lepel* **music** *Hans Zimmer* **cast** *David Eberts, Faye Dunaway, Klaus Maria Brandauer, Ian Richardson, John Nettleton, Martin Obernigg*
Running time: 105 mins
US release: Vestron, Dec 22, 1988
UK release: Vestron, Apr 14, 1989

BUSINESS AS USUAL

Blatant political polemic and pure entertainment rarely make comfortable screen bedfellows but this committed, low-budget, drama of sexual harassment in Liverpool nearly made it. That is thanks to the passion of first-

time director Lezli-An Barrett and a cast of committed actors who, if unable wholly to flesh out the characters, do manage to elevate the enterprise beyond mere agitprop. **QF**
Director/script Lezli-An Barrett **producer** Sara Geater **execs** Menahem Golan, Yoram Globus **camera** Ernest Vincze **editor** Henry Richardson **design** Hildegard Betchler **music** Paul Weller **cast** Glenda Jackson, John Thaw, Cathy Tyson, Mark McGann, Eamon Boland, James Hazeldine, Buky Armstrong, Stephen McGann, Philip Foster, Natalie Duffy, Jack Carr, Mel Martin
Running time: 89 mins
US release: Cannon, Oct 21, 1988
UK release: Cannon, Sep 11, 1987

BUSTER

The 1963 Great Train Robbery and its aftermath are revisited in a further example of the British cinema's enthusiastic raking-over of the headline events of a generation ago. *Buster* has a predominantly comic tone which does not sit altogether comfortably with its basis in an actual (and violent) crime, or with the screenplay's pop-sociological gestures towards treating the 'them and us' divide. The film does, though, possess a lively surface and benefits from Phil Collins's fluent performance as the cheeky chappie version of train bandit Buster Edwards; and the sequences devoted to the Mexican exile of Edwards and his wife convey a bracing whiff of the vulgar and misanthropic. **TP**
Director David Green **producer** Norma Heyman **execs** Frank Giustra, Peter Strauss **script** Colin Shindler **camera** Tony Imi **editor** Lesley Walker **design** Simon Holland **music** Anne Dudley **cast** Phil Collins, Julie Walters, Larry Lamb, Stephanie Lawrence, Ellen Beaven, Michael Attwell, Ralph Brown, Christopher Ellison, Sheila Hancock, Martin Jarvis, Clive Wood, Anthony Quayle
Running time: 102 mins
US release: Hemdale, Nov 23, 1988
UK release: Vestron, Sep 16, 1988

BUY AND CELL

This trash is so obvious that the pun in the title defuses in advance any surprise its unfortunate makers may have intended for us. Robert Carradine, the least talented member of that family who's apparently convinced that trying to look like Rick Moranis will enhance his charisma (probably true), is a stocks and shares man taking a bum rap and making out in the Pen by doing guess what. This tediously slow comedy-drama mixes up a non-statement

about greed with the, by now routine, comedy clichés about psychopathic violence and homosexual rape that are the genre's lifeblood. About average for any film that dares to include Malcolm McDowell in its credits. **PB**
Director Robert Boris **producer** Frank Yablans **exec** Chris Band **script** Ken Krauss, Merrin Holt **camera** Daniele Nannuzzi **editor** Bert Glatstein **design** Giovanni Natalucci **music** Mark Shreeve **cast** Robert Carradine, Michael Winslow, Malcolm McDowell, Lise Cutter, Randall 'Tex' Cobb, Ben Vereen
Running time: 91 mins
US release: TWE, Jan 27, 1989

BATMAN

For 50 years now the Dark Knight has been battling against crime in his comic-strip world, appearing first as a silent creature of the night who hunted down criminals with an almost vampiric quality. During the 1940s, the daytime *alter ego* was introduced – millionaire Bruce Wayne – along with the gallery of villains that still menace him to this day: the Joker, the Penguin and the Riddler.

Batman went back in time to confront prehistoric monsters, and even travelled to outer space, accompanied by another hero in tights, Superman. But the grit went out of the character with the arrival of the television series, whose theme tune has now become the anthem for American pop culture of that era.

The Caped Crusader had stepped in front of the cameras before, having appeared in two Saturday morning cinema adventure serials. Restricted by their tight budget, hammy acting and crass special effects, these efforts do not remain fondly in memory.

William Dozier wanted a prime-time TV series that would attract both adults and children; he found it with *Batman*. The camp, almost vaudevillian style of the script and the 'POW', 'BAM', 'BIFF' fight scenes inadvertently inspired the comics to follow the same lines, leading to a loss of respectability from which the character did not recover until 1986.

Then Frank Miller, a young Californian who venerated Raymond Chandler and hard-core detective fiction, set out to restore the myth to its former glory. His four-part Batman opus, *The Dark Knight Returns*, placed its embittered super-hero amid nightmarish urban jungles populated with psychopaths and adolescent terrorists, investing this legend among comics with an adult, contemporary sensibility.

Miller's work bolstered the faith of Jon Peters and Peter Guber, who had optioned the rights to make a *Batman* film towards the end of the 1970s and then spent most of this decade trying to get it made. Once the man in the bat outfit was firmly established as again a public favourite, the film received a green light from Warner Bros.

Tim Burton, brought in after the success of his first foray into film directing, *Pee Wee's Big Adventure*, was determined to bring his own vision of the concept to the screen. He saw Batman and the Joker as two men who are adults, yet living in a childlike world of confused reality where the dangerous sides of their imaginations are allowed to become all too realistic. Forced to grow up too fast, they find solace in mythological archetypes: Batman as the masked avenging angel (the Scarlet Pimpernel, Zorro, the Lone Ranger), the Joker as a cantankerous harlequin.

Burton makes his Batman a force to be reckoned with. Gone are the cloth capes and floppy felt ears of the 1940s serials, gone are the bright blue leotards and unconvincing cowls of the 1960s TV series; Batman is now a lethal fighting machine, clad in bullet-proof body armour with an arsenal of weapons that are formidable to even the most maniacal of terrorists. The urban rot of Gotham City has an adversary that will not go down without a fight.

Gotham City (splendidly designed by Anton Furst, who also created the ravishingly expressionist sets of *Full Metal Jacket* and *The Company of Wolves*) is a crumbling artifice comprising Fritz Lang's *Metropolis*, 1940s Manhattan and Hieronymus Bosch. A sleazoid journalist (Alexander Knox) and a *femme-fatale* photographer Vicki Vale (Kim Basinger) join forces to demonstrate the existence of a six-foot creature whose extra-curricular activities include the decimation of the city's criminal fraternity, while dressed up as a cross between Count Dracula and a giant bat.

Against this grim, sombre, nocturnal guerrilla stands Jack Napier (Jack Nicholson), hoodlum and sexual rival to gangland Carl Grissom (Jack Palance). Napier's inadvertent transformation, by way of a set-up at a chemical factory, produces an acid-scarred, progressively more psychotic and flamboyant sociopath, the Joker – whose creation and ultimate dissolution have more to do with the new boy in town, Batman (alias millionaire Bruce Wayne), than he might ordinarily presume.

Batman is the stuff of Gothic romance. Its premise, however you look at it, is patently comic and absurd. Two men, both in need of therapy, both garishly adorned, battle for media and tabloid hegemony over a morally and fiscally bankrupt palatial slum. Tim Burton's Gotham is a world where this fundamentally mad duo engage in combat – the one dressed in functional black leather, the other cavalier and garish.

Evocative of such modern action thrillers as *Robocop*, the *Dirty Harry* cycle and *Manhunter*, Sam Hamm and Warren Skarren's screenplay is suffused with similar moral ambiguities and thematic underpinnings. Paul Verhoeven's cyborg owed much to Miller's saga, and whilst created to enforce laws (that Batman ignores), the more mechanical he became, the more he was aware of his humanity. Dirty Harry becomes less human and less moral in response to what happens to him; Keaton's masked avenger, whether in rubber leotard or tuxedo, is similarly a walking anomaly. He has no special powers but, like *Manhunter*'s cop Will Graham, teeters upon that narrow edge that divides right from wrong, reality from illusion – in the process mimicking the enemy to become that which he despises.

Batman is introduced as the ultimate formidable prowler, turning up in the pre-credits sequence as an animated gargoyle and threatening a thug with his moral edict, 'I own the night'. He is a dangerous guy with a mad rich-kid's toys – a voice-activated Batmobile that turns into an armoured car, a utility belt replete with tear-gas, spear-guns and other lethal accessories.

Jack Nicholson's Joker enjoys being bad with a childlike innocence and exuberance designed to compensate for his pre-pubescent introduction to delinquency and evil. He greets his mistress Alicia (Jerry Hall) with the casually-announced news of his transformation (sitting in his favourite chair in her apartment, dressed in smoking jacket, slippers, sipping a Martini): 'Honey, you wouldn't believe what happened to me today.' He confronts the mobster who framed him and helped turn his skin chalk-white and seaweed green with the stoicism, 'Death's quite liberating, you have to think of it as therapy . . . as you can see,' (pointing to his perpetual grin before shooting the man to bits), '. . . I'm much happier.'

This Joker is lethal, a homicidal maniac, whose idea of fulfilment is to go on network TV to pitch his product – a deadly nerve-gas (mixed into domestic household products) that contorts its victims' features, provoking a hideously paralytic facial grin. For recreation Nicholson defaces all the paintings in an art gallery, all except an agonized portrait that Jack can relate to.

This criminal is shot in the face by his own bullets (they ricochet off Batman's cape) before plunging into a vat of acid – he similarly knows that in New York, everyone can be a celebrity if they try hard and are weird enough. And that includes conversing with charred, electrocuted corpses or stabbing criminal rivals through the throat with razor-sharp pens.

Batman never disintegrates into farce. The hero's odyssey to find the murderer of his parents leads him to a finale when (after he has curtailed the Joker's media circus with gimmicks that include nerve-gas-filled balloons and dollar bills inscribed with the clown's face) he arrives in the bell-tower, planning not to arrest but to *murder* the Joker. Nicholson's hallucinatory world prevails when he puts on a pair of spectacles and facetiously appeals to Keaton's good nature; 'You wouldn't hit a man with glasses . . . I say you made me, so you have to say I made you? How childish can you get?' he exclaims before Batman beats him to a pulp.

Batman is more than a re-stylized Western or grown-up cartoon. It is a profound fairy-tale. Neither Nicholson's Joker, nor Keaton's idealized lantern-jawed action hero is totally in line with the comic book's ethos, but then Burton's universe is his own. Only a totally narrow-minded Bat-fan would resent Burton's development of his own mythology, borrowing elements from every phase of the legend (the 1940s serials, tiny bits of the 1960s TV show, the 1980s re-awakening).

Re-established and revived, the future for the caped crusader must surely be assured as the money comes pouring in to Warner's coffers. Inevitably the sequels will appear in rapid succession, becoming progressively more disappointing until the bubble finally bursts. But Batman is now ready to take on the new decade, and perhaps survive for another 50 years.

MARKUS NATTEN

THE BIG BLUE

E ven with seven TV channels, the French still adore movies. Few releases are not regarded as an *événement*. Fewer still merit this attention. Therefore, when one has its director, two stars *and* composer on the cover of the best-selling TV guide magazine – and the film is not even on TV – that movie has to be an event-plus. *Le Grand Bleu* swims on as a major cultural, social and clearly unfathomable phenomenon in France and other francophone territories. Everywhere else it sank with all hands.

The four mecs in blue were posing because it was time for Cannes 1989 – which meant *Le Grand Bleu* was one year old. And still alive and well and packing not just one cinema (like the eleven years of *Emmanuelle* on the Champs-Elysées or a decade of *One Flew Over the Cuckoo's Nest*) but numerous theatres on national release.

To be precise, the film on display is a second version – A Grander Blue. It is director Luc Besson's cut. Not that which opened Cannes in 1988. Not the version so rapidly beached in Britain. Certainly not the one cut to shreds by know-it-all Hollywood, which insisted, among other absurdities, on re-scoring Eric Serra's ethereal music with Bill Conti brass.

David Lean had to wait some 26 years before he could add a Spiegel-shorn 22 minutes back to his masterwork, *Lawrence of Arabia* (which ironically opened the Cannes festival in 1989). Luc Besson got his way about restoring 25 minutes of self-cut *Bleu* footage after about 26 weeks. Despite its cool reception at Cannes ('self-styled, overblown sea saga' in the *Hollywood Reporter*, 'soggy banality' according to *Variety*), the movie had soul. It also had feet – well, flippers.

In the short Besson cannon, I prefer his first, brave, glorious feature, *Le Dernier Combat*, shot in black-and-white and without dialogue. It's a far greater achievement than the show-off *Diva* from his media-twinned rival Jean-Jacques Beineix. *Subway* proved Besson's potential, despite an incredibly weak hero in Christopher Lambert.

Le Grand Bleu is *Subway* relocated. The other-worldly hero is stronger – in script, on screen. Besson again deals with a subculture, under-sea as opposed to underground life on the Métro. Both movies share the same bravura flair for the bizarre.

Unlike Richard Corliss in *Time* ('talented young director in over his head'), I had no objections to Besson making a personal film. He had earned the right in my book to weave a story (better in the long version) around his own love of deep-sea diving and treasured experiences with dolphins.

No one, certainly not Besson, expected it to become – and so rapidly – a

colossus of French cinema. And no one, certainly not Besson, seems to know why – not exactly. *'Le Grand Bleu,'* he says, 'is the name of another universe – so profound it becomes impenetrable.'

Spielberg's *Jaws* worked wonders even in the mid-American farming belt and other global communities that never see the sea, much less a shark. *Le Grand Bleu* has more than swimmers and dolphinists worshipping at Besson's altar. My own daughter is among the congregation, even though, in line with the family tradition, she never puts her head in, much less *under*, the water.

What then could attract Delphine at 19 to a film about a man (who isn't Richard Gere) in love with the sea, his diving rival, his quirky American girl friend and, above all, dolphins?'

'Everything!' she says. 'The feelings. The atmosphere. The guys. Their rivalry. Their love for each other and for nature. And, *bien sur*, Eric Serra's music. It's the first film I've loved so *completely*. I've seen it four times and will return again . . . and again. Each time I come out of it, I am dizzy, I feel great and sad and don't quite know where I am.'

She is not alone. In its first year, *Le Grand Bleu* has been seen by more than eight million French ticket buyers. A quarter of them having returned for the *version longue*.

'Three hours is too long,' considered Besson. 'I'm never happy with any film I see that's over two hours long – but the short version frustrated us all, the actors and the crew. I wanted to have at least one copy of the full version. I also thought it might interest some cinephiles. Then the Rex cinema asked to show it . . .'

Opening day at the Rex, not only one of the biggest Paris cinemas but also a youthful haven (it houses the annual screaming match known as the Paris Fantasy and Horror Movie Festival), caused queues, eight to ten thick, around the block, bringing traffic to a much-headlined halt. Cinema queues are not uncommon in Paris. But . . . before midday? Every day!

Besson was away at the time, shooting his fourth feature, with its mock title, *Nikita*. He filmed an introduction to his new cut of *Le Grand Bleu*. With his blonde-streaked spiky hair attracting eyes from his bulky body, he resembled a shy, diffident rock-group leader as he thanked his fans for the film's enormous success. He was cheered. The film, now running at two hours and 50 minutes, was interrupted several times with more cheers for new scenes and old and, in the *Rocky Horror* tradition, with audiences joining in with the dialogue.

The new cut meant a new poster, with not one but countless dolphins this time. Plus a second and third album (two with dialogue snatches) of the Hollywood-scorned score. They are all best-sellers. So are the T-shirts and the book. No longer a phenomenon, the movie is an industry.

Even so, eight million people? That's a lot of bums on seats. A sudden mass love of dolphins is hardly reason enough for the success.

Admittedly, the French seem to love animals – wild beasts and family pets

– with even greater gusto than the English. Or, as per most things in France, they certainly talk a lot about doing so. (Different story in the summer when family dogs, cats and the odd rabbit are flung out of speeding cars *en route* to the South.) The other big 1988 winner proved to be about bears. And Jean-Jacques Beineix, launched first and rapidly overtaken by Besson, attempted to regain the upper hand by borrowing Besson's theme (he borrowed a Besson actor last time) for a film about a couple in love with . . . circus lions!

It doesn't matter how many dolphins populate the new poster, they are just half the story. The true dolphin is the character played by Jean-Marc Barr. He's devoted to marine life, diving deep within it (without oxygen) and ultimately choosing to take to the sea forever more – leaving Rosanna Arquette on the quayside. Even given the usual vicissitudes of an Anglo directed by a foreigner, Rosanna was at her amateur-night worst, embarrassingly over the top. She was the only fishy part of the movie.

If Besson cannot – as yet – solve the 'ear' problem of directing actors in English (not every French director is Louis Malle), he does understand cinema. His often breathtaking imagery, linked to drama, comedy and action tempo, leaves Lelouch's camera flurries and Beineix's pretensions gasping. If the short-form story didn't altogether work, it was in trying to make landlubbers *feel* (rather than being told about) the apparent bliss of an Atlantis lifestyle.

More importantly, better than most current French directors, Besson also understands the public, or that section of it which has become his faithful following. 'He uses the kind of spiritual language their generation needs,' suggests Jean Reno, who has acted in all four Besson movies. 'Between Besson and youth there's been a long, mysterious *connivence* that can only be explained by psychoanalysis or . . . mysticism.' Which makes him sound like the director Beineix thinks he is!

Besson, then, has become something of a god for French youth. His flippered-heroes, Jean-Marc Barr and Jean Reno have become superstar idols. Both Serra and Reno are part of *Nikita*, which brings back other Bessonites: Jean-Hugues Anglade and Richard Bohringer. And, in Arquette's place, Luc's lady, Anne Parillaud.

As the idols talk, Besson looks on. He is secretive: in the Paris showbiz village where everyone knows who's with who, news that Besson had fathered a daughter only leaked out two years after *l'événement* – when he dedicated *Le Grand Bleu* to her.

'If,' says Besson, 'the first ten years of my life have powerfully impregnated this movie, I'm convinced the ten months of shooting will surely influence the next picture I make.' Maybe Hollywood will leave that one alone.

TONY CRAWLEY

CADDYSHACK II

Ten years after the main event comes a sequel that makes the original look good. It's yet another gross-out comedy celebrating the closing of the American mind with 90 minutes of below-par golf and sex jokes, punctuated by brief (very brief) cameos from the more successful members of the original cast (except Bill Murray, who was too busy embarrassing himself in *Scrooged*). Chevy Chase plays Chevy Chase, only without the charm; the rest of the cast mugs energetically, but ultimately the acting honours are stolen by the gopher. Inept, tiresome and very loud. **TW**
Director Allan Arkush *producers* Neil Canton, Jon Peters, Peter Guber *script* Harold Ramis, Peter Torokvei *camera* Harry Stradling *editor* Bernard Gribble *design* Bill Matthews *music* Ira Newborn *cast* Jackie Mason, Dyan Cannon, Robert Stack, Dina Merrill, Chevy Chase, Dan Aykroyd, Randy Quaid, Jessica Lundy, Jonathan Silverman, Chynna Phillips, Brian McNamara
Running time: 93 mins
US release: Warner, Jul 22, 1988

CALL ME

A wooden Patricia Charbonneau leads this laughable attempt at an erotic thriller, involving telephone sex, a murderous cop and a wimpish admirer of Charbonneau who gets his kicks from oranges. A brooding Stephen McHattie reprises his B-movie rôle as a world-weary street urchin forming a tentative alliance with the eternally-confused heroine, who staggers through poorly-shot and clumsily-edited chase scenes with vapid indifference. A sequence involving oranges was cut from the UK print, reducing the film's one attempt at an erotic sequence to a rather messy jump cut and a wet T-shirt. The concluding chaos through a deserted warehouse is shot with such imprecision that any atmosphere is dissipated in meaningless angles and club-footed tension. Both as eroticism and action this is a tedious failure. **SD**
Director Sollace Mitchell *producers* John E. Quill, Kenneth F. Martel *execs* Mitchell Cannold, Steven Reuther, Ruth Vitale *script* Karyn Kay *camera* Zoltan David *editor* Paul Fried *design* Stephen McCabe *music* David Frank *cast* Patricia Charbonneau, Stephen McHattie, Boyd Gaines, Sam Freed, Steve Buscemi, Patti D'Arbanville
Running time: 98 mins
US release: Vestron, May 20, 1988
UK release: Vestron, Dec 2, 1988

CAMERON'S CLOSET

Convoluted plotting prevents this curious horror movie from exploring any of the issues it initially raises. Ten-year-old Cameron, encouraged by his father to expand his psycho-kinetic powers, unwittingly summons a demon who proceeds to annihilate all those who know of its existence. The closet, traditional hiding place for every child's bogeyman, becomes an atmospheric middle-ground between Hell and the child's suburban environment. Peripheral characters are dispatched in virulently macabre fashion (one has his eyes burnt out and is flung through a window), but once the monster, The Deceptor, makes his scheduled appearance, its unimpressive nature tends to reduce proceedings to a mechanistic struggle to dispatch the creature back the way it came. The power of a child's imagination is potentially the underlying theme, with its sense of absolute good and evil, but the hollow freneticism of the demon's malevolent activities becomes increasingly the film's formulaic concern. **SD**
Director Armand Mastroianni *producer* Luigi Cingolani *exec* George Zecevic *script* Garry Brandner, from his novel *camera* Russell Carpenter *editor* Frank De Palma *design* Michael Billingham *music* Harry Manfredini *cast* Cotter Smith, Mel Harris, Scott Curtis, Chuck McCann, Leigh McCloskey, Kim Lankford, Gary Hudson, Tab Hunter
Running time: 87 mins
US release: SVS, Jan 27, 1989
UK release: Medusa, Dec 2, 1988

CAMILLE CLAUDEL

'I lived for your *Burghers of Calais*, now I'm going to live for myself!' cries Isabelle Adjani, hurtling off into the dark night of the soul after her fling with Rodin (Depardieu). Début director and ex-cameraman Bruno Nuytten gives us three hours of romantic agony as *l'art* and *l'amour* battle it out. If Camille Claudel, sculptress, madwoman and sister of Paul, had not existed, Adjani would have had to invent her. Indeed, for the most part, she does; coming on like *The Return of Adele H.*, as her shredded, beautiful heroine howls through the Paris streets, hell-bent on occupancy of the asylum in which Camille did indeed end up. A substantial hit in its native France - where they like tormented artists - the film promises to be a substantial miss everywhere else. **HK**
Director Bruno Nuytten *producer* Christian

Fechner **script** Nuytten, Marilyn Goldin, from book by Reine-Marie Paris **camera** Pierre Lhomme **editor** Joëlle Hache, Jeanne Kef **design** Bernard Vezat **music** Gabriel Yared **cast** Isabelle Adjani, Gérard Depardieu, Laurent Crevill, Alain Cuny, Madeleine Robinson, Philippe Clevenot, Katrine Boorman, Danièle Lebrun, Maxime Leroux, Jean-Pierre Sentier, Roger Planchon, Aurelle Doazan
Running time: 174 mins
UK release: Cannon, Apr 7, 1989

CHANCES ARE

Cybill Shepherd's return to films sparkles only intermittently. In this reincarnation comedy, her character unfortunately has none of the sprightly malice that can set off her loveliness so appealingly. Robert Downey Jr., the spirit of her long-dead husband, arrives to find her settled into sexless early middle age. Her best friend, Ryan O'Neal, has long desired her but never dared declare himself. She falls for Downey, accepting that he's as near as she'll ever come to the dear departed. The twist at the end strains credulity, but no more than the twist at the start. **BM**
Director Emile Ardolino **producer** Mike Lobell **execs** Andrew Bergman, Neil A. Machlis **script** Perry Howze, Randy Howze **camera** William A. Fraker **editor** Harry Keramidas **design** Dennis Washington **music** Maurice Jarre **cast** Cybill Shepherd, Robert Downey Jr., Ryan O'Neal, Mary Stuart Masterson, Christopher McDonald, Josef Sommer, Joe Grifasi, Susan Ruttan, Fran Ryan, James Noble
Running time: 108 mins
US release: Tri-Star, Mar 10, 1989

CHECKING OUT

David Leland comes to America and lays an egg. His comedy of hypochondria stars Jeff Daniels as a young exec. who becomes irrationally convinced he's about to die of a heart attack. He goes over the edge when his best buddy drops dead before delivering the punchline of this joke, 'Why don't Italians have barbecues?' In his dementia, Daniels spends a fortune on useless self-help gizmos, threatens his marriage to Melanie Mayron and jeopardizes his future with the firm. Throughout, he seeks to solve his late friend's riddle. (The answer isn't worth the price of admission, so here it is: 'Because the spaghetti keeps falling into the fire.') **BM**
Director David Leland **producer** Ben Myron **execs** George Harrison, Denis O'Brien **script** Joe

Eszterhas **camera** Ian Wilson **editor** Lee Percy **design** Barbara Ling **music** Carter Burwell **cast** Jeff Daniels, Melanie Mayron, Michael Tucker, Kathleen York, Ann Magnusson, Jo Harvey Allen, Felton Perry, Ian Wolfe, John Durbin, Allan Havey
Running time: 93 mins
US release: Warner, Apr 21, 1989

CHILD'S PLAY

This variant on the killer-doll movie is nowhere near as provocative or suspensful as the definitive example of this sub-genre, Alberto Cavalcanti's episode in the 1945 film _Dead of Night_, although a respect for the narrative conventions of vintage horror-tales, assisted by developmentss in animatronics, render _Child's Play_ effective fun. A gargantuan toy emporium is the opening scene's setting for serial-killer Brad Dourif's transmigration into the body of a doll, an item later purchased by single mum Catherine Hicks for her young son. Both, of course, are unaware of the voodoo practitioner latent in the cuddly toy whose homicidal inclinations manifest themselves in such anti-social gestures as murdering the baby-sitter. Holland's direction never concedes to the ridiculousness of the premise, and melodrama is employed to sustain one's interest in the obstreperous, diminutive Terminator. **MN**
Director Tom Holland **producer** David Kirschner **exec** Barrie M. Osborne **script** Don Mancini, John Lafia, Holland **camera** Bill Butler **editor** Edward Warschilka, Roy E. Peterson **design** Daniel A. Lomino **music** Joe Renzetti **cast** Catherine Hicks, Chris Sarandon, Alex Vincent, Brad Dourif, Dinah Manoff, Tommy Swerdlow, Jack Colvin
Running time: 87 mins
US release: UA, Nov 9, 1988
UK release: UIP, Jun 2, 1989

CHOCOLAT

Following the plethora of British films about the declining days of empire, _Chocolat_ is a delicate and affecting French variation on the same theme. The significantly-named France returns to the Cameroons, and flashes back to childhood, when her amiably gullible father was District Commissioner, and something was almost going on between her bored mother (Boschi) and the black houseboy (de Bankolé). The film avoids melodrama, making a virtue out of its lack of dramatic incident, and concentrates on meaningful moments, quiet

comedy and eccentric characters. By comparison with *The Kitchen Toto*, which it resembles in many ways, it is masterfully subtle and suggestive, and benefits from a non-judgemental approach to all its characters. Finally, *Chocolat* is just as it is titled - rich, sweet and surprisingly filling. **KN**
Director Claire Denis **execs** Alain Belmondo, Gérard Crosnier **script** Denis, Jean-Pol Fargeau **camera** Alain Alazraki **editor** Claudine Merlin **design** Thierry Flamand **music** Abdullah Ibrahim **cast** Isaach de Bankolé, Giulia Boschi, François Cluzet, Jean-Claude Adelin, Laurent Arnal, Jean Bediebe, Jean-Quentin Chatelain, Emmanuelle Chaulet, Kenneth Cranham, Jacques Denis, Cécile Ducasse, Clémentine Essono, Didier Flamand, Essindi Mindja, Donatus Ngala, Edwige Nto Ngon a Zock, Philemon Blake Ondoua, Mireille Perrier
Running time: 105 mins
US release: Orion Classics, Mar 10, 1989
UK release: Electric, Apr 21, 1989

THE CHOCOLATE WAR

Robert Cormier's widely-read 1974 tale of schoolboy evil is here faithfully recorded. Brother John Glover heads a Jesuit school's fund-raising chocolate sale, and he's willing to cut moral corners to get better results. A gang of schoolboy pranksters, headed by Machiavellian Wally Ward, enmeshes Everykid Ilan Mitchell-Smith in their plot, first to sabotage the sale, then to overfulfill the norm. Ostracized, Mitchell-Smith finally exacts tainted revenge in a bizarre boxing match. The chilling story has nothing to do with the just-ended cycle of Hughesian high school hijinks movies, everything to do with *Lord of the Flies*. **BM**
Director/script Keith Gordon **producer** Jonathan D. Krane **script** Gordon, from book by Robert Cormier **camera** Tom Richmond **editor** Jeff Wishengrad **design** David Ensley **cast** John Glover, Ilan Mitchell-Smith, Wally Ward, Doug Hutchison, Adam Baldwin, Brent Fraser, Bud Cort
Running time: 100 mins
US release: MCEG, Jan 27, 1989

CLARA'S HEART

A long way after *Gone with the Wind*, Whoopi Goldberg plays a Mammy type in this light drama of a young boy's acquisition of wisdom. As in all such stories, Neil Patrick Harris is a perfect brat at the start, and why not? His parents are filthy rich and they're splitting up. While taking a break in the islands, his Mom finds the most darling Jamaican maid (Goldberg), and she brings the woman back to the States. Harris too falls under Goldberg's spell and soon is speaking in patois and singing island ditties. Harris's eventual betrayal of their friendship doesn't faze the weary Goldberg, who is spot-on in a non-comedic rôle. **BM**
Director Robert Mulligan **producer** Martin Elfand **exec** Marianne Moloney **script** Mark Medoff, from novel by Joseph Olshan **camera** Freddie Francis **editor** Sidney Levin **design** Jeffrey Howard **music** Dave Grusin **cast** Whoopi Goldberg, Michael Ontkean, Kathleen Quinlan, Neil Patrick Harris, Spalding Gray, Beverly Todd, Hattie Winston
Running time: 108 mins
US release: Warner, Oct 7, 1988
UK release: Warner, Jun 2, 1989

CLEAN AND SOBER

This occasionally downbeat look at chemical abuse is overlong but thankfully devoid of slick paeans to sobriety. It follows the inadvertent rehabilitation of Michael Keaton, a seemingly compassionless executive who intially checks into a detox programme only to escape creditors and police investigations into his involvement in a possible murder. Inevitably sentimental, it's nevertheless realistic in its documentation of the imbiber's recovery and ends up a non-polemical anti-drug movie that graciously sidesteps the allegorical superfluities of such just-say-no narratives as *Bright Lights, Big City* or the offensively preachy *Less Than Zero*. Keaton's character is morally ambiguous enough to make one wonder whether he'll make it or not. **MN**
Director Glenn Gordon Caron **producers** Tony Ganz, Deborah Blum **exec** Ron Howard **script** Tod Carroll **camera** Jan Kiesser **editor** Richard Chew **design** Joel Schiller **music** Gabriel Yared **cast** Michael Keaton, Kathy Baker, Morgan Freeman, M. Emmet Walsh, Brian Benben, Luca Bercovici, Tate Donovan, Henry Judd Baker
Running time: 124 mins
US release: Warner, Aug 10, 1988

COCKTAIL

Tom Cruise's army vet hoping to make it in the big city may not be from Vietnam, but that's about it for originality here. He finds it tougher out there than he expected and becomes a hot shot cocktail barman who climbs to superstar (superbar?) status under the tutelage of cynical Bryan Brown, sleeps with the prettier members of the supporting cast and

falls in love with the wasted Miss Shue in time for a Dreadful Warning finale as she gets pregnant and his best friend dies because he never read *How To Become a Millionaire*. It all ends happily, with Cruise fighting his way into the girl's father's penthouse, beating up the doorman and eloping to live in poverty and happiness - running his uncle's bar and delivering bar-room poetry to his unborn child - in the most nauseating ending of the year. Bryan Brown's very amusing performance almost justifies seeing the film, but Cruise's limited range (he smiles an awful lot in this one), Heywood Gould's supposedly autobiographical script and Donaldson's surprisingly bland direction all combine to scupper the film's potential. **TW**
Director Roger Donaldson **producers** Ted Field, Robert W. Cort **script** Heywood Gould, from his novel **camera** Dean Semler **editor** Neil Travis, Barbara Dunning **design** Mel Bourne **music** J. Peter Robinson **cast** Tom Cruise, Bryan Brown, Elisabeth Shue, Lisa Banes, Laurence Luckinbill, Kelly Lynch, Gina Gershon, Ron Dean
Running time: 103 mins
US release: BV, Jul 29, 1988
UK release: Warner, Jan 20, 1989

COCOON: THE RETURN
This follow-up to Ron Howard's elegant fantasy brings back to earth, for a short visit, the group of elderly protagonists who, by following a group of aliens to their home on Antarea, successfully evaded the human frailties of disease and senility they might otherwise have fallen victim to. Reproducing practically every moment from the first movie, *The Return* also restates its central dilemma, and thus has to confront problems not raised by the original. The utopian regimen of Antarea really needs more narrative explication to assist the audience in their understanding of why the senior citizens would even consider rejecting their paradisaical alien retirement zone to contemplate an alternative existence on Earth a place where old people don't even get decent pensions, let alone immortality. **MN**
Director Daniel Petrie **producers** Richard D. Zanuck, David Brown, Lili Fini Zanuck **script** Stephen McPherson **camera** Tak Fujimoto **editor** Mark Roy Warner **design** Lawrence G. Paull **music** James Horner **cast** Don Ameche, Wilford Brimley, Hume Cronyn, Jack Gilford, Steve Guttenberg, Maureen Stapleton, Jessica Tandy, Gwen Verdon, Elaine Stritch, Courtney Cox

Running time: 116 mins
US release: Fox, Nov 23, 1988
UK release: Fox, May 26, 1989

COHEN & TATE
Eric Red scripted the ingenious road movie-cum-chiller *The Hitcher*, and as writer-director here, he utilizes a similar combination of genres, though within an ostensibly more realistic framework. The duo of the title are professional murderers, detailed to kidnap a small boy who has witnessed a gangland débâcle, and the action covers the single night of the threesome's inevitably unfinished journey back to base. Despite some over-reliance on dialogue in the earlier passages, the film sustains a keen edge of tension, particularly in the set-piece episode of negotiating a police road-block, and the pared-down construction makes it satisfyingly reminscent of bygone thrillers by the likes of Don Siegel and Phil Karlson. **TP**
Director/script Eric Red **producers** Antony Rufus Isaacs, Jeff Young **camera** Victor J. Kemper **editor** Ed Abrams **design** Davis Haber **music** Bill Conti **cast** Roy Scheider, Adam Baldwin, Harley Cross, Cooper Huckabee, Suzanne Savoy
Running time: 85 mins
US release: Hemdale, Jan 27, 1989

COLD FEET
'Clunky' doesn't do justice to the level of awfulness perpetrated by Robert Dornhelm's post-modern Western about an unholy trinity of petty crooks smuggling a cache of gems across the Rio Grande in the belly of a race-horse. Novelists McGuane and Harrison wrote an intermittently funny but incoherent script, and someone persuaded Sally Kirkland (her character infatuated with laconic Keith Carradine) to compress her bodacious 40-something into a series of micro-minis that would shame a stripper. You have to admire her pluck, and Tom Waits's as an unloved psycho who's hammier than Kevin Kline in *A Fish Called Wanda*. **GF**
Director Robert Dornhelm **producer** Cassian Elwes **exec** Cary Brokaw **script** Tom McGuane, Jim Harrison **camera** Bryan Duggan **editors** David Rawlins, Debra McDermott **design** Bernt Capra **music** Tom Bahler **cast** Keith Carradine, Sally Kirkland, Tom Waits, Bill Pullman, Rip Torn, Kathleen York, Macon McCalman, Bob Mendelsohn, Vincent Schiavelli, Amber Bauer, Tom McGuane, Jeff Bridges

Running time: 91 mins
US release: Avenue, May 19, 1989

DISAPPOINTMENT

COLORS

Director Dennis Hopper *producer* Robert H. Solo *script* Michael Schiffer *camera* Haskell Wexler *editor* Robert Estrin *design* Ron Foreman *music* Herbie Hancock *cast* Sean Penn, Robert Duvall, Maria Conchita Alonso, Randy Brooks, Grand Bush, Don Cheadle, Gerardo Mejia, Glenn Plummer, Rudy Ramos, Sy Richardson, Trinidad Silva, Charles Walker, Damon Wayans
Running time: 121 mins
US release: Orion, Apr 15, 1988
UK release: Rank, Nov 11, 1988

COMING TO AMERICA

This stilted fairy tale of an African prince travelling to New York in the guise of a poor man to find a bride who will want him for his charming personality rather than his cheque book, is little more than a vehicle for Eddie Murphy's supposed vaudevillian talents. John Landis, still suffering from a star-fixation, plugs for anonymity and an enormous budget. Murphy, who wrote the story, has a field day as he steps away from the virile black stud image to lampoon sitcomesque ethnic images, such as barber-shop braggards or lecherous beauty show hosts. Quite what was intended to emerge from this cutely wholesome collision of make-believe with the New York borough of Queens is not evident. While Murphy dominates the screen with his various cameos, his leading rôle is banally inadequate, removing a desperately-needed central performance that might have held the film together, instead of letting it drown under a welter of character sketches. **SD**
Director John Landis *producers* George Folsey Jr., Robert D. Wachs *execs* Mark Lipsky, Leslie Belzberg *script* David Sheffield, Barry W. Blaustein *camera* Woody Omens *editors* Malcolm Campbell, Folsey *design* Richard MacDonald *music* Nile Rodgers *cast* Eddie Murphy, Arsenio Hall, John Amos, James Earl Jones, Shari Headley, Madge Sinclair, Eriq La Salle, Allison Dean, Paul Bates, Louie Anderson, Clint Smith, Vanessa Bell
Running time: 117 mins
US release: Paramount, Jun 29, 1988
UK release: UIP, Jul 29, 1988

THE COMMISSAR (Komissar)

Alexander Askoldov's first and, to date, last film was made in 1967, then shelved by Soviet authorities. It takes a simple tale - a Commissar takes time off from the Civil War to lodge with a Jewish family and bring forth an unwanted baby - but elaborates its initially crude life/death dichotomy (the Commissar announces her pregnancy immediately after ordering the execution of a deserter) into an extraordinary interplay of images from life for the poor-but-happy family group and the relentless march of war. A performance of vordless impassivity from Nonna Mordyukova, whose inner conflicts are explored through surreal scenes of war, is set against the expressive gestures of Rolan Bykov, a fountain of words as the muddled, life-loving, resigned father of six. A near-abstract use of sound and Alfred Schnittke's strident score heighten the film's emotional impact. **JP**
Director Alexander Askoldov *producers* V. Levin, V. Grigorev, L. Prilutzkaya *exec* Gorky Studios *script* Askoldov, from novel In the Town of Berdichev by Vasily Grossman *camera* Valery Ginsburg *editors* V. Isayeva, N. Loginova, S. Lyashinskaya *design* Sergei Serebrennikov *music* Alfred Shnittke *cast* Nonna Mordyukova, Rolan Bykov, Raisa Nedashkovskaya, Vasily Shukshin
Running time: 108 mins
UK release: Artificial Eye, May 12, 1989

CONSUMING PASSIONS

Sold to the public as 'a tale of greed, lust and death by chocolate,' this bizarre satire on corporate indifference takes a whimsical play by Monty Python siblings Michael Palin and Terry Jones, broadens it out-in pursuit of a wider audience and misses by several miles. Jonathan Pryce, adorned by bow-tie and contemporary cynicism, is the innovative marketing man who capitalizes upon the unexpected results that follow when several company employees are tipped into a vat of candified sludge and metamorphosed into cannibalistic sweetmeats. Tyler Butterworth, already in thrall to Vanessa Redgrave's libido, becomes embroiled in a scheme to perpetuate sales of the sweet. Redgrave is funny, Pryce isn't and Butterworth just stands there. **MN**
Director Giles Foster *producer* William Cartlidge *script* Paul D. Zimmerman, Andrew Davies, from play Secrets by Michael Palin, Terry Jones *camera* Roger Pratt *editor* John Grover *design* Peter Lamont *music* Richard Hartley *cast* Vanessa

Redgrave, Jonathan Pryce, Tyler Butterworth, Freddie Jones, Sammi Davis, Prunella Scales, Thora Hird, William Rushton, John Wells, Timothy West, Mary Healey, Andrew Sachs, Bryan Pringle
Running time: 98 mins
US release: Goldwyn, Apr 6, 1988
UK release: Vestron, Oct 28, 1988

THE COUCH TRIP

Dan Aykroyd is in his element as an asylum-refugee on the loose in Beverly Hills. Escaping from a strait-jacket by impersonating his shrink, Aykroyd takes a job in Los Angeles, subbing for radio sex therapist Charles Grodin. To the consternation of the tight-buttocked Grodin, Aykroyd's profane directness sends ratings soaring. Matthau proves his comic deftness in an extended cameo as a pseudo-religious headcase whose best moment involves sucking jelly out of doughnuts with a straw. Stunts like taking hundreds of callers to a ball game ('Nymphomaniacs in bus three with me!') and lines like bit player Walter Matthau's 'A man never stands so tall as when he stoops to pet a plant' give *The Couch Trip* a more than adequate laugh count. But comedy of this sort always sacrifices its inclination for social comment - 'Well, I thought I was mad but people on the outside are just as crazy' - to sight gags and ironic facial expressions. **MN**
Director Michael Ritchie **producer** Lawrence Gordon **script** Steven Kampmann, Will Porter, Sean Stein, from novel by Ken Kolb **camera** Donald E. Thorin **editor** Richard Harris **design** Jimmy Bly **music** Michel Colombier **cast** Dan Aykroyd, Walter Matthau, Charles Grodin, Donna Dixon, Richard Romanus, Mary Gross, David Clennon, Arye Gross, Victoria Jackson, Chevy Chase
Running time: 98 mins
US release: Orion, Jan 15, 1988
UK release: Rank, Jul 22, 1988

THE COURIER

Dublin as a not so fair, and disappointingly anonymous, city is the background for a stereotyped crime yarn, with Gabriel Byrne as the white-suited king of the dope pedlars, eventually (and to the surprise of nobody) meeting fate by being shot on a fire escape and crashing on to the pavement from a great height. Even Ian Bannen as the lugubrious tec. on his trail cannot breathe any life to speak of into an undertaking disfigured elsewhere by a particularly objectionable display of gratuitous sadism entailing a broken bottle jabbed into a stool-pigeon's face. **TP**
Directors Joe Lee, Frank Deasy **producer** Hilary McLoughlin **execs** Neil Jordan, Nik Powell, John Hambley, Michael Algar **script** Deasy **camera** Gabriel Beristain **editors** Derek Trigg, Annette D'Alton **design** David Wilson **music** Declan MacManus (Elvis Costello) **cast** Gabriel Byrne, Ian Bannen, Cait O'Riordan, Kevin Doyle, Mary Ryan, Michelle Houlden, Mark Flanagan, Andrew Connolly, Patrick Bergin, Anne Enwright, Padraig O'Loingsigh, Lucy Vigne Welsh
Running time: 85 mins
US release: Vestron, Jun 2, 1989
UK release: Palace, Feb 19, 1988

COUSINS

Joel Schumacher ably remakes the 1975 French comedy of infidelity *Cousin, Cousine*, using North American ethnicity as a stand-in for Gallic spirit. Ted Danson and Isabella Rossellini meet when her mother marries his uncle. Their spouses' affair brings them together, and they satisfy their honour by first attempting to be friends and then by remaining apart. Naturally, neither stratagem works and eventually they are lovers. Like *Moonstruck*, *Cousins* pays attention to the lives of the lovers' extended families, allowing Sean Young, Lloyd Bridges and others to pepper the film with funny moments. **BM**
Director Joel Schumacher **producer** William Allyn **exec** George Goodman **script** Stephen Metcalfe, from film Cousin, Cousine by Jean-Charles Tacchella **camera** Ralf D. Bode **editor** Robert Brown **design** Mark S. Freeborn **music** Angelo Badalamenti **cast** Ted Danson, Isabella Rossellini, Sean Young, William Petersen, Lloyd Bridges, Norma Aleandro, Keith Coogan, Gina de Angelis
Running time: 110 mins
US release: Paramount, Feb 10, 1989

CRACK IN THE MIRROR

The advocates of High Definition Video as a replacement for 35mm film, who last hitched their hopes to *Julia & Julia*, really don't seem to be having any luck. Whether or not HDV is responsible for the blandness of the images here, they are of a piece with the tawdriness of the film's drugs morality tale. Debt-beleaguered Robby Benson is handed an unlikely two-week assignment as stand-in for a drugs baron (Gray). Dramatic potential in the fact that Gray's being hunted by gun-wielding mafiosi is wasted in a display of how much white make-

up is required to indicate the physical decline of a dealer who tastes his goods. Benson must, in fact, have used up the production's whole supply since his fiancée retains a perfect complexion even while dipping heavily into the crack supply, falling into bed with rival amours and generally going to pieces. The abrupt psychological transformations, hysterical over-acting and unresolved plot strands will put the fear of crack into no one. **JP**
Director Robby Benson **producers** Fred Berner, Jubran Jubran **execs** Denie Bieber, Jubran Jubran, Michael Marrone, Barry Rebo, Tomio Taki **script** Robert Madero **camera** Neil Smith **editor** Alan Miller, Craig McKay **design** Rueben Freed **music** Nile Rodgers **cast** Robby Benson, Danny Aiello, Tawny Kitaen, Kevin Gray
Running time: 95 mins
US release: Triax, Feb 3, 1989
UK release: Blue Dolphin, May 26, 1989

CRAZY LOVE (Love is a Dog from Hell)

Adapted with greater success than its predecessors from the booze-inspired works of Charles Bukowski, Dominique Deruddere's first feature is an impish, beautifully-crafted vision of male rites of passage. It begins in 1955 with twelve-year-old Harry discovering the sweaty reality of female flesh, moves to 1962 when devastating acne removes him further from blissful consummation, and concludes in 1976 with the drink-sodden hero at last united with the blonde princess of his dreams - a fresh corpse. Quietly disturbing in the way it finds beauty in corruption, as well as slyly humorous *Crazy Love* heralds a new Belgian talent. **DT**
Director Dominique Deruddere **producers** Erwin Provoost, Alain Keytsman **exec** Provoost **script** Marc Didden, Deruddere, based on The Copulating Mermaid of Venice, California *and* other work by Charles Bukowski **camera** Willy Stassen **editors** Ludo Troch, Guido Henderickx **design** Herbert Pouille, Erik Van Bellegh.m **music** Raymond Van Het Groenewoud **cast** Josse De Pauw, Geert Hunaerts, Michaël Pas, Gène Bervoets, Amid Chakir, François Beukelaers, Florence Béliard, Carmela Locantoire, Karen Vanparys, Doriane Moretus, An Van Essche, Kathleen Seret
Running time: 97 mins
US release: Cineplex, Mar 11, 1987
UK release: Mainline, Mar 10, 1989

CRIMINAL LAW

'Don't hold back on the rain-machine, boys, and let's hit them with the *film noir* atmospherics!' The weather is the most action-packed thing in this Brit-directed US thriller, in which lawyer Gary Oldman (plus American accent) has to defend murder suspect Kevin Bacon. But, in mid-case, he finds irrefutable proof of Bacon's guilt. So what should he do? Carry on as normal? Or abuse lawyer-client trust and show the evidence, ensuring that Bacon fries? Difficult choice, especially since he can hardly hear himself think through the rain and thunder. As directed by Martin Campbell, the film is strong on style, shakier on substance and plausibility. But Oldman helps, giving a deft transatlantic tweak to his anguished-spiv Brit persona. **HK**
Director Martin Campbell **producers** Robert Maclean, Hilary Heath **execs** John Daly, Derek Gibson **script** Mark Kasdan **camera** Philip Meheux **editor** Christopher Wimble **design** Curtis Schnell **music** Jerry Goldsmith **cast** Gary Oldman, Kevin Bacon, Karen Young, Joe Don Baker, Tess Harper, Ron Lea, Karen Woolridge, Elizabeth Sheppard, Michael Sinelnicoff
Running time: 117 mins
US release: Hemdale, Apr 28, 1989

CROSSING DELANCEY

Joan Micklin Silver's first feature in over a decade finds her on antique territory with this precious, genteel comedy about Jewish social manners. The impish Amy Irving is infatuated with a roguish writer. However, thanks to an irascible matchmaker (a heavily made-up Sylvia Miles), she is also the subject of a pickle-maker's affections. The film's myopic world view is peopled with over-familiar stereotypes, such as Irving's mother, a sprightly middle-aged crone. A moral tale of passionless love, Micklin Silver's whimsical love story emerges as a twee, pallid imitation of a short story by Isaac Bashevis-Singer, displaying neither heart nor conviction. It's a disappointment from a director whose *Chilly Scenes of Winter* offered such a precise analysis of obsessive love and desperate emotional entanglements. **SD**
Director Joan Micklin Silver **producer** Michael Nozick **exec** Raphael Silver **script** Susan Sandler, from her play **camera** Theo Van de Sande **editor** Rick Shaine **design** Dan Leigh **music** Paul Chihara **cast** Amy Irving, Peter Riegert, Reizl Bozyk, Jeroen Krabbé, Sylvia Miles, Suzzy Roche, George Martin, John Bedford Lloyd, Claudia

Silver, David Pierce, Rosemary Harris
Running time: 97 mins
US release: Warner, Aug 24, 1988
UK release: Warner, Apr 7, 1989

CRUSOE

This revisionist version of Defoe's casually racist classic centres on Crusoe's journey from slave trader to liberator through a *Hell in the Pacific*-style relationship with a cannibal warrior. Both Quinn and Sapara turn in finely-rounded performances; the script is humorous and manages a few genuine surprises; the Scope photograpy captures some memorable images and highlights the best storm sequence in years, but ultimately the film's brevity counts against it. All the memorable set pieces are there, but there is too little between them for us to become emotionally involved with Crusoe, no matter how much our liberal sympathies may approve of his final act of redemption. An honourable attempt nonetheless, and a vast improvement on Deschanel's first feature, *The Escape Artist*. **TW**
Director Caleb Deschanel *producer* Andrew Braunsberg *script* Walon Green, Christopher Logue, from Daniel Defoe's novel Robinson Crusoe *camera* Tom Pinter *design* Velco Despotovic *music* Michael Kamen *cast* Aidan Quinn, Ade Sapara, Elvis Payne, Richard Sharp, Colin Bruce, William Hootkins, Shane Rimmer
Running time: 91 mins
US release: Island, Mar 31, 1989

A CRY IN THE DARK

'A dingow stole mah bibey!' Yes, it's Meryl Streep again. This time Hollywood's leading accent junkie hits the Antipodes. Playing Lindy Chamberlain of the famous Dingo Baby case, Streep provides an object lesson in how a carefully studied performance with immaculate accent can be as dead as the bad movie it appears in. More like a police report with pictures than a living drama, Fred Schepisi's film moves through events - baby's disappearance, the nation's shock (everybody likes dingoes down under), Lindy's seemingly no less shocking impassivity, hubby's religiosity - and never breathes life into any of them. The real-life story was complex and filled with resonances about male attitudes towards women in Australia; shame about the movie. **HK**
Director Fred Schepisi *producer* Verity Lambert *execs* Menahem Golan, Yoram Globus *script* Robert Caswell, Schepisi, from book Evil Angels

by John Bryson *camera* Ian Baker *editor* Jill Bilcock *design* Wendy Dickson, George Liddle *music* Bruce Smeaton *cast* Meryl Streep, Sam Neill, Bruce Myles, Charles Tingwell, Nick Tate, Neil Fitzpatrick, Maurie Fields, Lewis Fitz-Gerald
Running time: 121 mins
US release: Warner, Nov 11, 1988
UK release: Cannon, May 26, 1989

CYBORG

Another tired, messy and very cheap *Terminator* ripoff aimed directly at the video shelf, this time it's up to Jeane-Claude Van Damme to save mankind from the usual genetic engineeering conspiracy by kicking a lot of people in the head (and various other places) whilst facing the kind of incredible odds that have foregone conclusion written all over them. Pyun's lethargic direction seems intended to destroy what is left of his reputation and make Michael Winner films look good by comparison; he succeeds on both counts. A bad, boring movie - and not even a funny one. **TW**
Director Albert Pyan *producers* Menahem Golan, Yoram Globus *script* Kitty Chalmers *camera* Philip Alan Waters *editors* Rozanne Zingale, Scott Stevenson *design* Douglas Leonard *music* Kevin Bassinson *cast* Jean-Claude Van Damme, Deborah Richter, Vincent Klyn, Alex Daniels, Dayle Haddon, Blaise Loong, Rolf Muller, Haley Peterson, Terri Batson
Running time: 85 mins
US release: Cannon, Apr 7, 1989

COLORS

I f there had been a swear box on the set of *Colors*, the filmmakers would have got their money back before the picture came out. Although the script is credited to Michael Schiffer, the dialogue feels as if it was improvized by sub-normal morons with vocabularies limited to a fairly small number of conjugations and noun formations of ʾie verb 'to fuck'. (Actually, since half of the film's cast are Hispanic, it frequently comes out 'fock'.)

There is nothing new in screen profanity − Brian De Palma's *Scarface* scored high on the F-word meter − but the non-stop fuckin' fuck count of *Colors* rapidly goes beyond the realms of gritty realism, turning the whole thing into a bizarre comedy of repetition.

There's a difference between a disappointing film and a bad one. By anyone's standards − its ridiculous profanity aside − *Colors* is not such a bad movie. Robert Duvall, cast as Bob Hodges, a streetwise Los Angeles cop who specializes in gang-related crimes, is as good as he always is, taking a fairly standard, grizzled, fatherly-policeman rôle, and giving it the kind of effortless individuality he has previously brought to such underwritten leads as the country-and-western has-been of *Tender Mercies* and the Air Force martinet of *The Great Santini*. Sean Penn, cast as Danny McGavin, the aggressive rookie cop partnered with Hodges, is more disciplined than usual, and plays well with Duvall. But when we bought our tickets, we were expecting more than just another tough cop buddy movie.

The film was sold as being the first major screen exploration of the street gang subculture of Los Angeles − previously touched upon in such oddities as *Boulevard Nights* and *Assault on Precinct 13* − and the ongoing war between the Crips and the Bloods, whose colours are blue and red respectively. The two factions are indistinguishable but they are nevertheless sworn to fight each other to death. Many of the articles that appeared in the press at the time of the film's release concentrated on its factual basis, and the rising number of gang-related crimes of violence in LA, where disadvantaged urban whites, blacks and Hispanics turn on each other with machine guns, and the police are hopelessly outnumbered by the hoods.

Expectations were raised by the involvement of Dennis Hopper, whose career since he appeared in *Rebel Without a Cause* has run in parallel with shifts in youth culture. Having modelled himself on James Dean, Hopper had the example of the star's early death to make him pessimistic about the possibility of youthful revolt. The emblematic characters he plays in his own films − the hippy biker in *Easy Rider*, the Hollywoodian in the jungle in *The Last Movie* and the traumatized father in *Out of the Blue* − all die. Given this background, he would seem to be the ideal candidate to make a shattering movie about the self-destructive no-hopers in the Crips and the Bloods, whose violence rises from terminal poverty and is tragically misdirected at themselves rather than towards any revolutionary or constructive end. *Colors* could have been the *Easy Rider* of the late 1980s, with Lou Diamond Phillips, perhaps, as one of the hard men of the gangs. After all, Sean Penn had been a competent juvie psycho in *Bad Boys* and *At Close Range* and could have carried off the gang leader rôle pretty well. In this scenario, the cops in the story would have been like the rednecks in the earlier film; barely glimpsed representatives of repression who would step in with pump shotguns to put a brutal and tragic end to the outlaw heroes.

But, in his need to make amends to Hollywood for the 1971 catastrophe of *The Last Movie* – deemed unreleasable by its major studio backer, Universal – Hopper seems to have felt obliged to Orion, his employers this time round, to deliver an ordinary commercial product. Given the chance to make a movie about street gangs, it is especially perverse that *Colors* should emerge as yet another film in which a wise veteran cop tames a young hothead, and the duo overcome their differences to concentrate on doing the job at hand. Clint Eastwood's Harry Callahan set the trend for this scenario in his team-ups with a Hispanic (Reni Santoni in *Dirty Harry*), a woman (Tyne Daly in *The Enforcer*) and a Chinese-American kung-fu kicker (Evan Kim in *The Dead Pool*), and we have had a straight-gay cop team (*Partners*), several black-and-white cop teams (*Lethal Weapon, Running Scared*) and, recently, such bizarre variations on the theme as *Saigon/Off Limits* (a black and a white cop, but in Vietnam), *The Presidio* (military and civilian cops), *The Hidden* and *Alien Nation* (human and alien cops), *Red Heat* (Russian and American cops) and *K-9* (human and dog cops).

Like *Mississippi Burning* and *Alien Nation*, *Colors* starts out with a fascinating, intriguing and potentially explosive premise and then goes back on it by delivering yet another cop team-up movie. Just as some audiences felt frustrated that Alan Parker was more interested in Gene Hackman and Willem Dafoe's contrasting law enforcement methods than in the civil rights battles of the 1960s, and sci-fi fans were fed up when Graham Baker neglected the genuinely offbeat idea of the forced integration of boat people from outer space into alien society in favour of James Caan and Mandy Patinkin exchanging wisecracks between car chases, anyone who went to *Colors* believing all the publicity about a film which lifted the lid off LA street gangs was due for a severe let-down. In fact, the 'fuckin' fucker' dialogue apart, all the gang sequences in the film could have been snipped from *Hill Street Blues*, which showed the ins and outs of American street gangs. Indeed, Hopper even called in Trinidad Silva, Hill Street's 'Jesus Martinez', to play another, rather less distinctive, Hispanic gang leader.

In addition to the arguments between the easy-going Hodges, who relies on his community contacts and reasonable nature to solve the crimes, and McGavin, whose gung-ho, head-kicking approach gets him nick-named 'Pacman' on the street, the film keeps the pot boiling through a ridiculous relationship between Sean Penn and Maria Conchita Alonso, who plays a sweet Chicano girl who falls in love with the young cop but is understandably upset when he brutally sprays ozone-unfriendly paint into her graffiti-artist cousin's face. Alonso, a likeable screen presence, is no more nor less well-served by her rôle in this supposedly serious and important film than she was by her part opposite Arnold Schwarzenegger as the token woman in *The Running Man*. She comes on and distracts the hero from violence for a few seconds, and they exchange banal dialogue about his macho way of life, and then she gets kicked out of the plot so that the action can rev up again for the finale. In contrast to most of the other cop-team movies of the current cycle, *Colors* reverts to the old ending whereby the grizzled veteran gets shot down in the line of duty and his young protégé is transformed from callow youth to a replica of his former mentor. Again the effect is to push the gangs into the background and to make this even more a film about two cops and their relationship, not with the community, but with each other. Duvall dies bravely in Penn's arms, and Alonso doesn't get a look-in.

It's all quite competently done: the knives clash; the cars crash; the fuckin' dialogue fucks; the sub-machine guns chatter; the knuckles crunch into faces; the hordes of gang extras go down amid plentiful bullet squibs, and the good guy cops chase their gang member quarry energetically over vacant lots. But the gang characters are one-note stereotypes − either beautiful young martyrs or hard-bitten psychopaths with bad teeth and tattoos − and are never given any screen parity with the cops. In the 1980s, we could probably expect no less − Hollywood wouldn't want a repeat of the kerfuffle over the last wave of youth gang movies (*The Warriors, The Wanderers*), which were accused of glamorizing juvenile delinquency − but one wonders what the Dennis Hopper who made *Easy Rider* and *The Last Movie* would think of a film that is essentially a publicity job for the noble and dedicated regular Joes of the Los Angeles Police. The old Hopper used to *hate* the pigs, and here he is glorifying them. A good film about LA gangs remains to be made, and we can all fuckin' fuck ourselves fuckin' motherfuckers that we fuckin' are. Fuck.

KIM NEWMAN

DA

Hugh Leonard's imaginative rewrite of his popular play retains the sprightly humour of the original but loses its pathos. Martin Sheen is a middle-aged New Yorker who returns to Ireland to bury his father, Barnard Hughes. The old man keeps popping up and reminding Sheen of heart-warming and hilarious episodes from his early years. In the play the son despairs of ever reconciling his feelings toward 'Da', but here Sheen merrily transports the old ghost to New York. Hughes is adorable and Sheen is an adequate straight man. **BM**
Director Matt Clark **producer** Julie Corman **execs** William R. Greenblatt, Martin Sheen, Sam Grogg **script** Hugh Leonard, from his play **camera** Alar Kivilo **editor** Nancy Nuttal Beyda **design** Frank Conway **music** Elmer Bernstein **cast** Barnard Hughes, Martin Sheen, William Hickey, Karl Hayden, Dóreen Hepburn, Hugh O'Conor
Running time: 102 mins
US release: Film Dallas, Apr 29, 1988
UK release: Premier, Apr 21, 1989

DOG

DANGEROUS LIAISONS

Director Stephen Frears **producers** Norma Heyman, Hank Moonjean **script** Christopher Hampton **camera** Philippe Rousselot **editor** Mick Audsley **design** Stuart Craig **music** George Fenton **cast** Glenn Close, John Malkovich, Michelle Pfeiffer, Swoosie Kurtz, Keanu Reeves, Mildred Natwick, Uma Thurman, Peter Capaldi, Joe Sheridan, Valerie Cogan, Laura Benson
Running time: 120 mins
US release: Warner, Dec 21, 1988
UK release: Warner, Mar 10, 1989

DARK EYES (Oci Ciornie)

An ingenious conflation of several Chekhov stories, Nikita Mikhalkov's film gives Marcello Mastroianni every comic and romantic opportunity to play his patented rueful roué character. The kept man of Silvana Mangano, Mastroianni capers through his wife's parties and ploughs through her friends. Retreating to a mud-bath spa, he meets Elena Sofonova. This time it's for real, and Mastroianni finds himself following Sofonova to her all-but-inaccessible home in Russia. Many promises are made, but none are kept, and Mastroianni is left with his memories. The film's tone is elegiac, interrupted by snickers. **BM**
Director Nikita Mikhalkov **producers** Silvia

D'Amico Benedico, Carlo Cucchi **script** Alexander Adabashian, Mikhalkov, with collaboration from Suso Cecchi D'Amico, based on short stories by Anton Chekhov **camera** Franco Di Giacomo **editor** Enzo Meniconi **design** Mario Garbuglia, Adabashian **music** Francis Lai **cast** Marcello Mastroianni, Silvana Mangano, Marthe Keller, Elena Sofonova, Vsevolod Larionov, Innokenti Smoktunovski
Running time: 118 mins
US release: Island, Sep 26, 1987
UK release: Curzon, Jul 15, 1988

DAUGHTER OF THE NILE (Niluohe Nüer)

The gigolos, criminals-turned-entrepreneurs and gangsters remain at the fringes in this story of Taipei youth, seen through the eyes of Yang Lin, a fan of the comic strip alluded to in the title. A largely passive character, she pines vainly for the boy whose relationship with a gangster's moll precipitates most of the film's bloody action. Complicit in her brother's crimes, she's keeping his money in her bank account, but can never influence what he, or others, get up to. Long shots through windows reflect her spectator's view of things and a sense of helplessness that leads to barely-expressed despair. A film so unsentimental could not expect to do great box office, but its elliptical telling and compassionate visuals make for an impressive piece of cinema. **JP**
Director Hou Hsiao-Hsien **producer** Li Xianchang, Zhang Huakun **execs** Cai Songlin, Wang Yingjie **script** Zhu Tianwen **camera** Chen Huai'en **editors** Liao Qingsong, Chen Liyu **design** Liu Zhihua, Lin Ju **music** Chen Zhiyuan, Zhang Hongyi **cast** Yang Lin, Gao Jie, Yang Fan, Xin Shufen, Li Tianlu, Cui Fusheng, Wu Nianzhen, You Anshun
Running time: 84 mins (originally 91)
UK release: Artificial Eye, Apr 21, 1989

THE DAWNING

Yet another end-of-innocence picture, this time set in Ireland in the days leading up to the Troubles. A young girl, engaged to a retired English officer, becomes fascinated with a stranger who appears in her beachside hut one day, and who may, or may not, be her father. Anthony Hopkins is excellent, while Rebecca Pidgeon makes a promising début and Hugh Grant's OTT Englishness works well for a change. Despite one marvellously funny sequence – when the local Sinn Feiners try to commandeer a car from a pair of elderly spinsters – it's a somewhat inconclusive affair,

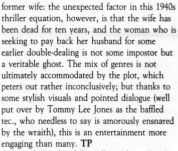

rather like *Ryan's Daughter* shot on a shoestring with television in mind. **TW**
Director *Robert Knights* **producer** *Sarah Lawson* **exec** *Graham Benson* **script** *Moira Williams, from novel* The Old Jest *by Jennifer Johnston* **camera** *Adrian Biddle* **editor** *Max Lemon* **design** *Mike Porter* **music** *Simon May* **cast** *Anthony Hopkins, Rebecca Pidgeon, Jean Simmons, Trevor Howard, Tara MacGowran, Hugh Grant, Ronnie Masterson*
Running time: 97 mins
UK release: Enterprise, Oct 21, 1988

DEAD BANG

Don Johnson, unhappily separated from wife and kids, crosses the country on the trail of a cop-killer and a bunch of white supremacists who worship Hitler and plan to change the way things are run in the US.
Director *John Frankenheimer* **producer** *Steve Roth* **exec** *Robert L. Rosen* **script** *Robert Foster* **camera** *Gerry Fisher* **editor** *Robert F. Shugrue* **design** *Ken Adam* **music** *Gary Chang, Michael Kamen* **cast** *Don Johnson, Penelope Ann Miller, William Forsythe, Bob Balaban, Frank Military, Tate Donovan, Tim Reid*
Running time: 105 mins
US release: Warner/Lorimar, Mar 24, 1989
UK release: Warner, Jun 23, 1989

DEAD CALM

This feisty seagoing thriller is culled from the source novel for Orson Welles' never-completed *The Deep.* Holidaying in the Pacific, Sam Neill and wife have their lives taken over by a mystery survivor from a drifting schooner. Has he killed his comrades? Might he kill again? And when Sam goes off to investigate the schooner, should he leave his wife alone with the human enigma? Welles might have done more to play up the Pandora's Box of plot twists that follow; but the story keeps us guessing and gasping, and Dean Semler's photography is knockout. **HK**
Director *Phillip Noyce* **producers** *Terry Hayes, Doug Mitchell, George Miller* **script** *Hayes, from novel by Charles Williams* **camera** *Dean Semler* **editor** *Richard Franci-Bruce* **design** *Graham (Grace) Walker* **music** *Graeme Reville* **cast** *Sam Neill, Nicole Kidman, Bill Zane*
Running time: 96 mins
US release: Warner, Apr 7, 1989

THE DEAD CAN'T LIE

A run-down private eye is hired by a wealthy layabout to cope with harassment from his former wife: the unexpected factor in this 1940s thriller equation, however, is that the wife has been dead for ten years, and the woman who is seeking to pay back her husband for some earlier double-dealing is not some impostor but a veritable ghost. The mix of genres is not ultimately accommodated by the plot, which peters out rather inconclusively; but thanks to some stylish visuals and pointed dialogue (well put over by Tommy Lee Jones as the baffled tec., who needless to say is amorously ensnared by the wraith), this is an entertainment more engaging than many. **TP**
Director/script *Lloyd Fonvielle* **producer** *David Latt* **execs** *Gerald I. Isenberg, Keith Addis* **camera** *Michael Chapman* **editor** *Evan Lottman* **design** *Carol Spier* **music** *George Clinton* **cast** *Tommy Lee Jones, Virginia Madsen, Colin Bruce, Kevin Jarre, Denise Stephenson, Frederic Forrest*
Running time: 98 mins
UK release: Cannon, Feb 10, 1989

DEAD ON ARRIVAL (D.O.A.)

The team who gave us Max Headroom now turn their attention to an updating of the classic 1949 *film noir,* in which the victim of a fatal but slow-acting poison spends his last hours unravelling the mystery of his murder. The setting has been moved rather improbably to the groves of academe, and the changes to the plot prove increasingly detrimental as the dénouement nears. Earlier, though, the movie puts an arresting post-modern gloss on the protocols of the 1940s thriller, with pyrotechnically overwrought visuals set off by some ultra-knowing dialogue, and manages to accomodate Dennis Quaid's mannerisms with reasonable comfort. **TP**
Directors *Rocky Morton, Annabel Jankel* **producers** *Ian Sander, Laura Ziskin* **script** *Charles Edward Pogue, based on 1949 screenplay by Russell Rouse and Clarence Greene* **camera** *Yuri Neyman* **editors** *Michael R. Miller, Raja Gosnell* **design** *Richard Amend* **music** *Chaz Jankel* **cast** *Dennis Quaid, Meg Ryan, Charlotte Rampling, Daniel Stern, Jane Kaczmarek, Christopher Neame, Robin Johnson, Rob Knepper, Jay Patterson, Brion James, Jack Kehoe, Elizabeth Arlen*
Running time: 97 mins
US release: BV, Mar 18,1988
UK release: Touchstone/Warner, Mar 3, 1989

DEAD POET'S SOCIETY

Some 14 years after *Picnic at Hanging Rock,* Peter Weir invests another scholastic drama –

this one set in a Vermont boys' college in 1959 – with uncontrollable natural forces. Here the muse is an unorthodox English master (Williams) inspiring his charges to 'seize the day', whereupon a gang of them steal to a cave for midnight poetry readings. The movie lapses into bathos when one boy (Leonard) who's filled with thespian dreams, disobeys his martinet father, leading to tragedy. Williams, however, is commendably restrained and the Whitmanesque mood prevails, Weir proving once again that he is brilliant at harnessing landscape to meaning. **GF**

Director Peter Weir **producers** Steven Haft, Paul Junger Witt, Tony Thomas **script** Tom Schulman **camera** John Seale **design** Wendy Stites **music** Maurice Jarre **cast** Robin Williams, Robert Sean Leonard, Ethan Hawke, Josh Charles, Gale Hansen, Dylan Kussman, Allelon Ruggiero, James Waterson, Norman Lloyd, Kurtwood Smith, Carla Belver, Leon Pownall
Running time: 128 mins
US release: BV, Jun 2, 1989

THE DEAD POOL

The premise for this turgid and unsuspenseful Dirty Harry vehicle, and its execution by director Buddy Van Horn, fail to sustain the level of interest elicited by the more enigmatic *Tightrope*. Liam Neeson is an amusing, obstreperous horror movie director whose game of celebrity victim-guessing is taken to inevitably macabre extremes. With nary a mugger or rapist in sight, Steve Sharon's screenplay attempts to replicate the slasher movie formula, seemingly unaware that the Harry character is too invincible to arouse any suspicions that he won't get his man. Perhaps the fact that assailants fall to the ground immediately *before* their extermination, and that Eastwood probably made this picture only in order to procure financing for *Bird*, are the most frightening things about this movie. **MN**
Director Buddy Van Horn **producer** David Valdes **script** Steve Sharon, based on characters created by Harry Julian Fink, R. M. Fink **camera** Jack N. Green **editor** Joel Cox, Ron Spang **design** Edward C. Carfango **music** Lalo Schifrin **cast** Clint Eastwood, Patricia Clarkson, Liam Neeson, Evan C. Kim, David Hunt, Michael Currie, Michael Goodwin, Darwin Gillett
Running time: 91 mins
US release: Warner, Jul 13, 1988
UK release: Warner, Apr 14, 1989

DEAD RINGERS

Director David Cronenberg **producers** Cronenberg, Marc Boyman **execs** Carol Baum, Silvio Tabet **script** Cronenberg, Norman Snider, from book Twins by Bari Wood, Jack Geasland **camera** Peter Suschitzky **editor** Ronald Sanders **design** Carol Spier **music** Howard Shore **cast** Jeremy Irons, Geneviève Bujold, Heidi von Palleske, Barbara Gordon, Shirley Douglas, Stephen Lack, Nick Nichols, Lynne Cormack
Running time: 115 mins
US release: Fox, Sep 23, 1988
UK release: Rank, Jan 6, 1989

DEADLY PURSUIT (Shoot to Kill in US)

Although blessed with some spectacular scenery, and one marvellous stunt that involves Tom Berenger swinging on a rope over a gaping chasm, this outdoor action thriller never makes up its mind what sort of film it wants to be. Citified black cop Sidney Poitier and white mountain guide Berenger are unwillingly teamed up as they track down a psychotic killer who has joined up with a party of suspicious character actors on an outward-bound holiday. Halfway through the film, the whodunnit aspect is summarily ditched as the culprit kills off most of the supporting cast and a less intriguing chase takes over. *Deadly Pursuit* pushes all the right buttons, and Poitier makes a welcome return to heroism as a very agile 60-year-old, but there's a ho-hum blandness that kills the tension, and once the film gets out of the woods and into the city, the excitement dwindles away completely amid a TV-movie-style finale. **KN**
Director Roger Spottiswoode **producers** Ron Silverman, Daniel Petrie Jr. **exec** Philip Rogers **script** Harv Zimmel, Michael Burton, Petrie **camera** Michael Chapman **editors** Garth Craven, George Bowers **design** Richard Sylbert **music** John Scott **cast** Sidney Poitier, Tom Berenger, Kirstie Alley, Clancy Brown, Richard Masur, Andrew Robinson, Kevin Scannell, Frederick Coffin
Running time: 110 mins
US release: BV, Feb 12, 1988
UK release: Touchstone/ Warner, Jul 1, 1988

DEAR AMERICA

Bill Couturie's harrowing documentary may be the best film yet about Vietnam. Using the

plainest of techniques – the letters home by soldiers read out over war or casualty footage – the tragedy of Vietnam 'comes home' in every sense. Men who survived, men who died, men maimed or wounded all put their thoughts and torments, tears and fears, into everyday language. Although the letters are read out by an all-star cast, real feeling is never sacrificed to the rhetoric of showmanship. The understatement is overwhelming. **HK**
Director Bill Couturie *producers* Couturie, Thomas Bird *script* Richard Dewhurst, Couturie *editor* Stephen Stept *music* Todd Boekelheide *voices* Tom Berenger, Ellen Burstyn, Willem Dafoe, Robert De Niro, Brian Dennehy, Kevin Dillon, Matt Dillon, Robert Downey Jr., Michael J. Fox, Mark Harmon, John Heard, Harvey Keitel, Elizabeth McGovern, Judd Nelson, Sean Penn, Randy Quaid, Martin Sheen, Kathleen Turner, Robin Williams
Running time: 87 mins
US release: Taurus, Sep 16, 1988

DEATH JAPANESE STYLE
(Osohiki – The Funeral in US)
Solemnly magnificent comedy on the Japanese way of dying by Juzo (*Tampopo*) Itami. A family gathers to honour a late-lamented member and gets involved in yards of po-faced protocol, several dubious off-the-coffin incidents (involving sex and food) and a general air of earnest, spiralling bewilderment. Highlights include a masterly variation on the *Ben Hur* chariot race (how to pass a TV dinner from car to car in the pouring rain); a slyly hilarious teach-yourself video on How To Behave at a Funeral: and a scene involving eel and avocados that no *Tampopo* fan should miss. **HK**
Director/script Juzo Itami *producer* Seigo Hosogoe *execs* Yasushi Tamaoki, Yutaka Okada *camera* Yonezo Maeda *editor* Akira Suzuki *design* Hiroshi Tokuda *music* Joji Yuasa *cast* Tsutomu Yamazaki, Nobuko Miyamoto, Kin Sugai, Shuji Otaki, Ichiro Zaitsu, Nekohachi Edoya
Running time: 124 mins
US release: New Yorker, Oct 23, 1987
UK release: Electric/Contemporary, Oct 28, 1988

DEATH OF A SALESMAN
Arthur Miller's play was revived in 1984 on Broadway with Hoffman scoring a personal triumph in the lead. Schlöndorff films this on one minimal set, around which the camera elegantly revolves. It's full of well-played scenes in which the characters cry, make painful revelations and hug each other. Hoffman has to work too hard, via old-age mannerisms and superb make-up, to turn himself into the battered old loser, whereas Fredric March in the 1951 film version just had to slump his shoulders and *be* Willy Loman. It's brilliant stage acting, but the camera's close-ups show all the workings behind the central performance. Everyone else comes across just as well on film as they must have done on stage. **KN**
Director Volker Schlöndorff *producer* Robert F. Colesberry *script* Arthur Miller, *adapted by* Michael Rudman *camera* Michael Ballhaus *editor* David Ray *design* Tony Walton *cast* Dustin Hoffman, Kate Reid, John Malkovich, Stephen Lang, Charles Durning, Louis Zorich, David S. Chandler, Jon Polito, Kathy Rossetter, Tom Signorelli, Linda Kozlowski, Karen Needle
Running time: 136 mins (180 mins for TV)
UK release: Artificial Eye, Aug 26, 1988

THE DECEIVERS
A boisterous tale of life among the officer classes, *The Deceivers* traces the adventures of the sort of native-shooting patriotic British Empire chaps who are normally depicted in sepia or on the labels of Camp coffee. Set in 1825, the film comes across as a rousing historical epic, with a dutiful captain (Brosnan) taking time off from his recent marriage to investigate the Thuggee cult - ritualistic Indian stranglers who murder and rob their victims in ceremonial veneration of the evil goddess Kali. Director Nicholas Meyer never ridicules the premise, but the piece is an under-achiever. What might have been a fascinating insight into the psyche of a British Army officer when infected with an alien ideology is transformed into another tribute to *The Four Feathers*. **MN**
Director Nicholas Meyer *producer* Ismail Merchant *exec* Michael White *script* Michael Hirst, *from novel by* John Masters *camera* Walter Lassally *editor* Richard Trevor *design* Ken Adam *music* John Scott *cast* Pierce Brosnan, Saeed Jaffrey, Shashi Kapoor, Helen Michell, Keith Michell, David Robb, Tariq Yunus
Running time: 103 mins
US release: Cinecom, Sep 2, 1988
UK release: Enterprise, Sep 23, 1988

DEEPSTAR SIX
This underwater re-telling of *Alien* is competently done but still rates pretty low on the thrills meter. The monster from the deep looks like a certain sort of automatic car wash, and its murderous visitations are too heavily

signposted to shock. The idea of the Thing Growing Inside is transmuted rather pathetically into a lady crew member's gestating baby. A couple of nuclear explosions may not destroy the beastie, but it's just too obvious that the nascent nuclear family will make it back to the top. JP
Director Sean S. Cunningham *producers* Cunningham, Patrick Markey *execs* Mario Kassar, Andrew Vajna *script* Lewis Abernathy, Geoff Miller *camera* Mac Ahlberg *editor* David Handman *design* John Reinhart *music* Harry Manfredini *cast* Taurean Blacque, Nancy Everhard, Greg Evigan, Miguel Ferrer, Nia Peeples, Matt McCoy, Cindy Pickett, Marius Weyers
Running time: 99 mins
US release: Tri-Star, Jan 13, 1989

DIARY FOR MY LOVES (Napló szerelmeimnek)

The second instalment of Márta Mészáros' autobiographical trilogy is more complex, and less affecting, than the first, *Diary for My Children*. The adolescent Julí (Czinkóczi), so stolid and obstreperous that she sometimes seems simply bored, shuttles between Moscow, where she's a film student, and the apartment of her hated foster mother in Budapest. She has some strong scenes with a wrongly imprisoned 'good' Communist, and the search for her father provides a degree of narrative drive, but Mészáros' casualness about establishing shifts in locale or mood, and failure to link newsreel footage to dramatic events, make for a film that appears muddled, at least to non-Hungarian audiences. JP
Director Márta Mészáros *exec* Mafilm/Budapest Studio *script* Mészáros, Éva Pataki *camera* Nyika Jancsó *editor* Éva Kármentő *design* Éva Martin *music* Zsolt Döme *cast* Zsuzsa Czinkóczi, Anna Polony, Jan Nowicki, Irina Kouberskaya, Mari Szemes, László Szabó, Pál Zolnay, Adél Kováts, Erzsébet Kutvölgyi
Running time: 130 mins
UK release: Artificial Eye, Feb 17, 1989

HIT

DIE HARD

Director John McTiernan *producers* Lawrence Gordon, Joel Silver *exec* Charles Gordon *script* Jeb Stuart, Steven E. de Souza, from novel Nothing Lasts Forever by Roderick Thorp *camera* Jan De Bont *editors* Frank J. Urioste, John F. Link *design* Jackson DeGovia *music* Michael

Kamen *cast* Bruce Willis, Bonnie Bedelia, Reginald Veljohnson, Paul Gleason, De'voreaux White, William Atherton, Hart Bochner, James Shigeta, Alan Rickman, Alexander Godunov, Bruno Doyon
Running time: 132 mins
US release: Fox, Jul 15, 1988
UK release: Fox, Feb 3, 1989

DIRTY ROTTEN SCOUNDRELS

Michael Caine and Steve Martin for once play to their strengths, as two tricksters working the same patch of the Riviera. Yet there's too little interaction between them to make sparks fly. The wild-eyed Martin, starting as an amateur, learns fast from the complacent older man – instruction mostly involves playing his teacher's mad brother to frighten away those with thoughts of marriage. By the time the two lock horns over a suspected millionairess, they're clearly an even match. Martin's impersonations are so crazy he really could be improvising his way out of defeat, while his rival's smug self-assurance marks him down as the eventual loser. In the end, of course, they both lose out to another's super-scam and one has to acknowledge just how tired this plot seems. JP
Director Frank Oz *producer* Bernard Williams *execs* Dale Launer, Charles Hirschhorn *script* Launer, Stanley Shapiro, Paul Henning, from 1964 film Bedtime Story by Shapiro, Henning *camera* Michael Ballhaus *editors* Stephen A. Rotter, William Scharf *design* Roy Walker *music* Miles Goodman *cast* Steve Martin, Michael Caine, Glenne Headly, Anton Rodgers, Barbara Harris, Ian McDiarmid, Dana Ivey
Running time: 110 mins
US release: Orion, Dec 14, 1988
UK release: Rank, Jun 30, 1989

DISORGANIZED CRIME

Directorial début for Jim Kouf, who wrote the screenplay for Stakeout, in which Rubén Blades and Lou Diamond Phillips are hired to rob a bank in Montana.
Director/script Jim Kouf *producer* Lynn Bigelow *execs* Rob Cohen, John Badham *camera* Ron Garcia *editor* Frank Morriss, Dallas Puett *design* Waldemar Kalinowski *music* David Newman *cast* Hoyt Axton, Corbin Bernsen, Rubén Blades, Fred Gwynne, Ed O'Neill, Lou Diamond Phillips, Daniel Roebuck, William Russ
Running time: 101 mins
US release: BV, Apr 14, 1989

DISTANT THUNDER

Maladjusted Vietnam vet movies didn't become

a genre until *Rambo*, but the character types were fixed in *Coming Home* and *Can't Stop the Rain* back in the 1970s: the impotent Jon Voight and the soul-destroyed Nick Nolte. Rick Rosenthal's movie has John Lithgow in the Voight part and several minor bent-brains sharing the Nolte part. Some 20 years after being traumatized in the jungle, gentle Lithgow collects ferns in the Northwest woods and his murderous buddies shoot intruders. Ralph Macchio is Lithgow's long-lost son who seeks to re-establish contact but runs into the runamucks. **BM**

Director Rick Rosenthal **producer** Robert Schaffel **exec** Richard L. O'Connor **script** Robert Stitzel **camera** Ralf D. Bode **editor** Dennis Virkler **music** Maurice Jarre **cast** John Lithgow, Ralph Macchio, Kerrie Keane, Reb Brown, Janet Margolin, Dennis Arndt, Jamey Sheridan, Tom Bower
Running time: 114 mins
US release: Paramount, Nov 11, 1988

DISTANT VOICES, STILL LIVES

Director/script Terence Davies **producer** Jennifer Howarth **exec** Colin MacCabe **camera** William Diver, Patrick Duval **editor** Diver **design** Miki van Szanenberg, Jocelyn James **cast** Freda Dowie, Pete Postlethwaite, Angela Walsh, Dean Williams, Lorraine Ashbourne, Sally Davies, Nathan Walsh, Susan Flanagan, Michael Starke, Vincent Maguire, Antonia Mallen, Debi Jones, Chris Darwin, Marie Jelliman, Andrew Schofield, Anny Dyson, Jean Boht
Running time: 84 mins
UK release: BFI, Oct 14, 1988

DOIN' TIME ON PLANET EARTH

Charles Matthau (son of Walter) makes his directorial début with this witless camp pastiche. A teenage misfit (Strouse), reviled by his ultra-suburban family, seeks an escort for his brother's wedding via a computer-dating agency and is revealed, through his answer to their questionnaire, to be an extra-terrestrial. Strouse is helped to return home by two psychedelic alien counsellors who inevitably assert that, in order to remember the identity of his planet, he needs to lose his virginity. **MN**

Director Charles Matthau **producers** Menahem Golan, Yoram Globus **script** Darren Star **camera** Timothy Suhrstedt **editors** Alan Balsam, Sharyn L. Ross **design** Curtis A. Schnell **music** Dana

Kaproff **cast** Nicholas Strouse, Hugh Gillin, Gloria Henry, Hugh O'Brian, Martha Scott, Timothy Patrick Murphy, Isabelle War, Paula Irvine
Running time: 85 mins
US release: Cannon, Sep 16, 1988

DO THE RIGHT THING

Director/producer/script Spike Lee **camera** Ernest Dickerson **editor** Barry Alexander Brown **design** Wynn Thomas **music** Bill Lee **cast** Danny Aiello, Ossie Davis, Ruby Dee, Richard Edson, Giancarlo Esposito, Roger Guenveur Smith, Sam Jackson, Joie Lee,Spike Lee, Bill Nunn, John Turturro, Rosie Perez, Paul Benjamin, Frankie Faison, John Savage
Running time: 130 mins
US release: Universal, Jun 30, 1989
UK release: UIP, Jun 23, 1989

DREAM DEMON

Just when Clive Barker seemed set to spark a renaissance in home-grown British horror, along comes this crass piece of low-rent Gothic which has neither the gratuitous zeal nor the visceral accoutrements of its American counterparts. Inevitably plagiarizing the dream-time emanations of Elm Street's adolescent victims, *Dream Demon* crawls from one over-telegraphed 'shock' sequence to the next in its efforts to provide insight into post-pubescent rich bitch Jemma Redgrave's nocturnal hallucinations, the majority of which revolve around her imminent marriage to lantern-jawed Falklands hero (Greenstreet). Director Harley Cokliss's pretensions to surrealistic psycho-drama are manifest in heavy-handed visual scares, also involving a bizarre plot featuring Kathleen Wilhoite as a sleazy American and a vaudevillian turn from Nail and Spall. But where is the demon alluded to in the title? It must have absconded, to avoid appending its name to this heretical horror movie. **MN**

Director Harley Cokliss **producer** Paul Webster **execs** Jonathan Olsberg, Nik Powell, Peter Watson-Wood, Timothy Woolford **script** Christopher Wicking, Cokliss **camera** Ian Wilson **editors** Ian Crafford, David Martin **design** Hugo Luczyc-Wyhowski **music** Bill Nelson **cast** Jemma Redgrave, Kathleen Wilhoite, Timothy Spall, Jimmy Nail, Mark Greenstreet, Susan Fleetwood, Annabelle Lanyon, Nickolas Grace
Running time: 89 mins
UK release: Palace, Oct 14, 1988

THE DREAM TEAM

Actor Michael Keaton continues a career in which bonanza movies beginning with B – Beetlejuice, Batman – alternate with duds beginning with almost anything. This one starts with a plot premise you wouldn't wish on your Actor Michael Keaton continues a career in which bonanza movies beginning with B – Beetlejuice, Batman – alternate with duds beginning with almost anything. This one starts with a plot premise you wouldn't wish on your least favourite filmmaker. Four mental patients are separated from their doctor during a trip to a baseball match, and have wacky adventures all over town. If this 'Let's laugh at the loonies' plot were not tasteless enough, how about the passel of over-the-top performances? Stephen Furst says little but fears much, Christopher Lloyd fusses over details, Peter Boyle strips and preaches at the slightest provocation and Keaton tends to act out hostility. Not so much a dream team, more a nightmare package from Tinseltown. **HK**
Director Howard Zieff **producer** Christopher W. Knight **exec** Joseph M. Caracciolo **script** Jon Connolly, David Loucka **camera** Adam Holender **editor** C. Timothy O'Meara **design** Todd Hallowell **music** David McHugh **cast** Michael Keaton, Christopher Lloyd, Peter Boyle, Stephen Furst, Dennis Boutsikaris, Lorraine Bracco, Milo O'Shea, Philip Bosco, James Remar, Jack Gilpin
Running time: 113 mins
US release: Universal, Apr 7, 1989

THE DRESSMAKER

One has become used to British 'features' that could have been made for TV. This slice-of-life in WW2 Liverpool is something else, a putative feature that so completely fails ever to get to the point or exploit its potential for black comedy it might be one episode from an ongoing series. The claustrophobic atmosphere of life in back-to-back housing is nicely evoked and there are richly-nuanced performances from Billie Whitelaw and Joan Plowright, as sisters respectively fun-loving and repressed, but John McGrath's script fails to explore its central plot strand – teenager Jane Horrocks' infatuation with a no-good American GI. This is another literary adaptation more concerned to convey a sense of the source book's 'texture' than to fulfil its potential as a movie. The film ends abruptly just as things start to become interesting. **JP**
Director Jim O'Brien **producer** Ronald Shedlo

exec John McGrath **script** McGrath from novel by Beryl Bainbridge **camera** Michael Coulter **editor** William Diver **design** Caroline Amies **music** George Fenton **cast** Joan Plowright, Billie Whitelaw, Jane Horrocks, Tim Ransom, Pete Postlethwaite, Pippa Hinchley, Rosemary Martin
Running time: 91 mins
US release: Euro-American, Jan 6, 1989
UK release: Rank, Jan 6, 1989

⬭ TURKEY

DROWNING BY NUMBERS

Director/script Peter Greenaway **producers** Kees Kasander, Denis Wigman **camera** Sacha Vierny **editor** John Wilson **design** Ben Van Os, Jan Roelfs **music** Michael Nyman **cast** Bernard Hill, Joan Plowright, Juliet Stevenson, Joely Richardson, Jason Edwards, Bryan Pringle
Running time: 119 mins
UK release: Recorded Releasing, Sep 2, 1988

DANGEROUS LIAISONS

L ETTER 176: The Baroness de Billson to the Marquise de Merteuil. Madame, having long been one of your most devoted followers, it falls to me to be the bearer of tidings that will make you gnash your teeth. On the other hand, you may well bust a gut laughing, since we know your sense of humour is amusingly warped. How delightful it is to recall the smallpox scar make-up that you wore on your last visit to Paris! How we chortled when that mischievous Choderlos de Laclos fellow put it about that this hideous disfigurement was divine punishment for your outrageous behaviour.

This is the gist of what I have learned. Do you remember persuading the Viscomte de Valmont to deflower the Volanges girl before the little slut could be married off to that ungrateful ex-lover of ours? Shortly after you retired from the public eye in order to compose your memoirs, many of the letters pertaining to this intrigue fell into the hands of a bounder named Christopher Hampton who, since he was a playwright, made a play out of them. His attempts at capturing your inimitable essence were surprisingly effective, though a natural bias towards his own gender resulted in the wretched Valmont being elevated perilously close to the status of hero. Instead of his well-deserved demise being the consequence of sheer ineptitude with the *épée*, it was made to appear that he was a romantic suicide. His deathbed confession was presented as a moral triumph, instead of as an act of cowardice and reprehensible betrayal of those sterner ideals to which he professed adherence whenever it suited his purposes.

Had it been left at that, my dear Marquise, you would have had little cause for complaint, especially as you yourself were portrayed by a certain Miss Lindsay Duncan as a charming creature of great beauty and amorality. But alas, the play proved such a success that it has been made into a motion picture, and it is here that I fear you have been sorely misrepresented.

Firstly, and in my opinion disastrously, you are played by Miss Glenn Close, who formerly achieved notoriety as the psychotic harpy in *Fatal Attraction*. Miss Close is, of course, lumbered with the baggage from this rôle, so that there are many filmgoers who see you as nothing more than a frustrated matron, a pitiable bitch to be booed and hissed like a music-hall villain. Miss Close, moreover, though she might conceivably be considered handsome in an impoverished backwoods community which prizes sun-darkened skin and freckle-faced candour above aristocratic elegance, is singularly lacking in sex appeal. Indeed, she looks positively *plain* when placed alongside Miss Michelle Pfeiffer, the actress who has been cast as your chief rival and object of Valmont's absurd puppy-crush – the nauseating Madame de Tourvel. What with her bruised lips and moist eyes and voice all a-tremble, my dear, it is no contest; no man in his right mind, not even

the ridiculous Valmont, would *ever dream* of casting such a cupcake aside as a favour to that imposter being passed off as yourself. To those of us who have had the honour of knowing you, Madame, this ludicrous deception stretches credulity too far.

As for Valmont, he is portrayed by Mr John Malkovich as a leering satyr, launching himself at women with a vulgar abandon that would get him banned from every respectable drawing-room in the land. Valmont had his faults, certainly, but lack of *savoir faire* was not one of them. Nor was lack of subtlety. Whenever Mr Malkovich and Miss Close tell untruths or utter *double entendres* in the presence of those not privy to their schemes, they smirk and twitch as if in the grip of Tourette's Syndrome, thus alerting us to their duplicity.

I could go on. I could mention the American accents which, although one is not averse to this New World way of speaking *per se*, are more redolent of *thirty something*-style-let-it-all-hang-out than of sexual intrigue *à la* eighteenth-century French aristocracy. I could tell you of the strangely underdressed châteaux, or of the perambulations that everyone takes in the gardens whenever Mr Stephen Frears gets bored with the great indoors and feels he should demonstrate that he is directing a *film* and not a *stage play*. Walk? In the *garden*? And run the risk of sullying one's pale skin with a plebeian suntan?

I could complain about the lack of social or economic context which makes your boast of avenging your sex seem no more than a half-hearted nod towards late twentieth-century feminism, or about the filmmaker's yellow-bellied concessions to popular sentiment, or about the inattentiveness to appearance in a story which is *all about* appearance. Instead, cast and crew have gone on record (and critics have backed them up) as saying it is somehow a good thing that the gorgeous, elaborate costumes are barely given the time of day. I know, and I know that *you* know, Madame, that to be a successful *poseuse*, one must always be aware of the discrepancy between appearance and actuality.

Madame, I urge you to take action. If necessary, we could retrieve your letters and promote our own version of events, this time with a more suitable actress in the leading rôle. Some 15 years ago, Faye Dunaway might have done you justice. Today, we might have . . . who? Geneviève Bujold? Catherine Deneuve? As for the director, we might hire Ridley Scott, who I am told can be pretty nifty with the matching accessories.

Or how does Milos Forman grab you? Madame, I fear I bring more bad tidings. Even as I write, Mr Forman is preparing to unveil his own interpretation of your story. His title, alas, does not bode well. He plans to call it – brace yourself, Madame – *Valmont*.

ANNE BILLSON

DEAD RINGERS

Jean Renoir once said something to the effect that a director's oeuvre constitutes one vast movie in which the individual films are variations on its grand theme. On a more mundane level, in contemporary Hollywood one might say that producers make the same film again and again, only varying the menu slightly by employing different directors and writers. Hence the proliferation of sequels; virtually any generic film that has a modicum of success is promptly extended to a part two. It's a practice that is particularly rife in the current cycle of horror films. At last year's Sitges Festival of Fantasy Cinema, the main cinema was overshadowed with hoardings and posters advertising films with titles in which numerals outscreamed words: *Hellraiser II*, *Short Circuit 2*, *Critters 2*, *Nightmare on Elm Street 4*, *Fright Night 2*. At the press conference held after a screening of *Dead Ringers*, David Cronenberg distanced himself from this trend, declaiming that whatever it was, *Dead Ringers* was not *The Fly II*.

In fact, Cronenberg is an *auteur* in the sense intended by Renoir. His films are clearly variations rather than mere duplications of each other, and it is relatively simple to sketch out a thematic and stylistic map of his concerns. What is significant about *Dead Ringers* is that it marks a decisive shift in the director's career. His earlier films (*Shivers*, *Rabid*) were amongst the most visceral ever made – showing the human body in revolt against itself. Then came The *Brood* and *Videodrome* which shatter the mind/body duality with characters who externalize feelings and neuroses as physical manifestations (*The Brood*) or alternatively (*Videodrome*) so completely lose any sense of self that their very bodies can be penetrated by material objects (the video cassette that the villains insert into the vaginal slot that appears in James Woods' stomach, the gun that grows onto his hand).

His remake of *The Fly*, in which two physical and intellectual identities share the same body, could have been even more visceral in effect. Instead, Cronenberg treats Jeff Goldblum's mutation as a voyage of discovery, with Goldblum as both the voyager and wryly philosophical commentator on the changes in lifestyle he undergoes.

Dead Ringers is, like *The Fly*, a special effects film, but whereas the earlier outing is a graphic demonstration of SFX technology – we see Goldblum's Seth Brundle 'become' a fly – *Dead Ringers*, for the most part, hides its effects. For the story to work we have to believe that Beverly and Elliot Mantle are identical twins. The effects, necessary to allow Jeremy Irons to play both parts, have to be 'invisible'. Also, the Mantles and Brundle are presented differently. Brundle, before he is seduced by Veronica Quaife and literally discovers the pleasures of the flesh, is a failure; the Mantles at the beginning of the film are successes.

The cost of Brundle's success is change – he mutates into something else; the cost of the destruction of the delicate equilibrium underpinning the lives of the Mantles is separation and introversion. In contrast to the simple grotesqueries of the earlier versions of *The Fly*, which presented their man-flys as horror film monsters, Cronenberg graphically shows us Seth Brundle's gradual transformation. *Dead Ringers* is even more relentless. Its logic is that of a dream, hence the slow-motion dreamlike quality of many of the sequences and the plot's speedy dismissal of the Bujold character once she has made her fatal intervention.

The plot is simplicity itself. Identical twins Beverly and Elliot run the world-famous Mantle fertility clinic. But, although physically identical, their emotional and intellectual identity is shared. Elliot is the front man, the fundraiser, and Beverly the researcher. Together they are a whole person, individually nothing. Each compensates for the other. Enter Bujold's Claire Niveau who presents them with an intellectual problem. A 'trifurcate' (an invention of Cronenberg's), she has three cervixes and accordingly cannot conceive. More significant is the emotional problem she poses when Beverly, who regularly accepts Elliot's sexual leavings, falls in love with her. For the first time Beverly finds his emotional needs satisfied outside the enclosed universe he and Elliot share. In one of the film's few visceral scenes, Beverly has a nightmare in which Claire literally separates Elliot and himself by biting through the umbilical cord joining them.

From here on it's all downhill. To calm Beverly's fears about separation from Elliott and to create a shared world, Claire introduces him to drugs and so sets about the inevitable destruction of the Mantles. Her body can intellectually and emotionally stimulate the brothers but she cannot replace either one for the other.

At the root of this, of course, is the matter of the sexual identity. Hence the non-gender-specific names, the way Beverly initially acts as a surrogate wife to Elliot's sexual/social/economic achiever, the early scenes in which the young Mantles discuss the sexual difference between the males and the females with a solemnity only available to children and the Mantles' profession as gynaecologists – explorers and facilitators of the moment of birth. From this perspective, Claire is a straightforward female fantasy figure. Having made a man (rather than a dependent person) of Beverly, she then (literally) withdraws from the relationship (and the plot), causing Beverly to collapse into infantile jealousy (he makes an abusive phone call to the location of the film she is engaged upon). To this view of the film one could add the misogynistic twist provided by the instruments of torture which Beverly invents and attempts to use on one of his clients as a revenge on womankind for Claire's desertion of him.

But such a view is too simple and one-dimensional. Sexuality may be an essential component of identity, but what Cronenberg examines is the inadequacy of the body (male in *Dead Ringers*, female in *Rabid* and *The Brood*) to deal with the questions of 'Who am I?' *Dead Ringers* is a relentless film, but not in the manner of slasher films like *Halloween* where, several cadavers on, the villain's sexual lack is made manifest by his death/castration at the hands of a female (usually characterized as a tomboy type) who is symbolically given a penis in the form of a knife, chainsaw, etc. By contrast, the trajectory of *Dead Ringers* is almost pre-sexual. Their social (and economic) identities having failed them, the Mantle brothers end their lives in a bizarre reversal of the very separation that allowed them to spring forth from the womb. Returned to their wholly private universe, they 'experiment' on each other (at the cost of Elliott's death) in an attempt to physically rediscover the Siamese link that ended with their entry into the world.

The main part of the film's narrative deals with Beverly's desertion of Elliot, and the twins' subsequent attempts to re-establish the delicate balance of their shared identity (through a synchronized drug-taking programme in which one takes uppers while the other is on downers). But Elliot too is allowed his moments of identity crisis. His lover, like Claire, encourages him to leave his brother, but to no avail. And, though initially presented as the dominant partner in the relationship, Elliott is as much in need of Beverly as Beverly of him. Thus, in the one moment of sexual activity in which we see him, he asks the two prostitutes to distinguish themselves when servicing him by calling him Beverly and Elliot respectively.

The unremitting pessimism of *Dead Ringers* makes it a hard film to 'enjoy'. But, if its dreamlike images and structure are unpleasant to contemplate, its view of the body as a vessel inadequate to contain the emotional needs of the intellect it carries remains powerful. The pain of the Mantles twins is of separation from each other, the pain the audience can share is of the isolation we all feel once set adrift in a world in which there are no reassuring fixtures or relationships to touch base with. Or, as Cronenberg himself put it succinctly in an interview: 'I am, therefore I fear.'

PHIL HARDY

DIE HARD

s there an effective response to international terrorism? It's a question that has troubled more than one US administration. The disastrous attempt by marines to rescue hostages from Tehran helped ensure the end of Jimmy Carter's regime. With Ronald Reagan gone from the White House, the stench from the Irangate affair and the activities of hatchet man Ollie North continue to dog George Bush and his team. The explosion of an American plane over Lockerbie at the end of 1988 confirmed the reach of the terrorist's trigger finger and the inability of governments to protect populations from their murderous intent.

Die Hard provides a fantasized resolution to this highly complex problem. The story is austerely basic. European terrorists-turned-robbers take over a Japanese corporation's headquarters in Century City, Los Angeles. A cop (Bruce Willis), visiting his estranged wife (Bonnie Bedelia), is trapped with her in the building. He picks off the Europeans one by one, as they wait for FBI terrorist procedure to shut off the electricity and unwittingly open the corporation's vault, containing $645 million in bonds.

The film is dominated by the grandiose presence of Nakatomi Plaza, a skyscraper with huge sheets of glass, hi-tech consumer-friendly gadgetry and tastefully swish décor. With the key action located inside the building, the set concentrates the film's focus on Willis's decimation of the terrorists' ranks. Everything in the film is geared towards this end, with the strongest tensions located in the explicit contrasts between the cop and the lead villain.

The antagonism between Willis and chief terrorist Alan Rickman is expressed through the contrasting images they present. Middle-class New Yorker Willis scarpers around, decidedly coarse, bare foot, wearing an increasingly tatty vest. He appears uncomfortable with anything vaguely contemporary or upmarket. Planes make him acutely nervous and he chooses to ride in the front of a limo with the chauffeur.

Rickman's profile is graced by swept-back hair, a flowing coat, the ubiquitous filofax and an appreciation for expensive clothes. The decadence with which Rickman so suavely surrounds himself – with its implicit connection to big business – is tactile and reptilian. One can almost smell the expensive cologne. His sartorial flair is equated with depravity.

The values of the terrorists are shown as superficial and vacuously style-conscious (Rickman's colleagues look like male models auditioning for a Jim Steinman rock opera). Terrorist political dogma has been replaced by the values of fashion. While Willis is the honest macho American trying to come to terms with his wife's successful career, Rickman's Germanic exactitude and seductive, glib cruelty draw on the image of a Gestapo killer.

The success of *Die Hard* is partly explained by the way it uses these contrasts in the narrative. The terrorists, with their European cultural arrogance, grossly underestimate the resourcefulness and iron will of the ordinary American cop, who fearlessly plays out the rôle of cowboy. Over the radio, Rickman chides Willis, 'Just another American who saw too many movies as a child. Another orphan of a bankrupt culture who thinks he is John Wayne, Rambo, Marshall Dillon.' Willis expresses a preference for Roy Rogers' sequined shirts and signs off 'Yippie kai ai motherfucker.'

The American public, powerless in the face of terrorism and angered by the humiliating revelations of Irangate, is provided through *Die Hard* with a face-to-face battle between the might of the all-American hero and the cold-blooded, valueless terrorists.

The balletic style of the camera work and the highly-choreographed violence – Rickman's sidekick, Alexander Godunov, moves like a ballet dancer – build an escalating pattern. The momentum starts to develop when the Mercedes carrying Godunov and the truck containing the rest of the terrorists sweep into the building. With graceful, flowing movements, the European hit squad waft through Nakatomi Plaza as though posing for a *Vogue* fashion spread. This visual style emphasizes the deep-rooted fears in America and the West that international terrorism arouses; terrorism as an uncontrollable, external force that arrives without warning, mercilessly seizing power and dispatching lives without hesitation.

While Rickman's malevolent band are glorified bank robbers, their use of ruthless terrorist tactics, executing hostages solely to make a point, generates the necessary malice to fuel the narrative's isolation of them as cold-blooded ciphers for any group of anonymous terrorists.

The gang's financial motive serves to stoke the hostages' anger at their false political posturing. It is at this level that *Die Hard* predictably finds Rickman's bunch an easy target. When Rickman, continuing the masquerade as a terrorist, lists his demands of freedom for terrorist prisoners in return for the release of hostages, one group he mentions is Asian Dawn. Godunov mutters 'Who?' 'I read about them in *Time* magazine' says Rickman.

The casting of Willis is clearly a master stroke, designed to give the film a light sense of realism which makes its resolution that much more satisfying. Building on his winsomely idiosyncratic performance in the *Moonlighting* TV show, he lacks the Austrian cruelty of blow-up doll Arnold Schwarzenegger or the steroid simplicity of Sylvester Stallone. The brutality of the rôle, both in terms of his suffering (pulling glass out of his feet) and vicious, street fighting style, is stolidly set against the flashy Europeans with their hi-tech weaponry. The hero's fleshy vulnerability makes the human stakes more emotionally plausible than a Schwarzenegger action-man vehicle.

The film often displays less than credible acrobatic feats by Willis, but the

implausibility of the action is overriden by *Die Hard*'s frenetic pacing, marked by noisy exchanges of gun fire. Fast, brutal editing backs up Willis's physical presence as a one-man action equivalent of a high-powered American football team – brutal, sweating, out for blood and unstoppable. High fashion and cowboy nonchalance fight it out in skyscraper Valhalla.

Die Hard's success is finally due to the solution it presents to the terrorist problem. By marginalizing in astute stereotypes the peripheral characters (the greasy TV reporter, the robotic FBI men, the blow-hard police chief), the film concentrates on its core business, the eradication of terrorists. As they swept in, so they are swept out. Willis's survival and triumph is supposedly America's. A fantasy, but one grounded solidly in modern day tensions, arguably *Die Hard* is the crowning celluloid achievement of the Reagan era.

STEPHEN DARK

DISTANT VOICES, STILL LIVES

B ombs fall. Babies are born. Lives are lived and lost. The old Britain wrestles with the new in the raw Northern streets. Place: Liverpool. Time: any and every year between the war's end and the beginning of the Brave New 1950s. Dad's the one with glowing eyes and swollen cheekbones. He's all right except when he beats the kids or gives Mum a walloping. Mum's the one with the warm voice and frazzled hair and face like a walnut. She's a survivor – she needs to be with him around. Then there's son Tony; strong as an ox and just as dependable. And daughters Maisie – that's the dark-haired one – and Eileen. Eileen's a right card. She's always the loudest one at a sing-song and thick as thieves with best friends Monica and Jingles. She's getting married to that solid young Dave. He'll keep her in line. High time too.

British cinema too has been growing up in the 1980s. But even in a decade studded with Brit Renaissance gems, Terence Davies' *Distant Voices, Still Lives* looks like being the Koh-I-Noor diamond. The film took the 1988 Cannes International Critics Prize and two other top festival accolades. Normally sober, even normally drunk, critics unpacked long-mothballed superlatives.

The movie is a mirror held up to the emotions of a joyful and horrifying childhood. It is Davies' portrait, moving but never misted by sentimentality, of his own warring parents and his oldest brother and two oldest sisters. (Davies was the youngest of ten children born to a poor Liverpool family.)

What makes it a modern film? It's a film about memory, but it's also a film about making a film about memory. Davies stuffs the movie with deliberately exposed pieces of grammar and homage. You're aware of the artifices of film lighting. You're aware that each crane-shot is a crane-shot. You're aware that a camera tracking from a wedding reception hall into a gulf of darkness then into a candlelit church then into more darkness and then along a terraced street is a geography-defying *coup de cinéma*. And you're aware of the recurring door-frame motif, *Searchers*-style, distancing and contextualizing the memory of family or friends.

But none of this awareness of style and technique vitiates the film's emotional impact. One reason is that its material is not dead but overpoweringly alive. For Davies, the past is not a 'foreign country' in the sighing, elegiac sense that has lately infected all those costume pix about the British Raj. For Davies, the past is guerrilla territory – not a sedate outpost of our existential empires but a Vietnam of the mind. There, emotions are not languidly picked over with a calf-gloved hand; they come out of the shadows, raw and ungloved, and pick *you* over.

This *sturm-und-drang* approach to the cinema of autobiography was prefigured in Bill Douglas's trilogy: *My Childhood, My Ain Folk* and *My Way Home*. But Douglas's way with memory was bleak, ironized and hieratic. His films were

pictures from The Family Album You Never See, graphic with remembered rage or grief, but still Then rather than Now.

Davies' past is now. And it has a universal resonance because it has a fearless specificity. Ten minutes into the film you realize how unnerving its originality is. Scenes are not there to illustrate points. There is no 'message' in the jagged tableaux of memory Davies is throwing at us, like pieces of broken glass. A boy smashes a window and screams and swears into the unanswering interior. Next shot, he is standing dead still and bloody-handed and talking quietly to his Dad. One moment we are with the family after Dad's death. The next we are with them years before. There are no syntactical signposts to guide us. The ripple-dissolve is dead: the mute, brute cut is the new grammar.

The characters likewise form a mosaic made out of rupture and contradiction. Dad (Pete Postlethwaite) is stoical and long-suffering: Dad is a raging bully who beats his wife and children. Dad is a kind-hearted chap who puts out a stocking on Christmas Eve: Dad is a maniac who pulls the table cloth and crockery off the table for no reason and screams at Mum to come and tidy. Dad lies grey-faced and white-sheeted in hospital: Dad is suddenly at the front door, black-faced and brooding. Dad is loved and venerated: Dad is loathed and feared.

Most films – or books or plays – about childhood lay a patina of adult understanding over the incomprehension of the child's mind. But Davies' movie isn't like that. It suggests not only that children cannot understand what is happening around them (even the near-grown-up children depicted in the film), but that adults looking back cannot understand what happened to them either. That indeed there *is* no understanding. There is only a sense that the family is by turns an inexhaustibly rich microcosm and an unbearably grim parody of all the ideas and emotions, hopes and quests, by which we later live.

The chief quest is for love. *Distant Voices*, part one of Davies' diptych movie, gives us the three childrens' struggle for love inside and outside the family. Part two, *Still Lives* is set two years later and was filmed two years later. It has the two sisters married (one unhappily) and the brother about to be. Dad is dead, and individual memories puncture the long central scene of a gathering of friends and family in the local pub.

Although Davies refuses to make life easy by 'explaining' childhood, the movie is never random in either structure or substance. Progressively in part one, we and the characters try to fathom the mystery of love; love as something that can be bought – early scenes tintinnabulate with the clink of coins thrown or swapped between parents and children; love as a vertiginous gamble – 'Taking a chance on love' croons the soundtrack over a scene of Mum (Freda Dowie) perched on a high window-sill cleaning an outside pane (and the same song continues smoothly into the next scene, of Dad savagely beating Mum); and love as blind faith or blind devotion – 'I want me Dad' sobs Dad-battered elder sister Eileen (Angela Walsh) at her wedding, as she crumples into her brother's arms.

In part two, Eileen's search for love has developed a split personality; marital disillusion coexists with maudlin, vicarious fantasy. One moment she is leading the pub singalong in a rendering of 'I Killed Nobody but My Husband'. The next she is sobbing her heart out at *Love Is a Many Splendored Thing*, awash at the big screen's version of all the emotions she's failed to find in marriage.

The movie has its own version of this constant seesaw between hope and hopelessness. It never levels out at a sustained mood, and it shows the volatility of a world in which despair and happiness can each be a springing-off point for the other. Eileen weeps for Dad at her own wedding. And her brother Tony (Dean Williams) stands alone on the family door-step, sobbing with grief, at his wedding party.

Conversely, Davies' camera mimics the process by which joy can grow out of darkness. Three crane-shots in the film are unforgettable. In one the camera rises mysteriously, magically to the second-floor bedroom window of the family's terraced house at night, and then the shot changes, almost imperceptibly, into a reverse interior of the window glowing with daylight, as we hear a softly murmured voice-off ('I loved the light nights'). Another shot levitates from a rain-huddled dome of umbrellas to the rooftop poster for *Love Is a Many Splendored Thing*, followed by a low glide (as smooth and numinous as the packing-cases shot in *Citizen Kane*) over the sniffling, raptured audience.

And the movie's finest grace-note is one that wills a deliberately enigmatic slippage in time. Late in part two, the camera turns away from an injured Tony's hospital bedside, rises to gaze out of a rain-streaming window and then re-descends to discover a new group of sympathizers around the bed and a palpably-changed emotional temperature. We're aware that hours could have passed, or days, or weeks, in a few seconds of camera life.

Distant Voices, Still Lives is post-modernist cinema just as the Paris Pompidou Centre building is post-modernist architecture. The visual devices and creative 'plumbing', far from being tucked away, are on open display. So are the aural devices. Most of the 40-odd songs, instead of being seamlessly incorporated or discreetly 'lost' as part of the soundtrack, are sung straight at us by the characters: with no accompaniment and no 'justification' in terms of narrative. It's a simple, preposterously bald device, and it works. The characters lay their hearts on the table, and we, grateful and astonished, accept the gesture.

HARLAN KENNEDY

A version of this article appeared in *Film Comment*.
Reprinted with permission. © Harlan Kennedy, 1989

DO THE RIGHT THING

I n the sticky, sub-tropical New York summer of 1989, debate raged over the social and political implications of *Do the Right Thing*. Most of the arguments focused on Spike Lee's moral responsibility – or lack of it – as a provocative black filmmaker depicting a series of incidents that culminate in the death of a black youth at the hands of the police, and a race riot in the economically depressed Bedford-Stuyvesant section of Brooklyn.

A *Village Voice* film supplement offered judgements on the film that ranged from the supportive ('as worthy a landmark as any of the next wave of black cinema') to the sceptical ('the sort of rancid fairy-tale one expects of a racist'). The *New York Times*, not to be outdone, printed excerpts from a round-table discussion involving, among others, Paul Schrader ('I think the film is marked by extraordinary restraint and responsibility') and Bronx State Supreme Court Judge Burton B. Roberts ('What worries me is whites are going to look at this movie in an unthinking fashion and suddenly increase fear, hate, whatever for the black community').

For the record, the *Voice*'s J. Hoberman and the *Times*'s Vincent Canby, critics usually as opposed ideologically as they are aesthetically, both championed Lee's film, but the Cannes jury snubbed it for the weaker meat of *sex, lies and videotape*.

Meanwhile, in its opening weekend, *Do the Right Thing* grossed nearly $3.6 million from multi-ethnic audiences in 353 venues; *Great Balls of Fire*, bowing simultaneously on four times as many screens, made only $250,000 more, and only *Batman* achieved a higher per-screen average. American movie-going habits are an unreliable barometer for a film's quality, but Lee's film was clearly doing something right.

The film is set in 'Bed-Stuy' on the hottest day of the year, a fact never in doubt from the opening credit sequence of Rosie Perez – Latino Girlfriend, Tina, of pizza delivery boy Mookie (Lee) – strutting her stuff to Public Enemy's incendiary 'Fight the Power', right through to the conflagration which finally swallows Sal's Famous Pizzeria. A variegated collage of accidents and meetings acted out by black, white, yellow and coffee-coloured workers and residents broiling in the heat, *Do the Right Thing* gives a fresh meaning to the expression 'melting pot'.

The perspiring denizens include two homeboys, the wired-up Buggin Out (Giancarlo Esposito) and the dangerous goofball, Radio Raheem (Bill Nunn), with his vast, reverberating beatbox; soused oldster Da Mayor (Ossie Davis), who saves a kid from running in front of an ice- cream van and flirts with crotchety Mother Sister (Ruby Dee); three bar-room philosophers who have taken refuge in the street and moan and laugh about everyone and each other; and a stuttering, retarded hawker (Roger Guenveur Smith) of photos bearing the double image of Martin

Luther King and Malcolm X (from whom Lee will offer apparently contradictory quotes about violence at the end of the film). Then there is Mister Señor Love Daddy (Sam Jackson), the local DJ and omniscient dispenser of omens – 'The colour of the day is black' – and wisdom; whose storefront console is his personal Olympus.

The tinderbox on this block is Sal's; its proprietor (Danny Aiello) a small-time but self-made Italian-American who wants to leave his business to his reluctant, bickering sons, the racist Pino (John Turturro) and the milder Vito (Richard Edson). They have a love-hate relationship with Mookie who's diligent in giving them advice about their attitudes, but slothful in delivering their slices; he's more inclined to bunk off to cool down the inflamed Rosie (neglected mother of his son) with discreetly placed ice cubes. Mookie may be the conscience of the movie, but his eventual outburst against Sal – inciting the black riot – is complicated by the (sexual) possessiveness he shows to his sister, Jade (Joie Lee, sister of Spike), when Sal welcomes her in his store.

By now, the day has nearly expired in its own heat. Radio Raheem has duelled with some schoolkids; a fire hydrant has offered a midday shower and been used as a water cannon on an uptight white motorist; a white gentrifier (John Savage) has run his cycle over Buggin Out's sneakers and been hassled going up his steps. But when Buggin Out orders a boycott of Sal's because there are no photos of black brothers among the Pacinos and De Niros framed on the wall, and Raheem turns up his beatbox on Sal's counter, the pressure cooker explodes. After witnessing Sal's demolition of his radio, Raheem goes berserk and is strangled by the cops. It's Mookie who throws a garbage can through Sal's window and, the morning after it has been torched to the ground, insists on getting his pay from Sal in the film's ambiguous coda.

A comedy which lurches into tragedy, *Do the Right Thing* is also anti-racist agitprop and funky, galvanizing entertainment which, in its rap-acious rhythms and tumultuous urban panoramas, makes giddy vie ing. As the atmosphere percolates, Aiello does an outrageous De Niro schtik; Lee sends an embassy from each race in front of the camera for a snarling racist diatribe; and when Radio Raheem invades Sal's, his face threatens to burst the screen. Whatever accusations can be levelled at *Do the Right Thing*, for sheer visual inventiveness it ghetto-blasted the summer's megabudget exercises in self-congratulatory comic-strip machismo from the theatres.

Do the Right Thing is the first time Lee has used white actors. Unlike *She's Gotta Have It* and *School Daze*, films by Lee which made no concessions to white audiences, this latest does not examine black 'isms' and schisms. Nor does it absolve black people from prejudice, even though Lee will not contemplate the notion of black racism: 'White people can't call black people racist. They invented that shit,' he has said.

By the end of the film, the black community has taken a stand of solidarity, but is this in the cause of 'Afro-fascist chic', as the *Voice* put it? Or is the Bed-Stuy

neighbourhood actually resisting violence? *Do the Right Thing* was partly inspired by the Howards Beach tragedy of December 1986 when one of the black youths chased from a Queens pizzeria by white kids was struck and killed by a car; it was filmed at the time of a media circus surrounding a case in which a black teenager, Tawana Brawley, alleged that she was abducted, beaten and raped by white racists. Even as *Batman* wheeled out a half-satirical, half-affectionate lookalike of Mayor Ed Koch, Lee was anticipating the release of his film as a salvo against Koch – widely recognized as having polarized racial groups in the city – during the 1989 mayoral elections.

New York Magazine's political correspondent, Joe Klein, meanwhile contended that 'Spike Lee's reckless new movie' could damage black mayoral candidate David Dinkins. Notwithstanding *The Thin Blue Line*, movies have seldom changed the course of history. For whatever ends, Lee inscribed both Howards Beach ('Cowards Beach' is shouted by the mob torching Sal's) and the Brawley case ('Tawana told the truth' appears as graffiti) in his film, but with as much ambivalence as the forlorn, unsettling ending when Sal and Mookie face off – the pizza man to contemplate his ruin, his former employee to take the money and run. It's a sheepish conclusion, having more to do with day-to-day survival than the clenched leather fist of Black Power. As the camera cranes back over the block, already struggling into fresh life, Lee is letting the movie and its temper cool out. The final quotes: from Martin Luther King, deploring violence, and from Malcolm X, advocating self-defence, are instantly self-cancelling, but until the promised 'kinder, gentler' America finally materializes, *whatever* needs to be done must, perforce, be the right thing. That's the realistic message of one of the most courageous movies of the 1980s.

GRAHAM FULLER

DROWNING BY NUMBERS

There is no getting away from it: Peter Greenaway has established himself as someone to reckon with in European cinema. The film that made his name, *The Draughtsman's Contract*, was highly English, in both use of landscape and its deployment, albeit in period terms, of that most native of genres, the detective story. Greenaway moved on in *A Zed and Two Noughts* and *The Belly of an Architect* to become a Common Market moviemaker.

At the same time, he has increasingly abandoned narrative; in a statement to accompany *Z.O.O.* (beware of filmmakers bearing statements) he went so far as to maintain that 'cinema is too rich and capable (*sic*) a medium to be merely left to the story-tellers.' But what, one asks, is he going to replace them with? Some might say that his subsequent work has increasingly rendered such a query rhetorical.

Drowning by Numbers sees Greenaway back in the English countryside after his Continental excursions, but finds him showing no inclination to turn away from what some might call the cerebral and abstract, and others the fey and whimsical. At the same time, the film does possess a sort of narrative basis, in the rather lurid shape of a tale of sex and murder. The French title of *The Draughtsman's Contract* is translated as *Death in an English Garden*, and here we are regaled with a series of deaths and watery graves along the highways and byways of deepest Suffolk.

On the face of it, this is an exercise in *comédie noire*, with a woman, her daughter and her grand-daughter putting paid to their spouses – in the first case, on grounds of infidelity; in the latter two, for not much more reason than that the ladies find them a bore. All three women (they are played by Joan Plowright, Juliet Stevenson and Joely Richardson) rejoice in the name of Cissie Colpitts. The appellation was previously met in Greenaway's *The Falls*, but it is hard to say what light that may throw on its multiple manifestations here. At any rate, the three Cissies contrive to get away with their activities to the extent of enlisting the collusion of the even more peculiar local coroner (Bernard Hill), and with a roundabout sort of inevitability, he winds up as their final victim.

Needless to say, there is no question here of an organic narrative, in even the most fantasticated vein; rather, the events of the 'plot' serve as a pretext. But a pretext for what? A satire, perhaps, of Anglo-Saxon attitudes and sexual appetites? Certainly there is plenty of self-conscious bawdiness, starting with an ungainly display of frontal nudity in the sequence where the eldest Cissie's husband larks about with his *inamorata* in, of all things, a tin bath. But the determined oddity of demeanour, of which this is a fair sample, is apt to render satire inoperable, since it dispenses with any behavioural yardstick.

Fair enough, it might be retorted, but what is being aimed at here is the creation of a closed world of the imagination. The trouble is that this throws up the crucial requirement that such a world bids you enter, or at least challenges you to do so. And in *Drowning by Numbers*, the annotation of the bizarre goings-on is all so owlish and arch and (although here we are in the realms of the subjective) so unfunny: for example, when the coroner retires to bed unwell, he calls for a large bowl of chocolate pudding to settle his stomach.

By extension, there is a plethora of game-playing, with the dramatic action (barely perceptible as it may be) supplanted at frequent intervals by demonstration of such pastimes as 'dead man's catch' and 'hangman's cricket': it comes as no surprise when we are told of the latter that it would take all day to learn the rules. Again, it is not just that these seem precious, but that they contain no discernible relevance to any controlling design, at least beyond the sense in which the meaningless names echo the all-pervading preoccupation with mortality; at one point, we are even treated to the spectacle of Richardson and the ill-fated object of her desire getting to grips alongside the corpses of two unfortunate cows. And the margins of the film are decorated with such delights as a girl in grotesque fancy dress being run over by a car, or the coroner's young son, who has earlier conducted an amateur circumcision on himself, hanging himself with her skipping rope.

Undeniably, some of this is arresting to the eye, thanks to the luminous cinematography of Sacha Vierny, and to the ear as well, thanks to Michael Nyman's score. On the other hand, the performances often seem awkwardly directed, compounding the affected quality of the dialogue and with it the overall sense of being stranded in a labyrinth. There is, it should be said, a thread of a kind leading through the labyrinth, in the shape of an ostentatiously planted series of the numbers one to 100; and an unconscionably long time it seems before the 100 signals impending release, via end-titles in which credits for an entomologist and a pyrotechnics expert may offer some intimation of the recherché character of the undertaking as a whole. It is debatable, however, whether anything could adequately intimate the depths of tedium the film managed to plumb for at least one spectator.

Perhaps, given the high esteem Greenaway's work is accorded in some quarters, it must simply be designated as an acquired taste. What can be said with confidence, however, is that for those not won over by his earlier pictures, *Drowning by Numbers* is highly unlikely to turn into a road to Damascus. Oh, and kindly pass the chocolate pudding.

TIM PULLEINE

EARTH GIRLS ARE EASY 👍

Julien Temple's amiably goofy satire of life among the Valley Girls of Los Angeles plops Jeff Goldblum's spaceship into Geena Davis's swimming pool. Goldblum is blue and furry, so the first thing Davis does is have him depilated and cosmeticized. Goldblum and his two primary-colour mates, also re-made to look like surfer dudes, go out on the town and have an hour's worth of predictable culture-clash adventures. Temple succumbs to his taste for tacky song-and-dance several times too often. The story is short of gripping and the characters offer no surprises; so all we have to watch is bright-lit décor, and that isn't quite enough. **BM**

Director *Julien Temple* **producer** *Tony Garnett* **script** *Julie Brown, Charlie Coffey, Terrence E. McNally* **camera** *Oliver Stapleton* **editor** *Richard Halsey* **design** *Dennis Gasner* **music** *Nile Rodgers* **cast** *Geena Davis, Jeff Goldblum, Julie Brown, Jim Carrey, Damon Wayans, Charles Rocket, Michael McKean*
Running time: 100 mins
US release: Vestron, May 12, 1989

EDGE OF SANITY

This version of the Dr Jekyll and Mr Hyde story cynically tries to cash in on the Jack the Ripper centenary as well. After freebasing on cocaine (as a result of experiments with monkeys), Anthony Perkins turns into a debauched Mr Hyde who stalks streets and brothels in search of potential victims.
Director *Gérard Kikoine* **producers** *Edward Simons, Harry Alan Towers* **exec** *Peter A. McRae* **script** *J. P. Felix, Ron Raley* **camera** *Tony Spratling* **editor** *Malcolm Cooke* **design** *Jean Charles Dedieu* **music** *Frederic Talgorn* **cast** *Anthony Perkins, Glynis Barber, Sarah Maur-Thorp, David Lodge, Ben Cole, Ray Jewers, Jill Melford, Lisa Davis, Noel Coleman*
Running time: 90 mins
US release: Millimeter, Apr 14, 1989

EIGHT MEN OUT

A sports film about not winning was always going to be a tough nut to swallow. John Sayles' account of the 1919 Black Sox Scandal, when the nation's top ball players threw the World Series as revenge on their meanie manager, can't get over the fact it's such a sorry tale: having been ripped off by the gamblers, the players were then driven out of the game. The script is so scrupulous in painting in individual motivations for the characters, and chronicling the details of what happened, that it plods even when trying to stir the emotions. One longs for the players to get back into their game and, when they do, there are more thrills in a few minutes than in the rest of the film. After *Matewan*, you might have thought Sayles knew how to make us angry at the exploiters. **JP**

Director *John Sayles* **producers** *Sarah Pillsbury, Midge Sanford* **execs** *Barbara Boyle, Jerry Offsay* **script** *Sayles, from book by Eliot Asinof* **camera** *Robert Richardson* **editor** *John Tintori* **design** *Nora Chavooshian* **music** *Mason Daring* **cast** *John Cusack, Clifton James, Michael Lerner, Christopher Lloyd, John Mahoney, Charlie Sheen, David Strathairn, D. B. Sweeney, Don Harvey, Michael Rooker, Perry Lang, James Read, Jace Alexander, Gordan Clapp, Richard Edson, Bill Irwin, Michael Mantell, Kevin Tighe, Studs Terkel, John Anderson, John Sayles*
Running time: 119 mins
US Release: Orion, Sep 2, 1988

18 AGAIN!

Was this movie necessary? Among America's four significant recent movies about mind-body switches between men of different generations, Paul Flaherty's is the most obviously unoriginal. The claim to uniqueness here is that the switch occurs not between father and son, but between grandfather and grandson! Charlie Schlatter is the boy who takes over gramps's mind after an auto crash, and George Burns is the senior citizen who becomes 18 again. The other movies in this narrow genre have relied mostly on following the older (and more famous) body as it flounders through boyhood, but here George Burns is neglected in favour of too many flat jokes featuring the forever-smiling Schlatter. **BM**

Director *Paul Flaherty* **producer** *Walter Coblenz* **execs** *Irving Fein, Michael Jaffe* **script** *Josh Goldstein, Jonathan Prince* **camera** *Stephen M. Katz* **editor** *Danford B. Greene* **design** *Dena Roth* **music** *Billy Goldenberg* **cast** *George Burns, Charlie Schlatter, Tony Roberts, Anita Morris, Miriam Flynn, Jennifer Runyon, Red Buttons, George DiCenzo, Bernard Fox, Kenneth Tigar*
Running time: 100 mins
US release: New World, Apr 8, 1988
UK release: Entertainment, Oct 7, 1988

84 CHARLIE MOPIC

Written and directed by Vietnam vet Patrick
Duncan (creator of HBO's *Vietnam War Stories*),
84 Charlie Mopic offers a harrowing grunt's-eye
view of a seven-man reconnaissance mission,
through the unblinking, first-person lens of a
one-man motion-picture unit. Lacking the hype,
heroism and bombast of Hollywood 'Nam',
Duncan's edgy (that is, hand-held) docu-drama
pans out, from a study of guerrilla warfare
waged by seasoned tourists, rookies and a
would-be corporate raider, into a rueful analysis
of the 'Why We Are Fighting' imperative.
Trimmed of the metaphoric fat that Coppola,
Cimino, Stone and Kubrick have accustomed
us to, this is the candid camera of
Vietnamerican movies and perhaps the most
honest yet. **GF**
Director/script *Patrick Duncan* **producer** *Michael
Nolin* **camera** *Alan Caso* **editor** *Stephen Purvis*
design *Douglas Dick* **cast** *Jonathan Emerson,
Nicholas Cascone, Jason Tomlins, Christopher
Burgard, Glenn Morshower, Richard Brooks, Byron
Thomas*
Running time: 95 mins
US release: New Century/Vista, Mar 22, 1989

ELVIRA, MISTRESS OF THE DARK

Elvira, for those who haven't been exposed to
her US TV appearances, is a horror movie
hostess - she interrupts old movies like *It
Conquered the World* with campy jokes and
stupid *double entendres*. In this movie spinoff,
our heroine, who resembles Morticia Addams
in a very low-cut dress, is fired from her TV
job and goes to the town of Fallwell,
Massachusetts, to collect her inheritance.
There, she is made an outcast by the moral
majority and comes into conflict with her evil
uncle over possession of a book of magical
recipes. The uncle conspires with the town's
many killjoys to revive the ancient New
England custom of witch-burning, and it begins
to look as if Elvira isn't going to achieve her
only ambition and bring her tassel-swinging act
to Las Vegas. Elvira is obnoxious and
uninteresting; at once a caricature of the nubile
woman and entirely sexless; and unable to do
anything once she's liberated from her two-
minute appearances between imaginative Z-
movies this film unwisely sneers at. There are
the occasional good lines ('If I'd wanted your
opinion, I'd have beaten it out of you') but it's
mostly sub-*Munsters* trash. A fine performance
by W. Morgan Sheppard as the villain goes to
waste. **KN**

Director *James Signorelli* **producers** *Eric Gardner,
Mark Pierson* **exec** *Michael Rachmil* **script** *Sam
Egan, John Paragon, Cassandra Peterson* **camera**
Hanania Baer **editor** *Battle David* **design** *John De
Cuir Jr.* **music** *James Campbell* **cast** *Cassandra
Peterson, W. Morgan Sheppard, Daniel Greene,
Susan Kellermann, Jeff Conaway, Edie McClurg,
Kurt Fuller, Pat Crawford Brown*
Running time: 96 mins
US release: New World, Sep 30, 1988
UK release: Entertainment, Mar 31, 1989

ERNEST SAVES CHRISTMAS

The second adventure of the inimitable klutz
Ernest P. Worrell (Varney) - a more
cosmetically-ravaged, but no less frenetic, dumb
nephew to Pee Wee Herman - whose initial
sleeper hit, *Ernest Goes to Camp*, introduced
Americans to the hapless world of this Stateside
Norman Wisdom for the crack era. Worrell, a
charmingly-naive human cartoon, gets to meet
Santa, satirize the cynical ineptitude of
Hollywood and naturally rescue Yuletide from
oblivion. **MN**
Director *John Cherry* **producer** *Stacy Williams,
Doug Claybourne* **execs** *Martin Erlichman, Joseph
L. Akerman Jr.* **script** *B. Kline, Ed Turner*
camera *Peter Stein* **editor** *Sharyn L. Ross* **design**
Ian Thomas **music** *Mark Snow* **cast** *Jim Varney,
Douglas Seale, Oliver Clark, Noelle Parker, Robert
Lesser, Gailard Sartain, Billie Bird, Bill Byrge,
Buddy Douglas, Patty Maloney*
Running time: 89 mins
US release: BV, Nov 11, 1988

EVERLASTING SECRET FAMILY

A young man (Lee) at a private school is
taught homosexual practices by a Senator and
taken to a secret family of boys who faithfully
serve their employers' sexual requirements. Lee
becomes involved with a judge, and the
Senator's son (Goddard). A rejuvenation expert
helps Lee stay young and he takes Goddard as
his lover. Out of this curious mishmash of fantasy and sexual intrigue emerges a convoluted
narrative whose Australian setting contributes
little. The precious, often absurdist, scenario
tinkers with various themes from sexual
development to Dorian Gray-like concern with
immortality. Yet the often farcical nature of the
sex scenes suggests a black humour wildly out
of kilter with the film's rather staid progression.
Drastically shifting from genteel rituals to ex-
travagantly camp humour to kitsch narcissism,
director Michael Thornhill is unable to find a
sympathetic level from which he can bring

some sense of cohesive identity to the eccentric dalliances of the script. **SD**
Director/producer Michael Thornhill exec Anthony I. Ginnane script Frank Moorhouse, based on his book camera Julian Penney editor Pamela Barnetta design Peta Lawson music Tony Bremner cast Arthur Dignam, Mark Lee, Heather Mitchell, Dennis Miller, Paul Goddard, Beth Child, John Clayton, Nick Holland, Bogdan Koca
Running time: 93 mins
UK release: Cannon, Nov 25, 1988

EVERYBODY'S ALL-AMERICAN

This thematically confusing film celebrates an anti-climactic 25 years in the lives of Louisiana celebrities – football hero Dennis Quaid and his naïve companion Jessica Lange. Quaid's sporting deity gets to score touchdowns, invest in a drinking saloon, go broke, consume beer and participate in male-bonding rituals, whilst the perpetually-pregnant Lange confides her frustration and loneliness to a third party (Hutton). Quaid retires to become a golf-club pro, Hutton becomes a writer and grows a moustache, and Lange, endowed with the gift of cynical resignation to her suburban fate, goes into business. For Taylor Hackford and writer Tom Rickman, football is a religious experience. Emotional subtexts, historical anecdotes and any sort of critical perspective on lives seduced and abandoned by a culture obsessed with sporting accomplishments necessarily give way to celebrations of The Game. **MN**
Director Taylor Hackford producer Hackford, Laura Ziskin, Ian Sander exec Stuart Benjamin script Tom Rickman, from book by Frank Deford camera Stephen Goldblatt editor Don Zimmerman design Joe Alves music James Newton Howard cast Jessica Lange, Dennis Quaid, Timothy Hutton, John Goodman, Carl Lumbly, Ray Baker, Savannah Smith Boucher, Patricia Clarkson
Running time: 127 mins
US release: Warner, Nov 4, 1988

THE EXPERTS

Ten years ago millions would have died for him, but now you can't give John Travolta away, as Paramount found to their cost after a disastrous opening for this straight-faced farrago. Travolta plays a fast-living New Yorker who's kidnapped by the KGB, along with nightclub owner Arye Gross, another 'expert' in what's hip in America. They are persuaded to open a US-style night venue deep inside Mother Russia, and it takes them some time to realize that what they're doing is training Soviet spies in American ways. The Russkies are so taken by what they learn that they defect promptly after crossing the border. In the production notes Travolta, who has turned down more good parts since his early burst of fame than most actors see in a lifetime, thanks Scientology for the new direction of his career. Now we know who to blame for his unbelievable, ever-smiling performance in this inept embarrassment. Avoid. **TW**
Director Dave Thomas producer James Keach execs Jonathan Krane, Jack Grossberg script Nick Thile, Steven Greene, Eric Alter camera Ronnie Taylor editor Bud Molin design David Fischer music Marvin Hamlisch cast John Travolta, Arye Gross, Kelly Preston, Deborah Foreman, James Keach, Charles Martin Smith
Running time: 83 mins
US release: Paramount, Jan 13, 1989

FAMILY VIEWING

Deliberately plotted like a dim-witted soap opera, this is a weird, perceptive satire on the way television and associated technologies kill off caring conversation and contact with nature. Hemblen is the demon: he video-records his love-making and cannot get it up without the intervention of a telephone prostitute. Aidan Tierney is the film's hollow hero. He's initially so out-of-touch that he casually presents a girl (Khanjian) with a tape of her mother's funeral as if it was a satisfactory substitute for being present at the event. It's when he discovers that scenes of his past are being taped over with sexual hijinks that he seeks to establish a real relationship with that catatonic grandmother and Khanjian. The subsequent rediscovery of his mother leads to a wonderfully cod ending. **JP**
Director/producer/script Atom Egoyan *camera* Robert MacDonald *editor* Egoyan, MacDonald *design* Linda Del Rosario *music* Mychael Danna *cast* David Hemblen, Aidan Tierney, Gabrielle Rose, Arsine Khanjian, Selma Keklikian, Jeanne Sabourin, Rose Sarkisyan
Running time: 86 mins
US release: Cinephile, Jul 29, 1988
UK release: Other Cinema, Sep 30, 1988

FAR NORTH

Sam Shepard's directorial début focuses on the bickerings that arise within a fractious family when the gruff old patriarch (Durning) orders his pregnant but unmarried daughter (Lange) to exact revenge upon the horse that has hospitalized him.
Director/script Sam Shepard *producers* Carolyn Pfeiffer, Malcolm Harding *camera* Robbie Greenberg *editor* Bill Yahraus *design* Peter Jamison *music* The Red Clay Ramblers *cast* Jessica Lange, Charles Durning, Tess Harper, Donald Moffat, Ann Wedgeworth, Patricia Arquette, Nina Draxten
Running time: 90 mins
US release: Alive, Nov 9, 1988

DISAPPOINTMENT

FAREWELL TO THE KING

Director John Milius *producers* Albert S. Ruddy, Andrew Morgan *script* Milius, from book by Pierre Schoendoerffer *camera* Dean Semler *editor* C. Timothy O'Meara, Ann V. Coates *design* Bernard Hides, Gil Parrondo *music* Basil Poledouris *cast* Nick Nolte, Nigel Havers, James Fox, Marily Tokuda, Frank MacRae, Aki Aleong, William Wise, Gerry Lopez, Marius Weyers, Elan Oberon, Choy Chan Wing
Running time: 117 mins
US release: Orion, Mar 3, 1989
UK release: Vestron, Jul 7, 1989

FATAL BEAUTY

When is this woman going to make a good movie? In her latest disaster, Whoopi Goldberg plays an unorthodox police-woman, *à la Beverly Hills Cop*, going after a drug-pushing villain with a German name (Yulin). Goldberg's character, inexplicably, has an Italian name. Ultra-WASP Sam Elliott plays a bodyguard with a Jewish name. Goldberg throws out multiple anti-man witticisms while following the trail of some bad dope that is knocking off yuppie snorters all over LA. The jokes and action in Tom Holland's film will entertain only those who thought *Dirty Harry* was soft on crime. **BM**
Director Tom Holland *producer* Leonard Kroll *script* Hilary Henkin, Dean Riesner *camera* David M. Walsh *editor* Don Zimmerman *design* James William Newport *music* Harold Faltermeyer *cast* Whoopi Goldberg, Sam Elliott, Rubén Blades, Harris Yulin, John P. Ryan, Jennifer Warren, Brad Dourif, Mike Jolly, Charles Hallahan, Neill Barry, Richard (Cheech) Marin, Ebbe Roe Smith, Belinda Mayne, Celeste Yarnall
Running time: 104 mins
US release: MGM, Oct 30, 1987
UK release: Enterprise, Feb 24, 1989

FEDS

Female buddy picture puts Rebecca DeMornay and Mary Gross into training for the FBI via multiple contests with the male majority.
Director Dan Goldberg *producers* Ilona Herzberg, Len Blum *exec* Ivan Reitman *script* Blum, Goldberg *camera* Timothy Suhrstedt *editor* Don Cambern *design* Randy Ser *music* Randy Edelman *cast* Rebecca DeMornay, Mary Gross, Ken Marshall, Fred Dalton Thompson, Larry Cedar
Running time: 91 mins
US release: Warner, Oct 28, 1988

A FEW DAYS WITH ME (Quelques jours avec moi)

Claude Sautet's film is either a riotous ensemble comedy or - if, like me, you didn't laugh - a sombre study of depression. Daniel Auteuil is heir to a chain of hypermarkets, but he has lost interest in life. Just out of an asylum, he goes to inspect the branch in

Limoges. He finds out that the store manager is stealing but becomes interested in the manager's maid, Sandrine Bonnaire. He woos her with his wealth and parties with her low-life friends. The store manager and his twin-set-and-pearls wife soon let down their hair, too. Through it all, Auteuil retains a vaguely constipated look. **BM**

Director Claude Sautet **producers** Alain Sarde, Philippe Carcassonne **script** Sautet, Jérôme Tonnerre, Jacques Fieschi, from novel by François Robin **editor** Jacqueline Thiedot **design** Carlos Conti **music** Philippe Sarde **cast** Daniel Auteuil, Sandrine Bonnaire, Jean-Pierre Marielle, Dominique Lavanant, Vincent Lindon, Thérèse Liotard, Danièlle Darrieux
Running time: 131 mins
US release: Galaxy, Apr 14, 1989

FIELD OF DREAMS

Phil Alden Robinson reaches for Frank Capra-style sentiment in this hymn to baseball as a symbol of the American Utopia and very nearly hits a homer. Kevin Costner is an Iowa farmer who one day hears a voice, 'If you build it, he will come.' Having puzzled out the message, he builds a baseball field at the edge of his cornfield, and Shoeless Joe Jackson (Liotta) shows up. Jackson is the great outfielder banned from baseball for his part in a 1919 gambling scandal. Soon Jackson's deceased team-mates arrive and Costner goes on further missions involving James Earl Jones and Burt Lancaster. Skirting the corn, the story builds towards an unexpected family reconciliation. **BM**

Director Phil Alden Robinson **producers** Lawrence Gordon, Charles Gordon **exec** Brian Frankish **script** Robinson, from book Shoeless Joe by W. P. Kinsella **camera** John Lindley **editor** Ian Crafford **design** Dennis Gassner **music** James Horner **cast** Kevin Costner, Amy Madigan, Gaby Hoffman, Ray Liotta, Timothy Busfield, James Earl Jones, Burt Lancaster, Frank Whaley, Dwyer Brown
Running time: 106 mins
US release: Universal, Apr 21, 1989

A FISH CALLED WANDA

Director Charles Crichton **producer** Michael Shamberg **execs** Steve Abbott, John Cleese **script** Cleese **camera** Alan Hume **editor** John Jympson **design** Roger Murray-Leach **music** John Du Prez

cast Cleese, Jamie Lee Curtis, Kevin Kline, Michael Palin, Maria Aitken, Tom Georgeson, Patricia Hayes, Geoffrey Palmer, Mark Elwes
Running time: 108 mins
US release: MGM, Jul 15, 1988
UK release: UIP, Oct 14, 1988

FIVE CORNERS

The Bronx in 1964 is the setting for Tony Bill's low-key movie - enlivened by such surreal touches as the killing of a spiteful teacher by an unknown archer - about a bunch of young adults, mostly misfits, trying to sort out their lives. Marvellous as usual, Jodie Foster is the realistic neighbourhood angel, loved by a cripple, protected by a strong, silent pacifist involved in the Civil Rights movement, and stalked by a sad psychotic (Turturro) who eventually throws his mad old Momma out of a window. Jodie and a penguin survive. Bill and writer John Patrick Shanley (responsible for Moonstruck) sympathize with, rather than judge, their characters and, despite the eruptions of violence, reflect poignantly on small people already overtaken by the cataclysmic events of the decade. **GF**

Director Tony Bill **producer** Forrest Murray, Bill **execs** George Harrison, Denis O'Brien **script** John Patrick Shanley **camera** Fred Murphy **editor** Andy Blumenthal **design** Adrianne Lobel **music** James Newton Howard **cast** Jodie Foster, Tim Robbins, Todd Graff, John Turturro, Elizabeth Berridge, Rose Gregorio, Gregory Rozakis, John Seitz, Kathleen Chalfant, Rodney Harvey
Running time: 94 mins
US release: Cineplex, Jan 22, 1988
UK release: Recorded Releasing, Mar 10, 1989

FLETCH LIVES

Are you sure, doctor? We may need a second opinion. In this sequel to hit Chevy Chase comedy Fletch, the quick-quipping journalist-sleuth moseys south to inherit a mansion. What should he stumble on there but racism, corruption and skullduggery among the Bible-belters? In short, business as usual. He certainly doesn't stumble on a good script. The only moment of comic take-off as the plot thickens to a standstill is our hero's dream on the plane: a Song of the South spoof with Chevy and chorus zip-a-dee-doo-dah-ing away among cartoon animals and mock-Tara mansions. One or two jokes follow. But mostly, with Michael Ritchie directing, it's all downhill. **HK**

Director Michael Ritchie **producers** Alan Greisman, Peter Douglas **execs** Bruce Bodner, Bob

Larson **script** Leon Capetanos, based on characters created by Gregory McDonald **camera** John McPherson **editor** Richard A. Harris **music** Harold Faltermeyer **cast** Chevy Chase, Hal Holbrook, Julianne Phillips, R. Lee Ermey, Richard Libertini, Randall 'Tex' Cobb, Cleavon Little, George Wyner **Running time:** 95 mins
US release: Universal, Mar 17, 1989
UK release: UIP, May 19, 1989

THE FLY II

Directed by former special-effects wizard Chris Walas, this uninspired sequel metamorphoses the emotional subtleties of David Cronenberg's profound biological parable into a blood-drenched teen monster-flick. The son fathered by the original's doomed lead scientist grows up into a confused, emotionally-perplexed mutant (Stoltz) whose lapses into vulnerability, assisted by love interest and research-lab assistant Daphne Zuniga, are merely plot points preceding a pyrotechnical pay-off. As a human, Brundlefly junior gets to act sentimental, fall in love and escape from the exploitative conglomerate who have locked him up to capitalize upon his future insectorial prowess. Stoltz follows a heavy dose of insectoid transformation with self-redemptive anger, which means he gets to squash the heads of various bad guys like raisins. **MN**
Director Chris Walas **producer** Steven-Charles Jaffe **exec** Stuart Cornfeld **script** Mick Garris, Jim and Ken Wheat, Frank Darabont, based on characters created by George Langelaan **camera** Robin Vidgeon **editor** Sean Barton **design** Michael S. Bolton **music** Christopher Young **cast** Eric Stoltz, Daphne Zuniga, Lee Richardson, John Getz, Frank Turner, Ann Marie Lee, Gary Chalk, Saffron Henderson, Harley Cross, Matthew Moore **Running time:** 105 mins
US release: Fox, Feb 10, 1989

FOR QUEEN AND COUNTRY

With a central character called Reuben (to make us think of Rambo?), this was probably sold to financiers as a British version of First Blood. But the script never makes up its mind whether it's about a black Falklands vet trying to square his experiences of racial harassment with recent gallantry on behalf of the nation, or a study of the crack problem on London's housing estates. Denzel Washington's failure to convey any sense of post-Goose Green trauma in the central rôle makes one think of Sylvester Stallone as a subtle actor. By turns curmudgeonly, charming and brooding, he's also written as a character who sees everything - murder, burglary, drug raids, bomb-making - but never gets involved. The filmmakers don't know how to prepare the dramatic high-points, nor what to do after they've passed, and the cut from a policeman's murder to a football supporter singing in the back of a taxi cab must count as one of the most bathetic in recent memory. **JP**
Director Martin Stellman **producer** Tim Bevan **script** Stellman, Trix Worrell **camera** Richard Greatrex **editor** Stephen Singleton **design** Andrew McAlpine **music** Michael Kamen **cast** Denzel Washington, Dorian Healy, Amanda Redman, Sean Chapman, Bruce Payne, Geff Francis **Running time:** 106 mins
US release: Atlantic, May 19, 1989
UK release: UIP, Jan 20, 1989

FRANTIC

Trouble in Paris for American Dr Harrison Ford when his wife is kidnapped on the eve of a medical conference. Whodunnit? Through an assault course of false trails, McGuffins, language perplexities and dead bodies, Ford sleuths. Roman Polanski proves that the minor career setback of The Pirates can now be forgotten. This is a major career setback. Diffuse, stilted, humourless and implausible, the movie seems the work of an exiled filmmaker dying from lack of Hollywood oxygen. **HK**
Director Roman Polanski **producers** Thom Mount, Tim Hampton **script** Gérard Brach, Polanski **camera** Witold Sobocinski **editor** Sam O'Steen **design** Pierre Guffroy **music** Ennio Morricone **cast** Harrison Ford, Emmanuelle Seigner, Betty Buckley, John Mahoney, Jimmie Ray Weeks, David Huddleston, Gérard Klein, Jacques Ciron, Dominique Pinon, Thomas M. Pollard **Running time:** 120 mins
US release: Warner, Feb 26, 1988
UK release: Warner, Sep 16, 1988

FRESH HORSES

If I have to look at Andrew McCarthy vacillating his way through one more movie - why, I don't know what I'll do. Here he and Molly Ringwald re-enact their momentous relationship in Pretty in Pink: will he or won't he? Again, she's a poor girl from the wrong side of the tracks, he's a priveligioso with a taste for slumming. Again, he has a best friend (Stiller) with an unhealthy interest in preventing him from following his impulse. Instead of suburbia, the two worlds are a college in Cincinnati and the sticks of

A FISH CALLED WANDA

RAIN MAN

WHO FRAMED ROGER RABBIT

DISTANT VOICES, STILL LIVES

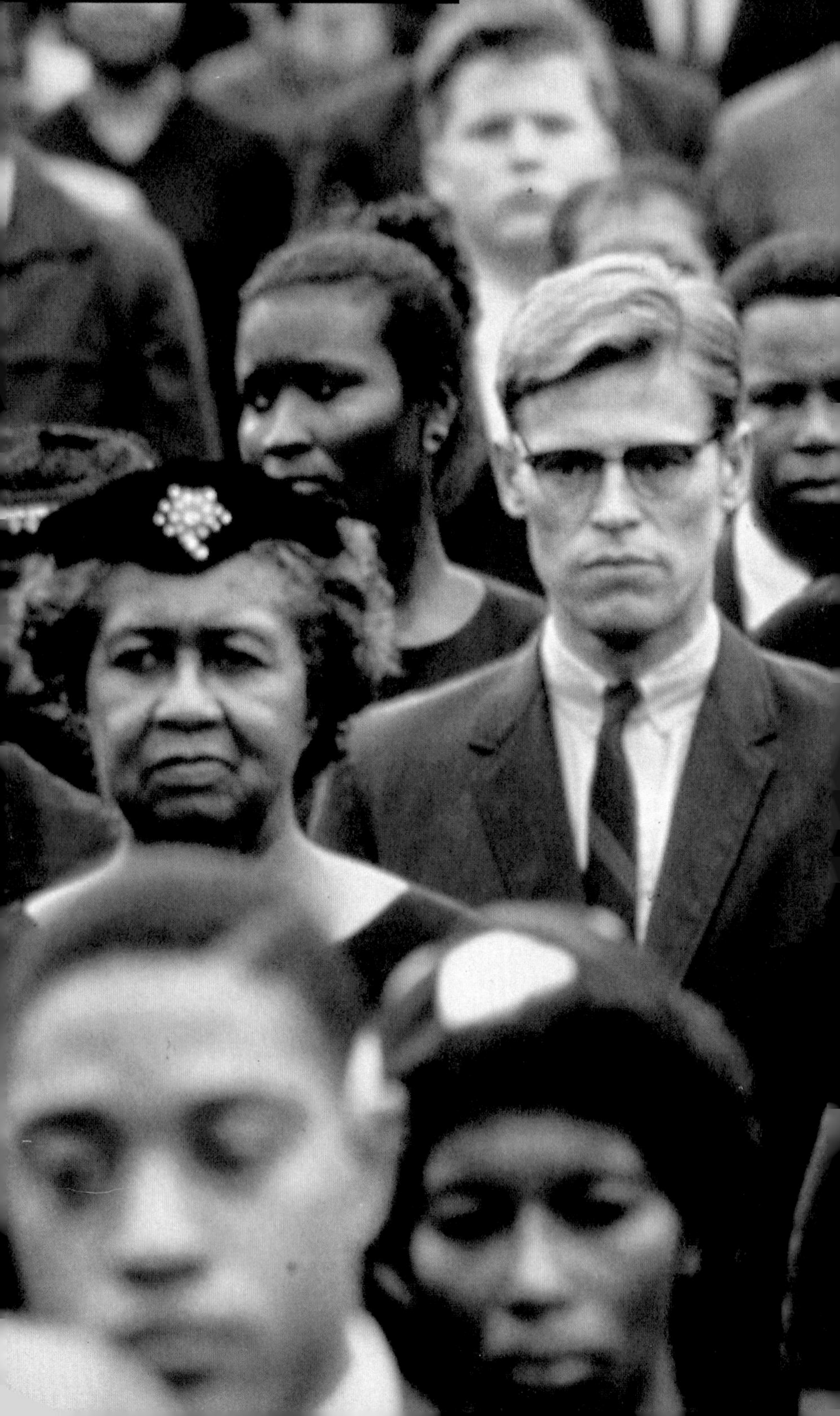

A WORLD APART

Kentucky. All this might have played better on stage in Larry Ketron's original version, but not with these one-note actors. **BM**
Director David Anspaugh **producer** Dick Berg **exec** Allan Marcil **script** Larry Ketron, from his play **camera** Fred Murphy **editor** David Rosenbloom **design** Paul Sylbert **music** David Foster, Patrick Williams **cast** Molly Ringwald, Andrew McCarthy, Patti D'Arbanville, Ben Stiller, Leon Russom, Molly Hagan, Viggo Mortensen, Doug Hutchison, Chiara Peacock, Marita Geraghty, Rachel Jones, Welker White
Running time: 105 mins
US release: Weintraub, Nov 18, 1988

FRIGHT NIGHT PART 2

Charley Brewster (Ragsdale), the teenager who joined forces with ham actor Peter Vincent (McDowell) to destroy vampire Chris Sarandon in *Fright Night*, is now in college, and has finally been persuaded by his shrink that the events of the first film were a hallucination. But, when the Sarandon character's sister (Carmen) shows up in town to exact revenge, the film has to go through the whole business of the heroes being convinced yet again that, yes, there really is such a thing as a vampire. As sequels go, this is just about par for the course: the story simply treads water while the actors from the first film who haven't had any better offers go through their schtick, and some new ones fail to make much of an impression. It is quite an achievement to leave an audience totally unmoved by a black, bisexual, mute, roller-skating, disco-choreographer vampire. Tommy Lee Wallace fails to bring any coherence to the material, which is as likely to yank in a gratuitous bowling sequence as it is to pull off a special-effects set piece. **KN**
Director Tommy Lee Wallace **producers** Herb Jaffe, Mort Engelberg **script** Tim Metcalfe, Migue' Tejada-Flores, Wallace, based on characters created by Tom Holland **camera** Mark Irwin **editor** Jay Lash Cassidy **design** Dean Tschetter **music** Brad Fiedel **cast** Roddy McDowall, William Ragsdale, Traci Lin, Julie Carmen, Jonathan Gries, Russell Clark, Brian Thompson, Merritt Butrick, Ernie Sabella, Matt Landers, Josh Rishman
Running time: 104 mins
UK release: Col/Tri-Star, Apr 7, 1989

THE FRUIT MACHINE (Wonderland in US)

Two gay teenagers witness a murder in a transvestite club in Liverpool, and are pursued by the perpetrator to Brighton. The early scenes have some of the vitality of the writer's

A Letter to Brezhnev, but once the setting shifts from Merseyside, a profusion of sub-plots and symbols buffet the picture all over the place. The rather four-square and academic style of direction hardly helps to paper over the credibility gaps. **TP**
Director Philip Saville **producer** Steve Morrison **script** Frank Clarke **camera** Dick Pope **editor** Richard Bedford **design** David Brockhurst **music** Hans Zimmer **cast** Emile Charles, Tony Forsyth, Robert Stephens, Clare Higgins, Bruce Payne, Robbie Coltrane, Carsten Norgaard, Kim Christie
Running time: 108 mins
US release: Vestron, Apr 28, 1989
UK release: Vestron, Oct 21, 1988

FULL MOON IN BLUE WATER 👍

Peter Masterson's clever comedy lets Gene Hackman add to his gallery of utterly believable ordinary Joes who triumph over small town woes. Here, he's a bar owner in a small Texas coastal town who's failing because his wife disappeared a year ago and he can't believe she won't come back. Greedy speculators covet Hackman's property and he doesn't seem to mind losing it. Ever-available bus driver Teri Garr tries to help, but unstable odd-job-man Elias Koteas panics when he pushes foul-mouthed stroke victim Burgess Meredith off the dock. **BM**
Director Peter Masterson **producers** Lawrence Turman, David Foster, John Turman **execs** Moshe Diamant, Eduard Sarlui **script** Bill Bozzone **camera** Fred Murphy **editor** Jill Savitt **music** Phil Marshall **cast** Gene Hackman, Teri Garr, Burgess Meredith, Elias Koteas, Kevin Cooney, David Doty, Gil Glasgow
Running time: 94 mins
US release: Trans World, Nov 23, 1988
UK release: Entertainment, Jul 7, 1989

FAREWELL TO THE KING

istory is made by remarkable men — some who even become kings while others make no more mark than a pebble in the sea.' *Farewell to the King* is the story of a man who fought a war for an empire which then enslaves his chosen people after the battle. And it is the story of a man who came to use him, learned to love him and went on to betray him. This should have been John Milius's masterpiece. Instead, it's a mess, albeit a magnificent one.

Pierre Schoendoerffer's classic novel *L'Adieu au Roi* had been Milius's pet project for more than 15 years, and it's not hard to see why. A bold philosophical reworking of Conrad's *Lord Jim*, set in WW2 Borneo, it tells of an American deserter, Learoyd (Nick Nolte), who is captured by headhunters and regains his courage to become their king, uniting the divided tribes and building a haven of peace amid a world at war. But the war arrives in the shape of an English botanist (Nigel Havers) who comes to enlist his aid against the Japanese — and undermine his authority in the process. He brings in experienced NCOs in the hope that the tribe will learn to recognize their authority instead of their king's — but they go native. He tries to sow the seed of doubt among them — only to find they have had these doubts already and have long discarded them. He finds himself drawn to Learoyd's authority and, when his life is saved by the self-styled Rajah, he is torn apart by the knowledge that one fine day he will have to betray him. And it is this knowledge that provides a real sense of emotional involvement, holding the movie together as everything falls to pieces around it.

John Milius may be one of the most talented screenwriters and directors of his generation, but the very things that make him stand out are the reasons he so rarely makes good films. Most of his best work has been writing for other directors (*Apocalypse Now*, *Jeremiah Johnson*, *The Life and Times of Judge Roy Bean*, uncredited work on *Jaws*); as a director and full-time maverick, he finds it hard to discipline himself and often goes off on self-indulgent tangents, whether they be pseudo-Nietzschean philosophical anecdotes or passages of beautifully-written but impossible-to-deliver dialogue. The latter is definitely *Farewell to the King*'s main problem. As its symbol of individuality, Learoyd is given a great many speeches outlining the philosophy of the jungle and the tribal ethos that are for the most part laughably poetic garbage (or just plain patronizing).

Strangely enough for such a personal film — and Milius regards the uncut version as his finest work — his main strengths are little in evidence. Famed for an ability to tell a story in a strikingly visual way, here he tends to regard exposition as an unpleasant chore to be got out of the way as quickly as possible so he can get on with the story, depriving Learoyd's journey from deserter to king of any real interest. Indeed, the first third of the film is so badly handled that enthusiasm nearly pales. Even his famed visual imagination seems to have deserted Milius in this section, as it does throughout much of the film. This may be due to a decision not to shoot in the CinemaScope that a story of this scale deserves. Milius is one of the few directors who knows how to use it to its full advantage; here he seems cramped by the size of the screen. Also, for all his reputation as a blood-loving warrior poet (the young Milius dreamt of being a samurai and wanted to go and die in Vietnam, but was turned down as constitutionally unfit), there is curiously little action in the film, and Milius often botches what little there is. A Japanese air raid on the village lacks either terror or the rush of adrenalin it should stimulate. And an early fight to the death between Learoyd and a Dyak rival is ruined by incessant narration (a persistent fault in the UK version).

What we do have is a mellower Milius, much more humanistic and forgiving than we've known in the past. Instead of revelling in the violence of a massacre of Japanese soldiers, he shows the emotional aftermath of the event on their killers. The dazed botanist tries to wash the blood off his hands only to find the river literally running with it, and Learoyd is so stunned by all the death that he refuses to take another life in a scene that chillingly takes place at the same time as the dropping of the first atomic bomb on Hiroshima. He even accepts the Japanese general who had earlier killed his family into the tribe as the war ends and a new one, against the British, begins. This Milius no longer takes joy in killing for killing's sake, as he did in *Conan*, but stops to count the cost and reason why. He shows a rare generosity of spirit and love for his characters that comes vividly across, although it often results in letting both stars get away with murder on several occasions. He also compromises the botanist's act of betrayal by allowing him to redeem himself. Like Sean Connery's Raisuli in Milius's finest film, *The Wind and the Lion*, this tale's ruler loses everything he has built − his village, his family, his kingdom − but ends the film a free man, forever a king in the minds of those who knew him.

Thematically, this is easily the most ambitious of Milius's films; yet it never fully explores the issues it raises and leaves too many loose ends. At times, Basil Poledouris's lyrical and passionate score seems to have a better grasp of the complexity of the material than Milius does. Some blame must attach to the extensive re-editing the film has undergone (three hour rough-cut, two-and-a-half-hour US running time, 117-minute version for Europe). The cuts certainly hurt. Nolte's gradual descent into madness as he finds himself being swallowed up by the jungle after watching his fellow deserters executed is gone; so we're straight into the raving nutter stuff. And Nolte is raving with a vengeance here.

The distributors must have known this was going to be a long film when they backed it − it was conceived with an intermission in mind − and, even if the uncut version did receive a poor audience response, if people are not willing to spend two and a half hours in the jungle with Nolte and Havers, why should they spend two?

If *Farewell to the King* suffers from lacking the will to pursue its own ideas to the full, it suffers more from lacking the imagination to pursue those it does in an original way. Whilst employing some witty and appropriate classical allusions (Learoyd avoids a war by persuading tribeswomen to withdraw their conjugal duties should the men fight), it is too obsessed with other directors' work – Kurosawa's films in general and David Lean's *Lawrence of Arabia* in particular. Two set pieces are lifted from Lean's film – a sequence where the botanist offers to kill a baby to avoid a blood feud between two rival tribes, and his later rescue by the king as he feverishly wanders under a fiercely-burning sun. Similarly, he tries to echo the haunting emotional resonance conveyed by the final moment of *Merry Christmas, Mr Lawrence* when the Englishman visits the condemned Japanese general in a vain attempt to bury his own guilt under the monstrosity of the other man's crimes. None of these scenes work because Milius does not attempt to do anything new with them. At one point, Learoyd's daughter says she wants to be just like him. 'No, you must be better,' he tells her. Unfortunately, Milius does not take this advice.

Yet *Farewell* has its moments of greatness. When Nolte becomes king, and after he saves the threatened baby's life by adopting it, Havers' admission, 'I have seen you do many things. Now I see you king,' sends a thrill through the body that briefly reminds one just how good Milius can be. He even pulls off one stunning coup as a moonlight ambush is thwarted by clouds and a brief rainstorm that obscures the Japanese while its intermittent lightning reveals the waiting warriors – a sequence that brings Dean Semler's excellent photography to the fore. He also manages to elicit fine supporting performances from James Fox, Marius Weyers, Gerry Lopez and Frank MacRae (looking for all the world like a black John Milius happily returning to the jungle). For all the clichés, for all the lack of imagination, for all the missed opportunities, you somehow find yourself forgiving Milius. You may shake your head at its simplicity and glance at your watch from time to time, but parts of the film stay with you long after it has finished.

In an exceptionally timid year, *Farewell to the King* is a genuinely ambitious film. It tries so hard for so much that, even as a failure, it is more worthy of attention than many a more successful film. If follies we must have, let them have the grandeur and intelligence of this farewell to a king.

TREVOR WILLSMER

A FISH CALLED WANDA

At the time of writing, *A Fish Called Wanda* has taken some $70 million in worldwide rentals, making it the most successful film of British origin for many years. For, although funded through a US studio, *Wanda* is in every other respect a British film, and much more so than the James Bond or Indiana Jones spectaculars which have used British technicians and studio space, but little else.

The story is only half the point, although its variations on a no-honour-among-thieves routine are ingeniously conceived and precisely structured, allowing plenty of room for comic set-pieces while never letting the pace flag too much. The basic plot could have come from any 'commercial' British film of the past 40 years – it is John Cleese's cynicism, wit and irreverence that provides the magic ingredient.

The film's opening deals swiftly with the relatively serious business of a successful bank-job, leading to betrayal and double-betrayal amongst a cynical gang that includes Wanda (Jamie Lee Curtis), her dangerously stupid lover Otto (Kevin Kline), who's later to be passed off as her brother, and hapless stutterer Ken (Michael Palin). The machinations of the plot require Otto, whose jealousy and aggression are tempered only by his stupidity, to masquerade as a camp gay in an effort to foil the suspicious Ken, while Wanda attempts to seduce her gang-leader's barrister, Archie Leach (Cleese), and thus dupe him into revealing the whereabouts of the bank haul.

Cleese's character blossoms in the presence of Wanda's unexpected admiration, and his impersonation of English reserve is the film's chief joy. And Lee Curtis does a nice job of reconciling her character's increasingly mixed feelings about hoodwinking the touchingly vulnerable Leach.

The plot splits in two as Wanda pursues Leach, pursued in turn by the increasingly manic Otto, and animal-loving Ken is sent to bump off an elderly witness to the crime (Patricia Hayes), ineptly slaughtering her pet dogs in the process. This latter section offers little in the way of plot or character development even though, as a set-piece, it works well – rather better than the long penultimate sequence which has Otto ramming chips up Ken's nose while eating his pet fish. The main plot unravels much more successfully as Wanda frees Leach of his viperish wife and finally his inhibitions, leading to a strip-cartoon climax that leaves virtue, or at least what passes for it in this film, triumphant.

When considering the *Wanda* phenomenon, all roads lead back to the enigmatic figure of John Cleese. A comic actor whose international status, even before *Wanda*, rivalled that of such top Americans as Steve Martin or Robin Williams, he is now established as a player whose presence in a film virtually

guarantees an audience.

The heart of the film's success lies in the determinedly independent stance of Cleese and his collaborators at the Python organization, Prominent Pictures. At the time of *Wanda*'s inception, the Hollywood industry, its eyes firmly set on the teen market, was gearing all comedy to the supposed tastes of the Californian adolescent. Cleese would have nothing to do with this and refused to countenance any form of studio interference in the creative aspects of his film. He was prepared to guarantee that the film would not exceed its relatively modest budget (something over $7 million) and, provided he kept to that side of the bargain, he did not expect to answer to anyone until the film was completed.

That creative independence was vital. While every aspect of the film was calculated to appeal to the widest possible audience, none of its elements suggested its future fortunes. Cleese's insistence on using 78-year-old Charles Crichton as director seemed perverse – the Ealing veteran had not worked in features for many years. In addition, neither of the imported stars were particularly bankable, although both undoubtedly played major rôles in *Wanda*'s success. Lee Curtis virtually reprises, with an extra dash of cynicism, her tart-with-a-heart performance from *Trading Places*. Cleese sensed in Kline a suppressed manic quality which suits the wild slapstick of his part. Palin relies largely on his native charm to make something out of the least well-written character.

Cynicism is a vital ingredient in *Wanda*. The plot may hark back to long-gone days of the Ealing comedies, but the violence, black comedy and dubious morality are thoroughly modern. *Wanda* is a brutal film, so much so in its early versions that major changes were made after early previews to soften characters and render the violence towards animals more cartoon-like. It seems that, while Cleese would brook no interference at the shooting stage, he was swift to act when previews showed resistance to some aspects of the film.

Despite the 1980s morality, *Wanda* does have an old-fashioned quality. Cleese's own character, as one would expect from someone named Archie Leach, harks back to the attractive diffidence of Cary Grant. And the film carries with it a very American notion of British character, using stereotypes and carefully-chosen locations to feed American preconceptions. Cleese's character (with undertones of Basil Fawlty more or less suppressed) is the reserved, gawky but ultimately plucky Brit beloved of the American imagination.

Into the nicely-updated recipe Cleese throws the Python ingredient, a blend of tastelessness and mild titillation which gives the proceedings an air of anarchy while not undermining the film's tight structure. Lee Curtis is on hand to provide the titillation, and although she receives little help from lighting which seems intent on making her look as ugly as possible, she manages her party piece with great competence – a kind of innocent sexiness that makes her forgiveable no matter what her character gets up to.

Many recent British comedies have foundered on notions of taste, either straining for a too self-consciously 'provocative' black humour, or running aground on the shores of feyness and whimsy. Cleese, through long experience of knowing what his international *Monty Python* audience responds to best, throws in enough blatant farce and Python-style silliness to keep his faithful audience without offending over-much those who think they don't like *Monty Python*. Untroubled by considerations of taste (except where it potentially affected commercial viability), Cleese is able to provide a superficially outrageous but never-threatening film. Very few audiences would be offended by anything in the film, but mostly they leave with a vague sense of having seen something rather naughty and perhaps a little dangerous.

This is partly why *Wanda* is not a favourite with highbrows or critics; it has very little in the way of style and cheerfully mixes in anything that might get a laugh, even to the extent of turning Otto into a virtual cartoon character by the end.

By no means insignificant too is the way that Cleese has refined his own screen persona, recognizing the potential for comic pathos in his gallery of pompous, impatient and physically inept heroes. He gives Leach (as well as the best lines) a vulnerability which is the stuff of all good comedy, and there is a genuinely touching quality about his scenes with Wanda. One can almost feel the audience willing him to break out of his straitjacket of Englishness. It's a fine piece of character writing: Cleese understands not only what is funny but also what is right for his character, a sureness of touch matched only by Woody Allen amongst current film comedy actors.

A Fish Called Wanda is a film contrived for international success. Probably only in Britain would such a degree of calculation be regarded with suspicion. There is a certain heartlessness about *Wanda*, a lack of spontaneity and freshness, and the film shows little of the compassion of Woody Allen or Bill Forsyth. Instead we have a film that knows its audience completely, and delivers exactly what is wanted, not to the lowest common denominator as in *Porky's* or a *Police Academy*, but rather in a way that tickles the intellect without being intimidating and provides belly laughs without being patronizing.

ADRIAN HODGES

JOHN CLEESE ON WANDA

Interviewed by Tony Crawley

W*anda* was fundamentally my idea and I had as much control as I think was good for me. That way, I didn't always have my own way. The film is better because of that. Everyone contributed. Jamie and Kevin wrote their rôles with me, making their characters more authentically American.

I'm not very good at writing love stories, or female rôles. Jamie is more experienced in love than I. You can take any scene in the film and I can say that the art director wrote that line, Jamie wrote that line, the assistant director wrote at least six lines. I'm proud of that. For example, it was Jamie's idea to have me naked in one scene. When I first thought it up, both of us were in the nude. Jamie said: 'That's not right! It's so much funnier if he's naked – because Wanda is always in control.'

In Holland, Sweden, Norway and Denmark, they seem to have a British sense of humour. My TV programmes go down better in Northern Europe than Germany, France, Spain and Italy – although the Spanish and Germans loved *Life of Brian*.

I've had two American wives. I've lived in America for nearly three years. More than half my friends are American. So, I'd always felt that English and American humour were the same. It isn't! As *Privates on Parade* and *Clockwise* proved, it is difficult to make English *jokes* about things that Americans understand. We cut or re-shot scenes to carefully explain things in *Wanda*, so Americans will know exactly what's going on. Once they understand – the sense of humour is very similar.

Making *Clockwise* was a useful experience. My character went into a public telephone box to make a call. The phone box didn't work. Neither did the next one, nor the next one. He became very frustrated. In England, this scene was very funny. In England, telephone boxes don't work! It didn't work in America, telephone boxes do work! Except in New York . . . where they laughed! That was a revelation. I'd never realized it was a cultural joke, relying on recognition and empathy with my character's frustration.

I realized years ago that when a man and woman are drawn together, it creates tension in the audience. Are they going to get together or not? Tension is wonderful for making people laugh. But if Archie ever got Wanda into bed, that tension would disappear. That's the real reason for never letting them get together.

I write unbelievably slowly! I'd go to Charlie Crichton's house and we'd sit – him at his desk and me in an easy chair with my feet up – and just talk about things that could happen. And very, very slowly, the story took shape. We'd tell the story to each other a lot of times. Then suddenly you'd get a good idea. Maybe one good idea in four or five sessions. And after two-and-a-half years of meeting three days a month, you have a lot of good stuff. Because we had given ourselves time.

Going through analysis has made my humour somewhat broader. If the therapy really works, you're able to experience feelings you previously denied. If you do that, two things happen. You become aware of more parts of yourself – and, therefore, you become a little more free, emotionally. What keeps you tight is hiding some feelings that your family taught you to be ashamed of. If you keep one feeling in, you keep them all in – you can't isolate just one. So as you become more free, you generally open up a little bit more.

The anti-Englishness speech comes straight from the heart. It's interesting that no one accuses me of racial prejudice! It would have been different if I'd done a similar speech about Italians, Belgians or Germans:

'Wanda, do you have any idea what it's like being English? Being so correct all the time, so stifled . . . by this dread . . . of doing the wrong thing? Saying to someone"Are you married!" and hearing, "My wife's left me this morning." Or saying, "Do you have children?" And being told "They all burned to death on Wednesday." You see, Wanda, we're all terrified of embarrassment. That's why we're so dead. Most of my friends are dead, you know. We have these piles of corpses to dinner . . .'

Americans laugh at it more than the English – but not more than Scottish audiences!

There's a lot of very nice things about England. A lot of rather gentle, kind people there. And there's still a sense of fair play. Maybe not so much in the big cities. I don't think I really understand England at the moment. The English are very often very intelligent and very free – in their heads. But emotionally they are very protective, very inhibited. They seem to be very frightened of the kind of direct emotional response. But they're changing. When I grew up, the idea, for example, of men touching each other affectionately, meant *awful* things. Even among parents and children, there was a big inhibition about ordinary affection and touching.

GENESIS

Adam delves, Eve spins and the Creation myth gets a repeat production, set in a crumbling ghost village. With Mrinal Sen's track record, there had to be Marxist resonances and there are. As our two heroes, outcast artisans, scrabble for survival among the gutted houses, they're betrayed not by the beautiful lady interloper (Azmi), but by the rich merchant who takes their pots and clothes to market and siphons off the profits. Anti-capitalistic message over-obvious; but performances potent and images eerily beautiful. **HK**
Directors/script Mrinal Sen **exec** Marie Pascale Osterrieth **camera** Carlo Varini **editor** Elizabeth Waelchli, Nadine Muse **design** Nitish Roy **music** Ravi Shankar **cast** Shabana Azmi, Naseeruddin Shah, Om Puri, M.K. Raina
Running time: 109 mins
UK release: Artificial Eye, Jul 8, 1988

GETTING IT RIGHT

Randall Kleiser admired 1960s British sex comedies so much he went to London and made one himself. The result, set today only in terms of the calendar, isn't quite up to The Knack but surpasses Smashing Time. Jesse Birdsall is a 30-year-old virgin until he meets rich twit Helena Bonham Carter, rich tigress Lynn Redgrave and poor hairdresser's assistant Jane Horrocks. The hairdresser she assists is Birdsall who, despite having a gay best friend, isn't gay himself - just very, very shy. Peter Cook is funny as the owner of the salon, and likewise Sir John Gielgud as Bonham Carter's nouveau riche father. **BM**
Director Randal Kleiser **producers** Jonathan D. Krane, Kleiser **exec** Rusty Lemorande **script** Elizabeth Jane Howard, from her book **camera** Clive Tickner **editor** Chris Kelly **design** Caroline Amies **music** Colin Towns **cast** Jesse Birdsall, Helena Bonham Carter, Peter Cook, Lynn Redgrave, Jane Horrocks, Richard Huw, John Gielgud, Pat Heywood, Judy Parfitt, Bryan Pringle
Running time: 102 mins
US release: MCEG, May 5, 1989

GHOST CHASE

A Hollywood in-joke adventure, hamfistedly aimed at the kiddie market, Ghost Chase is inept on every level, failing to click as a knockabout comedy, and floundering with the straight action adventure of protracted basement slug-it-out finale that takes place amid a cobwebbed set of torture instruments. Director Roland Emmerich also feels the need

to ladle an unengaging layer of non-stop disco pap over every scene, and edit in gratuitous shots of just about every billboard and trendy diner in Hollywood. The only genuinely weird touch comes when the hero asks the ghost whether he's met Boris Karloff in Heaven; no enlightening answer is forthcoming. **KN**
Director Roland Emmerich **exec** Ulrich Moeller **script** Emmerich, Thomas Kubisch **camera** Karl Walter Lindenlaub **editor** Brigitte Pia Fritsche **design** Ekkehard Schroeer, Sonja B.. Zimmer **music** Hubert Bartholomae **cast** Jason Lively, Jill Whitlow, Tim McDaniel, Paul Gleason, Chuck Mitchell, Leonard Lansink, Ian McNaughton
Running time: 89 mins
UK release: Medusa, Feb 10, 1989

GHOST TOWN

One of the more solid releases from Charles Band's now-demised Empire stable, Ghost Town mixes Western and horror ingredients. Offbeat, six-gun toting Deputy Frank Luz is supernaturally caught up in a High Plains Drifter-ish scenario. This time though it is the evil town that provides the spooks while the cop brings forth the disbelieving gasps. Enjoyable in its effective use of simple tricks, a possibly unintentional shortage of exposition contributes a mildly existential quality that seems appropriate. **PB**
Director Richard Governor **producer** Timothy D. Tennant **exec** Charles Band **script** Duke Sandefur, from story by David Schmoeller **camera** Mac Ahlberg **editor** Peter Teschner, King Wilder **design** Don De Fina **music** Harvey R. Cohen **cast** Franc Luz, Catherine Hickland, Jimmie F. Skaggs, Penelope Windust, Bruce Glover, Zitto Kazann, Blake Conway, Laura Schaefer, Michael Aldredge, Ken Kolb, Will Hannah
Running time: 85 mins
US release: Trans World, Nov 11, 1988

GHOSTBUSTERS II

There's a terrible feeling of we've-seen-it-all-before as the boiler-suited quartet of spectral annihilators trudge through their spook-busting exploits. They get together again in court, then pitch themselves against a demonic force intent on taking over the city by filling the river with ectoplasm, gathering the ghosts from the Titanic in the city centre and, in the finale, bringing the Statue of Liberty to life. The four Ghostbusters (Aykroyd, Murray, Raimis, Hudson) seem to be having a great time, but they don't bother trying to breathe life into the script. **AR**

Director/producer Ivan Reitman **execs** Bernie Brillstein, Joe Medjuck, Michael C. Cross **script** Harold Ramis, Dan Aykroyd **camera** Michael Chapman **editor** Sheldon Kahn **design** Bo Welch **music** Randy Edelman **cast** Bill Murray, Dan Aykroyd, Sigourney Weaver, Harold Ramis, Rick Moranis, Ernie Hudson, Peter MacNicol, David Margulies, Wilhelm Von Homburg
Running time: 102 mins
US release: Columbia, Jun 16, 1989

GHOSTS OF THE CIVIL DEAD

Set in a futuristic-seeming prison that looks like a backdrop from *Metropolis* or *THX 1138*, *Ghosts of the Civil Dead* is about an extraordinarily callous attempt to force prisoners into a revolt against their guards in order to justify repression. All the privileges and petty diversions that make prison life tolerable are removed and the guards are required to ignore the increasing violence of the inmates, with more and more outright psychopaths being introduced into the jail population. Director John Hillcoat avoids the usual clichés of the prison movie genre, and delivers the most upsetting entry in the cycle since *Brute Force*, by refusing to toe the traditional narrative line. It's horrifically violent, but not exploitative, and horrifically eloquent in its depiction of torture, repression and degradation. **KN**
Director John Hillcoat **producer** Evan English **script** Nick Cave, Gene Conkie, English, Hillcoat **camera** Paul Goldman **editor** Stewart Young **design** Chris Kennedy **music** Cave **cast** David Field, Mike Bishop, Chris de Rose, Nick Cave, Vincent Gil, Bogdan Koca, Kevin Mackey
Running time: 92 mins
UK release: ICA, May 12, 1989

GLEAMING THE CUBE

A fair idea for a TV movie gets turned into an embarrassing feature as a 'skateboard rebel' sets out to avenge the death of his adopted Vietnamese brother, with the aid of a hip-talking rebel cop who shouts at his superiors and impresses all the skateboarders with his amazing knowledge of skateboarding moves. Michael Tolkin's script never makes up its mind what it wants to be when it grows up, and Graeme Clifford's perfunctory direction lets the cast get away with murder: Bauer sneers a lot to prove he's cool and Slater seems under the delusion he's got the most pervasive smile since Tom Cruise (he even grins when he finds out his brother is dead!). About as much fun as falling off a skateboard, and a lot less exciting. **TW**
Director Graeme Clifford **producers** Lawrence Turman, David Foster **script** Michael Tolkin **camera** Reed Smoot **editor** John Wright **design** John Muto **music** Ray Ferguson **cast** Christian Slater, Steven Bauer, Min Luong, Art Chudabala
Running time: 105 mins
US release: Fox, Feb 17, 1989

GOOD MORNING VIETNAM

Robin Williams was Oscar-nominated for his incredible vocal gymnastics and sane-beneath-the-zany portrayal of real-life Armed Forces Radio DJ Adrian Cronauer - whose irreverent rock 'n' roll broadcasts earned him the adulation of the GIs and the wrath of the authorities in Saigon at the start of the Vietnam War. Indeed, the star never palls in Barry Levinson's comedy, and the scene in which Cronauer greets a convoy of troops is deeply affecting - less so his sentimental attachment to a Vietnamese girl and the schmaltzy interplay with her people. **GF**
Director Barry Levinson **producers** Mark Johnson, Larry Brezner **script** Mitch Markowitz **camera** Peter Sova **editor** Stu Linder **design** Roy Walker **music** Alex North **cast** Robin Williams, Forest Whitaker, Tun Thanh Tran, Chintara Sukapatan, Bruno Kirby, Robert Wuhl, J.T.Walsh, Noble Willingham
Running time: 108 mins
US release: BV, Dec 23, 1987
UK release: Touchstone/Warner, Sep 30, 1988

⬭ TURKEY

THE GOOD MOTHER

Director Leonard Nimoy **producer** Arnold Glimcher **script** Michael Bortman, from novel by Sue Miller **camera** David Watkin **editor** Peter Berger **design** Stan Jolley **music** Elmer Bernstein **cast** Diane Keaton, Liam Neeson, Jason Robards, Ralph Bellamy, Teresa Wright, James Naughton
Running time: 103 mins
US release: BV, Oct 7, 1988
UK release: Touchstone/Warner, Feb 10, 1989

GORILLAS IN THE MIST

Less cosmeticized than it could have been, this is a well-meaning biopic about Dian Fossey, intrepid preserver of endangered species of mountain gorillas in Central Africa, who died for her cause in mysterious circumstances. Sigourney Weaver emphasizes the real Fossey's

abrasiveness as she became increasingly rude to her fellow humans. But the script insists on an unlikely romanticized interlude with a visiting *National Geographic* photographer, as well as painting in accusatory arrows over the villains. Ultimately it is the gorillas themselves (the real ones almost indistinguishable from the Rick Baker creations) who are the crowning glory of the film, and Apted's direction is as properly in awe of them as any observer should be. **DT**
Director Michael Apted **producers** Arnold Glimcher, Terence Clegg **execs** Peter Guber, Jon Peters **script** Anna Hamilton Phelan, Tab Murphy, from the book by Dian Fossey and an article by Harold T. P. Hayes **camera** John Seale **editor** Stuart Baird **design** John Graysmark **music** Maurice Jarre **cast** Sigourney Weaver, Bryan Brown, Julie Harris, John Omirah Miluwi, Iain Cuthbertson, Constantin Alexandrove, Waigwa Wachira, Iain Glenn
Running time: 129 mins
US release: Warner, Sep 23, 1988
UK release: Warner, Jan 25, 1989

LE GRAND CHEMIN (The Grand Highway in US)

A village in Brittany 30 years ago is the setting for Jean-Loup Hubert's autobiographical movie about a nine-year-old uprooted from Paris and left with a friend of his mother while she has another child. The backwater scene is neatly, if a bit calculatingly, sketched in, and the tone modulates effectively between near-farce (the hostess's enigmatic husband, well played by Richard Bohringer, has to be brought back from the local bar in a wheelbarrow) and intimations of something more sinister in the couple's marital past. Less successful, however, is the shifting in viewpoint between the child's apprehension and a more Olympian detachment; this results in the implied reconciliation between Bohringer and his wife at the film's end being left rather up in the air. **TP**
Director/script Jean-Loup Hubert **producers** Pascal Hommais, Jean-François Lepetit **camera** Claude Lecomte **editor** Raymonde Guyot **design** Thierry Flamand **music** Georges Granier **cast** Antoine Hubert, Anémone, Richard Bohringer, Vanessa Guedj, Christine Pascal, Raoul Billery, Pascale Roberts, Marie Matheron, Daniel Rialet
Running time: 107 mins
US release: Miramax, Jan 22, 1988
UK release: Warner, Feb 24, 1989

GREAT BALLS OF FIRE

Jim McBride's old-fashioned biopic of Jerry Lee Lewis makes an infectious rock 'n' roll comedy, but somewhere along the line *Great Balls of Fire* was gelded. As a lovable hick with a surfeit of Southern arrogance, Quaid rides on his undeniable charm and energy, but there's only the barest hint of psychological complexity. Still, Winona Ryder, as his incredulous 13-year-old bride, and Alec Baldwin, as a perspiring Jimmy Swaggart, excel as do the late Trey Wilson as Sam Phillips and Michael St Gerard as a depressive Elvis. The songs, by the man himself, don't miss a beat. **GF**
Director Jim McBride **producer** Adam Fields **execs** Michael Grais, Mark Victor **script** Jack Baran, McBride, from book by Myra Lewis **camera** Alfonso Beato **editors** Lisa Day, Pembroke Herring, Bert Lovitt **design** David Nichols **music** Baran, McBride **cast** Dennis Quaid, Winon Ryder, John Doe, Stephen Tobolowsky, Trey Wilson, Alec Baldwin
Running Time: 108 mins
US release: Orion, Jun 30, 1989

GROUND ZERO

Colin Friels searches for some film shot by his newsreel cameraman father in the 1950s that could expose nasty secrets surrounding the British A-bomb tests in the Australian outback. This paranoia-conspiracy movie opens impressively with an irradiated plane, buried since 1953, being exhumed by decontamination suited zombies, but then gets into a somewhat protracted Hitchcockian build-up as the hero becomes involved in the machinations of vast agencies that are out to get each other. But once Friels becomes stranded in the desert with cracked and mechanical-voiced British veteran Donald Pleasence, things warm up again and the final revelations are well-handled. With a few stylish touches of hi-tech sophistry and Jack Thompson as the regulation untrustworthy government man, this emerges as a fine combination of message movie and nervous thriller. **KN**
Directors Michael Pattinson, Bruce Myles **producer** Pattinson **script** Jan Sardi, Mac Gudgeon **camera** Steve Dobson **editor** David Pulbrook **design** Brian Thomson **music** Chris Neal **cast** Colin Friels, Jack Thompson, Donald Pleasence, Natalie Bate, Simon Chilvers, Neil Fitzpatrick
Running time: 109 mins
US release: Avenue, Sep 23, 1988

THE GOOD MOTHER

Take a novel about a woman who abandoned career ambitions to care for her daughter, and is then dragged through the courts by her ex-husband, who's intent upon securing custody of their little girl. The questions raised by such a story are not the stuff of comic strips: What got the husband into such a vengeful mood? How would a woman react under that sort of pressure? What made the judiciary decide in *his* favour?

Adapting Sue Miller's *The Good Mother* for cinema called for sensitive treatment.But put the book into the hands of Touchstone Pictures, a studio noted for producing slick hits from processed scripts, and a director whose last film was the far-from-subtle *Three Men and a Baby*, and what do you get? For one thing, it's a film about grown-ups that could have been made by children. It's also a fairy-tale that goes wrong – the Queen doesn't recover her Princess – but whose makers don't seem able to turn that shift to dramatic effect. And, despite having the portentousness of a film with a Message, it's a picture that clearly doesn't know what it is trying to say.

The Good Mother, in short, exposes the hollowness at the heart of contemporary movie-making. It shows that, when the finest-tuned production machine in today's Hollywood turns away from formulaic comedies to deal with real emotions, real pain and real stories, it just can't cope. Although this is a film about a woman's despair, it didn't *have* to be so forlorn and mawkish – every moment of potential vibrancy smothered in phoniness.

Scriptwriter Michael Bortman seems to be under the impression that a contemporary audience can't deal with people looking unhappy on screen (if he's right, then there wasn't much point in trying to make this film). In fact, as any first-year literature student could tell you, take out the anger, frustration and misery, cut back the heights of passion and joy so that everyone appears *nice*, and you end up without any drama at all. More significantly – after all, this is supposed to be the *real* world – everything that happens on screen becomes inexplicable.

When Brian (James Naughton) arrives to serve a court order upon his ex-wife, there's been nothing in what's gone before to suggest his reasons. On previous visits to the family home, he's been the slightly guilty, cold ex-husband who walked out for another woman. And Anna (Diane Keaton) never gets to show how she feels about this event as she plods through the repetitious hell of social worker interviews and court proceedings, looking as if she's just been told she might have to get a tooth filled. Finally, however, she goes to pieces, but Keaton's stormy catatonics at this point have nothing to do with the rest of her performance.

'Why is Mr Dunlop doing it?', a psychiatrist asks Anna of her previous husband. 'Perhaps he's jealous in some way' is the reply. And that's about it for the film's

interest in a question that could have given some heart to this movie. You'd expect someone in Anna's position to query the motives of the man she used to share her life with, perhaps even offer up some insight from past experience. You might also imagine that a competent screenwriter would seize upon the opportunity provided by the question to explore some aspect of a modern divorce. But no. The events wash over the unthinking and seemingly unfeeling Anna, leaving the audience completely bemused.

What then is the film about? Looking around for an answer, you might seize upon the title's suggestion of an enquiry into what it means to be a 'good mother'. The problem is that the definitions of that concept offered by the film are limp. For Anna, it's someone who acknowledges she's never going to be a great pianist and washes bottles in a laboratory to earn some cash, but otherwise spends time with her little girl. For her ex-, it's someone who doesn't allow his child to sleep in the same bed as a copulating couple or touch her boyfriend's genitals. The two concepts are, of course, not mutually exclusive.

But without some sense of a conflict, how did anyone ever hope to build intrigue and suspense into the court scenes? Never before was judicial procedure presented to less suspenseful effect. Did that boyfriend (Liam Neeson) do wrong when he allowed the little girl, Molly, to satisfy her curiosity? He acknowledges to the judge he may have 'crossed the line', but he doesn't really believe it. Keaton concurs, even though she didn't really disapprove. After they've told their lies, you never get any hint as to why the judge makes the decision he does. The film might have made a point about lawyers who give bad advice, or a judge who had to be lied to. As it is, it doesn't seem to have anything to say about anything.

One obvious test of Anna's qualities as a mother, and the conflicting claims of her father, would be to see how Molly responds in the presence of either. But the screenwriters are so blind to the subject's dramatic potential that they let her slip out of sight. A psychiatrist goes into the witness stand to pronounce on Anna's strong bonding with her daughter, but the only scene Molly has with her mother following the abduction is played so flat there's no reason to think the girl is even aware her address has been changed.

Some light could have been thrown on Anna's doubts about her qualifications for maternity if we saw her interacting with her own mother. But, after being glimpsed momentarily in an opening scene, this obviously crucial figure just disappears. So complete is her evacuation from the script that I was waiting for an allusion to some dramatic car crash, or a plane that self-ignited on the tarmac.

This severing of Anna's parental roots is all the more perverse in that the film sometimes seems to be offering itself as a panegyric to the 'family'. The early scenes are set in a lakeside paradise, home to Anna's grandparents, where young and old gather for long, relaxed summers. Divorce wrecks such idylls, but the film then goes out of its way to avoid suggesting that staying together is a priority. When Anna goes to asks Gramps for money to pay for her court case, Granny

tells of the 15 years of real unhappiness she endured in her marriage. She may have come out the other side smiling but, when Grandfather does appear, he behaves in such a mean-spirited way that you wish for her sake she had given him up a long time ago. Similarly, the way Anna's husband behaves could never justify her fighting to keep him.

The film has a prologue which shows the young Anna being instructed in matters sexual and emotional by 'Baby', who is mother's sister but 20 years her junior. The fun-loving Baby gestates an illegitimate child and, shortly after letting her niece touch her swelling belly, things start to go wrong for her. Eventually she drowns in the lake.

Wages of sin indeed. What then are we to make of Anna's assertion that she modelled her life upon Baby? The statement surely doesn't explain her marriage to the passionless, humourless Brian. It's meant to refer to her relationship with Leo who, as an artist and a Celt, can offer just what uptight husbands cannot. Back at his studio on their first date, the couple fumble; she clings to the sheets and swathes of Elmer Bernstein music are laid across the soundtrack – the score is used to deaden the scene's emotional impact. The second time, she apologizes, 'I don't think I'm very good at it.' He offers to fix it. She spills some wine, writhes, reaches out and goes 'Oh!' Cue scenes of happy togetherness. That, apparently, is what it means to live up to Baby's shining example.

Perhaps the filmmakers thought that, by ascribing Anna's problems to her trysts with Leo, post-marital rather than extra-marital sex, they could tap into the puritan zeal that made a hit out of *Fatal Attraction*. If so, nobody told this to the screenwriter, who does a good job of establishing that what Anna needs at the beginning of the film is a good roll in the sheets, and that Molly's requirement is a happy mother and, possibly, a man about the house – a job that Leo fulfils more than adequately.

There are ideas in *The Good Mother* from which a decent film could have been forged, but they go off throughout this narrative like a series of damp squibs. Perhaps someone naïvely thought this was a 'serious' drama, which could cope with all the 'complexity' and 'contradiction'. One thing is certain. To judge by the number of lines and incident that come straight from Sue Miller's book, no one responsible for this production had any idea of their responsibility to rethink and re-structure the novel to dramatic and cinematic effect.

JAMES PARK

HAIRSPRAY

John Waters goes respectable without sacrificing bad taste in a film which has proved his most accessible yet (to a mainstream audience) and, sadly, was Divine's swansong. The big man rasps out his last lines as the outsize mom of plump newcomer Ricki Lake, whose Tracy Turnblad is desperate to become the queen of a TV teen dance shown in early 1960s Baltimore - and to dethrone the pampered daughter (Fitzpatrick) of Sonny Bono and a fantastically coiffured Debbie Harry. Waters slickly enfolds an integrationist theme as Lake champions the inclusion of black kids in the white supremacist show. Pia Zadora and Ric Ocasek (of The Cars) check in as a beatnik chick and cat, the soundtrack throbs, the hair explodes. Divine dances off into the sunset, and fat is beautiful. GF

Director/script John Waters *producer* Rachel Talalay *execs* Robert Shaye, Sara Richer *camera* David Insley *editor* Janice Hampton *design* Vincent Peranio *music* Kenny Vance *cast* Sonny Bono, Ruth Brown, Divine, Colleen Fitzpatrick, Jo Ann Havrilla, Michael St. Gerard, Debbie Harry, Ricki Lake, Leslie Ann Powers, Clayton Prince, Jerry Stiller, Mink Stole, Shawn Thompson, Ric Ocasek, Pia Zadora
Running time: 90 mins
US release: New Line, Feb 26, 1988
UK release: Palace, Jul 1, 1988

HALLOWEEN 4: THE RETURN OF MICHAEL MYERS

In this inevitably crass and disappointing follow-up to John Carpenter's original, director Dwight Little discards narrative explication and the search for new ideas in favour of a high body count, mucho carnage and the usual homicidal drivel. The re-introduction of suburban spectre Michael Myers is an insult to the Myers-less, Nigel Kneale-penned, second sequel. Could it be that Myers' psychosis stems from the fact that Freddy Krueger and Jason got to the counsellor before the young maniac and collected all the interesting personality foibles? Mikey has none. And if heroic shrink Donald Pleasence gets to buy a new yacht whenever he signs on for one of the instalments, and all you got was fan-mail from Motley Crue, you'd be tempted to violence too, wouldn't you? MN

Director Dwight H. Little *producer* Paul Freeman *exec* Moustapha Akkad *script* Alan B. McElroy, *from story by* Dhani Lipsius, Larry Rattner,

Benjamin Ruffner, McElroy *camera* Peter Lyons Collister *editor* Curtiss Clayton *design* Roger S. Crandall *music* Alan Howarth *cast* Donald Pleasence, Ellie Cornell, Danielle Harris, George P. Wilbur, Michael Pataki, Beau Starr, Kathleen Kinmont, Sasha Jenson, Gene Ross
Running time: 88 mins
US release: Galaxy, Oct 21, 1988

HANNA'S WAR

Jewish refugee Hanna trains to be a spy and lands in Nazi-occupied territory, where she is immediately captured and executed. With so many stories about the Jewish resistance to Hitler. why choose to film one where nothing actually happens? Although based on a true story, Menahem Golan's long-cherished pet project was so misconceived that not even the last-minute departure of Helena Bonham Carter from the title rôle could save it. Intended as a moving tribute to the human spirit, it runs through every WW2 cliché from cruel-to-be-kind RSM (Anthony Andrews in kilt and unbelievably bad Scottish accent) to the obligatory appearance of Donald Pleasence as a drooling Nazi torturer, with frightening lack of emotion or imagination. One of the few Cannon films to have been made with the best of intentions, it comes out no better than any of their other, numerous turkeys. TW

Director Menahem Golan *producers* Golan, Yoram Globus *script* Golan, *from books by* Hanna Senesh *and* Yoel Palgi *camera* Elemer Ragalyi *editor* Alain Jakubowicz *design* Kuli Sander *music* Dov Seltzer *cast* Ellen Burstyn, Maruschka Detmers, Anthony Andrews, Donald Pleasence, David Warner, Vincenzo Ricotta, Christopher Fairbank
Running time: 148 mins
US release: Cannon, Nov 23, 1988
UK release: Cannon, Oct 28, 1988

HANUSSEN

Brandauer gives a spellbinding performance as a shell-shocked WWI veteran, who gave up healing the psychological wounds of his fellow Germans in an army hospital to enjoy a spectacular stage career as a clairvoyant, only to find his more disturbing predictions being refashioned as Nazi propaganda. *Hanussen* at times plays like an epic and nightmarish *film noir* - Brandauer can predict political events but is powerless to prevent them; it is only at the hospital that he could achieve anything, but he is too much in love with the applause to go back. The result is a thoughtful reflection on man's inability to learn anything positive from his mistakes, or to prevent them occurring again. Its subtlety and insidious menace make *Hanussen* one of the most remarkable films of the decade. **TW**

Director Istvan Szabo *producer* Artur Brauner *script* Szabo, Peter Dobrai *camera* Lajos Koltai *editor* Zsuzsa Csakany *design* Jozsef Romvari *music* Gyorgy Vukan *cast* Klaus Maria Brandauer, Erland Josephson, Ildiko Bansagi, Walter Schmidinger, Karoly Eperjes, Grazina Szapolowska, Colette Pilz-Warren, Adriana Beidrzynska
Running time: 140 mins
US release: Col, Mar 10, 1989
UK release: Col/Tri-Star, Apr 21, 1989

HARD TIMES (Tempos Difíceis)

The austere black-and-white images and low-key performances in this adaptation of Dickens' novel to a present-day Portugal are contrasted provocatively with its profusion of dramatic incident. An orphan is taken into the household of the local factory owner; a school teacher's daughter enters a loveless marriage; a doleful worker struggles with his drunken wife, becomes a reluctant intermediary between his shop floor associates and management, and is set up with a robbery committed by the proprietor's son. Although self-conscious in its references to Bresson and Ozu, the visual style never seems derivative and, despite its period source, the film comes across as completely contemporary. **JP**

Director/script/producer João Botelho *exec* Manuel Guanilho, João Pinto Nogueira *camera* Elso Roque *cast* Henrique Viana, Julia Britton, Eunice Muñoz, Ruy Furtado, Isabel De Castro, Joaquim Mendes, Isabel Ruth, Lia Gama, Inês de Medeiros, Luís Estrela, Pedro Cabrita Reis
Running time: 96 mins
US release: Artificial Eye, Jun 2, 1989

HAUNTED SUMMER

'Lake Geneva welcomes Byron, Shelley and friends'. They still haven't taken the sign down after Ken Russell's *Gothic*. This time ex-Czech director Ivan Passer lenses the Romantic foursome's lake visit for Cannon. Scripted by John Lewis Carlino (*The Great Santini*), it's much more risible than Russell's version. While soft-focus photograpy turns the whole thing into a toilet-paper commercial, bouts of musical-beds romance alternate with Shelley's attempts to raise the tone of the occasion with some philosophizing. But even this is doomed. One

high-flying aria receives a long, judicious pause from Lord Byron, followed by the single word 'Bollocks'. Altogether, a new perspective on English literary history. **HK**

Director Ivan Passer *producer* Martin Poll *execs* Menahem Golan, Yoram Globus *script* John Lewis Carlino, based on novel by Anne Edwards *camera* Giuseppe Rotunno *editors* Cesare D'Amico, Richard Fields *design* Stephen Grimes *music* Christopher Young *cast* Philip Anglim, Laura Dern, Alice Krige, Eric Stoltz, Alexander Winter
Running time: 106 mins
US release: Cannon, Dec 16, 1988
UK release: Cannon, Apr 7, 1989

HAWKS

An energetic black comedy revolving around a fatalistic but good-humoured British lawyer (Dalton), whose wicked sense of cynicism rescues him from depression when an irreversible illness consigns him to a hospital ward. New arrival (Edwards) finds the going more traumautic since his now-deteriorating football-playing physique was formerly his professional salvation. Dalton decides to make their hopeless situation a shade more tolerable by absconding along with Edwards in an ambulance and heading for a final fling in the brothels of Amsterdam. Janet McTeer is the skeletal Plain-Jane who falls for Dalton in the prostitute-ridden environs where they meet, and ridicule towards her evolves into the couple's mutual attempts at emotional redemption. *Hawks* is a dramatic confection that sporadically gives way to cute stiff upper-lip moral exhortations and appears to be plagued with self-doubt, suggesting its makers feared audiences would not take the premise seriously. Sometimes, only sometimes, their attempts to alternate slapstick and character catharsis provide compensation. **MN**

Director Robert Ellis Miller *producers* Stephen Lanning, Keith Cavele *exec* Morrie Eisenman, Richard Becker *script* Roy Clarke, based on idea by Barry Gibb, David English *camera* Doug Milsome *editor* Malcolm Cooke *design* Peter Howitt *music* Barry Gibb, John Cameron *cast* Timothy Dalton, Anthony Edwards, Janet McTeer, Camille Coduri, Jill Bennett, Robert Lang, Pat Starr, Bruce Boa, Sheila Hancock, Geoffrey Palmer, Caroline Langrishe, Benjamin Whitrow
Running time: 109 mins
UK release: Rank, Aug 5, 1988

HEART OF MIDNIGHT

Something funny is going on in the nightclub that Jennifer Jason Leigh inherits from her uncle, and makes her home as refuge from a domineering mother. *Heart of Midnight* is built from a number of promising ideas that never come to anything very much. That's largely because the script doesn't sufficiently feed our uncertainties as to whether what we see happens in her mind or is the result of intervention by another force. Consequently there's no excitement to be gained from the process of finding out either what's happening behind the walls or what happened in her past. It's also partly the problem of having a character who so clearly starts on the other side of sanity - her first action is to grind a figurine into the sink - and never seems sufficiently interested in, or frightened by, the weird happenings. The film seems to be offering a message about the fruits (there are a lot of apples on display) of sexual decadence, but it's too muddled to hit its target. **JP**
Director *Matthew Chapman* **producer** *Andrew Gaty* **exec** *Jon Kurtis* **script** *Chapman, Everett De Roche* **camera** *Ray Rivas* **editor** *Penelope Shaw* **design** *Gene Rudolf* **cast** *Jennifer Jason Leigh, Denise Dummont, Gale Mayron, James Rebhorn, Sam Schacht, Frank Stallone, Brenda Vaccaro, Peter Coyote*
Running time: 105 mins
US release: Goldwyn, Mar 3, 1989
UK release: Vestron, Jan 27, 1989

HEARTBREAK HOTEL

Chris Columbus shows a Capraesque touch in this tale of a young small-town loser who finds the courage to realize his dreams when he kidnaps a portly Elvis from the tacky Las Vegan scene and tells him where he's going wrong. While there's more wishful thinking than acid in the humour and the film goes astray for the traditional Touchstone sentimental ending, it has a rare generosity and warmth for its characters that transcends the formula packaging. **TW**
Director/script *Chris Columbus* **producers** *Linda Obst, Debra Hill* **camera** *Stephen Dobson* **editor** *Raja Gosnell* **music** *Georges Delerue* **cast** *David Keith, Tuesday Weld, Charlie Schlatter, Angela Goethals, Jacque Lynn Colton, Chris Mulkey, Karen Landry*
Running time: 93 mins
US release: BV, Sep 30, 1989

HEATHERS

Director *Michael Lehmann* **producer** *Denise Di Novi* **exec** *Christopher Webster* **script** *Daniel Waters* **camera** *Francis Kenney* **editor** *Norman Hollyn* **design** *Jon Hutman* **music** *David Newman* **cast** *Winona Ryder, Christian Slater, Shannen Doherty, Lisanne Falk, Kim Walker, Penelope Milford, Glenn Shadix, Lance Fenton, Patrick Labyorteaux, Jeremy Applegate, Jon Matthews, Carrie Lynn*
Running time: 102 mins
US release: New World, Mar 31, 1989

HELLBOUND: HELLRAISER II

Clive Barker wrote the original story and acted as executive producer on this sequel to his successful directorial début. It starts off in a sort of Gothic lunatic asylum, and ends up in a papier-mâché hell, where a clutch of splendid, full-blooded monsters battle it out amongst themselves: the bad guys include a mad doctor (Cranham) who learns the secret of life-after-death when he gets a drill through the cranium, a wicked stepmother (Higgins) who is not only dead but skinless, and a clutch of leather-clad sado-masochists known as Cenobites. The plot gets chucked out of the window at an early stage, and one tires quickly of the vapid heroines, who spend a lot of time wandering through corridors. But as a weird fairy-tale, or as a series of imaginative splatter set-pieces with no particular logical link, this manages both to plumb new depths of ineptitude and soar to eye-popping new heights of radical anatomical reconstruction. **AB**
Director *Tony Randel* **producer** *Christopher Figg* **execs** *Christopher Webster, Clive Barker* **script** *Peter Atkins, from story by Barker* **camera** *Robin Vidgeon* **design** *Mike Buchanan* **music** *Christopher Young* **cast** *Clare Higgins, Ashley Laurence, Ken Cranham, Imogen Boorman, William Hope*
Running time: 96 mins
US release: New World, Dec 23, 1989
UK release: Premier, Jun 16, 1989

HER ALIBI

We're in *Romancing the Stone* territory here as dried-out pulp mystery writer Selleck finds himself living a real-life thriller when he offers the stunning Ms Porizkova an alibi after seeing her in court and becoming smitten. The question is, Is she really a murderer, and if so, will he be her next victim? Suspense is at an absolute zero due to lazy plotting; so the once-mighty Beresford concentrates on the comedy to good, though often predictable, effect without quite managing to convince that he hasn't botched up a good premise for a *film noir* in the process. **TW**

Director Bruce Beresford **producer** Keith Barish **exec** Martin Efland **script** Charlie Peters **camera** Freddie Francis **editor** Anne Goursaud **design** Henry Blumstead **music** Georges Delerue **cast** Tom Selleck, Paulina Porizkova, William Daniels, James Farentino, Hurd Hatfield, Ronald Guttman, Victor Argo, Patrick Wayne, Tess Harper
Running time: 94 mins
US release: Warner, Feb 3, 1989
UK release: Warner, May 12, 1989

THE HIDDEN

Jack Sholder's low-budget sci-fi *policier*, whilst heavily derivative of the work of James Cameron and John Carpenter, is sufficiently adept at imitating their strong narratives and liberal use of buddy-buddy heroics to ensure this 'alien in Los Angeles' pastiche hits its targets. Sceptical macho cop Michael Nouri is teamed with enigmatic Kyle MacLachlan, professedly a Federal agent, to investigate a series of inexplicable murders and robberies by seemingly-invincible, previously unimpeachable, citizens who suddenly drop dead after their arrest. What smoothly-ambivalent Nouri doesn't know, however, is that strange new colleague MacLachlan is in fact an inter-galactic vigilante who, armed with enterprising extra-terrestrial hardware, has arrived to wreak vengeance upon a prosthetically-sculpted villain who commutes from, and incubates in, the intestines of hapless Californians. Suitably tongue-in-cheek, *The Hidden* is effective pulp entertainment. **MN**

Director Jack Sholder **producers** Robert Shaye, Gerald T. Olson, Michael Meltzer **execs** Stephen Diener, Lee Muhl, Dennis Harris, Jeffrey Klein **script** Bob Hunt **camera** Jacques Haitkin **editor** Michael Knue **design** C.J. Strawn, Mick Strawn **music** Michael Convertino **cast** Michael Nouri, Kyle MacLachlan, Ed O'Ross, Clu Gulager, Claudia Christian, Clarence Felder, William Boyett, Richard Brooks
Running time: 96 mins
US release: New Line, Oct 20, 1987
UK release: Palace, Nov 25, 1988

HIGH HOPES

There's never any doubt where Mike Leigh's sympathies lie in this comic dissection of social class in contemporary London. They're a couple living in a high-rise. He's a motorbike despatch rider (Davis), she's a municipal gardener (Sheen). They have nice soft-left views, worry about whether to have babies, call a cactus Thatcher because she's a pain in the bum and take in strays, albeit reluctantly. More significantly, and unlike everybody else, they're reasonably content with their lot. By contrast, Granny's new neighbours sport names like Laetitia and Rupert Boothe-Braine: he's unable to remember what opera they saw the night before, she spends hours worrying about her skin. And Sheen's sister (Tobias) is one of life's fumblers, mistaking kitsch for quality and so knotted-inside she can't tell when she's causing embarrassment. The narrative structure is sometimes overly episodic, and allusions to the contrast between sex as procreation and as recreation never quite develop into a linking theme (and provoke the enquiry as to how Leigh's method of screenwriting-through-rehearsal/research could work with children in the cast), but there's so much wit and reality in the dialogue that you'll forgive this film anything. **JP**

Director/script Mike Leigh **producers** Simon Channing-Williams, Victor Glynn **exec** Tom Donald **camera** Roger Pratt **editor** Jon Gregory **design** Diana Charnley **music** Andrew Dixon **cast** Philip Davis, Ruth Sheen, Edna Doré, Philip Jackson, Heather Tobias, Lesley Manville, David Bamber, Jason Watkins, Judith Scott
Running time: 112 mins
US release: Skouras, Feb 24, 1989
UK release: Palace, Jan 13, 1989

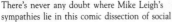

HIGH SPIRITS

Director/script Neil Jordan **producers** Stephen Woolley, David Saunders **execs** Mark Damon, Moshe Diamant, Edward Sarlui **camera** Alex Thomson **editor** Michael Bradsell **design** Anton Furst **music** George Fenton **cast** Peter O'Toole, Donal McCann, Mary Koughlan, Liz Smith, Steve Guttenberg, Beverly D'Angelo, Jennifer Tilly, Peter Gallagher, Daryl Hannah, Liam Neeson, Ray McAnally
Running time: 96 mins
US release: Tri-Star, Nov 18, 1988
UK release: Palace, Dec 9, 1988

HIGH TIDE

After the dull *Mrs Soffel*, Gillian Armstrong returned to Oz for another collaboration with

Judy Davis, who plays a no-hope back-up singer accidentally stumbling across her estranged teenage daughter, who never knew her true mother. Virtuoso photography and powerful performances - especially from newcomer Claudia Karvan - sustain the drama over some occasional weak scripting, and sentimentality is avoided in the clash of responsibilities and aspirations over three generations. **DT**
Director Gillian Armstrong **producer** Sandra Levy **execs** Anthony I. Ginnane, Joseph Skrzynski **script** Laura Jones **camera** Russell Boyd **editor** Nicholas Beauman **design** Sally Campbell **music** Peter Best **cast** Judy Davis, Jan Adele, Claudia Karvan, Colin Friels, John Clayton, Frankie J. Holden, Monica Trapaga, Mark Hembrow
Running time: 104 mins
US release: Tri-Star, Dec 18, 1987
UK release: Ritzy, Oct 28, 1988

HONEY, I'VE SHRUNK THE KIDS

When an inventor (Rick Moranis) zaps his teenage daughter, the boy next door and two young brothers with his latest invention, they are suddenly Lilliputians who – accidentally put out with the garbage – have to make an incredible journey through the backyard. There's nothing reductive about this exuberant Disney family comedy – with its friendly ant, three-story Lego bricks, and monstrous lawnmower – which delights not only in turning the garden into a prehistoric jungle but also in its wry observation of generational conflict. Moranis and Matt Frewer, the neurotically sporty neighbour, are terrific as dads preoccupied with their own adolescent fantasies. The movie was released in the US with *Tummy Trouble*, a dyspeptic cartoon short with Roger Rabbit and Baby Herman running amok in a hospital. **GF**
Director Joe Johnston **producer** Penny Finkelman Cox **exec** Thomas G. Smith **script** Ed Naha, Tom Schulman, from story by Stuart Gordon, Brian Yuzna, Naha **camera** Hiro Narita **editor** Michael A. Stevenson **design** Gregg Fonseca **music** James Horner **cast** Rick Moranis, Matt Frewer, Marcia Strassman, Kristine Sutherland, Thomas Brown, Jared Rushton, Amy O'Neill, Robert Oliveri
Running time: 86 mins
US release: BV, Jun 23, 1989

HORROR SHOW

This banquet of viscera is derivative of both the *Prison* and *Elm Street* cycles, but more enjoyable than either. Brion James, Central Casting's archangel of the psychologically disturbed, precipitates the splatter-quotient as a serial killer who, having sustained a visit to the electric chair, seeks revenge for his apparent death by hunting down the policeman responsible for his predicament. Lance Henriksen, as the cop, oscillates between paranoia, vengeance and frustration - the last resulting from James's ability to commute between dimensions. Both leads gleefully take part in the macabre set-pieces without sacrificing credibility. **MN**
Director James Isaac **producer** Sean S. Cunningham **script** 'Alan Smithee' (Allyn Warner), Leslie Bohem **camera** Mac Ahlberg **editor** Edward Anton **music** Harry Manfredini **cast** Lance Henriksen, Brion James, Rita Taggart, Deedee Pfeiffer, Aron Eisenberg
Running time: 95 mins
US release: MGM/UA, Apr 28, 1989

HOT TO TROT 🖑

What can you say about a film that advertises itself as 'The funniest talking-horse movie ever'? Not much, but you could try suing under the Trade Descriptions Act. Bobcat Goldthwait finds his office job on the line when he becomes involved with a foul-mouthed quadruped, much to the chagrin of boss Dabney Coleman. Will Bobcat keep his job? Will his four-legged friend sleep with an inflatable *horse*? Will the beautiful Miss Madsen ever make a decent movie? Who cares? Mr Ed would turn in his grave. **TW**
Director Michael Dinner **producer** Steve Tisch **script** Stephen Neigher, Hugh Gilbert, Charlie Peters **camera** Victor Kemper **editor** Frank Morris **design** William Matthews **music** Danny Elfman **cast** Bobcat Goldthwait, Dabney Coleman, John Candy, Virginia Madsen, Jim Metzler, Cindy Pickett
Running time: 83 mins
US release: Warner, Aug 26, 1988

HOTEL DU PARADIS

An ageing actor, typecast as a foreign villain in American thrillers and Bond movies, attempts to restore his self-confidence and his career by staging a Camus play, and becomes involved with the various residents of a hotel including: a runaway photographer, a theatre owner on the edge of insolvency and a film technician with prostate problems. Documentarist Jana Bokóva's first fictional feature mistakes a series of conversations for a movie and has pacing that would try the patience of a snail, but she shows a remarkable sympathy with her actors

that almost succeeds in making you forgive the over-indulgences. Fernando Rey turns in a marvellously understated performance in a rôle that at times seems too close to his own career for comfort. An elegant performance piece that goes nowhere but, thanks to Rey, goes there in style. **TW**
Director/script Jana Bokóva **producer** Simon Perry **camera** Gérard de Batista **editor** Bill Shapter **design** Patrick Weibel **music** Rodolfo Mederos **cast** Fernando Rey, Fabrice Luchini, Berangère Bonvoisin, Hugues Quester, Marika Rivera, Juliet Berto
Running time: 113 mins
UK release: Artificial Eye, May 5, 1989

HOTEL TERMINUS: KLAUS BARBIE, HIS LIFE AND TIMES

Marcel Ophuls turns the trial of war criminal Klaus Barbie into a lively, surprising and often entertaining piece of cinema. Lashing out in all directions behind a façade of bemused irony, he manages to cover almost every aspect of the bizarre case: exposing the collusion of the 'Allied' governments in Barbie's disappearance after the war, the willing collaboration of much of the French government and population in the racist purges, the irony of Barbie's defence (the kind of racially impure non-Aryan he so wantonly sent to the death camps acts as his lawyer) and the courage of the 'good neighbours' to whom the film is dedicated, who often risked their lives to save others. **TW**
Director/producer Marcel Ophuls **execs** John S. Friedman, Hamilton Fish, Peter Kovler **camera** Michael Davis, Pierre Boffety, Ruben Aaronson, Wilhelm Rosing, Lionel Legros, Daniel Chabert, Paul Gonon **editor** Albert Jurgenson, Catherine Zins
Running time: 267 mins
US release: Goldwyn, Oct 9, 1988

THE HOUSE ON CARROLL STREET

New York in 1951, at the height of the House Un-American Affairs Committee hearings, provides an evocative backdrop for this well-engineered suspense story, in which a journalist (McGillis) loses her job as a result of political intimidation, then finds herself witness to the workings of a conspiracy to smuggle ex-Nazis into the US, in which her chief persecutor (Patinkin, giving an admirably oily performance) proves to be the prime mover. With the plot building to a floridly melodramatic climax amid the rafters of Grand Central Station, this is a thriller which satisfyingly contrives to be

Hitchcockian in spirit rather than by flourishing spurious allusions. **TP**
Director Peter Yates **producers** Yates, Robert F. Colesberry **execs** Arlene Donovan, Robert Benton **script** Walter Bernstein **camera** Michael Ballhaus **editor** Ray Lovejoy **design** Stuart Wurtzel **music** Georges Delerue **cast** Kelly McGillis, Jeff Daniels, Mandy Patinkin, Christopher Rhode, Jessica Tandy, Jonathan Hogan
Running time: 101 mins
US release: Orion, Mar 4, 1988
UK release: Rank, Oct 21, 1988

HOW I GOT INTO COLLEGE

Savage Steve Holland's teen comedies have always been anarchic, yet true to life. This story, set amid the life-or-death struggle of the American college admissions process, has enough unforced sweetness and unexpected laughs to attract some adult audiences. Corey Parker is a good-natured semi-nerd who applies to a particular college because cheerleader Lara Flynn Boyle wants to go there. Anthony Edwards and Finn Carter are admissions officers at the college who win the internal debate over whether to accept marginal candidate Parker. Holland's most amusing sallies involve dramatizing those irritating entrance exam word problems. **BM**
Director Savage Steve Holland **producer** Michael Shamberg **script** Terrel Seltzer **camera** Robert Elswit **editors** Sonya Sones Tramer, Kaja Fehr **design** Ida Ransom **music** Joseph Vitarelli **cast** Anthony Edwards, Corey Parker, Lara Flynn Boyle, Finn Carter, Charles Rocket, Christopher Rydell, Brian-Doyle Murray, Tichina Arnold, Bill Raymond, Philip Baker Hall
Running time: 89 mins
US release: Fox, May 19, 1989

HOW TO GET AHEAD IN ADVERTISING

When Richard E. Grant isn't ranting his way through this movie, he's running around the garden half-naked. A hysterical diatribe, How to Get Ahead in Advertising sounds off about a 'conspiracy' but fails to offer any sort of coherent polemic, and largely wastes its central idea - a boil grows on ad man Grant's shoulder as he starts to nurse doubts about his profession. Since Grant's two personalities, as boil and well-meaning human being, both behave in such an extreme fashion, there's no contest between them, and neither character is ever sufficiently revealed to give the excrescence much value as metaphor. Robinson can write scenes and direct actors, but he can't structure

a script or orchestrate a movie. The final sequence, which suggests the whole thing is pitched against Robinson's former mentor, David Puttnam - a former ad man who runs a large country house and plays rousing music over the final moments of his films (including the Robinson-scripted *The Killing Fields*) - is as intensely irritating as the rest of this farrago. **JP**
Director/script Bruce Robinson ***producer*** David Wimbury ***execs*** George Harrison, Denis O'Brien ***camera*** Peter Hannan ***editor*** Alan Strachan ***design*** Michael Pickwoad ***music*** David Dundas, Rick Wentworth ***cast*** Richard E. Grant, Rachel Ward, Richard Wilson, Jacqueline Tong, John Shrapnel, Susan Wooldridge, Mick Ford
Running time: 95 mins
US release: Warner, May 5, 1989
UK release: Virgin, Jul 28, 1989

A HUNGARIAN FAIRY TALE (Hol Volt, Hol Nem Volt)

This witty satire takes its cue from a Hungarian law that assigns 'fake' fathers to children of unknown paternity. When the mother of one such is killed by a falling brick, the kid sets off for the address on his birth certificate and recruits the woman living there, a disaffected nurse, to his quest for a father. Meanwhile, the civil servant responsible for handing out false patronymics tires of his stupid task, burns all his records and travels to the same town. These three rebels against bureaucracy and conformism form a new family unit and flee on the wings of an eagle. The meaning of the more allegorical passages is necessarily opaque to non-Hungarians, but the good-humoured charm, brisk pace and sense of fun make for a subtly entrancing film. **JP**
Director Gyula Gazdag ***producer*** Mafilm-Objektiv Studio ***script*** Gazdag, Miklos Gyorffy ***camera*** Elemer Ragalyi ***editor*** Julia Sivo ***design*** Jozsef Romvari ***music*** Istvan Martha ***cast*** Arpad Vermes, Maria Varga, Frantisek Husak, Eszter Csakanyl, Szilvia Toth, Judit Pogany, Geza Balkay, Gabor Reviczky
Running time: 98 mins
US release: M.D.Wax/Courier Films, Dec 28, 1988
UK release: Pathé, Jun 30, 1989

HEATHERS

Now that the kids who loved John Hughes' simple-minded teen flicks a few years ago have grown up, they're drawn to films that are about teens but made for adults. Some of the year's most enjoyable pictures had adolescent casts playing to mature scripts: *Running on Empty* (a kid ready to outgrow his parents), *The Chocolate War* (playing cliques for keeps in a Catholic boys' school), and *Say Anything* (a misfit romance that's played realistically). A few teen flicks that failed the maturity test nevertheless gave a token nod towards thoughtful audiences, as in *Listen to Me* (a debate on abortion) and *Lost Angels* (a kind shrink who didn't have all the answers).

Heathers is a fast and ruthless satire that goes all the way into the hell known as high school. The film, although terrifically funny, is as disturbing a view of life among teens as was *River's Edge*. Coming on like nothing more than another comedy about conflicting classroom social strata, *Heathers* turns into a realistic vision of the classroom psycho across the aisle. The movie first honours all the conventions of the teen flick and then breaks through them to get at the laughs behind the horror behind the hijinks.

The title refers to a trio of self-assured girls who share an upscale name, Heather. They strut through Westerburg High School, dressed to kill, smirking cruelly at lesser mortals who wear the wrong brand of jeans, drive the wrong make of car or have the wrong kind of face. In the standard teen-flick scenario, these three would be humiliated picturesquely and the heroine would rule in their place, although more humanely.

Events turn out differently here because the heroine, Veronica (Winona Ryder), isn't the standard pretty-in-pink nerd seeking revenge. Veronica doesn't want to beat the Heathers, she wants to be a Heather. As a Heather-in-training, she's willing to learn the cruel games Heathers love to play. For instance, the Heathers enjoy croquet, especially when the opponent's ball gets knocked into the shrubbery. Veronica imagines her head in the about-to-go-flying position, but never considers renouncing Heatherism.

A typical Heather prank is directed at an inoffensive fat girl. As a sort of initiation, the Heathers require Veronica to forge a letter to this girl, from a dreamboat guy revealing his secret love for her. She goes all gooey on reading the note and when she finds out it was a hoax, she wants to kill herself. A momentarily repentant Veronica dissuades her and confides to her diary that she despises the Heathers' values and even wishes the Heathers' leader dead. This ambivalence leaves her open to the influence of newcomer J. D. (Christian Slater).

J. D. (read James Dean) is a loner by choice and a cynic by disposition. He's devilishly attractive, setting off by himself on his motorcycle, chuckling at the vainglorious antics of those who think they rule the school. When Veronica drifts into his orbit, he dazzles her with his indifference to all she holds dear and then shows her how easy it is to act out her most hateful thoughts, and laugh afterwards.

She imagines their campaign to purge Westerburg of conformism and consumerism will just be a series of harmless japes. J. D. has grander crimes in mind. Their first victim is the Heather-in-chief. She dies after ingesting kitchen cleaner – slipped in her drink by Veronica, who didn't realize her most secret wish would thereby come true. In too deep to back out now, Veronica agrees to forge a suicide note from the deceased: 'People think just because you're beautiful and popular, life is easy and fun. No one understood that I had feelings too.' The use of the word 'myriad' elsewhere in the note wins the approval of Heather's teachers, who were never aware she had – choke, sob – such a good vocabulary. The students are shocked to learn that the apparently shallow Heather actually harboured deep, depressing thoughts, and they mourn their former tormentor almost as a saint.

Westerburg's administrators, depicted throughout as witless relativists, foolishly encourage the media circus that ensues. The surviving Heathers – the new Heather supremo is an even worse witch than her predecessor – and other students seize the chance to grandstand for the TV cameras and chastise the usual suspects, uncaring parents. When parents are depicted in *Heathers*, they figure only as props in their own brie-and-BMW lifestyles. Veronica's parents are fixated on pâté. J. D. and his father have an arresting double act; the father calls J. D. 'Dad', and J. D. responds with 'Son'. In an understated touch typical of the film's indefatigable detailing, J. D.'s father is always seen playing with expensive adult toys, while J. D. goes about the adult business of executing his fellow students.

Once Heather is underground, J. D. and Veronica murder the school's two top football players. Again, Veronica only wanted a little light revenge against the boys for spreading rumours about her – she didn't know the gun J. D. gave her was loaded. The conspirators leave mineral water at the crime scene to back up the note Veronica composes, 'signed' by these two brutes, indicating they shared a love that dared not speak its name. Some at school are astonished, others nod sagely when it is revealed that such hyper-butch athletes were secretly gay. In Ohio, only deviants use mineral water – don't ask what they do with it!

Veronica decides that although she's hip-deep in blood, it's time to call a halt. J. D., however, is inspired to dream of grander mayhem, and only Veronica can stop his plot to blow up the school during a prep rally. This conventional reconversion-to-virtue finish is a typical 1980s loss of nerve. Like *Dr Strangelove*, the film should have climaxed with the end of the world, or at least the end of the world of Westerburg High School.

Funking the finale is a small blemish, however, beside the film's accomplishment in rising above the 'novelty' status to which its low budget might have relegated it. *Heathers* originated nearly a decade ago in Daniel Waters'

weekly column in his high school newspaper in Indiana. His script is a tight satire studded with stylized dialogue. Every scene has several gems, like Veronica's kiss-off to her clueless parents: 'Great pâté, but I have to motor if I want to be ready for that funeral.'

In the star-making rôle of J. D., Slater turns himself into a young Jack Nicholson. His smirking killer grin lends plausibility to the most perverse impulses. The drawling diction makes Veronica and the audience hang on every word. Knowing the comparison is doing him no harm, Slater has done his Jack act twice now, this time more aptly than in *Gleaming the Cube*. As Veronica, Ryder is intelligent enough to play the dumb side of her character convincingly. She somehow keeps the audience's sympathy even when Veronica is going along with the dirtiest of the Heathers' tricks.

Teen suicide has recently been a vogue issue in the US media, following numerous examples of multiple suicides among suburban high schoolers in places like Plano, Texas, and Sudbury, Massachusetts. 'Tabloid TV' has hopped on the topic, giving air time to ghouls, cranks and hand-wringers, thereby making sure that suicide receives maximum exposure as a romantic pre-voting-age alternative. Such glamorization is *Heathers*' target in the scene where a teacher counsels a student: 'Whether to kill yourself is one of the most important decisions a teenager has to make.'

Flippant lines like that drew howls from those critics ('scabrous morality', 'unprincipled viciousness') who felt teen audiences might misunderstand the film's anti-suicide message. A film that finds comedy in such a charged subject is dangerous, according to the guardians-of-society school of criticism. But how much more livid might such critics have been if the filmmakers had followed the original script, in which Veronica, overwhelmed by grief, killed herself. Instead, the film teases the audience, showing Veronica apparently committing suicide, but only as a ruse to keep J. D. guessing.

Despite the whitewash finale, in which J. D. gets his just desserts and Veronica befriends the fat girl she previously tricked, the film remains a clever attack on American society. In portraying the school's 'popular' crowd as storm troopers, the well adjusted wannabee as corruptible and the outsider as a homicidal maniac – and everyone's parents as pathetically out of touch – *Heathers* gets closer to reality than most realistic films.

BART MILLS

HIGH SPIRITS

T he ghost comedy has been raising our spirits in the cinema for as long as we've had trick photography; plus heroines with ear-perforating screams and directors who can bounce new life into old frissons. Any self-respecting spook collector, prowling screen history with his ectoplasm detector, knows the classics: *The Ghost Breakers, The Ghost Goes West, Heaven Can Wait*, as well as more recent spine-ticklers such as *Ghostbusters* and its sequel. Screams abound, giggles proliferate, sequels multiply. And now, 47 years after *Here Comes Mr Jordan*, here comes Mr Jordan.

Namely Neil of that clan; writer-director of *High Spirits* and now long-established as the white hope of Anglo-Irish cinema. Did ever a spook spoof come with higher credentials? Jordan behind the camera, Peter O'Toole in front, Alex Thomson lensing, Derek Meddings special FX-ing. And did any spook spoof then treat audiences to a more bone-crushing disappointment?

It is hard to pinpoint the cause of the damage. All we can make out amid the wreckage is some embattled script-work, umpteen sheets of knockabout Irish fiddle music and the smouldering comic reputations of some young American actors: Steve Guttenberg, Peter Gallagher, Beverly D'Angelo.

Movies, like aeroplanes, should carry their own 'black boxes'. We would then discover how a perky little plot about an Irish castle-owner (O'Toole) opening his pile to the public – complete with servants dressed as ghosts and Heath Robinson horror stunts – grew into an umpteen-million-dollar movie and then blew up in mid-air.

Initial inspection suggests imbalance of elements. A fatal mismatch exists between the film's high-performance special effects – equalling, even outclassing, *Ghostbusters* – and its low-performance comic knockabout. And on the acting side there's a no less grave imbalance; between the best thespian on view, Mr O'Toole, and just about everyone else.

Whenever we're with O'Toole and his silver-tongued drawl, the dialogue has wit and relish. His opening salvoes – spoken telephonically to the American millionaire trying to buy up the castle and whisk it to Malibu – bespeak a majestic Irish drunk born with a silver corkscrew in his mouth. Later, O'Toole gives a dandyish top-spin even to his insults: 'He's an unlovely combination of a son of a bitch and a rat's knackers' he baroquely muses of the American Croesus. And for connoisseurs of O'Toole enunciation, there's no choicer moment than his aside to a servant during a minor outbreak of poltergeist activity. 'Eamon,' he purrs, 'why are chunks of masonry (*sic*) floating about?'

Alas, there are 20-odd other speaking rôles in *High Spirits*, and no rival performer has O'Toole's flair for making bad lines seem good and good lines seem scintillating. His fellow Celts, entrusted with turning the castle into a DIY spook show, are the unfunniest bunch of stage-Irishers yet pushed before a camera. Many come with a limp or speech defect. Most deliver their dialogue as if shouting into a high wind. And their tendency to clatter frenetically about the screen on any cry of 'Action!' – from Plunkett-O'Toole or Jordan – suggest the film's movements were in the charge of that experienced choreographer, St Vitus.

Jordan seems to believe that stillness is the enemy of comedy. (He should study the slow-burn bravura of Laurel and Hardy: stillness can be the *secret* of great comedy.) So every comic crescendo in *High Spirits* is staged at breakneck speed, accompanied by gale-force rhubarbing and Irish fiddle music.

This is doubly counter-productive. Firstly, whenever the film slows down, it seems to have stopped completely: such is the law of contrasts. Secondly, none of the players – O'Toole apart, who takes his own time and makes his own laws – has leisure to craft a character in these hurricane conditions. D'Angelo and Guttenberg, our young American marrieds visiting Ireland for their second honeymoon, are hurled so fast into the fracas that they become marionettes, twitched whichever way the plot wants to twitch them. The race-against-time style makes their marital bickering ('Maybe if you made love more often, you wouldn't have all these headaches' etc.) seem cranky and ill-humoured rather than comical or endearing. As the movie proceeds, they, we and Mr Jordan fast succumb to the cinema's answer to executive stress; when the sense of humour is the first thing to go under the influence of a killing pace.

High Spirits puts us through so much forced-pace slapstick in its first half that even the later *Heaven Can Wait*-style whimsies – the eruption of a real ghost couple (Daryl Hannah and Liam Neeson) caught up in a crisis of the heart – can't restore our smiles. We're still in shock at the preceding overkill. We twitch in nervous apprehension that another four-poster-bed will rise, spin and fall 'hilariously' through several floors. That another ghost-frightened guest will plummet from his room – chortle chortle – into the courtyard fish pond. That the castle's 200-pound lady banshee will fly screaming through the air again and crash-land – ho ho – on the roof of an arriving charabanc. Or that another outbreak of Celtic fiddling will make us reach shakingly for our ear-plugs.

In minor mitigation, I did like the toy theatre sea-storm that turned into the real thing, lashing the audience with six-foot waves and giant-squid tentacles. I liked O'Toole. And I liked most of the special effects. But on the rest of the evidence, it's hard to like Neil Jordan when he's trying to be funny rather than when he's lyrical, macabre or mythopoeic (*Angel, The Company of Wolves*). Two hours of *High Spirits* and one nods in bleak accord with the Castle Plunkett guest who says 'This is the most pitiful supernatural shambles I've ever encountered.'

HARLAN KENNEDY

I'M GONNA GIT YOU SUCKA

Ultracool Jack Spade and his hip sidekicks
(Brown, Hayes and Casey) take on the Mr Big
of city crime in this sporadic, but often very
funny shafting of the blacksploitation movie of
the early 1970s. Aiming at the same audience
as *Hollywood Shuffle*, the film lacks Robert
Townsend's sure touch and runs out of steam
too soon, but it has more than enough great
moments to make up for it. **TW**
Director/script *Keenen Ivory Wayans* **producers**
Peter McCarthy, Carl Craig **execs** *Raymond Katz,
Eric L. Gold* **camera** *Tom Richmond* **editor**
Michael R. Miller **design** *Melba Farquhar,
Catherine Hardwicke* **music** *David Michael Frank*
cast *Wayans, Bernie Casey, Antonio Fargas, Steve
James, Isaac Hayes, Jim Brown, Ja'net DuBois*
Running time: 87 mins
US release: UA, Dec 14, 1988

INDIANA JONES AND THE LAST CRUSADE

Steven Spielberg returns to the gentler
adventure style of the first Indy production but,
unfortunately, we've seen much of it before.
Harrison Ford is after another religious relic,
the Holy Grail, and the villains are familiar
too: 'Nazis! I hate those guys!' as Ford says.
Lines draw themselves on maps in Saturday-
morning serial style as Ford zooms to Venice,
Turkey and even Berlin, where he obtains
Adolf Hitler's autograph in the film's funniest
section. Along for the ride is Sean Connery as
Ford's father, and the two actors exchange
much tiresome badinage along the lines of
'Junior –' 'Don't call me that, Dad.' **BM**
Director *Steven Spielberg* **producer** *Robert Watts*
execs *George Lucas, Frank Marshall* **script** *Jeffrey
Boam, from story by Lucas, Menno Meyjes, based
on characters created by Lucas and Philip Kaufman*
camera *Douglas Slocombe* **editor** *Michael Kahn*
design *Elliot Scott* **sfx** *ILM* **music** *John Williams*
cast *Harrison Ford, Sean Connery, Denholm
Elliott, Alison Doody, John Rhys-Davies, Julian
Glover, River Phoenix, Michael Byrne, Kevork
Malikyan, Robert Eddison, Richard Young, Alexei
Sayle, Alex Hyde-White, Paul Maxwell*
Running time: 127 mins
US release: Paramount, May 24, 1989
UK release: UIP, Jun 28, 1989

IRON EAGLE II

Glasnost meets *Top Gun* in this unlikely tale of
US and Russian pilots teaming up to destroy
an unnamed Arab power's nuclear bomb
factory (but it's definitely not Libya, even if its
dictator does wear a tea towel on his head and

act like all Three Stooges rolled into one).
Matters are complicated by back-room boys in
Washington trying to sabotage the mission, but
not in time to save us from a protracted finale
that seems to comprise stock footage from
USAAF recruitment ads. Last time the
Russians were the villains; this time it's the
producers. **TW**
Director *Sidney J. Furie* **producers** *Jacob Kotzky,
Sharon Harel, John Kemeny* **exec** *Andras Hamori*
script *Kevin Elders, Furie* **camera** *Alan Dostie*
editor *Rit Wallis* **design** *Ariel Roshko* **music**
Amin Bhatia **cast** *Louis Gossett Jr., Mark
Humphrey, Stuart Margolin, Alan Scarfe, Sharon
H. Brandon, Maury Chaykin, Colm Feore, Clark
Johnson, Jason Blicker, Jesse Collins, Mark Ivanir,
Uri Gavriel*
Running time: 100 mins
US release: Tri-Star, Nov 11, 1988
UK release: Guild, Mar 24, 1989

IT COULDN'T HAPPEN HERE

If anyone really needed a rock video reworking
of Derek Jarman's *The Last of England*, here it
is. The Pet Shop Boys indulge themselves by
using their songs as background to an
interminable, excruciating non-narrative ramble
through rainy, modern England, complete with
burning telephone boxes, and 1950s-styled
seaside postcards. In a moment of jaw-dropping
hubris, Neil Tennant juxtaposes his own lyrics
with extracts from Milton, and other highlights
include Barbara Windsor opening her mouth
with Dusty Springfield's voice emerging and
Joss Ackland impersonating either a blind
churchman or a motorway psycho-killer.
Probably the most difficult-to-sit-through film of
the year. **KN**
Director/producer *Jack Bond* **exec** *Martin Haxby*
script *Bond, James Dillon* **camera** *Simon Archer*
editor *Rodney Holland* **design** *Dillon* **music** *Neil
Tennant, Chris Lowe* **cast** *Tennant, Lowe, Joss
Ackland, Dominique Barnes, Neil Dickson,
Carmen Du Sautoy, Gareth Hunt, Barbara
Windsor, Nicholas Haley, Jonathan Haley*
Running time: 86 mins
US release: Liberty, Jun 17, 1988
UK release: Entertainment, Jul 8, 1988

JACKNIFE

Will you watch another drama about Vietnam vets who can't cope, even one as well acted as this? Robert De Niro plays a trout fisher, not a deer hunter this time, who takes himself to the brink of suicide in order to bring back a buddy, Ed Harris, whose combat memories are killing him. Kathy Baker is the sub-Streepian woman they left behind. The characters are such stock figures by now and the stagebound situation so trite that only performers as magnetic as De Niro and Harris could give it any life at all. David Jones, good as he is with actors, should pick his American scripts more carefully. **BM**
Director David Jones **producers** Robert Schaffel, Carol Baum **script** Stephen Metcalfe, from play Strange Snow **camera** Brian West **editor** John Bloom **design** Edward Pisoni **music** Bruce Broughton **cast** Robert De Niro, Ed Harris, Kathy Baker, Charles Dutton, Loudon Wainwright III
Running time: 102 mins
US release: Cineplex, Mar 10, 1989

JANUARY MAN

From the writer who brought you *Moonstruck* comes this self-destructing black comedy. A brutal serial killer is loose, in a city with enough oddballs on its hands already. Can puckish, unorthodox ex-detective Kevin Kline be lured back to solve the case? Will his politico brother Harvey Keitel help? And is there room in the plot for Susan Sarandon, Mary Elizabeth Mastrantonio and Rod Steiger blowing his top as Mayor? So many questions. In a movie with no discernible point or shape, there's room for everything: including so many style-swings (from *film noir* to slapstick) that we and director Pat O'Connor can only hang onto our seats and hope we make it to the end. **HK**
Director Pat O'Connor **producers** Norman Jewison, Ezra Swerdlow **script** John Patrick Shanley **camera** Jerzy Zielinski **editor** Lou Lombardo **design** Philip Rosenberg **music** Marvin Hamlisch **cast** Kevin Kline, Susan Sarandon, Mary Elizabeth Mastrantonio, Harvey Keitel, Danny Aiello, Rod Steiger, Alan Rickman, Faye Grant
Running time: 97 mins
US release: MGM, Jan 13, 1989
UK release: UIP, May 5, 1989

JIMMY REARDON (A Night in the Life of Jimmy Reardon in US)

Yet another coming of age story, this time set in early 1960s Chicago. But though William Richert is here revisiting the material of his autobiographical novel of some 20 years ago from the opposite side of the generation gap, this changed angle of vision doesn't prevent the resulting film from assuming an homogenized air. Most of the tried and tested elements are on view - the assorted peer group, the ambiguously sympathetic parents, the know-all kid sister - and although the semi-farcical plot generates some vitality, with the period trappings thankfully played down, a sense of over-familiarity prevails. **TP**
Director William Richert **producer** Russell Schwartz **execs** Mel Klein, Noel Marshall **script** Richert, based on his novel Aren't You Even Gonna Kiss Me Goodbye? **camera** John J. Connor **editor** Suzanne Fenn **design** Norman Newberry **music** Bill Conti **cast** River Phoenix, Ann Magnuson, Meredith Salenger, Ione Skye, Louanne, Matthew L. Perry, Paul Koslo, Jane Hallaren, Jason Court
Running time: 93 mins
US release: Fox, Feb 26, 1988
UK release: Enterprise, Sep 23, 1988

JOYRIDERS

Patricia Kerrigan, an abused young mother, leaves her children and heads for the countryside with a small-time thief (Connolly) in tow. With a particularly Irish melancholy, the film brings on a succession of one-scene characters who expose the hollowness of their dreams. One dance-hall sequence trots out, in rapid succession, Billie Whitelaw as a drunk obsessed with her Grand Ole Opry Days ('I got more dick than Elvis Presley had on him'); John Kavanagh as a lecherous manager who wants Kerrigan to hike up her skirts and parade in front of him; the customer who half-heartedly proposes marriage after one dance, and a group of depressed-looking dancers. An odd and uncomfortable attempt to match realism and whimsy, *Joyriders* is carefully made but ultimately uninteresting. And the cast keep being surprised by an unfortunate Irish script full of lines like 'It's the first toime in me loife Oi've got somet'in' to lose.' **KN**
Director Aisling Walsh **producer** Emma Hayter **script** Andy Smith **camera** Gabriel Beristain **editor** Thomas Schwalm **design** Leigh Malone **music** Hal Lindes, Tony Britten **cast** Patricia Kerrigan, Andrew Connolly, Billie Whitelaw, David Kelly, John Kavanagh, Deirdre Donoghue
Running time: 96 mins
UK release: Cannon, Apr 28, 1989

JUST ASK FOR DIAMOND

This trap for unwitting parents grossed barely
£10,000 at the box office before disappearing
without a trace, and taking with it all
possibility of anyone raising the money to make
a decent children's film in the UK. Cocky
teenage private eye Tim Diamond (the
charmless Dursley McLinden) and his smarter
brother Nick (the not-much-better Colin Dale)
are hired to look after a box of Maltesers. They
come up against dwarfs, fat men, nightclub
singers, sadistic metropolitan policemen and
other assorted Dashiell Hammett cast-offs,
played by a large array of blink-and-you'll-miss-
them TV favourites in a tiresomely drawn out
spoof that would shame most pre-school
television shows. **TW**
Director Stephen Bayly **producer** Linda James
script Anthony Horowitz, *from his novel* The
Falcon's Malteser *camera* Billy Williams **editor**
Scott Thomas **design** Peter Murton **music** Trevor
Jones **cast** Susannah York, Colin Dale, Dursley
McLinden, Peter Eyre, Nickolas Grace, Patricia
Hodge, Saeed Jaffrey, Roy Kinnear, Jim McManus,
Michael Medwin, Jimmy Nail, Bill Paterson
Running time: 94 mins
UK release: Fox, Dec 16, 1988

K-9

Yet another twist on the mismatched-buddy genre teams James Belushi with a dog to break a drug case, via numerous brawls and shootouts.
Director Rod Daniel *producers* Lawrence Gordon, Charles Gordon *exec* Donna Smith *script* Steven Siegel, Scott Myers *camera* Dean Semler *editor* Lois Freeman-Fox *design* George Costello *music* Miles Goodman *cast* James Belushi, Mel Harris, Kevin Tighe, Ed O'Neill, Jerry Lee, James Handy, Cotter Smith
Running time: 102 mins
US release: Universal, Apr 28, 1989

KAMIKAZE

Michel Galabru, an unemployed mad scientist obsessed with television, invents a Flash Gordon-style ray cannon which, when pointed at the screen, can kill anyone appearing live. When the smarmy link-men and women on afternoon TV start getting blasted in the middle of their announcements, rumpled flic Richard Bohringer gets on the case with the aid of a roomful of boffins, and sets out to track down the unknown killer. A throwback to the 1970s cycle of SF-tinged paranoia movies, which included *The Parallax View* and *Winter Kills*, as well as the French *Ecoute voir*, *Kamikaze* mixes bizarre assassination hardware and computerized complications with the traditional, down-at-heel strengths of the *policier* as it follows its two central characters through their own labyrinths. It's a fun movie, tinged with seriousness. Galabru is outstanding as the mad murderer, starting out as a sympathetic loser who wants to get back at the smug mannequins who simper all over his TV set, but turning into a major psychopath who whites his face, dresses up as a Mishima-style samurai and demonstrates extreme callousness. **KN**
Director Didier Grousset *producer* Luc Besson *exec* Louis Duchesne *script* Besson, Grousset *camera* Jean-François Robin *editor* Olivier Mauffroy *design* Dan Weil *music* Eric Serra *cast* Richard Bohringer, Michel Galabru, Dominique Lavanant, Riton Leibman, Kim Massee, Harry Cleven, Romane Bohringer, Etienne Chicot, Philippe Girard, Geoffroy Carey, Jean-Paul Muel, Philippe Landoulsi, Vincent Simenti, Beate Kopp
Running time: 89 mins
US release: Blue Dolphin, Apr 14, 1989

KANSAS

Contrivances abound in this twisted but dull combination road-buddy-caper-cornball-farming-romance State-of-the-Nation movie, in which Andrew McCarthy, making his way across the US to be at his best friend's wedding, meets up in a freight car with Matt Dillon, a farm boy gone bad who has been leaving a trail of petty crime through the Wheat Belt. Arriving in Dillon's home town during a parade, McCarthy finds himself co-opted for a bank robbery and, in the confusion, stashes the loot under a nearby bridge while rescuing the drowning daughter of the governor. Casting the callow McCarthy with the posey Dillon as mismatched crooks has the disadvantage that they have no screen chemistry whatsoever. Dillon is all method tics and outrageous outfits; McCarthy just mumbles amiably through another shallow, faintly repulsive pseudo-nice guy rôle. There's one good moment when Doyle's bimbo girlfriend asks him to autograph his 'Wanted' poster for her parents, but otherwise this is about as interesting as a stubble-burning tour of the dustbowl. **KN**
Director David Stevens *producer* George Litto *execs* Moshe Diamant, Chris Chesser *script* Spencer Eastman *camera* David Eggby *editor* Robert Barrère *design* Matthew Jacobs *music* Pino Donaggio *cast* Matt Dillon, Andrew McCarthy, Leslie Hope, Alan Toy, Andy Romano, Brent Jennings, Brynn Thayer, Kyra Sedgwick, Harry Northup
Running time: 113 mins
US release: Trans World, Sep 23, 1988
UK release: Entertainment, Nov 18, 1988

THE KARATE KID PART III

Venerable martial-arts whizz-kid (Macchio) gesticulates his way through another rites-of-passage teen pic, this time betraying and renouncing the stoic catechisms of his kung-fu mentor Miyagi (Morita) in favour of the brutal tactics employed by a rival - who's made a pile from dumping chemical wastes in Third World countries (yah booh hiss!) and is determined to revenge the team vanquished in Part II. Seeing as most of the Oriental profundities were explored in the first two movies, it's only Macchio's stupidity that keeps the plot stumbling through until the hero's final, inevitable victory. **MN**
Director John G. Avildsen *producer* Jerry Weintraub *exec* Sheldon Schrager *script* Robert Mark Kamen *camera* Stephen Yaconelli *editor* John Carter, Avildsen *design* William F. Matthews *music* Bill Conti *cast* Ralph Macchio, Noriyuki (Pat) Morita, Robyn Lively, Thomas Ian Griffith, Martin L. Kove, Sean Kanan

Running time: 111 mins
US release: Columbia, Jun 23, 1989
UK release: Col/Tri-Star, Jul 21, 1989

KING OF THE CHILDREN (Haizi Wang) 👍

Chen Kaige's third feature, consolidating his position as the premier *auteur* of China's fifth generation, concerns a footnote in the Cultural Revolution, but speaks volumes about human dignity and personal liberties. In 1976, an inexperienced young man is exiled to teach in a distant rural area, where the school is miserably ill-equipped and the old methods prove useless. Gradually he wins over his pupils to value learning as a means of self-expression. A film that could so easily have been sentimental melodrama is imbued with a fresh and poetic approach to the composition of sounds and images. **DT**
Director Chen Kaige *producer* Xi'an Film Studio *exec* Wu Tianming *script* Kaige, Wan Zhi, *from short story by* Ah Cheng *camera* Gu Changwei *editor* Liu Miaomiao *design* Chen Shaohua *music* Qu Xiaosong *cast* Xie Yuan, Yang Xuewen, Chen Shaohua, Zhang Caimei, Xu Guoqing, Le Gang, Tan Tuo, Gu Changwei, Wu Xia, Liu Haichen
Running time: 106 mins
US release: ICA, Aug 19, 1988

KINJITE (Forbidden Subjects)

Charles Bronson, having presumably run out of NY street-scum to sweep off the streets, is here transformed into a contemplative, angst-ridden LA cop assigned to stalk a notorious Latino pimp who has purloined the daughter of an eminent Japanese magnate. It so happens the Tokyo businessman also molested Bronson's daughter on the subway. *Kinjite*'s title derives from a traditional Japanese taboo towards sexual molestations, rape and other narrative stalwarts of Charles Bronson movies. Sufficiently exploitative to fulfil the requirements of a fetishistic B-movie, *Kinjite* is a low-brow deviant of the Paul Schrader school of catharsis through homicidal vigilantism (*Taxi Driver*). **MN**
Director L. Lee-Thompson *producer* Pancho Kohner *execs* Menathem Golan, Yoram Globus *script* Harold Nebenzal *camera* Gideon Porath *editors* Peter Lee-Thompson, Mary E. Jochem *design* W. Brook Wheeler *music* Greg DeBelles *cast* Charles Bronson, Perry Lopez, Juan Fernandez, Peggy Lipton, James Pax, Sy Richardson
Running time: 97 mins
US release: Cannon, Feb 3, 1989

THE KISS

In the age of AIDS, something fatally slimy could easily inhabit anyone's body - even your beautiful aunt's. In this horror fantasy, Joanna Pacula carries a snake-like monster within her that craves transmission to a family member. But it can only pass into another's body via a big wet kiss. Niece Meredith Salenger is the target of this sloppy assault, but first the infected Pacula must dispose of her sister and her niece's boyfriend. The monster is wisely kept behind closed lips most of the movie; for when it emerges at the end, it provokes laughter, not terror. **BM**
Director Pen Densham *producers* Densham, John Watson *exec* Richard B. Lewis *script* Stephen Volk, Tom Ropelewski *camera* François Protat *editor* Stan Cole *design* Roy Forge Smith *music* J. Peter Robinson *cast* Nicholas Kilbertus, Joanna Pacula, Meredith Salenger, Mimi Kuzyk
Running time: 101 mins
US release: Tri-Star, Oct 14, 1988
UK release: Col/Tri-Star, Jul 21, 1989

THE KITCHEN TOTO

Kenya was no place for a small native boy in 1950, with the Mau-Mau apt to murder your father, and your mother so needy she must send you off to labour in the kitchen of the police chief. Chief Bob Peck barely notices his kitchen toto as he struggles to stem the bloody rebellion. The boy's enchanting smile is seen less and less often as he gets sucked into the rebels' murderous designs, and the inevitable confrontation claims its innocent victims. Writer/director Harry Hook spends too much time at the edges of the real drama and fails to provide the leads with the character-defining scenes that might have made the story memorable. **BM**
Director/script Harry Hook *producer* Ann Skinner *execs* Menahem Golan, Yoram Globus *camera* Roger Deakins *editor* Tom Priestley *design* Jamie Leonard *music* John Keane *cast* Edwin Mahinda, Bob Peck, Phyllis Logan, Nicholas Charles, Ronald Pirie, Robert Urquhart, Kirsten Hughes, Edward Judd, Nathan Dambuza Mdledle, Ann Wanjugu, Job Seda
Running time: 95 mins
US release: Cannon, Jul 8, 1988
UK release: Cannon, Apr 29, 1988

KREUTZER SONATA (Kreitzerova Sonata)

One of Tolstoy's more concise short stories becomes a very long, very worthy and frequently very dull movie as a man meets a

stranger on a train and, with the aid of flashbacks, confesses to murdering his wife. Despite a good lead performance from Oleg Yankovsky as the cuckolded husband, the film never really holds the attention - aside from one truly surreal moment where a bedroom scene is accompanied by the throbbing pistons of an intrusive steam engine - or finds its own cinematic equivalent for Tolstoy's prose. **TW**
Directors *Mikhail Schweitzer, Sofia Milkina* **exec** *Mosfilm* **script** *Schweitzer, from the story by Leo Tolstoy* **camera** *Mikhail Agranovich* **editor** *Lyudmila Feiginova* **design** *Igor Lemeshev, Vladimir Fabrikov* **music** *Sofia Gubaidulina* **cast** *Oleg Yankovsky, Aleksandr Trofimov, Irina Seleznyova, Dmitri Pokrovsky*
Running time: 135 mins
UK release: Cannon, Feb 3, 1989

K

LADY IN WHITE

On Halloween night 1962, Haas is locked into a school cloakroom by the neighbourhood bullies, and sees a ghostly little girl, the first victim of a child-killer who has been terrorizing the community. *Lady in White* is a largely successful attempt to make a horror film for kids and there are several magical sequences that provoke shivers and enchantment. The film tries for too much in its mix of *Stand By Me*, *To Kill a Mockingbird*, *Moonstruck* and *The Uninvited* but, in the era of Jason and Freddy, it's a pleasure to find a chiller with any ambitions, let alone too many ambitions. The identity of the killer is as transparent as any of the film's superimposed spectres, and there's a touch too much Italian-American local colour in the film's account of Frankie's babbling, pasta-eating family. But the schoolroom stuff, the Bradbury-ish small town settings, the understated period recreation, and the gently melancholic ghost story work very well. **KN**
Director/script/music Frank LaLoggia ***producers*** Andrew G. La Marca, LaLoggia ***execs*** Charles M. LaLoggia, Cliff Payne ***camera*** Russell Carpenter ***editor*** Steve Mann ***design*** Richard K. Hummel ***cast*** Lukas Haas, Ken Cariou, Alex Rocco, Katherine Helmond, Jason Presson, Renata Vanni, Angelo Bertolini, Jared Rushton
Running time: 112 mins
US release: New Century/Vista, Apr 22, 1988
UK release: Virgin, Jun 16, 1989

THE LAIR OF THE WHITE WORM

Ken Russell's perversely brilliant romp through post-Hammer horror territory compensates for the inadequacies of its budget with a pantomime of evil ancient cults, nuns impaled on spikes and assorted blasphemous buffoonery. At the apex stands Amanda Donohoe as the lustfully vampiric Lady Sylvia Marsh who invests the comic revitalization of Bram Stoker's innocuous story with a camp vivacity. The film proves once again that Ken Russell is the king of gleefully repellent iconograpy, and also a man of profoundly Catholic taste. **MN**
Director/producer Ken Russell ***execs*** William J. Quigley, Dan Ireland ***script*** Russell, *from novel by* Bram Stoker ***camera*** Dick Bush ***editor*** Peter Davies ***design*** Anne Tilby ***music*** Stanislas Syrewicz ***cast*** Amanda Donohoe, Hugh Grant, Catherine Oxenberg, Peter Capaldi, Sammi Davis, Stratford Johns, Paul Brooke, Imogen Claire, Chris Pitt
Running time: 93 mins

US release: Vestron, Oct 21, 1988
UK release: Vestron, Mar 10, 1989

THE LAND BEFORE TIME

Before God created the wrist-watch, dinosaurs roamed the earth. And lo! They had no sense of time nor respect for normal human attention spans. And it happened that one dinosaur family, as drawn by animator Don Bluth, was cute and gambolling and pinkish-grey and went in search of the Great Valley (large and fertile), accompanied by much lolloping music. Onward, onward they trekked, through earthquake, bereavement (momma dinosaur snuffs it) and the antics of a funny pterodactyl. Finally they reach their goal: a vast, lush, empty space, untrod by other beings. (In this case it might be the movie auditorium.) A turgid brush-and-paint epic unleavened by wit or visual panache and sentenced to as certain an extinction as its subjects. **HK**
Director/design Don Bluth ***producers*** Bluth, Gary Goldman, John Pomeroy ***execs*** Steven Spielberg, George Lucas ***script*** Stu Krieger, *from story by* Judy Freudberg, Tony Geiss ***editors*** Dan Molina, John K. Carr ***animators*** John Pomeroy, Linda Miller, Ralph Zondag, Kuenster, Lorna Pomeroy, Dick Zondag ***music*** James Horner ***voices*** Pat Hingle, Gabriel Damon, Helen Shaver, Candice Houston, Judith Barsi, Will Ryan, Burke Barnes
Running time: 66 mins
US release: Universal, Nov 18, 1988

LANDSCAPE IN THE MIST

Another road movie from Theo Angelopoulos, with two children, brother and sister, setting off for Germany in pursuit of their (probably non-existent) father. The early sequences promise involvement, but despite some atmospheric locales, momentum all too rapidly peters out. The tone is more fantasticated than hitherto, but unfortunately this tendency goes hand in hand with a lack of narrative focus, a combination which achieves only masochistic glumness. **TP**
Director/producer Theo Angelopoulos ***script*** Angelopoulos, Tonino Guerra ***camera*** Giorgos Arvanitis ***editor*** Yannis Tsitsopoulos ***design*** Mikes Karapiperis ***music*** Eleni Karaindrou ***cast*** Michalis Zeke, Iania Palaiologuo, Stratos Tzortzoglou
Running time: 127 mins
US release: Artificial Eye, Jun 9, 1989

LAST RITES

Tom Berenger is a hip priest from an Italian American background who faces the sort of dilemmas that draw filmmakers to such subjects: loyalty to vocation against allegiance to (Mafia) family; maintaining vows of abstinence or submitting to physical desire. He finally crosses the border to escape the hoods on his trail, with lover in tow.
Director/script Donald P. Bellisario **producers** Bellisario, Patrick McCormick **camera** David Watkin **editor** Pembroke J. Herring **design** Peter Larkin **music** Bruce Broughton **cast** Tom Berenger, Daphne Zuniga, Chick Vennera, Anne Twomey, Dane Clark, Paul Dooley, Vassili Lambrinos
Running time: 103 mins
US release: MGM, Nov 18, 1988

DISAPPOINTMENT

THE LAST TEMPTATION OF CHRIST

Director Martin Scorsese **producer** Barbara De Fina **exec** Harry Ufland **script** Paul Schrader, from novel by Nikos Kazantzakis **camera** Michael Ballhaus **editor** Thelma Schoonmaker **design** John Beard **music** Peter Gabriel **cast** Willem Dafoe, Harvey Keitel, Barbara Hershey, Harry Dean Stanton, David Bowie, Verna Bloom, André Gregory, Juliette Caton, Roberts Blossom, Irvin Kershner, Gary Basrada, Victor Argo
Running time: 164 mins
US release: Universal, Aug 12, 1988
UK release: UIP, Sep 10, 1988

LAW OF DESIRE (La Ley del Deseo)

The first of Pedro Almodóvar's films to reach the UK is his seventh, made in 1986. The plotline may remind one of Fatal Attraction, but this version is flashy, intriguing, emotional and fun where the American blockbuster was formulaic, stilted and tedious. Kicking off with a classic Almodóvar grab-them opening − a boy simulates homosexual sex to encourage the occupants of a dubbing booth − Law of Desire shows what happens when the roundabout of change in relationships starts to go too fast, someone wants to stop the musical-chairs or people try too hard to defy fate and 'make' themselves. A film director (Poncela) goes home from a party with one boy, but doesn't want him to stay; says goodbye to his true love who's off to a small coastal village, and then finds himself sleeping with another. It's this third entry in the chain who makes a nuisance of himself and ends up committing murder.

This is a world where boys turn into girls, religious beliefs are acquired like packets in a supermarket and parents can be taken up or rejected by their young offspring. The ending is glorious melodrama, as policemen and spectators clamber up the scaffolding to where the pestilential lover (Banderas) lies dead and flames lick around the Madonna to which Poncela's brother-turned-sister (Maura) makes obeisance. **JP**
Director/script Pedro Almodóvar **producer** Ester Garcia **exec** Miguel A. Pérez Campos **camera** Angel Luis Fernández **editor** José Salcedo **design** Javier Fernández **cast** Eusebio Poncela, Carmen Maura, Antonio Banderas, Miguel Molina, Manuela Velasco, Bibi Andersen, Fernando Guillén
Running time: 101 mins
US release: Cinevista, Mar 29, 1987
UK release: Other Cinema, Nov 4, 1988

LEAN ON ME

John Avildsen's shamelessly manipulative film casts Morgan Freeman as the authoritarian principal of a nil-achieving inner city high school. With bullhorn and baseball bat he browbeats teachers and pupils alike, and succeeds in raising the school's pass rate on a 'basic skills' test (spell cat without a K). The question begged here is whether results could also be obtained with firmness but without throwing away the book at the kids. As Joe Clark, a real-life bully in Paterson, N.J., Freeman convincingly conveys monomania. Not so believable are the scenes in which he is the most compassionate educator since Sidney Poitier in To Sir With Love. **BM**
Director/exec John Avildsen **producer** Norman Twain **script** Michael Schiffer **camera** Victor Hammer **editors** John Carter, Avildsen **design** Doug Kraner **music** Bill Conti **cast** Morgan Freeman, Robert Guillaume, Beverly Todd, Lynne Thigpen, Jermaine Hopkins, Karen Malina White
Running time: 104 mins
US release: Warner, Mar 3, 1989

LA LECTRICE

Miou-Miou is relentlessly chirpy, even as she walks for the umpteenth time through the empty streets of Arles, in this clever-clever meditation on fiction and reality. Her recently-adopted profession, as a reader of books, leads her into the romantic fantasies of her clients. She shows her legs to the boy in a wheelchair, has an affair with a moustachioed businessman who goes off to Africa, takes a self-assured girl to the fairground despite her mother's

disapproval, and scatters carnations for the Russian princess celebrating Lenin's birthday. Finally she draws the line when summoned to the presence of a doctor, a judge and a policeman who want a recitation from de Sade. Michel Deville's admiration for Greenaway is recalled in formal compositions around beds and erotic closeups, but as with the British game-player, one is left with the question, What's the point? **JP**
Director Michel Deville *producer* Rosalinde Deville *script* Rosalinde Deville, Michel Deville, based on books by Raymond Jean *camera* Dominique le Rigoleur *editor* Raymonde Guyot *design* Thierry Leproust *music* Beethoven *cast* Miou-Miou, Régis Royer, Christian Ruché, Marianne Denicourt, Charlotte Farran, Patrick Chesnais, Brigitte Catillon, Clotilde de Bayser, Sylvie Laporte, Michel Raskine, Simon Eine, Christian Blanc, Maria Casarès, André Wilms, Jean-Luc Boutté, Bérangère Bonvoisin, Pierre Dux, Léo Campion
Running time: 98 mins
US release: Orion Classics, Apr 19, 1989
UK release: Curzon, Mar 31, 1989

LES PATTERSON SAVES THE WORLD

Barry Humphries may be one of the most talented live performers in Australia, but someone there should pass an Act of Parliament to keep him away from movies. AIDS, Arabs and toilet seats are the main targets in this hideously inept and genuinely tasteless comedy that uses ridicule to reinforce stereotypes rather than destroy them. The plot is a sub-standard demobbed James Bond affair, with Oz's nauseating cultural attaché sent to save the world from a social disease not a million miles from one currently killing thousands, with a little help from an amazingly unfunny Dame Edna Everage and a sad supporting rôle from the once-so-promising Pamela Stephenson. George Miller (the one responsible for *Snowy River*) doesn't so much direct as stand back and point the camera – the visual highlight is one of Sir Les's anal emissions catching light and torching an Arab delegate at the UN. A real bum-number. **TW**
Director George Miller *producer* Sue Milliken *exec* Diane Millstead *script* Barry Humphries, Millstead *camera* David Connell *editor* Tim Wellburn *design* Graham Walker *music* Tim Finn *cast* Barry Humphries, Pamela Stephenson, Andrew Clarke, Henri Szeps, Hugh Keays Byrne
Running time: 90 mins (originally 94)
UK release: Recorded Releasing, Oct 14, 1988

LEVIATHAN

It's just too soon to remake *Alien* again. George Cosmatos' adventure is perfectly serviceable but boringly predictable. Peter Weller is the hesitant commander of a group of undersea miners who come upon the wreckage of a Soviet ship and unwisely bring some genetically super-charged vodka on board. Daniel Stern is the first to succumb to the ichtheo-hominoid strain, which proceeds to absorb one after another of the crew members. Hector Elizondo plays the John Hurt scene, turning green as the thing bursts out of his chest. As in *Alien*, the ultimate villain is private enterprise, in the person of Meg Foster, who is righteously slugged by Weller when he gets topside. **BM**
Director George Pan Cosmatos *producers* Luigi De Laurentiis, Aurelio De Laurentiis *execs* Lawrence Gordon, Charles Gordon *script* David Peoples, Jeb Stuart *camera* Alex Thomson *editors* Robert Silvi, John F. Burnett *design* Ron Cobb *music* Jerry Goldsmith *cast* Peter Weller, Richard Crenna, Amanda Pays, Daniel Stern, Ernie Hudson, Michael Carmine, Lisa Eilbacher, Hector Elizondo, Meg Foster
Running time: 98 mins
US release: MGM, Mar 17, 1989

◁ DOG ▷

LICENCE TO KILL

Director John Glen *producers* Albert R. Broccoli, Michael G. Wilson *script* Wilson, Richard Maibaum *camera* Alec Mills *editor* John Grover *design* Peter Lamont *music* Michael Kamen *cast* Timothy Dalton, Carey Lowell, Robert Davi, Talisa Soto, Anthony Zerbe, Frank McRae, Everett McGill, Wayne Newton, Benicio Del Toro, Desmond Llewelyn, David Hedison
Running time: 133 mins
US release: UA, Jul 14, 1989
UK release: UIP, Jun 14, 1989

LICENSE TO DRIVE

This paranoid adolescent fantasy about failing the driving test initially promises a modestly charming light comedy with action. It's only a short while, however, before we realize the obsession with impressing women by the size of one's bonnet is not meant to be viewed critically. The pleasant moments are constantly vitiated by a persistent misogyny that appears deliberate. Some crappy rock music provides the basic ooze from which most of the whingeing and trivial concerns of this male-

orientated teen pic are inexorably brought to the surface. **PB**
Director Greg Beeman **producers** Jeffrey A. Mueller, Andrew Licht **exec** John Davis **script** Neil Tolkin **camera** Bruce Surtees **editor** Wendy Greene Bricmont **design** Lawrence G. Paull **music** Jay Ferguson **cast** Corey Haim, Corey Feldman, Carol Kane, Richard Masur, Heather Graham, Michael Manasseti, Harvey Miller, M. A. Nickles
Running time: 88 mins
US release: Fox, Jul 6, 1988

LIGHT OF DAY

Paul Schrader took a respite from his sexual and theological obsessions to make this unduly sombre family drama set in Cleveland, Ohio. A humourless character-study of a young factory worker (Fox) who moonlights as a guitarist in his sister's rock group, the film uses Fox's one-note bonhomie without revealing any additional gravity or depth. Despite a couple of interesting scenes with real-life musician Joan Jett, Fox's frustrated blue-collar character and the popular music themes don't make contact with any of Schrader's concerns. **MN**
Director/script Paul Schrader **producers** Rob Cohen, Keith Barish **exec** Doug Claybourne **camera** John Bailey **editors** Jacqueline Cambas, Jill Savitt **design** Jeannine Claudia Oppewall **music** Thomas Newman **cast** Michael J. Fox, Gena Rowlands, Joan Jett, Michael McKean, Thomas G. Waites, Cherry Jones, Michael Dolan
Running time: 107 mins
US release: Tri-Star, Feb 6, 1987
UK release: Rank, Jul 15, 1988

THE LIGHTHORSEMEN

Connoisseur of horse flesh Simon Wincer (*Phar Lap*) pays elaborate homage to the 800 cavalry of the Australian Light Horse in a superbly mounted re-creation of its famous charge on Turkish and German-held Beersheba in southern Palestine in 1917 – a turning point in the Allies' campaign in the Middle East. The human drama – about three 'mates' and a young volunteer (Phelps) who lacks the killer instinct and leaves their ranks for the field hospital and a nurse's embrace – is altogether less successful than in Peter Weir's sharper *Gallipoli*. There are some bathetic homoerotic scenes of naked riders romping with their horses in the sea and Anthony Andrews enjoys himself as a flamboyant British officer with a German name. Despite too many expository titles, the battle footage – a cacophony of clattering hooves and ringing harness against the backdrop of cannon – is truly thrilling. **GF**
Director Simon Wincer **producers** Ian Jones, Wincer **exec** Antony I. Ginnane **script** Jones **camera** Dean Semler **editor** Adrian Carr **design** Bernard Hides **music** Mario Millo **cast** Jon Blake, Peter Phelps, Tony Bonner, Bill Kerr, John Walton, Gary Sweet, Tim McKenzie, Sigrid Thornton, Anthony Andrews, Anthony Hawkins, Gerard Kennedy, Shane Briant, Serge Lazareff
Running time: 115 mins (originally 131)
US release: Cinecom, Apr 8, 1988
UK release: Medusa, Nov 11, 1988

LIKE FATHER, LIKE SON

This well-worn Hollywood plotline, in which a father and his teenage son switch identities, is an ideal vehicle for Dudley Moore. He's a heart surgeon, and his son (TV star Kirk Cameron) is a high school goof. One fix of a peculiar substance imported from an Indian reservation, however, and they've switched brains. Moore's body suddenly has a kid's brain – which has seemed to be the case anyway in most of his movies. He disrupts the hospital, while Cameron suddenly becomes a pompous know-it-all at school. Some scenes induce helpless laughter but too many fall very flat. Directed by TV veteran Rod Daniel, the movie will play better on the small screen. **BM**
Director Rod Daniel **producers** Brian Grazer, David Valdes **script** Lorne Cameron, Steven L. Bloom **camera** Jack N. Green **editor** Lois Freeman-Fox **design** Dennis Gassner **music** Miles Goodman **cast** Dudley Moore, Kirk Cameron, Sean Astin, Patrick O'Neal, Margaret Colin, Catherine Hicks
Running time: 99 mins
US release: Tri-Star, Oct 2, 1987
UK release: Col/Tri-Star, Dec 16, 1988

THE LION'S DEN (La Boca del Lobo)

This Peruvian film is gripping at first as it fills in the background to a massacre, but then fumbles the main event. The opening sequences show fear spreading through a group of soldiers despatched, with inadequate equipment and minimal strategy, to the mountains where Maoist guerrillas have already wiped out their predecessors. From terror grows a license to brutality against the native Indian population that leads to mass murder. Seen through the eyes of a career soldier (Vega) who remains aloof from racist indecencies and killing, the climax is a game of Russian roulette between Vega and his leader, which shows director Francisco Lombardi seemingly more interested

in exploitation (and imitation) than revelation. His stolid directing style is generally inadequate for the enormity of the events depicted. **JP**
Director *Francisco J. Lombardi* **execs** *Gerardo Herrero, Lombardi* **script** *Agusto Cabada, Giovanna Pollarolo, Gerardo Herrero* **camera** *José L. Lopez* **editor** *Jan San Mateo* **music** *Bernardo Bonezzi* **cast** *Gustave Bueno, Tono Vega, José Tejada, Gilberto Torres*
Running time: 116 mins
UK release: ICA, Jun 9, 1989

LISTEN TO ME

Seeking a new arena in which an unprepossessing teen could overcome the favourite and win the heart of his true love, Douglas Day Stewart hit upon college debating. Kirk Cameron comes from Nowhere, Oklahoma, but he has all the facts at his finger tips and all the jury-swaying arguments on the tip of his tongue. Jami Gertz, following the formula, initially hates him but winds up adoring him. The rôle of top kid from the right side of the tracks is played by Tim Quill and the irascible but soft-hearted coach is Roy Scheider. The film takes on a spurious seriousness when the subject of the climactic debate is abortion, but Stewart steers a timid middle course. **BM**
Director/script *Douglas Day Stewart* **producer** *Marykay Powell* **camera** *Fred Koenekamp* **editor** *Anne V. Coates* **design** *Gregory Pickrell* **music** *David Foster* **cast** *Kirk Cameron, Jami Gertz, Roy Scheider, Amanda Peterson, Tim Quill, George Wyner, Anthony Zerbe, Christopher Atkins*
Running time: 107 mins
US release: WEG/Columbia, May 5, 1989

LITTLE DORRIT
Part I: Nobody's Fault
Part II: Little Dorrit's Story

Nobody's Fault is the story of Arthur Clennam, newly returned to London from China in the 1820s to find his destiny still decreed by the religious mania and withered spirit of his crippled mother, and further tormented by the Circumlocution Office's appalling red tape before bad investment spirals him into the Marshalsea Debtor's Prison. The one bright spot in his life is his mother's seamstress, Amy, subject of *Little Dorrit's Story*, whose quiet determination and solicitude have succoured her father through his 23 years of incarceration at the Marshalsea – until Arthur effected their liberty. Christian Edzard's masterstroke in bringing Charles Dickens' teeming novel of corruption, capitalism and greed to the screen is in the overlapping of the two parts so that the suffocating world seen by Arthur is a place of hope and comfort for the unsentimental heroine. A great screen adaptation, as well as a cautionary fable for Mrs Thatcher's England, *Little Dorrit's* definitive performances – from a cast of 211 – include those of Derek Jacobi as Arthur, Sarah Pickering as Amy, the late Joan Greenwood as Mrs Clennam, Max Wall as the gnarled Flintwinch, and Alec Guinness as William Dorrit, the vain, feckless embodiment of shabby gentility. **GF**
Director *Christine Edzard* **producers** *John Brabourne, Richard Goodwin* **script** *Edzard, based on novel by Charles Dickens* **camera** *Bruno De Keyzer* **editors** *Oliver Stockman, Fraser Maclean* **design** *John McMillan, Peter Feroze, Mary McGowan, Charlie McMillan, Peter Seater, Hugh Doherty* **music** *Verdi, arranged by Michael Sanvoisin* **cast** *Derek Jacobi, Joan Greenwood, Max Wall, Patricia Hayes, Luke Duckett, Miriam Margolyes, Bill Fraser, Roshan Seth, Mollie Maureen, Diana Malin, Janice Cramer, Roger Hammond, Sophie Ward, Kathy Staff, Julia Lang, Pip Torrens, Graham Seed, John Savident, Brian Pettifer, John Hardin, Alec Wallis, Michael Meers, Edward Burnham, Harold Innocent, David Pugh, Alec Guinness, Cyril Cusack, Sarah Pickering, Amelda Brown, Daniel Chatto, Howard Goorney, Liz Smith, Gwenda Hughes, Celia Bannerman, Eleanor Bron, Michael Elphick, Simon Dormandy, Ian Hogg, Robert Morley, Alan Bennett, Brenda Bruce, Edward Jewesbury, Jonathan Cecil, Brian Poyser, Malcolm Tierney, Trevor Ray, Rosalie Crutchley, Betty Marsden, Paul Rhys*
Running time: 176 mins (part one), 181 mins (part two)
US release: Cannon, Oct 21, 1988
UK release: Curzon, Dec 11, 1987

LITTLE VERA (Malinkaiya Vera)

Just as the vaults seemed to have yielded the last of the masterpieces smothered by the post-Khruschev regime, along comes a Soviet film that suggests the beginning of a new spirit in the nation's filmmaking (seemingly mirroring, both in style and preoccupations, the 'new waves' of the early 1960s in Western Europe). It's a patchy effort, characterized by clumsy and repetitious use of *verité* devices and a script that doesn't know how to orchestrate its groundbreaking references to street-fights, alcoholism and teenage sex. Although Natalya Negoda is extraordinary as Vera, a knowing, sexy little dresser whose introduction into the

household of the sulky Sergei (Sokolov) splinters her rancorous family, leading to a somewhat melodramatic climax, some amateurish supporting performances mar the overall effect. Still, as a harbinger of things to come, *Little Vera* should be welcomed. **JP**
Director *Vassili Pitchul* **producer** *Mosfilm* **script** *Maria Khmelik* **design** *Vladimir Pasternak* **music** *Vladimir Matietski* **cast** *Natalya Negoda, Andrei Sokolov, Yuri Nazarov, Ludmila Zaisova, Alexander Niegreva*
Running time: 130 mins
US release: IFEX, Apr 14, 1989
UK release: Mainline, Jun 9, 1989

THE LONELY PASSION OF JUDITH HEARNE

Quietly directed by Jack Clayton, this very human drama centres on a heart-rending portrayal by Maggie Smith of the unloved Irish spinster, whose natural mirth was curbed in childhood by a selfish Victorian aunt (Hiller). Judith's tippling accelerates when the spivvy Americanized brother (Hoskins) of her landlady (Kean) courts and then discards her when he finds she's penniless. The title is ironic: her Catholic devotion is unable to help her in her hour of need, which makes her retreat from the well of madness utterly compelling. Clayton meanwhile delineates a grey cheerless Dublin peopled by mean-spirited middle-class citizens nursing their own disappointments. **GF**
Director *Jack Clayton* **producers** *Peter Nelson, Richard Johnson* **execs** *George Harrison, Denis O'Brien* **script** *Peter Nelson, based on the novel by Brian Moore* **camera** *Peter Hannan* **editor** *Terry Rawlings* **design** *Michael Pickwoad* **music** *Georges Delerue* **cast** *Maggie Smith, Bob Hoskins, Wendy Hiller, Marie Kean, Ian McNeice, Alan Devlin, Rudi Davies, Prunella Scales, Aine Ni Mhuiri*
Running time: 116 mins
US release: Island, Dec 23, 1987
UK release: HandMade/Virgin, Jan 6, 1989

LONG LIVE THE LADY! (Lunga vita alla Signora!) 👍

Ermanno Olmi serves a feast of a film: a fable of dreams and despotism set in a castle-hotel high amid Gothic mountains. A group of trainee waiters bow and glide at a bizarre banquet, prepared as if by Fellini (with frog soup and steamed sea monster) and presided over by a wizened crone who never speaks. As the plot's tragi-comic coils tighten, one young waiter (Esposito) dreams of romance and flight. Will the dream come true? Mervyn Peake settings and Federico F-style characters embellish a movie still unmistakably Olmi's;

charged with a luminous humanism and an insight into the secret dreams and masonic yearnings of youth. **HK**
Director/script/editor *Ermanno Olmi* **producer** *Giuseppe Cereda* **exec** *Marcello Siena* **camera** *Olmi, Maurizio Zaccaro* **music** *Telemann* **cast** *Marco Esposito, Simona Brandalise, Stefania Busarello, Simone Dalla Rosa, Lorenzo Paolini, Tarcisio Tosi, Alberto Francescato, Marisa Abbate, Luigi Cancellara, Giovanna Vidotto, Luca Dorizzi*
Running time: 106 mins
UK release: Artificial Eye, Sep 9, 1988

LOOSE CONNECTIONS

Maggie Brooks's script cleverly modulates a classic premise: Lindsay Duncan, who had intended driving to a feminist conference in Munich with two colleagues ends up instead being accompanied by a football supporter who represents everything she despises. But while it's easy to believe the stoney-faced Duncan and the flustered Stephen Rea wouldn't get on, it's impossible to accept the coming-together that such stories demand. The comic moments are in the scripting — Rea is arrested for vagrancy after a rainstorm demolishes his tent; later, he inadvertently sets fire to the jeep while tampering with the wiring — but Richard Eyre's flat direction can't overcome the uninspired casting. **JP**
Director *Richard Eyre* **producer** *Simon Perry* **script** *Maggie Brooks* **camera** *Clive Tickner* **editor** *David Martin* **music** *Dominic Muldowney* **cast** *Stephen Rea, Lindsay Duncan, Jan Niklas, Carole Harrison, Gary Olsen, Frances Low*
Running time: 99 mins
US release: Orion Classics, Jul 8, 1988
UK release: Virgin, Apr 14, 1984

LOST ANGELS

Beastie Boy Adam Horovitz is surprisingly sympathetic as the misunderstood juvenile in Hugh Hudson's ripoff of *Rebel Without a Cause*. Horovitz, confused by his parents' divorce, gets involved in his older brother's war against some local Hispanics. The boy's father turns him in to the police and his mother warehouses him in a behaviour-alteration clinic — a profit-making operation that fattens on insurance reimbursements. But Donald Sutherland is Horovitz's shrink; so he'll be OK. Although too few of the movie's plot strands unwind satisfactorily, the film does stand as an indictment of Los Angeles' me-first way of life. **BM**
Director *Hugh Hudson* **producers** *Howard*

Rosenman, Thomas Baer **script** Michael Weller
camera Juan-Ruiz Anchia **editor** David Gladwell
design Assheton Gorton **music** Philipe Sarde **cast**
Donald Sutherland, Adam Horovitz, Amy Locane,
Don Bloomfield, Celia Weston, Graham Beckel,
Patricia Richardson, Ron Frazier, Joseph d'Angerio
Running time: 116 mins
US release: Orion, May 5, 1989

LUCKY STIFF

A country cousin to the year's main
contribution to the cannibal genre, *Parents*, this
pastoral black comedy is a broad and cheery,
though none too ambitious, satirical foray.
Bulbous Joe Alaskey believes the ultimate cure
for his perpetual love-sickness has materialized
in delicious blonde Donna Dixon, who
seemingly reciprocates his romantic inclinations
when she takes him home to meet the folks for
a Yuletide feast. Anthony Perkins' direction is
amiable, extracting good-humoured laughs from
the eccentric characters without, regrettably,
exploiting the more intriguing aspects of the
premise. **MN**
Director Anthony Perkins **producer** Gerald T.
Olson **execs** Laurie Perlman, Pat Proft, Miles
Copeland, Derek Power **script** Proft **camera**
Jacques Haitkin **editors** Michael N. Knue, Tom
Walls **design** C. J. Strawn **music** Tom Jenkins,
Make Tavera **cast** Donna Dixon, Joe Alaskey, Jeff
Kober, Barbara Howard, Fran Ryan, Morgan
Sheppard, Leigh McCloskey, Elizabeth Arlen
Running time: 82 mins
US release: New Line, Nov 18, 1988

THE LAST TEMPTATION OF CHRIST

Take one story that changed human history. Take one novel that changed the way we see that story. And then take one Italian-American director whose best films — *Mean Streets*, *Taxi Driver*, *Raging Bull* — change the way we see the world around us. *The Last Temptation of Christ* is a movie whose fusion of talents should have resulted in an explosion somewhere over the Western world, showering fall-out over Christians and non-Christians alike. That the explosion never quite happened, that most of the noise came not from the movie but from self-appointed Jeremiahs riding the chariot of controversy, must be one of the major inquest topics for moviegoers in 1989.

The excitement that should have been *in* the movie happened around it. The burning visions of paradise or purgatory that Scorsese had conjured as modernist metaphor in other films remained stubbornly un-conjured here, even though closer to their iconographic source.

Heaven knows, if publicity and controversy could make a masterpiece, *The Last Temptation* had a head start. When not being threatened with fire or vandalism in Protestant Britain and America, the film found itself cast as red rag to papal bull in Catholic Italy.

But although Scorsese's film couldn't match the accompanying furore, it's in no simple sense a 'failure'. *The Last Temptation of Christ* is a long, earnest, demotic epic, full of dusty beauty and questing honesty. But it's also a film which falls short, after a two and three-quarter hour pilgrimage, of reaching whatever holy grail or philosophical 'Eureka!' it was seeking.

The dream-on-the-cross sequence, featuring Jesus making love with Mary Magdalene, which brought down the first God-squad thunderbolts, is the crucial anti-climax. The concept is dazzling: the execution is banal. The climactic revelation of 'Christ the human being', dreaming of the companionship of sex, marriage and the family, comes over less as a powerful humanist apocalypse than as an abruptly collapsed passion play. The scenery totters, the illusion falters.

It's all the sadder given the film's huge ambitions and long incubation period. Scorsese, who had been planning to film Nicos Kazantzakis' novel for over ten years, sets out his shingles on two fronts. Firstly, *The Last Temptation* is to show Our Lord as a man suffering human doubts, desires and frailties. Secondly, it is to relate him and his world to us today, giving us a plain-speaking, plain-feeling Christ for the 1980s.

Point one indicates the film's content, point two its means of expression. In both areas, Scorsese's struggles grow as the film progresses. The strongest scenes are the earliest, when the socio-historical 'reification' of Christ's story — making him a focused, credible human being in a focused, credible, contemporary world — is brilliantly successful. This Christ *is* a carpenter, earning an honest if tormented shekel from hewing Roman crosses. This Christ actually *does* know Mary Magdalene and her works. (The brothel scene, with Christ elbow-to-elbow among the waiting clients as Mary services each one in turn, is bold, literal and astonishing.) And this Christ believably wrestles both with his conscience and with Harvey Keitel's proto-terrorist Judas.

So potent are the early vibrations Scorsese sets up between Christ's society and our own that one might suspect the Wrath of the Airwaves was visited on the director for these scenes rather than the one elected as scapegoat. Where the latter (Christ's coition with Mary Magdalene) is chastely shot and inexplicit, there's a raw realism in scenes like the chasing of the money-changers from the temple that might well ruffle the conscience of any tax-free, send-your-cheque pulpiteer.

Instead the Christian Ayatollahs aimed their ammunition at a sequence whose very bathos is its own downfall. The dream on the cross highlights a void that has been growing throughout the film. The movie has no vision. In *Taxi Driver* or *Raging Bull*, Scorsese created a poetic setting where the characters' torments were embodied not just in their words but in their worlds. The steaming inferno of Travis Bickle's mind was all around him in the hellish mirror-image of New York. Jake La Motta's blunted monochrome soul, whose only intoxication was in the boxing ring, was in the film's plain black-and-white images, occasionally pixillated by slow-motion surrealism.

In *The Last Temptation*, Scorsese gives us an environment starved of symbolic or poetic inflection. Inner struggle is not mirrored in the landscape or imagery: those comprise an identikit Bible-land — dusty, beautiful and generic. As a result, there is no expressionist soil from which the culminating scenes of vision and longing can convincingly grow. Like other fantastical eruptions in the film — the Devil as a cobra, Christ pulling his beating heart from his chest — they are not suddenly heightened metaphor, but arbitrary conjuring tricks in an otherwise magicless show.

There is courage and ambition behind the movie. Scorsese must have known the film might both bomb at the box office and get bombed by the fundamentalists. Still, he gathered his cast and crew and schlepped off to Morocco for a six-month shoot. And he still argued, bravely, that far from being blasphemous, his portrait of Christ was reconcilable with the Bible's notion of the Son of God made man.

But although Scorsese the spokesman didn't falter, one suspects that at some point during the shooting Scorsese the filmmaker did. Gearing himself up for his coming media rôle as Serious Artist rather than Religious Vandal, he had to prove he wasn't painting moustaches on the New Testament. So caution replaced passion, and a bold, inventive dissidence was elbowed aside by a devout banality. Perhaps the 'last temptation' of Martin Scorsese was to be an earnest, respectable artist rather than a dangerous, lonely, high-reaching genius.

HARLAN KENNEDY

LICENCE TO KILL

The Bond films have generally been superb entertainments. The name evokes visions of spectacular stunts, beautiful girls, exotic locations and the odd striking image, all wrapped up in a cloak of wish fulfilment strong enough for the series to have withstood more than a quarter century of criticism and social change. Following the departure of Sean Connery, the hardware gradually took away the edge, leaving Roger Moore (who boasted a nice line in public school sadism in his earlier efforts) to quip his way through a series of ever more spectacular pantomimes as the character deteriorated around him. Worse still, rather than setting the pace, they began to imitate other films: most of the set pieces in *Octopussy* were relocated rehashes of those in *Raiders of the Lost Ark*, while *A View to Kill* borrowed its plot from the second half of *Superman*.

Just when all seemed lost, along came Timothy Dalton with a bold new Bond for the 1980s. In *The Living Daylights*, he returned the character to its darker roots in the Fleming novels. That was only the beginning, the producers announced; with *A Licence to Kill*, Bond would enter the 1990s with an emphasis on plot, characterization and a realistic villain drawn directly from the headlines. 'This time Bond bleeds' they boasted.

Perhaps they really meant that this time they would kill Bond once and for all. They certainly managed to wound him very badly; for *Licence to Kill* is a great idea, but a terrible movie. 007's ex-CIA pal Felix Leiter is hideously tortured, his wife raped and murdered, by a vicious South American drugs baron. The horrified Bond sets out to avenge him, running across government corruption and official disapproval – his licence to kill is revoked by his superiors – and political double-dealing. In pursuit of his vendetta, he finds himself driven to almost psychopathic acts of violence. This could have been one of the most radical and exciting reinterpretations of a cultural icon since the comic strip *The Dark Knight Returns* put the darkness and danger back into Batman. What we get, however, is a tired and undernourished script with a remarkably high body count and an unrelenting nastiness. The villain's mistress is given her lover's heart; Felix is half-eaten by a shark; a minion is crushed to death in a grinder; another is impaled on a fork lift; Anthony Zerbe is bloodily blown-up in a decompression chamber and a ninja is shot to pieces – nearly always off screen.

Despite complaints from the producers about a series of witty posters for *Nightmare on Elm Street 4* featuring its gloved anti-hero in a classic 007 pose, as Bond wanders through the film killing almost everyone he meets in increasingly unpleasant ways, *Licence to Kill* becomes almost a Freddy Krueger splatter movie without the splatter. Despite the corpses, the action sequences are uninvolving. There is no shortage of potentially lethal stunt work, much of it by Dalton himself,

but this never provokes any sense of danger.

More surprising still, bearing in mind the $36 million budget, is the low technical standard. Alec Mills' cinematography makes the least of every location, cruelly exposing the artificiality of the sets. John Glen's direction is so unimaginative that it is hard to believe he did such sterling work on *The Living Daylights* and *For Your Eyes Only*. Worse still is Michael Kamen's dismal score. His tendency to find a two-note sequence he likes and repeat it *ad infinitum* through any given scene only proves how underrated an asset is the contribution of regular composer John Barry (too ill to work on this one).

The performances vary from poor to indifferent. Whilst Desmond Llewelyn enjoys himself as Q and Carey Lowell shows some promise as the (marginally) smarter of the two Bond girls, Robert Davi and Anthony Zerbe are poor villains. And, despite having given the part of Felix Leiter a creditable shot previously in *Live and Let Die*, David Hedison makes no impact, rushing his scenes and depriving the movie of vital and much-needed emotional pull. Most worrying of all is Dalton's Bond, a lethargic and limited performance reminiscent of Moore at his worst. All the ground he gained on his previous outing has been lost, seemingly in the attempt to increase the film's appeal in the States, traditionally the Bond films' least important market.

Most of Bond's distinguishing characteristics are gone. Displaying no signs of class or intellect, he has become a mere killing machine. At first this works rather well – a sequence where Bond is offered a two-million-dollar bribe by the DEA agent who set up Leiter, only to throw the suitcase full of money at his stomach as he is precariously balanced on the edge of a shark tank, sends a chill down the spine – but the film never investigates the increasingly fine line between good and evil or the glimpses of schizophrenia that Bond's personal quest should hint at. It simply comes up with new ways to kill the bad guys. Even the promising notion of 007 allying himself with the drug lord and getting him to kill his partners by playing on his paranoia is soon discarded for a series of big explosions.

The producers' aim seems to have been to ensure that even a drunken truck driver from Pittsburgh could identify with Bond, in an effort to make the kind of money their American competitors do. By going for a new audience – which may not even exist if America's run of smash-hit comedy and family-orientated films is anything to go by – Messrs Broccoli and Wilson may well find themselves losing the audience they already have. At the public screening I attended, there were a lot of disgruntled Bond fans who felt the character they knew had been neutered. 'If that's what they think James Bond is, they might as well not bother' one was heard to mutter. And for the first time ever, when I saw the end credits promise 'James Bond Will Return', I wondered if that was such a good idea . . .

TREVOR WILLSMER

MAC AND ME

Mac is a pop-eyed little creature from outer space who looks as if he must have come from the same corner of the Universe as another, more distinguished, extraterrestrial. Vacuumed up into a US space probe and carried off to LA, he spends a goodly part of the movie *not* meeting up with the kid in a wheelchair who is obviously destined to become his buddy. The pre-credits sequence on a dessicated planet (E.T. as The Man Who Fell to Earth) has promise, but the sense of *déjà vu* that permeates the rest of the story makes this an item for undiscriminating kids only. The cynicism underlying the film's production is emphasized by blatant plugs for MacDonalds and Coca-Cola. **JP**
Director Stewart Raffill *producer* R. J. Louis *exec* Mark Damon, William B. Kerr *script* Raffill, Steve Feke *camera* Nick McLean *editor* Tom Walls *design* W. Stewart Campbell *music* Alan Silvestri *cast* Christine Ebersole, Jonathan Ward, Katrina Caspary, Lauren Stanley
Running time: 93 mins
US release: Orion, Aug 12, 1988
UK release: Guild, Jul 21, 1989

MADAME SOUSATZKA

Ruth Prawer Jhabvala's name on the credits suggests another 'literary' adaptation in the school of Merchant-Ivory (*Maurice, A Room With a View*). But here the Bernice Rubens novel has been updated from the 1960s to present-day, complete with references to property developers and soft indictments of commercialism, but without sufficient attention to the family background of the Indian boy that Madame's pupil has now become (he was Jewish before) or the characteristics of embittered piano teachers. Shirley MacLaine's performance seems aimed at winning prizes – she bangs her stick and shouts like a blind woman abandoned – rather than exploring the conflict between possessiveness and love for her young charge. The central dramatic conflict, as to whether the boy (Chowdhry) should please his mother by giving a public performance, or his teacher who says he's not yet ready, seems contrived, and John Schlesinger largely ignores the cultural conflicts set in motion when a boy brought up on Indian videos strives to master Chopin and Schumann. **JP**
Director John Schlesinger *producer* Robin Dalton *script* Ruth Prawer Jhabvala, Schlesinger, *from novel by* Bernice Rubens *camera* Nat Crosby *editor* Peter Honess *design* Luciana Arrighi *music*

Gerald Gouriet *cast* Shirley MacLaine, Navin Chowdhry, Peggy Ashcroft, Twiggy, Shabana Azmi, Leigh Lawson, Geoffrey Bayldon, Lee Montague, Robert Rietty
Running time: 122 mins
US release: Universal, Oct 14, 1988
UK release: Curzon, Mar 21, 1989

MAJOR LEAGUE

Police Academy meets *Eight Men Out* in this amiable baseball comedy that boasts an above-average cast and a few good jokes (though not many new ones), as coach Tom Berenger – displaying a nice comic touch – puts together the worst team imaginable in an effort to get relocated to Miami. It does nothing to advance the art of motion pictures, but it does make you laugh – which is all it sets out to do. And how many other movies this year offer the sight of a voodoo worshipper sacrificing Kentucky Fried Chicken? **TW**
Director/script David S. Ward *producers* Chris Chesser, Irby Smith *exec* Mark Rosenberg *camera* Reynaldo Villalobos *editor* Dennis M. Hill *design* Jeffrey Howard *music* James Newton Howard *cast* Tom Berenger, Charlie Sheen, Corbin Bernsen, Margaret Whitton, James Gammon, Rene Russo, Wesley Snipes, Charles Cyphers, Chelcie Ross, Dennis Haysbert, Andy Romano, Bob Uecker
Running time: 107 mins
US release: Paramount, Apr 7, 1989

A MAN IN LOVE (Un homme amoureux)

Diane Kurys sidesteps the overt autobiography of her previous features and goes for big screen romance in a slight story of movie star (Coyote) meets beautiful ingénue (Scacchi) in exotic Rome while making a film on writer Cesare Pavese. Her lead scores high on charisma and there are some sumptuous sex scenes, but the emotional core really comes from a beautiful cameo by Claudia Cardinale as Scacchi's mother. **DT**
Director/script Diane Kurys *producer* Michel Seydoux, Kurys *exec* Seydoux *camera* Bernard Zitzermann *editors* Joëlle Van Effenterre, Nathalie Le Guay, Michèle Robert, Valérie Longeville *design* Dean Tavoularis *music* Georges Delerue *cast* Peter Coyote, Greta Scacchi, Jamie Lee Curtis, Claudia Cardinale, Peter Riegert, John Berry, Vincent Lindon, Jean Pigozzi, Elia Katz, Constantin Alexandrov, Jean Claude de Goros
Running time: 111 mins
US release: Cinecom, Jul 31, 1987
UK release: Fox/Virgin, Jul 29, 1988

MANHUNTER

Director Michael Mann **producer** Richard Roth **exec** Bernard Williams **script** Mann, based on novel Red Dragon by Thomas Harris **camera** Dante Spinotti **editor** Dov Hoenig **design** Mel Bourne **music** Michel Rubini, The Reds **cast** William L. Petersen, Kim Greist, Joan Allen, Brian Cox, Dennis Farina, Stephen Lang, Tom Noonan
Running time: 119 mins
US release: DEG, Aug 15, 1986
UK release: Recorded Releasing, Feb 24, 1989

MANIAC COP

A serial killer, at large in New York City, turns out to be a uniformed cop. Not only that, but it looks like he's *dead* already . . . This exploitation quickie bears the imprimatur of its writer and producer – independent maestro Larry Cohen – but director William Lustig doesn't quite deliver the break-neck pace and improvisatory panache that this sort of story requires. Nevertheless, there are incidental pleasures a-plenty: lots of slam-bang violence, a solid supporting cast of great B-movie actors, the reliable Laurene Landon putting on her plucky-trooper act, and Bruce Campbell proving once again, as in *The Evil Dead*, that as the hero-in-peril he is second to none when it comes to having his head kicked in. **AB**
Director William Lustig **producer/script** Larry Cohen **exec** James Glickenhaus **camera** Vincent J. Rabe **editor** David Kern **design** Jonathan Hodges, Ann Cudworth **music** Jay Chataway **cast** Tom Atkins, Bruce Campbell, Laurene Landon, Richard Roundtree, William Smith, Robert Z'Dar
Running time: 85 mins
US release: Shapiro/Glickenhaus, May 13, 1988
UK release: Medusa, Feb 10, 1989

MANIFESTO

Yugoslav iconoclast Dusan Makavejev's flirtation with Cannon-financed Euro-production is a sorry mess. Filmed in his home country (in images of an undeniable beauty) with a multinational cast, and set in 1920, *Manifesto* concerns an ineffectual local revolution brought about in an eccentric Central European town by the arrival of a promiscuous heroine. For all its rumbustious good intentions, the result is rather like a firework display in which someone has forgotten the correct sequence of events. **DT**
Director Dusan Makavejev **producers** Menahem Golan, Yoram Globus **execs** Michael J. Kagan, Tom Luddy **script** Makavejev, inspired by story For a Night of Love by Emile Zola **camera** Tomislav Pinter **editor** Tony Lawson **design** Veljko Despotovic **music** Nicola Piovani **cast** Camilla Søeberg, Alfred Molina, Simon Callow, Eric Stoltz, Lindsay Duncan, Rade Serbedzija, Svetozar Cvetkovic, Chris Haywood
Running time: 96 mins
US release: Cannon, Jan 27, 1989
UK release: Cannon, Sep 2, 1988

MAPANTSULA

Made in South Africa with limited resources and under semi-clandestine conditions, *Mapantsula* is a brave stab at oppositional filmmaking, whose technical rough edges point up, rather than detract from, its sense of conviction. The film's strongest suit, in fact, is its unblinking stare at the surfaces of daily life in the township of Soweto. But while there is courage in taking for its black protagonist an unadmirable and even vicious spiv, the process of his eventual adoption of political commitment, at the possible cost of his life, is dramatized with no small degree of awkwardness, not least as regards the constant cross-cutting which the flashback structure dictates. **TP**
Director Oliver Schmitz **producer** Max Montocchio **execs** David Hannay, Keith Rosenbaum **script** Schmitz, Thomas Mogotlane **camera** Rod Stewart **editor** Mark Baard **design** Robyn Hofmeyr **music** The Ouens **cast** Mogotlane, Marcel Van Heerden, Thembi Mtshali, Dolly Rathebe, Peter Sephuma, Darlington Michaels
Running time: 104 mins
US release: Electric, Jan 13, 1989

MARRIED TO THE MOB

Jonathan Demme's insubstantial paean to Americana subtly lampoons gangster movies with its tale of a petit-bourgeois mobster widow (Pfeiffer) who tries to make a new life for herself away from the criminal hierarchies and confines of palatial Long Island. Her attempts are frustrated by the sexually-predatory surveillance of mafioso kingpin Dean Stockwell who, along with his possessively-maniacal wife Mercedes Ruehl, is the real star of this casserole of genres. *Married to the Mob* incorporates uncategorizable homages to ethnicity, blue-collar immigrant kitsch and seems insubstantial when set against such recent screwball forays as

the yuppie-bashing *Into the Night*, Scorsese's *After Hours* and Demme's earlier excursion into farcical angst, *Something Wild*. **MN**
Director *Jonathan Demme* **producers** *Kenneth Utt, Edward Saxon* **exec** *Joel Simon, Bill Todman Jr.* **script** *Barry Strugatz, Mark R. Burns* **camera** *Tak Fujimoto* **editor** *Craig McKay* **design** *Kristi Zea* **music** *David Byrne* **cast** *Michelle Pfeiffer, Matthew Modine, Dean Stockwell, Mercedes Ruehl, Alec Baldwin, Trey Wilson, Joan Cusack, Oliver Platt, Paul Lazar, Carol East, Ellen Foley*
Running time: 103 mins
US release: Orion, Aug 19, 1988
UK release: Rank, Jun 23, 1989

MASQUERADE

High noon in the Hamptons. And what's a pretty heiress like Meg Tilly doing in a murder plot like this? When not being persecuted by her evil stepfather or pestered by her policeman boyfriend, she's falling for devilishly-handsome yachting ace Rob Lowe. But Rob is not all he seems; or rather, he's more than he seems. Soon murder's afoot, director Bob Swaim is staging twist and counter-twist, and cameraman David Watkin is turning Long Island into gleaming Gatsby territory. Fun, menace and crazed ingenuity abound, even if plausibility doesn't. Still, who can resist a film that resolves its tangled tale by having a rat accidentally set off a propane-gas explosion on a yacht? **HK**
Director *Bob Swaim* **producer** *Michael I. Levy* **exec/script** *Dick Wolf* **camera** *David Watkin* **editor** *Scott Conrad* **design** *John Kasarda* **music** *John Barry* **cast** *Rob Lowe, Meg Tilly, Doug Savant, Kim Cattrall, John Glover, Dana Delany*
Running time: 91 mins
US release: MGM, Mar 11, 1988
UK release: UIP, Sep 30, 1988

MATEWAN

A familiar theme – (doomed) working class struggle – is transformed by John Sayles into a tale of escalating violence that culminates in a Western-style shoot-out. In the town of Matewan, West Virginia, striking miners join with scab immigrants to fight against the coal company and its allies – a compliant church and the local snoop. Sometimes Sayles' 'professional screenwriter' status shows in excessive contrivance but his deployment of suspense, skill in orchestrating a large cast, sensitivity to the interplay between immigrant cultures and eye for landscape revisions come right through to the devastating finale. **JP**
Director/script *John Sayles* **producers** *Peggy*

Rajski, Maggie Renzi **execs** *Amir Jacob Malin, Mark Balsam, Jerry Silva* **camera** *Haskell Wexler* **editor** *Sonya Polonsky* **design** *Nora Chavooshian* **music** *Mason Daring* **cast** *Chris Cooper, Will Oldham, Mary McDonnell, Bob Gunton, James Earl Jones, Kevin Tighe, Gordon Clapp, Josh Mostel, Ken Jenkins, Jace Alexander*
Running time: 130 mins
US release: Cinecom, Aug 28, 1987
UK release: Enterprise, Apr 14, 1989

MEMORIES OF ME

There's nothing more lovable in Hollywood's eyes than an old bastard who's about to croak. One-time TV star Henry Winkler's first film sentimentalizes a boorish father (King) whose New York surgeon son (Crystal) comes home to Los Angeles when he suffers an early heart attack. King and Crystal trade barbs for what seems like 17 reels before collapsing into each other's arms for another 17. JoBeth Williams is the girlfriend who, of course, can see what the two fellas can't – that they're exactly alike, no matter how estranged they are. Wise moviegoers will depart before the mariachi band plays 'Hava Nagila'. **BM**
Director *Henry Winkler* **producer** *Alan King, Billy Crystal, Michael Hertzberg* **execs** *Gabe Sumner, J. David Marks* **script** *Eric Roth, Crystal* **camera** *Andrew Dintenfass* **editor** *Peter E. Berger* **design** *William J. Cassidy* **music** *Georges Delerue* **cast** *Billy Crystal, Alan King, JoBeth Williams, Sean Connery, Janet Carroll, David Ackroyd*
Running time: 105 mins
US release: MGM, Sep 28, 1988

MESSENGER OF DEATH

What initially appears to be yet another run-of-the-mill Charles Bronson killer-thriller actually turns out to be an above-average mystery. Bronson investigates a series of killings in an isolated religious community in what seems at first an open-and-shut case, only to find something rather unpleasant lurking beneath the surface and, in the process, turning in one of his better recent performances. It's far from perfect and little effort is made to stretch its star's neglected potential, but after so many years of blowing away ethnic minorities in Michael Winner films, it's a welcome step in the right direction. **TW**
Director *J. Lee-Thompson* **producer** *Pancho Kohner* **execs** *Menahem Golan, Yoram Globus* **script** *Paul Jarrico, from novel The Avenging Angel by Rex Burns* **camera** *Gideon Porath* **editor** *Peter Lee-Thompson* **design** *W. Brooke Wheeler*

music Robert O. Ragland *cast* Charles Bronson, Trish Van Devere, Laurence Luckinbill, Daniel Benzali, Marilyn Hassett, Jeff Corey, John Ireland, Penny Peyser, Gene Davis, John Solari, Jon Cedar **Running time:** 90 mins
US release: Cannon, Sep 16, 1988

MIDNIGHT CROSSING

To high heaven, this one stinks. For a start, Faye Dunaway is a blind eye doctor. Her husband, Daniel J. Travanti, is a mild-mannered insurance man with a murderous secret. Travanti entices John Laughlin and Kim Cattrall to sail to an island off Cuba to reclaim some treasure left behind when Castro took over in 1959. On the voyage they meet old sea-dog Ned Beatty in the phoniest Robert Shaw part ever written. Soon after landfall, there are as many corpses as palm trees. Dunaway is the last one left, but things are not what they seem. Yes, with every scene, it gets worse. **BM**
Director Roger Holzberg *producer* Matthew Hayden *execs* Dan Ireland, Gary Barber, Gregory Cascante, Wanda Rayle *script* Holzberg, Doug Weiser *camera* Henry Vargas *editor* Earl Watson *design* José Duarte *music* Paul Buckmaster, Al Gorgoni *cast* Faye Dunaway, Daniel J. Travanti, Kim Cattrall, John Laughlin, Ned Beatty **Running time:** 96 mins (104 mins in US)
US release: Vestron, May 15, 1988
UK release: Vestron, Sep 30, 1988

MIDNIGHT RUN

This road movie struggles under the weight of its star billing to engender some charm into the antagonism between Robert De Niro's modern-day bounty hunter and his devious quarry, mafia accountant-turned-philanthropist Charles Grodin, but to little effect. Martin Brest's direction tends to lack focus or discipline, leaving De Niro to shuffle his way through a highly-mannered performance towards some understanding of Grodin's pedantic New Age values and colourless liberalism. The cross-country trek utilizes various forms of transport, but the changing landscape remains purely functional and the farcical pursuit of the ill-matched duo by the Mafia, the FBI and another bounty hunter undercuts what little tension the narrative can generate between the two characters. De Niro's performance style is more suited to Scorsese's coldly rational direction than Brest's heavy-handed, action-oriented camera work, leaving only Grodin's self-consciously prickly wimp to inject some fresh bile into the tepid narrative. **SD**

Director/producer Martin Brest *exec* William S. Gilmore *script* George Gallo *camera* Donald Thorin *editors* Billy Weber, Chris Lebenzon, Michael Tronick *design* Angelo Graham *music* Danny Elfman *cast* Robert De Niro, Charles Grodin, Yaphet Kotto, John Ashton, Dennis Farina, Joe Pantoliano
Running time: 126 mins
US release: Universal, Jul 20, 1988
UK release: UIP, Oct 7, 1988

THE MIGHTY QUINN

This diverting comedy-caper is one of the few movies to catch a Caribbean culture with any sensitivity. Denzel Washington proves his power as a leading man here, playing the squared-away-but-not-too-uptight police chief of an island colonized by the usual drug runners and CIA hit men. Robert Townsend is Washington's boyhood friend and rival in revelry who pops up almost magically throughout the story. Washington, as the title character, proves himself both as a crook-catcher and lover – even if his smooch with the white lady of the manor did get snipped from the final print. **BM**
Director Carl Schenkel *producers* Sandy Lieberson, Marion Hunt, Ed Elberg *execs* Dale Pollock, Gil Friesen *script* Hampton Fancher, *from* A. H. Z. Carr's *novel* Finding Maubee *camera* Jacques Steyn *editor* John Jympson *design* Roger Murray-Leach *music* Anne Dudley *cast* Denzel Washington, Robert Townsend, James Fox, Mimi Rogers, M. Emmet Walsh, Sheryl Lee Ralph, Art Evans, Esther Rolle, Norman Beaton, Alex Colon **Running time:** 98 mins
US release: MGM, Feb 17, 1989
UK release: UIP, Jun 16, 1989

THE MILAGRO BEANFIELD WAR

Illicit irrigation leads to endless troubles in a Hispanic-American community, with property developers bringing in Christopher Walken to restrain rebellion, the poor farmers deciding to stand behind their right to water the crops and the sheriff (Blades) caught between the two factions. Following his faceless directorial début, Robert Redford turned to potentially spikier material in John Nichols' well-liked novel, but the piece ended up as the epitome of Major Studio Liberalism, with the unfamiliar Latino players leavened by a sprinkling of box-office whites and the traditional view of suffering peasants as essentially happy souls who love nothing better than a laugh and a hoe-down dance. Melanie Griffith is unhappily cast as the

head villain's plump wife; John Heard is the token leftover 1960s radical gone-to seed; Sonia Braga overdoes the feminist agitator-cum-earth-mother rôle; Mexican comedian Carlos Riquelme dodders around in the company of an out-of-place ghost; Daniel Stern is a sociologist partnered with a pig in the happy ending; Richard Bradford and M. Emmet Walsh huff and puff nastily as the capitalist villains, and Christopher Walken does a soft-centred remake of his rôle in *Heaven's Gate* as the cowboy strong-arm-man who, along with everyone else, wimps out before the shooting really starts. Clogged with sub-plots and characters who seem to be in different films, *The Milagro Beanfield War* ultimately adds up to little more than a petty skirmish. **KN**
Director Robert Redford **producers** Redford, Moctesuma Esparza **exec** Gary J. Hendler **script** David Ward, John Nichols, based on Nichols' novel **camera** Robbie Greenberg **editors** Dede Allen, Jim Miller **design** Joe Aubel **music** Dave Grusin **cast** Rubén Blades, Richard Bradford, Sonia Braga, Julie Carmen, James Gammon, Melanie Griffith, John Heard, Carlos Riquelme, Daniel Stern, Chick Vennera, Christopher Walken, Freddy Fender, Robert Carricart, M. Emmet Walsh, Tony Genaro, Jerry Hardin
Running time: 118 mins
US release: Universal, Mar 18, 1988
UK release: UIP, Aug 19, 1988

MILES FROM HOME

Life on a farm is so boring, but there's a lot of it about. Richard Gere is the latest star to find that men of the soil in their duck-billed caps and scratchy overalls just look silly – especially when the only possible plot in American terms is 'How we gonna pay the mortgage on the farm?' Gere and his younger brother Anderson fail to make the payments on the farm; so they go on a bizarre revenge ramble through the countryside. Theatre director Gary Sinise substitutes long, silent closeups for character development and, for some reason, omits the violent ending he so slowly leads up to. **BM**
Director Gary Sinise **producers** Frederick Zollo, Paul Kurta **execs** Amir J. Malin, Ira Deutchman **script** Chris Gerolmo **camera** Elliot Davis **editor** Jane Schwartz Jaffe **design** David Gropman **music** Robert Folk **cast** Brian Dennehy, Jason Campbell, Austin Bamgarner, Larry Poling, Richard Gere, Kevin Anderson, Terry Kinney, Penelope Ann Miller, Helen Hunt, Moira Harris, John Malkovich
Running time: 112 mins
US release: Cinecom, Sep 16, 1988

UK release: Fox, Jun 30, 1989

MISS FIRECRACKER

Like her *Crimes of the Heart*, this new Beth Henley comic Gothic is peopled with characters too strong for its slender plot. Holly Hunter is a Mississippi plain-Jane, striving one last time to win her town's annual beauty-talent contest. One cousin, past winner Mary Steenburgen, is back home to crown the new victor and speak on 'My Life as a Beauty'. Other cousin Tim Robbins is home too, and half-wit Alfre Woodard hovers amusingly. Hunter does nothing halfway, from frizzing her hair to doing the splits, but the effort expended produces slightly too few laughs. **BM**
Director Thomas Schlamme **producer** Fred Bernler **execs** Lewis Allen, Ross E. Milloy **script** Beth Henley, from her play The Miss Firecracker Contest **camera** Arthur Albert **editor** Peter C. Frank **design** Kristi Zea **music** David Mansfield **cast** Holly Hunter, Mary Steenburgen, Tim Robbins, Alfre Woodard, Scott Glenn, Veanne Cox, Ann Wedgeworth, Trey Wilson, Amy Wright, Bert Remsen, Christine Lahti
Running time: 102 mins
US release: Corsair, Apr 28, 1989

MISSISSIPPI BURNING

Director Alan Parker **producers** Frederick Zollo, Robert F. Colesberry **script** Chris Gerolmo **camera** Peter Biziou **editor** Gerry Hambling **design** Philip Harrison, Geoffrey Kirkland **music** Trevor Jones **cast** Gene Hackman, Willem Dafoe, Frances McDormand, Brad Dourif, R. Lee Ermey, Gailard Sartain, Stephen Tobolowsky
Running time: 127 mins
US release: Orion, Dec 9, 1988
UK release: Rank, May 5, 1989

MR NORTH

The shadow of John Huston was very much over this project. Co-author of the screenplay and executive producer, he was only prevented by illness from acting a rich cameo part himself. Sad to say, the directorial grace he might have brought has not been passed on to son Danny, here making his feature début. Thornton Wilder's small-town story, set in 1926, deals with an ingenuous young man possessed of healing powers through his exceptional command of static electricity. The cast is mainly misdirected and the humane whimsy of the tale never takes off. **DT**

Director *Danny Huston* **producers** *Steven Haft,*
Skip Steloff **exec** *John Huston* **script** *Janet Roach,*
John Huston, James Costigan, from novel
Theophilus North by Thornton Wilder **camera**
Robin Vidgeon **editor** *Roberto Silvi* **design** *Eugene*
Lee **music** *David McHugh* **cast** *Anthony Edwards,*
Robert Mitchum, Lauren Bacall, Harry Dean
Stanton, Anjelica Huston, Mary Stuart Masterson,
Virginia Madsen, Tammy Grimes, David Warner,
Hunter Carson, Christopher Durang
Running time: 93 mins
US release: Goldwyn, Jul 22, 1988
UK release: Columbia/Tri-Star, Feb 17, 1989

THE MODERNS

Alan Rudolph and his co-writer, the late John
Bradshaw, seem to have got too close to this
long-nurtured project about Parisian art and
café society in 1926 to bring any wit to it. An
unengaging romantic plot – will enigmatic
American painter Nick Hart (pronounced 'art
naturellement) win back his trampy wife
(Fiorentino) from the chilly Chinese art-buyer
(Lone)? – runs alongside a sillier one about
forged masterpieces, involving Geneviève
Bujold's dealer and Geraldine Chaplin's
socialite. Still, Rudolph directs his stock
company with familiar affection; Wallace Shawn
and Kevin O'Connor amuse as the gossip
columnist Oiseau (forging his own demise) and
a soused, aphoristic Hemingway, and the entire
thing looks as if it's been cured in cigarette
smoke. **GF**
Director *Alan Rudolph* **producer** *Carolyn Pfeiffer*
exec *Shep Gordon* **script** *Rudolph, John Bradshaw*
camera *Toyomichi Kurita* **editors** *Debra T. Smith,*
Scott Brock **design** *Steven Legler* **music** *Mark*
Isham **cast** *Keith Carradine, Linda Fiorentino,*
John Lone, Wallace Shawn, Geneviève Bujold,
Geraldine Chaplin, Kevin J. O'Connor, Elsa
Raven, Ali Giron, Gailard Sartain
Running time: 126 mins
US release: Alive, Apr 15, 1988
UK release: Rank, Mar 10, 1989

MONKEY SHINES

'What if I was an animal, free to follow my
instincts?' 'That's what the devil is. Instinct –
animal instinct.' George Romero lets zombies
rest in peace for once and comes up with a
chilling and tragic portrait of the latent evil of
the human soul that knocks Cronenberg's
twisted gynos into a cocked hat. Abandoned by
friends, patronized by doctors and humiliated
by his family, quadraplegic Jason Beghe is given
a trained monkey with supernatural intelligence

to perform his household chores; but it also
sees his suppressed hatred and violence and acts
it out with devastating consequences. The
monster is not the monkey but Beghe's
subconscious and the horror derives not from
graphic violence but from his inability to
control events and, ultimately, his own feelings.
Transcending its pulp origins with a subtle,
almost casual, cinematic verve, *Monkey Shines* is
one of the best horror trips of the 1980s. **TW**
Director/script *George A. Romero* **producer**
Charles Evans **exec** *Peter Grunwald, Gerald S.*
?aonessa **camera** *James A. Contner* **editor**
Pasquale Buba **design** *Cletus Anderson* **music**
David Shire **cast** *Jason Beghe, John Pankow,*
Melanie Parker, Joyce Van Patten, Christine
Forrest, Stephen Root, Stanley Tucci, Janine
Turner, William Newman
Running time: 115 mins
US release: Orion, Jul 29, 1988

THE MONSTER SQUAD

Some revoltingly precocious schoolboys band
together to defeat Count Dracula, the
Werewolf, the Mummy and the Creature from
the Black Lagoon when these creatures emerge
from their various hidey-holes to launch an all-
out assault on Los Angeles. Frankenstein's
Monster also arrives on the scene, but turns
out to be a Good Guy. Like Fred Dekker's
début, *Night of the Creeps*, this is a none too
serious romp through horror film conventions.
It is debatable as to whether the age group at
which it is aimed will be familiar with the
classic creature features from which the
monsters are borrowed. **AB**
Director *Fred Dekker* **producer** *Jonathan A.*
Zimbert **execs** *Peter Hyams, Rob Cohen, Keith*
Barish **script** *Shane Black, Dekker* **camera**
Bradford May **editor** *James Mitchell* **design** *Albert*
Brenner **music** *Bruce Broughton* **cast** *André*
Gower, Robby Kiger, Stephen Macht, Duncan
Regehr, Tom Noonan, Brent Chalem, Ryan
Lambert, Ashley Bank, Michael Faustino
Running time: 82 mins
US release: Tri-Star, Aug 14, 1987
UK release: Columbia, Jul 15, 1988

MOON OVER PARADOR

This latterday variation on *The Prisoner of*
Zenda features a movie actor on location in a
Caribbean banana republic who is pressed into
impersonating the local dictator when the latter
drops dead at an inconvenient moment. The
result possesses neither the bite of satire nor the
momentum of farce, while the attempt at a love

interest between the actor and the strongman's mistress remains in the realm of bathos. A flashback structure, with the returned mummer recounting his experiences to a couple of cronies, tends to undercut suspense, but furnishes a pointed (if ill-advised) fade-out line when one of the listeners disbelievingly likens the narrative to something out of *Dynasty.* **TP**
Director/producer Paul Mazursky **script** Mazursky, Leon Capetanos, from story by Charles G. Booth **camera** Donald McAlpine **editor** Stewart Pappé **design** Pato Guzman **music** Maurice Jarre **cast** Richard Dreyfuss, Raul Julia, Sonia Braga, Jonathan Winters, Fernando Rey, Sammy Davis Jr., Michael Greene, Polly Holliday, Milton Gonçalves, Charo, Marianne Sägebrecht, René Kolldehoff, Paul Mazursky
Running time: 105 mins
US release: Universal, Sep 9, 1988
UK release: UIP, Jun 2, 1989

MOONWALKER
This multi-million dollar exercise in vanity filmmaking comprises an unconnected series of videos, shorts, concert footage and fanzine-style biography climaxing in a long drawn out sci-fi tale in which robot Michael saves a group of cute kids from a nasty criminal. Actually, they weren't in any danger until Michael turned up and dropped them in it. Despite an amusing claymation animation sequence set in a film studio (which inadvertently betrays the contempt Jackson feels for his fans) and a fine incidental score, it is all very tiresome.
Relegated to homevideo release in the US, *Moonwalker* cleaned up in UK cinemas. **TW**
Directors Colin Chilvers, Jerry Kramer **producers** Denis E. Jones, Kramer, Will Vinton, Jackson, Frank Dileo, Jim Blashfield **execs** Michael Jackson, Dileo **script** David Newman, from story by Jackson **camera** John Hora, Tom Ackerman, Bob Collins, Fred Elmes, Crescenzo Notarile **editors** David E. Blewitt, Mitchell Sinoway, Dale Beldin, Thomas C. Dugan, Paul Justman **design** Michael Ploog **music** Bruce Broughton **cast** Jackson, Joe Pesci, Sean Lennon, Kellie Parker
Running time: 93 mins
UK release: Warner, Dec 26, 1988

MYSTIC PIZZA
Female buddy films may be the next Hollywood genre. It's a shame, though, that Donald Petrie's effort to make a *Diner* for women simply flips the gender rôles, making the men into shallow sex objects. Still, there is plenty of comedy and honesty in this slight film about three young women who waitress at a pizza parlour in Connecticut. Julia Roberts is the beautiful one, strong enough to cope with the shortcomings of her yuppie beau. Lili Taylor is energetic and emotion-driven, unable to commit to her simple fisherman boyfriend. Annabeth Gish is the clever one, but naïve enough to lay down for a wishy-washy older man. The film's stronger character moments make up for the trite plot. **BM**
Director Donald Petrie **producers** Mark Levinson, Scott Rosenfelt **exec** Samuel Goldwyn Jr. **script** Amy Jones, Perry Howze, Randy Howze, Alfred Uhry **camera** Tim Suhrstedt **editor** Marion Rothman **design** Davi Chapman **music** David McHugh **cast** Julia Roberts, Annabeth Gish, Lili Taylor, Vincent D'Onofrio, William R. Moses, Adam Storke, Conchata Ferrell, Joanna Merlin
Running time: 104 mins
US release: Goldwyn, Oct 21, 1988

MANHUNTER

C op movies have got stuck in a rut. Either they're about a mismatched duo (*Lethal Weapon, Red Heat, Alien Nation*, etc.), or they involve a cop in an exotic environment: Chicago cops can be transferred to Los Angeles (*Beverly Hills Cop*) or Louisiana (*No Mercy*), working-class cops can wind up amidst the glitterati (*Someone to Watch Over Me*) or, in a not-so-rare mish-mash of every formulae that's on offer, black and white American cop buddies can find themselves cop-ping way out east in Platoon-land (*Saigon*).

Manhunter is different. Perhaps that's because director Michael Mann, having made a whole heap of dosh out of his rôle as mastermind of *Miami Vice*, which itself is a pretty formulaic (with the emphasis on 'pretty') cop-buddy series, has the emotional and financial security to go against the grain in his big-screen work. *Thief* (aka *Violent Streets*) was more than just a caper movie; *The Keep* was more than just a monster movie. Leonard Maltin's TV Movies and Video Guide justifies its low rating for the latter picture with the comment: 'Recommended only for connoisseurs of Strange Cinema.' *That* is a cause for *condemnation*?

Manhunter is more than just a cop movie; it is a film of such startling originality and stylishness that it stands head-and-shoulders above, not just other cop movies, but the rest of commercial cinema, whatever genre. This is one film which is a perfect fusion of sound and vision – a total Dolby experience, complete with nerve-shredding contributions from the likes of Shriekback and Iron Butterfly.

Much of the credit should go to Thomas Harris, whose novel *Red Dragon* provided the source material. Harris has dreamt up one of the edgiest heroes, and not one but *two* of the nastiest psychopaths ever to have graced or disfigured the printed page. The hero, Will Graham, is played by William Petersen, an actor (previously known for his rôle in *To Live and Die in LA*) who does indeed look as if he's got angst in his pants. He is a cop – a forensic investigator, to be precise – but he doesn't have a buddy, mismatched or otherwise. His fellow cops regard him with suspicion, because Graham is blessed, or cursed, with the ability to emphathize with the crazed serial killers he is assigned to track down. This talent doesn't exactly make for relaxed camaraderie, a couple of tubes of beer, back-slapping and boyish larks; even Graham thinks of himself as a freak, and he's trying his damnedest to be a regular guy. His last brush with a criminal mind almost cost him his life and his sanity, and now all he wants to do is settle down on the Florida Keys with his wife Molly and young son Kevin.

Mann, of course, is on home ground with Florida; pastel-coloured tones and lashings of blue seascape abound. But this domestic bliss is fractured by one of Graham's former colleagues; he wants to enlist him in the hunt for a maniac known as 'the Tooth Fairy', who has been butchering families, selected seemingly at

random, every full moon. Graham, against his better judgement, agrees to visit the Atlanta home of the Leeds family, latest victims of the (literal) lunatic. Mann, in his depiction of the scenes of carnage, shows an unusual restraint that is, perversely, ten times more horrible than if he had piled on the splatter. Like Graham, we are taken around the dead family's spacious, hi-tech house, almost like prospective buyers. It looks like a des. res., light and airy, but we see the blood stains, and we put ourselves in Graham's head even as he is inserting himself into the killer's and trying to imagine everything that happened. The corpses have already been carted off, but the horror lingers on.

Needing a kick-start, Graham picks up the scent of madness from a former quarry: Dr Hannibal Lecktor, now held in a psychiatric prison so shiny and white it might be a modern art museum. RSC actor Brian Cox plays Lecktor with a civilized malice so intense and creepy that the performance is in danger of dominating the rest of the film; it is no wonder that Harris returned to this character in *The Silence of the Lambs*, the sequel to *Red Dragon* which is already exciting curiosity as to who will direct and star in the film version.

'How did you catch me?' asks Lecktor. 'You had disadvantages,' replies Graham. 'What disadvantages?' asks Lecktor. 'You're insane,' replies Graham. But Lecktor has other ideas. 'The reason you caught me, Will, is that we're alike.' Graham flees from this intolerable notion, scurrying like a laboratory rat through architectural zigzags drained of all colour and life, back into the familiar shades of the real world. With matter-of-fact efficiency, as if it were the *only* thing to do, Lecktor goes about hitting Graham where it is likely to hurt him most: by placing his family, symbol of his longed-for normality, in jeopardy. For Lecktor and The Tooth Fairy turn out to be pen pals, and Lecktor drops Graham's address, in code, into the small-ads of scurrilous scandal rag the *National Tatler*.

It is somewhere around here, at the halfway stage, that we realize this is not shaping up to be a regular thriller plot. We realize this because we learn the Tooth Fairy's identity. He's Francis Dollarhyde – a shambling albino with a cleft palate. The manager of a film-processing laboratory in St Louis, he has been selecting his victims and casing their joints by watching the home movies that are mailed in to be developed. These, you will note, are the very same pieces of celluloid that Graham is now watching repeatedly in an attempt to pick up clues; both men are thus fingered as *just alike*, freaks and voyeurs.

The Tooth Fairy, on his murderous sprees, wears his dead grandmother's dentures – all the better to *bite* you with, my dear. This is not immediately apparent in the film, neither do we find out about the unhappy childhood which led him to murder. (Mann doesn't go in for flashbacks; he is concerned with the here and now, the surface and appearance of things.) Dollarhyde is obsessed with William Blake's 'The Great Red Dragon and the Woman Clothed with the Sun'. In his sick mind, killing is not murder but a process of *becoming*, both for murderer and victim.

In one of the most extraordinary scenes in the book, Dollarhyde goes to the Brooklyn Museum in New York and *eats* the Blake painting, but Mann leaves this out – maybe it would have looked too ridiculous, or maybe it was considered extraneous to the plot, or maybe it was thought art lovers would be offended. But Mann does retain the scene, another nod towards Blake, in which Dollarhyde takes his blind girlfriend, Reba McClane, to a tiger dentist, encouraging her to stroke the anaesthetized beast and to feel its enormous sharp teeth. (All the better to *bite* you with.) Dino De Laurentiis, whose company provided the backing, so loved this scene he wanted to call the film *Tiger* (he was loath to keep the title *Red Dragon* so soon after *Year of the Dragon*).

The Tooth Fairy sends Graham a billet-doux by despatching the sleazeback *Tatler* hack bouncing in a blazing wheelchair down the (zigzag again) ramp of an underground car park. This is the first, and most explicit, of only three killings that take place during the film. The second is a man who unwittingly, and innocently, incurs the murderer's wrath by acting in a friendly manner towards Reba McClane. Reba herself, marked out as the next victim, is saved in the nick of time, but not before Mann has whipped up the tension with a flurry of hi-tech gimmickry. Graham hits on the film lab connection and races to the rescue by Lear Jet, fixing on the killer's identity by a combination of deduction and portable fax machine.

The ending, somehow, brings no relief, even though the villain is blown away and the hero fetches up where he started – by the serene pastel waters of Florida. Will Graham has got away with it again, but he still has to live with the knowledge that he will never be one of the lads. And Mann's ending is sneaky; intentionally or accidentally, he changes it from the book's just enough to make the fadeout seem only a temporary respite. No buddies, and no exotic environment, unless you count the strange, uncharted territory of the human soul.

ANNE BILLSON

MISSISSIPPI BURNING

Alan Parker makes his films in anger. The screeds of venom scratched across *Pink Floyd The Wall* or *Midnight Express* first deadened the mind, then crushed out all feelings. And even a candy-floss subject like *Fame* could accommodate a heavy-handed scene drawing attention to social injustice and its director's sense of indignation.

Although Parker sometimes says he was inspired into movies by the work of Ken Loach, the British director of *Kes* and *Cathy Come Home*, he could never make films like Loach's. He's too much in love with operatic effects and the creation of 'atmosphere' to hit consistently at emotional truth. In consequence, while there's no doubting Parker's visual flair and facility with actors, his films often seem blatantly manipulative and pretentiously Gothic.

With *Angel Heart*, the expressionist visuals turned a pulp story into bombast, but Parker was always going to seem a better filmmaker when he got hold of a 'big' subject. *Mississippi Burning* makes the case. Here anger seems a relevant response, transforming his normal failings into strengths. Sometimes, it is true, Parker the Wrecker is on hand with his sledgehammer, but that force of fury also takes what could have been just another of this year's formulaic buddy-buddy cop movies, yoked to another series of dramatic contortions around recent historical events, and lifts the film right away from the limitations of either 'genre'.

Set in 1964, *Mississippi Burning* is a highly-fictionalized account of an FBI investigation into the murder of three civil rights activists, one black and two white, in the Deep South. The historical 'inaccuracies' provoked complaints from several quarters – the blacks should not have been shown as largely passive, and FBI officers just didn't behave that way. But when a filmmaker turns history into cinema he's aiming to address contemporary audiences – distortions are a necessary part of the package. The filmmaker's right to 'use' the past is not absolute, but Parker has made a film that's much more interesting than what some critics seemed to be demanding – an account of how grass-roots radicalism transformed the situation of blacks in the 1960s. *Mississippi Burning* brings out precisely the imperviousness of a Southern community to change – the intractability of economic and social oppression. At a time when the anti-liberal values of small-town America still seem in the ascendant, and when the Supreme Court is whittling away at the achievements of the 1960s, the film's underlying message is that all those battles have to be fought again, and much harder than before.

When Willem Dafoe and Gene Hackman put in their first appearance – two cops motoring into Mississippi – their character-defining banter may cause some gritting of teeth as viewers prepare for another series of exchanges on the way one cop hates the way the other picks his nose, eats his food or talks to girls. But this is not the film's opening, and the scene does not define its approach. Already we have seen images of apartheid (separate water fountains) and violence (a burning church and the murder of the three activists). If anything, the cut-and-thrust between the world-weary Anderson (Hackman) and the younger man, Ward, comes across as somehow irrelevant to what has just happened on the screen.

Ward believes that things can be changed. In a sense he represents the spirit of radical optimism, carrying liberal values to a community of bigots who don't like being told how to run their affairs. What he lacks is any understanding of the people he's working amongst. Anderson, by contrast, grew up in the South and knows about racial hatred from experience. He tells Ward of his father's justification for having poisoned a coloured neighbour's mule: 'If you ain't better than a nigger, who are you better than?' Having grown up with it, he's learned to accept it.

At first, it seems that Parker's instinct is to damn Ward, despite his idealism, as just an intellectual bereft of street sense. There's a ridiculous scene just after the investigative duo's arrival in town, when Ward not only ignores the lines in a segregated diner but puts some questions to a silent black kid, who is consequently treated brutally by the Ku Klux Klan. Two points are being made here – about the system of apartheid and the rule of fear – but a little less partiality on Parker's part might have made for a more authentic feel.

The antipathy gives way first to gentle mockery. Ward is the sort of policeman who would now try to solve crimes from behind a computer terminal. He tends to indulge in overkill (and could have been running the anti-terrorist show in *Die Hard*). When the local hotel refuses to accommodate FBI members, Ward orders his subordinate to buy up the place. When a marsh needs searching, he buses in naval reserves for an ultimately futile scour through the boggy waters. And when the car that the murdered boys were driving is found, a line of investigators recruited by Ward dip their fine-cut cloth into the river. Parker evidently wants us to laugh at these men in suits (Anderson cultivates a shirt-sleeves approach).

Not only does Ward not understand the people he's dealing with, he doesn't know how to elicit information from them. Anderson can identify the owner of a car by dropping into the hairdresser; Ward has to get on the line to Washington. But Anderson doesn't have his boss's determination to change things. He wants to extract the information by stealth, lock up the culprits and get out. There's a sense of powerlessness and failure rooted in Hackman's performance. It's only when he sees his hairdresser informant lying in a hospital bed, beaten to a pulp by her husband, that he accepts the need to go at the roots of racism. Ward has shown him what must be done, now he will show Ward how to do it.

Anderson's informant is the Deputy's wife (Frances McDormand) Mrs Pell. She could be the grown-up version of the little girl who spouts racist gibberish at Debra Winger in Costa Gavras' *Betrayed* – even now only dimly aware that what she's been hearing all her life may be wrong: 'You get told it enough times you believe it. You live it, breathe it, marry it,' she declares while preparing to reveal where the three bodies have been hidden. Here, where he shows the courage required to challenge a community's racist assumptions, Parker shows unwonted subtlety. As Mrs Pell leaves the street where a brutalized black's body has been dumped from a passing car, her hand on a black man's shoulder expresses solidarity. Caught by her husband as she plays with the child of a black neighbour, the nervous visual glances she casts in his direction shows how his racist hatred entwines with the loss of self-esteem her childlessness represents and results in her fear of him. At the end of the film, a battered survivor, she stands among the debris of her house, declaring, 'There's enough people around here know what I did was right.'

That belief may enable her to carry on in the town, but it doesn't change anything. The crime is solved – the Deputy and his co-conspirators all receive jail sentences – and the cops reach some degree of mutual understanding, but there's no sense of triumph, no sense that racism has been dispersed.

If Parker's début, *Bugsy Malone*, suggested he was a singing-and-dancing director, the chronicling of a character's descent into hell (a location later visited by Johnny Favourite in *Angel Heart*) in *Midnight Express* gave a truer insight into his emotional centre. Parker uses his anger to fight despair. His political hopes are dogged by nightmare. That's why his films sometimes get stuck in a cul-de-sac, as Parker sets about beating his own and the audience's heads against a wall. Anderson's violence – a heavy is hired to extract information from the mayor with threats of castration; a mock execution is staged to frighten one of the criminals into revealing the truth; Anderson goes after the Deputy with a razor blade – may not be truthful to the way FBI officers behaved in 1964 (and I'm pretty certain it's not Parker's recommended solution to all problems), but it's an honest account of how racist bigots make him *feel*. And it's what he sets out to convey to the audience with the repeated – some felt to the point of tedium – sequences of houses being burnt and blacks being beaten, cut or strung up from trees.

It's obviously not subtle cinema. And Parker seems blind to the fact that tough thinking can be as important as tough deeds. But, in the year of the buddy-buddy cop movie, *Mississippi Burning* was the one film that diverted the formulae into significant statement. And who can blame Parker if he wants to shout from the roof-tops his fury at the complacency of the times we live in? After all, anger *can* be a healthy emotion.

JAMES PARK

THE NAKED CELL

Never mind the docu-drama trimmings and the pseudo-Joycean monologues, this movie is pure sexploitation. Vicky Jeffrey plays the young lady with memory problems who finds herself locked up in a mental hospital after killing a man during love-making. Naturally, while so interned, she likes to take her clothes off and deliver long, moody, sexually-candid soliloquies. Pity the poor lady. And pity the poor filmgoer who goes to see this movie, prompted by the hype written by some critics about deep feminist statements. **HK**
Director John Crome **producer** Georgina De Lacy **exec** Laura Gregory **script** Berkeley Burdock **camera** Brian Herlihy **editor** Peter Dansie **design** James Dillon **music** Barry Guard **cast** Vicky Jeffrey, Richard Fallon, Jacquetta May, Yvonne Bonnamy, Jill Spurrier, Nicolas Lamb
Running time: 90 mins
UK release: Premier Releasing, Jul 8, 1988

THE NAKED GUN: FROM THE FILES OF POLICE SQUAD! 👍

Blink, and you might well have missed Police Squad!, the (extremely) short-lived TV show conceived and directed by the team which made Airplane!, and starring Leslie Nielsen as Lieutenant Frank Drebin, who can't seem to move without setting off some cataclysmic chain-reaction: a conflagration here, or an international incident there. The Naked Gun, in which Drebin is up against dastardly Ricardo Montalban's plot to assassinate Queen Elizabeth during a royal visit to Los Angeles, is the same mix as before: a mixture of sight gags and surrealism, groan-making puns, pratfalls and smutty innuendo, all packed so densely that it takes a second viewing even to begin to prise all the jokes apart. You could, if you were feeling mean-spirited enough, dismiss the humour as base or childish, but the result is so irresistible that, really, no excuses should be needed. **AB**
Director David Zucker **producer** Robert K. Weiss **execs** Jerry Zucker, Jim Abrahams, David Zucker **script** Jerry Zucker, Abrahams, David Zucker, Pat Proft **camera** Robert Stevens **editor** Michael Jablow **design** John J. Lloyd **music** Ira Newborn **cast** Leslie Nielsen, Priscilla Presley, Ricardo Montalban, George Kennedy, O. J. Simpson, Susan Beaubian, Nancy Marchand
Running time: 85 mins
US release: Paramount, Dec 2, 1988
UK release: UIP, Feb 10, 1989

THE NATURE OF THE BEAST

The title and opening subjective camera movements promise a horror story, but what follows is a far-from-gripping tale of unemployment, squabbling families and loss of hope among the inhabitants of a small textile town in Lancashire. Franco Rosso does himself no favours by deliberately reminding us of Ken Loach's Kes: a scene where the beast-obsessed youth says rude things to his sleeping grandfather, whom he loves, comes across as a misunderstanding of the scene where the bird-obsessed youth of the earlier film uttered expletives to his half-brother (Freddie Fletcher, here cast as the lad's father), whom he hated. Lynton Dearden's features are too inexpressive to convey the central character's emotional turmoil and the filmmakers never get close to making the 'beast' into effective allegory. **JP**
Director Franco Rosso **producer** Joanna Smith **script** Janni Howker, based on her novel **camera** Nat Crosby **editor** George Akers **design** Jamie Leonard **music** Stanley Myers, Hans Zimmer **cast** Lynton Dearden, Paul Simpson, Tony Melody, Freddie Fletcher, Dave Hill, Robert Kerr, David Fleeshman
Running time: 96 mins
UK release: Cannon, Nov 25, 1988

◄ FILM ►

THE NAVIGATOR

Director Vincent Ward **producer** John Maynard **exec** Gary Hannam **script** Ward, Kely Lyons, Geoff Chapple **camera** Geoffrey Simpson **editor** John Scott **design** Sally Campbell **music** Davood A. Tabrizi **cast** Bruce Lyons, Chris Haywood, Hamish McFarlane, Marshall Napier, Noel Appleby, Paul Livingston, Sarah Pierse
Running time: 91 mins
UK release: Recorded Releasing, May 12, 1989

NEW ADVENTURES OF PIPPI LONGSTOCKING

Flop kidpic based on the popular series of books about a fun-loving girl with magical powers and no respect for adult notions of good behaviour.
Director Ken Annakin **producer** Gary Mehlman, Walter Moshay **exec** Mishaal Kamal Adham **script** Annakin, from books by Astrid Lindgren **camera** Roland Smith **editor** Ken Zemke **design** Jack Senter **music** Misha Segal **cast** Tami Erin, Eileen Brennan, Dennis Dugan, Dianne Hull, George Di Cenzo, John Schuck, Dick Van Patten,

David Seaman Jr., Cory Crow, J. D. Dickinson, Chub Bailly
Running time: 100 mins
US release: Columbia, Jul 29, 1988

NEW YORK STORIES

Martin Scorsese assays comedy and nearly succeeds, Francis Coppola tries whimsy and gets covered in goo and Woody Allen returns to fantasy with hilarious results. This rare triptych started with Allen and should have stayed with him. In Scorsese's opening episode, Nick Nolte is an artist amusingly besotted with his youthful assistant. Coppola and daughter Sofia wrote his truly awful contribution, in which a little girl lives alone in a fancy New York hotel and wastes a lot of money bringing her globetrotting parents together. Allen stars in his own episode, in which his mother, the Jewish mother to end all Jewish mothers, hounds him from the sky above Manhattan. **BM**
LIFE LESSONS
Director Martin Scorsese **producer** Barbara De Fina **script** Richard Price **camera** Nestor Almendros **editor** Thelma Schoonmaker **design** Kristi Zea **cast** Nick Nolte, Rosanna Arquette, Patrick O'Neal, Jesse Borrego, Steve Buscemi, Peter Gabriel
LIFE WITHOUT ZOE
Director Francis Coppola **producers** Fred Roos, Fred Rucks **script** Francis Coppola, Sofia Coppola **camera** Vittorio Storaro **editor** Barry Malkin **design** Dean Tavoularis **music** Carmine Coppola **cast** Heather McComb, Talia Shire, Giancarlo Giannini, Paul Herman, James Keane, Don Novello, Selim Tlili, Carmine Coppola, Carole Bouquet
OEDIPUS WRECKS
Director/script Woody Allen **producer** Robert Greenhut **execs** Jack Rollins, Charles H. Joffe **camera** Sven Nykvist **editor** Susan E. Morse **design** Santo Loquasto **cast** Woody Allen, Mia Farrow, Julie Kavner, Mae Questel, Marvin Chatinover, Jessie Keosian, George Schindler, Bridgit Ryan, Mayor Koch
Running time: 123 mins
US release: BV, Mar 1, 1989

NICKY AND GINO (Dominick and Eugene in US)

This poor man's *Rain Man* starts low-key but ends up pulling hard on every available emotional lever, with Tom Hulce never quite at ease in the rôle of mental retard. Ray Liotta owes brother Hulce, who's putting him through medical school with the money he earns as a garbage collector. Most of the time, Liotta's a

loving brother, but he can also be an aggressive brute, and fears he's like the father who pushed his twin down the stairs. Already distraught by the complexities of life at home, Hulce is understandably upset when he witnesses the death of a young friend, but kidnapping the household's other baby marks too abrupt a transformation for a guy who can't kill a rat or deal with the hassle he gets on the street. The battalion of police mustered for the finale detract from the impact of the brother-to-brother revelations. **JP**
Director Robert M. Young **producers** Marvin Minoff, Mike Farrell **script** Alvin Sargent, Corey Blechman **camera** Curtis Clark **editor** Arthur Coburn **design** Doug Kraner **music** Trevor Jones **cast** Tom Hulce, Ray Liotta, Jamie Lee Curtis, Todd Graff, Mimi Cecchini, Robert Levine, Bill Cobbs, David Strathairn
Running time: 109 mins
US release: Orion, Mar 18, 1988
UK release: Rank, Mar 31, 1989

NICO (Above the Law in US)

Brutally humourless, Nico is distinguished only by its simplistic diatribe against clandestine CIA operations in Vietnam and South America. Ex-agency operative-turned-cop Steven Seagal discovers a CIA-approved plot to assassinate a State senator set to expose agency links with South American drug smugglers. Seagal, former model builder to the stars, has fashioned a vehicle unrelenting in its machismo addiction to karate fights, concrete facial tension and lovingly administered torture. Along with rather dubious revisionistic attitudes to the Mafia - Seagal sends his family away to be protected by portly Italian-Americans in sunglasses - Seagal's complete disinterest in following the law is buttressed hypocritically by his constant proselytizing against those who consider themselves above that law. Contemporary relevance is ignored in favour of a sleek, sadistic thriller, festooned with corpses and a brutalized mentality that wears down any emotional or political dimension. **SD**
Director Andrew Davis **producers** Steven Seagal, Davis **exec** Robert Solo **script** Steven Pressfield, Ronald Shusett, Davis **camera** Robert Steadman **editor** Michael Brown **design** Maher Ahmad **music** David M. Frank **cast** Steven Seagal, Pam Grier, Henry Silva, Ron Dean, Daniel Faraldo, Sharon Stone, Nicholas Kusenko, Joe V. Greco, Chelcie Ross, Thalamus Rasulala
Running time: 99 mins

US release: Warner, Apr 8, 1988
UK release: Warner, Nov 18, 1988

NIGHT ZOO (Un Zoo la nuit)

Jean-Claude Lauzon risks all in switching his sordid crime thriller into a lyrical love story between a father and son halfway through - the miracle is that he pulls it off. Vicious small-time hoodlum Marcel (Maheu), raped in prison prior to his release, returns to the ugly Quebec underworld where he is pursued by two bent cops on the hunt for some missing loot. Marcel is delivered from evil as, seeking to bring some joy into the days of his ailing, melancholy old dad (Le Bel), he takes him on a fishing trip in the mountains. Leaving the foul human menagerie behind, Lauzon even sends the pair on a hunting expedition to a zoo at night, but not even that contrived ending can spoil the tender mood which finally prevails in this bold offering from the Canadian new wave. **GF**
Director/script Jean-Claude Lauzon **producers** Roger Frappier, Pierre Gendron **camera** Guy Dufaux **editor** Michel Arcand **design** Jean-Baptiste Tard **music** Jean Corriveau **cast** Roger Le Bel, Gilles Maheu, Lynne Adams, Lorne Brass, Germain Houde
Running time: 115 mins
US release: Film Dallas, Mar 4, 1988
UK release: Hendring, Mar 17, 1989

A NIGHTMARE ON ELM STREET 4: THE DREAM MASTER

In this latest variation on Wes Craven's original theme, sleazy child-killer Freddy Krueger has been transformed from the genuinely frightening bogeyman of the first film in the series into a horror equivalent of James Bond - popping up in his victims' dreams with a would-be nasty wisecrack before dispatching yet another disposable teenager to a spectacular fate at the hands of the ingenious special effects department. The plot, in which Freddy's attempts to slaughter a new generation of Elm Street children are thwarted by a young girl with special dream powers, is no more than a threadbare excuse for sequences such as the one in which a fitness fanatic is turned into a cockroach, or for images such as the pizza made of shrieking human souls. Freddy's recent appearances on American television and in the toyshops would suggest he is now well on the way to becoming a malevolent variation on 'My Little Pony'. **AB**
Director Renny Harlin **producers** Robert Shaye, Rachel Talalay **execs** Sara Risher, Stephen Diener

script Brian Helgeland, Scott Pierce, from story by William Kotzwinkle, Helgeland, based on characters created by Wes Craven **camera** Steven Fierberg **editors** Michael N. Knue, Chuck Weiss **design** Mick Strawn, C. J. Strawn **sfx** Image Engineering - Peter M. Chesney, Larry Fioritto, Lou Carlucci **music** Craig Safan **cast** Robert Englund, Rodney Eastman, Danny Hassel, Andras Jones, Tuesday Knight, Toy Newkirk, Ken Sagoes, Brooke Theiss, Lisa Wilcox, Brooke Bundy
Running time: 92 mins (originally 93)
US release: New Line, Aug 19, 1988
UK release: Palace, May 5, 1989

976 - EVIL

Robert Englund's first foray behind the camera is a film that fits snugly into the generic definitions his *alter-ego*, Freddie Krueger, has been mercilessly carving out in the *Nightmare on Elm Street* series. The story of a bullied, disturbed boy (O'Bryan) latching on to a dial-a-death telephone service that imbues him with demonic powers, offers an intriguing perspective on the horror genre. O'Bryan's acts of revenge on those who humiliated him are executed with panache and the enclosed, insular sets are superbly lit in gloomy, neon colours, with Englund fashioning an eerie sense of the fantastic amid the twisted wreckage of the boy's relationship with his manic, alcohol-sated mother (Dennis). Never quite rising to the climactic scenes of suburban destruction, *976-Evil* is more successful in the intimate, painful moments, as when the boy tries to establish a relationship with his biker cousin's girlfriend, only to accidentally kill her. Pathos - a quality too often lacking in current horror output - is adroitly mixed with the darker menace of the phone service, which gleefully deals out power and death. In humanizing a staple horror narrative, Englund brings a gentle potency to a recently near-barren and exhausted genre. **SD**
Director Robert Englund **producer** Lisa M. Hansen **exec** Paul Hertzberg **script** Rhet Topham, Brian Helgeland **camera** Paul Elliott **editor** Stephen Myers **design** David Brian Miller **music** Thomas Chase, Steve Rucker **cast** Stephen Geoffreys, Patrick O'Bryan, Sandy Dennis, Jim Metzler, Maria Rubell, Robert Picardo, Lezlie Dean
Running time: 100 mins
US release: New Line, Mar 24, 1989
UK release: Medusa, Dec 9, 1988

1969 ⚑

Vietnam, civil rights, man on the moon, Woodstock, student rights, the awakening of political consciousness among American youth with all that to choose from, you'd think Ernest On Golden Pond Thompson could come up with something more interesting than this small-town drama that attempts to put the decade in microcosm through the lives of two teenagers, only to overdose on clichés and marketable nostalgia. Thereafter, it's Saturday Night Live goes to the 1960s as Kiefer Sutherland makes meaningful speeches that would make Groovy Wordbender cringe while Robert Downey freaks out on uppers and gets arrested in time for the whole town to rescue him when they realize how unfair the Vietnam War really is. **TW**
Director/script Ernest Thompson producers Daniel Grodnick, Bill Badalato exec Thomas Coleman camera Jules Brenner editor Michael Anderson design Marcia Hinds music Michael Small cast Robert Downey Jr., Kiefer Sutherland, Bruce Dern, Mariette Hartley, Winona Ryder, Joanna Cassidy, Christopher Wynne, Keller Kuhn
Running time: 90 mins
US release: Atlantic, Nov 18, 1988

NO MAN'S LAND

Charlie Sheen brings some credibility to this weak story, playing a Mephistopheles-like car thief entrancing the squeaky-clean rookie cop (Sweeney) despatched to infiltrate his gang. The anonymity of the camera work only serves to highlight the often static nature of the narrative in which Sheen lures Sweeney into the high life and almost persuades him to 'go native'. Sweeney is vacuous as the callow youth, but Sheen, with his tasteful yuppie affectations and twisted motivations, manages to produce some pace - injecting into his character a prowling, trapped sense of claustrophobia. But Werner constantly undercuts him with the mundanity of his imagery and the faltering development of the narrative. **SD**
Director Peter Werner producers Joseph Stern, Dick Wolf execs Ron Howard, Tony Ganz script Wolf camera Hiro Narita editor Steve Cohen design Paul Peters music Basil Poledouris cast Charlie Sheen, D.B. Sweeney, Randy Quaid, Lara Harris, Bill Duke, R.D. Call, Arlen Dean Snyder, M. Emmet Walsh
Running time: 106 mins
US release: Orion, Oct 23, 1987
UK release: Rank, Sep 23, 1988

OBSESSED

Apparently derived from real events, this variation on the vengeance formula achieves some originality in the way it plays with audience expectations. After a hit-and-run incident leaves a young boy dead, and legal technicalities allow the killer to remain free, the mother takes retribution into her own hands. Usually the basis for mindless fantasies of redress, the situation is instead used to question the validity of the mother's escalating acts of harassment. Kerrie Keane's portrayal of the disturbed parent and Saul Rubinek as the pathetic and terrified driver contribute to the film's unsettlingly ambivalent tone in this melancholic production. **PB**
Director Robin Spry producers Spry, Jamie Brown execs Neil J.P. Leger, Paul E. Painter script Douglas Bowie camera Ron Stannett editor Diann Ilnicki design Claude Paré music Jean-Alain Roussel cast Kerrie Keane, Daniel Pilon, Saul Rubinek, Lynne Griffin, Mireille Deyglun, Ken Pogue, Vlasta Vrana, Colleen Dewhurst, Alan Thicke, Leif Anderson
Running time: 103 mins
US release: New Star, Nov 4, 1988

OUT COLD

A thriller in the mould of Alfred Hitchcock's The Trouble with Harry, Out Cold confirms director Malcolm Mowbray's deftness at handling physical comedy – he previously did A Private Function. The tribulations of disposing of a frozen corpse (and one with a lollipop stuck to its forehead to boot) provide a series of hilarious set pieces. In this Mowbray is well served by his cast: John Lithgow's emotionally clumsy butcher (who thinks he's responsible for his partner's death); Teri Garr's sly femme fatale (the actual murderess) and Randy Quaid's powerfully venal private eye. The result is a great small film. **PH**
Director Malcolm Mowbray producers George G. Braunstein, Ron Hamady execs John Daly, Derek Gibson script Howard Glasser, George Malko camera Tony Pierce-Roberts editor Dennis M. Hill design Linda Pearl music Michel Colombier cast John Lithgow, Teri Garr, Randy Quaid, Bruce McGill
Running time: 91 mins
US release: Hemdale, Mar 3, 1989

THE NAVIGATOR

For some time now aliens have been dropping in on Hollywood. They may come to learn, like the gorgeous blonde in *My Stepmother Is an Alien* who is distracted from her mission by the discovery of sexual pleasure. Or they may come to teach, like the weird-headed creature in *Alien Nation* who dispenses lessons in racial tolerance to his cop buddy.

Such meetings between extra-terrestrial and humanoid offer filmmakers a vantage point to 'explore' the differences between cultures (while still casting the representative of the 'other' culture from the ranks of bankable stardom). There's a storehouse of culture-clash comedy to draw upon, and a battery of special effects to play with. But it's rare for films of this sort to give any sense of just how weird late-twentieth-century America might seem to outsiders, from whatever side of the temporal spectrum they arrive.

The aliens in Vincent Ward's *The Navigator* come not from another planet, but from fourteenth-century England. After tunnelling through to the other side of the globe, they arrive at contemporary New Zealand. By looking at that world through *their* eyes, Ward encourages *us* to look at today's urban civilization anew. His starting point was the question: How would such visitors react to a modern highway, with juggernauts pounding the tarmac in interminable procession? Initially perhaps they would be like children, enthralled by the wonder of the thing; quickly they would realize the danger, and how impervious are such motor-driven beasts to human intervention. In the film, that scene conveys the mix of wonder and terror, heaven and hell that makes up the twentieth-century experience of six visitors from mediaeval Cumbria.

Their journey has been inspired by the visions of Griffin (Hamish McFarlane), a nine-year-old boy. We are led into the make-believe that this rag-tag band have slipped through time, but Ward also makes clear that the main action is the boy's *re-telling* of the vision to his friends over a long night at the bottom of a mine. This explication seems unnecessary at first, a sort of apology for having led us into such a 'big' fiction. Ward must want us to think of the film's main story as reflecting *both* how the mediaeval mind might have imagined the modern world, if it had some of the necessary information, *and* how the returned traveller might elaborate upon the strangeness of what he had truly seen for the benefit of wide-eyed kids and innocents who had never yet gone beyond the bounds of their village. The point is that there is no single response to reality; it's our culture that decides *how* we see the world around us.

The film develops certain parallels between the situation confronting the Cumbrians and that of the New Zealanders. Both peoples attempt to fight off their contemporary plagues by isolating themselves from the rest of the world. As the

film opens, the fourteenth-century villagers await the return of Connor, who has been a long time away. He arrives, heavy with despair, to report the breakdown of social order: 'There are people no more than animals; you can trust no one.' Initially he believes that there is still time to take action, but that hope is promptly discounted by the sight of refugees, swollen with boils, being driven away by the terrified inhabitants of a neighbouring village. It is Griffin's vision that suggests a way to put a spike on the highest spire in Christendom – an action that could cause the plague to 'leap over' their village.

As the travellers leave their world, a skeleton passes across the moon. The image later connects explicitly to that of the Grim Reaper in a TV AIDS warning. Alongside, there is a report of nuclear stockpiles – a threat made manifest when some of the travellers see a nuclear submarine: a great whale that rises from, and then sinks back into, hissing water.

The point is not simply to make an obvious link between mediaeval Europe and contemporary New Zealand. There's a third, more persistent, image on the TV screen – a bird that leaps upon a running hare. This connects the two modern plagues to the natural world, which isn't so weird if you think of AIDS and nuclear energy as, like the Black Death, the explosive products of population growth and technological progress. These modern blights are something that cannot be simply dismissed as 'external' to the world we live in: they must be accepted in order that they can be challenged. Despair must be bolstered by faith.

For the time-travellers, what makes our modern world hellish is not the presence of sickness and death (which are kept out of view), but machines. The 'primitives' needed some sort of weird contraption to pound the earth and clear a way through to the other side, but there was a relation between it and the men who worked it. What's terrifying about those great lorries on the freeway, or the car that emerges from the dark to knock a man to the ground and then drive on, is their impersonality. And Connor, who sets off for the church on his own, sees a world of total horror, albeit one to which he is sensitized by illness. He meets no people, only these monstrous machines. As he stands in the middle of a rubbish yard, metal jaws lock and unlock above him. Pursued by a dumper truck, he makes his getaway on the front of a fast-moving train – his face contorted into an image of horrified distress.

These machines are turned by the mediaeval eye into forces of nature, and agents of terror. Human beings don't ever emerge from them, and the machines never respond to the men who pass in front of them. They have the force of the plague itself and, in the modern age, it is these machines that, like the plague in times before, turn people into beasts.

The one group of contemporary humans presented to the Cumbrians are benign, jovial and willing to assist the visitors (although they're not particularly inquisitive about *who* they are). Their gentleness seems so unrealistic that one has to keep on reminding oneself that they are the imagined creations of travellers

who don't really understand the profit motive: 'The church . . . is poor?' remarks a traveller in amazement when told why the workers had been unable to complete work on a spike for the church. These modern workers co-operate because the factory is to be closed down, and because they are almost encouraged by these strange visitors to take pleasure in the work.

Where the Cumbrians are earnest and filled with the urgency of their mission, the New Zealanders seem complacent. Their world is threatened, their livelihoods are about to be taken away; yet they happily amble about the forecourt of their soon-to-be-closed foundry. We don't know where they are heading or what their lives are like, but there's a smugness that seems like the beginning of self-defeat.

It's against that attitude that Ward seems to be angling himself as he confronts the contemporary Kiwis with these self-absorbed arrivals from another time-zone, and their quasi-childish ability to look at the modern world with a sense of wonder. A real time-traveller from a simple pre-industrial world would probably suffer instant breakdown in the face of the noisy, clanking mess of fumes and destitution, but when Martin (Paul Livingston), the philosopher among the travellers and the one who is dressed most like our image of mediaeval man, struggles out from the tunnel and gazes down upon the modern city, he remarks that, with so many lights glowing, this must be the 'good', the obverse of the plague-ravaged landscape from which they have come. The fact that the spire has been occluded by skyscrapers indicates that things are not so rosy but, as Martin reaches the church, the intense gaze he turns skywards indicates that he has retained the power to be amazed.

What stops modern man developing that state of mind, which is the precondition for accepting, and fighting, the plague, is an inability to see what *is* extraordinary. And that's because the strange is made banal by being so much present. When Griffin, whose vision has already led his band almost to the end of their journey, finds himself confronted by a bank of multiple TV sets, he loses his power to act as guide. Only when his eyes have been covered can he again see well enough to lead the troupe to his destination.

As Griffin gets closer to the church, he also becomes aware that one of their number will die – in his vision a gloved hand slips on the rungs of a ladder, a body falls through the air. Back at the village, realizing that the plague is upon him, his concern is to assure the villagers he will be its only victim. He accepts the sacrifice of his life to assure the survival of the community. It is not a modern attitude. As he shows the community's visionary passing away – the film's final image is that of his coffin floating in the water – Ward seems to chronicle the disappearance of those most important faculties – a sense of wonder, the power to dream, the willingness to work for the greater good. *The Navigator* shows us what we are, and what we lack.

JAMES PARK

PAPERHOUSE

Bold in ambition but curiously half-hearted in execution, Bernard Rose's directorial début doesn't hold a candle to Neil Jordan's *The Company of Wolves*, another British film about the fantasies of an unhappy, sickly girl hovering at the door into adolescence. After Charlotte Burke realizes her waking self can etch the contents of her dream house, an initial preoccupation with providing ice-cream, toys and whatever else its crippled boy resident desires, gradually gives way, as her fever rises, to darker thoughts and fears. Unfortunately, Rose can't handle actors and screenwriter Matthew Jacobs fails to develop any sense of real interchange between the two youngsters in the world of dreams. What should have been intriguing and moving ends up cold and affectless. **JR**
Director *Bernard Rose* **producers** *Sarah Radclyffe, Tim Bevan* **execs** *M. J. Peckos, Dan Ireland* **script** *Matthew Jacobs, from novel by Catherine Storr* **camera** *Mike Southon* **editor** *Dan Rae* **design** *Frank Walsh, Ann Tilby* **music** *Hans Zimmer, Stanley Myers* **cast** *Charlotte Burke, Ben Cross, Glenne Headly, Elliot Spears, Gemma Jones*
Running time: 92 mins
US release: Vestron, Feb 17, 1989
UK release: Vestron, Jun 2, 1989

PARENTS

Director *Bob Balaban* **producer** *Bonnie Palef* **execs** *Mitchell Cannold, Steven Reuther* **script** *Christopher Hawthorne* **camera** *Ernest Day, Robin Vidgeon* **editor** *Bill Pankow* **design** *Andris Hausmanis* **music** *Jonathan Elias* **cast** *Randy Quaid, Mary Beth Hurt, Sandy Dennis, Bryan Madorsky, Juno Mills-Cockell, Kathryn Grody, Deborah Rush, Graham Jarvis*
Running time: 82 mins
US release: Vestron, Jan 27, 1989

PARIS BY NIGHT

David Hare claims to have written this would-be thriller in six weeks; it shows. The story of a female politician who semi-accidentally murders the man she thinks is blackmailing her has obvious potential, but Hare's shoddy plotting kills off both plausibility and suspense; and without the forceful presence of Charlotte Rampling, the story's only 'strong' character, the film would be unwatchable. By failing to convey the textures of Rampling's life as a member of the European Parliament (everybody treats her as important, but we never understand why), Hare not only throws away the opportunities presented by the Eurocratic setting - a few cheap visual jokes are all we get - but raises doubts about how much credibility can be attached to the political pontifications he has scattered through the script. That so little is made of the night-time locations is a disgrace, but it's all too symptomatic of this city-hopping movie's lack of atmosphere. **JP**
Director/script *David Hare* **producer** *Patrick Cassavetti* **exec** *Edward R. Pressman* **camera** *Roger Pratt* **editor** *George Akers* **design** *Anthony Pratt* **music** *Georges Delerue* **cast** *Charlotte Rampling, Michael Gambon, Robert Hardy, Iain Glen, Andrew Ray, Jane Asher, Linda Bassett, Niamh Cusack*
Running time: 101 mins
UK release: Virgin, Jun 2, 1989

PASCALI'S ISLAND

An Aegean island early this century, when the Ottoman Empire was in its death throes, is the atmospheric setting for what starts out as a period thriller, then merges into a character study involving a Turkish spy (Kingsley) and an enigmatic Englishman (Dance) whose *soigné* exterior masks nefarious intentions. Both the ubiquitous leading players are better used than has sometimes been the case, and on the whole this is a witty and enjoyable demonstration of traditional narrative skills, though marred a bit by some overstated melodrama in the closing stages. **TP**
Director *James Dearden* **producer** *Eric Fellner* **exec** *Cary Brokaw* **script** *Dearden from book by Barry Unsworth* **camera** *Roger Deakins* **editor** *Edward Marnier* **design** *Andrew Mollo* **music** *Loek Dikker* **cast** *Ben Kingsley, Charles Dance, Helen Mirren, Stefan Gryff, George Murcell, Nadim Sawalha*
Running time: 104 mins
US release: Avenue, Jul 22, 1988
UK release: Virgin, Jan 13, 1989

PATHFINDER (Veiviseren/Ofelas)

The first film ever made in the Lapp language is a genuine wide-screen surprise. The hollow-eyed Tchudes come on as brutally and remorselessly as any horror-film monster, pursuing the boy (Gaup) whose family they have already killed, but writer-director Nils Gaup lays in sufficient fresh material from Northern legend to enliven any generic borrowings. And, despite some careless camera work, the snowy landscape is deployed to

impressive effect, particularly in a climactic sequence when the boy leads the Tchudes to their demise on a snow-swept rockface and the powerhouse killing-machines become desperate men struggling on the end of a rope. The script doesn't care enough about the community saved through the boy's actions to render the ending, when he's acknowledged to be their new 'pathfinder', as epiphanic as may have been intended, but this was one of the most refreshing movie experiences of the year. **JP**
Director/script Nils Gaup *producer* John M. Jacobsen *camera* Erling Thurmann-Andersen *editor* Niels Pagh Andersen *design* Harald Egede-Nissen *music* Nils Aslak Valkeapää, Marius Müller, Kjetil Bjerkestrand *cast* Mikkel Gaup, Ingvald Guttorm, Ellen Anne Buljo, Inger Utsi, Svein Scharffenberg, Helgi Skulasin, Knut Walle
Running time: 86 mins
UK release: Guild, Sep 23, 1988

PATTY HEARST

Paul Schrader's semi-documentary interpretation of the events surrounding Patty Hearst's kidnapping by a terrorist group, followed by her subsequent indoctrination and involvement in their criminal activities, is less personally motivated than his urban-revenge scripts (*Taxi Driver, Hardcore*) or his formalized dramatic essay on Japanese writer Yukio Mishima. Schrader finds absurd humour in the callous ineptitude of Hearst's captors, presenting her relationship with the self-obsessed terrorists, and their incessant posturing, with formalist precision. He constantly shifts from documentary candour to abstract montage to chillingly direct observation. The result is a consideration of Hearst's plight that fashions a non-judgemental essay on the mental vulnerability of an isolated individual. **SD**
Director Paul Schrader *producer* Marvin Worth *execs* Thomas Coleman, Michael Rosenblatt *script* Nicholas Kazan, based on book by Patria Campbell Hearst *camera* Bojan Bazelli, Stuart Barbee *editor* Michael R. Miller *design* Jane Musky *music* Scott Johnson *cast* Natasha Richardson, William Forsythe, Ving Rhames, Frances Fisher, Jodi Long, Olivia Barash, Dana Delany, Marex Johnson, Kitty Swing, Peter Kowanko, Tom O'Rourke
Running time: 104 mins (originally 108)
US release: Atlantic, Sep 23, 1988
UK release: Vestron, Apr 7, 1989

PELLE THE CONQUEROR (Pelle Erobreren) 👍

Denmark at the end of the last century. Bille August's award-festooned epic (Cannes *Palme d'or*, Best Foreign Film Oscar) sails into view, piloted by Max Von Sydow as a crusty Swedish emigrant bringing his son to a new life across the Baltic. Scenic, sentimental and slaloming through its appointed crises - Dad's drunkenness, boy's adult awakenings, droughts, deaths - August's film comes on at times like an overgrown soap-opera. But handsome photography and rich characterization work their spell, and Von Sydow is the film's lantern-jawed lynchpin: a chewy-vowelled codger who conjures genies from his bottle, in liquid form, and lives by swapping new delusions for old. **HK**
Director Bille August *producer* Per Holst *script* August, based on volume one of Martin Anderen Nexö's novel *camera* Jörgen Persson *editor* Janus Billeskov Jansen *design* Anna Asp *music* Stefan Nilsson *cast* Max Von Sydow, Pelle Hvenegaard, Erik Paaske, Björn Granath, Exel Ströbye, Astrid Villaume, Troels Asmussen, John Wittig, Ane Lise Hirsch Bjerrum, Sofie Gråböl
Running time: 160 mins
US release: Miramax, Dec 21, 1988

THE PERFECT MURDER

Adapted from his own novel by the very competent H. R. F. Keating, *The Perfect Murder* is awkward but intermittently endearing. Amjad Khan's roly-poly heavy is funny in his first scene, but becomes increasingly infuriating thereafter, and everyone else just gets a few skulking-and-sneaking scenes to make them seem suspicious. Naseeruddin Shah is fine as Keating's Indian sleuth, Inspector Ghote, who solves several tricky cases even though he has to be polite to all the rich suspects who refuse to answer questions and bow to the whims of his superiors no matter how stupid they may seem. However, Zafar Hai's direction is severely draggy and too often tries to turn the hero into an Inspector Clouseau figure with slapdash slapstick. There are 15 more Inspector Ghote mysteries: one hopes they'll keep Shah for the rest but sack everyone else. **KN**
Director Zafar Hai *producer* Wahid Chowhan *exec* Ismail Merchant *script* H.R.F.Keating, Hai *from novel by* Keating *camera* Walter Lassally *editor* Charles Rees *design* Kiran Patki, Sartaj Noorani *music* Richard Robbins *cast* Naseeruddin Shah, Stellan Skarsgard, Amjad Khan, Madhur Jaffrey, Ratna Pathak Shah, Sameer Kakkad, Vinod Nagpal, Dinshaw Daji, Dalip Tahil

Running time: 93 mins
UK release: Enterprise, Jul 1, 1988

PET SEMATARY

Based on Stephen King's bestseller, *Pet Sematary* concerns an animal graveyard built, like the Overlook Hotel in *The Shining*, on an Indian burial ground that has turned sour. Dad (Midkiff) is impressed when the family cat, despatched (by one of the gleaming juggernauts that dominate the rural routes) and duly interred, is resurrected - albeit as a mangy demon - and makes the mistake of planting his squashed two-year-old in the same place. Despite schlocky flashbacks and abysmal performances (except by creepy neighbour Gwynne and the tot), Mary Lambert's chiller fully comprehends the evil in children and comes up smelling of death and *Blue Velvet*, white picket fences and all. **GF**
Director Mary Lambert **producer** *Richard P. Rubinstein* **exec** *Tim Zinnemann* **script** *Stephen King, from his novel* **camera** *Peter Stein* **editor** *Michael Hill* **design** *Michael Z. Hanan* **music** *Elliot Goldenthal* **cast** *Dale Midkiff, Fred Gwynne, Denise Crosby, Brad Greenquist, Michael Lombard, Blaze Berdahl, Miko Hughes, Susan Blommaert*
Running time: 102 mins
US release: Paramount, Apr 21, 1989

LA PETITE VOLEUSE

Some 30 years after *Les Quatres cents coups* comes this tale of a sultry teenage femme kleptomaniac, scripted from an outline by Truffaut, but what might once have seemed fresh and challenging here seems calculated and contrived. Not that Charlotte Gainsbourg misses a beat in a careful performance as the parentless child who attempts to compensate for a lack of love with fantasy (cinema, inevitably), and seeks entry into the adult world through petty thieving and calculated loss of virginity. It's just that the film's makers never give the impression of trying to explore her predicament or say anything about its source. **JP**
Director Claude Miller **exec** *Jean-Rose Richer* **script** *Miller, Luc Beraud, Annie Miller from story by François Truffaut, Claude De Givray* **camera** *Dominique Chapuis* **editor** *Albert Jurgenson* **design** *Jean-Pierre Kohut-Svelko* **music** *Alain Jomy* **cast** *Charlotte Gainsbourg, Didier Bezace, Simon De La Brosse, Raoul Billerey, Chantal Banlier, Nathalie Cardonne, Clotilde De Bayser*
Running time: 110 mins
UK release: Pathé, Jun 23, 1989

PHANTASM II

This late retread of the late 1970s schlock hit, without any of the questionable virtues the original displayed, shows why we haven't heard much from Don Coscarelli in the intervening ten years. The Tall Man trashes towns, emptying out whole graveyards and turning victims into demonic munchkins. Meanwhile, two of his victims try to destroy him. *Phantasm's* grotesque imagery and death-obsession is reproduced on a bigger budget but with a very thin, unstructured narrative. The splatter-punk accoutrements of flying balls drilling into bodies and a priest hung by his own rosary are little more than indelicate viscera garnishing an empty plate. The one startling image, of a graveyard with every coffin disinterred, is hurried over as the narrative trudges towards its banal dénouement of vanquished villain returning for the hapless heroes. Coscarelli's failure to extend the original premise provides a fitting tombstone for the supernatural splatter-horror genre it arguably spawned. **SD**
Director/script Don Coscarelli **producer** *Roberto A. Quezada* **exec** *Dac Coscarelli* **camera** *Daryn Okada* **editor** *Peter Teschner* **design** *Philip J.C. Duffin* **music** *Fredy Myrow* **cast** *James Le Gros, Reggie Bannister, Angus Scrimm, Paula Irvine, Samantha Phillips, Kenneth Tigar, Ruth C. Engel*
Running time: 97 mins
US release: Universal, Jul 8, 1988
UK release: Guild, Jan 27, 1989

PHYSICAL EVIDENCE

A blackmailing mobster is found dead, and everyone concerned would like to pin the killing on beaten-up, frequently drunk, invariably suspended low-life cop Burt Reynolds. Theresa Russell, an ambitious public defender, takes up the case and tries to prove Reynolds' innocence. Unfortunately, he's the only person in town with more enemies than the deceased, and he's had a mental blackout about the evening of the murder. *Physical Evidence* follows *Suspect* in its focus on a committed lady lawyer whose personal life gets mixed up with the case she's working on, and while this one doesn't have as much slush as the Cher vehicle, it does have several too many unlikely plot twists. Director Michael Crichton, usually at home with sci-fi gadgetry and paranoia, pulls off a neat opening, with a would-be suicide discovering a corpse stashed under the bridge from which he wants to hang

himself, but thereafter fails to get much out of the *film noir* plotline, and is stuck with flavourless Canadian settings which suggest not so much mean streets as urban planning. **KN**
Director Michael Crichton **producer** Martin Ransohoff **exec** Don Carmody **script** Bill Phillips **camera** John A. Alonzo **editor** Glenn Farr **design** Dan Yarhi **music** Henry Mancini **cast** Burt Reynolds, Theresa Russell, Ned Beatty, Kay Lenz, Ted McGinley, Tom O'Brien, Kenneth Walsh
Running time: 99 mins
US release: Columbia, Jan 27, 1989

PIN

Tightly controlled from first to last, neither cast nor director allow this psychological thriller to slip into the self-parody that its bizarre obsessional theme might have provoked. David Hewlett and Cyndy Preston play it straight as a Cronenbergian pair of children whose education is conducted by Daddy throwing his voice into an anatomical model. A straightforward but consistent psychological structure is never allowed to trample over the considerable stylistic flair and sadly nostalgic reconstruction of a warped upbringing. **PB**
Director/script Sandor Stern **producer** Rene Malo **exec** Pierre David **camera** Guy Dufaux **editor** Patrick Dodd **design** François Seguin **music** Peter Manning Robinson **cast** David Hewlett, Cyndy Preston, John Ferguson, Terrance O'Quinn, Bronwen Nantel, Jacob Tirney, Michelle Anderson, Steve Bernarski
Running time: 102 mins
US release: New World, Jan 27, 1989

PINK CADILLAC

Directed by long-time Eastwood collaborator Buddy Van Horn, this low-octane comedy starring Clint as a greying skip tracer, pairs him so engagingly with Bernadette Peters as the ditzy young mom he pursues that you wonder why Warner Bros didn't customize them a vehicle before. The best moments have Clint in a series of disguises - clown's red nose, casino shark's gold lamé jacket - as he snares various cons and teams up romantically with Peters to retrieve her baby from her recidivist hubby and a bunch of backwoods neo-fascists led by psycho Michael Des Barres. If the title promises streamlined kitsch, it's a Rent-a-Wreck movie at heart, but still an agreeably dumb one. **GF**
Director Buddy Van Horn **producer** David Valdes **exec** Michael Gruskoff **script** John Eskow **camera** Jack N. Green **editor** Joel Cox **design** Edward C. Carfagno **music** Steve Dorff **cast** Clint

Eastwood, Bernadette Peters, Timothy Carhart, John Dennis Johnston, Michael Des Barres
Running time: 122 mins
US release: Warner, May 26, 1989

PLATOON LEADER

Michael *American Ninja* Dudikoff is his customary plank-like self as a rookie lieutenant thrown into the middle of a Nam firezone. Will he earn the respect of the surly grunts under his command? Who cares? This mish-mash reduces any understanding of the situation into a kind of sentimental battle-field pragmatism. Dudikoff practices his thousand-yard stare while the flesh flies in a technically proficient manner. The film demonstrates that Aaron Norris's directorial abilities are on a par with the acting achievements of brother Chuck. **PB**
Director Aaron Norris **producer** Harry Alan Towers **exec** Avi Lerner **script** Rick Marx, Andrew Deutsch, David Walker, from James R. McDonough's book **camera** Arthur Wooster **editor** Michael J. Duthie **design** John Rosewarne **music** George S. Clinton **cast** Michael Dudikoff, Robert F. Lyons, Michael De Lorenzo, Rich Fitts
Running time: 100 mins
US release: Cannon, Oct 7, 1988

THE POINTSMAN (De Wisselwachter)

In an unidentified location, a French-speaking *bourgeoise* alights from a train and finds herself stranded alongside an isolated signal box. There she strikes up a reluctant relationship with an almost mute pointsman, who protects her from the occasional visits of passing railwaymen. Jos Stelling's determinedly bizarre film promises a surreal encounter of cultural opposites, but as the proceedings provoke stranger imagery, so the narrative descends to banal resolutions. The film left most audiences mildly amused but not a little bored. **DT**
Director Jos Stelling **producer** Stanley Hillebrandt **script** George Brugmans, Hans De Wolf, Stelling **camera** Frans Bromet, Theo Van De Sande, Paul Van Den Bos, Goert Giltaij **editor** Rimko Haanstra **design** Gert Brinkers **music** Michel Mulders **cast** Jim Van Der Woude, Stéphane Excoffier, John Kraaykamp, Josse De Pauw
Running time: 96 mins
UK release: Vestron, Jul 15, 1988

POLICE ACADEMY 5: ASSIGNMENT MIAMI BEACH

'What is this, a moron convention?' asks a villain when presented with the *Police Academy* regulars (minus Steve Guttenberg).

Commandant Lassard (Gaynes) faces mandatory retirement, thanks to a scheming underling, and is sent to Miami where he is to pick up an award. He accidentally gets hold of a fortune in stolen diamonds and becomes the target of a gang of ruthless thieves. His loyal graduates - the tall one, the fat one, the psycho one, the one who does funny noises and the girl with large breasts - set out to save their boss. Alan Myerson, the so-called director of this dog, made a promising début in 1972 with *Steelyard Blues* and apparently hasn't had a good job offer since. **KN**
Director Alan Myerson **producer** Paul Maslansky **script** Stephen J. Kurwick, based on characters created by Neal Israel and Pat Proft **camera** Jim Pergola **editor** Hubert De La Bouillerie **design** Trevor Williams **music** Robert Folk **cast** Matt McCoy, Janet Jones, George Gaynes, G.W. Bailey, René Auberjonois, Bubba Smith, David Graf, Michael Winslow, Leslie Easterbrook
Running time: 90 mins
US release: Warner, Mar 18, 1988
UK release: Warner, Jul 15, 1988

POLICE ACADEMY 6: CITY UNDER SIEGE
Starting off with the vaguely promising notion of the criminal underworld of the city planning to invade all the positions of power, this sequel reaches the lowest depths of gutter-level humour. The ensemble cast seem exceedingly bored with the flat material into which they try valiantly to breathe life. **AR**
Director Peter Bonerz **producer** Paul Maslansky **script** Stephen J. Curwick **camera** Charles Rosher Jr. **editor** Hubert De La Bouillerie **design** Tho E. Azzari **music** Robert Folk **cast** Bubba Smith, David Graf, Michael Winslow, Leslie Easterbrook, Marion Ramsey, Lance Kinsey, Matt McCoy, Bruce Mahler, G. W. Bailey, George Gaynes, Kenneth Mars, Gerrit Graham
Running time: 83 mins
US release: Warner, Mar 10, 1989

TURKEY

POLTERGEIST 3
Director/exec Gary Sherman **producer** Barry Bernardi **script** Sherman, Brian Taggert **camera** Alex Nepomniaschy **editor** Ross Albert **design** Paul Eads **music** Joe Renzetti **cast** Tom Skerritt, Nancy Allen, Heather O'Rourke, Zelda Rubinstein, Lara Flynn Boyle, Richard Fire, Nathan Davis
Running time: 97 mins
US release: MGM, Jun 10, 1988
UK release: UIP, Sep 23, 1988

POWWOW HIGHWAY
Coming after a string of ill-fated, offbeat projects from Britain's HandMade Productions, *Powwow Highway* turns out to be a surprisingly mature and funny road movie about a pair of Native Americans on a quest to discover their cultural heritages. Becoming an almost mythical (but never pretentious) journey of self discovery, it is beautifully acted, especially by Gary Farmer as the road warrior, and photographed with a good eye for the characters' relations to the landscape. **TW**
Director Jonathan Wacks **producer** Jan Wieringa **execs** George Harrison, Denis O'Brien **script** Janet Heany, Jean Stawarz, from novel by David Seals **camera** Toyomichi Kurita **editor** James Austin Stewart **design** Cynthia Sowder **music** Barry Goldberg **cast** A. Martinez, Gary Farmer, Amanda Wyss, Joanelle Nadine Romero, Sam Vlahos, Wayne Waterman, Margo Kane, Geoff Rivas
Running time: 91 mins
US release: Warner, Mar 24, 1989

PRESIDIO
A string of strong scenes don't necessarily make a good film. Peter Hyams' connect-the-dots movie has a car chase (on San Francisco hills), a running chase (in Chinatown), a shootout in a cute location (a bottling plant), a drunken reminiscence on a roof-top, a punch-out in a bar, and a declaration of love under a suspension bridge. The picture that's not quite drawn involves the reconciliation of old enemies, army cop Sean Connery and city cop Mark Harmon, and their fluctuating feelings for Connery's flighty daredevil of a daughter, Meg Ryan. The perfunctory plot is a mere McGuffin: some suave conglomerate chiefs also smuggle diamonds. **BM**
Director/camera Peter Hyams **producer** D. Constantine Conte **exec** Jonathan Zimbert **script** Larry Ferguson **editor** James Mitchell **design** Albert Brenner **music** Bruce Boughton **cast** Sean Connery, Mark Harmon, Meg Ryan, Jack Warden, Mark Blum, Dana Gladstone, Jenette Goldstein
Running time: 97 mins
US release: Paramount, Jun 10, 1988
UK release: UIP, Jan 13, 1989

THE PRINCE OF PENNSYLVANIA
In this sincere, but rather dreary, piece of would-be gritty realism, Keanu Reeves is miserable because he's too intelligent and his family is falling apart around his semi-punk haircut. His Mom (Bedelia) is being regularly schtupped in the family caravan by a church-

going neighbour; his Pop (Ward) is a bigoted thug who refuses to sell a stretch of land the company wants to strip-mine, and his little brother is growing up boringly ordinary. Reeves, one of the kids from *River's Edge*, is an unsympathetic central figure, but he is indulged at the expense of such fine performers as Fred Ward, Bonnie Bedelia and Amy Madigan, all of whom do what they can with thin material. **KN**

Director/script Ron Nyswaner **producer** Joan Fishman **execs** Robert Shaye, Sara Risher **camera** Frank Prinzi **editor** William Scharf **design** Tony Corbett **music** Thomas Newman **cast** Fred Ward, Keanu Reeves, Bonnie Bedelia, Amy Madigan, Jeff Hayenga, Tracey Ellis, Joseph De Lisi, Jay O. Sanders, Kari Keegan, Demetria Mellott
Running time: 93 mins
US release: New Line, Sep 16, 1988
UK release: Palace, Mar 17, 1989

PRISONER OF RIO

Even more than *Buster*, *Prisoner of Rio* is suffused with criminal smugness. Paul Freeman as Ronald Biggs claims it was an injustice to sentence him to a 30-year stretch when 'murderers and rapists only get five years', and occasionally whines that he is still a prisoner in his exile, legally unable to get a job and thus forced to earn a living by giving interviews for pay and appearing in Australian coffee commercials. With footage of the Rio carnival to protract the murky mechanics of the kidnap-and-double-cross, Peter Firth and Steven Berkoff continue their run of heroically embarrassing rôles as hammy coppers out to kidnap Biggs. While it might be argued that Biggs has paid his debt to society for his original crime, his involvement as screenwriter in this ordeal of a film should be enough to convince any jury that he deserves at least another 30 years inside. **KN**

Director Lech Majewski **producer** Juliusz Kossakowski, Mark Slater, Andy Hybala **execs** Majewski, Eddie Egloff **script** Majewski, Ronald Biggs, Julia Frankel **camera** Alec Mills, Toca Seabra, Jaques Cheuiche, Richard Mosier **editor** Darren Kloomok **design** Oscar Ramos **music** Luiz Bonfá **cast** Steven Berkoff, Paul Freeman, Peter Firth, Florinda Bolkan, José Wilker, Zezé Mota, Desmond Llewelyn, Breno Mello
Running time: 105 mins
UK release: Palace, Dec 16, 1988

PUMPKINHEAD

The latest approved route for directing is via the special effects department; Stan Winston, best known for SFX on films like *Aliens* and *Predator*, makes his directorial début with what probably started out as an interesting idea, but has ended up a routine stalk 'n' slash pic. Lance Henriksen plays a backwoods farmer whose young son is accidentally killed by teens holidaying in the vicinity. With the help of a local hag, he summons an avenging demon who - surprise, surprise - corners the youngsters in a log cabin, chases them through the woods and picks 'em off one by one. The hick settings are never exploited and Henriksen's guilty about-face comes too late to liven things up. **AB**

Director Stan Winston **producers** Richard C. Weinman, Howard Smith **script** Mark Patrick Carducci, Gary Gerani **camera** Bojan Bazelli **editor** Marcus Manton **music** Richard Stone **cast** Lance Henriksen, Jeff East, John DiAquino, Kimberly Ross, Joel Hoffman, Cynthia Bain
Running time: 86 mins
US release: UA, Oct 14, 1988

PUNCHLINE

In this tragi-comic study of the victims, losers and winners of stand-up comedy, Tom Hanks plays a character whose acerbic talent in this field dictates poverty and a betrayal of his father's desire that he too become a physician. Like many comedians, Hanks has scant sense of self-worth, but his humanity is redeemed by a not so archetypal love-hate relationship with aspiring gagster and harassed house-wife Sally Field whom he reluctantly coaches for a competition in which they will both compete. *Punchline* is a confrontational drama that steadily progresses towards an emotional dénouement of sentimental reconciliation and culminates in a cathartic monologue from Hanks. **MN**

Director/script David Seltzer **producers** Daniel Melnick, Michael Rachmil **camera** Reynaldo Villalobos **editor** Bruce Green **design** Jack DeGovia **music** Charles Gross **cast** Sally Field, Tom Hanks, John Goodman, Mark Rydell, Kim Greist, Paul Mazursky, Pam Matteson
Running time: 122 mins
US release: Columbia, Sep 30, 1988
UK release: Col/Tri-Star, Apr 7, 1989

PARENTS

I n recent years, increasing attention has been focused on the so-called 'cult' movie
– thanks to mostly supercilious coffee-table books, TV series and video
distribution. The primary genre of the cult movie has always been the low-budget
horror film, and the mainstays have included such visceral horrors as *The Texas
Chainsaw Massacre*, *Night of the Living Dead* and *The Hills Have Eyes*; camp
horror comedies of the *Rocky Horror Picture Show* or *Pink Flamingos* variety and
such unintentionally hilarious 1950s disasters as *Plan Nine from Outer Space* or
Attack of the 50-Foot Woman.

For the most part, cult films are found, not made. Each *Night of the Living Dead*
requires a horde of faceless, pointless, ditchwater-dull 'ordinary' drive-in horror
films to give it context. Part of the appeal of the cult film is the joy of discovery,
the buzz of attending an exploitation double bill and finding that, while the A feature
is the competent *The Beast Must Die*, the unheard-of supporting picture is the
excellent *Sisters* from an unknown director called Brian De Palma. The true cult
movie comes from outside the mainstream, and is the product of an independent-
minded group of people who appreciate the freedom that a tight genre straitjacket
and a low budget allow them.

But cult movies have been so successful that some people are now setting out
to make them. Every Cannes or Mifed issue of *Variety* is now jam-packed with
ads for films with titles like *Stuff Stephanie in the Incinerator, Hollywood Chainsaw
Hookers* or *Rabid Grannies*. These are the knowing, wannabee cult movies, and
invariably they fail to live up to their packaging. By and large, they mix feeble
comedy, unconvincing gore and endless tedium to little effect.

The problem is that those who set out to make a cult movie usually end up
with a total nothing. Currently, too much horror cinema is infected with a slapstick
goriness that is the unfortunate legacy of fine films like *The Evil Dead, Re-Animator*
and *Dawn of the Dead*. It's rare to find anything as intelligent, frightening and
effective as the first wave of 1970s splatter movies. Horror in the 1980s too often
means either dispiriting retreads of the worthless *Friday the 13th* formula or
amiable, affectless, terminally imitative jokes like *Return of the Living Dead* and
Critters. Freddy Krueger is the patron saint of these subtly reactionary, settling-
for-less films, and his bandwagon threatens to roll like a juggernaut over a genre
that was formerly the province of the disreputable, the revolutionary and the
innovative.

In these circumstances, films are made and marketed as predigested cults,
and it is no surprise that so many would-be midnight movie hits are un-rented
and gathering dust in the forgotten racks of video corner shops. The camp
followers who set out to make movies as 'bad' as *Plan Nine* inevitably make

151

something technically better but totally negligible in every other way. It is a myth that bad films are non-stop hilarious entertainment, but it is true that the Best of the Worst are far more enjoyable than such carbon-copy losers as *The Toxic Avenger* or *Neon Maniacs*.

Still, the occasional genuine oddity does creep through, usually from an unexpected source. In recent years, *Trancers*, *Re-Animator*, *Bad Taste*, *Street Trash* and *Near Dark* have been real sleepers, appreciated by the horror *cognoscenti*. To that list, we can now add Bob Balaban's début feature, *Parents*, an untouted, inexpensive, minimally-released item that redeems the frequently despicable horror comedy genre and bravely goes against the thematic tide of 1980s horror. While big-budget horrors like *Poltergeist*, *The Lost Boys*, *Fatal Attraction* and *Child's Play* have been affirming the old values of heart and home, *Parents* fits in with a more interesting strain (*The Stepfather*, *White of the Eye*, *The 'burbs*, *The Applegates*), that goes against the grain by exposing those Reagan-Bush era virtues of middle-class family life as the root of all the world's evils.

Parents spins off from such classic sitcoms of the 1950s as *Ozzie and Harriet*, *Father Knows Best* and *Leave It to Beaver* by recreating a 1950s suburbia of tract homes, kidney-shaped coffee tables and canasta, and asking 'What's wrong with this picture?' Young Michael Laemle (Bryan Madorsky), the new kid on the block, is beginning to suspect that there's something wrong with his perfect Eisenhower-era parents. Nick Laemle (Randy Quaid) develops defoliants for the Toxico company, while his adoring wife Lily (Mary Beth Hurt) slaves over the cooker producing perfect meals. Michael is increasingly uncertain as to the ingredients of Mom's tasty meat dishes. 'We've been having leftovers every day since we came here, I'd like to know what they were before they were leftovers.'

It becomes clear that Nick might well be bringing home cadavers from work and turning them over to Lily for barbecuing. Miss Dew (Sandy Dennis), the child psychologist in Michael's school, is disturbed when Michael's picture of his family is a red-smeared image of monsters keeping a child in a box. She tries to investigate.

Of course, *Parents* isn't just about cannibalism. The really scary idea of the film is that grown-ups are alien creatures who have total power over children. Miss Dew, whom Michael doesn't class as a real grown-up ('real grown-ups don't get upset'), tries to find out what is wrong in the Laemle household and calls Lily in for an interview. In the film's most unnerving scene, the doctor asks Lily to tell her something about her child, and the immaculately coiffured woman is completely unable to come up with anything beyond 'he's not a big eater.'

Cannibalism has, not unaccountably, provided a rich source of sick humour for American horror cinema. Ivan Reitman's first feature, *Cannibal Girls*, Tobe Hooper's *The Texas Chainsaw Massacre*, Paul Bartel's stylishly sick *Eating Raoul* and such obscurities as *Motel Hell*, *The Folks at Red Wolf Inn*, *Microwave*

Massacre and *Deranged* are thick with jokes about lady's fingers, hunter's stew and conversational commonplaces like 'having someone special for dinner?' *Parents* is squarely in this tradition of carnivorous horror and, while it never descends to the tasteless depths of the notorious video nasty cannibal films, meat is central. Rarely has food been made to look so disgusting: Lily and Nick push burned hunks of dead flesh around on the barbecue and present Michael with groaning platters of congealed nastiness; livers are split open in close-up, and one image – a set of red-nailed female fingers pushing chunks of meat into the mincer – recalls nothing so much as the 'poundcake' inserts of hard-core pornography. In one of several nightmare sequences, Michael is attacked by a 16-foot length of German sausage that winds around him like a boa constrictor. But, as it was for Flanders and Swann (who used to do a song called 'Eating People is Wrong'), cannibalism is used by Balaban as merely a metaphor for more common abuses.

'*Parents*' says Bob Balaban, 'is not a horror film. It's really a comedy, a dark comedy about manners. I would call it a kind of social satire, if anything.' Certain American genre-oriented publications (*Fangoria, Cinefantastique*) have sneered at Balaban's description of his film, as if by refraining from an all-out bloodbath he were betraying the art form rather than being true to his own bizarre vision. The film does turn straight for a finale echoing those of *The Stepfather* and *White of the Eye* as parents and child engage in a bloody life-or-death struggle, topped by a cleverly downbeat final twist. However, it then extends the film's indictment of all-American images by sending the orphan off to live in a *Waltons*-style log cabin with his folksy grandparents who are, it is suggested, 'outsiders' too.

Director Balaban is best known as an actor: he has had strong supporting rôles in *Prince of the City, 2010* and *Dead Bang*. In *Parents*, from Christopher Hawthorne's screenplay, he has woven a bizarrely nostalgic fable with a darkly gruesome centre, decked out with period kitsch furniture and outfits. Cinematographer Robin Vidgeon, who also did *The Fly II* and *Nightbreed*, forsakes the foggy menace of most straight horror pictures for a hard-edged, illuminated postcard look that, like so many things about the film, has few precedents in recent cinema.

Young Madorsky doesn't quite click as the junior paranoid – although Juno Mills-Cockell is wonderful as his weird girlfriend, who claims to be an alien and enjoys playing doctors and nurses amid the suspicious parcels in the Laemle freezer – and the switch from sitcom to stabbing near the end is so unsettling that it's difficult for an audience to make the adjustment. For the most part, however, this is the perfect example of the genuine cult movie. Given a wide release on neither side of the Atlantic and ignored or abused by most Stateside critics – the British reviewers were a shade more perceptive – *Parents* has not yet built a reputation, but it should age well.

The film works because it doesn't play too broadly, and because of the performances from Randy Quaid and Mary Beth Hurt, two never-quite-made-it-as-stars players who here give performances that rank with their best work. They both have the sitcom smiles down pat and coo their way through the wholesome dialogue like refugees from a Disney family film, but with the barest of twitches that suggest all manner of insanity and degradation. Quaid's man-to-man speech with his son about not being afraid of the dark descends from *Father Knows Best* to *Psycho* in moments: 'You can be yourself in the dark,' he says, 'but there's one dark place you have to be careful,' he continues, pointing to his head. Hurt makes a lot out of creepy little details like slipping off one of her huge ear-rings to receive a telephone call. Until almost the finale, the film plays ambiguously with its young hero's imaginings, and the most suggestive sequence – in which he discovers his parents red-mouthed in their underwear late at night – has as much to do with any child's disturbed feelings about its parents' sex life as it does with flesh-eating ghoullery.

But the chief triumph of the film is its surreal sense of design. Even John Waters has never gone quite so far in his resurrection of the horrid excesses of 1950s chic. Wallpaper and curtains display matching patterns of wavy lines; Lily's dresses seem to have been starched with concrete; the front room is half-concrete like a nuclear bunker; turquoise triangular cushions adorn the couches; cars are huge and finned monstrosities; the soundtrack brims with hits like Sheb Woolley's 'The Flying Purple People Eater', The Big Bopper's 'Chantilly Lace' and Dean Martin's 'Memories are Made of This', and Hurt and Quaid sport matched simpers that could stand as the *Happy Days* generation's equivalent of the American Gothic stare. 'I was a kid in the 1950s,' says Balaban, 'and that's one of the reasons why I set the movie then, because outward appearances and being perfect were really so important then. The 1950s were about being homogenized. We were all supposed to think the same things. It was dangerous if you had beliefs that weren't just like everybody else's. And you had to look the same. God forbid you should have curly hair.'

KIM NEWMAN

POLTERGEIST III

Back in the mid-1930s, *Bride of Frankenstein* and *Dracula's Daughter* proved that sequels to hit horror films could be at least as good as the originals. Subsequently, we have had *Curse of the Cat People*, *Dawn of the Dead* and *Aliens* to give the lie to the assumption that the follow-ups have to be weak carbons churned out quickly to cash in on a hit. But what about *sequels* to sequels. What on earth can really be done with a Part Three?

Actually, in the 1930s and 1940s, *Son of Frankenstein* and *Son of Dracula*, while slightly hampered by formulae grown familiar, did a creditable job of keeping up the standards of their series. But since then, it's been downhill all the way. For a while, there was an asinine craze for making Parts Three in 3-D; a treatment meted out to *Jaws*, *Friday the 13th* and *Amityville*. The imaginative *A Nightmare on Elm Street, Part III: Dream Warriors* is probably unique in that it won back some of the ground lost by the execrable *Part II: Freddy's Revenge* – but, mostly, the best a sequel to a sequel can do is tread water and hope not to lose too much money.

Halloween III: Season of the Witch daringly junked all the apparatus of the first two films and tried, like John Boorman's *Exorcist II: The Heretic*, to be different, whereupon it was ritually slaughtered in the marketplace. And *The Final Conflict*, which should have been the most stirring film in the *Omen* saga, what with a grown-up villain and a literally apocalyptic finale, was a damp squib that showed how tired the filmmakers were of the whole thing. *Psycho III*, while entertaining, was not the unexpected gem that *Psycho II* turned out to be. And the forthcoming *Alien III* is going to have to be pretty original to sustain the momentum.

Poltergeist III was in a troubled position to start with, in that it was a sequel not only to the Tobe Hooper/Steven Spielberg *Poltergeist*, a well-crafted ghost story, but also to Brian Gibson's *Poltergeist II: The Other Side*, a dreadful piece of codswallop. Gibson's film, like all really terrible sequels, seemed to have been made by people who had either failed to understand, or even not bothered to see, the first film. The dazzling mix of magic, serious scares, childish whimsy, suburban humour and pop mysticism that made *Poltergeist* a hit – if not a horror classic – was replaced by ham acting, tired shock tactics and a muddled script. Worst of all, it tried to impose some sort of logic on the deliberately loose premise of the original by dragging in a new dead character, the evil Reverend Kane (Julian Beck), to function as an all-purpose villain, and a new live one, a mystic Indian played by Will Sampson, to provide pretentious spiritualist explanations of his rotten nature.

Beck and Sampson – like too many people involved in the series (notably

young actress Dominique Dunne) – died shortly after *Poltergeist II*, but that didn't prevent their plot threads being picked up for the third movie. Sampson's was left out, with all the ghostly twaddle going to screechy-voiced Tangina (Zelda Rubinstein), the midget medium who was annoying in the first movie and is a blazing nuisance in this one. And Kane was replaced by lookalike Nathan Davis to menace anew, although this time deprived of most of his monster worms, hobgoblins and *Outer Limits*-style demons, thanks to a reduced special effects budget. The press notes try to make something of the fact that the film unusually forsakes optical effects for conjuring stunts done live on the sound stage, but that also means forsaking some of the monstrousness that enlivened even *Poltergeist II* – in which the H. R. Giger-designed worm in a bottle of tequila came to life inside Craig T. Nelson, cueing an impressive monster-vomiting scene – in favour of hackneyed tricks with mirrors.

Little Carol-Anne Freeling (Heather O'Rourke) has survived her horrid experiences in the first two films and mysteriously grown hamster-like cheek pouches while living in a Chicago high-rise. Her aunt and uncle (Tom Skerritt and Nancy Allen) have taken her into their family – probably because Craig T. Nelson and JoBeth Williams, who used to be her parents, thought that the last film did enough damage to their careers and had their agents get them out of the series. Carol-Anne has problems at a school for 'gifted' (read 'fruitcake') children. The rotten reverend pops up as a ghostly window-cleaner and subsequently gets his jollies from tampering with the heating of the skyscraper so that ice develops everywhere. He also has a sideline in dropping child psychologists down elevator shafts. When a pair of very boring teenagers get dragged into a limbo under a puddle in the car park, it is up to auntie to get them back by reaffirming, with TV-movie-style sloppiness, how much she loves them all.

The first sequel made the mistake of trying to impose its own storyline on the unconnected events of the original film, and this one compounds the error by reducing all the manifestations of supernatural activity to yet another attempt by the villain to get the girl to 'take him into the light' (whatever that means!). At the end of this movie, Tangina sacrifices all for the brat by willingly going off with Kane in Carol-Anne's place, which ought to put a damper on further instalments. The film is long on irrelevances like the child psychologist's tirades, some teenage partying and life in a luxury high-rise, and only has one new idea – about people being in mirrors but not the real world – that it relentlessly hammers into the ground. Obviously, some painstaking work has had to be done with doubles, reverse sets and all-glass scenery, but it is too subtle to register much on the Sense of Wonder scale and not really a substitute for the leering monsters, killer trees, murderous playthings, living corpses, after-life light shows and exploding houses of the earlier films.

Gary Sherman, the director responsible, is one of those filmmakers who have never delivered on the promise of their first feature. In 1972, with the money he

156

had earned directing the New Seekers' Coca-Cola commercial ('I'd like to buy the world a coke . . .') he financed *Death Line* (aka *Raw Meat*), an astonishing little sickie which had Donald Pleasence investigating a series of murders on London's Piccadilly Line and discovering a nest of cannibals preying on commuters. The film was funny, gruesome, poignant and exciting, and at the cutting edge of the horror boom of the 1970s. Subsequently, Sherman turned out the competent action thriller *Vice Squad*, the muddled but interesting horror *Dead and Buried* and the dull *Wanted: Dead or Alive*, an action flick featuring Rutger Hauer. *Poltergeist III*, his first film for a Hollywood major, is the worst thing he has ever done, and he will have to come up with something incredible to regain the critical and commercial high ground.

'The original film had been suburban, the second was rural,' said Sherman, who compounded his sins by co-writing the screenplay with Brian Taggert. 'So I thought it would be really interesting to do *Poltergeist III* as a ghost film in a highly-congested metropolitan area. I pictured a high-rise building, and I guess that five or ten of the tallest buildings are in Chicago.' That's also the city where Sherman lives, so presumably his decision to set the film there might have had something to do with a desire to eat in his own kitchen every night as well. High-rise buildings have been used as settings for horror movies before – most notably David Cronenberg's startling début feature, *Shivers*. *Ghostbusters* and *Demons 2* also offered opportunities to have the scary stuff run riot through an ultra-modern environment. But this film takes no advantage whatsoever of the setting, especially by comparison with such a nail-biting near-contemporary as *Die Hard*. It even manages to fumble with the infallible business of characters dangling from windows 17 storeys above the ground.

Surely any screenwriter worth their salt would have given Carol-Anne a bad case of vertigo, rather than have her blithely sleep next to an exterior window high over the city. The characters here don't have any traits beyond their impeccably tailored costumings or the dictates of the dumb plotline. The dialogue throughout is laughable, and the actors shuffle through it with one eye on the pay cheque and the other on getting a decent part next time round. O'Rourke, who has to bear the dramatic weight of the film, frankly isn't up to it, whether appearing shrilly as herself or pretending to be possessed by the villain.

After the film's completion, twelve-year-old Heather O'Rourke became the fourth actor in the series to die, of a congenital birth defect that caused her intestines to rupture, and the film is dedicated to her. Undoubtedly the makers are sincere in their mourning, but one would hate to have *Poltergeist III* as a monument to one's memory.

KIM NEWMAN

RAGGEDY RAWNEY

Bob Hoskins' directorial début is well-meaning - it says war is horrid - and distinctive, but has a home-movie feel. To make an audience accept a story set in a never-never land requires the sort of attention to detail that isn't applied here. Also, casting British character actors as gypsies acquainted with evil spirits is like asking Arnold Schwarzenegger to play Hamlet. That said, Dexter Fletcher as the fugitive soldier who takes refuge amongst the travellers and is ascribed sufficient magic powers to be regarded as a 'rawney', shows flickers of his potential, and the naïveté underlying the whole enterprise could be seen as charming. **JP**
Director Bob Hoskins *producer* Bob Weiss *execs* George Harrison, Denis O'Brien *script* Hoskins, Nicole De Wilde *camera* Frank Tidy *editor* Alan Jones *design* Jiri Matolin *music* Michael Kamen *cast* Bob Hoskins, Dexter Fletcher, Zoë Nathenson, Zoë Wanamaker, J. G. Devlin, Ian Dury, Emma D'Inverno, Perry Fenwick, Steve Fletcher, Graham Fletcher-Cook, Gawn Grainger, Dave Hill, Ian McNiece, Rosemary Martin, Jane Wood
Running time: 102 mins
UK release: HandMade/Virgin, Jun 30, 1989

RAIN MAN

Director Barry Levinson *producer* Mark Johnson *execs* Peter Guber, Jon Peters *script* Ronald Bass, Barry Morrow *camera* John Seale *editor* Stu Linder *design* Ida Random *music* Hans Zimmer *cast* Dustin Hoffman, Tom Cruise, Valeria Golino, Jerry Molen, Jack Murdock, Michael D. Roberts, Ralph Seymour, Lucinda Jenney, Bonnie Hunt, Kim Robillard, Beth Grant
Running time: 133 mins
US release: UA, Dec 16, 1988
UK release: UIP, Mar 3, 1989

THE RAINBOW

Ken Russell returns to Nottinghamshire with this 'prequel' to his 1970 film *Women in Love*. He fills the screen with Lawrentian images of thundering horses, nymphs in ponds, swains breasting hillsides and, of course, the optical illusion of the title. His otherwise faithful adaptation of the last third of D. H. Lawrence's classic omits, however, a strong enough actress at the centre. Sammi Davis lacks the range to do more than stick her snub nose in the air and look cross when thwarted. Glenda Jackson as her mother and Amanda Donohoe as her co-nymph do more with less. We never get any sense from Davis of Ursula's struggle against the limitation of her roots or her uncompromising need to be free, and so, however honourable, we are left with just another costume drama with nude scenes. **BM**
Director/producer Ken Russell *execs* William J. Quigley, Dan Ireland *script* Ken Russell, Vivian Russell, from novel by D. H. Lawrence *camera* Billy Williams *editor* Peter Davies *design* Luciana Arrighi *music* Carl Davis *cast* Sammi Davis, Paul McGann, Amanda Donohoe, Christopher Gable, David Hemmings, Glenda Jackson, Dudley Sutton, Jim Carter, Judith Paris, Ken Colley, Glenda McKay, Molly Russell, Rupert Russell
Running time: 112 mins
US release: Vestron, May 5, 1989

RAMBO III

'I don't believe this' is the first utterance delivered here by the taciturnly bulging-muscled hero, and in the ensuing hour and a half the audience has ample opportunities to echo his words. The wild storyline about Rambo contriving all but single-handedly to snatch his old CO from a Soviet dungeon in Afghanistan is not enhanced by the casual logistics of the staging, and the protagonist's indestructibility is such that little suspense is generated, even at the crudest blood-and-thunder level. **TP**
Director Peter Macdonald *producer* Buzz Feitshans *execs* Mario Kassar, Andrew Vajna *script* Sylvester Stallone, Sheldon Lettich *camera* John Stanier *editors* James Symons, Andrew London, O. Nicholas Brown, Edward A. Warschilka *design* Billy Kenney, Austen Spriggs *music* Jerry Goldsmith *cast* Sylvester Stallone, Richard Crenna, Marc de Jonge, Kurtwood Smith, Spiros Focas, Sasson Gabai, Doudi Shoua
Running time: 102 mins (100 mins in UK)
US release: Tri-Star, May 25, 1988
UK release: Col/Tri-Star, Aug 26, 1988

RED HEAT

This East-West collaboration thriller is further evidence of Walter Hill's declining relevance to 1980s action cinema. The narrative recalls the superior *48 Hours*: a Russian cop works with a redneck Yank cop to capture a drug-pushing Russkie loose in the States. This is clearly a Hill film rather than a Schwarzenegger vehicle: the latter underplays his bulky Moscow officer rôle as against James Belushi's manic, cardboard slob. But the lack of connecting friction between the two pinpoints the film's indifference to exploring their contrasting perspectives on social and cultural values. The

villain (O'Ross) is a stubbled psycho-killer, who obsessively beats against spatial and physical limitations (mowing down anything that gets in his way). There are several impressive set pieces but very little else in the form of interesting narrative development or visual flair. **SD**
Director Walter Hill **producers** Hill, Gordon Carroll **execs** Mario Kassar, Andrew Vajna **script** Harry Kleiner, Hill, Troy Kennedy Martin **camera** Matthew F. Leonetti **editor** Freeman Davies **design** John Vallone **music** James Horner **cast** Arnold Schwarzenegger, James Belushi, Peter Boyle, Ed O'Ross, Larry Fishburne, Gina Gershon, Richard Bright, Brent Jennings
Running time: 103 mins
US release: Tri-Star, Jun 24, 1988
UK release: Columbia/Tri-Star, Jan 13, 1989

RED SORGHUM (Hong Gaoliang)
Director Zhang Zimou **producer** Xi'an Film Studio **exec** Wu Tianming **script** Chen Jianyu, Zhu Wei, Mo Yan based on stories by Mo Yan **camera** Gu Changwei **editor** Du Yuan **design** Yang Gang **music** Zhao Jiping **cast** Gong Li, Jiang Wen, Teng Rujun, Liu Ji, Qian Ming, Ji Chunhua, Zhai Ghunhua
Running time: 92 mins
US release: New Yorker, Oct 10, 1988
UK release: Palace, Feb 10, 1989

RENEGADES
Frenetically-paced thriller pitches Kiefer Sutherland, an undercover cop on the trail of a diamond thief, together with Lou Diamond Philips, hunting the murderer of his brother, who has made off with a relic sacred to his Indian tribe.
Director Jack Sholder **producer** David Madden **exec** James G. Robinson, Joe Roth, Ted Field, Robert Cort **script** David Rich **camera** Phil Meheux **editor** Caroline Biggerstaff **design** Carol Spier **music** Michael Kamen **cast** Kiefer Sutherland, Lou Diamond Phillips, Jami Gertz, Rob Knepper, Bill Smitrovich, Floyd Westerman
Running time: 106 mins
US release: Universal, Jun 2, 1989

THE RESCUE
Walt Disney meets Rambo in this workmanlike and tiresome Touchstone turkey about a group of brat-pack rejects journeying to Korea (the Communist one) to rescue their dads from the Yellow Peril when the Pentagon top-brass who sent them in on a secret mission won't help. Clichés breed faster than rabbits as, with the

help of the resistance, they find the courage to invade a neutral country and kill a lot of slant-eyes, with plenty of big explosions that look great in the trailer. **TW**
Director Ferdinand Fairfax **producer** Laura Ziskin **script** Jim Thomas, John Thomas **camera** Russell Boyd **editor** David Holden, Carroll Timothy O'Meara **design** Maurice Cain **music** Bruce Broughton **cast** Kevin Dillon, Christina Harnos, Marc Price, Ned Vaughn, Ian Giatti, Charles Haid, Edward Albert
Running time: 98 mins
US release: BV, Aug 5, 1988

RETURN FROM THE RIVER KWAI
This mess is sufficiently handicapped by its attempt to fit an action adventure plot into its 'true story' scenario for the inevitable comparison with David Lean's classic to seem an unfair encumbrance. Perversely, however, the filmmakers go out of their way to recall past precedent, both in the characterization of Edward Fox and through a subplot featuring Denholm Elliott as an unlikely vet-turned-commando. Also, shortly before leading a disastrous attack on a Japanese train, Elliott evokes the spirit of T. E. Lawrence - the appalling dialogue makes this one film which might come across better with subtitles. As the POWs are transported towards Japan by rail and sea, memories of Lean's film fade but the conflict between poetry-spouting Fox and sadistic Jap is so clumsily told that the film's claimed relationship to historical reality has to be laughed off the screen. **JP**
Director Andrew V. McLaglen **producer** Kurt Unger **exec** Daniel Unger **script** Sargon Tamini, Paul Mayersberg, based on book by Joan Blair, Clay Blair Jr. **camera** Arthur Wooster **editor** Alan Strachan **design** Michael Stringer **music** Lalo Schifrin **cast** Edward Fox, Denholm Elliott, Christopher Penn, Tatsuya Nakadai, Masato Nagamori, George Takei, Nick Tate, Timothy Bottoms, Michael Dante, Richard Graham
Running time: 101 mins
UK release: Rank, Apr 7, 1989

RETURN OF THE LIVING DEAD PART II
Although this re-run is occasionally involving, it's clear that no one involved was trying very hard to strike any sparks of originality from the familiar plot. A canister dropped from an army van in the environs of a cemetery revives the dead and turns a junior member of the population into a zombie. The opening of the graves can still cause a stir, as the young heroes

flee from the blood-hungry rabble, but the suspense hangs around only one crude question: What means of disposal will they use on this occasion? Given that a nuclear bomb did the job last time around, anything with less oomph is bound to seem a bit of a let-down, as is the case here. **JP**
Director/script Ken Wiederhorn **producer** Tom Fox **exec** Eugene C. Cashman **camera** Robert Elswit **editor** Charles Bornstein **music** J. Peter Robinson, Vladimir Horunzhy **cast** James Karen, Thom Mathews, Michael Kenworthy, Marsha Dietlein, Dana Ashbrook, Philip Bruns
Running time: 89 mins
US release: Lorimar, Jan 15, 1988
UK release: Guild, Feb 24, 1989

ROAD HOUSE

Beware any movie directed by a person whose first name is Rowdy. The culprit here, Rowdy Herrington, tries to romanticize the profession of dance-hall bouncer by casting Patrick Swayze as his lead thug and giving him the paradoxical motto, 'Be Nice'. Swayze arrives in a hick town in Missouri and sets things right in the sort of bar where the band plays behind bullet-proof glass, using martial arts and old-fashioned American fists. Ben Gazzara is the town's smirking Mr Big, another example of how business is always up to no good in Hollywood. **BM**
Director Rowdy Herrington **producer** Joel Silver **execs** Steve Perry, Tim Moore **script** David Lee Henry, Hilary Henkin **camera** Dean Cundey **editors** Frank Urioste, John Link **music** Michael Kamen **cast** Patrick Swayze, Kelly Lynch, Sam Elliott, Ben Gazzara, Marshall Teague, Julie Michaels, Red West, Sunshine Parker, Jeff Healey, Kevin Tighe
Running time: 114 mins
US release: UA, May 19, 1989

ROCKET GIBRALTAR

Three generations of a prosperous East Coast family gather to celebrate Burt Lancaster's 77th birthday. The patriarch, once a blacklisted writer, poet and teacher, suffers from a terminal disease; the grandchildren build a boat so that he can have a 'Viking' funeral. Otherwise, not much happens.
Director Daniel Petrie **producer** Jeff Weiss **execs** Michael Ulick, Geoffrey Mayo, Robert Fisher **script** Amos Poe **camera** Jost Vacano **editor** Melody London **design** Bill Groom **music** Andrew Powell **cast** Burt Lancaster, Suzy Amis, Patricia Clarkson, Frances Conroy, Sinead Cusack, John

Glover, Bill Pullman, Kevin Spacey, John Bell
Running time: 100 mins
US release: Columbia, Sep 2, 1988

ROOFTOPS

Robert Wise, director of *West Side Story* and *The Sound of Music*, returned to direction after an eight-year absence for this 'action romance with music and dance.' It's a story of youths who live atop abandoned tenements on Manhattan's Lower East Side and channel their frustrations into vigorous dance competitions.
Director Robert Wise **producer** Howard W. Koch Jr. **execs** Taylor Hackford, Stuart Benjamin **script** Terence Brennan, from story by Allan Goldstein, Tony Mark **camera** Theo Van de Sande **editor** William Reynolds **design** Jeannine C. Oppewall **music** David A. Stewart, Michael Kamen **cast** Jason Gedrick, Troy Beyer, Eddie Velez, Alexis Cruz, Tisha Campbell, Allen Payne
Running time: 95 mins
US release: New Century/Vista, Mar 17, 1989

THE RUNNER (Dawandeh)

A waif living on the edge of an Iranian gulf port rises from garbage picker to shoe-shine boy in Amir Naderi's autobiographical film.
Director Amir Naderi **exec** Fathola Dalili **script** Naderi, Behruz Gharibpur **camera** Firuz Malekzadeh **editor** Bahram Beyza'i **design** Gholam Reza Ramezani **cast** Majid Nirumand, Musa Torkizadeh, A. Gholamzadeh, Reza Ramezani
Running time: 94 mins
UK release: Electric, Jul 29, 1988

THE RUNNING MAN

More masochistic adventures from the Schwarzenegger superman factory, exploiting the actor's uneasy marriage between Neanderthal strength and Austrian deadpan humour in a poorly-delineated futuristic setting. Convicts play for life or death stakes in a game show where they are hunted down by bizarrely-costumed comic-book killers. Schwarzenegger, framed by a corrupt state, is forced to play. Under Paul Michael Glaser's business-like direction, the film mechanistically proceeds to exploit an already well-used narrative concept - future media will pacify the populace through violent entertainment. *The Running Man* adds nothing to Norman Jewison's *Rollerball*, and only the manic gestures of game-show host Richard Dawson create any kind of satirical resonance. **SD**
Director Paul Michael Glaser **producers** Tim

Zinnemann, George Linder **execs** Keith Barish,
Rob Cohen **script** Stephen E. de Souza, based on
novel by Richard Bachman (Stephen King) **camera**
Thomas Del Ruth **editor** Mary Roy Warner **design**
Jack T. Collis **music** Harold Faltermeyer **cast**
Arnold Schwarzenegger, Maria Conchita Alonso,
Richard Dawson, Yaphet Kotto, Jim Brown, Jesse
Ventura, Erland Van Lidth, Marvin J. McIntyre,
Gus Rethwisch, Prof. Toru Tanaka
Running time: 101 mins
US release: Tri-Star, Nov 13, 1987
UK release: Rank, Sep 23, 1988

RUNNING ON EMPTY

As in *Daniel*, Sidney Lumet tells a story of
what happens to the children when a couple of
radicals go too far into political action. Judd
Hirsch and Christine Lahti bombed a building
in their anti-war years, but somebody got hurt
and they spent the following two decades on
the run. Now their son River Phoenix is ready
to leave the nest to study music and he's also
in love with his music teacher's daughter,
Martha Plimpton. Do they hold on to him
forever or let him go and risk their safety? The
teen romance is treated as seriously as the film's
'problem', resulting in a typically gripping
Lumetian melodrama. **BM**
Director Sidney Lumet **producers** Amy Robinson,
Griffin Dunne **execs** Naomi Foner, Burtt Harris
script Foner **camera** Gerry Fisher **editor** Andrew
Mondshein **design** Philip Rosenberg **music** Tony
Mottola **cast** Christine Lahti, River Phoenix, Judd
Hirsch, Martha Plimpton, Jonas Arby, Ed Crowley,
L.M. Kit Carson, Steven Hill, Augusta Dabney
Running time: 116 mins
US release: Warner, Sep 9, 1988
UK release: Warner, Jul 28, 1989

R

RAIN MAN

It never rains but it pours. By Oscar time, 1989, *Rain Man* had taken $134 million at the US box office. Umbrellas were soon being unfurled for the $150 million mark. And who says only Spielberg and Lucas movies can break $200 million? All for a film about two long-lost brothers rediscovering themselves in road-movie America.

Hollywood has developed its own form of double act, in which, under the heading 'buddy buddy', wholesome platonic relationships evolve between two persons of the same sex. Amorous encounters with others, if they happen at all, are footnotes to the discarnate friendship between guy and guy or gal and gal.

The buddy-buddy movie never dies, it merely sleepeth. And 1989 looks like a major wake-up year, bringing us: *Twins*, with Schwarzenegger and DeVito; *Beaches*, with Midler and Hershey; *Mississippi Burning*, with Dafoe and Hackman; *Dead Ringers*, with Irons and Irons. Also entering the ranks were *Tequila Sunrise*, *Midnight Run*, *Red Heat*, *Nicky and Gino* and *Alien Run*.

Above all, we have *Rain Man*, which may be the most startling and unlikely money-spinner in Hollywood history. Here is a mental defective teamed up for two hours with a bumptious go-getter. Here is a film with no special effects, no sex, no violence, no 'love interest' and scarcely any plot. And how much money will it have made by the end of the decade? *E. T.*, watch out.

So what exactly is going on. Why all this now? Why, in 1989, is asexual bonding big business? Could be because we live in an age of moral hygiene, where the West has turned Right and America keeps loosening the buckles on its Bible Belt to contain its swelling piety? Buddyism appeals to this constituency because it speaks of strength through friendship, and love without the untidy convulsions of passion.

The renaissance of buddyism looks suspiciously like the latest instalment of Hollywood's exploration of Innocence. Some 18 months ago, we were being overrun by babies; every new comedy had something small, pink and noisy crawling across the carpet. Later it was age-swap films, in which adults took on the mental age of kids and vice versa. This trend produced one treat, *Big*, and a stream of turkeys. But it provided clear evidence that Dr Tinseltown, our mad scientist busy titrating public taste, firmly believed that the flavour of the era was Innocence.

In an age when our teeth rattle at the global imponderables around us – ozone destruction, incurable diseases, chemical weapons, Dan Quayle and the march of Islam – the invocation of innocence is a bromide that dissolves in the mouth while quelling our deadlier anxieties. No coincidence that two films with virtually identical plots dominated the New York box office in the US and the Easter box office in the UK.

That plot goes like this: an overgrown innocent, sheltered from the outside world all his adult life, is bounced into that world where he meets a sleazy, opportunist brother. Off they go on a road journey, during which the innocent shows his goodness and sweetness and intuitive capacity for survival, while the selfish, short-fused brother gradually comes round to loving him.

Meet *Rain Man* and *Rain Man*'s twin brother, *Twins*. Joined at the hip, these two mega-hits are late-1980s variants on the classic figuration of American buddy-buddy films. On the surface, Hollywood double acts – notably the comic ones, from Laurel and Hardy to Martin and Lewis – nearly always consist of a lovable innocent or idiot and a less lovable 'minder' or surrogate parent. But underneath that surface, reversals and contradictions lurk. The innocent often turns out to be wiser, brighter and more inspirational: the minder to be a bully or dullard with a smart-operator veneer.

Indeed it's the message of *Rain Man* and *Twins* that while maturity can provide and protect, innocence can reveal and redeem. The 'child of nature' Hoffman or the 'noble savage' Schwarzenegger come into their respective brothers' lives in the yuppie-dominated late-1980s and say: 'Life isn't a matter of screaming along in the fast lane. It's about caring and being cared for, helping and being helped, loving and being loved.'

No surprise that *Rain Man* and *Twins* launched themselves skyward at Christmas – the season of peace, love and goodwill. Months later, around Easter, the first-phase uncoupling took place. *Twins* started falling back to Earth while Oscar-boosted *Rain Man* kept powering on into Outer Space.

Its stamina may prove more startling than its first *éclat*. *Rain Man* has hit the jackpot because it links a reverberant buddy-buddy optimism to that stalwart box-office gimmick of our times, the twinning of two top male stars. In doing so, it becomes a pop Sermon on the Mount – 'Blessed are the poor, the backward, the inadequate, the reclusive, etc.' – rolled up into a box-office snowball with a dollop of Laurel and Hardy, a pinch of road-movie *wanderlust* and, most irresistible of all, a hero who in his unblinking, incorruptible innocence is humanity's closest answer yet to E.T.

The film's sentimentality is indisputable. But it's also well camouflaged, and the chief camouflager is Dustin Hoffman, who refuses to play his autistic hero according to the 'Teach Yourself Retard Acting' book. Instead of yawing his face and contorting his voice, in laboured mimicry of infantilism, Hoffman is abrupt, bird-like, *pizzicato*. He's also 'lovable' without cap-in-hand cuteness. He never goes for babyishness or helplessness. His performance endears us to Raymond through his efflorescence or idiosyncrasies, its other-worldliness and, in scenes like Raymond's statistical invocation of Quantas as the world's safest airline, its sheer comic timing.

If this movie were ever asset-stripped, the most valuable item by far would

be Hoffman. Just imagine *Rain Man* with an earlier Oscar-winning retard, Cliff Robertson's *Charly*: it would be throw-up time.

The second priciest asset would be director Barry Levinson, whose account of what he jettisoned from this project when he took it over from Steven Spielberg – from wacky chase scenes to lines like 'Know yourself, Charlie Babbitt' (Hoffman to Cruise) – suggests he may well have saved the film from being a bloated buddy caper smug with sententiousness. He may have made it grow into a movie which owes its popularity as much to what *isn't* formulaic – the subject of autism, Hoffman's acting – as to what calculatedly or crassly is: the high-concept casting, Tom Cruise's acting, the in-tune-with-the-times sexlessness.

Rain Man is a phenomenon no one could quite have seen coming. But with the help of hindsight its footprints clearly belong to the age in which it was born.

HARLAN KENNEDY

RED SORGHUM

ike *Yellow Earth*, the film which announced the arrival of a New Chinese Cinema, *Red Sorghum* opens with a wedding procession. The titles indicate shared concerns – the colour of landscape, rural life – and reflect the common experience of China's 'fifth generation' of filmmakers, bustled off to live and work among the peasantry during the Cultural Revolution.

But although Zhang Zimou was cinematographer on the first film and director of *Red Sorghum*, the two films offer very different approaches to their subjects. Chen Kaige presented an almost analytical look at the dour realities of peasant life; Zimou plunges us into a vortex of surging passion.

The wedding cavalcade in *Yellow Earth* kept the viewer at a distance; every image in *Red Sorghum* is cast to immediate emotional effect. The face of a girl, Nine (Gong Li), is prepared for her wedding. Placed inside the chair, she pulls aside her veil to reveal the angry, beautiful visage of an unwilling bride. The porters mock her for marrying a man who rots, their bawdiness and swaying movements adding to her misery. The music and the movement build to a crescendo, but are suddenly cut short by the sound of her tears. Like naughty boys caught in wickedness, they start to trot quietly and gently across the sandy terrain.

The film is told as a young man's imaginary reconstruction of his grandparent's past, a tale that 'not everybody believes anymore'. In the opening sequence Zimou repeatedly draws attention to one character, the only hired hand among the carriers, thus posing the dramatic question: How will the porter and the bride ever become man and wife? Immediately, events turn towards this outcome. A bandit threatens the procession, and is summarily despatched by the porter Yu (Jiang Wen). Nine walks calmly back to her chair, saying nothing. But she does glance at him. It is enough. She pulls down the screen but leaves her foot showing. He pushes that foot back, a gesture of love.

Zimou subtly charts an emotional trajectory for his two characters that counterpoints the main flow of the action. This is most apparent in a scene where the workers celebrate the arrival of the first sorghum wine, singing a gutsy song of the sort that peppers the narrative. As they chant, a figure appears in the distance. It is Yu. All look on in awe, and increasing anger, as he lifts up the vats of the new vintage, pisses in them, then scatters coal over the workers. But as he is alienating *them*, his transgressions are exciting *her*. By the time he is through, all she wants is to collapse into his arms.

Nine is an exceptional heroic presence, an indomitable creature of legend. She first reveals her mettle when she takes that calm, seductive walk back to her chair away from the would-be rapist's corpse. Seeing her huddled in the corner

of a bed with her scissors we know that her husband, Big Head Yi, could never hope to get the better of her. She casts aside traditional assumptions about respect for parents: 'I don't want a father like you. You traded me for a mule.' And when Yu arrives drunk to claim her, she first ejects him, then beats him, not flinching for one moment from his primal screams.

It is Nine and Yu's shared willingness to defy convention that draws them to each other. It is desire, Yu's for Nine, that leads to the disappearance of Big Head Yi – almost a magical event – and clears the way for her to establish authority over the wine-making process. When she tells the workers not to call her 'boss' – 'What's mine is yours too' – it would turn the film into cod propagandizing were the statement not so clearly sourced in a genuine sense of solidarity. The colour red is here almost stripped of its reference to party dogma, so that it can be reasserted as a metaphor for a life lived to the full. Once she has persuaded the workers not to leave, they burn the furniture of the old master and fling sorghum wine around the house to wash away his traces.

The sorghum and the sorghum fields are sources of magic. From the sorghum comes that luckless bandit whose surprise arrival sparked the romance between Nine and Yu. Passing back through the cornfields after four days of pseudo-marriage, Yu emerges to seize her. But while the sorghum wine can wash away the residue of sickness, it is useless as an explosive when placed in the path of the Japanese invaders, who are to kill Nine and devastate the sorghum fields.

Just as the efficacy of the wine has its limits, so things do not always favour rebellious individuals. Some critics have taken seriously Zimou's apology for the final section of *Red Sorghum*, which details the horrific cruelty inflicted by Japanese invaders on those who attempted resistance, and represented it as a rhetorical concession to the ideological commitments of the China Film Bureau. Such an argument presupposes some other (happier?) ending to the story, in which history does not intrude. But where is the mis-match between the main theme of the film – the desire that brings the lovers together – and its concluding section about the brutality committed by the Japanese which destroys them?

Earlier, after Yu has absconded in shame, he comes to a butcher's shop where the best beef is being saved for a bandit. Yu brawls with the bandit but is made to look foolish. The same bandit is later helpless when strung up by the Japanese. Forceful against one bandit, Yu is helpless against another. Capable of mocking Yu in his own context, the bandit can do nothing against a mighty army. However vital their élan, however great their courage, these individuals are powerless against an overwhelming force determined to crush the life out of them. The soldiers here may be Japanese, but they could as well be the Chinese troops sent in to drive their own people out of Tiananmen Square. *Red Sorghum* needs no apologies, but stands as a premonition of recent ghastly events, and an extraordinary piece of filmmaking.

JAMES PARK

SACRIFICED YOUTH (Quingchun Ji)

Another attempt to deal with the Cultural Revolution, *Sacrificed Youth* shows a family being dispersed from Beijing to various parts of the countryside and follows one of its members (Fengxu) as she adjusts to rural life.
Director *Zhang Nuanxin* **producer** *Zhao Yamin* **exec** *Li Ning* **script** *Zhang Nuanxin, based on short story by Zhang Manling* **camera** *My Deyuan, Deng Wei* **editor** *Zhao Qihua* **design** *Li Yonxin, Wang Yanjin* **music** *Liu Suola, Qu Xiaosong* **cast** *Li Fengxu, Feng Yuanzheng, Song Tao, Guo Jianguo, Yu Da, Yu Shuai*
Running time: 96 mins
UK release: Artificial Eye, Dec 9, 1988

SAIGON (Off Limits in US)

Back to Nam for *Platoon*'s Willem Dafoe, this time as an MP teamed with cool cat Gregory Hines in the harrowing investigation of a prostitute killer who's also a US army officer. The clichéd black/white/buddy-movie formula and a tepid romantic friendship between Dafoe and Amanda Pays' unshockable nun notwithstanding, this behind-the-lines thriller offers a peculiarly disenchanted appraisal of the American way of doing things in Saigon. With Scott Glenn chilling as the crazed Colonel who leaps out of a chopper, and excellent re-creation of life under fire at the notorious Khe Sanh airstrip, *Saigon* captures the mayhem and the madness with as much vibrancy, if less style, than the more acclaimed Vietnam combat movies. **GF**
Director *Christopher Crowe* **producer** *Alan Barnette* **script** *Crowe, Jack Thibeau* **camera** *David Gribble* **editor** *Douglas Ibold* **design** *Dennis Washington* **music** *James Newton Howard* **cast** *Willem Dafoe, Gregory Hines, Fred Ward, Amanda Pays, Kay Tong Lim, Scott Glenn*
Running time: 102 mins
US release: Fox, Mar 11, 1988
UK release: Fox, Jul 8, 1988

SALAAM BOMBAY!

This extraordinary début from Mira Nair sweeps aside the clichéd conventions of mainstream Indian cinema to observe the lives of the down-and-outs who inhabit the streets of Bombay. No songs, no lavish sets, no happy endings, precious little hope but an immense sense of humanity and compassion. The huge cast – mixing professionals with real-life pimps, beggars and addicts – are a marvel in a film with a vision and hard-edged style. **TW**
Director/ producer *Mira Nair* **execs** *Anil Tejani,*
Michael Nozik, Gabriel Auer **script** *Sooni Taraporevala* **camera** *Sandi Sissel* **editor** *Barry Alexander Brown* **design** *Mitch Epstein* **music** *L. Subramaniam* **cast** *Shafiq Syed, Raghubir Yadav, Aneeta Kanwar, Nana Patekar, Hansa Vithal, Mohnaraj Babu, Chandrashekhar Naidu, Chanda Sharma, Shaukat Kaifi, Sarfuddin Qurrassi, Raju Barnad*
Running time: 114 mins
US release: Cinecom, Oct 9, 1988
UK release: Mainline, Jan 27, 1989

SALOME'S LAST DANCE

This magnificently stylized piece of cinema from irrepressible, overgrown choirboy Ken Russell sets Oscar Wilde's scandalous play in a London brothel in 1892, where Wilde himself attends a performance arranged by Lord Alfred Douglas. Russell invests this Bacchanalian celebration with an aura of perverse chic, whisked into a delightful orgiastic frenzy by milque-toast Douglas (Stratford Johns) and coquettish newcomer, the elfin Imogen Millais-Scott. Dancing midgets, lusty eunuchs and semi-nude dancing girls augment this amusing Sadean novelty – another offering from industrious *auteur* Russell that repudiates the glib British filmmaking dogma that confuses great cinema with refined conversation and picturesque photography. **MN**
Director *Ken Russell* **producer** *Penny Corke* **execs** *William J. Quigley, Dan Ireland* **script** *Russell, from play by Oscar Wilde* **camera** *Harvie Harrison* **editor** *Timothy Gee* **design** *Michael Buchanan* **cast** *Glenda Jackson, Stratford Johns, Nickolas Grace, Douglas Hodge, Imogen Millais-Scott, Denis Ull, Russell Lee Nash, Alfred Russell, Ken Russell*
Running time: 89 mins
US release: Vestron, May 6, 1988
UK release: Vestron, Jul 1, 1988

SALSA

Even by bopsical standards, this is a pretty threadbare effort, in which an unappealingly bumptious youth gets on the nerves of friends and family in his desire to win a Salsa dance contest and thus a free trip to Puerto Rico. The movie mainly resembles a series of commercials for soft drinks or deodorants, then actually turns into an advertisement for TWA, with a lengthy dance routine constructed around a billboard promoting the airline. The only moment of slight surprise is afforded by the interpolation into the score of 'Blue Suede Shoes'. **TP**

Director Boaz Davidson *producers* Menahem Golan, Yoram Globus *script* Davidson, Tomas Benitez, Shepard Goldman *camera* David Gurfinkel *editor* Alain Jakubowicz *design* Mark Haskins *cast* Robby Rosa, Rodney Harvey, Magali Alvarado, Miranda Garrison, Moon Orona, Angela Alvorado, Loyda Romas, Valente Rodriguez, Daniel Rojo, Humberto Ortiz
Running time: 99 mins (97 mins in UK)
US release: Cannon, May 6, 1988
UK release: Cannon, Jul 22, 1988

SAY ANYTHING

This romantic comedy for mature teens stars John Cusack and Ione Skye as seemingly mismatched lovers in the summer after their high school graduation. Cusack has no ambitions whereas Skye is programmed for high achievement at a top college. In spite of this and disapproval of her loving father, John Mahoney, she discerns his hidden merits. Cusack gets his best-yet film part as a winning kid who knows how to express his feelings, if not his intelligence. **BM**
Director/script Cameron Crowe *producer* Polly Platt *exec* James L. Brooks *camera* Laszlo Kovacs *editor* Richard Marks *design* Mark Mansbridge *music* Richard Gibbs, Anne Dudley *cast* John Cusack, Ione Skye, John Mahoney, Lili Taylor, Amy Brooks, Pamela Segall, Jason Gould, Loren Dean, Joan Cusack
Running time: 100 mins
US release: Fox, April 14, 1989

DOG

SCANDAL

Director Michael Caton-Jones *producer* Stephen Woolley *execs* Nik Powell, Joe Boyd *script* Michael Thomas *camera* Mike Molloy *editor* Angus Newton *design* Simon Holland *music* Carl Davis *cast* John Hurt, Joanne Whalley-Kilmer, Bridget Fonda, Ian McKellen, Leslie Phillips, Britt Ekland, Daniel Massey, Roland Gift, Jean Alexander, Paul Brooke, Ronald Fraser, Alex Norton, Jeroen Krabbé, Keith Allen, Ralph Brown, Ken Campbell, Ian Cuthbertson
Running time: 115 mins
US release: Miramax, Apr 28, 1989
UK release: Palace, Mar 3, 1989

SCENES FROM THE CLASS STRUGGLE IN BEVERLY HILLS 👍

This is Paul Bartel's funniest-yet concoction of camp, knockabout, farce, irony, dry wit, dirty jokes and every other way to get a laugh in a dark room. Into a disgustingly rich household in Beverly Hills Bartel tosses such types as a relieved widow (Bisset), a bisexual houseboy (Sharkey), a houseboy who resists bisexuality (Beltran), a fat diet doctor (Bartel), the ghost of Bisset's hubby (Mazursky), a lusty neighbour (Woronov), her faithless ex-husband (Shawn) and others. Bartel keeps his *Scenes* moving quickly from style to style, ensuring that everybody will find something offensive or funny or both. **BM**
Director Paul Bartel *producer* J. C. Katz *execs* Amir J. Malin, Ira Deutchman *script* Bruce Wagner *camera* Steven Fierberg *editor* Alan Toomayan *design* Alex Tavoularis *music* Stanley Myers *cast* Jacqueline Bisset, Ray Sharkey, Robert Beltran, Mary Woronov, Ed Begley Jr., Wallace Shawn, Arnetia Walker, Rebecca Schaeffer, Barret Olivier, Edith Diaz, Paul Bartel, Paul Mazursky
Running time: 102 mins
US release: Cinecom, Jun 9, 1989

SCHOOL DAZE

Spike Lee's dispiritingly unfunny follow-up to *She's Gotta Have It* makes (for better or worse) absolutely no concessions to white audiences or to the demands of movie storytelling in its stop-start saga of life on a Southern black university campus. Glued together by musical numbers, *School Daze* pitches militant activists (led by Larry Fishburne's Dap) against the elitist Gamma Phi Gamma fraternity (led by Giancarlo Esposito's Big Brother Almighty), with pledging freshman Half-Pint (Lee) caught in the middle, and the light-skinned wannabees fighting it out with the darker Jigaboos among the women. If the film has a message, it's a call to black consciousness, but the most telling scene has Dap's boys confronting some working-class brothers out in the city. There's no resolution as such and very little fun, except a delicious dance duel between the female gangs on a hair-salon set. Not short of ideas, Lee has crammed them all in without bothering to impose a structure. **GF**
Director/producer/script Spike Lee *exec* Grace Blake *camera* Ernest Dickerson *editor* Barry Alexander Brown *design* Wynn Thomas *music* Bill Lee *cast* Larry Fishburne, Giancarlo Esposito, Tisha Campbell, Kyme, Joe Seneca, Ellen Holly, Art Evans, Ossie Davis, Spike Lee
Running time: 120 mins
US release: Columbia, Feb 12, 1988
UK release: Col/Tri-Star, Jul 22, 1988

SCROOGED

Director Richard Donner **producers** Donner, Art Linson **exec** Steve Roth **script** Mitch Glazer, Michael O'Donoghue **camera** Michael Chapman **editors** Fredrick Steinkamp, William Steinkamp **design** J. Michael Riva **music** Danny Elfman **cast** Bill Murray, Karen Allen, John Forsythe, John Glover, Bobcat Goldthwait, David Johansen, Carol Kane, Robert Mitchum, Nicholas Phillips, Michael J. Pollard, John Houseman **Running time:** 101 mins **US release:** Paramount, Nov 23, 1988 **UK release:** UIP, Nov 25, 1988

SEE NO EVIL, HEAR NO EVIL

Richard Pryor and Gene Wilder re-team hilariously as a blind man and a deaf man respectively, who collectively 'witness' a murder. The blind man heard the shot, the deaf man saw the legs of the murderess (Severance). Without demeaning the seeing-deprived and hearing-impaired, Arthur Hiller's film is a slapstick compendium of blind and deaf jokes (yes, Pryor drives a car; yes, Wilder gets steamed when people shout at him). Non-handicap jokes abound too. Severance is about to execute our two heroes, but first she grants Wilder's wish – a kiss. Pryor pipes up, 'I suppose a fuck is out of the question?' **BM** **Director** Arthur Hiller **producer** Marvin Worth **execs** Burtt Harris, Earl Barret, Arne Sultan **script** Barret, Sultan, Eliot Wald, Andrew Kurtzman, Gene Wilder **camera** Victor J. Kemper **editor** Robert C. Jones **design** Robert Gundlach **music** Stewart Copeland **cast** Richard Pryor, Gene Wilder, Joan Severance, Kevin Spacey **Running time:** 103 mins **US release:** Tri-Star, May 12, 1989

SEE YOU IN THE MORNING

Divorce Hollywood style. Jeff Bridges can't get on with beautiful wife Farrah Fawcett; so he divorces her. He falls in love with beautiful Alice Krige instead and soon she is Mrs Bridges II. The seasons change, but the movie's wisdom-through-tears blandness doesn't. Nor its taste for plonky piano music. Basing the film on his own marital vicissitudes, writer-director Alan J. Pakula seldom elevates the material above women's magazine-status. Even when the film focuses on the children caught in the crossfire its sentimental stoicism exasperates. Especially from a filmmaker who once had both rage and range (Klute, All The President's Men). **HK** **Director/producer/script** Alan J. Pakula **camera** Donald McAlpine **editor** Evan Lottman **design** George Jenkins **cast** Jeff Bridges, Alice Krige, Farrah Fawcett, Drew Barrymore, Lukas Haas, David Dukes, Frances Sternhagen, Heather Lilly **Running time:** 119 mins **US release:** Warner, Apr 21, 1989

LA SENYORA

Director Jordi Cadena deploys his eye for physical gesture and contrasts in décor to turn this otherwise familiar tale of sexual frustration into unsettling cinema. Silvia Tortosa is married off by her parents to a man whose obsession with cleanliness frustrates her physical longing. After indulging in necrophilia on his death bed, she moves to the country, but her would-be lover is drowned shortly before a planned consummation, and she takes up with a local peasant boy. The shift from dark, cluttered interiors to glowing rural landscapes, and from squabbling relatives to simple country-folk, is not the journey into the light she had planned. An increasingly embittered landowner, she blocks her lover's chance of marital happiness. Although Tortosa's face is not expressive enough to fully convey her transformation, careful pacing and an elliptical narrative sustain tension throughout. **JP** **Director** Jordi Cadena **producer** Jonni Bassiner **exec** Paco Poch **script** Cadena, Silvia Tortosa, based on novel by Antoni Mus **camera** José G. Galisteo **editor** Amat Carreras **design** Josep Mariá Espada **music** J. M. Pagán **cast** Silvia Tortosa, Hermann Bonnin, Luis Merlo, Fernando Guillén-Cuervo, Jeannine Mestre, Alfonso Guirao **Running time:** 103 mins **UK release:** ICA, Apr 21, 1989

SEPTEMBER

Famous as the movie that Allen shot with one cast and then re-shot with another, September marks the nadir of the great comic writer-director's intent to capture the spirit of Bergman and Chekhov. Claustrophobically set in one interior, the drama features a series of related characters wandering in and out to bemoan their dissatisfactions in love. Whatever Allen intended, it is the 'banal' figures who have all the vitality, and the insipid intellectuals who lead the audience to cheer on their anticipations of self-induced demise. The effect is indescribable tedium. **DT** **Director/script** Woody Allen **producer** Robert

Greenhut **execs** *Jack Rollins, Charles H. Joffe*
camera *Carlo Di Palma* **editor** *Susan E. Morse*
design *Santo Loquasto* **cast** *Denholm Elliott,
Dianne Wiest, Mia Farrow, Elaine Stritch, Sam
Waterston, Jack Warden, Ira Wheeler, Jane Cecil,
Rosemary Murphy*
Running time: 83 mins
US release: Orion, Dec 18, 1987
UK release: Rank, Jul 1, 1988

THE SERPENT AND THE RAINBOW

A Harvard anthropologist, seeking the secret
ingredient which can turn Haitians into
zombies, falls foul of black magic and the Ton-
Ton Macoute. Wade Davis's book, on which
the screenplay was based, was non-fiction, but
Wes Craven simply uses the framework of the
story, set in the days immediately prior to the
fall of Baby Doc, as a framework on which to
pin all manner of staple horror ingredients –
spooky cemeteries, being buried alive, walking
corpses, creepy-crawlies and snakes erupting out
of orifices. He also seizes the opportunity to
experiment further with the dream-versus-reality
scenario introduced into *A Nightmare on Elm
Street*. Here, it's merged with demonic
possession and what looks like straight-up
necromancy. It is to Craven's credit that, while
one is never sure whether one is watching
fantasy or reality, he maintains a strong enough
grip on structure to prevent the horrors lapsing
into anarchy. Sensitive male viewers should be
advised that there is a notably nasty torture
scene in which the villain hammers a nail
through the hero's scrotum. **AB**
Director *Wes Craven* **producers** *David Ladd,
Doug Clayborne* **execs** *Rob Cohen, Keith Barish*
script *Richard Maxwell, A.R. Simoun, based on
book by Wade Davis* **camera** *John Lindley* **editor**
Glenn Farr **design** *David Nichols* **music** *Brad
Fiedel* **cast** *Bill Pullman, Cathy Tyson, Zakes
Mokae, Paul Winfield, Brent Jennings, Conrad
Roberts, Badja Djola, Theresa Merritt, Michael
Gough, Paul Guilfoyle, Dey Young, Aleta Mitchell*
Running time: 98 mins
US release: Universal, Feb 5, 1988
UK release: UIP, Apr 21, 1989

THE SEVENTH SIGN

A portentous disaster of a movie that features
the Jesus-like presence of Jürgen Prochnow
warning the heavily-pregnant Demi Moore that
her child will be born without a soul and the
world will come to an end. Totally crucified by
the hollowness of its loudly apocalyptic script,
this 'the end of the world is nigh' hysteria

shudders forward like a stalled car. Moore
waddles along, suitably aghast at the various
natural phenomena that are hurled in her
direction. Much bible-bashing and biblical
nightmares later, Demi finds her faith and saves
the planet. Such inane dialogue as 'How can
someone who cares so little for life give life to
the world' suggests that the film was a dodo
from the start. While Prochnow's sorrowful,
haunting presence transcends the inanities he
strides through, director Carl Schultz struggles
for an expressionistic style that occasionally
brings forth an undercurrent of menace. But
the overblown self-importance of the narrative's
apocryphal leanings splinter any coherence he
tries to muster. **SD**
Director *Carl Schultz* **producer** *Ted Field, Robert
Cort* **exec** *Paul R. Gurian* **script** *W.W.Wicket,
George Kaplan (Clifford Green, Ellen Green)*
camera *Juan Ruiz-Anchia* **editor** *Caroline
Biggerstaff* **design** *Stephen Marsh* **music** *Jack
Nitzsche* **cast** *Demi Moore, Michael Biehm, Jürgen
Prochnow, Manny Jacobs, Peter Friedman, John
Heard, Akosua Busia*
Running time: 97 mins
US release: Tri-Star, Apr 1, 1988
UK release: Col/Tri-Star, Nov 18, 1988

SHAG

With its succession of retro-chic music, cars and
fashion, *Shag* is the latest in a line of teen
nostalgia films that stretches from *American
Graffiti* to *Dirty Dancing*. The direct inspiration
here is Glendon Swarthout's twice-filmed (and
twice-bungled) novel *Where The Boys Are*. *Shag*
resurrects the character types and plot
incidentals of the book, mixed in with familiar
bits and pieces from other teen movies, with
the result that the film seems like a greatest-hits
compilation album of the genre. We are
presented with a wild party that trashes an
elegant mansion; a crucial dance contest in
which the underdogs suddenly display amazing
footwork; the black maid who is always
wandering into rooms where teenagers are
clinching ('You is the horniest bunch of white
folks I's ever seen!'); a mean and macho rebel
who prods the soon-to-be-settled-down queen
out of her complacency; the self-involved teen
star who proves a disappointment to his gold-
digging fans; playful defiance of parental
authority; trips to the fairground and the local
lovers' lane, and the awkward but touching
relationship between two teens who realize they
aren't quite the geeks they think themselves to
be. In a young and lively cast, only Annabeth

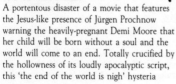

Gish really comes across well. **KN**
Director Zelda Barron **producers** Stephen
Woolley, Julia Chasman **execs** John Daly, Derek
Gibson, Nik Powell **script** Robin Swicord, Lanier
Laney, Terry Sweeney **camera** Peter MacDonald
editor Laurence Méry Clark **design** Buddy Cone
cast Phoebe Cates, Scott Coffey, Bridget Fonda,
Annabeth Gish, Page Hannah, Robert Rusler,
Tyrone Power Jr., Jeff Yagher
Running time: 98 mins
US release: Hemdale, May 12, 1989
UK release: Palace, Aug 12, 1988

SHAKEDOWN (See Blue Jean Cop)

SHAME

Small-town melodrama-cum-road movie with a
feminist slant, in which a woman lawyer from
the city stranded in an Outback hamlet
becomes caught up in a conspiracy of silence
and eventual violence over the rape of a
teenage girl. Vividly observed and vigorously
staged, this is, despite a tendency for things to
go over the top in the finale, an encouraging
instance of exploitation formulae put to
responsible use, and boasts an impressive
central performance by Deborra-Lee Furness.
TP
Director Steve Jodrell **producers** Damien Parer,
Paul Barron **script** Beverly Blankenship, Michael
Brindley **camera** Joseph Pickering **editor** Kerry
Regan **design** Phil Peters **music** Mario Millo **cast**
Deborra-Lee Furness, Tony Barry, Simone
Buchanan, Gillian Jones, Peter Aanensen
Running time: 92 mins
US release: Skouras, Jul 22, 1988
UK release: Other Cinema, May 5, 1989

SHE'S OUT OF CONTROL

Fathers often feel squirmy when their daughters
discover sex, but Stan Dragoti's comic
treatment of this sad complex is an insult to
fathers and daughters, let alone Electra and
Agamemnon. Tony Danza is a radio station
manager, a job that should put him on young
people's wavelengths. But, when his bookworm
daughter (Dolenz) metamorphoses into a teen
temptress with the help of Danza's own steady
(Hicks), he changes from doting Dad to
hyperactive spy, investigating her every
involvement. In the movie's one bright spot,
Wallace Shawn plays a psychologist and author
of 'Daddy's Little Girl', a guide to raising
daughters. Only too late does Danza discover
that Shawn has no daughters. **BM**
Director Stan Dragoti **producer** Stephen Deutsch

exec Robert Kaufman **script** Seth Winston,
Michael J. Nathanson **camera** Donald Peterman
editor Dov Hoenig **design** David L. Snyder **music**
Alan Silvestri **cast** Tony Danza, Catherine Hicks,
Ami Dolenz, Wallace Shawn, Dick O'Neill, Laura
Mooney, Derek McGrath, Dana Ashbrook
Running time: 95 mins
US release: WEG/Columbia, Apr 14, 1989

SHOOT TO KILL (See Deadly Pursuit)

SHORT CIRCUIT 2

TV fantasy director Kenneth Johnson takes a
break from such formulaic family-oriented series
as The Incredible Hulk and V to helm this
sequel to the cute-robot-that-is-almost-human
movie which originally starred Steve
Guttenberg and Ally Sheedy. Neither of the
original cast is present this time round, and the
heart-on-the-sleeve mentality is exchanged for
an insipid thriller style, stuffed full of gadgetry
and bungling criminals. The robot, curiously
now named Johnny Five, gets more of the one-
liners than last time and its attempt to
understand its mechanical nature is sometimes
poignant. Johnson, purely a journeyman, brings
little life to what is essentially a shopworn one-
joke wonder, with little if any real momentum
left in it. **SD**
Director Kenneth Johnson **producers** David
Foster, Lawrence Turman, Gary Foster **exec**
Michael MacDonald **script** S. S. Wilson, Brent
Maddock **camera** John McPherson **editor** Conrad
Buff **design** Bill Brodie **music** Charles Fox **cast**
Fisher Stevens, Michael McKean, Cynthia Gibb,
Jack Weston, Dee McCafferty, David Hemblen
Running time: 110 mins
US release: Tri-Star, Jul 6, 1988
UK release: Col/Tri-Star, Feb 10, 1989

SHY PEOPLE

Konchalovsky's fourth film for Cannon
describes a New York sophisticate travelling
with her degenerate daughter into the dark and
mysterious bayous of Louisiana to write about
her long-lost great uncle. What they find is his
dogged young widow (a commendably dignified
Barbara Hershey) and her trio of weird sons.
The culture clash is deafening, the tedium of
this estranged world all too palpable. **DT**
Director Andrei Konchalovsky **producers**
Menahem Golan, Yoram Globus **script** Gérard
Brach, Konchalovsky **camera** Chris Menges **editor**
Alain Jakubowicz **design** Stephen Marsh **music**
Tangerine Dream **cast** Jill Clayburgh, Barbara
Hershey, Martha Plimpton, Merritt Butrick, John

Philbin, Don Swayze, Pruitt Taylor Vince, Mare Winningham, Michael Audley, Brad Leland
Running time: 119 mins
US release: Cannon, Dec 4, 1988
UK release: Cannon, Jul 1, 1988

THE SICILIAN

Michael Cimino's film of the story of Salvatore Giuliano amounts almost to a hagio-pic. As portrayed by Christopher Lambert, the famous Sicilian bandit is a noble Robin Hood figure with an impossible dream (that of having Sicily join the US as an extra state) and palpably innocent of the well-documented atrocities that have been attributed to him. Moreover, he possesses the enviable ability to appear, after several weeks' roughing it in the mountain, as if his clothes had just been helicoptered in from Milan. Lambert once again shows himself to be an actor of endearingly small range; his scenes with Barbara Sukowa, as an American Duchess enamoured of his tough peasant's physique, are minor classics of howling embarrassment. But Cimino has not lost his sense of cinema, and the result is a wacko hotch-potch of awesome spectacle, cringe-making dialogue and bare-faced hamming – particularly from Joss Ackland, who romps away with the entire show as the gravel-throated *capo*. **AB**
Director Michael Cimino *producers* Cimino, Joann Carelli *exec* Sidney Beckerman *script* Steve Shagan, based on novel by Mario Puzo *camera* Alex Thomson *editor* Françoise Bonnot *design* Wolf Kroeger *music* David Mansfield *cast* Christopher Lambert, Terence Stamp, Joss Ackland, John Turturro, Richard Bauer, Barbara Sukowa, Giulia Boschi, Ray McAnally, Barry Miller, Andreas Katsulas, Michael Wincott, Derrick Branche
Running time: 146 mins (119 mins in US)
US release: Fox, Oct 23, 1987
UK release: Fox, Sep 2, 1988

SING

A downbeat neighbourhood of Brooklyn is about to lose its school. Do parents and teachers gather round to fight for its survival? Sadly, no. Seemingly their only concern is to ensure the school goes down in glory, after the best 'sing' ever. Nice little Jewish girl (Stern) is teamed up with a part-time mugger (Dobson) to direct the show, cueing yet another unlikely screen romance. It turns out he's the one with choreographic talent, thanks to mucho time spent in the local disco. True love, however, takes a bumpy ride, especially after he takes part in a raid on the diner run by Stern's

mother. Lorraine Bracco, who showed such promise in *Someone to Watch Over Me*, is horribly wasted here and, even if some of the dancing is great, it never lifts the proceedings above School of *Fame* filmmaking at its most basic. **JP**
Director Richard Baskin *producer* Craig Zadan *exec* Wolfgang Glattes *script* Dean Pitchford *camera* Peter Sova *editors* Bud Smith, Jere Huggins, Scott Smith *design* Carol Spier *music* Gay Gruska *cast* Lorraine Bracco, Peter Dobson, Jessica Stern, Louise Lasser, George DiCenzo, Patti LaBelle, Susan Peretz
Running time: 97 mins
US release: Tri-Star, Mar 31, 1989
UK release: Col/Tri-Star, Jun 9, 1989

'68

Revealing its low budget in the hole-in-the-corner aspect of sequences involving an open-air concert and a political rally, this look at the vicissitudes of a Hungarian émigré family in San Francisco is unfortunately all too low on inspiration as well. The college drop-out son who is the centre of attention never comes into convincing focus; several of the incidental figures are presented in terms of risible caricature, and political context chiefly resides in an endless succession of TV and radio news bulletins. **TP**
Director/script Steven Kovacs *producers* Dale Djerassi, Isabel Maxwell, Kovacs *camera* Daniel Lacambre *editor* Cari Coughlin *design* Joshua Koral *music* John Coppolina, Shony Alex Braun *cast* Eric Larson, Robert Locke, Sandor Tecsi, Anna Kukasz, Miran Kwun, Terra Vandergaw, Neil Young
Running time: 98 mins
US release: New World, Feb 26, 1988
UK release: Entertainment, Sep 9, 1988

SKIN DEEP

Blake Edwards' sex comedy may be his best work in recent years – and contains the funniest safe-sex scene to date – but still ends up, appropriately enough, being rather superficial. John Ritter plays yet another self-obsessed Californian writer sleeping his way through most of the supporting cast before seeing the light in time for yet another Dreadful Warning finale (wife leaves him, best friend dies). We never really care, despite Ritter's boy-next-door charm, but it's a painless couple of hours, and the luminous condom joke (the main selling point in the ad campaign) is almost worth the price of admission. **TW**

Director/script Blake Edwards *producer* Tony Adams *execs* Joe Roth, James G. Robinson *camera* Isidore Mankofsky *editor* Robert Pergament *design* Rodger Maus *cast* John Ritter, Vincent Gardenia, Alyson Reed, Joel Brooks, Julianne Phillips, Raye Hollit, Michael Kidd, Chelsea Field
Running time: 101 mins
US release: Fox, Mar 3, 1989
UK release: Fox, Jul 7, 1989

SLAVES OF NEW YORK

James Ivory, never one to raise many smiles, reproduces the milieu of Tama Janowitz's stories about struggling artists in lower Manhattan, but omits the humour. Bernadette Peters, about twice the age of Janowitz's heroine and far too pretty, can't afford Manhattan unless she keeps rooming with cretinous artist Adam Coleman Howard. She makes hats out of junk she finds in bins but has yet to make a commercial connection. Others in the gallery world push and thrive but Peters just cooks and irons for Howard. In a tacked-on resolution, she finally gets her millinery accepted and moves into a place of her own. **BM**
Director James Ivory *producers* Ismail Merchant, Gary Hendler *script* Tama Janowitz, *from her stories camera* Tony Pierce-Roberts *editor* Katherine Wenning *design* David Gropman *music* Richard Robbins *cast* Bernadette Peters, Adam Coleman Howard, Nick Corri, Madeleine Potter, Charles McCaughan, Chris Sarandon, Mary Beth Hurt, Mercedes Ruehl, John Harkins
Running time: 121 mins
US release: Tri-Star, Mar 17, 1989

SLIPSTREAM

This mish-mash of SF plot ideas offers us Bob Peck as an android on the run through a world devastated by environmental catastrophe. How do we know he's an android? Because he's wearing a suit and can heal cataracts while nobody's looking. He can also dance *à la* Fred Astaire and quote Byron. Bill Paxton snatches him from another bounty hunter and they're off through a variety of communities headed by former Oscar nominees. The filmmakers, however, lack both maps and meteorological charts. Whenever captor and captive are in the air, they hover above a barren desert. But when they land, they might be in a Turkish village, where the important people all speak English, or they might find themselves among green fields surrounded by trees and looking very much like England. The narrator, who doesn't have much else to do with what's going

on, belongs to a community which worships the wind (the Slipstream) and tries to kill off the android as an example of technology-gone-wild. Finally, almost everyone makes it to a place that looks like the British Museum, where most get their rocks off and Peck learns how to fall asleep. When will people learn that packaging together sparkling elements (although it's a long time since *Star Wars* for producer Gary Kurtz and star Mark Hamill) can never make up for a dumb script? **JP**
Director Steven M. Lisberger *producer* Gary Kurtz *execs* Nigel Green, William Braunstein, Arthur Maslansky *script* Tony Kayden, *from story by* Sam Clemens *camera* Frank Tidy *editor* Terry Rawlings *design* Andrew McAlpine *music* Elmer Bernstein *cast* Mark Hamill, Bob Peck, Bill Paxton, Kitty Aldridge, Eleanor David, Ben Kingsley, F. Murray Abraham, Susan Leong, Alkis Kritikos, Gay Baynes, Robbie Coltrane, Paul Reynolds, Rita Wolf, Roshan Seth
Running time: 102 mins
UK release: Entertainment, Feb 10, 1989

SOME GIRLS

One of MGM's most jinxed projects of recent years, and barely released in the States, Michael Hoffman's film turns out to be a smart, intelligent and often very funny movie about one of those weekends that just doesn't work out the way you planned. College student Dempsey goes to girlfriend Connelly's family home and finds her running hot and cold on him while he gets caught up with her two captivating sisters. If that isn't confusing enough, her father writes in the nude (clothes constrict his imagination), her mother is fiercely religious and their amazing house is Alice's wonderland relocated to an art gallery. Plot is not the strong point here; ambience and illusion are all as Dempsey's everyman tries vainly to make sense of a group of people who so deeply live their notions of art – even the sisters think they are Botticelli's Three Graces – that they can never quite grasp the real world. A genuine original. **TW**
Director Michael Hoffman *producer* Rick Stevenson *script* Rupert Walters *camera* Ueli Steiger *editor* David Spiers *cast* Patrick Dempsey, Jennifer Connelly, Sheila Kelly, André Gregory
Running time: 94 mins
US release: MGM, Sep 9, 1988

SOUR SWEET

From the director-producer team responsible for the taut, atmospheric *Dance with a Stranger*

comes this rambling story of a Chinese couple trying to make a go of things in contemporary London. What went wrong? Asking Ian McEwan to write the screenplay, for starters. He makes no attempt to develop the thrills potential of war between Triad gangs in London's Soho district; nor does he find any level at which to fuse the gangster theme to the film's central focus on a husband and wife setting up a takeaway food business in a desolate corner of the capital. Sylvia Chang is magnificent but Danny An-Ning Dun as her screen husband is so obviously a patsy (his financial problems drive him into the Triad maw, but he's unwilling to run cocaine for them) that there's no possibility of any chemistry between them. Despite some amusing reflections on divergent cultural attitudes, these never cohere into a consistent point of view. And McEwan thinks nothing of introducing crucial new ideas into the last ten minutes of the film. **JP**
Director Mike Newell **producer** Roger Randall-Cutler **script** Ian McEwan, based on novel by Timothy Mo **camera** Michael Garfath **editor** Mick Audlsey **design** Adrian Smith **music** Richard Hartley **cast** Sylvia Chang, Danny An-Ning Dun, Jodi Long, Speedy Choo, Han Tan, Soon-Teck Oh, William Chow, Shih-Chieh King, David K. S. Tse, Jim Carter, Philip Tan
Running time: 111 mins
US release: Skouras, May 12, 1989
UK release: Curzon, Feb 10, 1989

SOUVENIR

Christopher Plummer, a just-retired German-American pork butcher, makes a trip to Lascaud, the French village where he was stationed with the occupation troops during the war and had the big love affair of his life. There, he finds out what the SS really did to the population after he was transferred north. Between syrupy flashbacks to the young Plummer and his *fille* mooning in fields and humping in barns, the embittered old man staggers about feeling guilty and trying to unbend. This is a lazy, silly melodrama that takes an interesting premise and softens it to the point of pointlessness. In David Hughes' book, the Plummer character was actually guilty of war crimes, but here he is found elaborately innocent and depicted as just another victim of the Third Reich. Apart from that, a set of decent actors are stuck with unendingly trite dialogue in three languages, and too many of the plot's contrivances draw giggles. **KN**

Director Geoffrey Reeve **producers** Tom Reeve, James Reeve **exec** André A. Blay **script** Paul Wheeler, based on novel The Pork Butcher by David Hughes **camera** Fred Tammes **editor** Bob Morgan **design** Morley Smith **music** Tony Kinsey **cast** Christopher Plummer, Catherine Hicks, Michael Lonsdale, Christopher Cazenove
Running time: 93 mins
UK release: Curzon, Jan 6, 1989

SPELLBINDER

Why is it that films featuring witchcraft and devil worship always turn out to be so slavishly tied to the kind of conventions that were wrung dry by *Rosemary's Baby*? This story of Timothy Daly's deepening involvement with a coven of present-day American witches wastes a couple of decent creepy moments by submerging them in a 'surprise twist' story that makes itself glaringly obvious half-way through. A sense of horror is dissipated by the use of all those dreary chantings and silly hooded outfits that, along with the obligatory goat, succeed only in convincing us that the devil has a depressingly provincial idea of what constitutes a good party. The previous experience of director Janet Greek (*LA Law*, *Saint Elsewhere*) shows through in a production that has 'small screen' written all over it. **PB**
Director Janet Greek **producers** Joe Wizan, Brian Russell **execs** Howard Baldwin, Richard Cohen **script** Tracey Tormé **camera** Adam Greenberg **editor** Steve Mirkovich **design** Rodger Mauss **music** Basil Poledouris **cast** Timothy Daly, Kelly Preston, Rick Rossovich, Audra Lindley, Anthony Crivello, Diana Bellamy, Cary-Hiroyuki Tagawa
Running time: 98 mins
US release: MGM, Sep 23, 1988

SPICY RICE (Drachenfutter)

Young Pakistani meets young Chinese in Hamburg. Each says to the other 'Let's start a restaurant.' The consequence is they do. But things don't go to plan, and immigration officers have a surprise in store for them on opening night. *Sour Sweet* meets *My Beautiful Laundrette* in this graceful, grainy comedy of race manners from German ex-documentarist Jan Schütte. The central friendship is less interesting than the marginalia – oddball characters, quaint details of restaurant-business lore – but the film as a whole is still a piquant treat. **HK**
Director Jan Schütte **script** Schütte, Thomas Strittmatter **camera** Lutz Konermann **editor** Renate Merck **design** Katharina Mayer-

Wöppermann **music** *Claus Bantzer* **cast** *Bhasker,
Ric Young, Buddy Uzzaman, Wolf-Dieter Sprenger,
Ulrich Wildgruber, Frank Oladeinde, Louis Blaise
Londolz, Su Zeng-Hua, Circe, Peter Mertens*
Running time: 72 mins
UK release: Cannon, Jul 22, 1988

SPIKE OF BENSONHURST

Paul Morrissey's reactionary Mafia flick
concerns a pretty young boxer (Mitchell) whose
thing with the daughter of the Don (Borgnine)
results in his exile to Third World Brooklyn
and a stint busting crackhouses. When he steps
out of line again, he gets busted for good and
winds up a Mob lackey in the police. A long
way after *Flesh*, Morrissey's dispiriting take on
Saturday Night Fever lacks that film's power to
thrill and leaves its own cocky hero high, wide,
but no longer handsome. **GF**
Director *Paul Morrissey* **producer** *David
Weisman, Nelson Lyon* **exec** *Sam Grogg* **script**
Alan Browne, Morrissey **camera** *Steven Fierberg*
editor *Stan Salfas* **design** *Stephen McCabe* **music**
Coata Mundi **cast** *Sasha Mitchell, Erneste
Borgnine, Anne DeSalvo, Sylvia Miles, Geraldine
Smith, Antonia Rey, Rick Aviles, Maria Patillo*
Running time: 101 mins
US release: Film Dallas, Nov 11, 1988

SPLIT DECISIONS

Like a fixed fight, this old-fashioned boxing
movie takes a dive in the second half. The
sharp jabs of the early scenes dissolve into
tearful reconciliations and the inevitable
climactic ketchup applications. Craig Sheffer is
a top amateur middle-weight taking his father's
advice to save himself for the Olympics. But his
older brother is killed because he won't throw a
fight and Sheffer resolves to take his place in
the ring. Jennifer Beals, impressive in her one
early scene, is reduced at the end to yelling
'Eddie! Eddie!' from her ringside seat. Hackman
is also wasted as a one-note unyielding parent.
BM
Director *David Drury* **producer** *Joe Wizan* **script**
David Fallon **camera** *Timothy Suhrstedt* **editor**
John W. Wheeler, Jeff Freeman, Thomas Stanford
design *Alfred Brenner* **music** *Basil Poledouris* **cast**
*Craig Sheffer, Jeff Fahey, Gene Hackman, John
McLiam, Jennifer Beals, Eddie Velez*
Running time: 95 mins
US release: New Century/Vista, Nov 11, 1988

STAND AND DELIVER 👍

The story of a Hispanic mathematics teacher
who coaxes outstanding calculus exam results

from his initially reluctant and defiant class
makes surprisingly engrossing cinema. Based on
true events at Garfield High School in East LA
in the eighties, it features Edward James Olmos
as the unglamorous Jaime Escalante who speaks
to his kids in their own street vernacular and,
challenging and cajoling cool hoodlums like
Lou Diamond Phillips (*La Bamba*), demolishes
the theory that school is for sissies, eventually
instilling them with pride. Social deprivation,
racism, crime and negative family attitudes are
alluded to in passing, but collective and
individual endeavour win out as Olmos's high-
scorers baffle the authorities with their newly
developed skills. Ramon Menendez directs
tightly and engagingly throughout. **GF**
Director *Ramon Menendez* **producer** *Tom Musca*
exec *Lindsay Law* **script** *Menendez, Musca*
camera *Tom Richmond* **editor** *Nancy Richmond*
design *Milo* **music** *Craig Safan* **cast** *Edward
James Olmos, Lou Diamond Phillips, Rosana De
Soto, Andy Garcia*
Running time: 103 mins
US release: Warner, Mar 11, 1988
UK release: Warner, Nov 18, 1988

STAR TREK V: THE FINAL FRONTIER

Directed by William Shatner in a style derived
from his previous assignments on TV's *T. J.
Hooker*, this sequel attempts to invest its space-
Western storyline with the portentous religious
concerns of *Star Trek's* creator, Gene
Roddenberry. The space explorers are
disappointingly earthbound for the first half
hour, then kidnapped by a crazed, alien hippy
(he turns out to be Spock's Vulcan half-
brother) who proclaims pseudo-spiritual
stoicisms, commandeers the Enterprise and
takes the crew to a never-before visited planet
at the heart of the Galaxy in a search for a
mythical being. In the course of ensuing events,
Kirk engages in Ramboesque heroics, Spock
philosophizes intently and Scotty raises the
already-excessive slapstick quotient by walking
into doors and falling down incessantly. **MN**
Director *William Shatner* **producer** *Harve Bennett*
exec *Ralph Winter* **script** *David Loughery, from
story by Shatner, Bennett and Loughery based on
TV series created by Gene Roddenberry* **camera**
Andrew Laszlo **editor** *Peter Berger* **design** *Herman
Zimmerman* **sfx** *Bran Ferren* **music** *Jerry
Goldsmith* **cast** *William Shatner, Leonard Nimoy,
DeForest Kelley, James Doohan, Walter Koenig,
Nichell Nichols, George Takei, David Warner*
Running time: 106 mins
US release: Paramount, Jun 9, 1989

STARLIGHT HOTEL

Sleeping under the stars, that's what 'Starlight Hotel' means; though nodding off in the stalls is more the effect of this under-plotted Australian road movie. When teenager Kate (Robson) runs away from home to join job-hunting Dad in the faraway big city, she stumbles on a fellow drifter; ex-soldier Peter Phelps, who's wanted by the law after biffing a bailiff. Together they explore the Outback and their own 'inner space': they are, if you like, a down-under Bonnie and Clyde. If you don't like, there's little you can do. The pic wanders on for 93 minutes, etiolated and episodic, with only the stars to guide us and some lustrous photography. **HK**
Director *Sam Pillsbury* **producer** *Finola Dwyer, Larry Parr* **script** *Grant Hinden Miller, from his novel* The Dream Monger **camera** *Warrick Attewell* **editor** *Michael Horton* **design** *Mike Becroft* **music** *Andrew Hagen, Morton Wilson* **cast** *Greer Robson, Peter Phelps, Marshall Napier, Ian Brackenbury Channell, Alice Fraser, Patrick Smyth, Bruce Phillips, Elric Hooper, John Watson*
Running time: 94 mins
UK release: Recorded Releasing, Jul 8, 1988

STARS AND BARS

This is not one of those wonderful movies Europeans sometimes make about the United States. William Boyd's script follows the misadventures of a British art dealer despatched to the American South on the trail of a rediscovered Renoir. The film's vision of America has the authenticity of something filmed in Bray Studios. Working with a played-out plot device – the one about a valuable picture – the film's central character is uninteresting, and Daniel Day-Lewis is forced to draw on an off-the-shelf repertoire of 'embarrassed Englishman' gesticulations in order to keep the thing on the move. Half-hearted attempts to build in a romantic angle fall flat. One wishes Boyd would stick to what he does best, writing novels, and hand them over to someone else for adaptation. **JP**
Director *Pat O'Connor* **producer** *Sandy Lieberson* **exec** *Sheldon Schrager* **script** *William Boyd, based on his novel* **camera** *Jerzy Zielinski* **editor** *Michael Bradsell* **design** *Leslie Dilley, Stuart Craig* **music** *Stanley Myers* **cast** *Daniel Day-Lewis, Harry Dean Stanton, Martha Plimpton, Matthew Cowles, Joan Cusack, Maury Chaykin, Deirdre O'Connell, Will Patton, Steven Wright, Keith David, Lauri Metcalf, Lenne Headly, Kent Broadhurst, Rockets Redglare, Spalding Gray, Celia Weston*
Running time: 94 mins
US release: Columbia, Mar 18, 1988
UK release: Col/Tri-Star, Sep 23, 1988

STEALING HEAVEN

The story of philosopher Abelard's love for the beautiful scholar Heloise is one of the most moving of the Middle Ages, but you'd never guess it from this bodice-ripping Mills and Boon-inspired version of the tale. Kim Thomson and, particularly, Derek de Lint are wildly inadequate as the two leads, although Denholm Elliott as Heloise's outraged father and Bernard Hepton as a sympathetic Bishop try to compensate, giving better than Chris Bryant's bland screenplay deserves. Clive Donner's occasionally imaginative direction tries to give the film a sense of period its production designer seems unaware of, but he is constantly thwarted by the chocolate box photography that ultimately renders the ill-starred enterprise, like its ill-starred hero, ball-less. **TW**
Director *Clive Donner* **producers** *Simon MacCorkindale, Andros Epaminondas* **exec** *Susan George* **script** *Chris Bryant, based on novel by Marion Meade* **camera** *Mikael Salomon* **editor** *Michael Ellis* **design** *Voytek* **music** *Nick Bicat* **cast** *Derek de Lint, Kim Thomson, Denholm Elliott, Bernard Hepton, Kenneth Cranham, Patsy Byrne, Cassie Stuart, Philip Locke, Rachel Kempson, Angela Pleasence, Slavica Maras, Niki Hewitt, Yvonne Bryceland, Vjenceslav Kapurai*
Running time: 115 mins
US release: Scotti Bros, Apr 28, 1989
UK release: Rank, Apr 28, 1989

STEALING HOME

This sentimental regurgitation of *Summer of '42* charts the return to emotional stability of an ex-basketball player Billy Wyatt (Harmon), following the death of a charismatic female (Foster) whose sisterly love and guidance colluded with sport to compensate for the demise of his father. Affluent, upmarket Philadelphia is the location for the sexual awakening procured by young Willie (McNamara) and buddy (Ramis), as they are taught seemingly-invaluable life lessons by the rebellious Foster, who is both svengali, lover and fatalistic Madonna to man-child Willie. Harmon courageously dispels his image of sobriety through drunkenness and incessant tobacco consumption, but the self-indulgent confines of this predictable folk-tale are bittersweet to the point of nausea. **MN**
Director/script *Steven Kampmann, Will Aldis*

producers *Thom Mount, Hank Moonjean* **camera**
Bobby Byrne **editor** *Anthony Gibbs* **design**
Vaughan Edwards **music** *David Foster* **cast** *Mark
Harmon, Blair Brown, Jodie Foster, Jonathan
Silverman, Harold Ramis, John Shea*
Running time: 115 mins
US release: Warner, Aug 26, 1988

MY STEPMOTHER IS AN ALIEN

A lineal descendant of such 1960s sitcoms as
Bewitched and *I Dream of Jeannie*, this
unpretentious fantasy also owes a lot to Jerry
Lewis's finest movie, *Visit to a Small Planet.*
Dan Aykroyd is an over-zealous astronomer
who successfully makes contact with a hitherto
undiscovered planet. Kim Basinger, a
voluptuous extra-terrestrial, responds eagerly to
his inter-galactic call. Guided by her talking
satchel, she marries Aykroyd in order to exploit
his astronomical skills and fulfil her sinister
plan. The narrative is threadbare and
formulaic, the direction perfunctory, and
although the film can still be enjoyed for its
pop-culture references and inevitable 'fish out of
water' jokes, it's a depressingly lackadaisical
effort. **MN**
Director *Richard Benjamin* **producers** *Ronald
Parker, Franklin R. Levy* **execs** *Laurence Mark,
Art Levinson* **script** *Jerico Weingrod, Herschel
Weingrod, Timothy Harris, Jonathan Reynolds*
camera *Richard H. Kline* **editor** *Jacqueline
Cambas* **design** *Charles Rosen* **music** *Alan
Silvestri* **cast** *Dan Aykroyd, Kim Basinger, Jon
Lovitz, Alyson Hannigan, Joseph Maher*
Running time: 108 mins
US release: Weintraub, Dec 9, 1988
UK release: Col/Tri-Star, Apr 28, 1989

STICKY FINGERS

A lively divertissement which, in blending a
celebration of modish bohemianism with the
materials of stylized farce, is somewhat
reminiscent of the 'way out' comedies of the
1960s. The plot, involving two aspiring female
musicians who find themselves custodians of a
huge cache of underworld money, may be on
the arbitrary side. But the handling of the set
pieces, like a wild interlude in a gambling club,
is assured. Feminist spectators may, though, be
inclined to view the movie's depiction of its
heroines as unduly stereotyped, notwithstanding
the fact that both writers and director are
women. **TP**
Director *Catlin Adams* **producers/script** *Adams,
Melanie Mayron* **exec** *Jonathan Olsberg* **camera**
Gary Thieltges **editor** *Bob Reitano* **design** *Jessica*

Scott-Justice **music** *Gary Chang* **cast** *Helen Slater,
Melanie Mayron, Danitra Vance, Eileen Brennan,
Carol Kane, Loretta Devine, Stephen McHattie,
Christopher Guest, Gwen Welles, Shirley Stoler*
Running time: 97 mins (88 mins in UK)
US release: Spectrafilm, May 6, 1988
UK release: Virgin, Sep 2, 1988

TURKEY *OF THE YEAR*

STORMY MONDAY

Director/script/music *Mike Figgis* **producer** *Nigel
Stafford-Clark* **camera** *Roger Deakins* **editor**
David Martin **design** *Andrew McAlpine* **cast**
*Melanie Griffith, Tommy Lee Jones, Sting, Sean
Bean, James Cosmo, Mark Long, Brian Lewis,
Derek Hoxby, Heathcote Williams, Prunella Gee,
Guy Manning, Alison Steadman, Al Matthews*
Running time: 93 mins
US release: Atlantic, Apr 22, 1988
UK release: Palace, Jan 20, 1989

A SUMMER STORY

How could even a blond barrister forsake the
lovely, rosy-cheeked Imogen Stubbs for the
straight-laced Sophie Ward? The answer, which
would probably tell you everything you need to
know about the emotional deficiencies of the
middle-class English male, isn't delivered in this
tale of ill-fated romance between weak-willed
James Wilby and the country lass he meets on
a walking holiday in Devon. Set in 1902, the
story is told with some zest, and the scenes of
communal sheep-shearing and rustic revelry are
almost worth the price of admission, but
tedium sets in as Wilby hovers indecisively in
Torquay, where he's gone to raise some cash,
and hides from the lover who comes searching
for him. The wonder is that anyone thought
this story worth retelling for a contemporary
audience. **JP**
Director *Piers Haggard* **producer** *Danton Rissner*
script *Penelope Mortimer, based on short story by
John Galsworthy* **camera** *Kenneth MacMillan*
editor *Ralph Sheldon* **design** *Leo Austin* **music**
Georges Delerue **cast** *Imogen Stubbs, James Wilby,
Ken Colley, Sophie Ward, Susannah York*
Running time: 96 mins
US release: Atlantic, Aug 11, 1988
UK release: Warner, Oct 28, 1988

SUNSET

Hollywood, 1929. The biggest cowboy star in
town, Tom Mix (Willis), is cast in a movie
about the life of frontier marshall Wyatt Earp.
As a publicity stunt, oldster Earp (Garner) is

brought to town by clown-cum-tycoon Alfie Alperin (McDowell). Earp and Mix size each other up, but soon get plunged into a complicated murder case awash with floozies, blackmailers, gangsters, crooked cops and near-libellous depictions of historical figures. Earp and Mix, a pair of old frauds considerably more interesting and less endearing than the characters played here, come off pretty well, but otherwise Edwards goes out of his way to be nasty about Hollywood legends, particularly in his traducing of the McDowell character's obvious real-life original. A terrific idea has been turned into a terrible movie. If *Sunset* is at all watchable, it's down to Garner, but the film keeps tripping up, thanks to Edwards' maladroit direction. He shoots off in all directions, cutting from badly-staged slapstick to brutal violence with no regard for tone. A major disappointment. **KN**

Director/script Blake Edwards **producer** Tony Adams **camera** Anthony B. Richmond **editor** Robert Pergament **design** Rodger Maus **music** Henry Mancini **cast** Bruce Willis, James Garner, Malcolm McDowell, Mariel Hemingway, Kathleen Quinlan, Jennifer Edwards, Patricia Hodge, Richard Bradford, M. Emmet Walsh, Joe Dallesandro, Andreas Katsulas
Running time: 107 mins
US release: Tri-Star, Apr 29, 1988
UK release: Col/Tri-Star, Dec 16, 1988

SWEET HEARTS DANCE

Robert Greenwald's drama with light laughs recounts the broken marriage of grown-up high school sweethearts Don Johnson and Susan Sarandon. Much to the shock of their old buddy, school principal Jeff Daniels, Johnson decides he's been married too long and goes off to live in his construction company's trailer. Daniels, meanwhile, is beginning a romance with Elizabeth Perkins. In the pattern of Alan Alda's *The Four Seasons*, the film skips from holiday to holiday. Yes, there is ice-skating, and yes, the ice is too thin to support everybody. The tentative reconciliation at the end is as unmotivated as the initial break-up, but there are some enjoyable moments in between. **BM**

Director/exec Robert Greenwald **producer** Jeffrey Lurie **script** Ernest Thompson **camera** Tak Fujimoto **editor** Robert Florio **design** James Allen **music** Richard Gibbs **cast** Don Johnson, Susan Sarandon, Jeff Daniels, Elizabeth Perkins, Kate Reid, Justin Henry, Holly Marie Combs
Running time: 101 mins

US release: Tri-Star, Sep 23, 1988
UK release: Col/Tri-Star, Mar 24, 1989

SWITCHING CHANNELS

This fourth screen version of the Hecht-MacArthur war-horse *The Front Page* explicitly remakes Howard Hawks' *His Girl Friday*, which transformed the ace reporter who wants to quit into a woman formerly married to her scheming editor. Burt Reynolds and Kathleen Turner, who take over from Cary Grant and Rosalind Russell, lack the rapport displayed by their predecessors, while Christopher Reeve is amusing as the heroine's dispensible fiancé. The change from print journalism to television goes for nothing since the basic mechanics of the old play are retained more or less intact, with photocopier substituted for roll-top desk as a place of concealment for the escaped prisoner. Ned Beatty and Henry Gibson are value for money in small rôles, but Ted Kotcheff's direction is bland. **KN**

Director Ted Kotcheff **producer** Martin Ransohoff **exec** Don Carmody **script** Jonathan Reynolds, based on play The Front Page by Ben Hecht, Charles MacArthur **camera** François Protat **editor** Thom Noble **design** Anne Pritchard **music** Michel Legrand **cast** Kathleen Turner, Burt Reynolds, Christopher Reeve, Ned Beatty, Henry Gibson, George Newbern, Al Waxman, Ken James, Barry Flatman, Ted Simonett, Anthony Sherwood, Joe Silver, Charles Kimbrough
Running time: 105 mins
US release: Tri-Star, Mar 4, 1988
UK release: Rank, Nov 4, 1988

SCANDAL

Scandal is the name of the game. No one wants to back the film. It can't be the script, it must be the establishment. Emily Lloyd won't play Mandy Rice-Davies. It can't be that she doesn't want to take her clothes off, she's just sold out to Hollywood. The Americans want to give it an X-rating (porno houses only). They just think it's smut, they don't realize it's art (but you can see the uncut version at your local Odeon).

The Palace Pictures bandwagon – the people who gave you *High Spirits* and *Absolute Beginners* – strikes back, straddling both the salivating tabloid press and the I'm-more-radical-than-you-are arts shows and listings magazines, secure in the knowledge that this is a once-in-a-lifetime opportunity to have their cake and eat it. If the critics like it, they'll take the bows. If they don't – well, with a Tory-controlled press, they would say that, wouldn't they? If only Palace could put some of the passion they devote to their media campaigns into their productions, they just might come up with a decent movie.

As an exercise in marketing, it's a masterpiece and has the box office to prove it. As a film, it's yet another example of British cinema at its most British; impeccably acted, shot like a Sunday evening TV show and paced like a House of Lords debate. Indeed, it resembles nothing so much as a Private Member's Bill – long, excessively verbose and so littered with compromise that it leaves the main issues untouched amid a welter of trivia. As political cinema, it's a non-starter. As drama, it's pedestrian. As black comedy, it's painfully unfunny. As sexploitation, it's limp.

And yet no British film in recent years has had a story with so much potential – a rich, untapped vein of deceit, betrayal, sexual hypocrisy, political and media manipulation as well as the ever-popular British pastimes of snobbery and social climbing. All this, combined with an opportunity to examine recent history in the light of current social and political trends (and scandals). So what went wrong?

The cast do what is expected of them – John looks hurt and Joanne Whalley-Kilmer shows off her bum for her art. That they leave the emotions untouched is the fault of Michael Thomas's screenplay, which seems unable to decide whose story it wants to tell. The film's intention is to clear the unfortunate and pathetic Stephen Ward's name *à la 10 Rillington Place*, but it sometimes opts instead for a platonic love story between Ward and Christine Keeler *à la Douglas Sirk*. John Profumo hardly gets a look in.

Did I neglect to mention that the film is the story of the Profumo affair? Well, so does the film for the best part of its first hour, during which it tells us about these two birds, Christine and Mandy, who have a smashing time with the likes of Peter Rachman (What? You didn't know he was the most notorious slum landlord of the

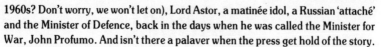

1960s? Don't worry, we won't let on), Lord Astor, a matinée idol, a Russian 'attaché' and the Minister of Defence, back in the days when he was called the Minister for War, John Profumo. And isn't there a palaver when the press get hold of the story.

How did they get hold of it? Well, if you must know, Stephen Ward – he's the nice society osteopath who introduced her to all these famous people – threw Christine out of his flat when one of her ex-boyfriends fired shots at the front door. Anyway, Profumo said he didn't do anything, then said he did; everyone blamed Ward, so he killed himself. Oh yes, and the government collapsed. The lights go down and everyone leaves the cinema, nodding sagely that the story should be told and pretending not to mind that the nude scenes really were tastefully done.

Scandal has to be one of the shoddiest big budget features ever made in Britain. An ambitious shot of Keeler stifling a yawn over Profumo's shoulder is ruined by sloppy execution. Mandy Rice-Davies' notoriously publicity-conscious retort to Lord Astor's denial of impropriety – 'Well, he would say that, wouldn't he?' – is so flatly delivered compared to the vivacity Bridget Fonda brings to the rest of her all-too-brief scenes that you would swear they printed an out-take by mistake. Panning shots are frequently too blurred to decipher and the film's unimaginative use of colour reflects neither the garish Eastmancolor of 1960s cinema nor the drabness of the period. Michael Caton-Jones' bland and characterless direction only comes briefly to life for a stunning final slow-motion shot of a cigarette falling from the dead Ward's hand and tumbling to the floor – but its emotional effect is immediately dissipated by the irrelevant Dusty Springfield/Pet Shop Boys single that follows.

Not to say that *Scandal* doesn't want to be a decent film when it grows up, but it is just too aware of possible legal reprisals to break any new ground (or even any old ground) and too enamoured of Hollywood melodrama to want to. It misses its mark as tragedy because, as with *Dangerous Liaisons*, we are given no sense of a world outside these people, or of the political stagnation and decay of the era that played a much more important rôle in the government's downfall than Profumo's peccadilloes. A mediocre title montage contrasting Harold Macmillan with Ken Dodd just doesn't cut it, but it's about as far as the film dares go. Even *Absolute Beginners*, for all its neon and stereotyping, had a better sense of time and place. *Scandal* doesn't even offer nostalgia.

TREVOR WILLSMER

SCROOGED

f any one film can be said to sum up Hollywood's year, it must be *Scrooged*, Paramount and CAA's multi-million dollar contribution to the commercialization of Christmas. You can just imagine Mike Ovitz in his office, licking his wounds after David Puttnam blew the original *Ghostbusters II* deal. Bill Murray just wants to do something with biting social relevance, but every studio in town wants him in just another ghost comedy. Outside it's as cold as Burbank gets. Christmas trees and street-corner Santas only rub in the misery. His secretary says he's acting like a real Ebeneezer Scrooge – lighten up, it's Christmas.

Hey, wait a minute – that's it. *A Christmas Carol*. Ghosts, social relevance, ghosts, plenty of cameos and more ghosts. Bill can't play English, so let's set it in America, let's set it now (more social relevance). Let's make Scrooge an evil TV vice-president, the kind of guy to fire his staff on Christmas Eve. Let's make it an attack on the deterioration of 1960s values. Let's make it an attack on the commercialization of Christmas. Hell, we can clean up the Christmas market and make millions.

And lo it came to pass. How low is hard to believe.

The main problem with *Scrooged* is not that the jokes aren't funny – they often are – or that its cast is not amiable, or even that the idea is a bad one. But it's a sloppy production trying to hide an even sloppier production-line script under a lavish budget. It starts off sublimely, the Paramount logo giving way to Santa's workshop. Suddenly psychos raid it with automatic machine guns blazing. All seems lost when Lee Majors appears blowing away the bad guys as Mrs Santa reloads ('You've been a good boy this year, Lee.'). It's a trailer for 'The Night the Reindeer Died', the latest sicko ratings-boosting commission from Frank Cross (Murray). But this is only his production-line stuff – the jewel in his crown is to be a star-studded live version of *A Christmas Carol*, to be broadcast around the world on Christmas Day. To make sure no one misses it, he promotes the show with a series of trailers so sickeningly violent that at least one little old lady is terrified into a heart attack. Great – front-page publicity you just can't buy. Then, all of a sudden, the jokes end and the plot begins, heralded by the appearance of Cross's deceased partner John Forsythe to announce the impending visits of three ghosts, each with a neater line in special effects than wit. Christmas Past is now a nauseatingly demonic cab driver (David Johansen); Christmas Present is Carol Kane, who quickly outstays her welcome doing her Rocky Balboa impersonation of a sugar-plum fairy with a vicious right hook who gives the forces of good a bad name; and finally Christmas to Come, a special effects creation which at least comes close to the nightmarish conception of Dickens.

En route we meet his neglectful parents, his old girlfriend, (Karen Allen, feeding the homeless), a cute down-and-out (Michael J. Pollard) as well as his underpaid secretary and her mute child. Amid all this tinsel, only Robert Mitchum shines as Murray's charmingly pixillated boss. Obsessed with the notion of TV programming for dogs and other domestic animals ('Think of the viewing figures.'), he inspires the film's best moments as he persuades his heir apparent to cast mice as Santa's reindeer: when it is discovered that the antlers won't stay on, Cross retorts 'Have you tried staples?' Believe me, it is one of the film's best moments. Everything ends in the kind of embarrassing finale that ruins many a lesser career, with Murray ad-libbing a completely zonked-out diatribe against television, department stores and commercials direct to camera. It's not anarchic, it's not funny, it's not even well-argued, it's simply incomprehensible waffle.

The film's biggest problem is that it is exactly what it is satirizing, a cynically-contrived money-making (or in this case money-losing) machine that resembles nothing so much as the vulgar production it revolves around. It ignores its most interesting paradox, where Cross's career rapidly loses ground to the criminally under-used John Glover as his compassion and humanity is restored, and it never finds an equivalent social or political context to Dickens beyond 'the poor will always be with us.'

Dickens' Christmas is no chocolate-box affair but a lewd, hideous time when the elements do their worst to the under-privileged. Scrooge was a victim of a heartless society who joined their ranks to escape pain. Frank Cross, by contrast, is simply a victim of his own desire for success. Dickens' festive season envelops a nightmare city where beggars freeze to death – which, to be fair, *Scrooged* re-creates in Pollard's demise – whilst Tiny Tim is a child dying horribly of polio because his father cannot afford to keep him alive in a society with no National Health Service.

Here, all the chill of these outrages is diluted as Pollard is resurrected for the sing-a-long finale and the mute child learns to talk via a miraculously-discovered love of Cross. But then, Dickens isn't one of Michael Ovitz's clients; so it's okay to give him short shrift.

It would be charitable to ignore director Richard Donner's contribution, if only because he has done sterling work in the past at revitalizing moribund genres but, as in *The Toy*, his inability to direct comedy adds a nail in the coffin of this overlong and sorely-misjudged enterprise. If nothing else, *Scrooged* should stand as everlasting proof, if proof be needed, that even a good cast, a talented crew and a lot of money cannot compensate for a bad script (courtesy of Mitch Glazer and Michael O'Donoghue) with no life of its own and no end but making money. But you can bet there'll be a lot more where this came from.

TREVOR WILLSMER

STORMY MONDAY

tormy Monday belongs to the *film noir* sub-genre developed by Wim Wenders, but here the sleuthing dwindles into mooching around, and the plot collapses into angst about alienation, the system, the awful effect of American friends on the British natives, cultural decay, cultural renovation, businessmen, the Establishment and Mrs Thatcher.

Tommy Lee Jones is a suave, vicious American tycoon, bent on buying prime redevelopment sites in Newcastle-upon-Tyne. He hires a London gang to scare jazz-loving nightclub-owner Sting, and ace party-girl Melanie Griffith to sweeten the city councillors. However, she has turned clean, decent, honest and truthful, and has fallen for a soulful, drifting Irish prole (Sean Bean). The lovers encounter a visiting Polish jazz band – Solidarity supporters hauled in to demonstrate a politically-correct combination of patriotism, socialism, union community-spirit and swinging cosmopolitanism, in contrast to the gangster spirit of business big or little and the sad ineffectiveness of our politically-unorganized loners. But an American time-bomb kills the lead jazzman, and greedy treachery/moral paralysis cows the locals.

As a synopsis this could look like hot stuff, mingling highbrow and thick-ear. And it's an exceedingly *pretty* film, playing off shrill yellow factory-smoke against shrill blue sky, sultry neons against dark blue night. Never mind the *déjà vu*, the style still does ring true. (Even if a colour-match between wallpaper and shirt is so exquisitely self-conscious it sets your teeth on edge.)

Newcastle takes on the glitter and glow of a modern city. On our right, international corporations wipe local colour off the map. On our left, cosmopolitanism is a rainbow coalition, with socialist Slavs continuing jazz where American blacks left off. Although art movies have been worrying about alienation/new roots for 30 years (ever since a French heroine spoke English with a Japanese pick-up in a nightclub named 'Casablanca' in *Hiroshima Mon Amour*), this tale does illustrate a new aspect of a worldwide process.

What went so badly wrong?

David Puttnam once wondered why good British scripts had become so very hard to find, and this concoction is a useful instance of the reasons why. Good dramatic scripts pursue a fascination with the unpredictability of human reactions: their twists and U-turns, their paradoxical flip-flops, their permutations of contradictions. Never mind if it's still the same old story, a stream of different details can make it new. (Compare the three versions of *The Postman Always Rings Twice*.) But all this requires careful script construction.

That's something Hollywood never forgot. But when the trad British cinema

collapsed in the 1960s, few artistically ambitious young *auteurs* learned the secrets of 'the well-constructed film'. Sometimes, they infatuated themselves with *Nouvelle Vague*-style 'spontaneity', not noticing how *classically* Truffaut and his friends wrote their scripts. Often, university mis-education read stories as philosophical generalizations, thus desensitizing students to stories as streams of surprises. The basis of worthwhile art, however, is frank portrayal of disorderly experience.

Earlier leftist thought could spark fine dramatic writing (e.g. Sartre, Graham Greene). But as a rule-of-thumb, the more anti-bourgeois young British films are, the more stereotyped their characters, the more yawn-inducing their plots and the more simple-minded their politics.

Stormy Monday has heavy-duty stars: Melanie Griffith (the *Something Wild* girl), Tommy Lee Jones (the croupier in *The Big Town*) and Sting. Its actors are all tooled up for twists, turns, uncertainties. But this plot *conceals* their talents within characters as rigid as plaster-casts, or should I say cement overcoats. We have our All-Ugly American, our predictably treacherous British capitalist, our Just Vague hero, our Reformed heroine, our Idyllic Ethnic Community.

The politics which call this film's tune are the left-wing equivalent of pre-war letters by irascible Colonels to *The Times*, only this film substitutes the International Gangster-Capitalist Conspiracy for their obsession with the International Bolshevik conspiracy. Its big threat to Solidarity is an American bomb. (Yet American, and Polish-American involvement *supported* Polish unionism, and it's the communist conservatives who had the treacherous weapons – police machine-guns – and murdered people.) As for the association of US finance, when it renovates capital-starved Britain, with beat-em-up 'gangsters', it's as daft as having a Japanese hi-fi firm take Britain over by kung-fu. (Especially after 15 years of British 'gangsters' buying US corporations hand over fist.)

This film does have some fine details, like the closing shots of a bright and lively marching band, strutting along American style. But its deep-eyed gloom crimps and cramps that too. For our innocent proles, American high-stepping is Bad. But if US-style jazz is okay for Poles, what's so wrong about US-style majorettes for Geordies? I'd bet my last red cent, that had this film shown the slightest interest in traditional prole pastimes (dog-fighting, Bingo . . .), or practical prole attitudes (like not necessarily preferring criminal-fringe nightclubs to job-generating redevelopments), it would have despised them as disgustingly reactionary/capitalist/tasteless too.

Writer-director Mike Figgis is one more promising talent hamstrung by a typically British mixture of snobbery, puritanism and leftier-than-though Arty Socialism. If these directors could get past their dreary dogmas to make stories which *test* their faith, they might well make something rich and true.

RAYMOND DURGNAT

THE A-Z OF FILMS

TAFFIN

Pierce Brosnan is an unshaven Irish macho man who dropped out of the seminary but still carries his vocation around with him in his work as a strong-arm debt collector. When his peaceful home town is threatened by property developers who want to build a chemical plant, he dithers for a long time before deciding to take on the company hard-men. If Brosnan saw this as a consolation prize for losing the rôle of James Bond, he's as bad a judge of scripts as he is of razor blades. With its ridiculous characterizations, laughable dialogue and basically stupid storyline, *Taffin* is the dullest excuse for a thriller to creep out of someone's tax shelter money for years. As befits the traditional image of Ireland as a land of drunks, most of the key scenes take place in pubs. **KN**
Director Francis Megahy **producer** Peter Shaw **exec** Allan Scott **script** David Ambrose, based on Lyndon Mallet's book **camera** Paul Beeson **editor** Rodney Holland **design** William Alexander **music** Stanley Myers, Hans Zimmer **cast** Pierce Brosnan, Ray McAnally, Alison Doody, Jeremy Child, Dearbhla Molloy, Jim Bartley, Alan Stanford, Gerald McSorley
Running time: 96 mins
US release: MGM, Feb 26, 1988
UK release: Vestron, Nov 11, 1988

TALK RADIO

Eric Bogosian's scabrously-cynical radio host is a martyr to his own notions of fatuous controversy in this indictment of the American media's shock tactics. A glorified DJ's gleeful and vindictive exploitation of numerous callers' raw news is an apocalyptic cabaret set in a Dallas radio station. Adapted from actor/writer Eric Bogosian's stageplay of the same name, the film version of *Talk Radio* is supplemented with documentary details taken from the life and murder of Alan Berg, and vilifies the self-perpetuating dark evangelism of shock broadcasters, and the sinister, sometimes fatal, repercussions that ensue when intimate conversation is turned into consumer entertainment. The confrontational slanging-matches are marshalled by Oliver Stone with a flair far exceeding that displayed in *Platoon* or *Wall Street*. **MN**
Director Oliver Stone **producers** Edward R. Pressman, A. Kitman Ho **execs** Greg Strangis, Sam Strangis **script** Eric Bogosian, Stone, from play by Bogosian, Tad Savinar **camera** Robert Richardson **editor** David Brenner **design** Bruno Rubeo **music** Stewart Copeland **cast** Eric Bogosian,

Alec Baldwin, Ellen Greene, Leslie Hope, John C. McGinley, John Pankow, Michael Wincott, Zach Grenier, Anna Levine, Robert Trebor
Running time: 110 mins
US release: Universal, Dec 21, 1988

THE TALL GUY

A lot of good ideas go to waste in this clumsily written and directed British comedy whose central problem is scripter Richard Curtis's inability to stick to a theme. He makes a lot of fuss about Goldblum's hay fever at the beginning, as if it's of character-defining importance instead of just a device to get Goldblum to fall in love with a nurse (Thompson). The potential of his relationship as straight man to Rowan Atkinson is never developed, and the satirical barbs launched against an Andrew Lloyd Webber-style production of *The Elephant Man* don't justify the time they take up on the screen. Despite some fun moments, it's a distressingly unmoving experience. **JP**
Director Mel Smith **producer** Paul Webster **execs** Linda Agran, Nick Elliott **script** Richard Curtis **camera** Adrian Biddle **editor** Dan Rae **design** Grant Hicks **music** Peter Brewis **cast** Jeff Goldblum, Emma Thompson, Rowan Atkinson, Geraldine James, Emil Wolk, Kim Thomson, Harold Innocent, Anna Massey, Joanna Kanska
Running time: 92 mins
UK release: Virgin, Apr 14, 1989

TAP

The pleasure to be derived from watching Gregory Hines put his tap shoes into action is somewhat diminished by the phoniness of the story offered here. A case for preferring authentic tap to the contemporary stage version is amiably presented by Sammy Davis and his still-hoofing old mates, but their argument for authenticity is hard to square with the synthesized disco performance that brings Hines's talents to a young public at the film's climax, and also puts a stop on his flirtation with crime. Because he never seems comfortable with the thieves who want to lure him away from dance, Hines's dilemma never has any weight and the script's easy recourse to clichés doesn't help: after Hines (deliberately) blows a Broadway audition, he flings his shoes into a river; torn between art and Mammon, he articulates his frustration by flinging to the floor the dishes he's supposed to be washing. **JP**
Director/script Nick Castle **producer** Gary Adelson **exec** Francine Saperstein **camera** David

185

Gribble **editor** Patrick Kennedy **design** Patricia Norris **music** James Newton Howard **cast** Gregory Hines, Suzzanne Douglas, Sammy Davis Jr., Savion Glover, Joe Morton, Dick Anthony Williams, Terrence McNally, Sandman Sims, Bunny Briggs, Steve Condos, Jimmy Slyde, Pat Rico
Running time: 110 mins
US release: Tri-Star, Feb 10, 1989
UK release: Col/Tri-Star, Jun 16, 1989

TAPEHEADS

Rock and its videoclip fish thrive on put-ons and improvisations, but William Fishman's film takes these tendencies to unfunny lengths. Tim Robbins and John Cusack are a pair of ne'er-do-anythings who decide they might as well be the next monster-rock video production team. Then they find some whacked-out old Soul artistes and plot to make them huge again. They pursue these goals witlessly and relentlessly through a plot that's like the least edifying video you ever were chained in front of. **BM**
Director Bill Fishman **producer** Peter McCarthy **exec** Michael Nesmith **script** Fishman, McCarthy **camera** Bojan Bazelli **editor** Mondo Jenkins **design** Catherine Hardwicke **music** Fishbone **cast** John Cusack, Tim Robbins, Doug McClure, Connie Stevens, Clu Gulager, Mary Crosby, Katy Boyer, Lyle Alzado, King Cotton, Don Cornelius
Running time: 97 mins
US release: Avenue, Mar 17, 1989

A TAXING WOMAN (Marusa no Onna)

Juzo Itami makes intensely Japanese social comedies that nevertheless travel very well. In this paper-chase comedy-drama, the star of all his movies, wife Nobuko Miyamoto, is a zealous, almost pitiless, investigator with the tax police. After terrorizing some peculating amusement parlour operators, Miyamoto decides to go after big game: limping property swindler and 'adult motel' operator Tsutomu Yamazaki. But she becomes more entangled with this engaging crook than she bargained for. The tax woman's 'raiddu' on Yamazaki's HQ is a tense and funny sequence involving over 100 actors. **BM**
Director/script Juzo Itami **producers** Yasushi Tamaoki, Seigo Hosogoe **camera** Yonezo Maeda **editor** Akira Suzuki **design** Shuji Nakamura **music** Toshiyuki Honda **cast** Nobuko Miyamoto, Tsutomu Yamazaki, Masahiko Tsugawa, Yasuo Daichi, Eitaro Ozawa
Running time: 127 mins

US release: Original, May 13, 1988
UK release: Artificial Eye, Nov 18, 1988

TEQUILA SUNRISE

Director/script Robert Towne **producer** Thom Mount **exec** Tom Shaw **camera** Conrad L. Hall **editor** Claire Simpson **design** Richard Sylbert **music** Dave Grusin **cast** Mel Gibson, Michelle Pfeiffer, Kurt Russell, Raul Julia, J. T. Walsh, Arliss Howard, Arye Gross, Gabriel Damon, Garret Pearson, Eric Thiele, Tom Nolan
Running time: 115 mins
US release: Warner, Dec 2, 1988
UK release: Warner, Mar 31, 1989

THE TERRORISER (Kongbufenzi)

The opening scenes of this Taiwanese film suggest another working-over of contrasts between writing - a novelist (Cora Miao) complains to her husband of writer's block - and action - a hoodlum (Wang An) escapes from police gun-fire. However, the film builds the parallels between these two femme fantasists into a complex jigsaw of narrative fragments, and in the process throws into question the lines of division between fantasy and reality: the telling of stories - Wang An's prank phonecalls, Cora Miao's novels - can 'do' things to people while the action of a 'terrorist' is just fantasy writ large. The process by which Edward Yang links the shards of contemporary urban life into a complex mosaic is unsettling, fascinating and, in its reliance on observed scenes, totally cinematic. **JP**
Director Edward Yang **producer** Xiao Ye **exec** Xu Guoliang **script** Xiao Ye, Yang **camera** Zhang Zhan **editor** Liao Qingsong **design** Lai Mingtang **music** Weng Xiaoliang **cast** Cora Miao, Li Liqun, Jin Shifie, Gu Baoming, Wang An, Liu Ming, You Anshun, Ma Shaojun, Huang Jiaqing
Running time: 109 mins
UK release: ICA, Feb 24, 1989

THEY LIVE

John Carpenter's action fairy tale is a critique of capitalist America's indifference to poverty and the homeless which purposelessly descends into a formulaic B-movie rendition of the same dramatic substance as the TV thriller V. The film's poorly-characterized lead is a drifter (Piper) who exemplifies the American blue-collar Everyman when he inadvertently alights upon a conspiracy to establish corporate extra-terrestrial hegemony over the Earth. This

revelation is precipitated by sunglasses which display the residents of LA, more often than not, as skeletal inter-galactic vampires desirous to subvert the world's human values with inducements of money - expounding a catechism of conformity, competition and success. It all ends in chases-down-corridors and machine-gun battles. **MN**
Director John Carpenter **producer** Larry Franco **execs** Shep Gordon, André Blay **script** Frank Armitage, from short story Eight O'Clock in the Morning by Ray Nelson **camera** Gary B. Kibbe **editor** Gib Jaffe, Frank E. Jimenez **design** William J. Durrell Jr. , Daniel Lomino **music** Carpenter, Alan Howarth **cast** Roddy Piper, Keith David, Meg Foster, George Flower, Peter Jason, Raymond St. Jacques
Running time: 93 mins
US release: Universal, Nov 4, 1988
UK release: Guild, Jun 23, 1989

THE THIN BLUE LINE

True-life thriller, or trial by cinema? Errol Morris's riveting documentary raises as many questions as it answers. Sleuthing through a miscarriage of justice - the conviction of Randall Adams for a policeman's murder he (seemingly) didn't commit - Morris presents his case through a movie-mosaic. Interviews with key figures, including Adams and the probable killer, are set alongside stylized re-enactments of the murder. Part fact, part hallucination - a gun twisting slow-motion into firing position, a milk-shake flying balletically through the night air - the movie tells us there *are* no final truths: the more you uncover, the more still lie waiting. Mesmerizing. **HK**
Director Errol Morris **producer** Mark Lipson **exec** Lindsay Law **camera** Stefan Czapsky, Robert Chappell **editor** Paul Barnes **design** Ted Bafaloukos **music** Philip Glass
Running time: 101 mins
US release: Miramax, Aug 26, 1988
UK release: ICA Projects, Mar 17, 1989

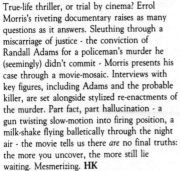

DISAPPOINTMENT

THINGS CHANGE

Director David Mamet **producer** Michael Hausman **script** Mamet, Shel Silverstein **camera** Juan Ruiz Anchia **editor** Trudy Ship **design** Michael Merritt **music** Alaric Jans **cast** Don Ameche, Joe Mantegna, Robert Prosky, J. J. Johnston, Ricky Jay, Mike Nussbaum, Jack Wallace
Running time: 100 mins

US release: Columbia, Oct 21, 1988
UK release: Col/Tri-Star, Feb 24, 1989

36 FILLETTE (See Virgin)

THREE FUGITIVES

Disney raids France again, backing Francis Veber's remake of his Les Fugitifs. Nick Nolte and Martin Short assume the big bruiser and weaselly shrimp rôles created by Gérard Depardieu and Pierre Richard. Short, the world's worst bank robber, botches a heist and randomly chooses Nolte, a just-paroled bank robber, as his hostage. Short's tiny daughter, mute since her mother died, joins them on the lam. Nolte and Short bicker and make up, bicker and make up, a double act that is funnier to watch than to describe. The late Kenneth McMillan stands out as a senile vet who treats the wounded Nolte as a dog. **BM**
Director/exec/script Francis Veber **producer** Lauren Shuler Donner **camera** Haskell Wexler **editor** Bruce Green **design** Rick Carter **music** David McHugh **cast** Nick Nolte, Martin Short, Sarah Rowland Doroff, James Earl Jones, Alan Ruck, Kenneth McMillan
Running time: 96 mins
US release: BV, Jan 27, 1989

TIGER WARSAW

Patrick Swayze returns to his home town some 15 years after departing in a blaze of controversy, drugs and violence, and upsets everyone in his family all over again. His loving Mum (Laurie) wants to forgive and forget, but his soon-to-be-married sister (McDonnell) doesn't want the thug putting off her new fiancé. The near-senile Dad (Richardson) takes a taxi to the nearest sporting goods store and buys a pump-action shotgun. Meanwhile, Tiger is demonstrating that he's a changed man by starting a meaningful relationship with an old girlfriend, getting a job, crying a lot, having his beard shaved and doing his best to look like an appealing puppy-dog. Swayze and Laurie don't appear in a scene unless they can have glycerine in their eyes, and everyone else is similarly inclined to choking back deeply-felt emotions. Despite all-round good acting, this is a drab, blurry movie, put out by a producer-director who has declared an intention 'to make quality films that deal with adult human emotions' but who has no idea how awful that sounds. **KN**
Director/producer Amin Q. Chaudhri **exec** Navin Desai **script** Roy London **camera** Robert

Draper **editor** *Brian Smedley-Aston* **design** *Tom Targownik* **music** *Ernest Troost* **cast** *Patrick Swayze, Piper Laurie, Lee Richardson, Mary McDonnell, Barbara Williams, Bobby DiCicco, Jenny Chrisinger, James Patrick Gillis*
Running time: 93 mins
US release: Sony, Sep 2, 1988
UK release: Recorded Releasing, Sep 23, 1988

THE TIME OF DESTINY

The makers of *El Norte* again treat family relationships within a context of external imperatives, but this time on a canvas broadened to encompass the WW2 Italian campaign, and novelistically elaborated to take in vendetta and obsessional behaviour. The plotting may be somewhat ramshackle, and William Hurt is none too happily cast as the Basque immigrant's son seeking to avenge his unloving father's death. But the central love affair is treated with a Borzage-like intensity of feeling, and the melodramatic appurtenances, culminating in a set-to atop a bell tower, possess a baroque flourish worthy of the same tradition. **TP**
Director *Gregory Nava* **producer/script** *Anna Thomas* **execs** *Carolyn Pfeiffer, Shep Gordon* **camera** *James Glennon* **editor** *Betsy Blankett* **design** *Henry Bumstead* **music** *Ennio Morricone* **cast** *William Hurt, Timothy Hutton, Melissa Leo, Stockard Channing, Megan Follows, Francisco Rabal*
Running time: 118 mins
US release: Columbia, Apr 22, 1988
UK release: Rank, May 12, 1989

TO KILL A PRIEST

Co-production cock-up of the year. As directed by Agnieszka Holland, the story of Poland's Father Popieluszko - his life and untimely death at the hands of secret police - comes on like a potboiler by Jerzy Le Carré or Andrzej Ambler. France's Christopher Lambert (priest) and America's Ed Harris (killer) hack their way through yards of banal plotting and B-movie dialogue, and the international enterprise is rendered yet more esperanto by the presence of Brits Joanne Whalley and Joss Ackland. Another instant write-off for the David Puttnam Columbia production slate. **HK**
Director *Agnieszka Holland* **producer** *Jean-Pierre Alessandri* **script** *Holland, Jean-Yves Pitoun* **camera** *Adam Holender* **editor** *Hervé de Luze* **design** *Emile Ghigo* **cast** *Christopher Lambert, Ed Harris, Joss Ackland, Tim Roth, Timothy Spall, Pete Postlethwaite, Cherie Lunghi, Joanne*

Whalley, David Suchet, Charles Condou
Running time: 117 mins
UK release: Col/Tri-Star, Nov 18, 1988

TORCH SONG TRILOGY

Imagine *Terms of Endearment* with laughs, emotion, a plot, something to say and characters you care about and you're halfway there. Fierstein plays gay drag artist Arnold in this splendid adaptation of his own award-winning off-Broadway play - and takes us on a rollercoaster ride of romance, comedy, politics and raw emotion that could move even the most heartless homophobe (although that didn't stop many Stateside cinemas from refusing to play the film for fear of a post-AIDS moral backlash). Anne Bancroft forgets the movie star routine that has sunk so many of her recent films to give a ferocious performance as Fierstein's mother, constantly attempting to 'reform' him rather than come to terms with his lifestyle; Broderick gives a brave and ultimately heart-breaking portrayal of Arnold's lover, whilst Brian Kerwin almost steals the show as a nervy, uncomfortable bisexual torn between his desires and 'respectability'. In a year of compromises and low ambition, *Torch Song Trilogy* stands out as a bold and brilliant beacon of illuminating light. **TW**
Director *Paul Bogart* **producer** *Howard Gottfried* **exec** *Ronald K. Fierstein* **script** *Harvey Fierstein, based on his play* **camera** *Mikael Salomon* **editor** *Nicholas C. Smith* **design** *Richard Hoover* **music** *Peter Matz* **cast** *Harvey Fierstein, Anne Bancroft, Matthew Broderick, Brian Kerwin, Karen Young, Eddie Castrodad, Ken Page, Charles Pierce, Axel Vera*
Running time: 118 mins
US release: New Line, Dec 14, 1988
UK release: Palace, May 19, 1989

TRACK 29

Sexually neglected by her hubby (Lloyd), a doctor more interested in model trains and being spanked by a thick-lipped nurse (Bernhard), North Carolina housewife Linda (Russell) daydreams about the long-lost son she bore at 15 after a fairground seduction - and he comes to life as an English delinquent (Oldman) returning to claim his American birthright and fulfil her psychotic Oedipal fantasies. Dennis Potter's script, full of digs at America, revisits his theme of the 'stranger outside the door who's really inside your head' and gives Nicolas Roeg plenty of opportunities to crosscut through time, memory and an imagined past and present. Not without *longueurs* the result is spiteful, sexy and funny whenever Russell and Oldman are together - two pouting grownups striving to get back to the playpen. **GF**

Director Nicolas Roeg **producer** Rick McCallum **execs** George Harrison, Denis O'Brien **script** Dennis Potter **camera** Alex Thomson **editor** Tony Lawson **design** David Brockhurst **music** Stanley Myers **cast** Theresa Russell, Gary Oldman, Christopher Lloyd, Colleen Camp, Sandra Bernhard, Seymour Cassell, Leon Rippy, Vance Colvig, Kathryn Tomlinson

Running time: 90 mins
US release: Island, Sep 19, 1988
UK release: HandMade/Recorded Releasing, Aug 5, 1988

TREE OF HANDS

A film about a woman (Shaver) who takes in the child her loopy mother (Bacall) has kidnapped, and is then pursued by a sinister, blackmailing chauffeur (Firth) and the child's gun-crazy stepfather (McGann), really should have had audiences sitting on the edge of their cinema seats. This, however, is a 'British thriller', determined to kill the potential for suspense with half-baked reflections on mother-child relationships, excessive narrative clutter, shoddy plotting and too many scenes of hysteria. Helen Shaver as recipient of the battered bairn, and Kate Hardie as its proletarian source, are both as good as they could be given the lack of real ambition behind this TV-financed production. **JP**

Director Giles Foster **producer** Ann Scott **script** Gordon Williams, from novel by Ruth Rendell **camera** Kenneth MacMillan **editor** David Martin **design** Adrian Smith **music** Richard Hartley **cast** Helen Shaver, Lauren Bacall, Malcolm Stoddard, Peter Firth, Paul McGann, Kate Hardie, Tony Haygarth, Phyllida Law, David Schofield, Amanda Dickinson

Running time: 89 mins
UK release: Cannon, May 12, 1989

TRUE BELIEVER

Maybe not in Presidential campaigns, but in movies it's okay to take a strong pro-civil liberties stand. Wearing a curly grey ponytail, James Woods is a burned-out leftish lawyer reduced to getting drug dealers off on technicalities. Wide-eyed Robert Downey Jr. joins his practice and re-awakens Woods' idealism. Woods takes on the DA, seeking to expose his plot to imprison an innocent man for the greater good of jailing drug dealers. Woods is his usual frayed-nerve self in Joseph Ruben's gripping, if somewhat predictable, courtroom drama. **BM**

Director Joseph Ruben **producers** Walter F. Parkes, Lawrence Lasker **exec** Peter Rosten **script** Wesley Strick **camera** John W. Lindley **editor** George Bowers **design** Lawrence Miller **music** Brad Fiedel **cast** James Woods, Robert Downey Jr., Yuji Okumoto, Margaret Colin, Kurtwood Smith, Tom Bower, Miguel Fernandes, Charles Hallahan

Running time: 103 mins
US release: Columbia, Feb 17, 1989

TUCKER: THE MAN AND HIS DREAM

It's something of an achievement to transform an obvious downer – like the tale of how Preston Tucker's dream project, 'The car of tomorrow, today', was stymied by the automobile giants – into a splashy, upbeat paean to family life, group creativity and the maverick visionary. But the resolute cheerfulness in the face of adversity also turns this fairy-tale into schmaltz. Jeff Bridges' immutable smile may reflect George Lucas's desire to pitch the project to a mass audience (who can't, it's assumed, cope with complexity) or Francis Coppola's attempt to project himself as the eternal optimist (he has encouraged comparisons between the collapse of Tucker's enterprise and that of his own Zoetrope Studios), but an air of dishonesty hangs over every scene. Technically, *Tucker* is an outstanding piece of filmmaking, but that makes its thematic superficiality all the more regrettable. Martin Landau as Tucker's beleaguered financial manager and Dean Stockwell's impersonation of Howard Hughes, in the film's only truly intriguing scene, make a more lasting impression than the lead performer. **JP**

Director Francis Ford Coppola **producers** Fred Roos, Fred Fuchs **exec** George Lucas **script** Arnold Schulman, David Seidler **camera** Vittorio Storaro **editor** Priscilla Nedd **design** Dean Tavoularis **music** Joe Jackson **cast** Jeff Bridges, Joan Allen, Martin Landau, Frederic Forrest, Mako, Elia Koteas, Christian Slater, Lloyd Bridges, Nina Seimaszko, Anders Johnson, Dean Stockwell, Corky Nemec, Anders Johnson, Marshall Bell, Don Novello, Jay O. Sanders, Peter Donat

Running time: 111 mins
US release: Paramount, Aug 12, 1988
UK release: UIP, Nov 18, 1988

TWINS

Twins is essentially a one-joke film, the premise of which can be pitched in a single line: Schwarzenegger and DeVito are twins. All the rest is padding: a subplot about industrial espionage, and some tiresome romantic scenes featuring what must be two of the most unrewarding female rôles in recent cinema (Preston and Webb wear ra-ra skirts and high heels, get their bottoms fondled, and that's about it). Ivan Reitman directs with a total lack of comic timing or pace, and it is left to the two leads to inject some pizzazz into the proceedings, which they manage to do with admirable professionalism and charm. No one who has been following Schwarzenegger's career with anything approaching attentiveness is likely to be surprised by the ease with which he takes to comedy; unlike musclemen of the Stallone school, he has always shown a tendency to send himself up. **AB**
Director/producer *Ivan Reitman* **execs** *Joe Medjuck, Michael C. Cross* **script** *William Davies & William Osborne, Timothy Harris & Herschel Weingrod* **camera** *Andrzej Bartkowiak* **editors** *Sheldon Kahn, Donn Cambern* **design** *James D. Bissell* **music** *Georges Delerue* **cast** *Arnold Schwarzenegger, Danny DeVito, Kelly Preston, Chloe Webb, Bonnie Bartlett, Marshall Bell, Trey Wilson*
Running time: 112 mins
US release: Universal, Dec 9, 1988
UK release: UIP, Mar 17, 1989

TEQUILA SUNRISE

R obert Towne easily ranks among the most noteworthy American screenwriters of the past two decades. Perhaps best known for the pastiche melodrama of *Chinatown* and the raw emotional directness of *The Last Detail*, he also has a reputation as a script 'doctor' or fixer, of the sort enjoyed in an earlier generation by Ben Hecht. Some of his credits have been on essentially conventional films, but conventionality of form need be no bar to distinctive achievement. There are, therefore, no necessary grounds for concern in the fact that the material of *Tequila Sunrise*, which Towne has directed from his own script, certainly stays close to a commercial norm, with drug smuggling and undercover police operations (yes, again) to provide the violence, and some triangular romance to bring in the sex.

Where *Tequila Sunrise* primarily proves disappointing is in its lack not of ambition but of flair or even functional efficiency as a piece of storytelling. From a writer of Towne's standing, it comes as a surprise that the 'back story' – how narcotics cop Kurt Russell and supposedly reformed cocaine dealer Mel Gibson were once teenage confederates; how the latter's life was saved in jail by a Mexican 'connection' (Raul Julia) – should emerge with so little clarity or point. Much worse, though, is the clumsiness with which the foreground narrative proceeds, taking fully 120 minutes to retail what an episode of *Miami Vice* could get through in less than half the time.

The two constituent parts of the story remain frustratingly separate: on the one hand, there is the cops and robbers stuff about the law's shadowing of Gibson and the latter's ambiguous position vis-à-vis Julia (who initially turns up in the guise of a policeman, although anyone even slightly acquainted with this kind of fiction will instantly recognize his real identity); on the other, the entanglement of both Russell and Gibson with a glamorous restaurateur (Michelle Pfeiffer). Given the perfunctoriness of the movie's thriller aspects, at least until a profusion of chases and explosions sets in during the final half-hour, it is on the romantic complications that attention is mainly brought to bear.

Towne may imagine that the laconic sparring owes a debt to Howard Hawks, and just occasionally there is a line or gesture which summons up such a legacy. There is a nice moment when Pfeiffer offers Russell some lip-gloss as a satirical way of lubricating his tongue-tied reticence. By and large, though, the flippancy and concealed soulfulness would barely pass muster in the most mechanical latter-day buddy movie. Nor would Hawks, or any other old Hollywood pro, have tolerated the kind of long-winded speechifying that occurs here at the drop of a hat, most stultifyingly in the case of the long scene in the restaurant bar in which Russell recapitulates the state of the parties. Indeed, when Julia at one point tells Russell, 'You go to a great deal of trouble to explain an inconsequential event,' it is hard to resist the feeling that he is delivering a judgement on the screenplay in general.

The attempts at hip humour (Julia inveigling Gibson into a table tennis match as the police net seems about to close in on them) are a good deal less than spontaneous. And as for the sentimental ballast provided by Gibson's relationship with his tiresome know-all of an infant son, the less said the better.

Qualities of style in the realization might, of course, lift the movie free even from such shortcomings as these. But while Towne has enlisted some prestigious collaborators – Richard Sylbert as production designer, Conrad Hall as cinematographer – *Tequila Sunrise* seems to possess little more in the way of visual invention than some arty silhouette effects, and one of those fantasticated love-making scenes, set in and out of a sauna, which does not even stop short of some rippling upside-down reflections. The locations are no more than statutory, and even the designer chic of costumes and trappings wears a half-hearted air, prompting not much more of a response than mild bewilderment at how Russell's white shirts retain their pristine crispness throughout his hectic working and amatory round.

In all the circumstances, it is hardly surprising that the performances have a tentative feel to them, variously affected (Gibson), blank (Pfeiffer and Russell) or stolid (Julia). The sharpest character drawing, in fact, comes from J. T. Walsh as Russell's opposite number in the FBI; but it is only too representative of the film's failure to spring any surprises that this figure, dishonourable and double-dealing, should be the nearest the movie comes to possessing an outright villain.

And it is here that the doubts about *Tequila Sunrise* assume a different complexion. The absence of tension, in either character or incident, may be discouraging; the long passages of explanatory dialogue tend to belie the movie's authorship. But over and above objections of this sort lies the question of the picture's choice of a hero; for it is very much as a hero that Gibson is treated, to the extent that in the final fade-out he and Pfeiffer go into an ecstatic clinch while Russell looks on with rueful approval. Gibson may be an ex-dealer, but there is no sense of his having undergone a reformation, nor any suggestion that the story's events have afforded him a purgative experience. Rather the reverse, in fact: he is absorbed all the more comfortably into a bland, homogenized realm of fantasy.

Coming from a writer whose work has at its best powerfully dramatized states of ambiguity within the formulae of popular fiction, the sad thing about *Tequila Sunrise* is that its disposition of the still potentially viable components of a traditional crime thriller should fail to arrange them into any effective pattern of moral revelation, let alone amoral provocation.

TIM PULLEINE

THINGS CHANGE

S cions of the American Dream, David Mamet and Sam Shepard have each written successful screenplays examining its corrosion: Mamet (*The Postman Always Rings Twice, The Verdict, The Untouchables*) bringing a cynical gloss to familiar genres and situations; Shepard (*Paris, Texas* and *Fool for Love*) as a cowboy poet borne back into the tragic past and forward into an unresolved future. They should write more if they are to continue their involvement with cinema, because little in the films they have recently directed suggests that either of these celebrated playwrights has found a new vocation.

Far North, Shepard's directorial début, is about a bunch of feisty, eccentric women in rural Minnesota avoiding the order of their paterfamilias, a hospitalized farmer, to shoot the old family horse that threw him. Despite the presence of Jessica Lange and Tess Harper as sisters reconciled by a silly nocturnal adventure, Shepard is no Beth Henley when it comes to delineating the dreams that motivate women, and the pacing of the movie is as leaden as its *mise en scène*.

But I would prefer a weekend in *Far North*'s wintry feminine wilderness to five minutes in a luxury hotel on Lake Tahoe with Gino (Don Ameche) and Jerry (Joe Mantegna). This isn't squeamishness about opulent vulgarity on my part, but rather a growing antipathy for the ascetic, bloodless touch Mamet has so far applied to his films as a director, of which *Things Change* is the second. His first, *House of Games*, was highly praised; yet I must admit to being underawed by its elaborate scam-ology, schematic structure, pseudo-*noir* stylization and unremitting coldness.

It is with the clinical precision of a surgeon dissecting the human mind that Mamet, known for his perfectionism, lays out the action of his movies, even though *Things Change* is less clever-clever and cerebral than its predecessor, and the bonding of the two protagonists gives it a heart. A poor, guileless shoeshine man in Chicago, Gino dreams of returning to his native Italy with a fishing boat when he retires. Picked up by two hoods and taken to their boss, Mr Green, he's promised the money to realize this dream if he agrees to spend a few years in jail in place of a senior *mafioso* who's guilty of murder.

Agreeing to do it, Gino is placed in the care of Jerry, a bungling mobster on probation, who recklessly decides to treat the old man to an idyllic last weekend of freedom in Tahoe. There they are pampered by the hotel staff, gamble in the casinos, and revel with a pair of chorus girls. Jerry is begrudgingly drawn to Gino's quiet dignity and simple wisdom, and the same qualities persuade a local Don that Gino must be a Mafia VIP and a kinsman; he invites him to his home where Jerry is horrified by the arrival of Mr Green for a high-ranking pow-wow. But Gino extricates them from this crisis, from police arrest at a police station and, finally, from the climactic run-in with Frankie, a Chicago hood who has told Jerry he must execute Gino instead of taking him to court. Restored to his little shop, Gino has relinquished his dream of the Mediterranean but gained an assistant, Jerry.

'The essential nature of a drama is a dream,' Mamet has said, and there is, indeed, a dreamlike hyper-reality to *Things Change*, as with *House of Games*. Mamet is lauded for his exploration of American low-life milieux, and his ear for street vernacular and the hustlers who use it, but his sets are obsessively antiseptic. I wonder if he has ever looked at Jonathan Demme's pictures, and savoured their shopping-mall chic and Third World exotica. Hygienic to a fault, *Things Change* gleams like a corporate property, but the rottenness in the Mafia boardroom is never fully exposed.

The essence of the film, in any case, is not its pristine texture, but its slight, serpentine narrative, which keeps threatening to leave Gino and Jerry stranded at the mercy of Mr Green and his hoods. Every time disaster looms, 'things change', with a heavy reliance on coincidence (the chorus girls, for example, lend them the money to escape) and contrivance, and usually at the behest of optimistic Gino rather than sullen Jerry.

In *House of Games*, the scam with which Mike (Mantegna) duped Dr Ford (Lindsay Crouse) hinged on his exploiting the chinks in her emotional armour, especially her need to be possessed sexually – the conman's innate cunning defeating the psychologist's textbook methods. In *Things Change*, it's not a mental chess game that ensues, either for the characters or the audience, but a moral one, no matter that Mamet still telegraphs each manoeuvre and the financial transaction – or 'deal' – that accompanies it.

In this he is well-served by his actors, not that you really think they would bleed if they were shot. There is one astonishing image of Mantegna, as Jerry waits in the busy kitchen of the Tahoe Don's lakeside palace and bitterly contemplates the mess in which he has landed himself – a reverie of silent desperation. Ameche keeps us guessing as to whether he is the sage fool or the fount of all wisdom. It's Gino's code of honour, and his insistence on keeping his part of a deal that has been struck by Mr Green to betray him, that enables him to get by and finally ruins the scam. Using, without irony, the same words that Mr Green used to him ('It's a big man who knows the value of a small coin'), Gino passes Green's token of 'trust', a Sicilian coin, onto his new friend, the Tahoe Don, who gives him a quarter and the phone number Gino calls for deliverance when he is about to die.

As each plot twist is twisted, however, Mamet takes us further and further from the film's moral sensibility and the touching friendship which has both embarrassed Jerry and redeemed him. Emotion is finally sacrificed for a stratagem – Frankie takes the rap – and the movie ends, literally, with a noncommittal shrug as Gino and Jerry get down to polishing shoes for the rest of their lives. The moral order is restored, sort of, and the fishing boat sinks on the imaginary horizon. It seems to me that another American dream has been dismantled and another fast one pulled by David Mamet, a director who knows the value of a small scam, but not the necessity of making an audience laugh, cry, or care about his characters.

GRAHAM FULLER

UNDER SATAN'S SUN (Sous le soleil de Satan)

A determinedly solemn film, lacking the realist vigour characteristic of other Pialat pictures, *Under Satan's Sun* nevertheless exerts a hypnotic power in its fractured telling of a country priest's confrontation with evil. Sandrine Bonnaire and Gérard Depardieu are convincing as lost souls struggling with inner torment. He is a cleric obsessed with the idea of holiness who meets Satan; she is a woman lost on her path of evil and remorse. **JP**
Director Maurice Pialat *exec* Claude Abeille *script* Sylvie Danton, based on novel by Georges Bernanos *camera* Willy Kurant *editor* Yann Dedet *design* Katia Vischkof *music* Henri Dutilleux *cast* Gérard Depardieu, Sandrine Bonnaire, Maurice Pialat, Alain Artur, Yann Dedet, Brigitte Legendre, Jean-Claude Bourlat, Jean-Christophe Bouvet, Philippe Pallut, Marcel Anselin
Running time: 98 mins
US release: Alive, Mar 22, 1989
UK release: Cannon, May 6, 1988

THE UNHOLY 👎

'Somebody around here just hates priests,' says detective Ned Beatty to Ben Cross, 'you could be number three.' Certainly looks like it. Unlucky Father Ben has hit one of those American parishes big on death, demonology and special effects. The local nightclub has a line in Satanic sacrifice and, back in the rectory, blind priest Trevor Howard keeps saying things like 'You are the one!' or 'At last, Desiderius!' No one knows what he means, least of all the audience, who, when not puzzling over the plot, have to hold on to their stomachs as one emetic effect succeeds another. **HK**
Director Camilo Vila *producer* Matthew Hayden *execs* Frank D. Tolin, Wanda S. Rayle, Duke Siotkas *script* Philip Yordan, Fernando Fonseca *camera* Henry Vargas *editor* Mark Melnick *design* Fonseca *music* Roger Bellon *cast* Ben Cross, Hal Holbrook, Jill Caroll, William Russ, Trevor Howard, Claudia Robinson, Ned Beatty
Running time: 102 mins
US release: Vestron, Apr 22, 1988
UK release: Vestron, Mar 3, 1989

VAMPIRE'S KISS

Cruising the singles bars of a Gothicized Manhattan, uptight literary agent Nicolas Cage is vamped by a luscious pick-up (Beals) and, in the belief that he is turning into Nosferatu, terrorizes - and finally rapes - his Hispanic secretary (Alonso) as revenge. An excoriating comedy on misogyny, sexual harassment in the workplace and economic supremacy, writer Joseph Minion's companion piece to *After Hours* takes the yuppie nightmare movie to a sneering, genre-twisting conclusion. Cage, though, is bitingly funny as the hysterical would-be Dracula who has to buy his fangs in a joke shop. **GF**
Director Robert Bierman *producers* Barry Shils, Barbara Zitwer *script* Joseph Minion *camera* Stefan Dzapsky *editor* Angus Newton *design* Christopher Nowak *music* Colin Towns *cast* Nicolas Cage, Maria Conchita Alonso, Jennifer Beals, Elizabeth Ashley, Kasi Lemmons, Bob Lujan, Jessica Lundy
Running time: 103 mins
US release: Hemdale, Jun 2, 1989

VERONICO CRUZ (La Deuda Interna)

Notwithstanding its political significance as an Argentinian/British co-production, Pereira's first feature disappoints as a film about the Falklands war told from the losing side. The script takes the familiar humanist route in its simple story of an earnest young teacher befriending a boy whose absent father turns out to have 'disappeared' after joining a forbidden workers' organization. In turn, the boy becomes another victim of the fascist state when it emerges he served on the Belgrano. Pereira achieves a slow-burning 'art' movie while never coming to grips with the importance of what is off-screen. **DT**
Director Miguel Pereira *producer* Julio Lencina, Sasha Menocki *script* Eduardo Leiva Muller, Pereira *camera/editor* Gerry Feeny *design* Kiki Aguiar *music* Jaime Torres *cast* Juan José Camero, Gonzalo Morales, René Olaguivel, Guillermo Delgado, Don Leopoldo Abán, Ana Maria Gonzales
Running time: 96 mins
UK release: Recorded Releasing, Dec 2, 1988

VIBES

A museum keeper (Goldblum) and a beautician (Lauper) meet at an Institute for Psychic Research where their paranormal powers are tested. Both are approached by a charmingly transparent conman (Falk) and suckered into a trip to Ecuador in search of an Incan Lost City, a treasure beyond anyone's wildest dreams and a source of incredible mystic power. *Vibes* comes off like a mediocre episode of a good television series: the characters are likeable and well-played, and the basic premise is sound, but the specifics of this particular story never really fall into place. There are good jokes, pretty South American locals, and one hopes the returns are good enough to warrant a sequel in which these nice people will have something worthwhile to do. The supposedly awesome finale is even sillier than that in *The Golden Child*, and too much of the rest is just xeroxed from *Romancing the Stone*. **KN**

Director *Ken Kwapis* **producers** *Deborah Blum, Tony Ganz* **exec** *Ron Howard* **camera** *John Bailey* **editor** *Carol Littleton* **design** *Richard Sawyer* **music** *James Horner* **cast** *Cyndi Lauper, Jeff Goldblum, Julian Sands, Googy Gress, Peter Falk, Michael Lerner, Ramon Bieri, Elizabeth Peña, Ronald G. Joseph*
Running time: 99 mins
US release: Columbia, Aug 5, 1988

VICE VERSA

This entrant in the 1988 body-swap mini-genre features an obnoxious marketing executive in a toy firm who switches body with his brattish son. Old-fashioned Hollywood morality, courtesy of British writers Ian LaFrenais and Dick Clement, is mixed with nostalgia to create this blandly juvenile entertainment. Judge Reinhold has a lot of fun with the physical confusions of the rôle, but the darker elements that the body-swap concept throws up, such as the physical freakishness of growing up and the yearnings of adults to vicariously enjoy childhood pleasures, are treated in such burlesque form that any undercurrents are obliterated with heavy-handed farce and a sickly sentimentality. The fantastic is treated literally, not psychologically, and the elegiac pining of *Big* is totally absent from this family movie. **SD**

Director *Brian Gilbert* **producers/script** *Dick Clement, Ian LaFrenais* **exec** *Alan Ladd Jr.* **camera** *King Baggot* **editor** *David Garfield* **design** *Jim Schoppe* **music** *David Shire* **cast** *Judge Reinhold, Fred Savage, Corinne Bohrer, Swoosie Kurtz, David Proval, Jane Kaczmarek*
Running time: 98 mins
US release: Columbia, Mar 11, 1988
UK release: Col/Tri-Star, Jul 29, 1988

VINCENT - THE LIFE AND DEATH OF VINCENT VAN GOGH

This highly personal tribute to Van Gogh uses copious extracts from letters to his brother, the paintings themselves, images of locales associated with the artist, and various more expressionist effects, plus (the least successful element) snatches of reconstruction. While rather too long and diffuse to serve its purpose, and with John Hurt's voice rather incongruously recognizable on the soundtrack, this is not only a work of evident commitment, but one which reveals intriguing insights into the imaginative world developed in Cox's other movies. **TP**

Director/camera/editor *Paul Cox* **producer** *Tony Llewellyn-Jones* **exec** *Klaus Selinger* **script** *Cox, based on the letters of Vincent Van Gogh* **design** *Richard Stringer, Neil Angwin* **voice** *John Hurt*
Running time: 99 mins
US release: Illumination, Mar 16, 1988
UK release: Artificial Eye, Oct 28, 1988

VIRGIN (36 Fillette in US)

Catherine Breillat's provocative look at how a teenage girl deals with the loss of her virginity carries the mark of truth. Beginning with a set of ill-disciplined, unsympathetic characters, Breillat gradually focuses in on the burgeoning attraction between bored, aggressive 14-year-old Lili and bored roué Maurice, who are finally left to face each other's bodies in a Biarritz hotel. The tensions arise from her reluctance to make the big sacrifice, and his resigned complicity in her forestalling his desire. Superbly acted by the two principals, Breillat's film puts all previous modish or embarrassed attempts at this subject well out of competition. **DT**

Director *Catherine Breillat* **producers** *Emmanuel Schlumberger, Valerie Seydoux* **exec** *Pierre Sayaf* **script** *Breillat, from her novel* **camera** *Laurent Dailland* **editor** *Yann Dedet* **design** *Olivier Paultre* **cast** *Delphine Zentout, Etienne Chicot, Olivier Parnière, Jean-Pierre Léaud, Berta Dominguez*
Running time: 88 mins
US release: Circle, Jan 6, 1989
UK release: Electric, Feb 17, 1989

WALKER

Alex Cox's agitprop allegory of Reagan's intervention in Central America re-creates the imperial degradations of Colonel William Walker (Harris), a deluded disciple of Manifest Destiny who invaded Nicaragua with a small band of mercenaries in 1855 and proclaimed himself president of a brutal 'democracy'. Featuring Cox's travelling stock company of actors and rock stars (plus Marlee Matlin as the colonel's fiery deaf-and-dumb fiancée) and shot on Nicaraguan locations, *Walker* Wurlitzer's slick satirical screenplay and emerges as a wayward, half-indulgent mess from a director unable to relinquish the half-baked spaghetti Western theatrics he tested out in the awful *Straight to Hell*. **GF**
Director Alex Cox *producers* Lorenzo O'Brien, Angel Flores Marini *script* Rudy Wurlitzer *exec* Edward R. Pressman *camera* David Bridges *editors* Carlos Puente Ortega, Cox *design* Bruno Rubeo *music* Joe Strummer *cast* Ed Harris, Richard Masur, Rene Auberjonois, Keith Szarabajka, Sy Richardson, Xander Berkeley, John Diehl, Peter Boyle, Marlee Matlin, Alfonso Arau
Running time: 95 mins
US release: Universal, Dec 4, 1987
UK release: Recorded Releasing, Mar 31, 1989

WAR REQUIEM

Derek Jarman's visualization of Benjamin Britten's *War Requiem* contains many of the director's usual obsessions - handsome soldiers at the mercy of the war machine, Britain's patriotic obsessions made tawdry - as well as developing scenes from the life of Wilfred Owen, the WWI poet whose works the composer combined with the Latin liturgy to make his text. The inspiration on display is undercut by a long montage of gut-wrenching footage from many of this century's wars. **DT**
Director Derek Jarman **producer** Don Boyd **exec** John Kelleher **camera** Richard Greatrex **editor** Rick Elgood **design** Lucy Morahan **music** Benjamin Britten **cast** Nathaniel Parker, Tilda Swinton, Laurence Olivier, Patricia Hayes, Rohan McCullough, Nigel Terry, Owen Teale, Sean Bean
Running time: 93 mins
UK release: Anglo International, Jan 6, 1989

WARLOCK

An enjoyable supernatural adventure which borrows from *The Terminator* and *Highlander*, and which is tackier than either (the special effects are basic, to say the least), but which forges its own territory out of the paraphernalia of witchcraft lore. Sands is profitably cast against type as the sadistic villain who sidesteps being burned at the stake by fleeing across time from seventeenth-century Boston; he has a field day casting a hex on a modern-day Los Angeles waitress ('rentum oscularum tormentum' he ominously intones) or making a flying potion by boiling down the fat of an unbaptized child. Grant is the witchfinder who follows him across time and space to prevent him from gathering pages of the Grand Grimoire. Packed with the sort of dialogue in which characters say 'Let us tarry not' instead of 'Let's go', and striking a nice line between tension and humour, this is definitely superior hokum. **AB**
Director/producer Steve Miner *exec* Arnold Kopelson *script* David Twohy *camera* David Eggby *editor* David Finfer *design* Roy Forge Smith *cast* Richard E. Grant, Julian Sands, Lori Singer, Kevin O'Brien, Richard Kuse, Juli Burkhart, Chip Johnson, David Carpenter, Anna Levine
Running time: 102 mins
UK release: Medusa, Jun 2, 1989

THE WASH

Michael Toshiyuki Uno's admirably strong-minded domestic comedy/drama is unusual among American films in that the star is a sour old codger who doesn't go all mushy and lovable in the end. The man and his wife (Mako and Nobu McCarthy) are separated after 40 years of marriage. The only thing holding them together is McCarthy's weekly visit with Mako's clean laundry. McCarthy is coming out of her shell at last, finding happiness with a pleasant widower, while Mako is indifferent to a waitress who is attracted to him. Mako eventually breaks down and begs McCarthy to return, but it's too late. **BM**
Director Michael Toshiyuki Uno *producer* Calvin Skaggs *exec* Lindsay Law *script* Philip Kan Gotanda *camera* Walt Lloyd *editor* Jay Freund *music* John Morris *cast* Mako McCarthy, Nobu McCarthy, Patti Yasutake, Marian Yue
Running time: 93 mins
US release: Skouras, Aug 17, 1988

WATCHERS

Fur Face, a genetically-altered canine, escapes from a top-secret government lab and is soon engaged in combat with The Outsider, a mélange of ape, dog, bear and alligator. Adapted from a considerably more horrific novel, *Watchers* oscillates between being a formulaic splatter movie, intermittently absorbing elements from Stephen King's *Cujo*,

and a sentimental foray into Lassie/Benji territory as it traces the relationship between a lovable canine and pugnacious teen lead Corey Haim (who, after *Silver Bullet* and *The Lost Boys*, seems destined to be hailed as the C. Thomas Howell of the drive-in horror movie). Only the villainous Michael Ironside confers any stylistic grace upon this crass foray into the malevolent-animal horror sub-genre. **MN** *Director* Jon Hess *producer* Damian Lee, David Mitchell *exec* Roger Corman *script* Bill Freed, Lee, *from novel by* Dean R. Koontz *camera* Richard Leiterman *editor* Bill Freda, Carolle Alain *design* Richard Wilcox *music* Joel Goldsmith *cast* Corey Haim, Barbara Williams, Michael Ironside, Lala, Duncan Fraser, Blu Mankuma, Colleen Winton, Norman Browning
Running time: 92 mins
US release: Universal, Dec 2, 1988
UK release: UIP, Jun 9, 1989

WE THINK THE WORLD OF YOU

Ill-matched gay couples are a new staple of the English cinema. Throw in a dog and you've got all the clichés covered. Yet Colin Gregg's film is a relatively fresh account of how love can dwindle into possessiveness and be deflected into indifference. It's the early 1950s and upper-middle-class Bates loves working-class Gary Oldman. But when Oldman goes to prison, Bates gradually transfers his love to Oldman's dog, battling Oldman's wife (Barber) and mother (Smith) for custody. It's all very funny-pathetic, anchored by Bates' sympathetic portrayal of frustration and repression. **BM** *Director* Colin Gregg *producer* Tommas Jandelli, Paul Cowan *script* Hugh Stoddart, *from novel by* Joseph R. Ackerley *camera* Mike Garfath *editor* Peter Delfgon *design* Jamie Leonard *music* Julian Jacobson *cast* Alan Bates, Gary Oldman, Max Wall, Liz Smith, Frances Barber, Sheila Ballantine
Running time: 94 mins
US release: Cinecom, Dec 22, 1988

HIT
OF THE YEAR

WHO FRAMED ROGER RABBIT

Director Robert Zemeckis *producers* Robert Watts, Frank Marshall *execs* Steven Spielberg, Kathleen Kennedy *script* Jeffrey Price, Peter S. Seaman, *from* Gary K. Wolf's book Who Censored Roger Rabbit? *camera* Dean Cundey *editor* Arthur Schmidt *design* Elliot Scott, Roger Cain *animator* Richard Williams *music* Alan Silvestri *cast* Bob Hoskins, Christopher Lloyd, Joanna Cassidy, Stubby Kaye, Alan Tilvern,

Richard Le Parmentier, Joel Silver, Betsy Brantley *voices* Charles Fleischer, Kathleen Turner, Amy Irving, Lou Hirsch, Mel Blanc, Morgan Deare, Mae Questel, Tony Anselmo, Joe Alakey, June Foray, Richard Williams, Wayne Allwine, Russi Taylor, Tony Pope, Cherry Davis, Peter Westy, Frank Sinatra
Running time: 103 mins
US release: BV, Jun 24, 1988
UK release: Warner, Dec 2, 1988

WHO'S HARRY CRUMB?

Watching John Candy make a complete ass of himself may cause some to chortle; others it drives up the wall. Here he plays a private dick whose adoption of disguises - a punk with frizzy hair swinging in a windowcleaner's cabin outside the window of a copulating couple; a Hungarian visiting the beauty parlour from which a girl has been kidnapped; an Indian air conditioning repair man - produces some reasonably funny moments. But the plot is just too predictable: Candy fails to recognize that his employer is the kidnapper, and marks down as the criminals those who wish to murder the kidnapped girl's father. After a while, one begins to wish he could get a few smarts together instead of rampaging around like the blind man in the glass shop - destroying model boats, prehistoric relics and tropical fish. **JP** *Director* Paul Flaherty *producer* Arnon Milchan *exec* John Candy *script* Robert Conte, Peter Martin Wortmann *camera* Stephen M. Katz *editor* Danford B. Greene *design* Trevor Williams *music* Michel Colombier *cast* John Candy, Jeffrey Jones, Annie Potts, Tim Thomerson, Barry Corbin, Shawnee Smith, Valri Bromfield, Doug Steckler, Renee Coleman, Wesley Mann, Fiona Roeske
Running time: 98 mins
US release: Tri-Star, Feb 3, 1989
US release: Col/Tri-Star, Jul 7, 1989

TURKEY

WILLOW

Director Ron Howard *producer* Nigel Wooll *exec* George Lucas *script* Bob Dolman *camera* Adrian Biddle *editors* David Hanley, Michael Hill, Richard Hiscott *design* Allan Cameron *music* James Horner *cast* Val Kilmer, Joanne Whalley, Warwick Davis, Jean Marsh, Patricia Hayes, Billy Barty, Pat Roach, Gavan O'Herlihy, David Steinberg, Phil Fondacaro, Mark Northover, Kevin Pollak
Running time: 125 mins
US release: MGM, May 20, 1988
UK release: UIP, Dec 9, 1988

WINTER PEOPLE

As in *Witness*, Kelly McGillis plays a single mother in an isolated community who shelters a fugitive city man. In Appalachia, the clans are feudin', and McGillis has made the mistake of loving a man from the wrong clan. While her guest (Russell) constructs a fancy clock for the town, she must make a Sophie-like choice or see the feud erupt into murder. McGillis's face and stature make her a natural as the primitive madonna. The material is sometimes a little Lil' Abner-ish, and Lloyd Bridges seems out of place in a rural patriarch, but for the most part Ted Kotcheff casts a believable spell. BM
Director *Ted Kotcheff* **producer** *Robert H. Solo* **script** *Carol Sobieski, from novel by John Ehle* **camera** *François Protat* **editor** *Thom Noble* **design** *Ron Foreman* **music** *John Scott* **cast** *Kurt Russell, Kelly McGillis, Lloyd Bridges, Mitchell Ryan, Amelai Burnette, Eileen Ryan, Lanny Flaherty, Don Michael Paul, David Dwyer, Jeffrey Meek*
Running time: 110 mins
US release: Columbia, Apr 14, 1989

WITHOUT A CLUE

This slapstick variation on the Baker Street Legend turns all the elements of the Sherlock phenomenon upside down, reducing Holmes to a fiction whose 'reality' is impersonated by a boozy, lascivious, thespian buffoon (Caine) acting under instructions from the real genius, John Watson (Kingsley). What starts as a satirically-enterprising exercise declines into a version of 'Carry On Conan Doyle' with characters walking into doors and falling into lakes, augmented by sexual innuendo and peepshow comedy only occasionally more creative than *Police Academy*. Caine himself is reduced to a stunt double with lines in an attempt to rescue the plot from farcical drollery. He really can't have been first choice for the part - it must have been Benny Hill. MN
Director *Thom Eberhardt* **producer** *Marc Stirdivant* **script** *Gary Murphy, Larry Strawther* **camera** *Alan Hume* **editor** *Peter Tanner* **design** *Brian Ackland-Snow* **music** *Henry Mancini* **cast** *Michael Caine, Ben Kingsley, Jeffrey Jones, Lysette Anthony, Paul Freeman, Nigel Davenport, Pat Keen, Peter Cook, Tim Killick, Matthew Savage*
Running time: 107 mins
US release: Orion, Oct 21, 1988
UK release: Rank, Apr 28, 1989

WIZARD OF LONELINESS

Nobody in this movie set in Vermont looks like a Vermonter, but otherwise Jenny Bowen's film of John Nichols' novel about the civilizing of an unhappy boy is true to what life might have been like in wartime New England. After the death of his mother and the enlistment of his father, embittered Lukas Haas arrives at the home of his grandfather (Randolph). Haas gradually rises above his own problems as he sees others dealing with theirs. His aunt Lea Thompson deals compassionately with the deserter living rough in the woods who was once her sweetheart. Uncle Lance Guest struggles against the guilt he feels at not fighting Hitler. It's a stirring ensemble drama with an epiphanic one-word ending. BM
Director *Jenny Bowen* **producers** *Thom Tyson, Philip Porcella* **script** *Nancy Larson, from novel by John Nichols* **camera** *Richard Bowen* **editor** *Lisa Day* **design** *Jeffrey Beecroft* **music** *Michel Colombier* **cast** *Lukas Haas, Lea Thompson, Lance Guest, John Randolph, Dylan Baker, Anne Pitoniak*
Running time: 110 mins
US release: Skouras, Sep 2, 1988

WIZARD OF SPEED AND TIME 👎

Mike Jittlov functions as a virtual one-man band on this odd undertaking, and turns it into something resembling a Valentine to himself. A would-be farcical plot of surpassing witlessness, about an independent filmmaker struggling against every conceivable professional vicissitude, serves as a pretext to showcase the achievements of special effects technicians. But the tiresome fantasy of the film within the film hardly seems calculated to justify any assumptions about the intrinsic fascination these are deemed to exert, while the constant resort to fast motion and similar devices means the viewer is likely to be left with watering eyes as well as sorely-tried patience. TP
Director/script/editor *Mike Jittlov* **producers** *Richard Kaye, Jittlov, Deven Chierighino* **exec** *Don Rochambeau* **camera** *Russell Carpenter* **music** *John Massari* **cast** *Jittlov, Richard Kaye, Paige Moore, David Conrad, Steve Brodie, Mohn Massari, Gary Schwartz, Frank LaLoggia*
Running time: 98 mins
UK release: Medusa, Dec 17, 1988

FILM

WOMEN ON THE VERGE OF A NERVOUS BREAKDOWN (Mujeres al Borde de Un Ataque de Nervios)

Director/script Pedro Almodóvar **producer** Agustin Almodóvar **camera** José Luis Alcaine **editor** José Salcedo **music** Bernardo Bonezzi **cast** Carmen Maura, Antonio Banderas, Fernando Guillén, Julieta Serrano, Maria Barranco, Rossy de Palma, Kitty Manver
Running time: 98 mins
US release: Orion Classics, Nov 11, 1988
UK release: Rank, Jun 16, 1989

WONDERLAND (See The Fruit Machine)

WORKING GIRL

Perfect entertainment for any secretary who ever wanted to unseat her boss, this fairy-tale takes Melanie Griffith from sexually-harassed typist to an office-of-her-own, via the bed of Harrison Ford, some rôle-playing and a cool idea for a deal. In a sense, it's another body-swap drama, except that the witch played by Sigourney Weaver ends up on the street rather than in the secretarial pool. Melanie Griffith just doesn't look like someone who's hungry for success, nor does she provide many clues as to how it took so long for her to discover aspirations (and talent). The background story may intend some answers, but it's messily told and, combined with Weaver's abrupt transition from devious double-crosser to hysterical shrew, turns an intriguing premise into farce. **JP**
Director Mike Nichols **producer** Douglas Wick **execs** Robert Greenhut, Laurence Mark **script** Kevin Wade **camera** Michael Ballhaus **editor** Sam O'Steen **design** Patrizia von Brandenstein **music** Carly Simon **cast** Harrison Ford, Sigourney Weaver, Melanie Griffith, Alec Baldwin, Joan Cusack, Philip Bosco, Nora Dunn, Oliver Platt, James Lally, Kevin Spacey, Robert Easton, Olympia Dukakis
Running time: 113 mins
US release: Fox, Dec 21, 1988
UK release: Fox, Mar 31, 1989

FILM

A WORLD APART

Director Chris Menges **script** Shawn Slovo **camera** Peter Biziou **editor** Nicolas Gaster **design** Brian Morris **music** Hans Zimmer **cast** Barbara Hershey, Jodhi May, David Suchet, Jeroen Krabbé, Paul Freeman, Tim Roth, Linda Mvusi, Yvonne Bryceland, Albee Lesotho, Nadine Chalmers, · Carolyn Clayton-Cragg, Merav Gruer
Running time: 113 mins
US release: Atlantic, Jun 17, 1988
UK release: Palace, Aug 26, 1988

WHO FRAMED ROGER RABBIT

T he stars of comedy films are normally expected to at least exist, if not to be funny. The star of *Who Framed Roger Rabbit* is unique in that he fits into neither category. Not since *The Man Who Never Was* has somebody so unamusing and so non-existent done so well at the box office; and *The Man Who Never Was* wasn't supposed to be funny.

Roger Rabbit is a witty charge through the history of cartoon films, avoiding all the smug pitfalls that those tributes which seek to supersede their progenitors usually leap at. You don't have to know that the Daffy Duck in the piano duel sequence is Daffy Duck as he was originally drawn – or that the waiters in the same scene are the penguins from *Mary Poppins*, or that Bugs Bunny is shown as a complete bastard because he is a complete bastard – to enjoy *Who Framed Roger Rabbit*. It's funny anyway; spotting the references just adds to the fun.

But Roger Rabbit – the rabbit – is not funny at all. He may tickle the viewer if the viewer is a particularly devoted fan of Gene Wilder or the TV work of Lou Costello, but for most people Roger Rabbit is a squealing mess of jangling nerves and flailing arms with a notably irritating squeaky voice and a tendency to over-react in the most ordinary domestic situations. His best line – that he can do things 'only when it's funny' – is great because it becomes instantly apparent to this viewer that nothing this rabbit does *is* funny. The circumstances of his life are funny – he is married to the most glamorous cartoon character ever and nobody can understand why; he is a huge movie star; he is made to wear ludicrous red dungarees – but Roger is not.

This is one of the fine things about the film. A large part of the interest centres around the old *noir* cliché of the broken-down private eye. Bob Hoskins will not work with Toons because a Toon killed his brother; naturally he is called upon to save a Toon. And not a sensible, smart Toon such as Bugs Bunny, nor even someone as personally appalling and great as Porky Pig, but the most neurotic character in the history of animated films. Roger Rabbit is completely incompatible with Hoskins; he cries all the time, makes tactless enquiries about the death of Bob's brother and completely nauseating bids for Bob's attention, and generally irritates the private eye as much as he irritates us. After that, all we can do is tolerate this rabbit which, ultimately, we do. Tolerate, become slightly fond of, even, but find funny – no.

The ramifications for a sequel or even a serial are fraught. Being fictional, a cartoon character may thrive for decades, immune to McCarthyism and hippyism and *auteur* theory. It may end up as an etiolated, unfunny nightmare, like the current Bugs Bunny, but all it has to do is to be popular and it will live. It needn't be pleasant; Yosemite Pete, Daffy and Donald, the Roadrunner – these are some of the rudest, most anti-social characters ever and yet on they go, cursing us and the day we were born, and as popular as the Care Bears scum. But a cartoon character, if it claims to be funny, has to *be* funny, and Roger Rabbit couldn't make a Tasmanian Devil laugh.

Arguably, this is completely unimportant. After all, there is nothing remotely funny about the Care Bears, the Smurfs, the infinite cartoon versions of Fraggle Rock and Muppet Babies and the remade/remodelled Yogi Bear and Bugs Bunny serials, but they're still immensely popular. Immensely popular with pre-teens, true, who like the cartoons because they bought the toys, but big names in cartoons for all that. Roger Rabbit has followed the marketing route ever since his inception with useless Roger Rabbit toys and Roger Rabbit bibs and infant sweatshirts in every shop; in that respect, his future is assured. So why should anyone care about the career prospects of an imaginary rabbit? Even if Roger Rabbit existed, would it matter if he turned into another mass-produced, low-budget, computer-generated Saturday morning kids' TV yawn?

Normally, no, but for the fact that *Who Framed Roger Rabbit* is the first genuinely funny cartoon film in a very long time. It is more than a brilliant pastiche of the ideas and comedy of the great pre-WW2 Warner and Disney animators. One has to remember that when Robert Zemeckis, the director, went to his animators and in effect promised them a free imaginative hand in the film, with no 'creative' input from the multinationals who own the characters, they were fiercely sceptical. More than any other sector of the film industry, animators are kept on a tight leash. *Roger Rabbit* allowed them to go crazy in a way not seen for decades. In that sense, the film is a tribute to the animation of the past, because it's full of the attitude of those times, the Tex Avery and Chuck Jones attitude. It's an attitude you can find in a few non-animated films still, from *Hairspray* to *Repo Man*, but *Roger Rabbit* is the only mainstream cartoon film which is contemporary and is as funny as the old stuff.

So it could be a way forward for animated comedy; it certainly should be. Roger Rabbit – the rabbit – may not exist and may not be funny, but *Roger Rabbit* – the film – is hilarious. If the makers of *Who Framed Roger Rabbit* go the way of Saturday morning cartoons, then animated comedy could end up down the dumper. Remember – this sort of stuff is only good when it's funny.

DAVID QUANTICK

WILLOW

magination can often seem the most dispensable item on a Hollywood producer's balance sheet. Behind the commercial and critical failure of *Willow* lies an industry that seems increasingly to rely more on the factory-style production of photographic illusions, than on the creative abilities of writers and directors.

Willow tries to plaster over the yawning gaps in its narrative with special effects. Instead of enhancing the narrative, these displays of state-of-the-art technology knock sideways the delicate balance between acting and artificially-rendered imagery, continuously grinding the narrative's progress to a series of exclamation-marked stops.

The plot is quite simple. Little person Willow (Warwick Davis) is given the task of protecting a baby with special powers from the murderous clutches of evil Queen Bavmorda (Jean Marsh). Her daughter Sorsha (Joanne Whalley) hunts down the baby but falls in love with Willow's reluctant sidekick, Madmartigan (Val Kilmer). The three, with the help of a rag-tag army of rebels and fairies, defeat the wicked witch. It's a tale of good triumphing over evil, seen from the perspective of a little person, Willow. The community of Bilbo-Bagginsesque Nelwyns, to which Willow belongs, forms a link with a fairy-tale world full of dwarfs and midgets.

There are striking similarities between the characters of this film and producer George Lucas's *Star Wars* trilogy. Featured in both are child-like goodness (Luke Skywalker/Willow), dark malice (Darth Vader/Bavmorda), family links between good and evil (Skywalker-Vader/Sorsha-Bavmorda), a likeable rogue (Hans Solo/Madmartigan) and a knockabout romance between rogue and headstrong princess (Solo-Leia/Madmartigan-Sorsha). Horses replace space fighters, castles stand in for death stars, magic for The Force. The comparisons are so numerous that one begins to feel Lucas has merely reworked the myths developed in his first success.

But while *Star Wars* revived the near-extinct science-fantasy genre, *Willow* dramatically fails to breathe life into epic fantasy. The intention was to create a fairy tale seeped through with early European mythology. And myth was to be mixed with history: research was conducted into Celtic pre-Roman Britain in the hope that this would give the film an earthy, rustic ambience on a visual and thematic level. Records of the Celtic lifestyle helped source costumes, weapons and set pieces such as the village fête, while Arthurian myths of knights and Druidic magic were also exploited.

The director of *Willow* was Ron Howard, who acted in Lucas's *American Graffiti* and made his own breakthrough as a director with *Night Shift*, the mortuary caper film featuring Michael Keaton which demonstrated an admirably adroit mixture of good and bad taste. *Splash* and *Cocoon* showed him developing a forte for comedic fantasy, but the latter film also revealed a worrying inability to integrate special effects-generated imagery convincingly with a human interest story.

In *Cocoon* crusty octogenarians are offered the fountain of eternal life by aliens. While sequences depicting the mundane existence of the elderly inhabitants of an old people's home demonstrated Howard's sharply-defined observation of human frailties, static shots of spaceships and floating aliens hindered the narrative's exploration of the limits of mortality. Only sequences evoking the release experienced by the physically-rejuvenated protagonists successfully blended fantasy with social observation.

Willow's script by Bob Dolman, a TV writer penning his first feature, betrays many of the film's fundamental flaws. Dialogue is inanely functional. Characters are hurriedly sketched out. And, while the accoutrements of fantasy (dwarfs, knights, witches, huge castles and magic) and Biblical imagery (shades of Moses when the baby is found in river rushes) are scattered through the script, there is no underlying mythological structure to knit them all together. *Willow*'s thematic and visual echoing of so many different stories underscores the failure to create its own identity.

Lucas and Howard seem to have had little interest in the quality of dialogue, seeing the script as a framework from which an epic fantasy could be drawn. During preproduction they screened *Excalibur* for its dynamic battle scenes, *Darby O'Gill and the Little People* for its depiction of leprechauns, and an early version of *Baron Munchausen* for the epic nature of its fantasy. The duo were particularly attracted by the visual immediacy of Kurosawa's *Ran* which they wanted to draw on to achieve a similar sense of scale. Such wilful eclecticism suggests an indecisiveness as to the visual impression the film should make.

Still Howard had much to work with. Not least was Warwick Davis's Willow and the opportunity to bring a human dimension to cinematic fairy-tales. The script also featured several strong female characters, including Sorsha, Bavmorda's daughter brought up as a man, and Fin Raziel, the white witch who suffers various animal tranformations before realizing her elderly human form.

Howard's skill in handling actors is reflected in the quiet authority of Davis's performance. Jean Marsh's Bavmorda (which reprises her rôle in *Return to Oz*) has Gothic elegance and an upstaging sense of presence that suggests a more fruitful direction the film could have taken. However, Joanne Whalley's masculine knight, Sorsha, is one of the film's major disappointments – a potentially-powerful rôle suffocated by clichéd romanticism.

Howard's partial success with performances did not extend to containing the overwhelming presence of special effects (and the substantial budget that provided it), or achieving a sense of epic grandeur and scale. Occasionally Howard's better judgement shines through. There's an early sequence where Willow first meets Madmartigan, locked up in a cage suspended above the ground. The scene delicately conveys the Nelwyn's courage and trepidation in the face of the comparatively freakish large soldier, placing within a human scale the daunting task facing Willow as he cautiously ventures out into the war-shrouded adult-sized world.

But the script became less a framework for such quizzically gentle confrontations than a blueprint for a fusillade of special effects. Perhaps this was inevitable. As a George Lucas production, rather than a Ron Howard movie, a substantial part of the budget was allocated to expensive technology. The film included 400 effects shots, created by ten SFX crews from Lucasfilm's subsidiary, Industrial Light and Magic.

Howard lacks any sense of visual scale or grandeur. He can direct performances with sensitivity to nuance and gesture, but scenes of 300 extras masquerading as an army are largely wasted in terms of the film's supposed pretensions to epic scale. There is a lack of conviction in the battle scenes. The only truly effective sequence in the film – and the one original idea in the script – features horses erupting out of the ground and storming Bavmorda's castle, intimating a sense of the epic fantasy which *Willow* aimed for but so brutally missed.

The blazing mechanical artistry of special effects exploding in all directions across the screen, from braziers coming to life to Bavmorda vaporizing into an apparition of scarlet smoke, reduced the film to a noisy, overlong video game, squeezing out any form of internal cohesion the frail narrative could muster, by its sheer physical presence.

The film's weaknesses inevitably bring into question the contemporary relevance of Lucas's cinematic vision. *Star Wars* successfully encased a marriage of futuristic hardware and old-fashioned romantic values. *Willow*'s attempt to achieve this same mixture using sword and sorcery relied too much on individual impressive special effects and not enough on a compact narrative. Money, in the form of special effects, was thrown at any and all problems in the hope that, like mud, some of it would stick.

And perhaps Howard just wasn't the right choice for director. He was nicknamed 'executive producer in charge of directorial affairs' by the crew on *Willow*, reflecting his seemingly marginal involvement in a film which seeks to create wonder through an interpretation of magic as something generated by special effects. This devastating misconception can be traced to Lucas rather than Howard. To achieve Lucas's conception of the film, Howard's strengths as a director became trampled beneath the weight of the machinery required to create *Willow* as Lucas had conceived it.

STEPHEN DARK

WOMEN ON THE VERGE OF A NERVOUS BREAKDOWN

W omen on the Verge of a Nervous Breakdown is the sort of film that British critics just can't deal with. The pace is too fast, the plot too much motivated by a sense of fun and the 'messages' lie concealed too far beneath a bubbling surface.

By the same token, although I've heard some Americans complain that the Spanish film is too much like homegrown fare, it's easy enough to predict the sort of hash Hollywood will offer up as the 're-make' (just consider what happened when *Trois hommes et un couffin* became *Three Men and a Baby*). They'll straighten out the lines, blunt the edges and emphasize emotions to the point of insincerity -- transforming everything that sparkles in the original into silliness.

For British middlebrows, the slapstick-pop sensibility that Pedro Almodóvar had already shown to be his natural terrain in *Law of Desire*, *Matador* and *What Have I Done to Deserve This?* presents problems. They might echo the words of the cop who, having listened to Pepa (Carmen Maura) accounting for a day's highly-charged emotions in her Madrid apartment, declares, with ineffable seriousness, 'I get the feeling you're pulling my leg.' And they don't want to give the time of day to a story that's knitted together from a series of coincidences: the boy who comes to look over Pepa's flat just happens to be her ex-lover's son; the lawyer Pepa consults on behalf of a friend is her ex-lover's new mistress; the plane that the lawyer and the lover are taking to Stockholm is the flight that Pepa's friend Candela knows is going to be hijacked. But these pieces of narrative glue are of a piece with a plot that is fired up by its crazy zestfulness, where everything is weird but you accept it because it is also, in a sense, true.

The American mainstream *can* cope with pop when, as in such recent offerings as *Earth Girls Are Easy* or *My Stepmother Is an Alien*, there's never any danger you'd confuse the characters on the screen with real people. But that's what makes *Women on the Verge* such an astonishing delight. Without ever ceasing to amuse, or becoming callous towards his characters, Almodóvar takes you right into the pain and the frustration of a group of women whose problem is men and the pain they cause. ('Don't call me a pain. I'm feeling vulnerable,' one character miserably declares.) A simple shot of the film's heroine standing on an empty street at dawn as the lights go out, which speaks volumes for her inner emptiness, is the sort of thing that just doesn't seem to happen when Americans turn to 'farce'.

Feminists may resent the film's implication that what these women partly live for, get dressed up for, wait for and dream of, is men, especially since these men really are worthless and treacherous shits (even a lovable taxi-driver shows signs of cowardice when he's confronted by a challenge). The lowest of the males is Pepa's ex-lover Ivan who, like her, dubs romantic films for a living, and whose smooth-toned voice may well be his only attraction. At the film's opening, the already lovelorn Pepa dreams Ivan is mouthing sweet nothings of love to a parade of girls. He clearly doesn't mean a single word. And it's when his institutionalized ex-wife Lucia hears him, in a Hollywood movie, telling a woman he loves her, that she casts off her amnesia, makes a satisfactory pretence of sanity, and sets off in pursuit of him.

Pepa wants Ivan back (in the beginning, at least) but, although she keeps hearing that wretched voice on her answering machine, there's never a chance to confront him. She's a sassy woman for the most part: you can tell from the way she carefully flings a cigarette into the flames that consume her bed before turning the hose on to it. But the frustration caused by her weak-kneed lover's skill in avoiding her unlooses a few screws: she flings phones out of the window, only to repent a few seconds later as the vain hope revives inside her that he will ring. She bundles all the useless gifts she received from him into the suitcase he's asked her to pack: 'Who would think of giving a duck as a present' she says to make it quite clear we know she's realistic about his faults. She spends the night watching the places he might come to. And 'sick of being good', she spikes the deep-red gazpacho she intends him to drink with a heavy dose of barbiturates. And she never seems to mind how many bruises she acquires in this frenetic bustle. After all, no one else in this world is too embarrassed to display emotional scars; she can always dust herself down and get on with things when the need arises.

Pepa is the sort of woman who takes in strays – her terrace, home to chickens and rabbits, is compared to Noah's Ark – and when other distraught females arrive on her doorstep, less capable of dealing with *their* romantic problems, she gets herself together enough to help them out. Candela is distraught because her lover has turned out to be a Shi'ite terrorist who was using her apartment as a base, and she fears the police may be after her. And Marisa, who turns up with the son of Pepa's ex-lover, soon realizes from the interest he shows in the luscious Candela that her fiancé is just a pint-sized version of Ivan.

'Why are men like that?' exclaims Candela. It is their failure to understand which unhinges the younger woman, making Candela successively tearful, suicidal and susceptible (to Carlos's passion for kissing). She heals easily, of course, but when in the full flood of despair she makes the sort of scatty connections that bring film dialogue to life: 'I couldn't face my parents. It's bad enough that I became a model' she declares while contemplating a term of imprisonment.

Pepa, by contrast, understands her man too well; the problem is that she can't get hold of him. If she could, she knows she'd win him back. He knows it too; that's why he's out of the door before she can get him on the telephone, and hides in

phone boxes when he sees her approaching. For Pepa *is* the sort of woman you'd imagine a weak man would run away from; she's too organized, too clear about what *she* wants. Perhaps it's part of Ivan's charm that he *knows* he's weak. When the lawyer he's running away with reproaches him for this failing, he angers her by refusing to deny it. You think she's going to dump him but in fact she just accepts it.

These women are so unhinged by their need for a man, however worthless, that you might suspect Almodóvar was laughing at them. Instead, the director accepts these emotional upsets as part of life. What makes *Women on the Verge* such a joy to watch, especially when compared to the cold and calculating comedies that Hollywood has been offering up recently, is Almodóvar's evident affection for these people. You might imagine he identifies with the taxi driver who's always there to take Pepa on her missions in search of Ivan, and has everything in his car his customers might need. Or at least he thinks he has until a weeping Pepa makes a request he can't satisfy. 'Why didn't I think of eye-drops. What a 'dope' he declares in evident irritation as tears start to roll down his own cheek.

I know some people who found *Women on the Verge* less sexy than Almodovar's earlier films, even though Pepa and everyone else are clearly on heat the whole way through this movie (there's nothing casual about the scene in which she burns her bed). Even as Candela lives in terror of arrest, and Pepa tries to track down Ivan, the two of them are trying out costumes, smartening themselves up and preparing for the next round in the sex war. And although her purpose may be murder, Lucia is at it too, though her garb dates back 25 years, to the time before her breakdown. (I wish she had retained that weird tiger skin-patterned hat that looked like an inverted waste-paper basket.)

On TV, Pepa plays the mother of a killer (we see a funny commercial in which she promotes a washing powder by showing its efficacy in washing out bloodstains). In reality, she calls upon her taxi driver to pursue the gun-wielding Lucia to the airport. After she's saved Ivan's life, she realizes she doesn't even want to tell him her one important piece of news. That she saves for Marisa, who's slept through most of the movie, after a bout with the spiked gazpacho, and dreamt her way through more sexual pleasure than anyone else has been able to secure. It's to her that Pepa confides news of her pregnancy, in a moment of calm making us feel she's discovered that perhaps . . . for a while . . . she can make it on her own.

Watching *Women on the Verge* makes you realize just how lifeless and formulaic other film comedy has become. You'd have to go a long way back to find anything so fresh, so zippy, so observant of people's ticks and habits. For once, when you laugh, you're laughing at life rather than plot construction or clever-clever dialogue. And Carmen Maura; she's a star. Any re-make that doesn't have her in it isn't even going to be worth switching on the TV for.

JAMES PARK

A WORLD APART

Could anything seem to promise less than a British movie that's based on a true story and deals with a serious issue? The description conjures visions of Darling Dickie accepting yet another award for a wildly over-long, persil-white account of a saintly saviour of an oppressed majority. You know it's boring, but the cause is so worthy you dare not criticize the film for fear of social ostracism.

A World Apart is set in South Africa, but *Cry Freedom* it is not. Thanks to an autobiographical script by Shawn Slovo, direction by Chris Menges and a series of amazing performances, it is a truly cinematic and emotional experience.

Based on the life of the anti-apartheid journalist Ruth First (Slovo's mother, here called Diana Roth), the film revolves around the 13-year-old Molly's struggles to come to terms with the consequences of her mother's political commitment. Initially this only means waiting around the office for her to finish work, putting up with snide glances from friends' parents and wondering when her father will come back from his frequent trips 'away'. He never does.

But soon Diana's involvement with the ANC leads to her imprisonment under the infamous 90 Days Detention Act. Respectable white society takes its vengeance on Molly: friends avoid her while their parents openly assault her; teachers attempt to gain her confidence to spy on her and the family begins to split apart as prison visits are constantly arranged and abruptly denied. Her mother is finally released into house arrest only after attempting suicide – and it is upon learning about this last desperate act that Molly finally confronts her with all the resentment she feels about her lonely and loveless childhood.

The style of *A World Apart* is deceptively simple. The opening is even a little dull, as Molly hangs around the office, bored and irritable with her mother's constant delays; but we are getting to know these people (a strange habit to get back into when every other movie seems to open with a big scene to keep the audience hooked). The film never loses its human focus. Even in the few set pieces – funerals, protest marches, a mass arrest at a black church – the leads are kept in the foreground by a director more interested in reflecting on how these events touch the participants than in playing soldiers with the extras.

A World Apart tells us a lot about life in South Africa for both black and white, and the sacrifices people make in their struggle for freedom. It does so not through speechifying or choreographed massacres but by recounting the casual brutalities that touch its characters. A party is invaded by the police, complete with attack dogs and photographers, because the white host is serving alcohol to blacks. Molly and her mother are stopped during a strike because they carry black passengers in their car. 'Jeez man, what kind of a mother are you?' one of the policemen asks

on seeing the girl there. It is a question that is echoed throughout the film.

All that Molly learns of her mother's cause she learns from others. From the maid, Elsie, she picks up the lyrics of 'Nkosi Sikelela Afrika', the ANC anthem'; from Elsie's charismatic brother, Solomon, comes an alternative history of the country to that taught at school. And it is Solomon who hands her the colours of their cause and ultimately brings Molly and her mother back together. Her mother never explains anything. She's too busy with her work. It is this inability to integrate her beliefs with her family life that torments Diana during her detention, and it is this weakness that her interrogator plays upon, when he accuses her of wasting her life and 'playing Joan of Arc as an excuse for being a lousy mother!' until she is brought to the edge of madness.

As her resolve gradually deteriorates, so does the family. Grandmother has a nervous breakdown and Molly is despatched to board at school, her resentment gradually growing. Like her mother, she becomes too deeply hurt to even hope. The apartheid apparatus seems set against the family, as if the system's future depended on the destruction of the very institution it claims to be founded on. But it fails. The family does not fall apart, and Molly and her mother stand united at the funeral of yet another black martyr in the film's final and most moving moments. And it is here that the film lets loose its final bombshell: a caption informs us that Ruth First was herself assassinated on 17 August 1982.

Chris Menges' unobtrusive style never overwhelms the emotions of the film, but subtly delineates them with such natural assurance that it is hard to believe this is his first time in the chair, after more than a decade as a leading cinematographer. In an age of video directors with more interest in dazzling the eye than in telling a story, communicating an idea or engaging rather than manipulating the feelings of an audience, it is a striking achievement.

Menges' skill with actors combines with Shawn Slovo's subtly understated screenplay to produce dense and complex characterizations. Jodhi May's Molly, a breathtakingly natural performance, is smart, intelligent and likeable, and whilst you may admire her mother's principles, Barbara Hershey's playing makes it clear she is not the easiest woman in the world to live with. Similarly, David Suchet's interrogator is no neo-Nazi bully, but is constantly frustrated by Diana's inability to see his reasoning. Linda Mvusi manages to steer the rôle of Elsie away from cliché into a fully-rounded human being, whilst Albee Lesotho as her brother Solomon instils his portrait with a simple matter-of-fact decency that makes his final scene – involuntarily swallowing to stop the blood in his throat from choking him as a security officer circles him – all the more powerful, throwing the humiliation and savagery of political torture into stark relief.

A World Apart will stand for years to come as a passionate testament to Shawn Slovo's love for her mother, and to the cause for which she died.

TREVOR WILLSMER

THE YEAR MY VOICE BROKE

Adolescent rites of passage, in a raw little New South Wales township in the early 1960s, are crossed with Gothic intimations over the mystery surrounding the orphan girl at the centre of a teenage romantic triangle. The mixture is not altogether successful, with the revelation of the town's guilty secret seeming somewhat facile. But the foreground observation effectively combines sentiment and satire, and the film as a whole is marked by a reassuring sense of concern for its characters. **TP**

Director/script *John Duigan* **producers** *Terry Hayes, Doug Mitchell, George Miller* **camera** *Geoff Burton* **editor** *Neil Thumpston* **design** *Roger Ford* **cast** *Noah Taylor, Loene Carmen, Ben Mendelsohn, Graeme Blundell, Lynette Curran, Malcolm Robertson, Judi Farr, Tim Robertson, Bruce Spence, Harold Hopkins, Anja Coleby*
Running time: 105 mins
US release: Avenue, Aug 25, 1988
UK release: Palace, Apr 28, 1989

YEELEN (Brightness in US)

This mesmerizing tale of a young African (Kane) in flight from his father, a practitioner of black magic with murderous intent, is also a rites-of-passage story. The father - boorish, brutal and mean-spirited - wants to maintain his monopoly over magic powers; Kane discovers that he must sacrifice himself to destroy his father and ensure the next generation has access to knowledge. Initially unaware of the enormity of his mission, he sends fire and bees to drive away an attack on the village where he takes refuge but, when asked to cure the chief's wife of barrenness, he sleeps with her instead and fathers a child. Souleymane Cissé's ability to involve one in his characters, while seemingly avoiding none of the complexities of an alien belief system, is true magic. For viewers jaded by too many retellings of the Oedipus tale, Cissé opens the door to a new source of mythic vitality. **JP**

Director/producer/script *Souleymane Cissé* **camera** *Jean-Noël Ferragut* **editor** *Dounamba Coulibaly, Andrée Davanture, Marie-Catherine Miqueau, Jenny Frenck, Seipati N'Sumalo* **design** *Kossa Mody Keita* **music** *Michel Portal, Salif Keita* **cast** *Issiaka Kane, Aoua Sangare, Niamanto Sanogo, Balla Moussa Keita, Soumba Traore, Ismaila Sarr'*
Running time: 104 mins
US release: Cinecom, Apr 14, 1989
UK release: Artificial Eye, Oct 21, 1988

YOUNG GUNS

The plastic Peter Pans known as The Brat Pack resurface in a Western. Emilio Estevez, as a psychotic Billy the Kid, leads such peer luminaries as Charlie Sheen and Kiefer Sutherland on a revenge trip, after the murder of an English rancher. But in Christopher Cain's crudely-obvious reworking of Sam Peckinpah's gritty, pseudo-realistic 1970s pictures, the contemporary fashion for cowboy regalia (dusters, boots and neckchiefs) dominates the film's visual codes, rather than any narrative elements of the Western genre itself. The presence of such contemporary whiskered stalwarts as Harry Dean Stanton and Jack Palance fails to provide any genre sensibility. Equally, the squeaky-clean features of the brat packers ripping it up in traditional Western style destroy any contemporary allusion to the psychosis of teenagers who worship guns. The Western is rendered as a slick youth-cult vehicle complete with rock soundtrack, sounding an undeservedly tawdry death knell for the genre. **SD**

Director *Christopher Cain* **producers** *Joe Roth, Cain* **execs** *John Fusco, James G. Robinson* **script** *Fusco* **camera** *Dean Semler* **editor** *Jack Hofstra* **design** *Jane Musky* **music** *Anthony Marinelli, Brian Banks* **cast** *Emilio Estevez, Kiefer Sutherland, Lou Diamond Phillips, Charlie Sheen, Dermot Mulroney, Casey Siemaszko, Terence Stamp, Jack Palance, Terry O'Quinn, Sharon Thomas, Geoffrey Blake, Alice Carter, Brian Keith, Tom Callaway, Patrick Wayne, Harry Dean Stanton*
Running time: 107 mins
US release: Fox, Aug 12, 1988
UK release: Vestron, Jan 6, 1989

AWARDS

EVENT	CATEGORY	WINNER

THE ACCIDENTAL TOURIST

NY Critics	Picture	Lawrence Kasdan
Oscar	Supporting Actress	Geena Davis

THE ACCUSED

Oscar	Actress	Jodie Foster
Golden Globe	Actress	Jodie Foster

UNE AFFAIRE DE FEMMES

Venice	Actress	Isabelle Huppert

AU REVOIR, LES ENFANTS

BAFTA	Director	Louis Malle
European	Screenplay	Louis Malle

BABETTE'S FEAST

BAFTA	Foreign Film	Gabriel Axel
London Critics	Foreign Film	Gabriel Axel
London Critics	Actress	Stéphane Audran

BAGDAD CAFE

César	Foreign Film	Percy Adlon
César	European Picture	Percy Adlon
Golden Bug	Foreign Film	Percy Adlon

THE BEAR

César	Director	Jean-Jacques Annaud

BEETLEJUICE

Oscar	Make-up	Ve Neill, Steve La Porte, Robert Short
National Critics	Actor	Michael Keaton

BIG

Golden Globe	Actor/Comedy	Tom Hanks
LA Critics	Actor	Tom Hanks

THE BIG BLUE

César	Music	Eric Serra

212

EVENT	CATEGORY	WINNER
BIRD		
Golden Globe	Director	Clint Eastwood
NY Critics	Supporting Actress	Diane Venora
Oscar	Sound	Les Fresholtz, Dick Alexander, Vern Poore, Willie D. Burton
BLACK RAIN		
Cannes	Technical Prize	Shohei Imamura
BULL DURHAM		
WGA	Screenplay	Ron Shelton
CAMILLE CLAUDEL		
César	Film	Bruno Nuytten
Berlin	Actress	Isabelle Adjani
César	Actress	Isabelle Adjani
César	Photography	Pierre Lhomme
César	Art Direction	Bernard Vezat
César	Costumes	Dominique Borg
CAMP THIAROYE		
Venice	Special Grand Prix	Ousmane Sembene, Thierry Faty Sow
CHOUANS		
César	New Actor	Stéphane Freiss
CLEAN AND SOBER		
National Critics	Actor	Michael Keaton
A CRY IN THE DARK		
NY Critics	Actress	Meryl Streep
Cannes	Actress	Meryl Streep
DANGEROUS LIAISONS		
WGA	Adapted Screenplay	Christopher Hampton
Oscar	Adapted Screenplay	Christopher Hampton
Oscar	Costume Design	James Acheson
Oscar	Art Direction	Stuart Craig, Gerard James
DEAD RINGERS		
Genie	Film	David Cronenberg, Mark Boyman

EVENT	CATEGORY	WINNER
LA Critics	Director	David Cronenberg
Genie	Adapted Screenplay	David Cronenberg, Norman Snider
Genie	Actor	Jeremy Irons
NY Critics	Actor	Jeremy Irons
LA Critics	Supporting Actress	Geneviève Bujold
Genie	Cinematography	Peter Suschitzky
Genie	Art Direction	Carol Spier
Genie	Editing	Ronald Sanders
Genie	Score	Howard Shore

EMPIRE OF THE SUN

BAFTA	Cinematography	Allan Daviau
BAFTA	Music	John Williams
BAFTA	Sound	Charles L. Campbell, Lou Edemann, Colin Charles, Robert Knudson, Tony Dawe

EVENING BELLS

Berlin	Special Jury Prize	Wu Ziniu

FATAL ATTRACTION

BAFTA	Editor	Michael Kehn, Peter E. Berger

A FISH CALLED WANDA

Oscar	Supporting Actor	Kevin Kline
BAFTA	Actor	John Cleese
BAFTA	Supporting Actor	Michael Palin

GORILLAS IN THE MIST

Golden Globe	Actress	Sigourney Weaver
Golden Globe	Score	Maurice Jarre

A HANDFUL OF DUST

BAFTA	Supporting Actress	Judi Dench

HIGH TIDE

National Critics	Actress	Judy Davis

HOTEL TERMINUS

Oscar	Documentary	Marcel Ophüls

HOUSE OF GAMES

London Critics	Film	David Mamet

EVENT	CATEGORY	WINNER
London Critics	Script	David Mamet

——I LOVE, YOU LOVE——

Berlin	Director	Dusan Hanak

——ITINERARY OF A SPOILT CHILD——

César	Actor	Jean-Paul Belmondo

——JESUS OF MONTREAL——

Cannes	Jury Award	Denys Arcand

——LANDSCAPE IN THE MIST——

Venice	Silver Lion/Direction	Theo Angelopoulos

——THE LAST EMPEROR——

BAFTA	Film	Jeremy Thomas
BAFTA	Costume	James Acheson
BAFTA	Make-up	Fabrizio Sforza

——LA LECTRICE——

César	Supporting Actor	Patrick Chesnais

——LEGEND OF THE HOLY DRINKER——

Venice	Golden Lion	Ermanno Olmi

——LITTLE DORRIT——

LA Critics	Picture	Christine Edzard
LA Critics	Supporting Actor	Alec Guinness

——THE LONELY PASSION OF JUDITH HEARNE——

BAFTA	Actress	Maggie Smith

——MADAME SOUSATZKA——

Venice	Actress	Shirley MacLaine
Golden Globe	Actress	Shirley MacLaine

——MARRIED TO THE MOB——

National Critics	Supporting Actress	Mercedes Ruehl
NY Critics	Supporting Actor	Dean Stockwell
National Critics	Supporting Actor	Dean Stockwell

——THE MILAGRO BEANFIELD WAR——

Oscar	Original Score	Dave Grusin

——MILK AND HONEY——

Genie	Original Screenplay	Glen Salzman, Trevor Rhone

——MISSISSIPPI BURNING——

Oscar	Cinematography	Peter Biziou
Berlin	Actor	Gene Hackman

EVENT	CATEGORY	WINNER
THE MODERNS		
LA Critics	Supporting Actress	Geneviève Bujold
MYSTERY TRAIN		
Cannes	Artistic Contribution	Jim Jarmusch
THE NAVIGATOR		
Australian Film Institute	Film	Vincent Ward
NUOVO CINEMA PARADISO		
Cannes	Special Jury Prize	Giuseppe Tornatore
OBSESSED		
Genie	Supporting Actress	Colleen Dewhurst
PELLE THE CONQUEROR		
Oscar	Foreign Language Film	Per Holst
Golden Globe	Foreign Language Film	Per Holst
European	Actor	Max Von Sydow
European	Young Actor	Pelle Hvenegaard
PUNCHLINE		
LA Critics	Actor	Tom Hanks
Golden Globe	Actor/Comedy	Tom Hanks
RAIN MAN		
Oscar	Film	Mark Johnson
Golden Globe	Film	Mark Johnson
Berlin	Golden Bear	Barry Levinson
Oscar	Direction	Barry Levinson
DGA	Director	Barry Levinson
Oscar	Original Screenplay	Ronald Bass, Barry Morrow
Oscar	Actor	Dustin Hoffman
Golden Globe	Actor	Dustin Hoffman
REVOLVING DOORS		
Genie	Supporting Actor	Remy Girard
Genie	Costume Design	François Barbeau
RUNNING ON EMPTY		
LA Critics	Actress	Christine Lahti
SEX, LIES AND VIDEOTAPE		
Cannes	Golden Palm	Steven Soderbergh
Cannes	Actor	James Spader

EVENT	CATEGORY	WINNER

A SHORT FILM ABOUT KILLING

European	Film	Krzysztof Kieslowski

THE SUMMER OF AVIYA

Berlin	Silver Bear	Eli Cohen

TALK RADIO

Berlin	Outstanding Achievement	Eric Bogosian

THINGS CHANGE

Venice	Actor	Don Ameche, Joe Mantegna

TIME OF THE GYPSIES

Cannes	Direction	Emir Kusturica

TOO BEAUTIFUL FOR YOU

Cannes	Special Jury Prize	Bertrand Blier

TRAVELLING NORTH

London Critics	Actor	Leo McKern

TUCKER

NY Critics	Supporting Actor	Dean Stockwell
National Critics	Supporting Actor	Dean Stockwell
Golden Globe	Supporting Actor	Martin Landau
BAFTA	Production Design	Dean Tavoularis

MY TWENTIETH CENTURY

Cannes	Camera D'Or	Ildiko Enyedi

THE UNBEARABLE LIGHTNESS OF BEING

National Critics	Picture	Saul Zaentz
National Critics	Director	Philip Kaufman
BAFTA	Adapted Screenplay	Jean Claude Carrière, Philip Kaufman

THE VANISHING

European	Supporting Actress	Johanna ter Steege

LA VIE EST UN LONG FLEUVE TRANQUILLE

César	First Feature	Etienne Chatiliez
César	Screenplay	Etienne Chatiliez, Florence Quentin
César	Supporting Actress	Hélène Vincent
César	Young Actress	Catherine Jacob

EVENT	CATEGORY	WINNER
WHO FRAMED ROGER RABBIT		
Oscar	Film Editing	Arthur Schmidt
Oscar	Sound Effects Editing	Charles L. Campbell, Louis L. Edemann
BAFTA/Oscar	Visual Effects	Ken Ralston, Richard Williams, Edward Jones, George Gibbs
WINGS OF DESIRE		
LA Critics	Foreign Film	Wim Wenders
European	Director	Wim Wenders
European	Supporting Actor	Curt Bois
WOMEN ON THE VERGE OF A NERVOUS BREAKDOWN		
NY Critics	Foreign Film	Pedro Almodóvar
European	Young Film	Pedro Almodóvar
Venice	Screenplay	Pedro Almodóvar
European	Actress	Carmen Maura
WORKING GIRL		
Golden Globe	Comedy Film	Douglas Wick
Golden Globe	Supporting Actress	Sigourney Weaver
Golden Globe	Actress/Comedy	Melanie Griffith
Oscar	Original Song	Carly Simon
A WORLD APART		
NY Critics	Director	Chris Menges
BAFTA	Original Screenplay	Shawn Slovo

TALKING BEHIND THE CAMERA

Compiled by Tony Crawley

It's up to us to provide better quality movies.
Lloyd Kaufman, producer of Stuff Stephanie in the Incinerator

Directing is more fun with women – everything is!
Ingmar Bergman

It's all downhill from here.
Steven Soderbergh, 26, on winning Best Film at Cannes, 1989 for sex, lies and videotape

Peter Pan didn't have courage. I'm trying to grow up.
Steven Spielberg

All films are subversive.
David Cronenberg

Alan Parker's problem is that he pretends to be a Marxist but he's actually a Fascist.
Mississippi Burning *writer Chris Gerolmo*

I am different . . . I was once described by one of my critics as an aesthetic fascist.

Oliver Stone I didn't like. But then nobody likes Oliver. He's just an aggressive man like me – but he hasn't got my sense of humour.
Alan Parker

We expected criticism with this film and, actually, I welcome it.
Hugh Hudson on Lost Angels

It's been re-cut and it's a mess. They'd have done much better to get a chimpanzee for post-production.
David Leland on his Hollywood début, Checking Out

There are two types of animals roaming the Hollywood jungle. Those who do the screwing, those who get screwed. You have to try and ensure you're one of the former.
Bruce Robinson

People associate me with, let's say, delicate movies. But I'm a vulgarian, as well. That doesn't mean I go around breaking wind but I love the idea of making people laugh.
Pat O'Connor

Tabloid journalism in Britain is great training ground for Hollywood. If you can survive there, Hollywood is not the great nest of sharks you think it's going to be.
William Davis, co-writer of Twins

It's more a case of my life reflecting my movies than my movies reflecting my life.
Francis Coppola

Spielberg's office is the biggest Taco Bell in the world. Its cost. No man can say.
John Milius

When you're in your teens you vow to never lie about your age. When you get to my age, you wish you had.
Verity Lambert

It doesn't matter to me how big or small a movie is, whether you've got 20,000 people in front of the camera or just one, as long as they're doing the right thing. The only problem with bigger films is the politics that surrounds them. That's when the nightmare starts.
Neil Jordan

Have a go. Anybody can do it.
Alan Parker on directing

If you can drive a car, you can direct a movie.
John Landis

Pauline Kael is the Rambo of film critics.

... a demented bag-lady.
Alan Parker

Unfortunately, directors never see their films for the first time.
Jerry Schatzberg

Actors are the ones who are important. I keep telling my crew: These people are on the screen, you are not.
Louis Malle

A bad director is like a bad date.
Dustin Hoffman

Cats gotta scratch. Dogs gotta bite. I gotta write. I'm obsessed with obsessions.
James Elroy, author of Cop

I'm almost prepared to think that what the American movies want to be about is fucking and shooting and that you're simply fighting city hall to write about anything else.
Thomas McGuane, novelist and scenarist of Cold Feet

In many movies, including *Platoon*, war looks like fun. In reality, a dead body is a very ugly thing and it's hard to carry. Life isn't cheap and I wanted to rub that in the audience's face.

It wasn't half the work I was led to believe.
First-time director Patrick Duncan on 84 Charlie Mopic

To make the movies I made in Hollywood, it's like a gift. And sometimes they even pay me for it.
Martin Scorsese

THE US YEAR

I n a year of shake-up among the majors and shake-out among the minors, financial fat-cats fought to buy Hollywood's solid gold-plated properties as well as its hastily painted false fronts. Meanwhile, audiences flocked in record numbers to see what the glitter machine had to show.

Conglomerate-sized financial strength is the new *desideratum*. While many a would-be mini-major foundered from lack of deep pockets and the muscle to make the right connections, the traditional majors lurched toward becoming all-round media companies. Studios have long sought vertical integration – a finger in every pie from production to playoff's final flicker. Now they're broadening themselves through alliances with other purveyors of information and entertainment.

Rupert Murdoch's Twentieth-Century Fox is seen as the model for Hollywood's new rôle as a piece on the international media chessboard. The year's biggest move in this new direction was the battle for control of Time Inc. waged by Warner Bros and Paramount. Less spectacularly, Quintex bought United Artists from Kirk Kerkorian, and Giancarlo Parretti rummaged through various moribund properties after rescuing Cannon. Sony may yet become a player in Hollywood: it sniffed after MGM/UA and was reported as coveting Universal's parent, MCA, or Coca-Cola's Columbia unit.

Disney led all the studios in market share during 1988. Thanks in part to *Who Framed Roger Rabbit*, it took 20 per cent of the box office as against 14 per cent the previous year. Paramount, which had led in three of the preceding four years, recovered top place the following summer, fuelled by *Indiana Jones and the Last Crusade*. And while Fox owner Rupert Murdoch was busy buying Triangle Publications for $3 billion, his studio ticked over nicely with hits like *Big* and *Die Hard*.

MARRYING TIME

Warner Bros' film business prospered, but the company made more headlines on the financial pages than in entertainment. The studio's eventful year began with its purchase of Lorimar Telepictures for $675 million. Warner picked up the pieces after Lorimar's chairman Merv Adelson made too many money-losing films to realize his dream of building a new major on the basis of his success in TV production. Lorimar had lost $83 million in its last year before being gobbled up. Adelson, however, won't be crying. He got $4.8 million to go away, plus Warner shares worth £33 million.

Some eight weeks after digesting Lorimar, Warner agreed to combine with Time and create a $10 billion all-media giant. In addition to its strength in magazines, Time owns premier pay-cable outlet Home Box Office and numerous broadcast properties. Bunting was hung and flags were waved as Time and Warner sought to ensure an okay from Washington by noting that America needed big combines to fight off the nasty Germans (Bertelsman), French (Hachette) and Australians (Murdoch) – not to mention the Japanese (Sony). But it turned out that the biggest threat to 'Time-Warner' was 'Paramount-Time'.

Paramount's higher bid for Time, which moreover was a cash offer rather than a stock swap, had been foreshadowed. Paramount's parent, Gulf and Western, shed a financial subsidiary known as The Associates to carve itself down into solely a media company and, in recognition of this refocusing, dropped the G&W name in favour of Paramount. The war chest from its Associates sale, plus backing from Citibank, enabled Paramount to leap upon Time's unsuspecting neck.

RIPE FOR PICKING

The divine command that struck Warner and Paramount at the same time – concentrate on the media business and concentrate hard – was also heard by those who follow Orion, Columbia and Universal.

Orion's stock soared while its profits stayed flat (a piddling $14 million on revenues of $470 million). The smart money thinks Orion is ripe for a takeover because the investor who owns 72 per cent of the company's stock, John Kluge, may find cashing in more attractive than remaining friends with chairman Arthur Krim.

Universal, although it seemed perfectly secure on its own until recently, suddenly seemed small, forlorn and lonesome without a major corporate protector. Controlled by ageing chairman Lew Wasserman, who might be vulnerable to take-the-money blandishments, Universal seemed to be another prime takeover candidate.

The logic in the rumours surrounding Columbia was that Coke isn't clued in closely enough to the media business to keep Columbia competitive, and thus might be willing to get out at the right price. In this scenario, Coke was just priming its movie properties for sale when it wrapped its 100 per cent Columbia ownership and 40 per cent Tri-Star stake into a combined 49 per cent and then, a year later, folded the two entities into one. Sony was the whisperers' favourite potential bidder following its initial American foray – the acquisition of CBS Records.

In some other countries, the selling off of a national asset such as Hollywood might raise a stink; in America it's just business. The industry was created by immigrants, why not let immigrants buy it back? David Puttnam, former chairman of Columbia Pictures, warned from his new Warner-backed base in London, 'There are precise parallels between the Detroit of the mid-1970s and the Hollywood of the mid-1980s.' For now, though, Japanese money has remained mostly on the sidelines.

HUSTLING THE MGM SHELL

Kirk Kerkorian had been dangling his MGM/UA holdings in front of potential buyers ever since he profited handsomely by selling them to Ted Turner and then buying most of them back three years ago. A $100 million deal, that would have spun off 25 per cent of MGM to a triumvirate of producers, collapsed two weeks after it was announced. Two weeks was just long enough for the trio to have a good look at the books and realize that MGM was little more than a shell, Turner having retained the library and Lorimar having taken over its studio property. It didn't even have people any more, as MGM/UA chairman Lee Rich, MGM chairman Alan Ladd Jr. and UA chairman Tony Thomopoulos had departed for pastures new.

Having gutted his properties, Kerkorian hired an investment banker, Jeffrey Barbakow, to sell them. Sony considered buying them for up to $1 billion but backed off when Kerkorian tried to hold back rights to the MGM name and logo. Giancarlo Parretti briefly imagined MGM/UA as part of his new Cannon-Pathé empire. Thomopoulos found an angel in Monaco, Elizabeth Dickerson Industries, to put up $1 billion, but Kerkorian refused that offer. Finally, another newcomer, Christopher Skase, signed on the dotted line. Skase's Quintex Group, an Australian broadcaster and resort owner, bought most of the assets of MGM/UA for a net cost of around $600 million, and will operate the studio as United Artists Pictures. Kerkorian retained his beloved MGM name and logo, plus MGM's TV production company, which could become the nucleus of yet another incarnation of that mangy old lion which once boasted 'more stars than there are in heaven.'

STUMBLING MINI-MAJORS

MGM/UA had been a loss-maker since Kerkorian resumed ownership in 1986, but its value to Quintex apparently lay in its infrastructure and know-how. These hard-to-value intangibles are just what would-be mini-moguls Menahem Golan and Dino De Laurentiis had been unable to buy quickly enough to stave off their respective companies' collapse. Golan's Cannon and De Laurentiis' DEG both relied too heavily on their bosses' seat-of-the-pants intuitions. The two companies lacked the personnel and traditions for the second opinions, follow-through and relationship-tending that represent the justification for the 30 per cent distributors' fees that the studios require. Major stars and big-hit directors shunned DEG and Cannon, which found themselves churning out B-pictures that few Americans could be induced to see. DEG, which financed its films by preselling ancillary rights and wound up relying on domestic rentals that never materialized, went down more quickly than Cannon only because the Israeli cousins could borrow against their foreign interests.

Nevertheless, Cannon lost hundreds of millions and writhed through a prolonged death agony of missed debt payments and forced sales of assets before Giancarlo Parretti swooped down like Superman Six to keep the company out of bankruptcy, with cash infusions totalling a quarter of a billion dollars. The olive oil merchant's son and one-time waiter at the Savoy proceeded to cut an astonishing swathe through Hollywood's undergrowth, bidding for virtually every snake in the grass. He seemed to be bankrolled by Credit Lyonnais, which had oddly enough financed most of the bankruptcy candidates Parretti was now seeking to 'save'. Was it a case of the blind backing the blind?

Parretti bid $139 million for foundering New World Entertainment, a small company with big losses that he planned to make the base for his American operation. But NWE left Parretti at the altar, preferring a $145 million offer from Ronald O. Perelman's Andrews Group. Perelman is the raider who six months before had sold Technicolor to Britain's Carlton Communications. Parretti also bid and re-bid for DEG before losing this tattered property to Carolco, which promised to eviscerate it immediately.

Having lost these bids, Parretti remained flush enough to arrange new lives for jobless aliens Golan and De Laurentiis. Both got big backing to produce movies for Parretti. Golan lost no time in waving around a slate of a dozen films he'll make immediately through his 21st

Century Film Corp., though his ties with Parretti were quickly cut. Parretti made one deal that seemed to be sticking: hiring Alan Ladd Jr. to head Pathé Entertainment with a four-year 14-picture contract. Warner Bros will release Ladd's Pathé films, recalling the Warner-Ladd Co. tie of the early 1980s.

Other mini-majors also stumbled. Weintraub Entertainment Group had trumpeted its $461 million backing when it was formed but landed in financial trouble after releasing only three films. It turned out that much of its nest egg was only promises and lots of the rest was for future delivery. The company managed to lose $40 million in 1988 on revenue of $48 million. And Vestron, the video company that jumped into production with *Dirty Dancing*, failed to bottle lightning a second time and suffered the indignity of losing its bank loan (although it later obtained a smaller facility from another institution).

THE SURVIVORS
A few of the larger independents prospered. Hemdale stayed in business despite John Daly's 'sue me' style. A typical complaint against Hemdale was lodged by Gene Hackman, who alleged that a complex deal settling Vestron's suit against Hemdale unfairly caused his income from *Hoosiers* to be reduced. Hemdale responded that Hackman should have accepted its settlement offer.

Carolco, focusing on internationally appealing muscle-and-blood pictures like *Rambo III* and *Red Heat*, paid whatever it cost to get them in the can and still came out ahead. *Rambo III*'s price tag was $63 million, making it one of the most expensive American films ever made (among the year's releases, *The Adventures of Baron Munchausen* was the second most extravagant, going $20 million over budget.)

Joseph Roth's Morgan Creek, preferring low-cost films like *Young Guns* and *Major League*, succeeded through negotiating creative deals. For films it releases through Fox, for instance, Morgan Creek pays the $6 million or so print-and-advertising costs, thus ensuring the films a first-class launch. In return for this reduced exposure, Fox waives its 30 per cent distribution fee.

GRABBING THE CASH
While the dinosaurs were re-positioning their limbs and juggling their millions, the movie-making mice down below had never before worked so productively. Although the number of actual bums on seats in America has remained steady for 30 years, Hollywood's US box office gross in 1988 soared to a record $4.46 billion and continued at a record-setting pace into 1989. America's per-capita moviegoing rate of 4.4 contrasts with Britain's 1.4. Even in Canada, the average person saw just 2.8 movies in 1988. A breakdown of America's gross showed that comedies took a stronger share of the box office as action-adventure declined – which is another way of saying that Eddie Murphy made *Coming to America* instead of another *Beverly Hills Cop* movie, and Arnold Schwarzenegger turned up in *Twins*.

The homevideo business now grosses $10 billion a year, and cassette sales of individual films like *E.T.* can bring in $300 million (of which director Steven Spielberg personally took $75 million). And American films are dominating foreign cinemas as never before – while correspondingly, foreign films are being crowded out of American cinemas (the only exceptions being 'foreign' movies with American stars, like *A Fish Called Wanda*). At the same time, Hollywood managed to lower its average 'negative' costs to $18.1 million from $20.1 million ('negative' means all pre-release expenses). In this recital of good business news, the only worrying note was the 5.6 per cent rise in the cost of releasing movies: for most major pictures, the budget for prints and advertising now runs into eight figures.

Protecting Hollywood's money-making apparatus was a major motivation when it came to negotiating labour contracts. Dealing from strength, the studios were able to withstand a 23-week strike by the Writers' Guild, forcing the writers to give back some previously-won income and to accept token rises in other income areas. Although the long strike hobbled America's TV networks, it was just a blip to the film studios, while the writers lost an estimated $100 million in work. In the following months, the studios proved equally able to dictate terms to other unions: the actors settled without a whimper; the craft unions gave back such hard-won benefits as overtime pay for weekend work, and even the hard-nosed Teamsters crawled back behind the wheel after a four-week strike, giving management most of what it had demanded.

The studio bosses showed more generosity when negotiating with themselves. Seven- and eight-figure stock options and golden parachute deals are *de rigueur* today. Forget salaries. Disney chairman Michael Eisner received a paltry $750,000 in salary for 1988, and even his performance-based bonus of $6.8 million wasn't much of a thrill, because he took down $32.6 million in profits from the sale of Disney stock he was allowed to buy for a pittance under a stock option plan. Unless Disney somehow suddenly trips over its tail, Eisner stands to rake in equivalent amounts until the end of the century.

Stars continued to do all right. Bruce Willis, a come-lately with a hit TV show (*Moonlighting*), got $5 million for *Die Hard*, even though Fox failed to put his picture into its print ad for the film. Al Pacino, who hasn't been in a hit for years, was promised $4 million plus a percentage for a film, *Carlito's War*, that he wound up not making.

Some had to sue for their cash. Raquel Welch received $10 million after an appellate court upheld an earlier award compensating her for MGM firing her from *Cannery Row* in 1980. A jury awarded Timothy Hutton a similar amount from MGM for its cancellation of a 1983 film, *Roadshow*, without paying him the $1.5 million he was due under his pay-or-play contract. The big individual winner in the year's court proceedings was Melissa Matheson (Mrs Harrison Ford); an arbitrator awarded her five per cent of the merchandizing income from *E. T.*, which she wrote, right down to specifying the creature's telescopic neck and glowing heart. No money changed hands when Disney sued the Academy of Motion Picture Arts and Sciences for using its Snow White character, without permission, on the Oscar show. Disney withdrew its suit after the Academy apologized for letting camp-loving Alan Carr depict Snow dancing a lewd duet with actor Rob Lowe.

CHANGING OFFICES

More than half the studios shook up their executive suites. MGM/UA lost its three top men just before the Quintex buy: Lee Rich, who wound up with an independent deal at Warners; Tony Thomopoulos, ditto at Columbia, and Alan Ladd Jr., to Pathé. Fox president Leonard

Goldberg left after 28 months in the job, during which he brought the studio up to third in box-office share from sixth when he arrived. Fox chairman Barry Diller will share Goldberg's job with Goldberg's former subordinates. Universal's production president Sean Daniel left to head the Geffen Co.'s film division. Casey Silver took over. Paramount chief of production Ned Tanen was replaced after four years by George Lucas's one-time publicist, Sid Ganis. Tanen is remaining at the studio in an 'advisory' rôle. In an old-fashioned management struggle at Columbia/Tri-Star, the winner was Dawn Steel, baby in the office and all. Tri-Star president David Matalon vanished into executive vice-president land when Tri-Star was made a Columbia subsidiary, and new Tri-Star president Jeff Sagansky reports to Steel. Soon after this reshuffle, Burbank Studios, which Columbia shares with Warner, announced it would build a day-care centre.

BART MILLS

WE KNOW WHERE WE'RE GOING

The Growth of the Brit-American Movie

Visitors to the Cannes Film Festival are accustomed to attention-grabbing displays from producers who hope to get their movies noticed amidst the schlock and the occasional masterpiece being projected from booths up and down the Rue d'Antibes. But even the most Cannes-worn must have been perplexed by the British display at the 1989 event.

How were they *meant* to react to a parade of vintage cars winding their way down the Croisette after a journey through France? Two of the automobiles had indeed appeared in 'British' films on display in the Palais: a Roller in David Lean's *Lawrence of Arabia*, a Jag in *Scandal*. But was this really a way to tell the world how exciting, fresh and relevant are the nation's films – the sort of thing that might have kids queueing around the block in Rio, Auckland and Kyoto?

Perhaps the rally had more to do with promoting the interests of Shell UK, which sponsored the event, than pitching British pictures to international buyers, but why then did the industry allow itself to be hijacked by a cars-are-beautiful philosophy, which could only reinforce the old idea that British films are hung up on nostalgia. Let's have more scripts on the empire's glory days, the wonderful 1960s and jolly aristos in their country castles.

Like everyone else nowadays, the nation's film industry is obsessed with self-promotion. British Screen's director Simon Relph recently asked some advertising agencies to come up with a concept for promoting Britpix: they offered only blank faces or well-worn stereotypes. And screenings have been organized to the regional press in the hope that, seeing they were good, the journos would urge cinema managers to screen some British films, and audiences would take a look. Unfortunately, such events cannot hope to give the impression that British filmmakers know where they are heading, or provide the sense of excitement that is missing from the films.

A few years back, something interesting did seem to be afoot. The Stateside success of two low-budget pictures, *My Beautiful Laundrette* and *A Letter to Brezhnev*, suggested a future for movies about contemporary Britain which had a satirical edge. Both creatively and economically this movement dried up even more quickly than such manifestations of creative energy usually do. The team responsible for *Laundrette* followed with the flabby bombast of *Sammy and Rosie Get Laid*, and writer Frank Clarke's *The Fruit Machine* lacked the verve of its predecessor. And, although Mike Leigh's *High Hopes* this year created the same sort of critical stir as the earlier films, the moanings of its financiers about the small returns available from the US suggested that the time for such pictures had passed.

228

The British film industry needs to be making films that are rooted in its own themes and problems alongside pictures pitched at the international market. No longer content to lure audiences into a richly-textured narrative, today's indigenous films aim for the quick-grab effect and the striking premise – but the follow-through that might make these ideas thrill never arrives. Brave ideas become not-so-sweet nothings: the advertising executive with a vengeful boil on his neck (*How to Get Ahead in Advertising*); the sickly child whose drawings control the world of her dreams (*Paperhouse*); the European parliamentarian who accidentally kills the man who's blackmailing her (*Paris by Night*); the chocolate confectionery that's improved when three employers get into the mix (*Consuming Passions*).

These disappointments are, on one level, just further evidence of the failure of British screenwriters to grasp the essentials of film narrative – how to lay out their themes, develop characters and sustain audience interest. But they are also films so full of evasions, so unwilling to confront the challenges presented by their own subject matter, so reluctant to present an audience with imagery that thrills, that one has to look deeper for the source of the problem.

But why is it that sometimes filmmakers seem able to make many ideas sing; but then produce a succession of flabby pancakes? At the beginning of this decade, a certain amount of creative energy came from the fact that producer David Puttnam and Goldcrest Films on the one hand, Jeremy Isaacs and Channel 4 TV on the other, presented a vision (however limited) of what British films could be. Filmmakers might reject both visions, but that very act was stimulating to the creative juices. Isaacs is now a TV personality running an opera house, and Puttnam is doing his own thing. Nobody else has moved into the vacuum, and the present set-up doesn't generate the same energy; it's just too bitty and incoherent. Even more than before it's the setting up of the deal that absorbs all the energy as those well-fingered scripts are circulated to several tarnished pots of gold, in the hope that a little dust from each one may make up the budget of a film.

Local finance sources are increasingly fragmented. BSB, a new satellite distribution company, channelled a small portion of its image-conscious millions to British pictures (the rest, of course, going to line the pockets of the US majors). The BBC announced it would invest £500,000 apiece in a number of independent pictures. And, although their willingness to invest has been undermined by changes in their tax position and prospective shifts in the structure of independent television, such TV companies as LWT, Granada, Thames/Euston, TVS and Scottish TV *have* been putting up money for features. But none of these financing sources seem to have any sense of what they are doing, beyond imitating what Channel Four did half a decade ago, and somehow positioning themselves to exploit the new era in television.

Producers have had to deal with the hardening of the US market as the companies with whom the Brits had been developing relationships either went to the wall or cut back on 'foreign' production. The sort of advances being paid a few years back are no longer to be found for low-budget, indigenous films, and companies like Zenith and Working Title, which built their reputations in that area, have had to rethink. They now want to make bigger films angled more firmly at the mainstream. £3 million is now talked about as the minimum budget for a British film with any chances of making it, whereas a few years back some were coming in at just over £1 million. The higher figure is not a lot of money by US standards, but what it means for local producers is that they *have* to score in the States. And that means changing the nature of the films that are made.

Some idea of how far things have changed can be seen from what has happened to Goldcrest Films, the company that, under different management, redefined the notion of a 'British' film in the early 1980s by doing the opposite of what EMI Films had been doing in the previous decade. But the new Goldcrest is committed, like EMI was in the past, to making 'American' films, and it seems largely uninterested in fostering British talent (the lights that failed?) apart from the obvious 'international' names. Local helmer Mike Hodges was despatched to North Carolina to direct Jason Robards and Rosanna Arquette in *Black Rainbow*, while the company's executives were seeking an American writer for *Killing Time*, the story of a woman journalist's trek from Atlanta to Miami with a man who turns out to be a serial killer.

Other companies, aware of the dangers involved in making American films from a British base, remain keen to exploit local themes and talent. But they also need those dollars. The newly fashionable solution is the Brit-American picture, a film rooted in British subject matter (definitely not mid-Atlantic) but with a heavy ladling of American content. It's a hybrid plant with many antecedents – Yanks were stalking through British pictures even before *The Ghost Goes West* in 1935 – but the new strain seems set to become the predominant mode of locally-financed production. That's hardly surprising in the year that provided a flagship in *A Fish Called Wanda*, a film carefully tailored to the US audience with its Yankee cast and alertness to American ideas about the English.

Current production slates are packed with examples of this new breed, although one doubts whether their scripts will match John Cleese's piece for careful honing. Zenith is preparing *After You've Gone*, about black musicians from New York on a trip to London. Working Title is pitching in with *Chicago Joe and the Showgirl*, in which Kiefer Sutherland plays an American officer who served in Britain during the Second World War and was hanged. That WW2 will prove a rich source of Brit-American subject matter is further indicated by the fact that David Puttnam is making *Memphis Belle*, about an American bomber crew operating out of the UK.

On paper, such projects seem like a clever solution to the problem of how British film producers can survive in a world dominated by American distribution companies. But they can also cause creative schizophrenia. Several recent films show foreign subject matter twisting the narrative in the wrong direction and undermining the best intentions of writers and directors.

High Spirits is set in Ireland, but it shares problems with many British films. Neil Jordan initially sets up a film that has Peter O'Toole at its centre – a gangly aristocrat, boozy and preoccupied with thoughts of suicide, who's in trouble over a mortgage secured from tough American financiers. It's all up with his strange household unless he can find some way to lure over the American tourists. So far so good. But once Steve Guttenberg arrives with his awful wife in tow, and two ghostly star-crossed lovers start passing through the walls of time, the film Jordan has established so well becomes submerged under *Beetlejuice*-style effects and crazy pitches towards the US mainstream. O'Toole wanders in occasionally to make a speech and remind us of the film that might have been.

Stormy Monday is unsettled from the beginning by the fact that its premise – a British city being taken over by American businessmen in league with local gangsters – seems out-of-touch with the realities of the international business community. Everything about writer-director Mike Figgis's feature début seems skewed by the phoniness of his central idea: he can't make the Irish Sean Bean's relationship with American Melanie Griffith ring true, and he seems unable to root his themes in the key characters; all because he's constantly being distracted by his 'big theme' – the supposed corruption of English society and values by an alien (American) import. And Figgis seems unconscious of the irony involved in making a film critique of the British municipal authorities' submission to American economic and cultural imperialism that itself uses all the hand-me-down clichés of Hollywood, albeit to little effect.

Those Americans kept popping up all over the place. In *Dream Demon*, the nice little English virgin troubled by nightmare visions of her imminent marriage is accompanied through her horrors by a black-haired American (who turns out to be English after all). In *Dealers*, a go-for-it British answer to *Wall Street*, the lady who usurps the place Paul McGann thinks is rightfully his and ends up flying away with him in his private plane, just happens to be an American (Rebecca DeMornay). And it's another expatriate (Helen Shaver) who gets landed with a kidnapped baby by her loopy mother in *Tree of Hands*.

And American performers intruded into the cast of films that couldn't possibly have justified their presence on other than financial grounds. Denzel Washington, as a Falklands vet returned to a drug-infested council estate, could never begin to look as if he might once have belonged. Bridget Fonda, looking pretty in *Scandal*, and Glenne Headly, struggling to be a tough mother in *Paperhouse*, had such problems with their accents that one wondered how often the producers had regretted their casting decisions. Only Jeff Goldblum turned out a winner, as the relaxed comic hero of *The Tall Guy*.

The demands of financiers, and the increasing difficulty of finding them, obviously explains the presence of so many American performers, and possibly also the predominance of Brit-American themes. But producers seem to lose their judgement when it comes to assessing a project with British and American angles. It's not difficult to see why. The relationship between the two countries provides them with the questions that bedevil their working lives. How can the 'indigenous' be reconciled to the imperatives of an American- dominated market? How can one adapt Hollywood's narrative forms to British themes? And it's these preoccupations that lead them away from their potential audience. The producer sees America as a threat, a danger and a suffocating presence when most of their intended audience probably welcomes US culture for sometimes displaying energy, vitality and freshness (as the producer probably does when he or she goes home and puts a video in the machine).

It's not a problem that involves only the Anglo-American relationship. British filmmakers aren't very good at dealing with any sort of culture-clash themes. Americans have the advantage of thinking that the US is, for the most part, a wonderful place. British filmmakers are more likely to share the sentiments of Archie Leach in *A Fish Called Wanda*, feeling that the native culture is, like its films, insipid and repressive. Set immigrants from another culture against the Brits, and you touch off an inferiority complex that makes filmmakers tentative, edgy, nervous. Take *Sour Sweet*, for example; its makers didn't seem to know enough about Chinese culture to act as anything other than observers, but nor could they extract any significant insights from the contrasts with the British way of doing things.

Films work when their makers can tap the source of their characters' passion. It must mean something that the only 'British' film of the year which set off any emotional firecrackers didn't actually have any Brit characters in it, but was set in South Africa and dealt exclusively with South Africans (albeit acted by English, American and African performers). Drawing upon the autobiographical experiences of screenwriter Shawn Slovo, and its director's background as a documentarist, *A World Apart* lacked for nothing in passion, commitment and flair.

There may be several good films in the works that explore the relationship between British and American culture, but the well cannot be very deep. Of course the interflow between American and British (and European) cultures since WW2 has been interesting. And the politics of a declining American Empire and the spreading tentacles of its business interests naturally throw up some gripping stories. But given the lack of conviction that British writers (apart from John Cleese) and directors have brought so far to these themes, one feels that producers who embrace them are voluntarily tying one hand behind their back. And when the seam runs dry, then producers will have to face up to the fact that the world really is an awful lot larger than the stretch of land and water connecting Heathrow to JFK.

Two producers on whom that message is not lost are David Puttnam and Jeremy Thomas, both sufficiently bankable in their own right to make pictures wherever, and with whomsoever, they wish. Alongside his *Memphis Belle* Britpic, Puttnam is preparing a thriller set in Bulgaria, a romantic comedy around events in a small Latin American town and a picture about a Hungarian conductor's efforts to stage an opera with a multinational company in Paris. Thomas's pictures are set in the Far East, Latin America and the weird world of William Burroughs' *The Naked Lunch*, and draw upon the talents of such interesting directors as Jonathan Demme, David Cronenberg, Bernardo Bertolucci, Nic Roeg and Chen Kaige. Puttnam's financing structure was built around his long-term relationship with Warner Bros. Jeremy Thomas relies rather on a group of European distributors, although the financial underpinnings come from the Japanese.

Do the set-ups established by Thomas and Puttnam have any real significance for the broader British production industry? Perhaps one will have to wait and see whether the structures hold, and the films actually work. Puttnam was quoted in the trade press as suggesting his formula would lay to rest 'all the problems of the British industry once and for all . . .', but it's difficult to see that the relaunch of Enigma did anything more than solve the problems of one Mr Puttnam (and those of the writers, directors and others associated with him). Having run a film studio, albeit for a short time, carefully nurtured a relationship with Warner Bros. over many years, and produced a fair number of hit films, he *deserves* that sort of backing. That doesn't make things much easier for his contemporaries with less impressive track records, or talented juniors starting up the ladder.

Thomas and Puttnam have taken off above the tacky little sweatshop that is the British film industry. They can go wherever they want, picking ideas and directorial talent wherever they grow. What's refreshing is that they're both relatively independent of the concerns of mainstream Hollywood, but savvy enough about the international market to make films that just might work. It may be that, as Puttnam has suggested, they're laying the seeds for a European film industry that will one day act as a significant counterweight to the might of Hollywood. But given the puniness of the efforts so far made in Strasbourg and Brussels to nurture cinema in the European Community, and the continuing problem of language that a Puttnam-sponsored film like *To Kill a Priest* emphasizes, it's difficult to see the dream turning quickly to reality. For the moment, as one scans the list of future projects from Enigma and Thomas's Recorded Picture Company, it's depressing to see how few interesting *ideas* have come from Britain, where only a few years back a 'renaissance' was said to be in progress, and how little the pool of native talent has to offer these European super-producers.

JAMES PARK

PERFORMING LIPS

Compiled by Tony Crawley

Acting is a bum's life. Quitting is a sign of maturity.
Marlon Brando

All right, I'm young, I'm beautiful – but you don't have to hate me.
Sean Young

When I was a young actor, I won countries. Now I get the girl.
Anthony Quinn

I'm not God. I have no answers. I just speak my ideas.
Klaus Maria Brandauer

I'd much rather be playing bridge than making a bad movie.
Omar Sharif

I'll get married one day. But first we have to save the earth.
Kenneth Branagh

An actress is someone with no ability who sits around waiting to go on alimony.
Jackie Stallone, Sly's mother

What's happened to the questions they used to ask in the old days, like your favourite colour . . . like, you know, What's your favourite food?

I don't know where the world would be without art.

If I can't find some humour in my work – even in my image – that would be terrible.
Sylvester Stallone

Before we shot that kissing scene in *The Front*, Woody Allen said to me; 'I'm going to give you only one lip when we kiss. Because if I give you two, you'll never live through it.'
Andrea Marcovicci

People ask me how I liked working with a talking horse in *Hot To Trot*. Hey, I've worked with Steve Guttenberg – what's the big deal.
Bobcat Goldthwait

Behind every successful man you'll find a woman – who has absolutely nothing to wear.
James Stewart

Do people treat me differently now? Well, all my jokes seem to have become a *lot* funnier.

TV, for the most part, bores the shit out of me. TV is not about quality work as much as it is about selling things.
Bruce Willis

I suppose many people don't even know if I'm still alive – well, perhaps I'm not.
Douglas Fairbanks Jr.

I felt it was time I did something for fish. They're so special but people take them for granted and it's not fair. Fish are so under-rated these days. Especially sand dabs. All of them really. I could go on and on about it. I do, actually. People say to me, 'Don't go on about fish today, please, Jack.' And I say, 'Just tell me one thing – can you breathe underwater?' And, of course, I have them there.
John Cleese

He's surrounded by a world of adoring acolytes, most of whom are desperate not to offend him. Not being on the payroll, I can be as rude as I like.
Mrs Sting, actress Trudie Styler

I've got a filthy mouth but it's my only sin.
Eddie Murphy

It thrills me that one day my grandchildren may see their grandmother in her little half-slip and bra – seducing a monster.
Susan Sarandon on her cult movie, The Rocky Horror Picture Show

Sometimes I look at my skin and say, 'Oh, my God, it doesn't look so good – I have to have more sex!'
Model-turned-actress Paulina Porizkova

Being good in bed means I'm propped up with pillows and my mom brings me soup.
Brooke Shields

The new actors are great. Charlie Sheen is a gentleman; his parents must've raised him right. Tom Cruise is a real prince. And they're all so disciplined. Not as wild as our group was. No booze, no drugs. These guys are athletes!
Tom Berenger

Mel Gibson is God's gift to a director. But he tells the worst jokes in the world.
Richard Donner

After everything he did to his body, this man should be dead.
Haskell Wexler on pal Dennis Hopper

People can be very cruel. They don't mean to be. They just don't regard celebrities as real. And I guess, in some ways, we're not.
Don Johnson

I turned down dinner with Mickey Rourke. Because he's a star! To me, a star is inaccessible, mysterious, an impossible dream – and should stay that way. Adjani's a star. Deneuve's a star. Not me.
Miou-Miou

Arnold's very strong-willed, his concentration is almost supreme. But he does have a major weakness. During shooting, I got anything I wanted when I gave him vanilla ice-cream – his parking space, his wife, anything!

It's not everyday you get to embrace Arnold Schwarzenegger in a motel room. It's like holdin' on to a moose.
Danny DeVito on Schwarzenegger

Arnold Schwarzenegger has great courage. More than once, he campaigned for me and then returned home each time to face his in-laws.
President George Bush on Conan The Republican, married into the Kennedys

I don't just look for difficult rôles. The hardest rôle for me would be something I had no interest in . . . in the worst script ever written. Now, that *would* be a challenge.
Dustin Hoffman

It reminded me of *Star Wars* with camels.
Bruce Willis on the restored Lawrence of Arabia

I'm not doing *Ghostbusters II* for the dramatic challenge, that's for sure.
Sigourney Weaver

Before I make a film, I always dream I'm showing up on the set naked and everybody else has clothes on. I don't know what the scene is and it's my cue and I just don't know what the fuck is happening. All I know is I'm there without my clothes on and I don't know why.
Theresa Russell

I never wanted to be a man. I feel sorry for them.
Glenn Close

My liveliness is based on an incredible fear of death. Most people are afraid of death, but I really *hate* it.
Mel Brooks

When you're in a TV show, something does happen to you. You get an overinflated sense of your own importance. You think you know all the answers. You don't even know the fucking *questions*.
Tom Hanks

I didn't know what I was doing. It was completely bonkers.
Uma Thurman on The Adventures of Baron Munchausen

The difference between English and American humour is $150 a minute.
Eric Idle

ERIC BOGOSIAN

One of the most chilling moments in *Talk Radio* comes when Eric Bogosian's loudmouthed left-wing talk-show host is sitting at the mike and putting down a Holocaust doubter by citing the Star of David that he picked out of the dust when he visited Dachau. Although he claims to have the religious artefact in his hand, proof that he's just a deceitful media-jackal arrives when the camera pans down to reveal he's only holding a coffee mug. It is this kind of moment that Bogosian is obsessed with crystallizing in his work.

With the believe-me-believe-me-not face of a born liar and the half- mad glint of someone wasted by either too much falsehood or too much honesty, he straddles the divide between ethnic bogeyman and traditional incorruptibility, jolting Hollywood with a dose of real-life ambiguity in an era of too many smooth-faced white young Anglo-Saxon Protestant leading men. Only Bogosian could play the part he created in *Talk Radio*, the liberal radio chat-show host who overdoses on his own notoriety. The film, directed by Oliver Stone, is based on a play Bogosian co-wrote and starred in off Broadway three years ago.

'We're watching a *prima donna* coming to the end of his rope,' Bogosian says of the character. 'The movie is about a guy whose big mouth gets him in a jam. He doesn't want to know who's out there listening. In the end, though, he comes face to face with what he's really doing.'

Bogosian's demolition of his character's ego is echoed in his own, self-aware admission that he too is 'a *prima donna* making a living from selling social commentary in the mass media.' Up until now, the masses weren't buying. In the late 1970s and early 1980s he used to perform his terrifying brand of comedy in New York theatres that were not so much underground as subterranean, gaining a reputation as the comic no act wanted to follow. His persona as the political torturer describing how much pain and damage a cigarette can cause to a human being, or his desperately pleading child adopting the prejudices of an undemonstrative invisible father to gain his love, confronted audiences with the same sense of power, shock and intense discomfort as a sledgehammer between the legs.

Bogosian came closer than any of his contemporaries to the over-used and abused label of 'the new Lenny Bruce' with his unrelenting, undeniably honest material that refused to let either his audience or himself off the hook, but with one crucial difference – no one laughs. Bogosian turns his comedy into something like political theatre or a highly disciplined form of performance art. In an intimate space, he offers no escape from his presence: he seems to be the one baring his soul, but in the end you are the one whose self has been stripped naked while he walks away, perfectly in control.

The confrontation and verbal self-immolation of his stage persona is carried over into his first major screen rôle, as the doomed and damned radio phone-in host who strips away the comfort of listeners' prejudices or the hypocrisy of their liberalism, devoting himself to the mediocrity of their empty lives and paying the price for it.

Barry Champlain is Bogosian's most offensive character. His station manager says he is 'just a suit salesman with a big mouth'. Barry is rude to callers, often hanging up on them in mid-sentence. When people call in to agree with him, he's apt to keep them off balance by launching into a neo-fascist tirade. Barry will say anything on air to upset people, because outrage builds ratings and ratings make Barry a star.

What happens to Barry does not surprise those who know about Denver talk-show host Alan Berg, murdered by a right-wing hate group in 1984. (Another fictionalized version of Berg's death was the basis of Costa-Gavras's film *Betrayed*.) Oddly, Bogosian wrote his first version of *Talk Radio* in 1984 before he had heard of Berg. 'At first I was more interested in the callers, and I wanted a mellow guy. Then I realized you can't watch a guy who's mellow for an hour or two. So I made Barry rock 'n' roll.'

When the film version came to be made, Bogosian was determined to remain part of the package. 'People came up to me saying, "We'll give you a lot of money, we'll rip the insides out of the material and we'll give the part to a star." ' Bogosian wound up taking less money, allowing a smaller-scale production ($4.5 million) that 'doesn't cop out'.

Stone and Bogosian expanded the play from its original *Swimming to Cambodia*-style theatrical constrictions (one actor, one desk, one mike, one rant) to a moody, cantankerous tirade that indicted both the character and the American media's propensity to parlay social commentary into ratings-busting controversy.

Since the play brought Bogosian up from the underground, he has taken his scabrous style onto TV in a slightly cleaned-up version of his one-man show, *Drinking in America*, in which such characters as an agent, a hoodlum and a TV evangelist ramble on boozily. He forces the audience to not simply love or hate him, but to re-evaluate their own duplicities

Getting people's backs up isn't just a job for this man, it's a vocation. It's difficult to speculate how a mainstream sensibility will assist him to expand his artistic empire – whether Hollywood, now that it beckons, will nurture or destroy this pugnacious brat who can be crass or charming, vulnerable or vindictive.

Today, Bogosian says, 'I'm trying now to give myself a break a little bit, even though I don't come from the airbrush-your-face school of acting. I'm not the angry, insane guy Barry is.'

BART MILLS

MICHELLE PFEIFFER IN *MARRIED TO THE MOB*

AND IN *DANGEROUS LIAISONS*, RIGHT

NATASHA RICHARDSON IN *PATTY HEARST*

JODHI MAY IN *A WORLD APART*

ERIC BOGOSIAN IN *TALK RADIO*

FOREST WHITAKER IN *BIRD*

JEREMY IRONS IN *DEAD RINGERS*

LIAM NEESON IN *HIGH SPIRITS*

GEENA DAVIS

et me look into the crystal ball. Yes, I see a tall, slim, gleaming statuette. It is an Oscar. And yes, my dear, you will win it for your sixth feature film, as Best Supporting Actress, in 1989. But there will be troubles before that. In your early films you will act opposite Dustin Hoffman in drag and Michael Keaton wearing rotting teeth and mildew. And, in another picture, Jeff Goldblum's ear will fall off before your eyes. But never fear. Your strange, reposeful beauty will win you the Gene Tierney sex appeal franchise for the 1990s. To the delight of Hollywood gossip writers, you will become the constant companion of he whose ear fell off. And you will be in work until, and possibly beyond, the year 2000.'

With half-a-dozen movie appearances and an Oscar tucked away so far, Geena Davis makes the clairvoyant's lot an easy one. It is hard to see how Hollywood won't form itself into a human ladder to let her ascend into stardom. As indicated by Madame Astrolabia, our expert on the stars (formerly Secretary for Forward Planning to the Reagans), Davis has triumphed over a run of the weirdest movies and male leads Filmdom could fling at her.

In *Tootsie*, she survived a comedy of transvestism. In *The Fly*, she co-starred with the man of her dreams, who at the time was vomiting over everything, coming apart at the limbs and turning into a housefly. And in *Beetlejuice*, she stood by while the movie's special effects, otherwise known as Michael Keaton, whirled, whizz-banged and exploded all around her.

But no wonder she got those rôles. She can look pixillated, wide-eyed and serenely agog like no other actress. Her bemusements are beatific. Her astonishments are seraphic. Her full mouth can gape in wonder while pursing childlike at the corners. Her voice is 'soft and low, an excellent thing in woman.' And she can mirror whole stories in her eyes: 'reacting' to them without seeming to react at all. She may be the least actressy actress to have hit Hollywood in years.

Davis's flair for playing characters who can't be fazed – a form of sanity which is also a form of loopiness – fits her for her Oscar-winning rôle in Kasdan's *The Accidental Tourist*. Muriel Pritchett, dog trainer, single mother, scatterbrain and pest, is the life force in a romantic comedy where Davis's reactions must for once be directed at too little happening around her rather than too much. William Hurt's menopausal hero is a study in 'non-acting' so subtle and funny that not even Davis could match it. So for once she 'acts'; encouraged no doubt by a filmmaker keen on having strong women in his movies (Kathleen Turner in *Body Heat*, Glenn Close in *The Big Chill*).

The result, like many Oscar-winning performances, is less interesting and more of a 'turn' than Davis's less actressy rôles. But never mind. It's another stage in

241

her ongoing portrait of unfazeable American womanhood; and the statuette will help push into stardom an actress who seems able to make a fresh, loose, camera-friendly modernity blend in with invocations of the past. (There's a touch of 1930s screwball charm, school of Hepburn, and also of 1940s *film noir* mystery: she's got Tierney's face and at times the low purr of Stanwyck in the voice.)

But Geena Davis at best remains un-Hollywoodish. Maybe she owes it to a New England background. Born in *Beetlejuice* country – Wareham, Massachusetts – she studied at Boston University and then acted for the Mount Washington Repertory Theatre Company. Modelling brought her into *Tootsie*, she followed up with *Fletch* and *Transylvania 6-5000*, and the rest has been rapid history.

By far the best Davis performance to date has been in *The Fly*. She's only off-screen in four scenes of Cronenberg's shocker, and during the rest she has to evolve through three phases. One, brash scepticism. (After all, she's a working newswoman, with a raincoat, a tape-recorder and a hardboiled smile; so what's this stuff about 'teleportation'?) Two, growing love and empathy as crazy Jeff gropes towards a place in scientific history. Three, grief and horror as the boyfriend grows hairs, sheds ears, throws up over the doughnuts and behaves in ways that would make any less lovestruck woman reach for the Mafu spray.

Davis gets every phase in the movie right. 'Designer phone booths, ve-ry cute' she clucks at first sight of the giant teleportation pods: no one puts humbug or mumbo-jumbo over on this girl. In the first part of the film, Davis – a walking lesson in deportment anyway – scarcely bends from the perpendicular. She's poker-backed, cool and sassy. Only the sometimes wayward eyes, moving from side to side, or the off-guard eyelids, which drift down beguilingly to half-mast, sketch a vulnerability to come.

Later, Davis's changes are wondrous to observe. The voice warms and the manner unbends as love and science beckon. Later still, the excitement communicates itself to her like a fevered trance: she's caught in its rays like a rabbit in headlamps. Later still, as Jeff Goldfly comes unstuck and begins to resemble something stirring on a butcher's slab, Davis has almost no dialogue to play with apart from 'Oh God no!' (scream), 'Oh no please don't!' (sob), 'Oh please no!' (gulp shriek), 'Oh Seth no!' (gurgle), 'Oh no!' (sob scream).

She wins by never letting go of the character's master-key; which is that love and revulsion are locked inextricably in battle right to the end. When the pathetic beastie shredded in the teleporter (formerly Mr Goldblum) points the gun she's holding to his blood-tattered head, we feel every beat and whimper of her agony. For this actress hasn't once during the film given us Hollywood histrionics.

Nor has she done so yet in any other film. Long may the record hold. Long may Tinseltown keep Geena Davis busy.

HARLAN KENNEDY

JEREMY IRONS

ow, boys, pay attention! Shoulders back, stiff upper-lip primed, that's the stuff. We here at the True Brit Academy of Performing Arts aim to turn out top-hole troopers. Which brings me to the sad case of Irons, Jeremy: the Old Boy who only a few terms ago was being held up as the epitome of the Romantic Leading Man. Seldom, if ever, have careers been launched to such a chorus of hurrahs. A swift double innings: the TV adaptation of *Brideshead Revisited* (*et in Arcadia ego* and all that), followed by *The French Lieutenant's Woman* opposite Meryl Streep – whose Olivieresque aptitude for accents places her firmly in the Honorary Brit Category. Jeremy conducted himself with admirable restraint and decorum, and he showed off his nervous good looks. He was even dubbed The Thinking Woman's Crumpet.

But, oh dear! We have realized that, although the Polish film director Jerzy Skolimowski was a London resident, a Pole is a Pole is a Pole. In other words, not *British*. And here was Jeremy Irons in *Moonlighting* as a Pole (and a working-class Pole to boot) and not even playing his Polish accent up for all it was worth. Dear lord, it looked almost as if he were *living* the rôle instead of *acting* it out in the correct British manner. Had his association with Meryl taught him *nothing*?

For a while, we thought it merely a temporary lapse. He was back on course with *Betrayal*, a stirring tale of adultery in Hampstead. But the next thing we knew, he was sneaking off to Europe, *and* without a chaperone. There were red faces when we saw *Swann in Love*, I can tell you. That it should have been directed by a German was bad enough, but here was our most promising pupil playing (gulp) a *Frenchman*, in a story written by a froggy Jew. *And* doing frightfully un-British things to some Italian bint; the very thought of it renders me almost speechless.

If only we'd been firmer with him, insisted he stop all this nonsensical fraternization with foreigners, he might even now be counted as One of Us. He would be making a comfortable living, thank you, playing uppercrust heroes, or fine upstanding gentlemen with starched collars in some of those beautifully nostalgic costume pictures of which we British are rightfully proud.

We thought *The Mission* was a step back in the right direction. Admittedly he was playing a Jesuit, and much of the filming took place in the sort of exotic jungle setting which positively encourages a chap to go native, especially when the hot sun goes to his head and the local gals aren't wearing blouses. But we thought he was safe with old Putters and, indeed, Jeremy seemed happy enough afterwards to fly the British flag on Broadway in a Tom Stoppard play. (There are those troublemakers who maintain that Stoppard isn't an Englishman. I ask you.)

How could we have guessed at what would follow? We heard he was playing

twins. Aha, we thought, *The Comedy of Errors*. Who better than the Bard to curtail Jeremy's urge to roam and take risks? The director was to be some Canadian chap, name of Cronenberg. Can't say I'd heard of him, and his name sounded suspiciously Germanic, but at least his passport was Commonwealth, and the c.v. sounded promising: *Scanners*, one imagines, was all about an appeal to raise money for a hospital, and *The Fly* was evidently some sort of National Geographic nature special.

Mea culpa: screening *Dead Ringers* in the village hall was not a good idea. I knew as soon as the vicar's wife fainted and had to be helped outside by some of the senior prefects that we were in trouble, and that was only the first five minutes. No sooner was the film underway than women were lying on their backs with their legs apart, and Jeremy was peering at their – ahem – private parts. He was drinking too much, and taking drugs, and getting up to all sorts of kinky stuff with this froggy slut, and wandering around in his underpants, and generally letting the side down with his snivelling. And he was doing all this *twice* over, because he was playing twins. I'll grant you it was dashed clever; these fellows were called Elliot and Beverly Mantle, and even though they looked as alike as two peas in a pod, Jeremy somehow managed to give each of them a totally distinctive character, and mannerisms, and facial expressions, so that you always knew which was which, even when one of the twins was impersonating the other.

But why oh why did they have to be *gynaecologists*? Why couldn't they have been lawyers, or something in the City? Cronenberg said he thought that an American Method actor might have had trouble in the dual rôle, and that the English style of acting, which is theatre-based and which stresses discipline, was the way to go about it. It has always been rumoured that there are plenty of foreign filmmakers lurking out there, ready and willing to tempt England's finest with the sort of rôles that encourage them to let it all hang out and make spectacles of themselves. It is all a plot to undermine English values. Boys, let this be a lesson to you.

ANNE BILLSON

MICHAEL KEATON

M ichael Keaton can play the handsome, vaguely-enigmatic lead, or he can be a comedic pit-bull terrier. The angular eyebrows, the pugnacious smirk and those frenetic eyes betray intelligence and suggest a wide range of acting possibilities. Born in Pittsburgh, Pennsylvania, Keaton dropped out of Kent State University, and later worked off-screen on *Mr Roger's Neighborhood* – a chat show for children. Disenchanted with technical duties and the show's hyper-friendly male host, he moved on to LA. There, after an unsuccessful stab at stand-up comedy (Keaton's characters have never been joke-machines) and selected TV appearances, he exploded onto the screen in 1982's black comedy, *Night Shift*.

As the accomplice to a financial analyst-turned-morgue attendant, Keaton's shaggy hipster Bill Blaze was not the sort of guy who embraced complacency. Dictating opportunistic ideas for improvized get-rich-quick innovations into a tape-recorder Blaze strutted around the office of straight man Henry Winkler with the kinetic zeal of a human peacock. Driving a hearse disguised as a limo service, Keaton's first major rôle identified him as a little man with big ideas, the most viable of which was *Night Shift*'s essential premise – a plan to lease hookers out of the city morgue. He seemed to know he was funny and, having taken that for granted, believed he was unstoppable.

Keaton's humour has always relied on that intangible balance between good and bad taste. In *Gung Ho*, he provokes a violent confrontation between the two warring automobile factory tribes – Japanese and American – prompting a bigger rift between cultures when, after myriad attempts to prove American superiority, he simply raises an eyebrow, shifts into a defiant posture of bemused malignancy and gently taunts his Japanese rival: 'Well, who lost the big one then?'

After languishing in a string of unsuccessful comedies (including the gang-land pastiche *Johnny Dangerously*, and comedy thriller *The Squeeze*) along came Tim Burton's *Beetlejuice* to bring Keaton back to prominence. This time Keaton was not forced to subordinate his persona to a rôle that demanded likeability. When his character Betelgeuse's head spontaneously gyrates on its shoulders, he stops to complain glibly, 'Don't ya hate it when that happens?' as if it were (to would-be clients, the newly-deceased astral homebodies Geena Davis and Alec Baldwin) an ordinary occurrence, which, of course, it is for him.

Beetlejuice took Keaton back to the time before stereotypical good-guy comedy engulfed him. He was the strange and uncouth monster who had been expelled from human congress and, left abandoned to his own devices, created his own reality, one where there are no parameters, no caution or reason. In the process, Keaton's antagonist got to break some heavy rules of comedy in a dissonant farce

that was funny because it was organic, imperfect, at times incomplete.

Keaton went on to play the irredeemable alcoholic junkie of *Clean and Sober*, a yuppie embezzler who seeks refuge in a 21-day detoxification programme for other than the obvious reason, and in the process recovers a new respect for himself by purging not only the chemicals, but also the more reprehensible aspects of his character.

This pilgrim's progress was neither didactic nor sanctimonious – and Keaton's scabrous irreverence ensured that this foray into 'serious', mature, leading-man status transcended the moral-inflections of what could have been, without Keaton, merely another 'just say no' paean to abstention. *Clean and Sober* brought about a re-evaluation of Keaton's undervalued diversity as a performer.

After working with Tim Burton on *Beetlejuice*, some sort of reunion was always on the cards, but his casting as Batman was a surprise. What's ironic about the ensuing hate-mail and indignation is that, whilst various factions conspired to denigrate his artistic credibility (the comic-book fans who loved the original comic but hated the TV show seemed to equate Keaton only with the scatterbrained wise-guy of *Mr Mom*), Bob Kane, the character's creator, made it abundantly clear that, if not Keaton, comedian Dan Aykroyd was his idea for the schizophrenic Dark Knight of Gotham City, while producers Jon Peters and Bill Guber publicly contended they had always wanted someone like Bill Murray.

Keaton's Batman had much in common with his rôle in *Beetlejuice*. Both are a mass of mimetic shadows manipulated only by the performer's imagination. The pivotal scene attesting to how this diminutive actor stood the entire super-hero concept on its head occurs when Bruce Wayne, accompanied by reporter and love-interest Vicki Vale (Kim Basinger), witnesses the massacre of a whole contingent of Gotham's criminal underworld, along with some citizens who are held at gunpoint by the Joker and his gang. Keaton's Wayne freaks out, cognizant of his rôle as a child spectator forced to watch his parents gunned down by a thug and powerless to do anything. Even now, because he has nowhere to change, he can't become Batman; he can't save the victims. These touches, these gestures, unmask the true Caped Crusader in Keaton – anarchic behaviour manifesting itself alternately as psychological paranoia and vengeful self-perpetuating heroism.

Trivial fancies like *Mr. Mom* will no longer prove as satisfying as they once were to Keaton. Always vigilant and always sceptical, his characters really don't care what society thinks. They are obviously crazed, but in the most appealing manner possible. This renewed abrasiveness parallels his migration from early rôles that were embodiments of Everyman to the province of subversion.

Take a look at a picture of him. Michael Keaton's eyes will show you where his mind and thoughts are. Take a look while you have the chance, because this lunatic has escaped to take over the asylum.

MARKUS NATTEN

JODHI MAY

Britain is one of the few countries in the world where children are taught to act: more than 30 stage schools across the country are filled to bursting with budding Bonnie Langfords who make up in volume for what they lack in subtlety, charm or talent. As a result, the UK has some of the worst child actors in the world.

It was rumoured at one point that Warner Bros, before coming upon ordinary schoolboy Christian Bale, so despaired of finding a suitable young lead for *Empire of the Sun* that they contemplated changing the character's sex to make things easier. Even if the story is apocryphal, it does seem indicative of the majority of British child performers. Therefore, the emergence of a talent as obvious and unforced as Jodhi May's seems little short of miraculous. Even more so when one discovers that May *did* study acting, at the Anna Scher Theatre School.

Picked from some 3,000 girls to play the lead in *A World Apart*, the anti-apartheid drama directed by Chris Menges, May's part as Molly Roth, a girl coming to terms with the emotional effects of her journalist mother's arrest under the infamous 90 Days Detention Act, calls for a wide range of emotions. The success of the film depends on her rôle – she appears in almost every scene – and there are so many dramatic moments written into the script that it would have been easy to overplay it. Anything less than brilliance and the film fails.

Much of the film's passion derives less from the incidents than the playing. When Elsie, the black maid, teaches Molly the lyrics of the ANC anthem, 'Nkose Sikelela Afrika', there is no additional dialogue, just words sung in a foreign language; but the life and depth of understanding May brings to the scene is amazing. Accepting rather than understanding its meaning, she sings it as a way of deepening her bond with Elsie. There is a sense of joy, of fun and an underlying sadness that cannot be contrived by just a writer or director. Later, she meets Elsie's brother in a brief scene that boasts little dialogue beyond perfunctory politenesses, but still manages to project a sense of warmth and easiness that she cannot feel with her mother, subtly drawing attention to the parallels between the politically and the emotionally dispossessed without succumbing to the temptation to turn Molly into a saint in the process.

Indeed, she can be downright unpleasant at times, as at the 'family' breakfast after her mother's arrest where she reprimands her grandmother for sitting in her absent parents' seats. 'That's where mum sits,' she tells her grandmother. Grandmother moves: 'That's where dad sits,' is her surly retort. May shows where such behaviour comes from. Molly is so engrossed in her own pain that she is oblivious to the pain she causes those around her.

May's ability to convey a range in her pain is striking: when her best friend

247

says she was wondering when Molly would return to school after her mother's arrest, she very simply responds, 'Didn't try very hard to find out,' with all the desperate pleasantness of a recovered invalid who received no get-well-soon cards but daren't let the disappointment show for fear of losing a friendship. Rather than play pain with a capital P, she tries to hide it, at first gradually trying to let it out through simple remarks until there is no one to turn to and it becomes too much to bear. Even then, she tries to hold it back, doing little – tightening her chin, concentrating her gaze, tensing up in an attempt not to shake – thus making her few eruptions all the more powerful and believable for their violent frustration.

Like the best American child performers, May has the ability to appear perfectly natural on screen and react rather than overact. She is also able to listen and react differently to different people: to her friend Yvonne she is conspiratorial, out of a sense of fun; to her headmistress she is withdrawn because of her isolation; to her mother contrary because of her resentment; to Elsie obedient out of need. Molly is a character who refuses to be summed up easily – she is intelligent and compassionate and she wants to learn about people, but she can be moody, introspective and rude. She has increasingly less patience with a cause she knows is right but which she wants to go away so that she can lead her own life.

For once, you can actually believe that this is a character who had a life before the film started, and will have one after it has finished. You care about her and believe in her. May not only carries the early scenes in the film, where little is said or done, but manages to translate them into something of real substance, building an emotional reservoir that makes the shockwaves of the finale, where Molly demands her mother's love, reverberate all the more profoundly. It is the most violent scene in the film as Molly vents all the hurt and confusion she has ever felt, tearing apart old wounds in an attempt to heal the new ones. It's a scene filled with pitfalls for the unwary, but May pulls it off with a confidence and assurance that would shame most experienced adult performers.

Whilst Jodhi's talent is undeniable, good rôles are rare for young actresses and casting directors are reluctant to let them grow up. Although she now has moved to one of the larger theatrical agencies, the tendency to regard any talented child performer as a nine-day-wonder, coupled with her unorthodox looks (not enough freckles for the good ship lollipop, too friendly for the exorcist) could count against her. But some people are just too talented to ignore, and Jodhi May is certainly one of them.

TREVOR WILLSMER

LIAM NEESON

Pray silence for a miracle. Actor Liam Neeson is breaking forth from the chrysalis of mute-and-macho supporting rôles and becoming a multi-coloured movie butterfly. Hallelujah. In the past twelve months, Irish-born Liam has lent a loony, logorrhoeic presence to *The Dead Pool*, as chief murder suspect and part-time movie director, and an overpowering Celtic charisma to *The Good Mother*, as a life-force sculptor tried for child abuse.

So Liam Neeson *can* talk and act. Good heavens. There we were all those years thinking – unless we had seen him on stage at London's National Theatre (*Translations*) or in his native Ireland (*One Flew over the Cuckoo's Nest*, *Streamers*) – that he was an actor whose skills were confined to looking like Saint Sebastian and talking like Harpo Marx.

Not for naught was Neeson's first American TV appearance in a drama called *Sworn to Silence*. In his early screen rôles, he seemed typecast for Trappist integrity or taciturn machismo. In *Duet for One*, he was a bit of off-the-street rough for Julie Andrews. In *The Mission*, a black-robed Neeson hung about for hours of screen time, speechless and surplice-to-requirements. In *A Prayer for the Dying* and *High Spirits*, he tersely pursued Mickey Rourke and Daryl Hannah across the movies' respective maps. And in *Suspect*, his first title rôle, he was a deaf-and-dumb Vietnam veteran accused of murder. 'Carl Anderson is the American nightmare' warbles public defender Cher, as poor Liam spends most of the movie in the dock, with hanging head and zero dialogue.

After these formative experiences, the actor could well have handed in his Pinewood and Hollywood dinner pails and returned to the live theatre. But Neeson has a star quality that stands out through his haloed hangdog rôles, and even through the eye-blink epiphanies – waving spear, broadsword or flintlock – in *The Bounty*, *Excalibur* or *Krull*.

You can recognize the actor in these films by his ability to look as if he wants to be somewhere else. Even while he puts heart-and-soul into the rhubarbing or weapon-wielding, a far-off gleam ennobles the visage. Only true stars can manage this trick, and they tend to end up being put on the mountain peaks they silently aspire to.

But it often takes a catalyzing piece of cross-casting to get a good actor noticed. Neeson has much in common with his *Mission* co-star, Jeremy Irons. Athough good at radiating goodness, he can suffer from the tautologies and low tension of typecasting. Irons was perfect and boring in *The Mission*; Neeson was perfect and boring in *Lamb*. As an Irish teacher-priest on the run with a bullied kid, Neeson was sensitive, finely-honed and a touch anodyne. But put either of them in an unlikely rôle – Irons in *Dead Ringers*, Neeson in *The Dead Pool* and *The Good*

Mother – and sparks fly from the abrasion of opposites.

Neeson has a high time in the latest Dirty Harry epic. In a thriller so pulpy that everyone else sinks up to the knees, Neeson's porno filmmaker and murder suspect is heroically over-the-top. While his never-never-land accent intrigues the ear (what is it meant to be? Australian, cockney, both?), his Catherine-wheel physical pyrotechnics enthrall the eye. Lighting the blue touch-paper to the tousled hair and martyred stoop of *Suspect*, he turns hippie passivity into crazed Bohemianism. Strutting amid the movie lights, he is a limey Sternberg, a loon in Lotus-land. And his funniest moment suggests a paranoia so deep-seated even its owner is hardly conscious of it. Who does he think is trying to frame him, Clint asks Liam. 'Could be anyone' replies Liam, thinking about it: 'My agent, my producer, my stars, my writer . . .'

But *The Dead Pool* is playtime stuff compared to *The Good Mother*. Almost everything goes wrong in this Disney-Touchstone stab at an 'adult' subject, except for Neeson himself. As the fiery sculptor accused of abusing girlfriend Diane Keaton's little daughter, Neeson takes over the screen. Someone certainly had to. Oscillating between magazine weepie and feminist encyclical, the movie wholly defeats star Keaton and director Leonard ('Out, damned Spock') Nimoy.

But Neeson's magnetism engulfs his scenes. He makes this life-force Michelangelo, though novelettishly-conceived, seem both an amatory hustler and a wholehearted human being. As Pauline Kael enthused, he 'takes a new cliché – the artist as ideal, sensual man – and plays it with such rhythmic ease that you hardly question it.' And even when this sculptor-hunk ends up in court, condemned to frowning silence as if in a re-run of *Suspect*, Neeson's flair for portraying grace under pressure keeps his inner motor ticking. You keep looking at Neeson, although he's 'expressing' nothing: you seldom look at Keaton, although she's expressing everything.

Destiny is weird in Moviedom. Maybe Neeson's flair for all-male quietude and his sculpted Roman looks – the brow and nose of a Caesar, the reposeful stoop of a Botticelli Mars – will prove somewhat time-warped for modern tastes. In an age when feminism has questioned many junk clichés in the Sexual Casting department, including that of the 'strong silent male', Neeson has to go on proving he's more than a roll-on-roll-off virility symbol.

The move to Hollywood already seems a good idea. Out there, crazy filmmakers get crazy casting notions; especially with actors they haven't yet got a handle on. If Neeson can go on stretching his range beyond the easy-option rôles the Irish and British cinema kept giving him – saintly worker-priests, IRA toughies, human wallpaper for sword-and-sorcery flicks – he may soon stretch himself all the way to stardom. It's within his reach.

HARLAN KENNEDY

MICHELLE PFEIFFER

She possesses the most exquisite face in modern American cinema. Not that it is desirable to define Michelle Pfeiffer's effulgent beauty without considering the warmth, vulnerability, reticence and tenacity that she radiates off-screen and on. Pfeiffer defies a prosaic response. In the flesh, as in still photographs, her face may haunt but it seldom comforts. She smiles wanly for the press, as if some wound is being inflicted. From what she says about doing publicity for her films, this seems to be true. Like Garbo, Pfeiffer might want to be alone, except that she needs a movie camera to liberate her, and therefore needs us.

For an American, especially a highly visible one who has recently joined the élite of Hollywood actresses, Pfeiffer is disarmingly retiring, a star renowned, professionally, as a complex blend of honey and grit, whose tendency to self-deprecation seems sincere.

If you can imagine the risky emotional journey made by a gorgeous Mafia widow who turns her back on a life of soiled luxury in suburban Long Island to start over again as a hairdresser's help (son and dog in tow) in grungy, funky Lower East Side Manhattan, then you might find a clue to the real-life transformation made by Michelle Pfeiffer. She admits an affinity for Angela DeMarco, the character she plays in *Married to the Mob*, Jonathan Demme's sweet and bloody post-modern parable about gangsters, materialism and true feelings. And you can see what attracted her to the film, the eleventh she has made since 1980. It is the first rôle that allows her to lose her 'golden girl' identity without becoming an ice-queen, a bitch, a witch or a princess. But the film *is* a contemporary fairy tale and she *does* let her hair down – in this case, a mane of dark, gypsyish curls she cultivates to put the licentious local Don (Dean Stockwell) and his jealous wife (Mercedes Ruehl) off her trail. Pfeiffer has never been more relaxed, even as she's whisked off, in a sassy red-and-white polka dot frock, to a samba club by the gentle FBI man (Matthew Modine) who's supposed to be staking her out.

Once just another identikit pretty blonde hanging around with surfers on the beaches of Southern California, Pfeiffer may not be quite sure how she became serious, ethereal, and even a touch melancholic, let alone a star. Her flat, sometimes inaudible undertone is rippled by expressions of girlish incredulity, but she has a reputation for stubbornness. Certainly, Pfeiffer's career is a testament to endurance. The second of four children born to the wife of a heating and air-conditioning contractor, she took court-reporting classes and was working as a checkout girl in a supermarket, going nowhere fast when, at 18, she decided to become an actress. But first, reluctantly, she became a beauty queen – Miss Orange County – and secured that all-important Hollywood commodity, an agent.

251

Then came the long, hard slog through commercials and acting classes and, finally, a rôle – a rather thankless one – as a sorority bimbo in the TV series *Delta House*. Some dumb movie rôles followed before her breakthroughs as the flamboyant Pink Lady in *Grease II* and as Al Pacino's elegant but deep-frozen, coke-sniffing wife Elvira in *Scarface*. It was as the ripest of Jack Nicholson's three wild-haired sorceresses (alongside Cher and Susan Sarandon) in *The Witches of Eastwick* that Pfeiffer became a star.

She says she has no idea how she's viewed by the Hollywood decision-makers today – 'The reasons you choose to do a picture are varied, but the most important thing is the text' – or what her screen image is: 'If other people's image of me is anything like my own, then they must be very confused. I'm a different person everyday.' That chameleonesque quality, that lack of centre, might sound ideal for movies, which demand an actor to be a quick-change artist. However, there was a common denominator to Pfeiffer's characters in her three 1988 films.

If, in *Married to the Mob*, Angela was a born-again social virgin, delivering herself from a corrupt lifestyle, in Robert Towne's *Tequila Sunrise* her sophisticated LA restaurateur – caught between Kurt Russell's cop and Mel Gibson's reformed drug-runner – is an even more chaste, emotionally empty woman until, that is, she's warmed up by Gibson. The seduction of Pfeiffer's virtuous Madame de Tourvel, in Stephen Frears' *Dangerous Liaisons*, is both more literal and agonizing. In each rôle, abandonment itself – not simply the man who inspires it – brings Pfeiffer fulfilment (and, in *Liaisons*, destruction), and yet she does not use her sexiness as a weapon; she is never less than kind. Nor is her on-screen goodness a posture, although it may limit her in future. It is difficult – but tantalizing – to imagine her, these days, as a *femme fatale*. 'I'd quite like to play a wildly sexy rôle,' she confesses, 'as long as it isn't *just* wildly sexy.'

Since *Liaisons*, she has completed *The Fabulous Baker Boys*, singing in a band with Jeff and Beau Bridges, and played Olivia in *Twelfth Night* in Central Park. She is the quietest of stars, but not tranquil. Happy to be animated before the dark, anonymous masses, in person she is shy and cautious because too many journalists have pondered her private life. One thing is certain, that her acting ability is now considered as important an asset as her looks. For, as Jonathan Demme admits, 'She is so fascinating to look at that it takes a while to get beyond that. She's just so damned smart, and yet you find yourself addressing this unbelievable face. In the end, playing Angela didn't even scratch the surface of her potential. We'll be moved by her in a variety of ways over the years.'

GRAHAM FULLER

NATASHA RICHARDSON

Big things might have seemed inevitable from the daughter of Vanessa Redgrave and Tony Richardson. What a bummer, then, to launch your cinema career by taking on the Mary Shelley rôle in Ken Russell's *Gothic*. Since the likes of Gabriel Byrne and Julian Sands sank into its gloomy swamp without trace, it would have been unfair to judge Richardson's own non-impact on the strength of it. Unfortunately, more was to come. As Alice Keach in *A Month in the Country* she was an ethereally sweet and repressed figure who drifted in and out of the action with a performance wholly in keeping with the production's overall restraint and minimalism.

But, after her recent performance in the title rôle of Paul Schrader's *Patty Hearst*, the jury can only return with a positive verdict. The heiress and kidnap victim remains an enigma for those who followed the events of her abduction in February 1974. Snatched by the idiosyncratic terrorist group, the Symbionese Liberation Army, six weeks later she was photographed participating in an armed robbery. After eventual capture and the deaths of most of the SLA, Hearst was convicted of bank robbery despite evidence of emotional damage and brainwashing at the hands of her captors.

Schrader apparently wanted a 'piano-mover' or an actress to carry the rôle on which the film bases its totally subjective account of events. What had to be conveyed was a plausible vision of a confident, privileged young American woman taken into an alien world where her personality was destroyed by threats and disorientation. From this demolished person, somehow a survivalist core allows her to accommodate the alien influences, transforming herself into Tania, urban terrorist.

It is a subtle achievement from Richardson who teases not only those within the film who attempt to define her identity, but also the viewer hoping to solve the question of the real Patty. Commenting on the rôle, Richardson says, 'The part has extraordinary emotional range, big emotional gear changes, from total, childlike submission to a strong woman struggling for her life and identity in a completely bizarre and terrifying situation.'

On the technical side, Richardson perfected a West Coast accent in such a way as never to lose control of it through the most demanding nuances of the performance. From laughing college graduate to whimpering victim she retains a faultless command over her vocal inflections – crucial to a film in which voiceover and dialogue are the chief bearers of identity for the first 30 minutes.

What is impressive is that Richardson's impact is made through such an economy of movement and gesture. The survivor avoids, rather than engages, eye contact; submission and compliance are not positions that admit the conventional scene-stealing repertoire. Whereas her presence in *A Month in the Country* seemed merely passive, here we are shown a woman who may, or may not, be brainwashed; what Richardson does is to maintain our sense of ambiguity about whether she is, or is not, acting the rôle her tormentors have mapped out for her. This remains an overriding concern of the film; eventually, alienated from Federal authorities, the speculating public, parents and captors, she is understood only as the object of conflicting fantasies of class and sexuality.

According to one's position she is class enemy or helpless young woman, brainwashed victim or urban terrorist: Richardson conveys the impression of emotional states ranging from misery to grace, never allowing her abject condition to eradicate the spark of guile and adaptability that will keep her alive as she plays the rôles allocated to her.

Despite the sensational elements of the events that took place – bank robberies, shootouts, bombings – Schrader eschews the use of genre conventions, preferring instead to adopt an elliptical and perfunctory approach to material that most others would have played upon for all it was worth. The burden of the film's interest falls relentlessly upon Richardson, all events being filmed within the perspective of Patty Hearst's memories of the period. It is one of the most interesting performances in recent memory.

Whether or not Natasha Richardson has the presence to become any sort of star is hard to say – the charismatic quality of conventional stardom would have worked against this particular achievement – but her acting ability is unquestionable, leaving the viewer with the memory of a complex persona and giving an unsentimentally dignified substance to a shadowy and difficult subject. It is amusing to speculate on the usefulness of being her mother's daughter, given Vanessa Redgrave's alleged brainwashing activities with the Workers' Revolutionary Party but, ironies aside, if she has been indoctrinated, it is with the desire to act. The family background has, according to her, caused her to be 'acutely aware of what is not so good and what you should strive for.' If *Gothic* was not so good, *Patty Hearst* was well worth the strife. And her performance as Offred in Volker Schlöundorff's upcoming film of Margaret Atwood's *The Handmaid's Tale* should be worth looking out for.

PETE BOSS

FOREST WHITAKER

f you want to make it as a black actor, you've got to be sharp and funny, or you've got to be tough. Making them laugh is your best chance. Alternatively, you might be the darker side of a mismatched cop team, or the stocky hunk whose aggression and loud mouth start a riot. If you can tap dance, like Gregory Hines, you just might get your own movie. But if you're after playing soft and vulnerable rôles, forget it.

While Forest Whitaker may have sometimes tried to make people smile, he must have known long ago he'd never crack it. And he hasn't the musculature for bully rôles. Indeed, sometimes in the past five years he must have wondered just where his career could go. Unless, that is, some fortune teller told him Clint Eastwood would give him the chance to stagger and blow through a two-and-a-half-hour homage to Charlie Parker.

His strategy to date has involved hopping onto whatever film came his way (including the recent martial arts item *Bloodsport*) and then making sure he got himself noticed. Even if that involved the most disreputable tactics, like rolling his eyes and waving his arms – generally drawing attention to himself like a kid in a school play signalling to his half-blind grandmother in the back of the stalls.

In *Stakeout* he's a mismatched cop in the B-team, sidekicking to Dreyfuss and Estevez. But Whitaker's gangly body and expressive face push the others into the background whenever they're all together. Seeing his rivals return from a run-in with some fish, he remarks upon the pungent odour, screws up his face, then beams a smile and laughs. He's nicknamed 'Chuckles' and, whereas his companion needs a dog and a cigar to define his identity, all Whitaker has to do is unbutton his body and shake it.

Whitaker gets more screentime in *Good Morning Vietnam*, but this time he's eclipsed by the bundle of comic lightning that passes through the Armed Forces radio station. As minder to Robin Williams' Adrian Cronauer, Whitaker is the small-town boy – awkward, nervous and so amazed at Cronauer's pluck that he can't begin to disapprove.

With these lightweight parts, Whitaker is all over the place. It's as if he's hunting for resonances in the script that just aren't there. He seems happier in *Platoon*, showing for once that he could keep his body still. Whitaker's Big Harold is not one of the boys; he comes from the country and he's more thoughtful than the rest. When Martin Sheen's character is hurt, it's Big Harold who consoles him. And later, while the rest of his mates fast-talk their way around a massacre, Whitaker quietly intrudes with a reminder of the awfulness of what has happened: 'I don't know, brothers, but I'm hurting real bad inside.'

Until *Bird* came along, Whitaker's showpiece was in Martin Scorsese's *The*

Color of Money, as the pool hustler who takes Paul Newman for a ride. An actor acting someone acting, he runs through the whole of his repertoire. Huddled over the table, he spins a hard-luck story and recounts working in the 'psych' department – this calls for a stare, a closing of the eyes, a lowering of the eyebrows. He blows a shot, puts his hands over his eyes, stands awkwardly with his hands on his hips and rubs his eyes. Then he starts to score. 'This is bullshit' he exclaims as he waves his stick in the air like an amateur would. It's an unsettling performance, for Newman and the audience.

What you'd never know from any of this is whether Whitaker could build a character from the ground up. Sure he can roll his eyes and disport those long limbs. Sure he can say a line and strike an emotional chord. But could he really capture the spirit of Charlie Parker – a brilliant jazz musician and a total charmer, a man who hurt everyone he came close to and who fucked up his own life?

It's a job that's made all the harder by a script that moves backwards and forwards through Parker's life. Without much narrative development to go by, it's Whitaker who has to tell us when Parker is jammed full of heroin or can't get hold of the stuff, whether his music is filling him with joy or he's screwing up in pain. It's Whitaker who has to tell us something about the effect his music has on people, and why they loved him.

A brief introduction presents Parker's horn-playing to us. Then *Bird* plunges into the emotional thicket with a scene between Parker and his wife (Diane Verona) which ends with his attempted suicide. He takes his self-pity to his hospital bed as well as the physical discomfort (he has ulcers) that makes him fling himself on another patient: 'Can't you see I'm in pain here.'

With so much of the picture focusing on Parker's pain, it's difficult to understand the affection his friends, and his long-suffering wife, have for him. Desperate for drugs, he looks like a kid who's deliberately forcing himself to stay awake. And most of the time he really is childlike, sending an endless stream of distraught telegrams to his wife when he hears of his daughter's death, even while he's being pumped full of smack by his mistress. But when he does get a chance to play the cool seducer or to make us smile by turning a trumpet man into Albino Red, the Blues singer, Whitaker is all lit up. And when he's playing that horn, he not only shows he's absorbed, which would be easy, but the rolling eyes indicate a musical imagination in vibrantly good order.

It's as well that Whitaker goes out with a bang. He mocks the doctor's questions with his retort: 'Sometimes I have a little sherry before dinner.' Then he sits down in front of the television, laughs uproariously and dies. The scene almost makes up for the maudlin tone cast over the rest of the movie, showing that Whitaker can play the light as well as the dark, and that he's got a range which someone ought to tap into soon.

JAMES PARK

BOOKS

By Phil Hardy, Timothy Gee, James Park, Markus Natten

STAR TURNS

RICH: The Life of Richard Burton
Melvyn Bragg (Hodder and Stoughton)

Unlike too many screen biographers, Melvyn Bragg writes as if he's actually seen the films his subject played in, and has thought about the relation between the performances and the rest of the life that he recounts. Burton's career is often told as a story of promise wasted: he could have been a great Shakespearian actor but ended up meandering through some very bad films. Bragg points out that the late 1940s were a bad time for a performer of Burton's grand temperament to be launched on the film industry; native filmmakers were collapsing into gentility and Hollywood also sought to soften his impact. By the time Britain's New Wave took flight, and Burton took the lead rôle in Look Back in Anger, he was arguably too old for the part. But the fact that the actor walked away from a lucrative deal with Warner Bros to do the latter film enables Bragg to clear his subject of the charge that he only went where the cheques were fattest, even though, as a working-class boy from an insecure background, the pursuit of prosperity was important. Bragg portrays the bigness of the man in prose whose vigour reflects that of its subject.

PAUL ROBESON
Martin Bauml Duberman (Bodley Head)

Paul Robeson was a man born out of time. On a trip to Moscow in the early 1930s, he talked to Sergei Eisenstein about playing the rôle of Toussaint L'Ouverture in a film on the black Haitan revolutionary. It's a shame the picture wasn't made since it would have given Robeson the opportunity he longed for to portray a positive image of the black man. For the most part, his rôles left him angry and disappointed, generally feeling he had been duped by producers willing to pander to his vision of black pride just to get his image on their screen. Robeson's most bitter diappointment was with Sanders of the River where Zoltan Korda's early footage and music recordings convinced the actor that his part as the African

chief Bosambo would convey the truth about African culture. The resulting film was, in fact, a glorification of British imperialism. The one picture he was happy with was a smaller UK effort, The Proud Valley, about an unemployed black American who finds his way to a job as a Welsh miner. Martin Duberman reveals that Robeson felt a sense of spiritual kinship to the people of Wales, identifying with their sense of ethnic pride and radical politics. Robeson withdrew from films in 1942, had a triumphant run on Broadway in Othello, but for the rest of his life was harassed by the House Un-American Activities Committee and the FBI which, stupidly, considered this proud titan as 'one of the most dangerous men in the world'. Duberman's enormously well-researched book records a tragic end – the fervour banked down by electro-shock treatment and sedatives.

JAMES MASON: A Personal Biography
Diana de Rosso (Lennard Publishing)

ODD MAN OUT
Sheridan Morley (Weidenfeld & Nicolson)

The open season in James Mason biographies appears to have started. Fortunately, the two specimens so far 'bagged' are not duplicates one of the other and neither of them is of the 'warts and all' school, where warts are all and the rest nothing. It is a reasonable guess that the season has yet to get into full swing.

Diana de Rosso, half-sister to Mason's first wife Pamela, admits frankly that she has seen only a few of his films, but she does achieve much the more detailed portrait of Mason the man. In her version, Mason's life reads like the story of Job. He started out with the familiar cultural aspirations associated with an upper-middle-class family and a public school/Cambridge university education. From his first-hand encounters with the realities of film-making in Britain during and just after WW2, he was driven to such a state of frustration and exasperation that he made his contempt known in published articles.

When Mason arrived in Hollywood, he found a much higher volume of production but, if anything, an even more arrant philistinism. His own efforts at initiating projects, which had begun in England with *I Met a Murderer*, consistently failed to attract either critical or commercial attention. Miss de Rosso draws an agonizing picture of the star's isolation. He was living in a place he despised, and in his marital home even though the marriage had long since broken down. Always shy and gentlemanly, he was unable to take decisive action to restore a degree of equilibrium to his own life. It was not until Pamela instituted divorce proceedings that things began to change. The legal wranglings lasted four years and he left America with nothing but the clothes he was wearing. In addition, he faced heavy maintenance payments for his children.

Back in Europe, his only recreation was work. Although not by nature gregarious, he seems to have found reassurance in being part of a film unit. On his last venture into film production, with Michael Powell on *Age of Consent*, he met the Australian actress Clarissa Kaye. She became his second wife and the last 13 years brought Mason a contentment he had never previously experienced.

In his opening paragraphs, Sheridan Morley claims that previous experience as a biographer has satisfied him that 100 interviews are sufficient 'to complete some sort of jigsaw.' This method proves unsatisfactory when applied to James Mason. It may be sufficient to consider David Niven's career as the sum of the films in which he appeared; it will not do with Mason who needs to be understood in terms of his struggles to improve the subjects chosen as film material.

Harry Andrews provided Miss de Rosso with a cherishable anecdote about Mason during the production of *Julius Caesar*. As they were about to start shooting the scene in which Brutus has the line 'Let's carve him as a dish fit for the gods', Sir John Gielgud recalled that on one occasion at Stratford, Andrews had got the line wrong and said 'Let's carve him as a fish dish for the gods'. James Mason, an inveterate giggler, ended up corpsing on every take until finally Mankiewicz had no alternative but to abandon shooting for the day. That fleshes out the picture: highly intelligent, gentlemanly, reserved – and a great giggler. What an irresistible combination.

ELIZABETH TAYLOR, A CELEBRATION
Sheridan Morley (*Pavilion*)

As the subtitle makes clear, this is a book about Elizabeth Taylor the woman and it is laudatory rather than scurrilous. That said, the book is surprisingly interesting. Morley may have no special insight to offer us concerning Elizabeth Taylor, preferring instead to dwell on his rather inconsequential meetings with the star, but he tells her story well. The section on her marriage to Mike Todd (which is usually glossed over in favour of her more [melo-] dramatic relationship with Richard Burton) is particularly revealing.

VIVIEN LEIGH
Hugo Vickers (*Hamish Hamilton*)

Hugo Vickers attempts to justify this new account of Vivien Leigh's stormy life and astonishing career with the claim that she was 'almost certainly more interesting than hitherto presented,' but I'm not sure he adds anything of significance to Alexander Walker's previously published biography. New information has been unearthed about her parents, and Vickers provides an interesting chronicle of Leigh's friendship with her first husband, which continued long after she had ditched him for Sir Larry. But amidst the carefully-presented information there is little that enlarges one's understanding of an evidently full-blooded woman. Vickers may tell us what she did, but he doesn't convey who she was.

ROBERT MITCHUM
George Eells (*Robson*)

In this straightforward Hollywood biography, Eells doesn't get very far beyond the smokescreen of languor and professionalism behind which Mitchum has always hidden: 'It was good but dull. Still I got ten days work and to wear a suit and speak with some authority. So what the hell,' is Mitchum's account of his performance in *The Last Tycoon*. Similarly, if you're looking for insights into the key films Mitchum worked on (*Pursued, Out of the Past, The Lusty Men, Night of the Hunter*) they are few and far between. But what one does get is an inkling of the difficulties of building a career in Hollywood, first as a contract player in that most marginal of studios, RKO, and then independently from the mid-1950s onwards. A plodding book perhaps, but useful.

YOUNG KATE
Christopher Anderson (*Macmillan*)

Despite its title, *Young Kate* focuses primarily on Katharine Hepburn's parents, whose crusades read like a roll-call of the century's liberal causes: votes for women, birth control and public acknowledgement of the scourge of syphilis. Their eldest daughter says 'I've had a pretty remarkable life, but compared to my mother and father, I'm dull.'

Campaigning became a way of life for the Hepburn children, and the family background helps to explain why Katharine should have chosen Bernard Shaw's *The Millionairess* for her only appearance on the West End stage. It can also be detected in some of the rôles she has played on the screen, such as the socialite in *The Philadelphia Story*. Nothing however can account for the variety; from *Bringing up Baby* to *Suddenly Last Summer*, from *The African Queen* to *The Madwoman of Chaillot*. Katharine Hepburn may consider herself dull in comparison to her parents, but this is false modesty.

PAUL AND JOANNE
Joe Morella, Edward Z. Epstein (*W.H. Allen*)

Paul Newman was a 'bankable' screen actor long before the word was used in this context. The Oscar for best actress went to Joanne Woodward in 1958. Both have enjoyed long and distinguished careers and have used their public position to further charitable and liberal causes.

This book places the emphasis on their careers, with each film, teleplay and theatrical presentation methodically followed through from inception to public reception. The Newmans' colleagues have generally been intelligent, articulate people and they contribute telling comments. The authors' frequent references to the fact that the Newmans have kept their family life private bears witness to their frustrated search for more material. With Paul Newman's racing career, they are able to provide a lot more detail.

The title implies that the book is about a partnership. In fact it is about the separate careers of two actors who happen to be married. When they have appeared in the same film, the fact is recorded and left at that. A comment from Joanne Woodward on being directed by her husand seems revealing: 'I kept thinking it must be like the rapport Bergman

had with his actors,' but we learn little more than that.

CHER
J. Randy Taraborrelli (*Sidgwick & Jackson*)

Cherilyn Tarkisian's transmutation from one half of a singing duo of the 1960s to impressive actress in *Come Back to the Five and Dime, Jimmy Dean, Jimmy Dean* and *Silkwood* is one of the more interesting stories of contemporary stardom. J. Randy Taraborrelli's book provides some clues to explain the success of this bid for serious-actress status, chronicling the bumps she passed over – at one point she was doing a show with her ex-husband while married to a heroin addict who had just tried to divorce her – and showing how the outrageous approach to clothes reflects the insecurities that she brings into her acting.

DEBBIE: MY LIFE
Debbie Reynolds, David Patrick Columbia (*Sidgwick & Jackson*)

This is an all-American story, about Mary Frances from El Paso, Texas who gets into the movie business at the close of the studio contract era and ends up with a husband, two wonderful children and many dear friends. Its pages are studded with familiar names: Louis B. Mayer, she records, stood up when she first went into his office, but Jack Warner did not. Her first serious boyfriend was Robert Wagner, who was 'classy'. Henry Hathaway gave her hell on *How the West Was Won* but quickly came to adore her and ended up writing in extra scenes to keep her on the movie.

A wealth of material is shovelled in indiscriminately. That is the book's shortcoming. It is by turns a nineteenth-century morality tale, a twentieth-century success story and a ringside report on the silver age of the screen. At almost 400 pages, the narrative is over-long. At the outset Debbie Reynolds tells her readers she has tremendous energy and stamina. She goes on to demonstrate both. The reader who can emulate her will not go unrewarded. There is an excellent index.

REMEMBERING CHARLIE: The Story of a Friendship
Jerry Epstein (*Bloomsbury*)

Inevitably this is rather more about Jerry Epstein, aspiring film and theatre director, than the generous and endlessly curious man with whom he worked and played. That said, it does contain some revealing nuggets: Charlie would moan, mutter and grunt at the cinema if he didn't enjoy a film; he argued with Constance Collier over his view that *Othello* was a play about sex, and that Desdemona should be seen as a girl whose virginal exterior barely concealed fires smouldering within. Epstein is also revealing about the incredible snottiness of the British film establishment. In London to find stages on which to shoot *A King in New York*, Epstein discovered that Britain's greatest gift to cinema was viewed as a 'mere music-hall comic'. The photographs from the set of *Limelight* are particularly good, and there are some more intimate pictures of the Chaplin family in Switzerland, where he took refuge from the House Un-American Activities Committee.

CRAWFORD'S MEN
Jane Ellen Wayne (Robson)

Its title notwithstanding, this unappealing book is an account of Crawford's personal life. Forsaking the familiar stories of Crawford the child-beater for more prurient ones of her romantic and sexual liaisons, the book churns through the career of its subject, dishing out innuendo after innuendo; she made a pass at Marilyn Monroe, her many affairs were rumoured to include Spencer Tracy, etc. etc. Badly written and with remarkably few named sources, beyond Crawford herself, Jane Ellen Wayne's book misses an opportunity to explore the career of Crawford in terms of the complex compulsions that were clearly at work.

THE UNABRIDGED MARILYN
Randall Riese, Neal Hitchens (Corgi)
NORMA JEAN: A Hollywood Love Story
Ted Jordan (Sidgwick & Jackson)
MARILYN MONROE: The Body in the Library
Graham McCann (Polity Press)

Books about Marilyn Monroe come so thick and fast, and from so many directions, that an encyclopedic guide to the gossip, the trivia and the 'academic' arguments is overdue. In *The Unabridged Marilyn* you can look up her diseases and her operations, find out how long were her various honeymoons and learn that on a picnic in 1962, the blonde goddess ate cold steak sandwiches. It's an unfeeling way to dissect a life, and the authors don't provide

much help in distinguishing fact from fiction where that's a problem, but the result is a useful volume all the same.

Riese and Hitchens are dismissive of Ted Jordan's claims to have had a passionate affair with Marilyn. And so would anyone be after reading his book, *Norma Jean*. But although his account of a teenage romance lacks the sort of insights that convince one of its authenticity, it may be too much to expect someone recalling his passionate grapples with an ordinary girl who's now a myth to produce anything other than a string of clichés. There is some glimmer of plausibility in his repeated statements of perplexity in the presence of this 'screwy, maddeningly contradictory girl from the wrong side of the tracks,' but that doesn't make the book particularly interesting.

Graham McCann writes as a sociologist and devotes the latter part of his book to an apologia for the chauvinism of the growing volume of writing about her. His perceptions are accurate, although he makes some basic mistakes on matters of film history. The literature on Marilyn Monroe has now reached the stage of 'books about books'. McCann makes an interesting contribution to the sub-genre.

PETER LAWFORD: Hollywood, the Kennedys, the Rat Pack and the Whole Damn Thing
Patricia Seaton Lawford with Ted Schwarz (Sidgwick & Jackson)

Fact and fiction really are hopelessly muddled up in this very odd book, about a third-rate actor whose fame came largely from marriage into the Kennedy family – who ended up an impoverished drug addict and, according to his fourth wife, 'a sex addict who could no longer achieve an erection.' The opening section is a dramatic account of Lawford's early life. There follows a survey of all the more interesting people, such as Ronald Reagan and Frank Sinatra, with whom he was associated. From then on, until we reach Patricia Lawford's own attempt at self-expiation, we are treated to what one can only presume are the delirious reminiscences of a sick man: he didn't sleep with Elizabeth Taylor because of her thick thighs, was put off Marilyn Monroe by her messy room and witnessed John F. Kennedy, the President of the United States, taking photographs of his hero, the former British warlord Winston Churchill, stark naked on a

White House staircase with a bottle of port cradled in his arms. Still, one cannot help feeling sympathy for the book's author, a teenager Lawford married from his hospital bed and upon whom he inflicted his hang-ups.

BETTE DAVIS: An Intimate Memoir
Roy Moseley (*Sidgwick & Jackson*)

The one thing to be said for this book is that it's not as nauseating as one might be led to believe by the inside blurb, which promises the story of a friendship between a showbiz writer and a great actress which 'almost led them to the altar' (in fact only to secure Mosely a green card), or the photographs inside, which feature the two of them canoodling on the sofa. The text is reasonably illuminating about the life of a once-great actress who has alienated all her friends (one chapter is entitled 'Monster', and definitely put me in mind of *Sunset Boulevard*). But it casts an even more interesting light on the psychology of the determined fan, so overwhelmed that 'someone so famous, so admired, could become my friend' that he stayed in her circle for 15 years.

THE FILMS OF GREGORY PECK
John Griggs (*Columbus*)

Some biographers take years to gather the material for their books. John Griggs adopts a rather less labour-intensive approach. Choose your star, get a filmography and then interleave contemporary reviews, extracts from interviews and publicity handouts with synopses of every film he or she has been in. The plethora of similar accounts of stars in recent years confirm the essential soundness of the approach. Undeniably pedestrian, it has the clear advantage of providing a simple structure for the writer (and reader) and an ongoing question ('What is it that makes these films Gregory Peck films?') to play with. What is more, it fits the market, or rather a section of the market. If you want to know about Gregory Peck's films, rather than Gregory Peck, here they all are neatly bundled together. Considered from this perspective, John Griggs does a reasonable job: indeed the dullish but thorough account of Peck's films chimes rather well with Peck's screen image.

DIRK BOGARDE, THE COMPLETE CAREER ILLUSTRATED
Robert Tanitch (*Ebury Press*)

Much the same model is adopted for this survey of the career of Dirk Bogarde. What makes it more readable is its elegant design and the waspish tone in Tanitch's treatment of the lesser works in the Bogarde *oeuvre* (*Song Without End*: 'a superficial mix of romantic twaddle and vulgar exhibitionism'). All that's missing is a proper filmography, which really is the *sine qua non* of this type of book.

BRANDO, A BIOGRAPHY IN PHOTOGRAPHS
Christopher Nickens (*Columbus*)

You don't even get a checklist in this survey of Brando's life and times. Instead, as the subtitle states, you get a selection of photographs of Brando with paragraph-long captions indicating what was happening at the various stages of his career. The photos are fascinating, especially those of Brando as the manicured star, but there's not much meat in the sandwich.

LOUISE BROOKS, PORTRAIT OF AN ANTI-STAR
ed. Roland Jaccard (*Columbus*)

This laudatory account is given extra bite by the fact that its subject was closely identified with the amoral Lulu from Wedekind's play whom she impersonated in Pabst's film, *Pandora's Box*. That said, the book is terribly produced (most of the stills are muddy beyond belief) and palls in comparison to Brooks' own recent meditation on her career as Hollywood's bad girl.

DEAR ALEX: Guinness at 75
ed. Ronald Harwood (*Hodder & Stoughton*)
GUINNESS
Robert Tanitch (*Harrap*)

Neither of these books works particularly hard at honouring their subject. Harwood's introduction makes the obvious references to Guinness's chameleon tendencies, and follows with some rather inconsequential tributes from the likes of Peggy Ashcroft, Franco Zeffirelli and George Lucas. Robert Tanitch, by tracing the Guinness career through pictures and a rather thin commentary, does at least impress upon the reader the importance of theatre (and, latterly, TV) in a career which most will recall largely through the early screen performances. One quibble with the text: given that Guinness played Fagin in David Lean's *Oliver Twist*, why is it 'incredible' that the same director should have cast him as an Indian in *A Passage to India*?

TREVOR HOWARD: The Man and His Films
Michael Munn (*Robson*)

One has to admire the bravado of a writer who, having spent an hour with an actor and downed a couple of beers in his company, tries to spin out the interview into a full account of his life. Needless to say, the result is a little thin on real insights and one begins to wonder, after a while, whether Munn really is very interested in his subject. He repeatedly offers bland, and anti-climactic assurances that Howard was not a 'hellraiser' but doesn't provide any more interesting, alternative image of the man. Howard himself said: 'It's true I do enjoy myself. Possibly more than the average chap. That's to be expected after a hard film.' Between the assertion and the reality lies the man (and the actor) whom this book has largely ignored.

CARY GRANT
Charles Higham, Roy Moseley (*New English Library*)

Cary Grant is an ideal subject for a biography. He rose swiftly to star status in the mid-1930s and retained this position until he announced his retirement after the release of *Walk, Don't Run* in 1966. His range was limited, but fitted happily with the taste for 'screwball' comedies in the early years and matured naturally into the elegance that suited so well the films he made with Hitchcock and Stanley Donen. With the exception of *None But the Lonely Heart*, his one venture outside the area of light comedy, his career rarely faltered professionally.

A new element has been added to the file of press clippings and tape-recorded interviews in the Higham- Moseley formula for compiling a star biography. It may be called the Doheny factor and it has been only imperfectly incorporated into the traditional mixture. The Warner Bros' production records have been deposited at the Doheny Library of the University of Southern California. The authors are thus able to quote from the daily progress reports on the shooting of *Destination Tokyo* and, more significantly, *Night and Day*. On this film they record more instances of Grant's cantankerous, pedantic and sometimes irrational behaviour. But, armed with this information, they have not gone on to investigate whether this was an isolated episode, occasioned perhaps by disenchantment with the script, or a personal antipathy to director Michael Curtiz, or whether such behaviour was repeated on all the films in which he appeared. The account of

idyllic days shooting *To Catch a Thief* suggests there were no unwarrantable delays on that occasion. Perhaps he knew better than to try such tactics on Hitchcock. The contrast is intriguing. The on-screen image of Grant is relaxed and charming; off-screen, he could provoke his fellow actors and the film technicians to fury and hostility. This theme is raised but dropped almost immediately.

DOUBLE FEATURE
Terence Stamp (*Bloomsbury*)

In the third volume of his autobiography, Stamp describes his passage from overnight fame as the eponymous hero of Peter Ustinov's *Billy Budd* to his decision to abandon his career and set off for India, and the book is written very much as the story of a search for inner peace. Michael Caine's place as mentor is surrendered to the producer, James Woolf, whom Tel describes as 'the super-bright adult I'd always wanted in my life but had never had.' From there Stamp tumbles into his 'big' love affair with model Jean Shrimpton and, after that relationship self-destructs, gropes his way through a bout with drugs to discover the teachings of Krishnamurti. As with the two previous volumes, Stamp wins over the reader through his honesty but there's an occasional moment when the narrative seems a little too carefully constructed: after a stupid trip to the airport where he vainly hoped the Shrimp might materialize, he is held up by a crazy duo of highwaymen and returns home to contemplate suicide.

SCREEN LOVERS
Anne Billson (*Conran Octopus*)

Somewhere between the life and the films of a star, there's his or her image. These days that is traditionally captured in a glossy coffee table picture-book with a thin river of text. Such a book is *Screen Lovers*. What marks it out from most of its family is Anne Billson's text which, though slim, is argumentative and opinionated, giving the familiar images of Hepburn, Tracy, Gable, Grant and company a freshness that is appealing.

HEADS AND TAILS: The Film Portraits of Cornel Lucas
Cornel Lucas (*Lennard Publishing*)

As films have changed and journalists have become more intrusive, the idea that there should be a gap between the performers' lives and their public personae has largely faded. That may be why these photographic portraits of such icons as Katharine Hepburn, Marlene Dietrich, Laurence Harvey and Stanley Baker seem so much of another time. Lucas's sepia

portraits capture an intermediary state – the subjects are neither the performers on the screen, nor the individuals. As such, they are incredibly poignant.

TRIVIAL PURSUITS

WHO PLAYED WHO ON THE SCREEN
Roy Pickard (*Batsford*)
If you ever play the Silver Screen version of Trivial Pursuits then this is an essential reference book for you. It's an alphabetical listing of real and fictional characters, and the actors and actresses who have played them, which should satisfy most enquiries. It's only when you go deep into the B-movie that Pickard begins to slip up. Thus Philo Vance and Charlie Chan are in but not Boston Blackie (who appeared in some 22 movies) nor Mr Moto (who featured in nine). More surprisingly, Lemmy Caution (*Alphaville* and numerous other French films) fails to get an entry and the much-impersonated Buddy Holly is only represented by Gary Busey (*The Buddy Holly Story*). So there are omissions, but on the whole Pickard spreads his net wide and deep enough. And anyway the compilers of the questions for the Silver Screen edition will be using it, so they'll miss what slips through as well.

FOREIGN FILM GUIDE
Ronald Bergan, Robyn Karney (*Bloomsbury*)
VIDEO MOVIE GUIDE 1989
Mick Martin, Marsha Porter (*Ballantine*)
The handsomely-produced *Foreign Film Guide* will necessarily become an essential item on any film buff's shelf. The credits are sufficient; the synopses long enough to jog the memory and convey some impression of films only dimly recalled and the authors provide some critical perspective without trying to impose their views. The only reason for not buying it immediately is that the next edition may offer a directors' index.

What makes Mick Martin and Marsha Porter's guide to some 6,500 features currently available on video so useful are the indices, of both actors and directors. The book avoids the snottiness towards the innovative and adventurous displayed by some of its rivals,

although a family-orientated ratings system results in Turkeys being handed out to such films as John Boorman's *Zardoz*, John Waters' *Hairspray* and William Friedkin's *To Live and Die in LA*, with the latter being described as 'one of the bleakest cinema statements mankind ever produced.'

MOVIE TALK
David Shipman (*Bloomsbury*)
Out from David Shipman's card index come over 4,000 quotations about film people (not only the stars). The percentage of good ones is high, and *Movie Talk* should prove useful for party games involving movie buffs. More information about the source of the quotation might have been useful. After all, what is said at the wrap party may be very different from the comments made in the heat of the moment during shooting; an extract from a funeral eulogy may not tally with a remark made in the course of divorce proceedings. There is, however, an index through which one can trace each of Billy Wilder's entries. That has to be a good thing.

THE COMPLETE FILM DICTIONARY
Ira Konigsberg (*Bloomsbury*)
The film world is notably jargon-heavy. The East and West Coasts of the US have film industries which have developed more or less in isolation, and the British offshoot has been a further separate entity. Professor Konigsberg has chosen to tackle this massive accumulation of duplicated and triplicated technical language.

Within his formidable terms of reference, cataloguing the language of the creative, critical and business sides of the industry, he seems to be both accurate and comprehensive. In the matter of definitions, the Professor is hard to fault. It is when he goes on to explanations that his touch becomes less sure; indeed, the question arises whether they are necessary. For example, under 'MOS' we find 'Initials printed on a clapboard and appearing at the start of a take to indicate that the scene was shot without sound.' That is all that is needed. However, the entry continues: 'In the early days of sound films, technical personnel were often foreign-born and these initials stand for "mit out sound", the way such an instruction might have been spoken by a German director or member of the camera crew.' A mild little joke is completely lost in the ponderous telling.

ANIMATION: A Guide to Animated Film Techniques
Roger Noakes (*Macdonald Orbis*)

A prominent instructor and practitioner in the field, Noakes has written a fascinating textbook on animation which is probably too technical for enthusiasts wanting to understand the medium better. He starts with a summary of the history of animation from Emile Reynaud's unveiling of his Praxinoscope in 1880 to new developments in computer technology, then describes the industrialization of animation and includes references to Russian experimentation, advertising animation and the work of Disney, Max Fleischer and the other innovators. The

instructional sections of the book cover storyboarding, sound and image synchronization, stop-motion and cut-out animation.

THE TOP HUNDRED MOVIES
ed. John Kobal (*Pavilion*)

Take 81 critics from 22 countries, ask them for their Top Ten films and what do you get? Well, the obvious of course: *Citizen Kane* as the best film, *La Règle du jeu* as No. 2, etc. You also get a touch of madness (does Iain Johnstone really think that *A Fish Called Wanda* is the best film of all time) and a sense of the changing tastes of the times. *8½*, that darling of the 1960s notion of international cinema, is still up there (in fourth place), but Tarkovsky is otherwise pressing hard on Fellini's heels (with *Andrei Rublev* at 26 and *Mirror* at 64.) More surprisingly, there's no Godard. *Night of the Living Dead* gets in at 97, one place ahead of *Psycho* even. (Don't worry. Hitchcock also has *Vertigo* at 23, and *The Lady Vanishes* at 58). In short, this is like all list books, alternatively fascinating, boring and predictable.

OH HOLLYWOOD

EMPIRE OF THEIR OWN: How the Jews Invented Hollywood
Neal Gabler (*Crown/W.H. Allen*)

The story of how a group of Jewish clothiers and furriers built Hollywood from their penniless roots has been told many times before: movies were a new business they could thrive in without having to confront social prejudice; their retail backgrounds helped their sensitivity to public taste. What Gabler contributes is an account of how much their policies (particularly Louis B. Mayer's fawning before the House Un-American Activities Committee) were determined by fears of an anti-Semitic backlash, and how their desire for assimilation inspired the fantasized visions of an ideal America they fed to the public. Gabler gets close to what drove these very creative monsters, and makes one sympathize with their sense of cultural dislocation. He says that 'the Jews became the phantoms of the film history they had created, haunting it but never really able to inhabit it.'

THE ZANUCKS OF HOLLYWOOD: The Dark Legacy of an American Dynasty
Marlys J. Harris (*Crown/Virgin*)

Where monsters are abroad, there have to be horror stories. Darryl F. Zanuck was a Methodist rather than a Jew, but he had the energy, the creative flair and the sex drive that went with being a Hollywood mogul. What he knew nothing about was bringing up happy children and nurturing a sound dynasty – the third generation ends up in as much trouble with drinks, drugs and unrealizable aspirations as members of the Kennedy clan. Harris's book is a cautionary tale about what happens when too much money is combined with too little love. After being sacked from his job by his father, Richard produces *The Sting* and *Jaws*, but one sister dies an alcholic and the other is so estranged from her brother that she doesn't invite him to their mother's funeral party. In the end, it's the lawyers who benefit, and you can't help feeling that Zanuck litigiousness reflects their frustrated longing for affection. Early on, Darryl's estranged wife Virginia sues him in the hope they'll meet up in court and she'll get him to come home; he doesn't turn up and the case is settled *in absentia*.

Eventually, one case is fought over Darryl's will by his French girlfriend of 13 years, and another is started over Virginia's last testament on behalf of Richard's sons. The American nightmare.

A STAR IS BORN: The Making of the 1954 Movie and its 1983 Restoration
Ronald Haver (*André Deutsch*)

This is the record of an obsession; perhaps more accurately, of two obsessions. Ronald Haver's account of his labours in reconstituting the original version of *A Star Is Born* occupies the final 55 pages of the book. The account of the making of the film takes up just over 200 pages. It is an absorbing read.

We are left to imagine the upheavals in the accounts department as the original budget of $1.5 million escalated to the final cost of $5 million. On the other hand, the details of the pre-production meetings are set out in considerable detail, as well as the daily progress of the unit once the shoot finally got started. Inevitably, at the editing stage, the evidence peters out.

Ronald Haver clearly considers the cost and time spent on his restoration self-evidently justified. But was it? There is so much urgent work to be done in film preservation that the application of scarce resources to this project seems extravagant. And, once it had been established that the picture footage no longer existed, the work of reconstitution had a makeshift quality to it.

THE HISTORY OF THE MOVIES
ed. Ann Lloyd (*Macdonald Orbis*)

This volume began life as a weekly magazine, *The Movie*. When publication ceased, a comprehensive selection of articles and illustrations was published in a hardcover edition. That came out in 1982. This revised edition carries the story forward to 1988.

All the articles are unsigned, but included are contributions from practical filmmakers such as Bertrand Tavernier, Lindsay Anderson and Ray Harryhausen as well as critics and journalists. The coverage is enormously wide-ranging, though the central core of the book is essentially the story of English-language cinema. As with all the best film books, the illustrations deserve as much attention as the text. Both

colour and black and white reproductions are of a high standard.

THE HOLLYWOOD STORY
Joel Finler (*Octopus*)

This book lives up to the claims of its subtitle: 'Everything you always wanted to know about the American movie business but didn't know where to look.' Organizing his material through a series of interconnecting flow-charts, Finler has laid out the most authoritative map ever drawn of Hollywood. Here at a glance you can find a history of Warner Bros, the story of CinemaScope, lists of successful films and of creative personnel by profession and studio. The cost of this density of information is that *The Hollywood Story* is something to refer to rather than read. Nonetheless a marvellous book.

HOLLYWOOD AND THE BOX OFFICE 1895-1986
John Izod (*Macmillan*)

This useful synthesis of researches into the economic history of Hollywood focuses on the way shifts in this 'highly-organized and sophisticated industry' impact on the films produced. But its narrow focus excludes social factors and the personalities making creative and business decisions, as well as other cultural influences. For general readers, it will seem an unnecessarily limited view of the way the US movie-making machine has changed over the years.

THE DISNEY STORY
Richard Holliss, Brian Sibley (*Conran Octopus*)

Although reluctant to analyse the mystique behind Walt Disney, the spiritual ancestor of George Lucas and Steven Spielberg, and founder of an enormous business empire, this is a comprehensive history of the man, the studio, its output and its legacy.

Disney himself was born in Chicago in 1901. He was punished by his mother for his first attempts at art work when he drew pictures of a house and a pig on the homestead wall – portents of his fascination with family entertainment starring animals. Walt loved taking risks because he loved his medium, and he became a byword for populist family fun, inculcating several generations with a Norman Rockwell-like spiritual simplicity that instilled basic American middle-class values whilst revolutionizing children's entertainment.

Brian Sibley's text carefully charts the expansion of Disney's creative and business horizons. Not so cultist that it neglects the oft-recited history behind *Snow White and the Seven Dwarfs* (the world's first feature-length cartoon), Sibley and production-guide compiler Richard Holliss recount the embryonic origins of Goofy, Mickey, Donald et al., the setting up of theme parks and the corporation's initiation of the studio's adult arm, Touchstone Pictures. Exhaustive listings and credits are also included.

THE BFI COMPANION TO THE WESTERN
ed. Edward Buscombe (*André Deutsch*)

A desirable artefact for any armchair pioneer or outlaw, this is a veritable cornucopia of material on the Western, taking in its literary and celluloid incarnations as well as drawings, art and non-fiction. Copiously illustrated and meticulously researched, it includes historical pontifications on such subjects as revenge and the selling of cigarettes as well as extensive critiques of over 300 movies deemed thematically or culturally signficant. Out of this illuminating text, supplied by a coterie of critical luminaries, even the most rudimentary facts or morsels of trivia retain interest. An early view is repudiated that defined the genre's geographical parameters as 'West of the Mississippi, South of the 49th Parallel and North of the Rio Grande', with reference to Sam Peckinpah's *The Wild Bunch* (set in Mexico), *The Far Country* (set in the Yukon) and even Hopalong Cassidy's odysseys as far as China and Arabia. A robust tribute to a genre that avoids implying that it has been produced as an epitaph, the book's longevity is assured by its appeal to both the scholastic and the casual reader.

HOLLYWOOD'S VIETNAM
Gilbert Adair (*William Heinemann*)

This revised edition of Gilbert Adair's book takes the story from *Apocalypse Now*, where he previously ended, to Coppola's *Gardens of Stone*. Although the critical remarks on individual films are often perceptive and interesting, the book seems founded on a misapprehension. As others have done, Adair laments the slowness with which US filmmakers took up the War as a theme for drama, and then attacks the distortions that dramatization entailed. But movies deal in dreams and terrors, not pressing political issues, and one should not need to prescribe how quickly contemporary realities will become distilled into cinema. Adair's account might have been more interesting if presented against a broader perspective on America's response to what happened in South-East Asia. As it is, I'm not sure that it's very useful to talk about a 'Vietnam' that specifically belongs to Hollywood.

ELIA KAZAN: An American Odyssey
ed. Michel Ciment (*Bloomsbury*)

As with his books on Boorman and Kubrick, French critic Michael Ciment has here done an excellent job of combining text with images, although this time the words come almost entirely from Kazan himself – a collection of lectures, articles and working notes as well as such frank remarks on his past films as 'Don't blame this one on me. I don't.' Ciment recommends Kazan as one of the few American filmmakers who 'can express themselves about their art and combine action with thought' and, although the texts don't add much to what Kazan said in his autobiography, published last year, thanks to the illustrations, this is a useful companion volume.

COPPOLA
Peter Cowie (*André Deutsch*)

The chief value of Peter Cowie's book is as a reminder of how remarkable has been the career of this ageing movie brat, notwithstanding its vicissitudes and disappointments. But Cowie lacks the instincts of the biographer, and spends too much time on rather uninteresting accounts of the films. He illustrates sufficiently the importance to Coppola of family life and the sort of community he tried to establish at Zoetrope Studios, and shows how these concerns permeate the movies, but he doesn't convey how Coppola might justify the shifts in his approach to cinema, or how he feels about the setbacks he has endured. It would have been interesting to have more light thrown on his relationship with George Lucas, and the seeming conflict in Coppola's mind between his 'European' desire for aesthetic experiment and a personal 'vision', and an 'American' interest in technical gadgetry and the grand effect. And the significant question is not so much whether *Tucker* is, as Cowie seems to believe, a return to form but whether Coppola has learned enough from his Zoetrope tribulations to launch a new, and more effective, assault on Hollywood's way of doing things.

DARK DREAMS

In the epilogue to his authoritative survey of horror films between 1968 and 1988, Kim Newman reminds us that repetition and ridicule are the mark of a genre in decline. In the 1940s Universal sent Mother Riley and Abbott and Costello to do battle with Frankenstein and Dracula; similarly at present virtually every horror film is a sequel of a sequel. Although horror films are still being made in large quantities, the creative phase of the horror cycle has clearly come to a halt. Accordingly it's a good time to take stock and ponder the significance of the monsters and psychos who have stalked and slashed their way across our screens in recent years.

STAY OUT OF THE SHOWER
William Schoell (*Robinson*)

This is the least of the trio of obituaries. Schoell is clearly uneasy about his subject, though he's keen on celebrating the strained pleasure of the modern horror film. The result is an endless stream of paragraphs in which, having described a shocking scene in some detail, Schoell then backtracks ('Hooper lets the blood dry too quickly; such a wound would have bled for quite some time') and distances himself from the film under discussion ('The final section of the film, and perhaps the most distasteful . . .). Accordingly the most revealing, if not illuminating, section of the book comprises the chapters in which Schoell deals directly with the moral panic raised by modern horror films and attempts to argue that women are only stalked by slashers and psychos because 'that's the convention.' Unwilling to think deeply about the horror film, Schoell is unable either to see the threads connecting the films under discussion or their social dimension.

DARK ROMANCE
David J. Hogan (*Equation*)

Hogan is far more confident in his approach than Schoell. Taking his cue from Diane Arbus's comment, 'Someone once defined horror for me as the relationship between sex and death,' Hogan casts his net far wider and writes more forcefully. His account, for example, of Brian De Palma, a director whose work inspires varying degrees of hatred and cautious approval, is both measured and sound. It's only when Hogan broaches the big issues that he stumbles. For Hogan is also a fan and his history is really a catalogue. Thus once he's done the obligatory chapters on Universal, Dracula, Corman and so forth, Hogan rapidly

runs out of steam and adds little to what we already know. When he turns to his own obsessions (Barbara Steele and Edward D. Wood), it's another matter. The chapter on Wood, best remembered for the infamous *Plan 9 from Outer Space*, is far better than any previous accounts. He turns up beguiling nuggets of information – *Plan 9* was partially financed by a Beverly Hills Baptist Church, but only after Wood was baptized in the faith – and argues convincingly that, though Wood's films are terrible, he was an innocent rather than an awful filmmaker.

NIGHTMARE MOVIES
Kim Newman (*Bloomsbury*)

It's hard to over-praise Kim Newman's book. What marks it off from other attempts to come to terms with the modern horror film is the clarity of its organization of the material and the zest of the writing. Starting with an extended account of the seminal *Night of the Living Dead*, Newman outlines the various themes of the modern horror film (the rural massacre movie, ghost stories, remakes of 1950s' classics, weirdo killers in search of American teenagers, etc.) in telling, broad brush-strokes. Along the way he offers incisive capsule descriptions of films and sorts the wheat from the chaff: '*La Orgia de los muertos* is typical Spanish horror – silly, convoluted with occasional touches of telling surrealism'; 'Scott's contribution [to *Alien*] is an extension of his TV adverts – an accumulation of telling details that obscures illogicality.' Wisely Newman refrains from simplistic moralizing. Instead he grounds his account in the closely-related production cycles of the Hollywood majors and the independents in which indie box-office hits spawn imitations from both other indies and

267

the majors and inevitably directors either lose their flair as the budgets rise (John Carpenter), adapt (David Cronenberg) or, with great difficulty, remain independent (Larry Cohen).

JOE BOB GOES TO THE DRIVE-IN
Joe Bob Briggs (Penguin)

Many who could never be induced to expose themselves to such films as *The Grim Reaper*, *Basket Case* and *Don't Go into the Shower*, as well as others who have seen such pictures and rather wish they hadn't, could nevertheless enjoy this volume. Joe Bob Briggs writes about the pictures in much the same spirit as their makers must have made them. He revels in the vehicle crashes, decapitations, explosions and disembowellings; draws fine distinctions between various sorts of martial arts and declares exactly where he draws the line: 'I am opposed to power drills through the ear, machetes through the stomach, decapitations with barbed wire, flamethrower attacks and mutilation with a ball pen hammer, unless it's necessary to the plot.' Not many will rush around to their local video store after reading the book, but then seeing the movie is not going to be more fun than reading about it.

TRASH TRIO: Three Screenplays by John Waters
John Waters (Fourth Estate)

From the tips of his gold-lamé loafers upwards, venerated sleaze veteran John Waters is a filmmaker and writer who melts glib liberal standards of artistic decency with allusions to male rape, shit-eating, extreme sexual ambiguity and mass murder. This collection includes that grandfather of midnight movies, *Pink Flamingos*, the less popular but supremely perverse *Desperate Living* and *Flamingos Forever*, the unfilmed sequel of his unholy trinity which features necrophiles, a 400-pound black woman who rapes men when not wallowing in vats of jelly and a perverse menagerie of deviant groupies. Suggested to be read aloud in confessionals, while inhaling amyl nitrate.

LOST, LONELY AND VICIOUS: Postcards from the Great Trash Films
Michael Barson (Fourth Estate)

This collection of the promotional postcards for exploitation pictures is something of a cultural map of territory later explored by John Waters. Tag-lines such as 'Danger ... these girls are hot' (1954's *Jail Bait*) and 'Live Fast, Die Young

... the sin-steeped story of today's Beat Generation' evoke the sensibility that marketed the new devilish purveyor of vice, rock 'n' roll and a period where rebellion and teenage petulance were quickly appropriated by filmmakers and marketing men for hooligans and subversives to relate to, and for good kids to be repulsed by.

FANTASY AND THE CINEMA
ed. James Donald (BFI)

It may seem strange to find former hardline advocates of the *avant garde* reading Joe Bob Briggs, studying slasher films and wondering what they can learn from Ridley Scott's *Alien*, all in order to escape from the cul-de-sac to which theoretical debates that started in the mid-1970s had consigned them. But, as this intriguing reader reveals, the focus now is less on finding ways to 'expose' reality and the concealments of the 'classic realist text', than on deploying the uncanny, the grotesque, the magical and the surreal to unsettle and question the viewer's sense of perspective. This seems like a positive move towards accepting and exploiting what James Donald describes as 'the tackiness and the sublimity of cinema.'

FILM NOIR
ed. Alain Silver, Elizabeth Ward (Bloomsbury)
FILM NOIR
Bruce Crowther (Columbus)

In the 1940s, as the classic horror film began to parody itself, *film noir* emerged as an alternative means of dealing with the dark fears of the decade. It's not a point explored in Silver and Ward's new edition of their *Film Noir*. The book is valuable for its detailed credits, synopses and reviews of over 300 films, but it lacks any historical awareness and in no way extends our understanding of this subject. Although the introduction talks of *Black Mask*, the *femme fatale* and expressionistic visuals, the subsequent entries cover such a wide range of films that the very title of the book makes little sense. It's madness to include *Dirty Harry* and *The Kremlin Letter* and attempt to make a fully-fledged genre out of *film noir*, thus divorcing it from its times. *Harry* is a rogue cop movie that owes nothing either visually or thematically to *film noir*, while the cynicism of *Letter* is that of the spy movie. The recent spate of re-issues of the novels of a wide range of hardboiled crime writers, and remakes of classic *film noirs* (*The Postman Always Rings Twice*) and homages to them (*Body Heat*) testify to a renewed interest in crime literature and *film noir* in general. But what has shaped that interest is radically different from the forces seen behind the films of the 1940s and early 1950s.

What is needed is both a more considered and a more speculative approach in which visual style, themes and sources are carefully separated out and ideas rather than file cards are allowed to run wild. For instance, while Hammett and Chandler are clearly an influence on *film noir*, their episodic plotting and spare prose are the opposite of the tight plots and bravura style of most *noirs*. Similarly, it seems worth pointing out that even if we end *film noir* in the mid-1950s, the later films are visually less extravagant than those of the late 1940s and also less concerned with psychological states of mind. Perhaps a better approach would be to see *film noir* as a response to the horrors of a world at war and its immediate aftermath. In

film genre terms this would mean that *film noir* (like the science fiction cycle of the first half of the 1950s) emerged in the years between the decline of the horror film and its resurrection. But such thoughts are outside the concerns of the 17 contributors to *Film Noir*. They write in the manner of good librarians, seemingly unaware of what is in the film cans they catalogue so assiduously. Thus, the detailed credits are knowledgeable about the sources of the films but not of their varying importance, and the critical element of the entries is woefully ignorant of film history.

More straightforward is Bruce Crowther's *Film Noir*. A solid history of the sub-genre with stops along the way to discuss visual style, themes, actors and directors, the book touches all the bases without ever really explaining the fascination we have for the twisted universe of *film noir*.

BRITISH AND OTHERS

PIONEERS OF THE BRITISH FILM
John Barnes (*Bishopsgate*)

As this painstaking survey of the development of filmmaking in Britain reaches its third volume and the year 1898, the balance of interest begins to shift away from the manufacture of equipment towards the making of films. Streaking ahead of the others was R. W. Paul who built himself a studio in North London, started to concentrate on fictional subjects rather than 'actualities' and propagandized that 'the capacity of animated pictures for producing breathless sensation, laughter and tears' had hardly been realized. Concentrating the text on a single twelve-month period does produce a static narrative, but throws into focus just how much technical and creative innovation was underway.

REALISM AND TINSEL: Cinema and Society in Britain 1939–1945
Robert Murphy (*Routledge*)

Even in the 1950s, when a group of aspiring filmmakers berated British cinema for its timidity, they did so at the cost of ignoring the horror films being produced by Hammer Film Productions. Robert Murphy deals here with an earlier period, showing that, alongside the critically-respected 'realist films', the main

concern of British producers was with producing full-blooded movies for the mass market – analyzed here under the categories of costume pictures, melodramas, gangster films, morbid thrillers and comedies. The problem with this now-fashionable revisionism is that so many of the films resurrected for examination were poorly scripted and incompetently made, suggesting that the critic's scorn had to do with more than just prissiness. There are few films that transcend the division between tinsel and realism (Murphy instances *The Red Shoes*, *Blanche Fury*, *So Evil My Love* and *They Made Me a Fugitive*). Even so, the question remains as to whether a more sympathetic critical approach might not have helped to avert the decline into smugness that marked the films of the 1950s.

THE GOLDEN SCREEN: Fifty Years of Films
Dilys Powell (*Pavilion*)

Among those critics berated for their hostility to British cinema's more gutsy offerings, the *Sunday Times*'s Dilys Powell takes second place only to C. A. Lejeune on the *Observer*. Powell did indeed dismiss the Gainsborough hit, *The Wicked Lady*, suggesting that 'the hoary, the tedious and the disagreeable are married with an infelicity rare even in costume.' However, making allowances for the filtering process carried out by George Perry, most of her early reviews seem fair-minded enough. She expresses doubts about *A Canterbury Tale* or *La Belle et la Bête*, but leaves enough room for the reader to retort that the 'flaws' are the source of their pleasure. She could evoke the feel of a film and was often amusing as in her despatch from a screening of *Gone with the Wind* which reads: 'Sinking into a coma. This is tougher than pole-squatting.' She wrote sharply about British films in the 1940s because she wanted the native cinema to develop in ambition and competence, and clearly felt she had a rôle to play.

THE HIDDEN CINEMA: British Film Censorship in Action, 1913–1972
James C. Robertson (*Routledge*)

Dilys Powell turns up again in this history of British film censorship, and gets a rather bad press. She wrote a letter to the British Board of Film Censors, condemning their decision to pass *No Orchids for Miss Blandish*. She also supported the BBFC's ban on *The Wild One*, which kept the film from the British public from 1954 to 1967. The problem with writing about censorship is that, with changing values and circumstances, the righteous indignation of previous generations can seem silly. And although James Robertson clearly feels indignant about the number of films (many of them now recognized as classics) that the censors banned (500 from 1913 to 1970) or cut, his detailed case studies of particular projects show that the BBFC was, for the most part, an effective mediator between the repressive demands of government or the priggish middle-classes, and the liberalizing urges of filmmakers. Robertson is fair-minded enough to conclude his fascinating book by paying tribute to 'the dedication, exceptionally high calibre and long service of' BBFC personnel.

WHAT A CARRY ON
Sally Hibbin, Nina Hibbin (*Hamlyn*)

Although the *Carry On* films displayed a fine vaudevillian spirit, their centrality to British comedy during the 1960s and 1970s hardly indicates the existence of a vibrant film culture. They survived – 29 films over 20 years – because they were naughty without being dangerous and comprised 'the same thing over and over again', despite changes in background scenery. The series was launched shortly after

TV had begun making major incursions into British cinemagoing habits, and perhaps it was the offer of familiarity amidst the increasingly erratic efforts of producers to lure audiences into their theatres that kept them popular. In any case, producer Peter Rogers must be kidding himself when he says there will be more *Carry Ons*. Key performers such as Sid James, Kenneth Williams, Charles Hawtrey and Hattie Jacques have now passed to the other side; so any future *Carry On* would be a pale imitation. And surely it was more honest to go out with *Carry On Emmanuelle*, with its recognition that nod-nod, wink-wink was no longer enough.

ENIGMᴧ: David Puttnam, The Story So Far . . .
Andrew Yule (*Mainstream*)

Andrew Yule has been reasonably industrious in talking to most of the people associated with Britain's leading producer over the years, and he has put down what he heard, but he doesn't analyze what they say or follow through the ideas that are raised. How, for example, would Puttnam now measure himself against the inspirational discovery that Diaghilev 'didn't actually do anything himself, rather he caused it to be done?' How true is it that, as one of his associates remarks, he's 'interested in the *why* of a film, not the *how* of it' and how does that impact on the whole range of decisions a producer has to make? The answers to these questions are probably there in Yule's text, but he doesn't offer us a way through the minefield. He records Puttnam's self-doubts, without assessing how much strategy there was in their public airing. And, despite Alan Parker's puckish sniping from the sidelines, it's generally Puttnam's view of things that you get from this book – not a biographer's.

HULLABALOO IN OLD JEYPORE: The Making of The Deceivers
Ismail Merchant (*Viking*)

'This is all going down in the diary,' is a cry not infrequently heard in the course of film production. Sometimes it is a cry of mock despair, sometimes of defeat and sometimes simply a recognition of the rich vein of gossip that attends the making of every film. *Hullabaloo in Old Jeypore* is a rare instance of such a diary reaching the bookshops. Despite reservations about the author's prejudice, the eventful course of transferring John Masters' novel to the screen can be said to be entertainingly recorded.

Progress on the film was continually jeopardized by legal threats to halt shooting. The charge was that the film was promoting 'indecent portrayal which leads to immorality in public life,' and Merchant believes the instigator was one Bonnie Singh who had been disappointed in his expectations of a job in the production department. In this respect the problems that beset the production were unusual, in other respects, less so. It becomes apparent that Merchant had become so accustomed to working with James Ivory that he under-estimated the adjustment necessary for working with a new director and, coincidentally, a new production team.

The underlying tone of the narrative is that of the traveller recounting far-fetched tales. He has brought the photographs as well, all in full colour. The author appears in 16 of them; the director, Nicholas Meyer, in two, and in one of those he has his back to the camera.

CINEMA AND IRELAND
Kevin Rockett, Luke Gibbons, John Hill (Routledge)

When this book was started, its authors were optimistic about the prospects for indigenous Irish film culture. By the time of its publication, their hopes had been dashed. But then Irish filmmakers have always had a hard time. The films produced in the early years of the century were claimed as establishing 'a standard of interpretation that will bring to the markets of the world a product peculiarly our own which will receive a reasonable share of the world's patronage' but the native economy was too small to support a film industry and, until the setting up of the Irish Film Board in 1981, there were no subsidies for producers. The Board was closed down in 1987 just as it had begun to generate some interesting pictures, and it seems likely that the images of Ireland projected onto the world's screens will continue to be those imposed by foreigners – representing the country as either a rural backwater (the American preference), or a source of brutal violence (favoured by the British). The book's authors argue that an indigenous film culture could 're-work and challenge these same images without necessarily forfeiting international appeal.'

ITALIAN FILMS
Robin Buss (Batsford)

Robin Buss here explores the way Italian cinema has depicted Italy and Italian society. Focusing on the remarkable achievements of the nation's filmmakers over 20 years from 1955, he sees private TV as a 'real disaster' and shows how international co-financing has destroyed 'Italian' film culture, resulting in pictures that deal with inter-personal relationships and material possessions rather than the sort of social and political questions that fired the early films of Rosi, the Tavianis, Bertolucci and others. This important argument gets lost in a book that tries to cram too much into too small a space.

ROBERTO ROSSELLINI
Peter Brunette (Oxford)

So much critical debate has developed from, or raged around, the films of Rossellini, that this level-headed analysis of his films must be one of the most welcome books of the year. Instead of an attempt at a unifying interpretation of his work for cinema and TV, what's offered is a close reading of each film with an account of its background culled from anecdotal sources and Rossellini's many interviews. Unlike some, Brunette shows how high a level of intention the director brought to even his more conventionally-plotted films: in avoiding the poles of the overtly commercial or the *avant garde*, but always pushing at the boundaries of what was acceptable.

THE CINEMA OF APARTHEID
Keyan Tomaselli (Routledge)

Most recent films focusing on the issue of apartheid were shot in Zimbabwe, and the work of filmmakers within South Africa is little known. Not, it seems, that much has been missed. Keyan Tomaselli expresses his frustration at the failure of South African producers to make ambitious films exploring the explosive social and political situation in the country. Constrained by censorship, and made by directors who are cut off from the critical debates going on in Europe and black Africa, the majority of South African production has comprised either smug films for white audiences or micro-budgeted pabulum for blacks, produced with extraordinary condescension by white producers. Tomaselli is not over-optimistic about the prospects for a flourishing South African cinema.

OBITUARIES

Compiled by Trevor Willsmer
1 July 1988 – 30 June 1989

HARRY ANDREWS

Born in Kent, he acted on the stage in London and New York, only making his screen début at the age of 41, in *The Red Beret* (1952). This rôle typecast him for much of his career as the craggy, strong-jawed army type which he played in films such as *A Hill in Korea* (1956), *Ice Cold in Alex* (1958), *Too Late the Hero* (1969), *Battle of Britain* (1969) and in his best-known performance as the sadistic sergeant major in Sidney Lumet's *The Hill* (1965). His small rôles in such epics as *Alexander the Great* and *Moby Dick* (both 1956) led to more significant work on *Barabbas* (1962), *55 Days at Peking* (1962) and *The Charge of the Light Brigade* (1968) before the failure of *Nicholas and Alexandra* (1971), for which he provided one of many cameos, heralded the end of the genre. As film rôles got smaller – from a supporting part in *Equus* (1977) to two lines in *Superman* (1978) – he moved towards television work, guesting as Blake Carrington's father in an infamous episode of *Dynasty*.
Died Sussex, England, 6 March 1989, aged 77

HAL ASHBY

Born in Utah, he hitch-hiked his way to Los Angeles in 1950 and secured a job mimeographing scripts at Universal before moving to Republic, a company just outside the mainstream which produced the odd, quirky classic among mostly mediocre work – in many ways a model for Ashby's own career.

Having worked his way up from the print room to assistant editor, and having become a fully-fledged editor on *The Loved One* (1956), he won an Academy Award for editing *In the Heat of the Night* (1967) and served as associate producer on Norman Jewison's next two films, *The Thomas Crown Affair* (1968) and *Gaily, Gaily* (1969). Jewison sponsored his directorial début with *The Landlord* in 1970. His follow-up, *Harold and Maude* (1971), was a major career setback although it went on to gain cult status.

Ashby achieved both critical and commercial success with *The Last Detail* (1973), from a script by Robert Towne. After the writer and director had collaborated again on

Shampoo (1975), Ashby made his under-released biography of Woody Guthrie, *Bound for Glory* (1976). *Coming Home* (1978), probably his most accomplished film, was followed by the melancholy satire *Being There* (1979), which was another commercial success.

With the 1980s, his career went rapidly into decline, and his judgement of material became highly suspect, as witnessed by the dire *Lookin' To Get Out* (1982). After an attempted comeback in *Eight Million Ways To Die* (1986) which attracted a fine cast but was so uninvolving that they might as well have stayed at home, Ashby's reputation plummeted and ill health prevented him from working.
Died Malibu, California, 27 December 1989, aged 59

LUCILLE BALL

The most popular American TV comedienne of all time was the daughter of an electrician and a concert pianist. Discouraged by her teachers at acting school, she turned to modelling under the name of Diane Belmont. A series of ads for Chesterfield cigarettes caught the attention of Hollywood and, as a blonde, she moved from Columbia to RKO to MGM, taking bit parts in *Roman Scandals* (1933), *Top Hat* (1935), *Follow the Fleet* (1936), *Stage Door* (1937) and *Ziegfeld Follies* (1944) among more than 70 others; but it was as a red-head that she was to gain her first real taste of popularity when, in 1951, CBS decided to transfer her radio series, *My Favorite Husband*, to television. With husband Desi Arnaz as Ball's partner, *I Love Lucy* was born in 1951.

The show was an immediate success. By 1953, when her character gave birth, it was seen by 44 million viewers, and the couple signed a record $8 million no-cancellation two-year contract. Their success carried over to the big screen, with *The Long, Long Trailer* (1954) but, despite a few later flirtations with film, the demands of TV kept her from pursuing that side of her career. She made a final public appearance at the 1989 Academy Awards, wisecracking with Bob Hope, barely a month before her death.
Died Los Angeles, 26 April 1989, aged 77

LUCIEN BALLARD

One of the finest cinematographers, he started as an assistant on camera, cutting and direction at Paramount before becoming an operator and then associate cinematographer on Josef Von Sternberg's *The Devil Is a Woman* (1935). He moved to Columbia to work on a series of undistinguished pictures before a series of low-budget sleepers – most notably *The Raid* (1954) and the bleak *The Killing* (1956) – led to more intriguing assignments. He moved from a series of thrillers such as *Al Capone* (1959) and *The Rise and Fall of Legs Diamond* 1960) to work almost exclusively in Westerns (although he did go on to shoot the Blake Edwards comedy *The Party* in 1968), forming particularly strong relationships with Sam Peckinpah, Henry Hathaway and Tom Gries. It was Peckinpah's début, *Ride the High Country* (1962), that proved his skill at location colour and the widescreen format, using the warm autumnal tones that would distinguish much of their later work – *The Wild Bunch* (1969), *Ballad of Cable Hogue* (1970) and *Junior Bonner* (1972). With the exception of *True Grit* (1969), his work with Hathaway was less inspired but John Sturges' brooding *Hour of the Gun* (1967) and Gries's melancholy *Will Penny* (1967) proved that, with a good director, Ballard had few equals. Towards the end of the 1970s he worked less frequently, and made his swan-song in 1976 with two Westerns starring Charles Bronson – *Breakheart Pass* (1975) and *From Noon Till Three* (1976).
Died Rancho Mirage, California, 1 October 1988, aged 84

BERNARD BLIER

A portly actor (father of director Bertrand Blier), he appeared briefly on stage before making his film début in 1937 with *Heart of Paris*. His reputation soon grew through rôles in *Entrée des artistes* (1938), *Hôtel du Nord* (1938) and *Le Jour se lève* (1939) and he moved to character leads and supporting parts in numerous French and Italian pictures. He appeared in the 1955 version of *Crime and Punishment* and as Javert in the massive 1957 film of *Les Misérables* but, towards the end of his career, he found himself cast largely in international comedies such as *Catch Me a Spy* (1971) and *The Tall Blond Man with One Black Shoe* (1972).
Died Paris, 29 March 1989, aged 73

MERRITT BUTRICK

Although most of his short career took the form of guest rôles on US TV series such as *Hill Street Blues*, *Fame* and *Chips*, Butrick sprang briefly to the public's attention as Admiral Kirk's illegitimate son in *Star Trek II: The Wrath of Kahn* (1982) and its immediate sequel, *The Search for Spock* (1984). Other major rôles were not forthcoming and his career petered out after small parts in unsuccessful formula comedies such as *Zapped* (1982) and *Head Office* (1985).
Died Los Angeles, 17 March 1989, aged 29

JOHN CARRADINE (John Peter Richmond)

Making his acting début in 1921 with *Tol'able David*, his career took in Universal Gothic and De Mille spectacle, John Ford Westerns and aching social realism, roadshow epics and poverty row schlock.

'I have made some of the greatest films ever made, and a lot of crap too' he admitted, and who could argue with the tall, gaunt, supporting player of such films as *Jesse James* (1938), *Stagecoach* (1939), *The Grapes of Wrath* (1940), as well as *Sex Kittens Go to College*, *Satan's Cheerleaders* and *Psycho-a-go-go*?

He began his career as a scene painter and quick-sketch artist before making his stage début in a New Orleans production of *Camille* in 1925. He walked to Hollywood from New York, where he featured in a series of De Mille epics – *The Sign of the Cross* (1932), *Cleopatra* (1934) – and such Universal horrors as *The Invisible Man* (1933) and *The Bride of Frankenstein* (1935).

It was not until he collaborated with John Ford that he began to hit his stride. It was his striking portrayal of a doomed gambler clinging to his fading notions of honour in *Stagecoach* that led to further memorable collaborations on *The Grapes of Wrath*, *The Last Hurrah* (1958), *The Man Who Shot Liberty Valance* (1962) and Ford's swan-song *Cheyenne Autumn* (1964).

Despite proving himself in Shakespearian rôles and making his Broadway début in 1946, he never managed to secure decent leading parts in films, instead marking time in Westerns, horror sequels, wartime propaganda thrillers, even Tarzan movies, with the odd appearance in such mainstream features as *The Court Jester* (1955), *The Ten Commandments* (1956), *Around the World in 80 Days* (1956) and Nicholas Ray's *The True Story of Jesse James* (1956).

The 1960s and 1970s were not kind to his reputation. Although never out of work, there was no place for him in musical epics or the navel-gazing 'now' dramas that big studios saw as the solution to their problems. So he had to earn a living as an object of ridicule in the exploitation markets. Films such as *Munster Go Home* or *Won Ton Ton, the Dog That Saved Hollywood* were masterpieces compared to *Flesh Creatures of the Red Planet, Hillbillies in a Haunted House* and *Swastika Savages*. There were some gems – the dour undertaker stalking John Wayne's dying gunfighter in the elegiac Western *The Shootist* (1976); the werewolf with false teeth disillusioned with therapy in *The Howling* (1980) and the richly hammy parody of his horror days in *House of the Long Shadows* (1984); but for the most part the impression was of a talented actor limited by his unorthodox appearance and the myopia of casting directors. In later years he was eclipsed by his three sons: David, with whom he appeared in Scorsese's *Boxcar Bertha* (1972), Keith and Robert (all of whose careers, though encompassing lead rôles, threaten to follow a similar trajectory to his own). He nevertheless kept on working, perhaps as much out of habit as in the hope of something wonderful turning up.

Died Milan, Italy, 27 November 1988, aged 82

JOHN CASSAVETES

'I consider myself an amateur filmmaker and a professional actor' was Cassavetes' description of himself in the late 1960s. He gave more than a few great performances, dignified too many bad films with his presence and directed a series of highly individual independent features that alternately enthralled or infuriated.

The son of a Greek immigrant who made and lost a fortune in business, he enrolled in the American Academy of Dramatic Arts after graduating from college. A bit part in *Fourteen Hours* in 1951 led to his playing a series of juvenile delinquents on TV shows such as *Omnibus* and *The Kraft Theatre*. Soon he was playing them on the big screen in films such as *The Night Holds Terror* (1955) and *Crime in the Streets* (1956), broadening his range in Martin Ritt's brilliant *Edge of the City* (1957) and gaining enough of a reputation to win the lead in the short-lived TV detective series *Johnny Staccato* in 1959. Despite moody black and white photography, self-consciously hip dialogue

and a terrific jazz score, the show succumbed to clichéd plots.

Cassavetes used his salary from the show to support his first experimental feature, *Shadows* (1959). The rest of the budget was secured when he appealed for donations on Jean Shepherd's late-night radio show. Its raw-edged reality and remarkable sensitivity gained him enough attention to win a contract with Paramount as a writer-producer-director; but the result, *Too Late Blues* (1961), suffered from studio interference and was a pretentious disappointment. Cassavetes tried to work within the mainstream again on a drama about retarded children, *A Child is Waiting* (1963), drawing fine performances from Judy Garland and Burt Lancaster but, four months into production, producer Stanley Kramer had him replaced and re-edited the film, causing Cassavetes to disown it, and scaring most other majors off him in the process.

To finance his next feature, *Faces* (1968), he returned to acting and turned in brilliant portraits as one of Don Siegel's *The Killers* (1964), as the psychopathic convict Maggot in Aldrich's *The Dirty Dozen* (1967) and as the egotistical actor who sells his soul to the devil for a part in a Honda commercial in Polanski's *Rosemary's Baby* (1968). When *Faces* was finally released after a laborious process of piecemeal editing, it firmly established his improvisational way of handling actors.

Then it was back to acting to finance his next picture, appearing in such dross as *If It's Tuesday, This Must Be Belgium* and *Machine Gun McCain*. The latter introduced him to Peter Falk, who became a lifelong friend and a regular actor in his films, including the next, *Husbands* (1970). This often entertaining piece highlighted his over-indulgence (some said his reluctance to direct friends when they were no good), and for his next film, the likeable and touching romantic comedy *Minnie and Moskowitz* (1971), he tried a slightly more formal style.

With *A Woman Under the Influence* (1974), a microscopic examination of a wife's nervous breakdown centring upon a performance from Cassavetes' wife, Gena Rowlands, and *The Killing of a Chinese Bookie* (1976), his concentration on what seemed to be the non-events of the drama drove away some of his admirers. But *Gloria* (1980) found approval with the general public and Cassavetes went on to make *Love Streams* (1984). Despite cancer and heart trouble, the result of lifelong chain-smoking, he was planning new projects when he died.

Died Los Angeles, 3 February 1989, aged 59

GEORGE COULOURIS

Best known for his portrayal of the coldhearted banker Walter Parks Thatcher, the guardian of Citizen Kane, he was born in Manchester, made his London stage début in 1926 and went to New York in 1929. His screen début in *The Late Christopher Bean* (1935) made no impact and he concentrated on a stage career as part of Orson Welles' Mercury Theatre Group between 1933 and 1939. His rôle in *Citizen Kane* (1941) led to further supporting parts in *An Outcast of the Islands* (1951), *The Heart of the Matter* (1953) and *King of Kings* (1961), with Coulouris becoming a regular commuter between England and the States. In the 1970s the rôles became smaller – the corrupt doctor in *Papillon* (1973), the one member of the cast of *Murder on the Orient Express* (1974) who didn't do it and a cameo in *Shout at the Devil* (1976) that was cut out of the re-issue prints.

Died Hampstead, London, 25 April 1989, aged 85

MARIO CHIARI

He graduated in architecture but entered films in the 1940s as a writer and assistant to director Alessandro Blasetti, directing three undistinguished Italian documentaries before co-directing the superb Roman spectacle *Fabiola* with Blasetti in 1951. Despite co-writing the whimsical *Miracle in Milan* the same year and going on to direct one of the episodes of *Amori di mezzo secolo* (1954), his true talent lay in art direction and production design. At first working with Visconti and Fellini, he came to the attention of Hollywood in the 1960s via his work on Dino De Laurentiis' *War and Peace* (1956), the epic-cum-film-noir *Barabbas* (1962) and *The Bible* (1966). However, a brief spell on *Doctor Dolittle* (1967) did little to enhance his reputation, and he returned to the Continent where he continued to design for major directors until his retirement.

Died Rome, 9 April 1989, aged 79

T.E.B. CLARKE

One of the finest writers to work at Ealing Studios during the 1940s and 1950s, 'Tibby' Clarke began his career as a journalist, working his way up to the editorial staff of the *Daily Sketch*. It was not until 1944 that he wrote his first film, a documentary, and he went on to collaborate in a minor capacity on *Champagne Charlie* (1944), *The Halfway House* (1944), *Johnny Frenchman* (1945) and *Dead of Night* (1945).

In 1947 he was given the task of finding a story to fit an ending dreamt up by associate producer Henry Cornelius – hundreds of boys taking to the streets of London to sort out 'some sort of situation that only boys are really competent to handle.' The chance sight of a young boy walking through the street with his nose deep in a 'blood and thunder' comic provided the inspiration for *Hue and Cry* (1946).

On his way to some of British comedy's choicest moments, chance and an ability to listen provided inspiration: a news cutting, about the room in Canada where exiled Princess Juliana of the Netherlands gave birth during WW2 being designated Dutch soil to avoid a constitutional crisis, led to the impeccably realized *Passport to Pimlico* (1949); an old model of the Eiffel Tower in his drawer and the advice of three senior Bank of England officials on the best way to rob their place of employment provided the impetus to turn a serious crime drama into *The Lavender Hill Mob* (1951), while the origins of *The Titfield Thunderbolt* (1952) lay in a notice for volunteer plate-layers on a narrow-gauge line run by enthusiasts. However the poor response to the latter signalled the beginning of the end for Ealing. Everyone wanted an end to the petty restrictions and rationing of post-war Britain, everyone wanted to steal a million pounds, but not everyone wanted to run a railway.

Clarke sought work outside the studio, penning the execrable Benny Hill vehicle *Who Done It?* (1955) and the routine racetrack drama *The Rainbow Jacket* (1954), briefly returning to Ealing in 1957 for the pleasant but unexceptional Alec Guinness comedy *Barnacle Bill*. He adapted *A Tale of Two Cities* (1958) for Rank and *Gideon's Day* (1958) for John Ford, but the magic was definitely fading. Outside the friendly atmosphere of the studio, where colleagues would offer advice in the pub across the road, he delivered what was required of him – on Jack Cardiff's sombre *Sons and Lovers* (1960) and amiable entertainments such as Disney's *The Horse Without a Head* (1963) and *A Man Could Get Killed* (1966) – but lacked inspiration. After an uncredited rewrite of the unremarkable *Adam's Woman* (1970) and the 1971 NBC series *From a Bird's Eye View*, he decided to rest on his laurels and write his autobiography, the amusing *This Is Where I Came In*, published in 1974. He is mourned by bank clerks, railway buffs and eccentrics everywhere.

Died Surrey, England, 11 February 1989, aged 81

JACK CUMMINGS

Despite being the nephew of Louis B. Mayer, he started his career as an office boy at MGM, working his way up through the ranks to script boy, assistant editor and shorts director. After co-producing a series of features he went solo with the musical *Born to Dance* (1936). Its success led to his being offered all the musicals Joe Pasternak and Arthur Freed didn't want and paved the way to a 30-year career working with talents as diverse as Judy Garland, Freddie Bartholomew, Mary Astor, Frank Sinatra, Jimmy Durante, Esther Williams and Red Skelton.

Early hits such as *The Broadway Melody of 1938* and its sequel, and production-line fodder such as *Bathing Beauty* (1944) and *Three Little Words* (1950) gave him the experience needed to turn two low-budget back-lot productions for which the studio had minimal expectations into two of their biggest ever hits – *Kiss Me Kate* in 1953 (the first 3-D musical) and the following year's *Seven Brides for Seven Brothers*, the studio's first CinemaScope musical. Both films were still playing in theatres some 20 years after their release.

Other MGM hits included the musical drama *Interrupted Melody* (1955), *The Teahouse of the August Moon* (1956) and *The Last Time I Saw Paris* (1954). He left for Twentieth-Century Fox, where the disastrous 1959 remake of *The Blue Angel* was followed by unhappy experiences on *Can Can* (1960) and *Bachelor Flat* (1961). He returned briefly to an MGM in decline to co-produce Elvis Presley's biggest hit, *Viva Las Vegas* (1964), before retiring.

Died Los Angeles, 28 April 1989, aged 84

SALVADOR DALI

One of the most colourful characters of the twentieth century, his work in cinema was mostly less distinguished than the films he inspired (the pictures of Terry Gilliam most obviously). He studied art in Paris and Madrid, designing opera and ballets before his involvement in the surrealist movement led to a collaboration with Luis Buñuel. Together they wrote, directed and produced the classic short, *Un Chien Andalou* (1928), in which Dali also appeared. Its

shocking and bizarre images provoked outrage that ensured the film's notoriety spreading far beyond those few who actually saw it, and the two teamed up again in 1930 to co-write and direct *L'Age d'or*. With its bishops turning into skeletons and an infamous statue-sucking scene, it caused a riot among right-wing agitators at its first (and for a long time only) public screening.

Later, in 1945, Dali designed the vivid dream sequences for Hitchcock's psychological thriller, *Spellbound*. After the war, Dali exploited his own reputation shamelessly. His bizarre public image was milked on TV in everything from arts programmes to commercials. Many books, including *Abrige D'une histoire critique du cinéma*, turned up in his name, as did several paintings that were actually the works of students. Dali's wife persuaded him to sign blank canvases and sold the resulting works for a small fortune.

After an abortive attempt to film *Dune* in the 1970s, with Dali as the Emperor, and following the death of his wife, he became a recluse. His last public appearance came when he was rushed to hospital after accidentally setting fire to his bed.

Died Figueras, Spain, 23 January 1989, aged 84

IAN DALRYMPLE

An old-style British film producer, he was born into a distinguished family and educated at Rugby and Cambridge before going on to serve his apprenticeship as film editor (1924-5) and writer (1935-9) on films such as *The Citadel* (1938), *South Riding* (1937) and *The Lion Has Wings* (1939). The last led to his involvement with the Crown Film Unit at the Ministry of Defence during WW2, where he produced such classics as *London Can Take It* (1940), *Target for Tonight* (1941) and *Fires Were Started* (1942).

After the war, he formed Wessex Film Productions, producing such films as *Esther Waters* (1947), *The Wooden Horse* (1950) and *A Hill in Korea* (1956). Despite a bland script, the cast for the latter film included Stephen Boyd, Robert Shaw, Stanley Baker and Michael Caine: unfortunately for Dalrymple and Wessex, this was before any of them were famous. Dalrymple produced few solid hits and gradually drifted away from films.

Died London, 28 April 1989, aged 85

JIMMY EDWARDS

He made his first professional stage appearance in 1946 and went on to become a popular figure on radio through such shows as *Take It from Here*, *Educating Archie* and *The Glumms*. In *Whacko!* his Blimpish schoolmaster caught the public's imagination, leading to a TV series and a movie spin-off. But the film work was largely undistinguished and only *Three Men in a Boat* (1956) was memorable. Although the film rôles quickly disappeared, he continued to work in radio.

Died London, 7 July 1988, aged 68

FLORENCE ELDRIDGE (McKechnie)

Best known as a stage actress, she was the wife of Fredric March, with whom she often co-starred in films such as *The Studio Murder Mystery* (1929), *Les Misérables* (1935) and *Mary of Scotland* (1936). She survived her husband by 13 years.

Died Santa Barbara, California, 1 August 1988, aged 87

MAURICE EVANS

A versatile stage and screen actor equally at home in classical and drily comedic rôles, his career began at the age of seven when his father – a chemist, justice of the peace and amateur actor – cast him in adaptations of Thomas Hardy novels. However, it was some 20 years later that it really took off when his performance in the 1929 production of R. C. Sherriff's anti-war play, *Journey's End*, made him one of the most sought-after actors on the stage: ever the realist, he didn't give up his day job – running a dry cleaning business – stating that he had 'no intention of winding up starving in an attic.'

He joined the Old Vic in 1934 but was lured to Broadway the following year. He became an American citizen in 1941, joining the army in 1942. Assigned to the Army Entertainment Section in the Central Pacific, he staged more than 50 plays for the troops, the most popular an abridged version of *Hamlet*.

After the war he turned his new-found flair for production to commercial use, staging a series of Broadway hits such as *The Teahouse of the August Moon*, *Dial M for Murder* and *No Time for Sergeants*. Subsequent movie versions made him a near millionaire and led to a successful screen career playing character rôles in some minor 1950s films such as *The Story of Gilbert and Sullivan*, and some of the major films of the 1960s such as Polanski's *Rosemary's*

Baby and Franklin J. Schaffner's Norman drama *The War Lord*.

It was for Schaffner he gave probably his finest screen performance in the philosophical sci-fi allegory *Planet of the Apes* (1968), in which his baritone voice and passionate delivery as the politically pragmatic leader of the scientific community succeeded in illuminating the motives of his character, despite complex simian make-up. In the 1970s he found himself in competition for rôles with John Houseman and went into semi-retirement, playing occasional small rôle in comedies such as *The Jerk* (1979).

Died Rottingdean, England, 12 March 1989, aged 87

GEORGE FOLSEY

He started as an office boy to Adolph Zukor at Famous Players, moving through various other positions to become one of the earliest camera assistants and, in 1919, a cinematographer in his own right. From 1921 to 1932 he worked at Paramount, shooting the innovative *Applause* (1929) and the Marx Brothers' comedies The *Cocoanuts* (1929) and *Animal Crackers* (1930) before moving to MGM in 1934 where he worked on everything from melodramas to Andy Hardy and Dr Gillespie movies. His work on *Thousands Cheer* (1943), *The Clock* (1945) and *A Guy Named Joe* (1944) led to a series of musicals – *Meet Me in St Louis* (1944), *Ziegfeld Follies* (1944) and *Take Me Out to the Ballgame* (1949) among them – as well as *State of the Union* (1948) and *Adam's Rib* (1949). In 1954 he proved his mastery of the widescreen format with *Seven Brides for Seven Brothers* (1954) and the sci-fi classic *Forbidden Planet* (1956). He continued to work for the studio until his retirement.

Died Santa Monica, California, 1 November 1988, aged 90

MELVIN FRANK

Director, writer and producer, he wrote his first play, in collaboration with Norman Panama, while still at university in Chicago. The two friends moved to Hollywood in 1938, where they worked in radio as gag writers on the *Bob Hope Show* among others. They collaborated on a story for Hope's 1942 film, *My Favorite Blonde*, and went on to co-write *Thank Your Lucky Stars* (1943), *Mr Blandings Builds His Dream House* (1948) and *White Christmas* (1954). Later the two co-wrote, directed and produced

a number of films, including *Strictly Dishonourable* (1951), *Knock on Wood* (1954) and Danny Kaye's *The Court Jester* (1955), while Frank graduated to sole director's credit with *The Jayhawkers* (1959) and the ambitious but not entirely successful satirical musical *Li'l Abner* (1959), as well as producing and co-writing *The Road to Hong Kong* (1962) and *A Funny Thing Happened on the Way to the Forum* (1966). His biggest hit was *A Touch of Class* (1973), an extra-marital comedy that proved as strong on character as laughs, but public indifference greeted his attempt to re-create that success with *The Duchess and the Dirtwater Fox* (1976) and a re-teaming of *Class* stars Glenda Jackson and George Segal in the unexceptionable *Lost and Found* (1979). His last film, *Walk Like a Man*, was released in 1986.
Died Los Angeles, 13 October 1988, aged 75

GUNTER VON FRITSCH

Austrian born, he emigrated to the US where he became a film cutter at MGM in the 1930s, quietly building a reputation that led, in 1937, to his directing the influential *March of Time* documentaries. His attempt to broaden his horizons into features with the magical, psychological fairy tale *The Curse of the Cat People* (1944) was less successful: despite some moments of stunning originality and a powerful use of lighting, it ran way over schedule and, with no end in sight, producer Val Lewton handed the directorial reins to the film's editor, Robert Wise. Nonetheless, Von Fritsch went on to direct episodes of several US TV shows of the 1950s and 1960s, including '*77 Sunset Strip*, *Cheyenne*, *Flash Gordon* and *The Lawman*, before quietly retiring.
Died Pasadena, California, 27 August 1988, aged 82

GERT FRÖBE

His rotund and amiable figure will be best remembered by English-speaking audiences as possibly the finest Bond villain, Auric Goldfinger, but he also enjoyed a reputation as West Germany's favourite comic actor and was often compared favourably with Danny Kaye. The son of a rope-maker, he made his stage début in 1937. His career received a major setback when the Nazis closed all theatres and it was not until 1948 that he was to act again, making his film début with *Berliner Ballade*. His natural comic talent was quickly recognized and

he soon became a well-loved figure in German films.

He did appear in Elia Kazan's thriller *Man on a Tightrope* (1952) but it was not until the Bond film that he came to the general attention of American and English producers. In his hands, Goldfinger was as menacing as previous villains but with an added edge of dark humour that never slipped into the self parody of later master criminals: when Bond, strapped to a table with his private parts threatened by a deadly laser-beam, asks if Goldfinger expects him to talk, his simple reply, 'No, Mr Bond, I expect you to die,' is at once matter of fact, amusing and chilling, cutting through the inherent absurdity of the scene.

Despite a plethora of rôles in all-star vehicles, such as *Those Magnificent Men in Their Flying Machines* (1965) and *Chitty Chitty Bang Bang* (1968), which gave some small idea of his comic genius while straitjacketing it in bombastic Prussian stereotypes, most producers were never quite sure what to do with him. Cast either as a Nazi (as in *Triple Cross*) or a detective (the abysmal *Bloodline*) Fröbe's talents were generally wasted and he had to return to Europe for challenging parts, working with directors such as Visconti in *Ludwig* (1972) and Bergman in *The Serpent's Egg* (1977).
Died Munich, 4 September 1988, aged 75

SHEILA GRAHAM (Lily Sheil)

She was brought up in an orphanage before leaving to become a London showgirl and model. She moved to the US in 1933 and began a Hollywood gossip column in 1935, soon becoming one of a triumvirate of influential columnists, wielding not inconsiderable power over the lives of the aspiring and declining, alongside Louella Parsons and Hedda Hopper. Her four-year affair with F. Scott Fitzgerald (who modelled the heroine of his last, unfinished novel, *The Last Tycoon*, on her) led to her 1957 book, *Beloved Infidel*, which recounted their sometimes stormy relationship. This book was turned into a dull movie the following year and three more volumes of memoirs followed.
Died West Palm Beach, California, 17 November 1988, aged 84

JOHNNY GREEN

Born in New York City, he graduated in economics from Harvard but drifted into a job as a rehearsal pianist at Paramount in 1929. By the following year he was arranging and composing film scores, as well as pursuing a successful career as a nightclub bandleader. He was musical director at MGM for ten years from 1958, supervising such films as *It Happened in Brooklyn* (1947), *The Great Caruso* (1950) and *Brigadoon* (1954), sharing Oscars for his collaboration on *Easter Parade* (1948) and *An American in Paris* (1951). Further Oscars followed for *West Side Story* (1961) and *Oliver!* (1968) and, in addition to working on *Bye Bye Birdie* (1963), he scored and served as associate producer on *They Shoot Horses, Don't They?* (1969). He married twice, first to Betty Furness and then, in 1943, to MGM starlet Bunny Waters.

Died Beverly Hills, 15 May 1989, aged 80

STEPHEN GRIMES

He got his first film job as an assistant art director on John Huston's *Moby Dick* (1956) and, over the next 15 years, was either art director or designer on virtually all of the director's pictures, including his swan-song, *The Dead* (1987). He also worked on David Lean's *Lawrence of Arabia* (1962) and *Ryan's Daughter* (1970) and collaborated with such directors as Sydney Pollack, Peter Yates and Ulu Grosbard. His work on *Out of Africa* (1985) secured him an Oscar.

Died Positano, Italy, 12 September 1988, aged 61

CHARLES HAWTREY (Hartree)

He first rose to prominence after stage and radio work led to clever-dick schoolboy rôles in such Will Hay comedies as *The Goose Steps Out* (1942). Although never leading-man material, he was continuously in work and appeared in such classic British comedies as *Passport to Pimlico* (1949) and *Simon and Laura* (1955), as well as low-budget sci-fi pictures.

But his angular and unhealthy frame leapt into public consciousness as the most unique geek British cinema has ever offered. In the *Carry On* series, his extraordinary mix of physical repulsion (he often appeared clad solely in his underwear) and surreal verbal humour flourished in numerous bizarre guises – the inebriated Indian chief in *Cowboy* (1965), the magpie-like hiker in *Camping* (1969), the devil-in-a-skirt in *Up the Khyber* (1968) and Julius Caesar's randy father-in-law in *Cleo* (1964).

Off-screen, he was a colourful character – on one occasion during his mother's visit to a *Carry On* set, her cigarette fell into her handbag and set it on fire as he was in the middle of recounting an anecdote over his tea; without stopping, he simply emptied his cup into her bag and closed it.

Died London, 27 October 1988, aged 73

LUKAS HELLER

One of many German-born emigrés who worked in Britain and Hollywood, Heller soon earned a reputation for gutsy, fast-paced scripts with more depth than met the eye, but he pulled no punches through his work on the post-war racial drama *Sapphire* (1959), for which he wrote 'additonal dialogue'. This in turn led to his work on *Whatever Happened to Baby Jane?* (1962), making the start of a long relationship with director Robert Aldrich. Their collaborations included the morally-ambiguous forerunner of the disaster movie, *The Flight of the Phoenix* (1965), the spectacularly successful *The Dirty Dozen* (1967), the controversial black comedy *The Killing of Sister George* (1969) and the under-rated *Too Late the Hero* (1969), a WW2 drama with a gripping finale that tore apart notions of heroism, duty and honour with its tale of a group of ill-assorted allied soldiers on a Pacific island led by an incompetent idiot, fighting amongst themselves when their mission goes badly wrong. Its financial failure led to the end of their collaboration. Despite penning the excellent elegiac Western *Monte Walsh* (1970), his career petered out in the 1970s with his disappointing adaptation of a Sam Fuller story, *The Deadly Trackers* (1973), and a badly filmed, much rewritten version of the cult SF novel, *Damnation Alley* (1977). He worked uncredited on *Force Ten from Navarone* (1978) and, more recently, Walter Hill's *Extreme Prejudice* (1987), as well as on the script of the 1985 NBC telefilm *Hitler's SS: Portrait in Evil*.

Died London, 2 November 1988, aged 58

DOUGLAS HICKOX

London-born, he entered the industry as a production assistant at Pinewood Studios. Working his way up to second-unit directing, he went on to make documentaries for television before directing the film of Joe Orton's *Entertaining Mr Sloane* (1969). Despite being well received at the time, most of his further work proved disappointingly run-of-the-mill – the camp Vincent Price shocker *Theatre of Blood* (1973), the dull *Sitting Target* (1972), the ridiculous hang-gliding thriller *Sky Riders*

(1976) – with only the John Wayne comedy thriller *Brannigan* (1975) going down well with the public. The failure of the lavishly-mounted *Zulu Dawn* (1979), in which his cautious direction missed many of the opportunities the script and budget offered, led to his return to television and such miniseries as the lamentable *Sins* and *I'll Take Manhattan*, which seemed to cement his demotion to journeyman status.
Died London, 25 July 1988, aged 59

COLIN HIGGINS

An immensely talented but much wasted writer, he was born in New Caledonia to American and Australian parents. Working his way up through TV sitcoms and indifferent telemovies, his big break came when he sold his script for *Harold and Maude* (1971). The bizarre tale of a rich kid obsessed with death and his elderly lover, it was a huge flop at the time but was later recognized as the cornerstone of both his and director Hal Ashby's careers. It was not until *Silver Streak* (1976) that Higgins was to enjoy commercial success. Although critics recognized the importance of his contribution, it was only by selling his script for *Foul Play* (1978) at a reduced rate that he was able to convince Paramount to let him direct it. An energetic and enjoyable Hitchcock pastiche, *Foul Play* revitalized Goldie Hawn's dormant career and launched both Chevy Chase and Dudley Moore on the road to big-screen stardom. His *Nine to Five* (1980) made a fortune and he re-teamed with that film's co-star Dolly Parton for *The Best Little Whorehouse in Texas* (1982). The film was unsuccesful both critically and commercially, losing much of the warmth of the original show for flashy but heartless vignettes. It was Higgins' last major movie project.
Died Beverly Hills, 5 August 1988, aged 47

JOHN HOUSEMAN

Born in Bucharest and educated in France and England, he developed his interest in theatre after the Wall Street Crash wiped him out on the grain market. He directed his first stage show in 1934, collaborating with Virgil Thompson on Gertrude Stein's *Four Saints in Three Acts*. Further productions led to *Panic*, with the ambitious young Orson Welles in the lead, as well as the Welles-directed *Dr Faustus* in 1935. Welles and Houseman formed the Mercury Theatre in 1937. After their infamous radio production of *The War of the Worlds* in

the following year, both men headed for Hollywood; Houseman to become vice-president at David O. Selznick Productions. He resigned ten days after Pearl Harbor to join OWI as chief of overseas radio, taking time out in 1943 to act as producer at Paramount and, later, RKO.

He directed one of the first experimental programmes for CBS TV and, intrigued by the possibilities of the new medium, he went on to produce the classic shows, *The Seven Lively Arts* and *Playhouse 90*, which gave new directors such as John Frankenheimer and Franklin J. Schaffner their first big breaks. He produced such films as *They Live By Night* (1948), *Letter from an Unknown Woman* (1948), *The Bad and the Beautiful* (1952), *Julius Caesar* (1969), *Lust for Life* (1956) and *Two Weeks in Another Town* (1962).

His career took a new turn when he made his acting début in *The Paper Chase* (1973) as a tyrannical Harvard Law professor. The then 71-year-old John Houseman won an Oscar as Best Supporting Actor and carried the rôle over into a TV series. With his elegant, dignified manner and rich speaking voice, he found himself constantly in demand, turning in cameos for such varied productions as *The Fog* (1979), *The Naked Gun*, *Scrooged* and, his final film, Woody Allen's *Another Woman*.
Died Malibu, California, 31 October 1988, aged 86

JORIS IVENS

A pioneering Dutch documentarist, he made films in Italy, Cuba, Mali, Chile, Laos and Vietnam. His first pictures were impressionistic short studies but *Borinage* (1933), a denunciation of conditions in a Belgian mining region, displayed his political convictions.

In New York he established a production company with Ernest Hemingway, Lillian Hellman and John Dos Passos which made *This Spanish Earth* to publicize the Spanish Republican case in the US. Ivens left the US in the early 1950s, after he had been denounced as a communist, and settled successfully in the Dutch East Indies, Prague and Paris. *The Wind*, an evocation of his love of China, was premiered at the 1988 Venice Film Festival.
Died Paris, 28 June 1989, aged 90

ROY KINNEAR

A director once asked Roy Kinnear how he saw

the character he was going to portray in a film. 'Short, fat and stupid, because that's how I'm going to play him.' Playing short, fat and stupid made Wigan-born Kinnear one of Britain's most popular comic figures, enlivening many a dull film or television series. Although he made his film début in 1958, he first caught the public eye through his regular rôle in the classic, anarchic TV series *That Was The Week That Was*, where he imitated everyone from Harold Wilson to John Profumo.

Most of his film rôles were small – *The Hill* (1965), *How I Won the War* (1967), *Scrooge* (1970), *Willy Wonka and the Chocolate Factory* (1971) and *The Juggernaut* (1974) – and he continued to get his best opportunities on TV. His appearances in American films were also sporadic. He was in fellow Briton Marty Feldman's *The Last Remake of Beau Geste* (1977) and, most unusually, playing a variation on the Sidney Greenstreet 'fatman' rôle in Wim Wenders' *Hammett* (1982). It was while reprising his rôle as the dim-witted servant Planchet from Richard Lester's *The Three Musketeers* (1973) film in the sequel that he died, following a fall from a horse on the Spanish location. It was a sad end to a career in which his ebullient personality often triumphed over mediocre material.

Died Toledo, Spain, 20 September 1988, aged 54

HENRY KOSTER (Kosterlitz)

His early life is infinitely more interesting than his Hollywood career. Graduating from the Berlin Academy of Fine Arts in 1921, he became in turn a cartoonist, a commercial artist, a film critic and an agony aunt in a Berlin weekly, before going on to write, produce and direct publicity films in 1926. These earned him work as a writer for various Berlin studios, and he directed his first film, *Das Abenteuer einer schönen Frau*, in 1932. He was to direct in Budapest, Vienna and Amsterdam before moving to Hollywood, changing his name and working on a series of classic Deanna Durbin musicals such as *Three Smart Girls* (1936) and *One Hundred Men and a Girl* (1937) that were instrumental in saving Universal from bankruptcy. Leaving the studio in 1942 to pursue an independent career, his films were mostly undistinguished – with only the delightful invisible rabbit comedy *Harvey* (1950) and the not entirely successful Danny Kaye film of *The Inspector General* (1949) finding

much of an audience – until he moved to Fox in 1950.

More run of the mill features followed until he was given an adaptation of a Lloyd C. Douglas novel. Started in normal ratio, the resulting film *The Robe* (1953) was the first to be released in CinemaScope and briefly became the highest grosser of all time. Despite his visual uncertainty with the wide screen – he had a tendency to line his actors up in a row and have them talk across to each other – he gained a reputation for CinemaScope epics on a shoestring (second takes were not common practice on his sets) thanks to such films as *Desirée* (1936) and *A Man Called Peter* (1955).

As an independent, he remade *My Man Godfrey* (1957) and filmed the lavish Rodgers and Hammerstein musical *Flower Drum Song* (1962) before his career sank amid the dross of such execrable family comedies as *Take Her, She's Mine* (1963), *Dear Brigitte* (1965) and *The Singing Nun* (1966). Although he tried to interest studios in his own projects, generally unimaginative and lachrymose retreads of the early Durbin films, he found himself without a place in 1960s Hollywood and slipped grudgingly into retirement.

Died Camarillo, California, 21 September 1988, aged 83

MILTON KRASNER

He was cinematographer on his first film in 1933, working for various studios on production-line pictures before making his mark in 1944 with *The Woman in the Window*. His career really took off when he moved to Fox in 1950, where he worked on such black and white classics as *All About Eve* (1950) and *Monkey Business* (1931), before moving on to light many of the studio's prestige CinemaScope/De-Luxe colour productions such as *Three Coins in the Fountain* (1954), *Demetrius and the Gladiators* (1954) and *The Seven Year Itch* (1955). Soon his mastery of the format was in demand elsewhere, and he moved to MGM for some of his finest work, including the Cinerama production, *How the West Was Won* (1962), Vincente Minnelli's ill-fated remake of *The Four Horsemen of the Apocalypse* (1961), *Sweet Bird of Youth* (1962), *Two Weeks in Another Town* (1962) and on Nicholas Ray's unjustly ridiculed 1961 film *King of Kings* (shot in 70mm). Towards the end of the 1960s he became a freelancer working on Roger Corman's colourful *The St Valentine's Day Massacre*

(1967). He retired in 1968 after completing work on the Doris Day comedy Western *The Ballad of Josie*.

Died Woodland Hills, California, 16 July 1988, aged 84

SERGIO LEONE

'They call me the father of the Spaghetti Western. If so, how many sons of bitches I have spawned.' Sergio Leone, the master of the widescreen close-up and the man who made both Ennio Morricone's music and Clint Eastwood's poncho famous, was born in Naples. His father was an influential Italian film director and his mother an actress. So it was with no difficulty that he entered the film industry as an assistant on *Bicycle Thieves* (1948) and went on to work on more than 50 films, many of them American productions such as *Ben Hur*, *Helen of Troy* and *The Nun's Story*, before finally making it as a director on *The Colossus of Rhodes* (1960). This led to his directing the concurrent Italian version of Robert Aldrich's *Sodom and Gomorrah* (1962): the two men clashed violently throughout, but the experience provided the impetus his career needed to mount a low-budget production of his own, *Per un pugno di dollari*. Unable to afford James Coburn for the lead, he imported the co-star of the Western series *Rawhide*, Clint Eastwood, and filmed his Italian Western in the desert town of Almeria. Released in Europe as *A Fistful of Dollars* (1964), it's a radical reinterpretation of Western mythology and centres on a psychologically scarred monosyllabic hero little better than the villains. A sequel, *For a Few Dollars More* (1965), followed which took the darker elements of the original further with a frighteningly psychopathic villain and an ambivalent relationship between its two heroes. The third 'man with no name' film, *The Good, the Bad and the Ugly* (1966), was more ambitious still, setting the tale of an unholy trinity in search of buried treasure against a vivid depiction of the Civil War.

Its success led to Leone's first American film, *Once Upon a Time in the West* (1969), which imaginatively cast all-time nice guy Henry Fonda as a satanic killer. It established Leone's sweeping operatic style – its final gunfight lasts two reels with only two shots being fired (simultaneously) and its two protagonists hardly moving. The film was less successful than anticipated and Leone planned to move into production, preparing *A Fistful of Dynamite* (1971) for Sam Peckinpah and Peter Bogdanovich, only to find himself back in the director's chair when both dropped out.

He spent eight years preparing his biggest box of cinematic tricks, *Once Upon a Time in America* (1984), probably the last truly ambitious film of this decade. Telling the story of a small-time gangster trying to come to terms with the betrayal of his friends, the film became a mythic voyage of discovery moving back and forth in time between three decades to show the ways in which the past influences the present and memory is re-invented. With its dark characters, melancholy tone, shocking violence and a highly controversial rape scene, it was heavily cut and became a box-office disaster in the US.

Leone never quite got over its poor reception, and although the uncut version was successful in Europe, his attempts to film *The 900 Days* – the epic story of the siege of Leningrad – were constantly shelved, despite the involvement of *America* star Robert De Niro and producers Spielberg and Lucas. However, he was due to visit Moscow for talks on the project when he died. With him went an understanding of how to meld ideas, images, action and inaction, time and space into something extraordinary and unforgettable – pure cinema.

Died Rome, 30 April 1989, aged 60

JOHN LODER

Tall and aristocratically handsome, he was educated at Eton and fought in WW1. He made his movie début as an extra, gradually working his way up to leads and important supporting rôles in *The Private Life of Henry VIII* (1933), *Lorna Doone* (1934) and *Sabotage* (1936). After providing much needed comic relief to the 1937 version of *King Solomon's Mines*, he moved to Hollywood in 1939, playing leads in second features and less prominent rôles in *How Green Was My Valley* (1941), *Now Voyager* (1942) and *Gentleman Jim* (1942). In 1950 he returned to England and films such as *Gideon's Day* (1958) before retiring to the Argentine ranch of his fifth wife (the third was actress Hedy Lamarr). His autobiography, *Hollywood Hussar*, was published in 1977.

Died England, December 1988

JOSHUA LOGAN

Born in Texas, he was active in student

productions at Princeton alongside James Stewart, Henry Fonda and Margaret Sullavan. He made his mark on Broadway with *Annie Get Your Gun* and *South Pacific*. Further stage triumphs led to his being called to Hollywood where he directed the Marilyn Monroe drama *Bus Stop* (1956), the Brando comedy *Sayonara* (1957) and, inevitably, the movie version of *South Pacific* (1958). Despite a 'straight' adaptation of Marcel Pagnol's *Fanny* (1960), he was typecast as a director of musicals, and went on to hit an all-time low with the lavish *Camelot* (1967). Although it was a flop, that didn't stop its lyricist Alan Jay Lerner twisting Logan's arm into directing a reworking of his stage musical, *Paint Your Wagon* (1969). Filming was hell and Logan – a manic depressive who had to consume vast quantities of lithium to get through the protracted shoot – quarrelled with both Lerner and his star. 'Not since Attila the Hun swept across Europe leaving 500 years of total blackness has there been a man like Lee Marvin,' he is reported to have said. Although successful in Europe, the film never recouped its huge cost and Logan was so embittered by the experience that he never directed another film – finally taking revenge in his 1978 autobiography, *Movie Stars, Real People and Me*.
Died New York, 12 July 1988, aged 79

RAY McANALLY

Public recognition came late in life to this Donegal-born actor, despite first treading the boards as an amateur at the age of six, and becoming a professional scarcely ten years later.

In 1947 he joined Dublin's Abbey Theatre. Although he gained a reputation for being never out of work, be it in less than successful TV series such as *Churchill's People* or a couple of days' work on undistinguished features, it was not until 1986 that he came to prominence.

His fine performance as an embittered Protestant learning to forgive through the ridiculous petty rivalries and prejudices of two groups of old age pensioners in the Alan Bleasdale-scripted *No Surrender* (1986) was quickly followed by his powerful portrayal of the Cardinal caught between the will of God and political expediency in Roland Joffe's flawed *The Mission* (1986).

Many offers followed and, perhaps truer to his old habit of never turning work away than to his good judgement, he accepted most of them, leading to such regrettable experiences as *Taffin* (1988) in which he was powerless to overcome a low budget and an unambitious script. However, the rôle of the enigmatic father in the BBC's adaptation of John Le Carré's *A Perfect Spy* and his immensely charismatic Labour Prime Minister in an acclaimed and highly popular TV adaptation of *A Very British Coup* more than compensated, bringing him to the attention of a larger section of the public and earning more plaudits. He recently played the convict Magwitch in an HTV-Disney production of *Great Expectations*, and is featured in two forthcoming British movies, *Venus Peter* and *My Left Foot* as well as Robert De Niro-topliner *We're No Angels*.
Died County Wicklow, Ireland, 15 June 1989, aged 63

KENNETH McMILLAN

His career in TV, cinema and theatre spanned 30 years but it was in the 1980s that his burly, red face was first to reach public recognition following his appearances in *Little Miss Marker* (1980), *Whose Life Is It Anyway?* (1981), *Ragtime* (1981) and the dismal *Dune* (1984). Probably his finest performance was in the rôle of aging safecracker in *Pope of Greenwich Village* (1984), for which he shed 50 pounds to receive his first ever screen kiss.
Died Santa Monica, California, 8 January 1989, aged 56

IRVING MANSFIELD

He originally worked in public relations where, in 1943, he met and married the then aspiring starlet Jacqueline Susann before becoming a producer at CBS in 1946 on a series of variety shows; but it was when his troubled wife turned author that he hit the goldmine.

His production of her pulp pill-popping classic *Valley of the Dolls* turned out to be Twentieth-Century Fox's biggest hit of 1967. Although he had let the rights go to Fox for a minimal fee, through shrewd wrangling he managed to acquire five per cent of the profits and nearly a million dollars for the rights to the next Susann film, *The Love Machine* (1971). But audiences proved that once bitten, twice shy and the finished product's failure was instrumental in the breakup of his marriage. Further films and a second marriage followed but, unable to recapture his initial success, he slipped quietly into retirement.
Died New York, 25 August 1988, aged 80

RALPH MEEKER (b. Ralph Rathgeber)

He got his first big break by taking over the lead in the stage production of *A Streetcar Named Desire* from Marlon Brando but, despite his success in that and *Mister Roberts*, it was not until 1951 that he entered films. His performance as the ambiguous 'partner' who forces himself on James Stewart in Anthony Mann's *The Naked Spur* (1952) led to better rôles, including that of Mike Hammer in Aldrich's Cold War reworking of *Kiss Me Deadly* (1955) and as Rod Steiger's vengeful nemesis in Sam Fuller's *Run of the Arrow* (1956). Despite a fine performance as one of the doomed soldiers in Kubrick's *Paths of Glory* (1957), he found himself moving further down the cast list, initially in such successful films as *The Dirty Dozen* (1967), *The Detective* (1968) and *The St Valentine's Day Massacre* (1967), then in films which made less impact such as *I Walk the Line* (1970), *The Anderson Tapes* (1971), *Brannigan* (1975) and *Winter Kills* (1979). He shifted his focus towards TV, with guest appearances in many cop shows as well as such TV movies as the 1971 classic, *The Night Stalker*.
Died Woodland Hills, California, 5 August 1989, aged 67

ALAN NAPIER

This gaunt, dignified and politely English actor will doubtless be best remembered as the butler Alfred in the *Batman* TV series, but he trained at RADA and made his stage début with the Oxford Players in 1924. He moved to the US in 1939 and took small rôles in everything from Tarzan to Lassie movies, as well as *The Song of Bernadette* (1943), Val Lewton's neglected *Isle of the Dead* (1945), *The Great Caruso* (1950), *Julius Caesar* (1953) and *The Court Jester* (1955).
Died Santa Monica, California, 8 August 1988, aged 85

CHRISTINE NORDEN

British starlet Norden achieved brief screen fame as the *femme fatale* of such post-war British films as *Saints and Sinners* (1948), the fine psychological thriller *Mine Own Executioner* (1948) and *The Reluctant Heroes* (1951), but her fame was built more solidly on her spectacular 39-inch bust than her acting talents. Briefly one of the world's leading sex symbols, she inspired the infamous hymn 'Onward Christine's Shoulders', but was soon supplanted by such newcomers as Diana Dors and Shirley Eaton,

and by the mid-1950s she had disappeared from the screen. She married five times (her final husband, scientist George Heselden, dedicated his mathematical transformation group formula to her memory).
Died London, 21 September 1988, aged 63

MURIEL OSTRICHE

Although now little remembered, she was one of the most popular actresses of the early silent era, working for many of the most important early moving picture companies – Biograph, Pathé, Reliance, Carl Laemmle's Independent Moving Picture Co. and Vitagraph among many others. By 1913 her popularity had grown to such an extent that she was voted the second most popular actress in America (after Alice Joyce) by the Motion Picture Story magazine. The majority of her films – numbering more than a hundred – were one-reel comedies, many of which were either lost or destroyed with the advent of sound, which terminated her career.
Died 3 May 1989, aged 93

RICHARD QUINE

He was best known as a film director, but began his career as an actor (with a brief stint as a radio announcer), appearing mainly in musicals such as *Dames* (1934), *Babes on Broadway* (1941), *For Me and My Gal* (1942) and *Words and Music* (1948). Although he carried on as a performer until 1950, pausing only to serve with the US Coast Guard in WW2, he directed his first film, *Leather Gloves*, in 1948, sharing the task with his co-producer William Asher. He worked through the 1950s on a series of mostly unmemorable comedies, collaborating with Blake Edwards on several between 1952 and 1962. He gradually worked his way up to glossier productions and A-movie. budgets with such Kim Novak vehicles as *Bell, Book and Candle* (1958), *Strangers When We Meet* (1960) and *The Notorious Landlady* (1962); romantic dramas such as *The World of Suzie Wong* (1960) and slick comedies like the all-star *Sex and the Single Girl* (1964). His friendship with rising actor Jack Lemmon, who appeared in many of his early successes, stood him in good stead as his star rose, leading to his biggest hit, the misogynous black comedy *How To Murder Your Wife* (1964). However, despite the success of the lavish boardroom and bedroom soaper, *Hotel* (1967), he was unable to keep up the momentum and slipped into

misconceived misfires like *Oh Dad, Poor Dad, Mamma's Hung You in the Closet and I'm Feeling So Sad* (1966) before disappearing into undistinguished low-budget work.
Died Los Angeles, 10 June 1989, aged 68

KURT RAAB

Born in Czechoslovakia, he became a props master for stage and TV before beginning his collaboration with Rainer Werner Fassbinder. He worked on most of his films as either designer, assistant director or actor, taking the leads in *The Tenderness of Wolves* (1973) and *Satan's Brew* (1976). His only major non-Fassbinder credit was in Hans-Jürgen Syberberg's *Hitler: A Film from Germany* (1977). His last screen part was as an AIDS patient in Herbert Achternbusch's 1987 avant-garde film, *Wohin?*
Died Hamburg, 28 June 1988, aged 46

GILDA RADNER

One of the many comics who gained popularity on the legendary *Saturday Night Live* TV show, her talent made an uneasy transition to the big screen where, like many of her contemporaries, she found it hard to maintain an amusing character beyond sketch length. Her first major film (she had a walk-on part in *The Last Detail*), Buck Henry's *First Family* (1980), which cast her as the US President's nymphomaniac daughter, was a box-office failure and Mike Nichols' film of her one-woman show *Gilda Live* (1980) was barely released.

She was wildly miscast in the Hitchcockian comedy *Hanky Panky* (1982), but she worked well with (and later married) its star Gene Wilder, leading to a more successful collaboration on his *The Woman in Red* (1984). As the vengeful harpy of a secretary taking out her wrath on the menopausal hero, she contributed her best screen work. However, their follow-up with *Haunted Honeymoon* (1986) was less successful and turned out to be her final film.
Died Los Angeles, 20 May 1989, aged 42

MARGUERITE ROBERTS

Born in Nebraska, she worked as a model and then a news reporter before moving to Hollywood around 1926. Successively a secretary, a reader and then a screenwriter at Twentieth-Century Fox, her first script credit was on Raoul Walsh's *Charlotte Miller* (1933). As an MGM contract writer for 12 years, she

scripted *Honky Tonk* (1941) and *Dragon Seed* (1944) among many others. However, after being denounced to the House Committee on Un-American Activities in 1951, along with novelist husband John Sanford, she was put on the blacklist. Hired again in 1961 to write *Diamond Head*, she notched up further credits on such pictures as *Love Has Many Faces* (1964), *Shootout* (1971) and John Wayne-topliner *True Grit* (1969).
Died Santa Barbara, California, 17 February 1989, aged 84

HAROLD ROSSON

He began his incredible 52-year career as a bit part actor at Vitagraph. Over the next six years he took various jobs at independent studios and on Allan Dwann productions at Famous Players while holding down a full-time job as a stockbroker. From 1914 he concentrated on film work, also selling cinema tickets and working as a projectionist in Brooklyn. After a stint in Hollywood he moved to New York in 1915 to become a cinematographer and worked with Famous Players-Lasky and Paramount on the 1928 version of *Gentlemen Prefer Blondes*, *Trent's Last Case* and De Mille's bizarre comedy, *Madam Satan*, moving briefly to Fox in 1929 before becoming MGM's most valuable cinematographer on such prestige productions of 1932 as *Tarzan the Ape Man*, *Red Dust* and *Red Headed Woman*. In 1933 he eloped with Jean Harlow. The marriage only lasted eight months, but his career went from strength to strength. He was lent out to Alexander Korda for *The Ghost Goes West* (1935) and to David O. Selznick for *The Garden of Allah* (1936). After highly-praised work on *The Wizard of Oz* (1939), *Boom Town* (1944) and *Thirty Seconds over Tokyo* (1944), he was lent out to Selznick again for *Duel in the Sun* (1946) and went on to lens a series of classics back home at MGM – *On the Town* (1949), *The Asphalt Jungle* (1950) and *Singin' in the Rain* (1952). In 1953 he went freelance, working on *The Bad Seed* (1956), Dick Powell's claustrophobic submarine drama, *The Enemy Below* (1957), and the classic army comedy, *No Time for Sergeants* (1958). He made his final film, Howard Hawks's *El Dorado*, in 1967 after a period of semi-retirement.
Died Palm Beach, California, 6 September 1988, aged 93

MILTON SPERLING

He started life as a shipping clerk before

becoming a messenger boy at Paramount. After working in the script department at United Artists and becoming an associate producer at Edward Small Productions, he moved to Fox and became a writer on such forgettable fare as *Happy Landing* (1938) and *Here I Am a Stranger* (1939) before going on to produce three minor films. The war intervened and, from 1942-5, he served in the US Marine Corps, rising to the rank of Captain and being placed in charge of combat films such as *Tarawa* and *To the Shores of Iwo Jima*. After the war he established himself as an independent producer, releasing through major companies such as Warner Bros and turning out a lot of junk amidst the occasional low-budget classic – among them *The Enforcer* (1950), *The Court Martial of Billy Mitchell* (1955), *The Rise and Fall of Legs Diamond* (1960) and Sam Fuller's classic *Merrill's Marauders* (1962). His last major production was *The Battle of the Bulge* (1965) which he co-wrote and produced with Philip Yordan. One of the best of the mid-1960s war epics, it was only a moderate success and, although Sperling worked again with Yordan on the derivative *Captain Apache* (1971), he was unable to maintain the interest of the major studios and his career fell by the wayside in the 1970s.

Died Beverly Hills, 26 August 1988, aged 76

BOB STEELE (Robert Bradbury)

He made his screen début in silent two-reelers directed by his father, Robert North Bradbury, graduating to lead rôles in oaters such as *Davey Crockett at the Fall of the Alamo* and *Sitting Bull at the Spirit Lake Massacre*, reaching the peak of his popularity in the early 1930s as the cheerful hero who did all his own stunts in such imaginatively titled gems as *The Ridin' Fool*, *Rider of the Law* and *Riders of the Sage* before being edged out by the rise of the singing cowboy and into character rôles (such as the spiteful Curly in *Of Mice and Men*). He briefly regained his popularity with three 1940s' series – *Billy the Kid*, *Trail Blazers* and *Three Mesquiteers* – before going on to spend the tail end of his career playing small rôles (usually villains) in more prestigious productions such as *Rio Bravo* (1959), *Cheyenne Autumn* (1964), *Hang 'em High* (1967), *Rio Lobo* (1970), *The Skin Game* (1971) and Peckinpah's masterly *Major Dundee* (1965). In between he toured circuses and rodeos and made guest appearances in such classic TV series as *Gunsmoke*, *Rawhide*,

Cheyenne, Have Gun Will Travel and *F Troop*.

Died Burbank, California, 21 December 1988, aged 82

RAYMOND STROSS

Born in Leeds, he joined Columbia Pictures as a sales supervisor for the Midlands after leaving university but was drawn into legitimate theatre until, in 1948, he returned to films as a producer. Most of his films were traditional English fare, like *As Long as They're Happy* (1955) or *An Alligator Named Daisy* (1955), though a collaboration with Robert Aldrich on *The Angry Hills* (1959) led to his brief association with its star Robert Mitchum in a producing venture. The result, *A Terrible Beauty* (1960), was a shallow drama about the Irish revolution which failed to satisfy the prejudices of English or American audiences, and was barely released in Ireland. Stross went on to produce the powerful drama, *The Mark* (1961), which featured Stuart Whitman as a sex criminal trying to suppress his urges. Its modest success encouraged Stross to produce controversial subjects. Unfortunately, the divide between ambition and achievement was made only too apparent by *The Leather Boys* (1963), a hysterically funny attempt to remake *The Wild One* in central London with Rita Tushingham and Dudley Sutton in place of Mary Murphy and Marlon Brando. However, he was vindicated by the extraordinary success of his low-budget adaptation of D. H. Lawrence's *The Fox* (1967), starring his wife Anne Heywood, which outgrossed most of the big budget epics of its day as one of the first serious films to deal with lesbianism.

Died Beverly Hills, 31 July 1988, aged 71

ALDO TONTI

Born in Rome, he entered films in 1934 as a camera assistant, working his way up to camera operator on films such as Vittorio (son of Benito) Mussolini's classic fascist folly, *Scipio Africanus* (1937) – the Roman epic with the wristwatches and papier mâché elephants. He became a cinematographer in 1938, collaborating on numerous forgettable films before his work on Roberto Rossellini's *Ossessione* (1942) led to such films as *Europa 51* (1952), *La Lupa* (1953) and *Ulysses* (1954). The latter's wide release in America, combined with Dino De Laurentiis' determination to use local talent (that he didn't have to fly to Europe and put up in hotels) led to some impressive work

on *War and Peace* (1956) which in turn led to *Nights of Cabiria* (1956). However, his finest work was on *Barabbas* (1962), in which he pulled off a cinematic coup by filming the crucifixion during a total eclipse of the sun, one of the most stunning moments ever captured on film. Later films, including a brief excursion to Hollywood for John Huston's ill-conceived *Reflections in a Golden Eye* (1967), tended to waste his considerable talents and, although he continued to lens films on the continent, they were mostly lacklustre affairs.
Died Rome, 7 July 1988, aged 78

CHARLES VANEL

Born in Rennes, he left a naval academy in 1908 to join various amateur theatre groups, becoming a professional in provincial touring companies. He made his screen début in 1912, and for eight years alternated between French silent films and the Paris stage. However, it was on the screen that he was to have the most success. Aside from *La Belle équipe* (1936), much of his work was undistinguished and his appearance in Georges Clouzot's classic shocker *Les Diaboliques* (1954). Briefly catching Hollywood's eye, he appeared in Hitchcock's *To Catch a Thief* (1955) before gradually sinking from view in a series of unmemorable thrillers.
Died Cannes, France, 15 April 1989, aged 96

ROBERT WEBBER

He was one of the most reliable and easily recognizable character actors in American films. Following stage appearances in the early 1940s, his work in early television drama led to film rôles with *Highway 501* (1951). It was Sidney Lumet's *Twelve Angry Men* (1957) that really launched his screen career and he soon found himself taking prominent supporting rôles (often cast as an executive or a 'heel') in *The Sandpiper* (1965), *Harper* (1966), *The Dirty Dozen* (1967), *The Great White Hope* (1970), *Bring Me the Head of Alfredo Garcia* (1974) and *Midway* (1976). He is probably best remembered as a regular in Blake Edwards' comedies – the villain of *The Revenge of the Pink Panther* (1978), Dudley Moore's gay collaborator in *'10'* (1979) and the Hollywood journeyman of *S.O.B.* (1981).
Died Malibu, California, 17 May 1989, aged 64